Vodka Politics

VODKA POLITICS

Alcohol, Autocracy, and the Secret History of the Russian State

MARK LAWRENCE SCHRAD

OXFORD
UNIVERSITY PRESS

OXFORD
UNIVERSITY PRESS

Oxford University Press is a department of the University of Oxford.
It furthers the University's objective of excellence in research, scholarship,
and education by publishing worldwide.

Oxford   New York

Auckland   Cape Town   Dar es Salaam   Hong Kong   Karachi
Kuala Lumpur   Madrid   Melbourne   Mexico City   Nairobi
New Delhi   Shanghai   Taipei   Toronto

With offices in

Argentina   Austria   Brazil   Chile   Czech Republic   France   Greece
Guatemala   Hungary   Italy   Japan   Poland   Portugal   Singapore
South Korea   Switzerland   Thailand   Turkey   Ukraine   Vietnam

Oxford is a registered trademark of Oxford University Press
in the UK and certain other countries.

Published in the United States of America by
Oxford University Press
198 Madison Avenue, New York, NY 10016

CIP record is available from the Library of Congress

ISBN 978–0–199–75559–2

1 3 5 7 9 8 6 4 2
Printed in the United States of America
on acid-free paper

For my wife, Jennifer.
I have so many words to express so many things,
but none could hope to describe my love and appreciation
for who you are and all you do.

CONTENTS

NOTE ON PROPER NAMES

In this book, Russian names generally follow the British standard (BGN/PCGN) transliteration, with some alterations to accommodate the widely accepted English equivalents of familiar historical figures (for example, Tsar Nicholas and Tsarina Catherine, rather than Tsar Nikolai and Tsaritsa Ekaterina). To aid pronunciation, I have opted to change the Russian "ii" ending to a "y," and eliminate the Russian soft sign from personal and place names (so Maksim Gor'kii becomes Maxim Gorky). These alterations do not apply to the bibliographic references in the notes, which maintain the standard transliteration for those who wish to consult the original sources.

PREFACE

A book about Russia based on vodka? How's that going to sit with Russian readers? Well, when a *New York Times* article I wrote related to the subject found its way onto the Russian-language blogosphere, it certainly didn't take me long to find out: "Vodka? Hey, while you're at it, don't forget the bears and balalaikas" came one understandable rejoinder, drenched in the requisite sarcasm about gullible foreigners and their misguided perceptions about Russia. Dozens more jibes and sneers quickly followed.[1]

To be sure, confronting well-worn clichés is an uncomfortable business. Especially when unflattering broadsides are made against an entire nation, they prompt a response from both those outside and inside the group such stereotypes purport to describe. For insiders, the usual response to a hurtful platitude is to downplay or deny it. Sympathetic outsiders normally try to politely ignore it. Rarely do offended parties embrace a perceived insult, and rarer still does anyone stop to investigate and explore it.

Obviously, in studying Russia—its people, culture, politics, and history—we encounter just such a widely held and uncomfortable stereotype in the form of the hopelessly drunken Russian. People who can barely locate Russia on a map readily associate it with insobriety, while foreigners studying the Russian language surely know how to say "vodka" well before they even learn to say "hello."

Yet that image is not exclusive to foreigners: as the new millennium dawned, the All-Russian Center for the Study of Public Opinion (VTsIOM) asked actual Russian citizens what they considered the main symbol of twentieth-century Russia: vodka beat out not just bears and balalaikas, but also nesting dolls and even AK-47s for the top spot.[2] When it comes to perceived challenges for Russia's future, such concerns as "national security," "economic crisis," and "human rights" are routinely listed as national threats only by some ten percent of VTsIOM poll respondents. "Terrorism" and "crime" are consistently named around twenty-five to thirty percent of the time. The challenge that usually claims the top spot as Russia's most pressing challenge is "alcohol and drug addiction"—voiced by some fifty to sixty percent of respondents, year in and year out.[3] Still, while everyone knows alcohol is a major social problem, vodka's roots run so deep in Russian history and culture that simply acknowledging—much less unpacking and confronting—this endemic challenge seems somehow impolite, especially for an outsider.

Yet while virtually every developed country on earth put their so-called liquor question to bed a century ago, alcohol continues to bedevil high politics in Russia. For instance, in late 2011 and 2012, an unprecedented wave of popular opposition in Moscow nearly thwarted Vladimir Putin's return to a third term as Russia's president following four years as prime minister alongside his protégé Dmitry Medvedev. In his last major speech to the Duma—the lower house of Russia's parliament—before his re-inauguration, Putin highlighted Russia's precarious health and demographic situation as one of his administration's most pressing political challenges. "Without any wars or calamities," Putin said, "smoking, alcohol, and drug abuse [alone] claim 500,000 lives of our countrymen every year. This is simply a horrific figure." Unless Putin suffers from amnesia, these indeed-horrific figures should not have come as any surprise: he repeatedly lamented vodka's ghastly toll during both his first and second administrations (2000–2008) in almost the same language.[4]

Since Putin emerged on the political scene in 1999, Russian social indicators have unquestionably improved upon the unimaginable social devastation and economic demodernization in the years immediately following communism's collapse in 1991. The economy grew at some seven percent per year for an entire decade from 1998 to 2008 before getting hammered by the global financial crisis. Yet while the macroeconomic indicators were on the rebound, figures on Russian life expectancy more closely resembled sub-Saharan Africa than postindustrial Europe. Even today, the average teenage Russian boy has a *worse* chance of living to age sixty-five than do boys in failed states like Somalia and Ethiopia.[5] But unlike these desperate places, it isn't malnourishment or famine that is to blame—nor is it the errant bullets of civil war: it is vodka, pure and simple. With Russians consuming on average eighteen liters of pure alcohol per year—or more than twice the maximum amount deemed safe by the World Health Organization—in 2009 then-president Dmitry Medvedev called alcohol a "national disaster," ushering in a new attempt to combat the eternal Russian vice.[6]

Russia's tragic cultural weakness for vodka is often chalked up to the torments of the "Russian soul." But simply assuming that intoxication and self-destruction are somehow inherent cultural traits—unalienable parts of what it is to be Russian, almost down to the genetic level—is akin to blaming the victim. There is nothing natural about Russia's vodka disaster.

As I argue here, Russian society's longstanding attachment to the vodka bottle—and the misfortune that follows in its wake—is instead a *political* disaster generated by the modern, autocratic Russian state. Before the rise of the modern Russian autocracy, the people of medieval *Rus'* drank beers and ales naturally fermented from grains, plus meads naturally fermented from honey, and *kvas* naturally fermented from bread. If they were well-to-do, they imported wines fermented from grapes and berries. They not only drank beverages similar to those elsewhere on the European continent; they also imbibed similar amounts and in a similar manner. That all changed with the introduction of the very unnatural process of distillation, which created spirits and vodkas of a potency—and profitability—that nature simply could not match. Beginning in the sixteenth century, the grand princes and tsars of Muscovy monopolized the lucrative vodka trade, quickly promoting it as the primary means of extracting money and resources from their lowly subjects.

The state's subjugation of society through alcohol was not unique to Russia: even into the nineteenth century distilled spirits were instrumental in "proletarianizing" colonial Africa and subjugating the slaves of the antebellum United States—but nowhere did alcohol become a more intractable part of the state's financial and political dominance over society than in Russia's autocratic tsarist and Soviet empires, which has left disturbing legacies for the present and future of today's Russian Federation.[7] The moral, social, and health decay that resulted from plying the people with copious amounts of vodka could be easily overlooked so long as the treasury was flush and the state was strong. That the people's misery led them back to the tavern rather than forward to the picket line was an added benefit, at least as far as the stability of the autocratic leadership was concerned. In sum: vodka is only as natural as autocracy is natural—in Russia, they are woven together as part of the same cloth.

Does this mean that vodka is *everything* in Russia? Certainly not, but it is a lot of things. I don't claim to offer a monocausal explanation of Russian history: it would be the height of foolishness to claim that everything of political significance can be explained with reference to alcohol. Instead, I present vodka politics as an alternative lens through which to view and thereby understand Russia's complex political development. Think of it as beer goggles for Russian history—but unlike beer goggles that distort our perceptions, viewing history through the lens of vodka politics actually brings things into clearer focus. Vodka politics helps us to understand the temperament of Russia's famed autocratic leaders from both the distant and not-so-distant past and how they relate to their subjects. It highlights the significance of previously overlooked factors in major events in world history, including wars, coups, and revolutions. It fills in significant gaps in our understanding of politics and economics with Russian society and culture. It gives us new appreciation for the greatest works of Russian literature and casts stale understandings of Russia's internal dynamics in a completely new light. Finally, it may just help us confront the monumental challenges that these historical legacies of autocratic vodka politics present for a healthy, prosperous, and democratic future.

The Russian people today understand that they confront a huge problem with alcohol, and leaders across the political spectrum also begrudgingly admit that vodka is—quite possibly—the most serious problem facing their country. With so much to be gained in terms of both understanding the past and confronting the future, the benefits of addressing alcohol in Russia rationally and seriously far outweigh the risk of ruffling feathers and confronting a sensitive and uncomfortable stereotype or politely dismissing the topic as somehow too cliché. Scholars of all stripes and nationalities have done that for far too long already.

This surely isn't the first biography of vodka, nor will it be the last. Russians have been writing national histories of alcohol dating from Ivan Pryzhov's *Istoriya kabakov v Rossii* (*History of Taverns in Russia*) as early as 1868. Much of the subsequent popular literature on the topic—both in Russia and abroad— examines both the evolution and etymology of the drink we now know as vodka and tends to be rather superficial.[8] Far more rewarding are the works of professional historians, political scientists, sociologists, anthropologists, demographers, and public health experts who have dedicated their academic careers to understanding narrow slices related to the general history of alcohol in Russia. These include David Christian's *Living Water* (1990) dealing with the pre-emancipation Russian empire, Patricia Herlihy's *Alcoholic Empire* (2002) on late-imperial Russia, Kate Transchel's *Under the Influence* (2006) on the tumultuous years of communist revolution, Vlad Treml's *Alcohol in the USSR* (1982) on the postwar era, Stephen White's *Russia Goes Dry* (1996) on Gorbachev's anti-alcohol campaign, or Aleksandr Nemtsov's *Contemporary History of Alcohol in Russia* (2011) on the Soviet and post-Soviet legacies.[9] Unlike the more cursory social histories of vodka, I have built upon these and other more rigorous academic investigations—as well as unearthed additional primary source materials, including those in Russian, European, and American archives—to instead paint a political biography of alcohol in Russia by investigating how vodka is intimately tied to Russian statecraft across historical time periods: from Ivan the Terrible through the 2012 elections and beyond.

This book is neither meant to valorize alcohol nor maliciously lampoon Russian drunkenness. It is not an exercise in patronizing orientalism or anti-Russian hysterics—it is a recognition of the variety of ways alcohol influences and catalyzes political phenomena (and vice versa) in the context of Russian history. Even the idea of a political biography of alcohol is not unique to Russia. Indeed, W. J. Rorabaugh's influential *Alcoholic Republic* (1979) similarly recast

the early history of the United States in a new light: America was widely considered "a nation of drunkards" in the period when anti-British revolutionary
plots were being hatched in smoke-filled taverns. Even as early as the 1730s the
most successful newspaper in the American colonies, the *Pennsylvania Gazette*,
compiled a list of 220 colloquialisms for being drunk and also ran reports of
foreign attempts to deal with rampant drunkenness. The author of such pieces
was none other than the young Philadelphia printer and future founding father
Benjamin Franklin. Actually, most of America's vaunted founding fathers had
ties to alcohol, as winemakers, brewers, or distillers, with whiskey distiller
George Washington even becoming the iconic leader of the new country.[10] Yet
while every country has its own history with alcohol, perhaps in no other country is that relationship as enduring and intertwined with the culture, society, and
politics of the nation than in Russia. In the end, I hope that this book will instill
in others the same adoration and fascination with Russia—its people, politics,
history, and culture—that has motivated me for the past twenty years.

The writing of the manuscript occupied only the last three of those years—
though it seemed like far longer than that. For too long this project has taken
me away from my loving wife, Jennifer, and my children, Alexander, Sophia,
and Helena. I'm looking forward to baseball games, swimming lessons, and bike
rides with my family—all of which were put on hold for this book. My parents,
Dale and Paula Schrad, were always willing to bail me out on the home front
when the writing needed a kick-start, while my brothers Dan and Kent were
ready with sagacious advice and support. This project would be nothing without
my family—and neither would I, for that matter.

I'm also indebted to friends, colleagues, administrators, and students at
Villanova University—especially in political science and Russian studies—who
have provided feedback, camaraderie, and a wonderful and inclusive environ-
ment for our family. In particular, I benefitted tremendously from discussions
with Lynne Hartnett, Adele Lindenmeyr, Jeffrey Hahn, Matt Kerbel, Christine
Palus, Markus Kreuzer, Father Joe Loya, Miron Wolnicki, Boris Briker, Lauren
Miltenberger, David Barrett, Kunle Olowabi, Lowell Gustafson, Jack Johannes,
Bob Langran, Eric Lomazoff, Catherine Warrick, Catherine Wilson, Lara Brown,
Maria Toyoda, Jennifer Dixon, Daniel Mark, Shigehiro Suzuki, and Mary Beth
Simmons. Meanwhile, good friends Erasmus and Maureen Kersting were always
there to listen to my frustrations and gripes, even after hours. While Father Peter
Donohue, Father Kail Ellis, Merrill Stein and Taras Ortynsky provided institu-
tional support at different administrative levels, Steven Darbes, Shishav Parajuli,
and Max McGuire were instrumental for their research assistance. Villanova
University also provided a much-appreciated subvention to secure licensing for
the various photos used throughout the book. Yet more than anyone at Villanova
I owe a deep debt of gratitude to Steven Schultz, who diligently poured over

chapter upon chapter, draft upon draft—talking me through so many unexpected frustrations of writing for a wider audience. Thank you.

I feel blessed to have known Murray Feshbach—who plays a starring role in this book—as an advisor, mentor, and friend. Russia owes you a tremendous debt of gratitude for some five decades of tireless investigation; I owe you just as much in terms of guidance and inspiration.

Beyond my confines on the Main Line, I am thankful to a wide variety of scholars and friends who were gracious enough to endure my questions, impositions, or just provide friendly support, including Mark Steinberg, Mark Beissinger, Aleksandr Nemtsov, Nicholas Eberstadt, David Christian, Jim Sweigert, Richard Tempest, Kate Transchel, Robin Room, Martin McKee, David Leon, David Fahey, Charles King, Harley Balzer, Scott Gehlbach, Judy Twigg, Carol Leff, Emmanuel Akyeampong, Steve Trusa, Herb Meyer, Adrianne Jacobs, Anna Bailey, Dmitry Fedotov, Thomas Jabine at the Library of Congress, Jos Schaeken at the Birchbark Literacy project at Leiden University, Peter Maggs at the University of Illinois Law School, and Kristy Ironside, who saved me from making a separate transatlantic voyage to the archives in Moscow. Whether they know it or not, support and inspiration were often provided from afar by Vlad Treml, Jeremy Duff, Cliff Gaddy, Quinn Ernster, Daniel Treisman, Chris Walker, Clint Fuller, Lyndon Allin, Brian Varney, Tony Dutcher, Mark Adomanis, Anatoly Karlin, Sean Guillory, Duncan Redmonds, Jeff Williams, Tim Shriver, Dave Deibler and Barb Schilf, Steve Perry and the good folks at CPD, Fishbone, Templeton Rye, and Mitchell & Ness. Special appreciation goes to those active in the special needs community everywhere—both in the United States and abroad—for their often unheralded work with the vulnerable, the marginalized, and the brutalized. In a similar vein, much of my research in Russia would not have been possible without the kindness of Georgia and Andrew Williams and their charitable work with ROOF—the Russian Orphan Opportunity Fund. My experiences with disadvantaged orphans in Podolsk were truly life altering, as later chapters should make clear. Since many of the real victims of vodka politics are to be found in Russia's beleaguered orphanage system, it is only appropriate that a percentage of the proceeds from the sale of this book will go to ROOF.

Last but far from least, like its predecessor, *The Political Power of Bad Ideas*, this book would not have been possible without all of the tremendous, hardworking people at Oxford University Press. Foremost among them is my editor, David McBride, who has shared my vision and faith in the viability of this project from the get-go. I'd also like to extend my most heartfelt appreciation to the slate of anonymous reviewers who slogged through every line and every footnote of the manuscript: the project is much improved for your efforts.

Finally, it is necessary to say a thing or two about biases and motivations as a foreigner writing about a taboo subject like alcohol in Russia. I am certain that instead of confronting the arguments I put forth in the book some readers will jump to unfounded conclusions based solely on nationality. So let me clarify that my aim in writing this book is to promote the health, happiness, and prosperity of the Russian people, whom I have long admired and respected. My fascination with the topic grew even stronger while living in Moscow throughout the 1990s, when I first realized that an outsider's perspective means being able to see the forest for the trees when it comes to alcohol and Russian statecraft.

Others are sure to assume—again mistakenly—that my criticism of vodka's role in Russian politics and society is motivated by a personal distaste for alcohol. Having lived (and drunk extensively) both in Russia and the United States, I'll admit that I drink far more vodka than the average American and far more beer than the average Russian. This book ultimately may be criticized for many things, but it is certainly not a temperance tract by a puritanical teetotaler.

VODKA POLITICS

1

Introduction

Nikita Khrushchev was an oddly disarming fellow: five-foot-three and nearly as wide, with a face that seemed to be made from putty. With only four years of formal education, this former peasant somehow rose through the Soviet commissariat to become the unlikely successor to the blood-soaked tyranny of Joseph Stalin. The pudgy Khrushchev was the embodiment of contradiction: alternatively shrewd and shortsighted, secretive and straightforward, unassuming and pompous, optimistic and apocalyptic.

The world had never seen a Russian autocrat quite like Khrushchev. Before he rose to power in the early 1950s, Eurasia was ruled for centuries by commissars and emperors who were distant, cold, and inaccessible. Whether tsarist or communist, Russian leaders seemed omnipotent and actively supported an image of infallibility. Khrushchev, by contrast, was cursed with human frailty and imperfection, which were on full display for the world throughout the 1950s and 1960s.[1] From crushing popular opposition in Eastern Europe to banging his shoe at the United Nations, and even pushing the world to the brink of thermonuclear holocaust over Cuba, Khrushchev blundered from one fiasco to another. So it was understandable that, in 1964, the Politburo deposed the all-too-human Khrushchev in favor of the dour Leonid Brezhnev, returning to the traditional cold and distant Russian autocrat.

After being booted from power by his own Communist Party, "special pensioner" Khrushchev spent his autumn years in forced retirement at his dacha—a summer home west of Moscow. When not tending to his garden, or giving his guards the slip in order to stroll the banks of the nearby Moscow River in his telltale fedora and straining belt halfway up to his armpits, Khrushchev dictated his memoirs on a rudimentary tape recorder—providing invaluable perspectives from the only Russian autocrat to die peacefully out of office. Of the 1.5 million words that fell from Khrushchev's aging, meaty lips onto hundreds of hours of four-track, reel-to-reel tapes, the most fascinating tell of the importance of alcohol to the intrigues of Stalin's inner circle by one of the few who lived to tell the tale.[2]

Joseph Stalin is conventionally portrayed as a brutal dictator who in the early 1920s seized the reins of absolute power in the Soviet Union by outmaneuvering and purging his political opponents; a paranoid tyrant who fostered an all-encompassing personality cult and ruled the Soviet Union through fear, repression, and intimidation. Under him, untold millions would perish in labor camps, forced deportations, crash collectivization and industrialization, genocide and famine—all before sacrificing twenty-four million souls to Nazi Germany in World War II.[3] What must it have been like to be complicit in having the blood of millions on your hands? How do you walk the fine line between pleasing the master so that your head is not the next to roll and saving your sanity and your soul?

Through those scratchy tapes, Khrushchev's aging voice gives us a glimpse of life in Stalin's inner circle where, in good times and bad, the most pressing political questions were decided at the great leader's table. Early on in the 1930s Stalin was "simple and accessible."[4] Have a problem? Call Stalin directly. Or, better yet, go see him directly at his country dacha, where he'd sit out on the porch in the tepid summer air:

> They served soup, a thick Russian broth, and there'd be a small carafe of vodka and a pitcher of water; the vodka glass was moderate in size. You'd go in and say hello and he would say: "Want something to eat? Take a seat." And "take a seat" meant grab a soup bowl (the soup kettle was right there), fill a bowl for yourself, as much as you want, sit down, and eat. If you want something to drink, grab a carafe, pour yourself a glass, and drink it down. If you want a second drink, you decide that for yourself. The soul knows its own measure, as the saying goes. If you don't want to drink, you don't have to.[5]

But that was early on. Over time, the pressures of totalitarian dictatorship bore down on Stalin. In 1932, following a drunken public spat, his second wife died under mysterious circumstances, which sent Stalin into a bout of loneliness. The looming specter of war with Adolph Hitler—and the very real prospect of *losing* that war—sent him into ever gloomier depression.[6] Stalin grew dark. He drank more and more. Even worse, he began to force others to drink for his pleasure. As Khrushchev recalled, "At that time there were no dinners with Stalin at which people did not drink heavily, whether they wanted to or not. He evidentially wanted to drown his conscience and keep himself stupefied, or so it seemed. He never left the table sober and still less did he allow any of those close to him to leave sober."[7]

With the appointment of Stalin's sadistic hatchet-man, Lavrenty Beria, to the People's Commissariat for Internal Affairs (NKVD—precursor to the KGB), the once-pleasant Politburo dinners became steeped in terse competition to curry favor with the boss. Eternally suspicious of plots to do him in, Stalin used alcohol to keep his inner circle off balance: make his closest comrades (or potential rivals) drink to excess in order to draw out their honest opinions and lay bare their true intentions. If they were unable to control themselves, they would remain suspicious of one another and couldn't collectively topple his reign. "Stalin liked this," Khrushchev remembered. "He liked to set us against one another, and he encouraged and strengthened [our] baser inclinations."[8]

Throughout the 1940s and 1950s—from near-annihilation at the hands of the German Wehrmacht to boastful global superpower—Soviet high politics assumed the air of a college frat party with the devil. Either in the Kremlin or at Stalin's dacha, political decisions were made over drinking games and toasts of Russian vodka, Crimean champagne, Armenian brandy, and Georgian wine, beginning with the late-evening dinner and ending only with the dawn. Before attending to their assigned duties in the morning—or, more often, early afternoon—the Soviet leadership staggered outside to vomit or soil themselves before being borne home by their guards. As Yugoslav partisan Milovan Djilas ruminated after his Kremlin visits: "It was at these dinners that the destiny of the vast Russian land, of the newly acquired territories, and, to a considerable degree, of the human race was decided. And even if the dinners failed to inspire those spiritual creators—the 'engineers of the human spirit'—to great deeds, many such deeds were probably buried there forever."[9]

While Djilas *didn't* appreciate was that the members of Stalin's Politburo—the elite leaders of the Communist Party of the Soviet Union—were hardly willing participants in these dinners. Khrushchev's gravelly voice recounted how the inner circle loathed meeting with Stalin—due mostly to the drunken bacchanals:

> Almost every evening the phone rang: "C'mon over, we'll have dinner." Those were dreadful dinners. We would get home toward dawn, and yet we had to go to work. I would try to reach the office by 10:00 a.m. and during the lunch break take a nap because there was always the danger that if you didn't sleep and he called you again to come to dinner you would end up dozing off at his table. Things went badly for people who dozed off at Stalin's table.[10]

Foreign guests weren't spared either. After slicing up Eastern Europe with Adolph Hitler through the 1939 Molotov-Ribbentrop Pact, Stalin treated the delegation of Nazi foreign minister Joachim von Ribbentrop to an elaborate twenty-four course state dinner in the sumptuous Grand Palace of the Kremlin. For many of the visitors, it was the most remarkable event they had ever experienced.[11] But before anyone could eat, Soviet foreign minister Vyacheslav Molotov proposed a round of toasts to each and every member of the two delegations—twenty-two in all. Stalin exchanged a few words with each guest and clinked glasses. Having so "honored" each guest in turn, the now-sauced Germans sighed with relief and finally turned to eat—that is, until a visibly inebriated Molotov declared: "Now we'll drink to all members of the delegations who could *not* attend this dinner."[12] And on it went.

Of that fateful night, Ribbentrop recalled that the brown pepper vodka they drank was "so potent it almost took your breath away"—yet somehow Stalin seemed steady and unaffected. Tipsy, Ribbentrop stammered toward Stalin to express his "admiration for Russian throats compared with those of us Germans." The great dictator chuckled. Pulling the Nazi minister aside, Stalin revealed that his own cup held only a light Crimean wine, the same color as the "devilish vodka" he made everyone else drink.[13]

Perhaps the saving grace for foreign dignitaries was that—unlike the Politburo members—they didn't meet with Stalin regularly: the Nazi delegate Gustav Hilger later described the confrontation with Beria that erupted when Hilger refused to get drunk. "What's the argument about?" Stalin interrupted, later joking, "Well if you don't want to drink, no one can force you."

"Not even the chief of the NKVD himself?" Hilger pressed.

"Here at this table," replied Stalin, "even the NKVD chief has no more say than anyone else."

For the Germans, these confrontations underscored that the Soviet leadership was both unpretentious and unpredictable. Reflecting on how swiftly Stalin could swing from jovial to deathly serious, Hilger noted his "paternal benevolence with which he knew how to win his opponents and make them less vigilant."[14] Forcing others to drink until they lost touch with their senses was certainly useful for that.

Whether entertaining Stalin's erstwhile Axis allies at the outset of the war or his Allied allies during the war, alcohol was integral to high-level diplomacy. Three short years after the sodden Nazi delegation left Stalin's court, in August 1942, British prime minister Winston Churchill's delegation arrived only to endure the same treatment. These were the darkest days of World War II, and the British mission had intended to shore up relations with their new Soviet allies, who were then enduring the full force of the Nazi *blitzkrieg*. Churchill also broke the bad news that relief in the form of a second front in Western Europe would not be quick in coming. Having professed that the "drinking of alcohol before, after, and if need be during all meals and in the intervals between them" was his "sacred rite," Churchill seemed well prepared to confront the Kremlin's drunken bacchanals on their own terms.[15]

Still, the Soviets retained their home court advantage. "Nothing can be imagined more awful than a Kremlin banquet, but it has to be endured," recalled the British permanent undersecretary at the foreign office, Sir Alexander Cadogan. "Unfortunately, Winston didn't suffer it gladly."

Undaunted by the first banquet, before leaving Russia, Churchill requested a final audience with Stalin. At 1 a.m. on the morning of their departure, Cadogan was summoned to Stalin's private Kremlin residence, where he found the two leaders, now flanked by Molotov, in high spirits—feasting on all manner of food, a suckling pig, already having downed countless bottles of alcohol. "What Stalin made me drink seemed pretty savage: Winston, who by that time was complaining of a slight headache, seemed wisely to be confining himself to a comparatively innocuous effervescent Caucasian red wine." Still, according to Cadogan, the goodwill forged in that night of heavy drinking solidified the grand alliance that ultimately laid low the Nazi juggernaut.[16]

The Kremlin banquet scene was in full swing again when French president Charles de Gaulle arrived near the conclusion of the European war in December 1944. The jubilance of impending victory was tinged with unease over Stalin's looming drunkenness, as the great dictator presented a series of toasts to his circle—thirty by de Gaulle's count—each more chilling than the next.

To his rear army commander Andrei Khrulev (whose wife had recently been arrested under suspicions of conspiracy): "He'd better do his best, or he'll be hanged for it, that's the custom in our country!" This was followed by a joyous clinking of glasses and an understandably awkward embrace.[17]

To his air force commander Aleksandr Novikov: a "good Marshal, let's drink to him. And if he doesn't do his job properly, we'll hang him!" (Two years later, Novikov would be stripped of his rank, arrested, and tortured by Beria before being sentenced to fifteen years in a hard-labor camp.)[18]

Then there was Lazar Kaganovich, Khrushchev's mentor and mastermind behind Stalin's Ukrainian terror-famine of the 1930s that claimed millions of lives. During the prewar banquet with Ribbentrop, Stalin took special pleasure in making his Nazi guests squirm by celebrating a toast to the Jewish Kaganovich.[19] But by the end of the war, both the guests and the toasts had changed. Stalin proclaimed of Kaganovich: "a brave man. He knows that if the trains do not arrive on time—we shall shoot him!"

Could the uncomfortable de Gaulle have known that Kaganovich had sacrificed his own brother, Mikhail, to Stalin's bloodthirsty paranoia? "What has to be done must be done," Lazar coldly shrugged once informed that his brother had roused Stalin's suspicion. Mikhail was shot during the interrogation the following day. But that was at the outset of the war—like all the others, all Lazar could do now was endure such menacing toasts with a facade of good humor and an obedient clinking of the glasses.[20]

For any normal observer, much less a foreign dignitary such as de Gaulle, this was simply shocking. Reading the displeasure on his guest's face, Stalin put his hand on de Gaulle's shoulder and smiled: "People call me a monster, but as you see, I make a joke of it. Maybe I'm not horrible after all."[21]

On that evening, at least, Nikita Khrushchev avoided Stalin's ire, but such was not always the case. On other nights, Stalin cleaned his burning pipe by knocking it against Khrushchev's bald head before forcing the rotund, aging former peasant-turned-court-jester to drink glass after glass of vodka and perform the *gapak*, the traditional knees-bent Ukrainian folk dance, which caused him excruciating pain. Occasionally KGB chief Beria pinned the word *prick* to the back of Khrushchev's overcoat, which he would not notice until the company burst into rollicking laughter. Others left ripe tomatoes on his chair for Nikita to sit on. A proud and temperate man by upbringing, as with all of his compatriots, Khrushchev became a prodigious drinker for no other reason than to please Stalin. Sometimes he got so drunk that Beria had to help him to bed, on which he would promptly piss. As later biographers would note: "Awful as these sessions were, it was better to be there than not, better to be humiliated than annihilated."[22]

In his own words Khrushchev later recalled:

> He literally forced us to drink! Among ourselves we had brief discussions about how to bring the supper or dinner to an end more quickly. Sometimes before supper or dinner, people would say: "Well, what's it going to be today, will there be a drinking contest or not?" We didn't want to have such contests because we had work to do, but Stalin deprived us of that opportunity.... Stalin himself would just drink a glass of cognac or vodka at the beginning of the dinner and then wine.... Everyone felt repelled by this; it made you sick to the stomach; but Stalin was implacable on this matter.[23]

So is it any wonder that virtually every member of the Soviet Politburo of the 1940s was a drop-dead alcoholic? It was not because alcoholism was hardwired into their DNA but, rather, because they were products of a political system that compelled drunken excess. Stalin's inebriated inner circle, including Khrushchev, Beria, Molotov, Kaganovich, Georgy Malenkov, and Anastas Mikoyan was a collection of some of the most ruthless thugs the world had ever seen—yet all of them were made to drink against their will to keep them off balance and prevent them from plotting to topple the paranoid secretary general. "Stalin forced us drink a lot," Mikoyan confirmed in his memoirs, "apparently to loosen our tongues, so that we couldn't control what we said, and he would later know who was thinking what."[24]

According to one of Stalin's biographers, "Forcing his tough comrades to lose control of themselves became his sport and a measure of dominance."[25] The toughest of them all was Stalin's executioner, Lavrenty Beria—the sadistic head of the secret police who was notorious for cruising in his black limousine to select women (reportedly upwards of two hundred) from the streets of Moscow to be delivered to his apartment, where he would fill them with alcohol and rape them. When the tables were turned, however, Beria despised being forced to drink for someone else's pleasure. Still, not only did he drink, but he also made others do so out of servility to Stalin. Khrushchev's fading tapes recount Beria's predicament: "We've got to get drunk," said Beria, "the sooner the better. The sooner we're drunk, the sooner the party will be over. No matter what, he's not going to let us leave sober."[26] Like Beria, everyone tried their best to endure—or, better yet, avoid—Stalin's loathsome drinking bouts.

Not surprisingly, by the late 1940s the constant drinking caught up to Khrushchev, who began having kidney trouble. While Stalin was initially sympathetic to doctors' orders for Nikita to abstain from alcohol, Beria butted in that he too had kidney troubles but that he drank anyway, without a problem. "So I was deprived of my defensive armor (that I couldn't drink because of my bad kidneys): no matter, drink! As long as you're walking around, as long as you're alive, drink!"[27]

Others had different coping strategies. Khrushchev's wingman, Anastas Mikoyan habitually slunk away to steal a quick nap during the nightly revelry—before he too was ratted out by Beria. "Want to be smarter than the rest, don't you?" Stalin loomed: "see that you don't regret it later."[28] Khrushchev told how Mikoyan, along with Beria and Malenkov, even persuaded Kremlin waitresses to replace their wine with juice of the same color, that is, until Stalin's deputy Politburo candidate Aleksandr Shcherbakov exposed them. Khrushchev recalled:

> Stalin was furious that they were trying to deceive him, and he made things hot for Beria, Makenkov, and Mikoyan. All of us were angry with Shcherbakov because we didn't want to drink all of that wine. We drank to get Stalin off our backs, but we wanted to keep it down to the minimum as not to ruin our health and not become drunkards.[29]

Shcherbakov—Stalin's toady drunkard—died from a heart attack two days after the Nazi surrender, May 10, 1945, at the ripe old age of forty-four. While Stalin valorized him, Khrushchev and the rest of the circle "knew that he died from drinking too much in an effort to please Stalin *and not because of any insatiable urge of his own.*"[30] Likewise, Andrei Zhdanov—once thought of as Stalin's heir apparent—died less than three years later at fifty-two, to the end ignoring

STALIN AND HIS POLITBURO COLLEAGUES WALKING THE KREMLIN GROUNDS. 1946. From left, Anastas Mikoyan, Nikita Khrushchev, Joseph Stalin, Georgy Malenkov, Lavrenty Beria, and Vycheslav Molotov. Photo by Samari Gurari.

his doctors' frequent warnings to stop drinking. It was clear to all that this situation was disastrous both for their work and their physical health. "People were literally becoming drunkards, and the more a person became a drunkard, the more pleasure Stalin got from it."[31]

While the drunken Politburo meetings usually began at the dinner table, they rarely ended there. In the warm days of summer, when the northern sun shines well into the evening, the Politburo's dreadful dacha dinners often moved outdoors to take in the fresh air and serenity of the countryside. On such occasions, Khrushchev, along with Soviet major general Aleksandr Poskrebyshev, made a habit of pushing Soviet deputy defense commissar Grigory Kulik into a nearby pond. The bungling Kulik was fair game, since everyone knew that Stalin had long before lost respect for the "always half-drunk bon vivant" whose inept leadership on the Leningrad front in World War II allowed the Nazis to completely encircle Russia's second capital.[32] A bull of a man, the enraged and sopping wet Kulik would chase Khrushchev and Poskrebyshev around the entire estate before they ducked to hide in some nearby bushes. The drunken bootlick Poskrebyshev (by Stalin's daughter's account, also the most prodigious vomiter of the group) was pushed into the pond so frequently that the guards feared the Soviet leadership might drown and quietly had the lake drained. "If anyone tried something like that on me, I'd make mincemeat of them," Beria threatened, while Stalin simply beamed: "You're like little children!" By all accounts, this infantilism delighted Stalin.[33]

Like generations of tsars before him, as the self-styled patriarch of all Russia, "Uncle Joe" cultivated the father figure image. But of course a man only becomes a father when he has children. Just as with his inner circle, alcohol was instrumental not only in keeping Soviet society weak, divided, and off balance, but also reliant on the state, like children to a father.[34]

This, then, was the apprenticeship of Nikita Khrushchev. While he never cultivated the same sort of marionette theater among his own inner circle after succeeding Stalin, life in the viper pit weighed heavily on him until his last days:

> People might say that Khrushchev is washing dirty linen in public. But what can you do? Without washing dirty linen, there would be no clean linen. Clean linen gets its cleanness and whiteness by its contrast with dirty linen. Not only that; the conditions of Stalin's home life were closely interwoven with our work life. Apparently this is something that is almost inevitable when a country is actually being run by one person, and as a result, it's difficult to separate personal circumstances from public affairs.[35]

In the aging recordings of his memoirs, Khrushchev makes an important point: in autocratic governments, the personal and political are inexorably interwoven. It would be one thing if such drunken revelry went on day and night among in the peasants' *kabak* (tavern) or the bars of the urban factory workers, but it is a completely different matter when it happens at the highest ranks of government—and the government of one of the world's true superpowers. Moreover, if this sort of instrumental use of alcohol was an isolated event, then maybe we could be forgiven for dismissing it as some sort of minor, albeit chilling, footnote to world history. However, they sad fact is that Stalin's use of alcohol was not unique among Russian rulers—but was part of a very long and storied history. From the Romanov tsars through the Soviets and even into the post-Soviet period, the use and abuse of alcohol is crucial to understanding the dynamics of autocratic rule in Russia.

Just as Stalin used alcohol to keep his subordinates divided, fearful, confused, and off balance, so too the Soviet leadership continued a longstanding autocratic tradition of utilizing vodka to keep society in check: drunken, divided (atomized), and unable to mount a challenge to its power.[36] The communists, in particular, knew this well. Karl Marx and Friedrich Engels were explicit in condemning drunkenness as a consequence of capitalist oppression. Accordingly, Vladimir Lenin and the generation of revolutionaries that brought Bolshevism to Russia abstained from liquor in order to cast off the shackles of capitalist domination.[37] So it is more than a little ironic that the Soviet dictatorship, on behalf of the proletariat, enslaved the people with vodka even more than their bourgeois predecessors had.

That liquor could be used to keep the people drunk, divided, and passive is only one reason the autocracy came to rely on vodka; another is that the alcohol trade is incredibly lucrative. Distilled spirits like vodka are particularly cheap and easy to produce, so from the government's standpoint, being the bartender to an entire country of alcoholics has the added advantage of generating state revenues on a truly massive scale. Meanwhile, unlike many North Atlantic countries where the tavern was a raucous refuge from the prying eyes of the authorities, in Russia the drink trade was traditionally a government monopoly, so taverns and liquor outlets *were* the eyes and ears of the state. Taken together, preventing rebellion, providing defense, and extracting resources from society are three of the most vital aspects of statecraft. In Russia, however, these traditional functions are given an unusual twist, as none of them can be fully addressed without reference to alcohol.

Vodka has a very long political history, and it is no coincidence that the rapid expansion of the early Muscovite state occurred simultaneously with the harnessing of vodka's unmatched revenue potential. From the feudal and bourgeois eras of Russia's imperial past to its socialist and now post-socialist eras, vodka has been the keystone of state finance. In the early years, with Russian authority spread thin over a vast, yet sparsely populated landmass, the authorities farmed out the vodka tax—selling to the highest bidder the right to a total monopoly on the local liquor trade. In the interest of maximizing this vital and reliable income stream, the government increasingly looked the other way from the systemic corruption created by the system—the same corruption that bedevils Russia today. In fighting the abuses of the tax farmer and looking to secure ever-greater revenue for the treasury, the state attempted all manner of taxation, licensing, and monopoly regimes—using vodka to squeeze every last kopeck out of the weary peasantry. "The ways in which the state has obtained revenue from vodka have changed over the course of time," noted Soviet dissident Mikhail Baitalsky in the 1970s, "but the essential character of the vodka trade has not changed."[38]

Russian leaders—"great" and not-so-great—have come and gone. Through tumultuous, bloody, and revolutionary transformations, the Russian state has been built, destroyed, and rebuilt in different images. But through it all, the one constant has been vodka. At the height of Russia's tsarist empire in the eighteenth and nineteenth centuries, alcohol revenues constituted fully *one-third* of the entire operating budget of the Russian state—enough to cover the full costs of fielding and maintaining the largest standing army in Europe with enough left over to construct the royal family's opulent Winter Palace in St. Petersburg.[39] Even into the late twentieth century—when alcohol revenues were at best an afterthought to state finance in most European states—Soviet Russia was still reaping in the neighborhood of 170 *billion* rubles every year from vodka—over one-quarter of all the income to the Soviet state.[40]

"The financial interests of the state hold the producers of vodka in a grip no less powerful than that which vodka itself has on its consumers," the dissident Baitalsky concluded. "The state has never enjoyed such a fabulous income from the alcohol business as it enjoys today."[41] Indeed, for at least the past five hundred years the enduring strength of the Russian state itself cannot be understood without reference to alcohol.

Likewise, the persistently anemic state of Russian civil society has roots in vodka politics. Throughout the nineteenth and early twentieth centuries, temperance movements throughout Europe and North America provided one nexus of grassroots activism—along with the suffragist and labor movements— that cultivated a vigorous civil society. But not in Russia. Throughout Russian history, whether tsarist, Soviet, or post-Soviet, attempts to stem the flow of alcohol (thereby threatening the central pillar of the state), either through civic temperance organizations or top-down government initiatives on behalf of public health, were halfhearted at best and, at worst, were forcibly scuttled. Here too vodka politics is both cause and consequence—perpetuating the particular dynamics associated with Russian statecraft.

In anticipation of vodka's five-hundredth anniversary, Viktor Erofeyev, the accomplished Russian writer and son of Stalin's translator, penned an article— part lamentation and part tribute—to vodka, what he called "The Russian God." For a Russian, he wrote, the very mention of the word elicits a range of emotions—romanticization for some, consolation for others—but ultimately none are indifferent: "More than by any political system, we are all held hostage by vodka. It menaces and it chastises; it demands sacrifices. It is both a catalyst of procreation and its scourge. It dictates who is born and who dies. In short, vodka is the Russian god." And like any deity, vodka is wrapped in a sense of almost-mystical allure—a "pagan stupor" that calls to the lonely soul with a mix of lust and shame.[42]

Yet the impact of drinking is not borne simply by the individual enticed by vodka's siren song. Drinking is a social activity, and its effects—domestic violence and drunken driving to hooliganism and premature death—are social in nature. And inasmuch as these social impacts require government attention, the entire cycle of alcohol—from production and sales to consumption and effects—is fundamentally a political issue. Indeed, as Erofeyev suggested: "Vodka has taken control of the will and conscience of a substantial sector of the Russian population. If you add up all the time that Russians have devoted to vodka and gather together all the vodka-fueled impulses of the soul—the fantasies, the dreams, the weeklong binges, the family catastrophes, the shamefaced hangovers, the murders, suicides, and fatalities (favorite Russian pastimes include choking on your own vomit and falling out of a window)—it becomes clear that behind the official history of the Russian state there exists another dimension."[43]

This book seeks to uncover that dimension.

This, then, is nothing less than the secret history of the Russian state.

2

Vodka Politics

Just as vodka is the touchstone of Russians' social lives, *vodka politics*—encompassing both policy decisions to manipulate alcohol consumption and the influence of alcohol on political developments—is a central fulcrum of statecraft in Russia. Historically, vodka has been a main exchange point between Russian state and society, and just as vodka is simultaneously the solace of the downtrodden and the reason for their poverty, vodka is both one way the Russian state imposes itself on the individual and how society avoids the state. The might of the tsarist empire was largely built on vodka, and when the empire fell to the flames of revolution, vodka politics was partly to blame. Vodka helped keep the Russian people docile and passive, yet vodka has played a role in every Russian coup d'état and hastened every Russian revolution. Vodka has toasted international peace and helped bring Russia to the brink of war. Vodka has occasionally saved Russia from foreign invasion but, more often, hastened its military's defeat. And just as vodka politics facilitated the demise of the imperial Russian empire, a century later it helped do-in its Soviet successor as well. Vodka is not only the source of immeasurable revenue; it also is used as currency. After the collapse of communism, vodka facilitated the wholesale demodernization of Russian economy and society while unleashing a demographic catastrophe unlike anything before seen in the peacetime history of the world. In so many ways then, vodka politics is key to understanding Russia's tumultuous past, present, and future.

Today, Russia's greatest political challenge isn't terrorism, nuclear confrontation, or navigating the ever-changing global economic landscape—it is confronting the health and demographic crises produced by centuries of autocratic vodka politics. Before modestly rebounding in recent years, average male life expectancy in Russia during the 1990s fell to fifty-nine years—a level on par with Ghana. The primary culprit is unquestionably vodka. More than cardiovascular diseases, more than AIDS, more than tuberculosis or even cancer, study after study has laid the lion's share of the blame on vodka.[1] In announcing his anti-alcohol campaign in 2009, then-president Dmitry Medvedev bemoaned that, on average, Russians drank a "mind-boggling" eighteen liters of pure alcohol per year, roughly twice that of the United States and about ten liters more than what the World Health Organization considers healthy. In practical terms, this means that the normal Russian drinking man downs 180 bottles of vodka per year—or a half bottle per day...and that is the *average*.[2]

In the waning days of Soviet power, Mikhail Gorbachev withdrew military forces from the quagmire of Afghanistan, referring to the decade-long occupation as a "bleeding sore" on the underbelly of the Soviet Union: an unending drain on badly needed resources.[3] Over ten years in Afghanistan, the Soviets lost some fourteen thousand men. By contrast, directly or indirectly, Russia has lost more than four hundred thousand victims to alcohol *every year* since the collapse of communism, combined with life-expectancy figures for the average Russian man cratering at 57.6 years in 1994. Exhaustive health studies have concluded that Russia's vodka epidemic was the cause of *more than half* of all premature deaths in the 1990s. According to the country's foremost health experts, if you are a Russian, there is about a one-in-four chance (23.4%) that your death will have something to do with alcohol. No wonder Vladimir Putin consistently refers to Russia's resulting demographic crisis "the most acute problem facing our country today."[4]

In late 2009 the Kremlin finally took notice, outlining a dramatic plan to halve Russian alcohol consumption within ten years through a combination of alcohol-control measures.[5] In the meantime, health professionals both in Russia and abroad still investigate the wide array of negative implications of the demographic crisis: from a permanent drag on economic growth and the inability to field an effective standing army to social disarray and potential political disintegration.[6] To be sure, the consequences of Russia's addiction to alcohol are real, urgent, and truly a matter of life and death. However, such well-meaning government initiatives are doomed to fail without realizing that Russia's societal alcohol addiction is only a symptom of the Russian *state's* addiction to vodka revenues and the traditional role of vodka as an instrument of Russian statecraft—one that is a hallmark of autocratic rule.[7]

While the source of Russia's societal addiction to alcohol is to be found in autocracy, so too are the reasons for the state's persistent inability to do anything meaningful about it. Over centuries, generations of Russia's autocratic rulers nurtured society's dependence on alcohol. Such practices have become deeply rooted in Russian culture and are not easily—or quickly—altered. Weaning Russia from the bottle will take generations, requiring consistent efforts to change perceptions of the appropriateness of getting drunk, altering destructive drinking habits, and overhauling Russia's ramshackle healthcare infrastructure. However, since autocracies lack the legitimacy that comes from democratic procedures and guarantees of civil liberties, the Kremlin is under consistent pressure to deliver immediate (rather than long-term) results—to bolster its

legitimacy. It should come as no surprise then that generations of Russian autocrats—tsarist, communist, and post-Soviet—have initiated "crash" sobriety initiatives and that each and every one failed within the span of a few months or
years. Unfortunately, no matter how noble their aims, the government's current
efforts to slice Russian alcohol consumption by more than half by 2020 seems
doomed to repeat this failure.[8]

Alcohol And Autocracy In Russia

It may seem strange that a book on the political history of alcohol in Russia
should begin with Stalin and his inner circle. His reign marked neither the beginning of Russia's long and contentious political relationship with vodka nor the
height of Russia's alcoholism. But what we find in Stalin's Soviet Union of the
1920s through the 1950s is the merger of alcohol with the politics of authoritarian high-modernism, which most clearly illustrates the role of alcohol in the
autocratic Russian system.

Stalin inherited the vision of re-creating Russia from his revolutionary predecessor, Vladimir Lenin: the communist leader of the Bolshevik Revolution
in 1917. Not above using terror, Lenin orchestrated Red victory in a brutally
destructive civil war through the 1920s—which effectively dissolved the pre-
revolutionary societal order—only to suffer a series of strokes that led to his premature death in 1924. As Lenin and the Bolsheviks saw it, the revolution was not
simply the replacement of one ruling elite with another but an extreme makeover
of economics, society, and culture according to the communists' "high modern"
design. Forced collectivization and mechanization were to rationalize agriculture in the service of the state; crash industrialization and electrification were
to subjugate the totality of economic activity to the commands of the Soviet
leadership. This physical transformation was to be accompanied by a cultural
one: education, literacy, architecture, and city planning were all marshaled in
the interest of creating a "new man" embodying the social ethics that inspired
George Orwell's *1984*.[9] Ideally, under Lenin and Stalin, the new Soviet culture
was to promote modesty, punctuality, cleanliness, and sobriety—all great depar-
tures from the drunken, unwashed peasant produced by imperial Russia's hated
capitalist past.

Despite his monumental brutality and bloodletting—the relentless purges,
summary executions, gunpoint collectivization, famine, and mass deportations
to forced labor camps—Joseph Stalin surprisingly still has admirers both in
Russia and abroad.[10] Some point to his accomplishments: leading a technologi-
cally inferior military to victory over the Nazi juggernaut in World War II and the
simultaneous transformation of the Soviet Union from a war-ravaged, backward

agrarian society on the periphery of Europe to a global superpower rivaled only by the United States. Whether they know it or not, these apologists are high-lighting Stalin's role in confronting the central problem of statecraft: making a complex society legible to the political leadership.

In his classic work *Seeing Like a State*, Yale political anthropologist James C. Scott explains legibility as the government's arranging the population to sim-plify the classic state functions: taxation, conscription, and preventing rebellion. All states engage in these core functions, and the development of the modern nation-state can be read as a history of extracting of societal resources (taxa-tion and conscription), and neutralizing internal rivals.[11] Accordingly, many of the stories in the following pages highlight how alcohol has been used in the Russian state-building project: to bolster the economic and military resources of the state and to bludgeon internal dissent.

Under Lenin and Stalin, the Bolsheviks unveiled grandiose designs for the Soviet Union. Everything Stalin's regime created—from its military and govern-ment buildings to collective farms and factory towns—was done on a gigantic scale.[12] Yet a constant impediment to such high-modernist plans was the poverty and backwardness of a decimated countryside still recovering from decades of war, famine, and destruction. To ease recovery, Lenin made concessions to the overburdened peasantry in the form of his New Economic Policy (NEP) of the early 1920s, but he steadfastly refused to concede to alcohol and its corrupting influence on the new Soviet man. When confronted with the question of repeal-ing the nationwide prohibition that had been in force since the last Romanov tsar, Nicholas II, decreed it as a wartime measure in 1914, Lenin refused, claim-ing that despite the badly needed revenues it would generate, reviving the vodka monopoly would lead Russia "back to capitalism rather than forward to communism."[13]

As the economy slowly recovered under NEP, illegal distillation of home-brewed vodka—or *samogon*—flourished, as did drunkenness, assaults, absen-teeism in Soviet factories, and alcoholism within the communist party itself. Not only was such inebriety inconsistent with the vision of the new Soviet man, but the loss of billions of pounds of grain to illegal home distillation was unaccept-able economic leakage—especially for a leadership that demanded iron disci-pline if they ever hoped to repel the imperialist forces of global capitalism that were unrelentingly scheming to snuff out their great communist experiment.[14] While in 1923 Leon Trotsky—the firebrand founder of the Red Army—reso-lutely declared that there would be no concessions to alcohol, behind the scenes Trotsky's Politburo nemesis Stalin was hatching plans to do just that. Just as Stalin fully consolidated his might as the Soviet Union's unquestioned ruler, in 1925 he ended Lenin's "noble experiment" with prohibition and reinstated the traditional vodka monopoly in the name of state finance. Perhaps more than any other move, Stalin's sacrificing the "new Soviet man" to the economic interests of the state showed just how little difference there was between the proletarian Soviet autocracy and their bourgeois tsarist predecessors. The basic building blocks of statecraft transcend even the most revolutionary political upheavals, and in Russia, vodka politics is one of them.

Vodka Statecraft

All countries—democracies and dictatorships alike—extract resources from society, and most have utilized alcohol in that capacity. The foundation of the modern American state, for example, was built on taxes and tariffs on liquor. Indeed, immediately after passing the Bill of Rights, the very first item of business for America's founding fathers was raising alcohol revenues.[15] What makes Russian vodka politics different from the politics of alcohol in the United States or elsewhere in Europe is the longstanding legacy of autocratic government.

"In European culture," James Scott suggests, "the alehouse, the pub, the tavern, the inn, the cabaret, the beer cellar, the gin mill were seen by secular authorities and by the church as places of subversion. Here subordinate classes met offstage and off-duty in an atmosphere of freedom encouraged by alcohol."[16] Indeed, the American Revolution was itself born in dank taverns of England's thirteen colonies—away from the prying eyes of the British authorities. In the autocratic Russian context, however, the entire alcohol trade was controlled by the state, from production to sale in the local *kabak*, or "tsar's tavern," where even the tavern-keeper kissed the Orthodox cross to swear allegiance to the tsar.[17] As a consequence, not only were the lucrative alcohol revenues siphoned off to the benefit of the state rather than entrepreneurs, but also Russians were deprived of that space for association and potential dissent against the ruling order. Under the Soviets, this dynamic was compounded by a paternalistic Communist Party leadership that used the excessive drinking of functionaries and rank-and-file party members as grounds for public castigation and outright purges.[18] Here too, alcohol became another of the state's weapons over the individual. In short, while the general contours of statecraft are similar across countries, the particular manifestations in terms of Russian vodka politics are numerous, including not only generating revenue but also stymieing dissent and promoting autocracy.

Returning to his *Seeing Like a State*, Scott tries to understand why well-intended schemes to improve the human condition tend to go horribly awry. While he points the blame at statecraft and high-modernist ideology, that is only half of the equation: such human tragedies also require a determined authoritarian state and an incapacitated civil society, both of which are consistent hallmarks of Russia's storied history.[19] From Niccolò Machiavelli to Michel

Foucault, political philosophers have enumerated the instruments states have at their disposal to influence society.[20] And while democratic systems are considered more legitimate and hence less reliant on coercion to prevent rebellion, autocrats must utilize other mechanisms to keep society prostrate, off-balance, and unable to mount a challenge to power. I suggest that, in Russia, the process of autocratic state building atop a traditional spirit-drinking culture (as opposed to such lighter drinks as wine or beer) has created the particular dynamics—and tragedies—associated with vodka politics.

Although constantly overlooked or dismissed by scholars, vodka is undoubtedly key to understanding the political history of Russia from its origins in early Muscovy right through the present day. Accordingly, this book chronicles the long and often contentious relationship between the Russian people and their government over the bottle and the common good. Virtually every Russian leader has confronted the opportunities and challenges of vodka, and virtually ever major event of historical importance has been tinged with alcohol in some way. Having already peered into Stalin's inner circle, we'll continue to look at liquor's position in high politics, from the tsarist courts of Ivan the Terrible, Peter the Great, and Nicholas II straight through to Boris Yeltsin in the post-Soviet period (chapters 3, 4, 12, 17, and 19). But this book is more than just a political biography of the bottle—we'll explore the highly charged mystery of vodka's origins, why it came to occupy such a central place in Russian politics and society, and how vodka is inexorably tied to that other ubiquitous Russian malady, corruption (chapters 6, 8, and 15). To the degree that vodka became an instrument of state domination, I'll suggest how the liquor issue became a rallying point of organized resistance: from temperate peasants, revolutionaries, and Russia's celebrated writers of the nineteenth century through the Soviet dissident movement a century later (chapters 9, 10, 14, 16, and 17). I'll show how alcohol contributed to defeat in Russia's most infamous wars and may well have even started one (chapter 11). I'll examine vodka's catalyzing role in Russia's long history of coups d'état, from Catherine II's overthrow of her husband Peter III in 1762 through the failed hardline putsch that sought to ouster Mikhail Gorbachev in 1991 (chapters 5 and 19). I'll argue that vodka politics—namely, the misguided attempt to institute drastic "dry laws"—hastened the demise of both the mighty Russian empire and its Soviet successor (chapters 13, 17, and 18). Bringing the book into the present day, I'll untangle the legacy of Russia's autocratic vodka politics, which, when combined with the economic crisis of the post-communist transition of the 1990s, produced a wholesale demodernization of Russia and demographic catastrophe categorically unlike anything seen before in world history. After considering the enormous challenges that depopulation and alcoholization present for the Kremlin, I will consider how presidents Vladimir Putin and Dmitry Medvedev have tried to confront the "liquor question," and what—if anything—can and should be done, both now and in the future (chapters 20–24). It is my hope that this investigation will convince readers of the importance of vodka to understanding not only Russian culture but its history and politics as well.

Both in Russia and abroad, the heroic/tragic weakness for vodka is widely thought to be the defining cultural characteristic of Russians—a natural ethnic trait going down almost to a genetic level. But quaffing potent vodka is just about as natural as downing its distilled cousins kerosene or rubbing alcohol. Since ancient times, the Slavs of the forest, taiga, and steppe drank fermented ales, meads, and *kvas*. The far more potent distilled vodka arrived much later, as the yoke of the modern autocratic state. The one consistency that has united Russia's autocrats of the past five centuries—be they political reactionaries, radicals, or anything in-between—has been vodka politics. Vodka provided the financial foundation for the glorious expansion of the Russian empire and the might of its Soviet successor while also keeping political opponents and the Russian masses befuddled, divided, and docile. And when these political systems collapsed, vodka was there to make things worse—unimaginably worse.

Understanding the enduring link between autocracy and alcohol is crucial to confronting the legacies of both. Russia's storied addiction to vodka is not simply a social or cultural disorder; it is also a symptom of a deeper sickness—autocracy. It follows, then, that even in the post-Soviet period the repeated and unquestionably well-intentioned government efforts to wean Russians from the bottle will never fully succeed until the underlying illness—the autocratic system itself—is cured.

Vodka Domination, Vodka Resistance

Vodka politics is a pervasive feature of Russian autocracy—one that firmly embeds the state into culture, society, and private life. In normal settings alcohol is a respite: a temporary escape from the harshness of reality. Yet as a central pillar in Russian statecraft, apathy and disengagement further consolidate the power of autocracy. But if one cannot hide from state domination even in the bottle, what can can one do? One path would be to follow Lenin and the early Bolsheviks, who understood vodka as the means of domination of the capitalist class and abstained from all alcohol consumption in order to maintain their clarity of vision and purpose. The more brazen option is to speak truth to power by directly unmasking the dynamics of vodka politics for all to see.

Here again, the most telling examples come from the Stalinist era of totalitarian domination. While the cold wind howled beyond the Kremlin walls during Russia's long winter months, the Politburo's drunken party often retreated to the film room to screen the latest movies in Stalin's ever-growing personal collection of Russian and foreign movies—either imported for gold or captured as the spoils of war—usually until the dawn of the next day.[21] Boasting such cinematographic pioneers as Vsevolod Pudovkin, Grigory Aleksandrov, and Sergei Eisenstein, early Soviet films rivaled their Hollywood counterparts, and Stalin eagerly watched them all.[22] Stalin was the Soviet Union's top film critic and (with his inebriated entourage) the official censor for the entire domestic film industry. In Russia, acting and directing careers—and lives—were made or broken during Stalin's late-night screening room.

Unquestionably, Russia's greatest contribution to cinema was the master director Sergei Eisenstein. Even in today's Hollywood his litany of classic films, including *The Battleship Potemkin, Alexander Nevsky,* and *October* has solidified Eisenstein's place as one of the most influential directors in cinematic history.[23] His pioneering work with camera angles, montage, and film editing have inspired generations of filmmakers worldwide; while even Eisenstein's eccentric hairdo was emulated by David Lynch for the lead character in *Eraserhead.*[24]

In the darkest days of Russia's mortal struggle with Hitler, the world-renowned filmmaker unveiled his masterpiece *Ivan the Terrible,* which was commissioned by Stalin himself.[25] The historical epic chronicled the rise of the sixteenth-century tsar Ivan IV, who vowed to unite, strengthen, and defend Russia against its enemies, both from without and within. On screen, Ivan Grozny ("the Terrible") is a ruthless leader who wins the support of his Russian subjects by felling the khanate of Kazan and subduing the Polish and Livonian invaders from the west, in an obvious parallel to the Nazis. The movie was jingoistic propaganda: calling for a strong leader, national sacrifice, and defense of the motherland amid the horrors of World War II. Since the safest form of political discourse in any autocracy is to flatter the rulers,[26] Eisenstein did just that, allowing his commentary on the tragedy of autocracy to become perverted into an apology for it. Stalin loved the film, admitting that he saw much of himself in Ivan. Bold and decisive, a "great and wise ruler" with "strong will and character," Ivan the Terrible was presented as Stalin's quintessential Russian leader. It ate Eisenstein up inside that his artistic vision had been hijacked to serve the interests of the state. Essentially appointed Stalin's cinematic interpreter, the recalcitrant Eisenstein even won the Stalin Prize, first class, the country's highest award for cultural achievement— the Soviet version of the Oscar. At the awards ceremony, Eisenstein collapsed from a mild heart attack, which only strengthened his premonitions that he would die an early death at the age of fifty.[27]

Even before confronting his own mortality, the headstrong Eisenstein had long grappled with resisting the state's all-encompassing domination. At the height of Stalin's totalitarian terror, outright criticism would be professional suicide, yet he could not betray his principles. In 1943 Eisenstein decided to work himself to death, thereby choosing the only form of suicide that would preserve his creative vision.[28] While *Ivan the Terrible* portrayed the triumph of tyranny, the already planned sequel would embody its tragedy. Eisenstein was fearless and passionate in using his cinematic vision to speak truth to power, and he would do so by unmasking Stalin's brand of vodka politics.

By the end of World War II Eisenstein had completed his sequel, *Ivan the Terrible Part II: The Boyars' Plot*, in which a group of gentry boyars—the tsar's high-ranking inner circle of *oprichniki*—scheme to dethrone the tsar. The paranoid Ivan Grozny uncovers this plot by holding a drunken banquet where the intoxicated Vladimir Staritsky—Ivan's cousin and primary contender to the throne—informs the ruthless tsar of the boyars' plot to kill him, in the process sealing his own fate as well as that of the conspirators.

Serving as artistic leader of the most acclaimed Russian film studio, Mosfilm, fellow director Mikhail Romm was honored to be part of the group who viewed a sneak preview of the film as it neared completion. And it was Romm who was charged with breaking the Politburo's devastating reviews to Eisenstein:

> He asked us, "What's the matter? What's the problem? What do you mean? Tell me straight." But no-one dared to say directly that in Ivan Grozny could be felt a sharp reference to Stalin, in Malyuta Skuratov [the lickspittle head of Ivan's secret police] a reference to Beria, in the *oprichniki* a reference to his henchmen. And there was much more that we felt but couldn't say.
>
> But in Eisenstein's boldness, in the gleam in his eyes, in his defiant sceptical [*sic*] smile, we felt that he was acting consciously, that he had decided to go for broke.
>
> This was awful.[29]

Russia's most famous director had indeed gone for broke by using his cinematographic skills to highlight the tragedy of Russian tyranny, both past and present. Among themselves, other Soviet directors were understandably uneasy. In response to suggestions that *The Boyar's Plot* was a masterpiece and would have been a hit in the West, dramatist Vsevolod Vishnevsky sniped: "It would be 'Secrets of the Kremlin'" on show for the world to see.

"Either Eisenstein is naive, or—I don't know," added Ukrainian screenwriter and director Aleksandr Dovzhenko, "But such a film about such a Russia, the Kremlin—could serve as fantastic agitation against us."[30] To depict the tragedy of Russia's autocratic vodka politics was strictly taboo.

But Eisenstein did not back down. "'Taboo' is falsehood," he declared, "if you do something *with your heart's blood* you can say *everything*." Eisenstein even planned to disseminate his artistic condemnation of autocracy on the widest scale possible. "We shall have to have a lot of screenings—historians, writers, artists—and mass screenings, with thousands of people watching the film simultaneously, so that they will understand it better."[31] But before that could happen, it would have to first pass muster with Joseph Stalin himself.

Late on the night of March 2, 1946, Eisenstein's movie was shown to the Politburo—in their usual condition. At the end of the viewing, Stalin flew into a mad rage. "This is not a film, but some kind of nightmare!" His hangman Lavrenty Beria despised Eisenstein's masterpiece as "a bad detective story."[32] Stalin even berated the projectionist Ivan Bolshakov—who also happened to be chairman of the Committee for Cinematographic Affairs—using the *Boyars' Plot* to lash out at the entire Soviet film industry: "During the War we didn't have the time, but now we'll lick you into shape!"[33]

Did the depiction hit too close to home? Did Stalin object to the portrayal of Ivan's sadistic cruelty and inhumane repression for all to see? No—Stalin thought that Ivan's "ruthlessness" was fine, so long as the reasons for his cruelty were clear. The official resolution of the Central Committee of the Communist Party condemned the depiction of Ivan "as weak in character and lacking in

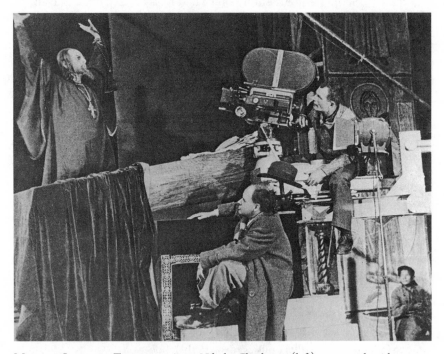

MAKING *IVAN THE TERRIBLE*. Actor Nikolai Cherkasov (left) portrays the title character. Sergei Eisenstein (seated, center) directs, as cameraman Eduard Tisse films. January 3, 1945. Source: RIA-Novosti/Mikhail Ozersky

willpower, something on the lines of Hamlet"—the character and tragedy of murder and high politics that Stalin famously loathed.[34] With this, the film was banned outright and Stalin was forced to rescind his earlier accolades for Eisenstein—something of a moral victory for Eisenstein the artist.

Along with other writers and critics, Romm concluded that the film was scrapped precisely due to the drunken feast scene, where the dictator is depicted as formidable (*grozen*) and cunning (*khiter*) in using alcohol to keep his entourage off guard. It was an attack on Stalin's cult of personality and a direct implication of Stalin's vodka politics. According to Romm, the dreadful "references to the contemporary situation could be sensed throughout the film, in the subtext of almost every episode."[35]

When informed of Stalin's condemnation of his film—a threat to both his life and livelihood—Eisenstein was surprisingly calm. He knew what the response would be. And while he was forced to ritualistically admit publicly that he (in the words of the Central Committee's official decree) "displayed ignorance in his depiction of historical facts," in private he decided to take the fight to Stalin. The great director requested—and received—a personal meeting with the great dictator.

At 11 p.m. on February 24, 1947, Eisenstein and Nikolai Cherkasov—the actor who portrayed Ivan the Terrible on screen—arrived at the Kremlin for a late-night meeting with Joseph Stalin, Vyacheslav Molotov, and Stalin's alcoholic commissar for ideology and culture, Andrei Zhdanov. The evening lasted well into the morning. The conversation was decidedly one-sided, with Stalin and his sycophants doling out equal parts tongue-lashing and history lecture. The usually diplomatic Eisenstein was unrepentant, much to the displeasure of Stalin. The following day he blithely remarked to friends: "Went to see Stalin yesterday. We didn't like one another."[36]

Throughout the standoff, the master filmmaker had unparalleled access to the very viper's nest he portrayed on screen. He took copious notes throughout the encounter. Eisenstein thought the outcome of the meeting was generally favorable: he was given a few years' time to reflect and prepare changes to *Part II* in order to appease Stalin, while this firsthand encounter only strengthened Eisenstein's resolve that his portrayal be accurate. "We'll hardly change a thing," he later told his co-workers. "It was an interesting meeting. I'll tell you some time ... "[37]

Perhaps Eisenstein was emboldened by his prophecy of an early death, which he envisaged for 1948—the same year he was to complete *Part II*. "What re-shooting?" Eisenstein asked his acquaintances. "Don't you realise that I'd die at the first shot? I can't even think of *Ivan* without feeling a pain in my heart."[38] Indeed, Eisenstein died before making any changes to *Part II*: victim of a second heart attack while defiantly filming *Ivan the Terrible, Part III* in 1948—as he predicted—at the age of fifty.[39]

Who Outdrinks Whom?

Stalin died of an agonizing brain hemorrhage in 1953, five years after Eisenstein's passing. Beria was arrested soon thereafter and charged with treason and terrorism. The trial allegations of Beria's rapes and drunken sexual exploits only added to his damnation, culminating in his summary execution—the parting shot that signaled the end of Stalinist terror.[40] It was left to the portly Nikita Khrushchev to confront Stalin's legacies. The personality cult, purges, forced collectivization, famines, and horror of the Stalin era were replaced by reforms and a thawing of Soviet society, culture, economy, and foreign affairs.

Five years after the curtain fell on Stalin, Beria, and Soviet totalitarianism, the curtain finally rose on *Ivan the Terrible, Part II*. Shown publicly for the first time in 1958, on the ten-year anniversary of Eisenstein's death, it met with national and international acclaim. His portrait of the patriotic emperor turned paranoid fratricidal murderer was dusted off and "rehabilitated"—much like Eisenstein's legacy itself—as an implication of the tragedy of tyranny, both past and present.[41] Confronting Stalin's brand of vodka politics became part of the nationwide catharsis of de-Stalinization under the peasant turned premier Nikita Khrushchev.

Though no longer steeped in terror, the alcoholic Kremlin traditions continued even after Stalin. During his decade in power, Khrushchev never passed up an opportunity to celebrate with a drink. Chinese premier Zhao Enlai even confided that, on occasion, "Khrushchev got me drunk," apparently to get him to divulge truths and enhance the Soviet bargaining position.[42]

By the 1970s even the Americans were preparing to confront vodka as part of what they saw as high-level Soviet negotiating strategy. When President Richard Nixon and Henry Kissinger visited Moscow in 1972 to finalize the Anti-Ballistic Missile Treaty, Leonid Brezhnev (whose own notorious alcoholism was born of his Stalin-era party upbringing) pushed for even greater concessions "while Kissinger was exhausted and Nixon drunk." In another instance, the American president joked that Brezhnev was trying to get his advisors inebriated during top-level arms control negotiations. Brezhnev apparently "played along" with this "gag" by constantly pouring ever-more vodka into Kissinger's glass.[43]

"The highest diplomacy does not consist of trying to drown differences in champagne and vodka toasts at feel-good summits," protested the straight-laced Soviet ambassador to the United States Anatoly Dobrynin, "but in finding ways to disagree without doing profound damage to an important strategic relationship." Apparently the sodden Brezhnev failed in this regard.[44]

Dobrynin described how the traditional high-level drinking backfired when visiting Nixon's California compound the following year. During a chance, late-night encounter in a hallway, the longtime Soviet ambassador was forced into "the most bizarre situation in all my years of diplomacy." Dobrynin became the uneasy translator for the American president as a whiskey-drunk Brezhnev grumbled about his nagging Politburo comrades before Dobrynin and Nixon were forced to carry the drunken general secretary to his bed.

"Anatoly, did I talk too much yesterday?" Brezhnev later asked.

Yes, he did, but Dobrynin reassured him that not everything was translated.

"Well done," Brezhnev replied. "Damn that whiskey, I am not used to it. I did not know I could not hold that much."[45]

Such anecdotes are fun to tell, but there are good reasons to do so beyond providing a voyeuristic glimpse into high-level diplomacy. For one, tensions between the steady Dobrynin and the sloshed Brezhnev foreshadow the surprisingly salient wet/dry divisions within both the Soviet leadership and Russian society. Second, theses anecdotes suggest how alcohol becomes intertwined with political power at the highest levels. Vladimir Lenin artfully summarized the central question of politics as *kto kovo?* Literally meaning "who whom?" it is often translated as "who wins out over whom?" or "who does-in whom?" When it comes to diplomacy, it would be more apt to ask "who outdrinks whom?" Finally, they give us greater insights into Soviet politics in the postwar era, when Russia's traditionally high levels of alcohol consumption soared to heights never before seen in Russia (or elsewhere)—the unshakable legacy of Stalin's reimposition of traditional autocratic statecraft.[46]

Whether in the Soviet Union of old or the Russian Federation of today, the more time you spend in Russia, the more you are struck by how important vodka is to Russian society and culture. Likewise, the more you look, the more you find vodka politics as a pervasive element of Russia's long and storied history. It is time to set aside well-worn cliches about Russia's alcoholism to address the reasons for it. Alcohol abuse is not hard-wired into the genetic code of Russians, but like the elites in Stalin's inner circle, Russians are victims of a system that has long cultivated—and to a staggering degree benefited from—social drunkenness. If Russia is a country of alcoholics, it's because the Russian autocratic state helped make it that way.

Only by unmasking the legacies of Russia's autocratic vodka politics can the primary contributors to a variety of Russian social, political, and economic problems be understood and confronted. This book lays bare the dynamics of vodka politics and the contentious relationship between the Russian state and society over health, revenue, and the common good throughout the imperial, Soviet, and even post-Soviet past with an eye toward a more prosperous future.

3

Cruel Liquor: Ivan the Terrible and Alcohol in the Muscovite Court

Sergei Eisenstein was a master of the historical epic. Virtually all of his films—from *The Battleship Potemkin* and *October* to *Alexander Nevsky* and his would-be *Ivan the Terrible* trilogy—depicted key events and leaders from the broad sweep of Russian history. Fortunately for storytellers such as Eisenstein, Russia's past is littered with both great triumphs and unspeakable tragedies; heroes and villains; eclectic personalities and majestic leaders. Perhaps had he lived beyond age fifty, Eisenstein would have chronicled not only Ivan the Terrible but also other so-called great leaders of Russia's past—such as Peter the Great and Catherine the Great—all the while highlighting the pervasiveness of alcohol in courtly intrigues throughout imperial Russia and the ubiquity of vodka politics as the historical basis of Russian statecraft.

Every tsar and tsarina worth his and her salt found alcohol both a convenient and necessary tool to use in strengthening the Russian state as it grew from an isolated principality to an expansive, multiethnic, multicultural, and multi-continental empire. Peter the Great not only forcibly dragged Russia out of the Middle Ages and into modern Europe; he also perfected the art of vodka politics within his court. Catherine the Great made Russia a major European power and a center of culture, but even she owed her position to vodka politics. Yet well before Russia became the global power it is today, it was a remote kingdom on the banks of the river Moscow. And while the growth of Romanov power was hardly smooth and uniform, vodka politics was there from the beginning.

Long before Ivan the Terrible was crowned tsar in 1547, before Martin Luther nailed his Ninety-Five Theses to the Wittenberg church doors in 1517, and even before Christopher Columbus set out to find new passages to the East Indies in 1492, the princes of Moscow had begun conquering neighboring principalities, consolidating their dominions through effective administrative institutions. The territory of Muscovy stretched from the Volga flatlands east to the Ural Mountains and north to the Arctic. In the west they did battle with the Lithuanians. In the south they rebelled against the Golden Horde, driving back the Asiatic Mongol invaders who had for centuries demanded tribute and subservience from the Slavs. Muscovy grew into a formidable power, as its grand princes adopted the symbolic Byzantine double-headed eagle—one looking east toward Asia, the other westward over Europe—simultaneously claiming the imperial heritage of Rome.[1]

The early Russian state had the economic resources to back up such audacious strategic and symbolic moves. The fifteenth century was a boom time for the elites of Moscow. The ancient wooden and limestone walls of the city's central fortress—or Kremlin (*kreml'*)—were replaced with solid brick, protecting gleaming new cathedrals and imperial palaces crafted by the finest Renaissance architects. Contrasted against the wrenching poverty of the peasants outside, the Kremlin court was opulent—characterized by a "barbaric grandeur" that mystified foreign visitors unfamiliar with Orthodox rituals.[2]

In the early sixteenth century the Austro-Hungarian baron Sigismund von Herberstein twice resided in the Kremlin palaces as the envoy from the Holy Roman Empire. Published in 1557, his extensive writings give us the earliest foreign account of the Russian court under the last Muscovite grand prince— Vasily III. Upon the Austrian's arrival, von Herberstein was given the traditional Russian invitation: "thou wilt eat bread [*khleb*] and salt [*sol'*] with us." The ceremonial breaking of bread and salt has deep roots in the traditional Russian lexicon, with *khlebosolny* being the Russian word for hospitality.[3]

The Kremlin guard led von Herberstein through torch-lit halls of cut stone adorned with magnificent tapestries to a banquet hall where he found the grand prince sitting on a magnificent throne, flanked by ranks of nobles: some in high fur caps, kaftans, or clad in white satin, each with a silver hatchet by his side. In the center of the hall stood a feast of magnificent proportions upon plates of purest gold, prepared by servers in thick robes embroidered with pearls and gems. Yet before the feast of roast swan, malmsey, and Greek wines began, the murmur in the hall hushed as Grand Prince Vasily raised his glass and spoke in a booming voice: "Thou art come from a great sovereign to a great sovereign; thou hast made a long journey. After receiving our favor and seeing the lustre of our eyes, it shall be well with thee. Drink and drink well, and eat well to thy hearty content, and then take thy rest that thou mayest at length return to thy master."[4]

Unsure of their new surroundings and unaccustomed to Byzantine cultural practices, the delegates from the royal house of Habsburg consummated the toast but were confused that the drink in their cups was not the traditional fermented beverages of Europe: not wine (*vino*), which the Russians learned from the Greeks of the Eastern Empire before the fall of Constantinople; not Scandinavian mead (*myod*) made from fermented honey, which came to Moscow by way of Novgorod and the Baltic trade in the tenth century; not European beers (*pivo*) and ales that had become the main alcoholic fare of Muscovy. Nor was the drink quintessentially Russian *kvas*, a beverage fermented from rye bread that was drunk even among Russia's ancient ancestors, the Sclavonians, almost since the time of Christ in the first century.[5]

Instead, their chalices were brimming with *aqua vitae*—water of life—distilled spirits.[6] Not quite the contemporary *vodka*—"little water" in Russian—consumed today, this stronger distilled alcohol, known to the Muscovite court as early as the fifteenth century, was plied by royal alchemists as a medicinal elixir. The inebriating qualities of this new drink were not lost on the Russian leaders of that day.

Once acclimated to the customs, opulence, and extravagance of the Muscovite court, foreign observers like von Herberstein quickly clued into the importance of liquor to palace intrigues. Indeed, even one of the first manuscript dictionaries of Russian compiled in the sixteenth century included the transposed English phrase *Gimi drenki okovitin*, or, "give me drink aqua vitae." Since very few native accounts of medieval Russia are available, such foreigners' accounts have proven invaluable to understanding early Russian history in general and the role of alcohol in particular.[7]

Von Herberstein's firsthand chronicles of the gluttonous and inebriated all-night banquets of the Muscovite court in the 1550s serve as distant echoes to the liquor surprise that awaited later foreign visitors von Ribbentrop, Churchill, de Gaulle, and Milovan Djilas to Stalin's court. Putting quill to parchment by candlelight, von Herberstein recounted how

> making people tipsy is here an honour and sign of esteem; the man who is not put under the table holds himself ill respected. The Muscovites are indeed masters at talking to others and persuading them to drink. If all else fails one other stands up and proposes the health of the Grand-duke, upon which all present must not fail to drink and drain the cup. After this they try to provoke toasts to the health of the Emperor and others. There is much ceremony about this drinking. The man proposing the toast stands in the middle of the room, his head bared, states what he desires for the Grand-duke or other lord—happiness, victory, health—and wishes that as much blood may remain in the veins of his enemies as drink in his cup. When he has emptied it he reverses the cup upon his head and wishes the lord good health. Or he will take upon a prominent position, have several cups filled, and distribute them with the motive for the toast. Then each goes into the middle of the room, drains his cup and claps it on his head.[8]

Von Herberstein found this practice just as bizarre as the generations of foreign dignitaries who followed did. Like subsequent visitors, von Herberstein too confessed his distaste for such drunken excess and sought any means to extricate himself from the uncomfortable customs, mostly "by pretending to be drunk or saying I was too sleepy to go on and had had my fill."[9]

While von Herberstein marveled at the opulence and omnipotence of his host Vasily III, the grand duke's hold on power was not as absolute as his stature implied. While the royal family was the political and spiritual core of Muscovy, other princely boyar families wielded tremendous economic and military power from their massive estates, while the Orthodox Church held such sway that it was often exempted from state regulations. With such internal rivalries, the grand prince depended as much on his courtly elites as they did on him. The Russian state of the late Middle Ages was at once both powerful and fragile—and Vasily knew it. During the last years of his reign, so as to dilute the opposition of competing nobles who had much to gain if one of Vasily's two brothers instead wrested the throne, the grand duke bestowed rank on a large number of boyars loyal to him and his infant sons.[10]

In the cold December of 1533, Vasily succumbed to a prolonged illness, leaving the grandeur and might of imperial Muscovy in the hands of his three-year-old son, Ivan. Intrigue abounded as competing clans grappled for power in an era of collective "boyar rule." Not above blackmail, torture, and murder, the Shuiskys, Glinskys, Belskys, Staritskys, and even the church engaged in a cutthroat battle for power and influence over the infant Ivan and his regency. Whenever one clan leader had his tongue cut out or was devoured alive by wild dogs, there was always a brother, uncle, son, or nephew to vow revenge on his behalf. There was no way to cut off all heads at the same time.[11]

"Our boyars governed the country as they pleased, for no one opposed their power," Ivan later recalled. Raised fatherless, "I adopted the devious ways of the people around me; I learned to be crafty like them."[12]

So it should come as little surprise that the boy who became Ivan "the Terrible" was devoid of a moral compass. At a time when political decisions were being made in his stead by constantly feuding elites, the child-prince gleefully tortured birds and tossed puppies from the high palace walls to be smashed on the courtyard pavement below.[13]

Ivan's bloodlust grew as a teen, as he hunted bears and wolves with an entourage of boyar teens whose families were no less affluent or respected than his. Having killed, feasted, and drunken to excess, the hunting party often set their sights on a different game: the local peasants. With heads full of drink, the carnivorous teens set upon unsuspecting villages: beating the peasant men and raping their daughters. Young Ivan reveled in the orgies of violence and debauchery—the wine, sweat, and blood—as much as his bestial pals, but Ivan never lost sense of his royal dignity as God's appointed servant on earth. "When he became drunk, when he fornicated, it was God who was getting drunk and fornicating, through him."[14]

In 1547 Ivan turned sixteen and was officially crowned, but instead of taking the traditional title of grand prince of Moscow he became the first to choose the title *tsar*—emperor of all Russia.[15] Knowing his vicious past, the court certainly heaved a collective sigh of relief when the young tsar announced he was giving up his drunken orgies in order to wed his beloved Anastasia—daughter of a lesser noble family. Within a few years, however, Anastasia mysteriously fell ill and perished. As Eisenstein portrays in his Stalin Prize–winning *Ivan the Terrible*, the tsar suspected a palace plot to poison his bride, which only deepened his paranoia. And much like Stalin's reaction to the sudden death of his own wife, the brooding tsar abandoned himself to loneliness, depression, and drunkenness. The fornication, sodomy, and unthinkable torture soon returned. Eliciting vengeance for both the suspect boyar class and whatever temperamental Almighty dared to smite the all-powerful tsar, Anastasia's death unleashed all of the base instincts of Ivan's childhood.[16]

While his conquering armies expanded the borders of the Russian state, the increasingly powerful and paranoid Ivan took pleasure in drunken debauchery, quiet prayer, and the slow and methodical torture of his would-be rivals at court. "The spurts of blood, the cracking of bones, the screams and rattles of drooling mouths—this rough cookery smelling of pus, excrement, sweat, and burnt flesh was pleasing to his nostrils," wrote popular French historian Henri Troyat. "He took such joy in the bloodbath that he had no doubt, in these moments of horror and ecstasy, that the Lord was at his side.... To him, prayer and torture were but two aspects of piety."[17]

Leading the heroic charge to topple the Khanate of Kazan on the Volga and the rebels of Udmurtia in the east, Ivan's confidant Prince Andrei Mikhailovich Kurbsky did the most to expand Russia's borders—and was wise enough to avoid being slowly dismembered himself for the tsar's sadistic pleasure. After leading Ivan's army to victory over the Livonians at Dorpat (in present-day Estonia), Ivan's general defected—fleeing to the nearby Kingdom of Poland. From the safety of his Polish asylum, Russia's first political refugee not only addressed vitriolic letters directly to the tsar, but in 1573 he also penned Russia's first historical monograph, the scathing *History of the Grand Prince of Moscow*.[18] Just as Nikita Khrushchev gave us an insider's view into the dictator's drunken Kremlin banquets, Kurbsky did the same, only four hundred years earlier:

> They begin with frequent feasts and drunkenness, from which all kinds of impurities sprang. And what did they add to this? Great beakers, pledged, in truth, to the devil, and beakers which were filled with extremely heady drink... and if they did not drink themselves into a

stupor, or rather a frenzy, then they added a second and a third beaker; and those who had no wish to drink or to commit such transgressions they adjured with great rebuke, while they shouted at the tsar: "Behold, this one here, and this one (naming him) does not wish to be joyful at your feast, as though he condemns and mocks you and us as drunkards, hypocritically pretending to be righteous!"[19]

Just as Khrushchev recounted how inebriety was forced upon the Soviet Politburo, so too was it forced on the court of Ivan the Terrible. "And with still more devilish words than these," Kurbsky continued, "they abused many men who were sober and moderate in their good way of life and habits, and they put them to shame, pouring those accursed beakers on them, with which they did not wish—or were quite unable—to become drunk, and they threatened them with death and various tortures, in the same way as they destroyed many people a little later for this reason."[20] The parallels with Khrushchev's descriptions of Soviet commissars transforming into toady drunkards could not be more clear.

Just as Stalin's henchmen were pumped full of alcohol for the leader's pleasure only to be borne home by their bodyguards, so too did guests at Ivan's table. "The obligation to do honor to all the cups sent by the Czar induced in some a stupor bordering on coma," says Troyat. "In their stomachs mead was mixed with Rhine wines, French wines, Malmsey, *kvas*, and vodka. And when they rose from the table to go home, it was not unusual for Ivan to send to their residences, as a token of friendship, more alcohol and food to be downed on the spot, in front of the officers who had brought it."[21] Not only did both tyrants appreciate liquor's effectiveness in maintaining control over their inebriated courtiers, but both were also wary of alcohol being used against them—regularly forcing subordinates to quaff what was in the leader's cup as a test for poison.[22]

Like the squeamish objections of Khrushchev, Beria, Mikoyan, and Stalin's other commissars, many of Ivan's boyars also resisted the drunken escapades. Those who refused were denounced—either secretly or openly—as foes of the tsar.[23] Consider Ivan's chancellor, Prince Mikhaylo Repnin, who once muttered that Ivan's drunkenness was unbefitting for God's chosen leader of Russia. Quietly stewing, the great tsar took note. The following Sunday during church vespers, Ivan's guards found Repnin deep in solemn prayer and unceremoniously hacked him to death beside the altar.[24]

Unlike Stalin's ominously threatening toasts, Ivan often dealt with his detractors more swiftly and directly. On another occasion, tired of being forced to drink round after round, one imperial boyar, Mochan Mitkov, finally snapped. Flying into a rage, Mitkov wagged his finger and denounced the "damned" (*okayannyi*) tsar to his face. Infuriated, Ivan rose from his throne, grasped the metal-tipped walking staff he kept by his side, and charged at Mitkov. Using the staff as a spear, the terrible Ivan ran him clean through, covering the banquet hall floor with blood. Collecting his wits and silently returning to his table, he left his henchmen to drag Mitkov's disemboweled and broken frame outside to finish him off.[25]

Having witnessed such gruesome events firsthand, the straight-laced commander Kurbsky wisely fled for his life. It is fitting that four hundred years later, Sergei Eisenstein began his scathing indictment of Stalinist autocracy in his film *Ivan the Terrible II: The Boyar's Plot* with Kurbsky's defection. Centuries before Eisenstein and Khrushchev, Kurbsky was the first to highlight the pervasive use of alcohol in Russian autocratic government.

Even without violence, Ivan found drunkenness a terrific instrument of blackmail against his underlings. While his drunken boyars feasted, sang, and uttered slanderous and shameful things, Ivan often ordered his scribes to write down their words. The next morning Ivan would confront his normally erudite, hungover yes-men with the damning transcripts.[26]

Eisenstein was hardly alone in underscoring the "deadly parallels" between Stalin and Ivan the Terrible. Both used terror as an instrument of state security and administration, both shared paranoid and homicidal personality traits, and both, it must be added, placed alcohol at the center of their statecraft as well as their personal lives.[27] When in 1925 Stalin revived the imperial vodka monopoly to extract additional resources for the Soviet state, he was following a path blazed by Ivan's monopolization of the *kabak*—or tsar's tavern— in 1553. Ivan was perhaps the first to realize the tremendous potential of the liquor trade. As Englishman Giles Fletcher wrote in 1591, the annual rent from these drinking houses "yeeldeth a large rent to the Emperours treasurie" on the order of a few thousand rubles annually from each establishment.[28] Their most effective use of alcohol, however, was keeping their rivals stupefied, suspicious, and divided.

As with Stalin, objecting to drinking was one of the offenses that drew Ivan's ire, often ending in the gruesome death of the nobleman and even his family. To replace the scores of elites who met such horrific ends, Ivan promoted from the ranks of the lesser nobility flunkies who never dared cross him and instead encouraged his debauchery. Sycophants such as Alexei Basmanov, Ivan's son Fyodor, Vasily Gryaznoi, and Malyuta Skuratov—who shared Ivan's lust for torture—became his closest advisors and most reliable drinking companions.[29] Together, these degenerate inebriates fed off one another, exploring new depths of drunkenness, cruelty, and depravity.

In the winter of 1564 Ivan suddenly and inexplicably abandoned Moscow, leaving to wander his lands aimlessly with his voracious, drunken entourage. After a long journey, they arrived at a small settlement north of Vladimir known as Aleksandrovskaya Sloboda, where the paranoid Ivan ordered an unofficial capital constructed—hoping for safety behind fortified ramparts, moats, and high walls. No one could enter or leave without Ivan's knowledge. At this new "court," Ivan created a new inner circle—the *oprichniki*—led by Skuratov, Basmanov, and others known for their loyalty, cruelty, and capacity for alcohol. With ranks eventually swelling to over six thousand, the *oprichniki* were above the law: commissioned to hunt down and sweep away Ivan's foes. Only the *oprichniki* could stand the piercing gaze of the tsar, and only with them did the demented Ivan finally feel at ease.[30] Having kissed the cross and taken an oath "not to eat or drink" with the Muscovite boyars of old—even if they were relatives—the drunken marauders ravaged the Golden Ring territories northeast of Moscow. Noblemen were either executed or exiled along with their families; crops, forests, and entire villages were set ablaze; peasant men and children were tortured; women were raped and killed in alcohol-fueled orgies. Leading the *oprichniki* was the bloodthirsty Skuratov, who even strangled the head of the Russian Orthodox Church, Metropolitan Philip II, to death with his own hands. No wonder the Skuratov character in Eisenstein's *Ivan the Terrible II* was seen as such an obvious parallel to Stalin's inebriate executioner and KGB head, Lavrenty Beria.

Behind the ramparts of Aleksandrovskaya Sloboda, the tsar—together with his teenage son and heir, tsarevich Ivan—led the slaughter. A typical afternoon began with public beheadings followed by private sessions of excruciating torture. In the evening the tsar, tsarevich, and their thugs received the blessings of (terrorized) priests before yet another drunken dinner feast. Ivan the Terrible was pleased that he had so much in common with his eldest son: they got drunk together, swapped mistresses, and enjoyed the same hobbies: whipping and roasting educated men, pouring scalding wine on ambassadors, and unleashing wild bears on unsuspecting monks, all for sport.[31]

While the thick walls of Ivan's unofficial capital protected him from outsiders, they could not defend him from his own drunken neuroses. In the growth of his bloodthirsty and headstrong son Ivan saw a new rival—one who had much to gain from his demise. By 1581 Ivan had wholly convinced himself that his son was plotting against him. In a subsequent fight between the two, Ivan swung at his son with his pointed staff. The tsar recoiled in horror to find that his pike had pierced his son's temple, which was gushing blood. Suddenly terrified to realize that he had just killed his son and the heir to the Russian throne, Ivan cradled the head of the tsarevich. For the last time regaining consciousness, the younger Ivan reportedly kissed his father's hands, muttering, "I die as your devoted son and the most submissive of your subjects."[32]

In the world-famous Tretyakov Art Gallery in downtown Moscow hangs Ilya Repin's famed *Ivan the Terrible and His Son Ivan*, which depicts the formidable

ILYA REPIN'S *IVAN THE TERRIBLE AND HIS SON*. Oil on canvas. 1885. State Tretyakov Gallery, Moscow.

tsar coddling the bloodstained and lifeless body of the tsarevich. In this moment, the eyes of the one who wrought so much horror on his people are themselves filled with dread, not simply for the death of a son—it is said—but also for the future and the end of the royal dynasty. When Ivan the Terrible met his inevitable end, the throne would now be left to his sickly and "weak-minded" son Fyodor, whom Ivan dismissed as "not fit to rule."[33] When Fyodor died without a male heir, the centuries-old Rurik bloodline died with him, ushering in Russia's first "Time of Troubles"—marked by Polish invasions, civil war, economic chaos, peasant revolts, usurpers, and impostors.[34] Of course it is doubtful that Ivan the Terrible foresaw such a collapse, but subsequent events highlight the importance of a strong leader as the linchpin holding together the political and economic institutions of the early Russian state. With the death of Ivan, that too was gone.[35] Yet while the autocracy itself would be compromised, the primacy of alcohol within the autocracy would endure.

In March of 1584 the weary and demented tsar—fat from gluttony and aged beyond his years from drink—collapsed over a chessboard in his quarters. There was at once a great outcry: doctors called for vodka and *aqua vitae* to revive him while others called for marigold and rosewater. It was all for naught: Russia's terrible drunken sadist was no more.[36]

Like all the grand dukes of Muscovy, the body of Ivan the Terrible is entombed in the Cathedral of the Archangel in the Kremlin. Yet unlike the graves of his predecessors, which litter the public sanctuary, Ivan's tomb is hidden from public view behind the grand iconostasis, where he lies in seclusion alongside his sons Ivan and Fyodor. Yet perhaps the most fitting epitaph of Ivan's life and reign is not on his grave, but in the writings of his confidant-turned-critic Andrei Kurbsky: "He did not force people to bring sacrifices to idols, but ordered them together with himself to be in concord with devils and forced sober men to drown in drunkenness, from which spring up all evil things."[37]

4

Peter the Great: Modernization and Intoxication

In the hundred years following the death of Ivan and the end of the Rurik dynasty, Russia's autocratic system plunged into chaos, only to slowly reemerge about a new royal family, the Romanovs. Through a succession of fragile leaders, Russia changed very little, before the late seventeenth century, when Peter the Great forcibly modernized Russia's medieval cultural practices and byzantine political and economic institutions, turning Russia into a formidable European military power and a true multinational empire. Yet while many valorize Peter's progressivism and modernism, one tradition that endured was the centrality of alcohol to Russian statecraft. In many ways, Peter had more in common with Ivan the Terrible and Russia's medieval past than the popular "modernizer" image would suggest.

Peter's father, Tsar Alexei Mikhailovich Romanov, ruled for thirty of those tumultuous years (1645–1676). His major accomplishments consisted of quelling riots and rebellions across the country, including a series of tavern revolts in 1648. A quiet, pious, and temperate leader, even he utilized alcohol to coerce his courtiers into desired behavior. The English court physician Dr. Samuel Collins noted that while the tsar drank very little wine, he took great pleasure in seeing his boyars "handsomely fuddled." From his throne in the banquet hall, Tsar Alexei "delivers out of his hand a *Chark* of treble or quadruble Spirits, which are able to take away his breath who is not accustom'd to them."[1] Those boyars who failed to attend morning prayer were unceremoniously "baptized"—dunked in water then forced to drink three draughts of vodka. Although the nobles detested, they rarely protested; instead they in turn made their foreign visitors and ambassadors as drunk as possible.[2]

Tsar Alexei's domestic tranquility was shattered by the death of his beloved wife Maria weeks after she bore him their thirteenth child. Understandably distraught, the tsar often left the cold, lonely palace to dine and drink at the warm houses of his close friends. Maybe the alcohol had gone to his head, but at the estate of his advisor Artamon Matveyev, Tsar Alexei became enraptured by Natalia Naryshkina—Matveyev's buxom servant who plied the sovereign with vodka and caviar.[3] In 1671 the two were wed, and the following year she bore him a son. While celebratory wines and fruits were distributed to military officers outside the Kremlin walls, inside the tsar himself poured the vodka for the nobles and officials, who toasted the health of the young Peter Alexeyevich Romanov.[4] An integral part of the alchemist's wares, vodka was among the elixirs of health and vitality that the tsar took regularly, and he ensured that his wife and children imbibed it regularly as well.[5]

With two older brothers—Fyodor and Ivan—ahead of him, it was unlikely that young Peter would ever ascend to the Russian throne. When the forty-seven-year-old Tsar Alexei died from a cocktail of ailments leading to kidney and heart failure, the nimble-minded, yet physically impaired Fyodor III was crowned tsar.[6] When he died at the age of twenty without a male heir, Russia was again thrown into crisis as the families of Alexei's first and second wives vied for power, with much of the outcome determined by a disgruntled group of palace guards known as the *streltsy*, or "shooters."

In the resulting Moscow Uprising of 1682, rival conspirators whipped up riots in the capital with rumors that the tsarevich Ivan had been strangled by the Naryshkin clan in order to place nine-year-old Peter alone on the throne. Joined by mobs of drunken peasants who rioted and looted Moscow, the *streltsy* mob burst into the Kremlin, slashing and hacking to death many powerful boyars, including his mother's former guardian Artamon Matveyev as well as two of Peter's uncles, who were butchered in the presence of the horrified tsarevich Peter. For days, Russia's feuding royal families—and the entire Russian government—were held hostage by the rampaging *streltsy*.

The Danish ambassador to Moscow, Butenant von Rosenbusch, recounted how the *streltsy* ransacked his residence on a false rumor that he was harboring a fugitive before hauling him through the riotous streets to the palace to plead his innocence. "God be praised! I am not guilty," protested the diplomat to his captors. "I have a clear conscience and do not doubt that as soon as I go to the castle you will let me go. Then if you will accompany me home again I will treat you to as much brandy [vodka] and beer as you like, but since the streets are full of your comrades who do not know anything about me you must take care that none of your men who meet me do me any harm."[7]

The *streltsy* agreed, and with this shrewd promise of alcohol, the terrified ambassador bought an escort of fifty bodyguards to lead him through the mob to the Kremlin. Once inside the Kremlin gates, von Rosenbusch suddenly stopped: a rival *streltsy* group dragged past the naked and beaten body of the fugitive the ambassador was accused of harboring. Continuing on to a packed palace square, von Rosenbusch was summarily dismissed and sent home by the recently widowed Tsarina Natalia Naryshkina and her daughter, the Princess Sophia.

Returning to his residence, the Dane's entourage had swollen to 287 thanks to rumors of the promises of alcohol. True to his word, the ambassador served them all as much vodka and beer as they could drink. Drunk on power and vodka, the *streltsy* then turned on their captive, demanding money. "Content us well, or we will leave no life in thy house. Dost thou not know that we have the power? Everything must tremble before us; and no harm can come to us for that."[8]

Even the royal family trembled before the mutinous *streltsy*, and like the ambassador they did everything possible to pacify them. To debunk the rumor that the tsarevich had been strangled, they presented Ivan V to the mob—alive and unharmed. They conferred upon the garrison the honorary title of "Palace Guard." Finally, in the courts and corridors of the royal palace, the *streltsy* were treated to liquor-adorned feasts at the rate of two regiments per day, receiving vodka from the hand of Princess Sophia herself, who stroked the egos of the truculent *streltsy* by lauding their loyalty and fidelity. Raising a toast to the princess, the inebriated rebels thus swore allegiance to her, and with vodka the uprising was subdued—and important lessons about the instrumental power of alcohol learned.[9]

A compromise was quickly brokered to reestablish order: the teenage Ivan V—beset by both physical and mental disabilities—and his ten-year-old half-brother Peter I would be crowned co-tsars, with Sophia ably acting as regent for both. Yet as Peter grew older and more ambitious, Sophia did not relinquish power willingly. Seven years after the 1682 uprising, while Peter was encamped with his loyal Russian armies at the Troitsk Monastery in Sergeyev Posad—the heart of the Russian Orthodox Church some forty-five miles northeast of Moscow—Sophia again turned to the *streltsy*. In 1689, while her frail brother Ivan V ladled out vodka to the soldiers, boyars, and other officials, Sophia gave an impassioned plea for their allegiance against her half-brother Peter.[10] All for naught—the boyars, the remaining *streltsy*, and even Ivan instead allied themselves with Peter. Sophia was arrested and forced to the convent at Novodevichy. Never interested in politics, the quiet Ivan V died in 1696, leaving Peter the sole tsar. Two years later, following another failed *streltsy* insurrection to place her on the throne, Sophia was forced to become a nun—this time flanked by one hundred armed guards. In a scene more reminiscent of Ivan the Terrible, the young Tsar Peter interrogated and condemned hundreds of *streltsy*. Determined to forever root out insubordination, he disbanded the *streltsy*. Scores of alleged conspirators were tortured, branded, hanged, beheaded, or broken on the wheel by the tsar's orders, frequently in his presence.[11] In Russia, the differences between "the Great" and "the Terrible" are less than one might think.

*   *   *

If all of the leaders of Russia past and present were to go round for round in a drinking contest, Peter the Great would undoubtedly be the last man standing. Surviving accounts suggest that Peter had a herculean capacity for both work and drink: reportedly downing thirty to forty glasses of wine daily, he was nonetheless lucid enough to enact sweeping domestic reforms and make Russia a formidable European power. According to these legends, even in his early teens Peter drank a pint of vodka and a bottle of sherry over breakfast, followed by about eight more bottles before going to outside to play.[12] Certainly such astronomical quantities should be met with some skepticism, as they far exceed the amount of liquor that would trigger death by alcohol poisoning. Still, it is clear that Peter was a heavy drinker, even by Russian standards.

By the time he wrested complete control of Russia from his sister Sophia, the teenage Peter already had an entourage of boyar princes, confidants, and advisors from his youth, which was spent primarily at the royal estate of Novo-Preobrazhenskoe northeast of Moscow. Like most boys, the young Peter played war games with his friends—but instead of toys, Peter and the sons of fellow nobles used *actual* soldiers in their military maneuvers. As Peter matured, so too did his band of warriors, and his Preobrazhensky and Semenovsky guards became the first and most accomplished regiments of the imperial Russian Army.[13]

Since his father died when Peter was only three and his mother was preoccupied with dynastic infighting, Peter's upbringing was left to his tutor, Nikita Zotov, and his governor, Prince Boris Golitsyn, who routinely took Peter to the so-called "German quarter"—the eastern fringe of Moscow that housed the city's settlers from Western Europe. It was there—surrounded by drunks and whores—that the young co-tsar learned to drink.[14]

Whether in the taverns of the German quarter, the garrison at Preobrazhenskoe, or the royal court in the Kremlin, Peter became fast friends with those who shared his intestinal fortitude, before appointing them to positions of power regardless of qualifications. Paul Yaguzhinsky, the son of Moscow's Lutheran church organist, met Peter in the German quarter, where he impressed the young tsar with his vivacity, work ethic, and capacity for strong drink. Peter made him Russia's first procurator-general. With his perennial good humor, Yaguzhinsky was "the only man in Russia who could stand before the Emperor, even in his worst moods, without trembling."[15]

Fyodor Apraksin served in the Semenovsky regiment. Uneducated, unable to speak foreign languages, and having never sailed at sea, Apraksin seemed an odd choice to head Peter's new admiralty that was crucial to Russia's naval ambitions. However, Peter's drinking companion was reported to have downed 180 glasses of wine in a three-day span—a (likely embellished) feat he repeatedly boasted to foreign ambassadors.[16]

From the rival Preobrazhensky regiment arose Aleksandr Danilovich Menshikov, a lowly, semi-literate soldier. Versatile, energetic, and loyal—Menshikov shared the tsar's sense of humor and immense capacity for alcohol, quickly becoming Peter's favorite. There is some suggestion that Peter and his "Aleksasha" were more than just friends: the Preobrazhensky chancellery hinted that the two "lived in sin." Moreover, in 1698, a drunken merchant was arrested for blurting out that Peter took Menshikov to his bed "like a whore."[17] Whatever their personal relationship, Menshikov became Peter's personal envoy and most trusted confidant.

Back in the German quarter, Peter met the gregarious Swiss mercenary François "Franz" Lefort, who became perhaps the greatest enabler of Peter's alcoholism. Lefort endeared himself to the young tsar by his frankness, unselfish friendship, outgoing personality, and legendary drinking abilities. Peter covered Lefort's debts, promoted him to positions of political importance, and even built him a palace in the German quarter. After long days of royal politics, Peter escaped nightly to Lefort's den, where he "soon found himself contentedly sitting in a haze of tobacco smoke, a tankard of beer on the table, a pipe in his mouth and his arm around the waist of a giggling girl." In 1692 the young (married) tsar took a warming to one of Lefort's concubines, Anna Mons—daughter of the German wine merchant. "The easy-mannered beauty was exactly what Peter wanted: She could match him drink for drink and joke for joke." She would become the tsar's mistress for the next eleven years.[18]

Lefort did much more than simply provide Peter with wine and women: he also coordinated Peter's so-called Grand Embassy of 1697–98—a massive dip-lomatic mission to Western Europe by 250 Russian ambassadors, officials, and attendants who accompanied the young tsar, who traveled incognito under the name Peter Mikhailov. During their European tour, Lefort met the German mathematician and philosopher Gottfried Wilhelm von Leibniz, on whom he made an indelible impression: "[Alcohol] never overcomes him, but he always continues master of his reason…no one can rival him…he does not leave his pipe and glass till three hours after sunrise."[19]

Historians have long highlighted just how significant Peter's impressions of Europe turned out to be: the shipbuilding and nautical expertise learned from Dutch shipbuilders and English admirals shaped Russia's naval ambi-tions; knowledge of European science, customs, and governance prompted Peter's westernizing reforms. Yet rarely do they mention the impressions Peter's entourage *left* on Europe, which often involved huge tabs for alcoholic feasts at all manner of inns, taverns, and guesthouses—and all left unpaid. In one day with Admiral Peregrine Osborne, the marquis of Cærmarthen—Peter's new-found English drinking companion, whom Peter rewarded with a monopoly on importing tobacco into Russia—local nobles marveled how the young tsar "drank a pint of sherry and a bottle of brandy for his morning draught; after that, about eight more bottles of sack, and so went to the playhouse."[20]

Upon their first meeting in 1697, English king William III ingratiated himself to the young tsar with the gift of an exquisite royal yacht. Yet their relationship ended badly when, at their final drunken banquet, Peter's favorite pet monkey (who always sat on the back of the tsar's chair) became agitated and attacked the king. More unpleasant surprises were in store for William even after his Russian guests departed—later receiving a bill from the aristocrats whose residences housed the raucous delegation during their stay. "The in-door habits of Peter and his retinue were, it appears from the estimates of damages, filthy in the extreme," concluded one government survey, chronicling the soiled linens, broken furniture and windows, and slashed curtains and paintings. The returning hosts were livid to find the destruction of their prized gardens, including a prized holly hedge—nine feet high, five feet thick and four hundred feet long—that had been perforated by wheelbarrows. "I can hear the laugh of Peter, as with brute force, stimulated by drink, he drove the wheelbarrow with Prince Menzikoff [sic] upon it, into the prickly holly hedge, five feet in thickness," ruminated one nineteenth-century writer.[21]

Upon returning to Moscow, Peter spent more evenings dining with Lefort than in the Kremlin palaces. Since his modest residence was too small to continually host the tsar's banquets, Peter commissioned a massive addition to Lefort's estate: a magnificent stone mansion replete with wine cellars and a banquet hall that could hold fifteen hundred drunken revelers. Much as Stalin had his dacha and Ivan had his fortress at Alexandrovskaya Sloboda, so too Peter created an unofficial capital and private counter court free of traditional Kremlin rules and conventions.[22]

From a fraternity of drinking companions, this motley collection of distinguished regents, retinues, youthful guards, and foreign adventurers evolved into Peter's "All-Mad, All-Drunken, All-Jesting Assembly," which openly mocked the traditions and mannerisms of the imperial court. Indeed, many in his raucous "Jolly Company"—foreigners and guards of low birth—would never have been allowed in the traditional court in the first place.[23] Whether at the imperial residence at Preobrazhenskoe, Lefort's clubhouse in the German district, or the noble residences of Moscow and later St. Petersburg, this "Jolly Company" traveled everywhere with Peter—drinking, feasting, and debauching, much to the horror of Russian conservatives.[24]

A typical drunken banquet at the mock court began around noon and often lasted for days. The good-natured Peter enjoyed seeing his friends drunk; the squeamish were considered suspect and lost the tsar's favor. Peter's toasts began immediately—starting with vodka followed by rounds of strong wines and English beers—served in massive glasses so that "every one of the guests is fuddled before the soup is served up."[25] As liquor unleashed their inhibitions, the revelers made grandiose speeches and raised innumerable toasts, each met with a blast of trumpets or artillery salvos over the cheers and fisticuffs of the rambunctious crowd. The more prodigious drinkers partied through the night in rooms strewn with the snoring bodies of those consumed by alcohol—who later emerged reanimated to drink and feast again.

Lampooning the ceremony and titles of the traditional court, Tsar Peter created a code of conduct for the masquerades at his new counter court—going so far as to personally beat his dearest Aleksasha Menshikov for forgetting to remove his sword before dancing. But the most dreaded penalty was the "Great Eagle"—a massive, ornate, double-handled goblet filled with 1.5 liters of vodka, to be downed on the spot. Many a visiting dignitary or lady of high standing watched in horror as besotted nobles were dragged home from the banquet by their inebriated lackeys after their turn with the Great Eagle.[26]

In the transition from drunken fraternity to counter court, many of the nicknames Peter gave his entourage were elevated to "official" titles based on their service at Preobrazhenskoe. In the play maneuvers of Peter's youth, a battle was waged between an "enemy" army led by boyar Ivan Buturlin against the defenders of the play fortress town of Pressberg, led by Prince Fyodor Romodanovsky—a horrible and cruel drunk who became one of Peter's most trusted followers. As a result, Peter dubbed Buturlin the "Polish king." Romodanovsky became known as the "king of Pressburg" and, later, "prince-caesar." These titles endured even into official correspondence, as Peter's letters to Romodanovsky were even addressed to "Your Majesty" or "My Lord King"—often signed "Your bondsman and eternal slave, Peter."[27]

Peter also mocked the powerful Russian Orthodox Church by creating the "All-Joking, All-Drunken Synod of Fools and Jesters," anointing his aging tutor Zotov as the "prince-pope," patriarch of Bacchus, to preside over the drunken heresy while seated atop a cask of vodka.[28] As in his counter court, Peter drew up rituals and ceremonies for the Drunken Synod, with the first commandment that "Bacchus be worshipped with strong and honorable drinking," meaning in effect that "all goblets were to be emptied promptly and that members were to get drunk every day and never go to bed sober."[29]

The group had their own "holy" book—a Bible hollowed out to carry several flasks of vodka. Lampooning the conclaves of Rome, Peter's "cardinals" were isolated and forced to drink until they answered a number of Pope Zotov's farcical questions about their respective families. Peter listened eagerly to the ribaldry, always noting "any hints of which it might be possible for him to make a vindictive use."[30] After three days and nights of heavy drinking, the doors of the conclave were thrown open. His holiness Zotov and the other hungover cardinals who stammered out were carried home on sledges while some never emerged at all. More than a few died from alcohol poisoning and instead needed to be borne to the *actual* church for interment. Their wakes demanded even more drinking.

The Drunken Synod even mocked the sacrament of marriage by arranging an elaborate wedding for Peter's "Royal Dwarf," Yakim Volkov. Peter had a deep affection for little people, and Volkov was at the side of the 6'7" tsar both in drinking contests and military conquests. For Volkov's wedding, Peter had prince-caesar Romodanovsky invite—or order—every *karlik* (or "dwarf," as was and is the commonly used term) across Russia to St. Petersburg to take part in the ceremony. On the big day, roughly seventy little people—all clad in fine European clothes ordered by Peter—made up the wedding train. The towering tsar himself held the wedding crown over the bride as the couple exchanged nuptials. During the reception the dwarfs sat at miniature tables in the center of the banquet hall while the full-sized guests looked on from the sides. They were served by a dwarf marshal, and the toasts were celebrated with salvos from miniature cannons. While such scenes easily offend our modern sensibilities, back then Peter, his courtiers, and foreign dignitaries all delighted in the spectacle of joyous dancing dwarfs stumbling and falling over drunk.[31]

The dwarf wedding, like the Drunken Synod, further blurred the lines between Peter's official world and his play one, since the same characters participated in both. Indeed, just as the Holy Synod was subordinate to the secular state power, so too the Drunken Synod was subordinated to the drunken court. In any case, through the alcoholic haze it was unclear where the mockery ended and the "real" government began.[32] For instance, an official letter of March 1706 from Peter in St. Petersburg to his confidant Menshikov was signed by Peter's compatriots in the Jolly Company: "the dog Lizetka, who affixed her paw, and the royal dwarf Yakim Volkov, who added that he had been given permission to be drunk for three days. The tsar signed himself 'Archdeacon Peter.'"[33]

Yet despite the constant flow of alcohol, Peter somehow always arose refreshed from the revelry to lead his country forward toward a new day—or at least another feast.

Very few could match Peter's pace, and even his best friends in the Jolly Company occasionally sought refuge from the flood of alcohol. At one celebration over heavy Hungarian wines, Menshikov was caught drinking a weaker Rhine wine, so as not to get drunk as fast. As a penalty for violating the rules, Peter made his favorite drink two full bottles of the heavier wine from the "Great Eagle," at which point Menshikov collapsed into a drunken stupor and had to be carried home while his wife and sister wept uncontrollably.[34]

During Russian holidays—from the spring carnival of Shrovetide to the winter feasts of Christmas and New Year's—the Jolly Company of eighty to two hundred revelers took this raucous party on the road: forcing themselves on the unsuspecting elites of Moscow and St. Petersburg. When caroling through the snowy streets in a caravan of sleighs each seating twelve to twenty, the group crowed off-key yuletide songs. If, in their drunkenness, any company member, besotted host, or innocent bystander forgot the tsar's rules, they were met with ceremonial blows from the knout or treated to the Great Eagle.[35] Peter even penned official rules for his hosts:

> Our intemperance means that we are sometimes so incapacitated that we cannot move from the spot and it may happen that we are unable to visit all the houses that we have promised to visit on a given day, and the hosts may be out of pocket as a result of the preparations they have made. Therefore we declare and firmly pronounce, on threat of punishment with the Great Eagle Cup, that nobody should prepare any food. And if we should deign to have a meal from someone, we shall communicate our orders in advance, and for confirmation we have signed this edict with our own hand and have ordered it sealed with the great seal of Gabriel.[36]

What was the reason for this bizarre behavior on the part of Russia's "great" leader? No one quite knows for sure. Contemporaries faulted his upbringing. Nineteenth-century scholars thought Peter needed to amuse his courtiers in his new capital of St. Petersburg. Some historians today view it as a testosterone-fueled cultural backlash against the overthrow of the (female) regency of Sophia, while others argue that institutionalizing such debauches was necessary to discredit medieval cultural practices and bring Russia into "modern" Europe.[37] When understood within the context of vodka politics and autocratic state building, with parallels in both Russia's modern and ancient history, Peter's drunken revelry seems less unusual and more of an enduring element of autocratic domination.

Indeed, bearing witness to the activities of Peter's Jolly Company both in the privacy of their counter court and in their public excursions, the Swedish dignitary John von Strahlenberg noted:

> Thus these Processions cause many sober People to get a Habit of Drunkenness, and some, who were treated in that Manner, died, the same Night, almost before they could reach their own Habitations. He likewise put the Inhabitants of *Muscow* under such Apprehensions, that no body durst to speak publickly any Thing against the *Czar*, or his Favourites; And when any Person was informed against, he was treated with the utmost Cruelty, and the informer rewarded.[38]

Peter's seemingly unusual antics were fully consistent with the Russian tradition of utilizing alcohol to keep both society and his inner circle off balance—using their drunkenness to extract useful information. Even in the midst of their revelry Peter drew out secrets from his drunken companions, making note mentally or in his pocketbook. Histories and firsthand accounts all concur that "he removed many a man out of the way who had revealed his mind in this manner."[39]

Alcohol was likewise an instrument in Peter's foreign policy portfolio. Grappling with Nordic powerhouse Sweden for a foothold in the Baltic in the Great Northern War, in 1703 Peter broke ground on his new capital—St. Petersburg—in the delta where the Neva River empties into the Baltic Sea.[40] The defining military victory, however, would not come until six years later at the Battle of Poltava (in present-day Ukraine), where Peter's modernized army put a decisive end to Sweden's territorial ambitions in Eastern Europe. Following their crushing defeat, the vanquished Swedes tendered their surrender to someone they thought to be the Russian tsar. Unbeknownst to them, the official delegation spoke not to Peter, but to his drunken "prince-caesar" Romodanovsky while a suspiciously tall "officer" stood silently to the side.[41]

Vodka could be even more instrumental than the military to Peter's territorial ambitions. With the Russians encroaching into his territory, Friedrich Wilhelm Kettler, the grand duke of Courland (present-day Latvia), agreed to wed Peter's niece Anna Ivanovna. Since her father—the co-tsar Ivan V—had died long ago, Peter assumed the role of father of the bride. In the frigid January of 1711 he threw a massive wedding feast rivaled only by the spectacle of the wedding of the Royal Dwarf Volkov earlier that winter—where Anna and Frederick were the uncomfortable guests of honor. The celebration following the royal wedding was even more surreal: the betrothed couple were ceremoniously served a massive pie, out of which popped two female dwarfs dressed in the height of French fashion who then read poetry and sang a minuet.[42] The uncomfortable duke—unaccustomed to such alcoholic absurdity—drank so much that he didn't simply get a hangover; he actually died. With this news, Peter claimed to oversee the administration of Courland in the name of his niece, thus effectively absorbing the duchy into Russia. Indeed, the "custom of immoderate drinking, which proved fatal to the duke of Courland, was taken advantage of by Peter, as well as by diplomatists in general, to promote their political objects. He compelled his guests, according to Russian usage, to drink brandy [vodka], that he might the more easily extract the secrets of his nobles and the foreign ambassadors, or destroy them."[43]

Foreign diplomats were not immune from Peter's vodka politics: he often plied them with alcohol until they too bore state secrets, passed out drunk, or just plain died. The Danish ambassador Just Juel tells of the tsar's servants forcing dignitaries to submit to the Great Eagle onboard his ship. Unable to dismiss

Peter's butler, the inebriated Juel scaled the foremast and hid among the sails. Learning of this, Peter himself climbed the mast of the tall ship with bottles of wine in his pockets and the Great Eagle in his teeth to force him to drink five rounds of penance together in his perch. On a separate occasion, Juel faked an illness to escape a "life-threatening" three-day victory celebration. Roused from his bed by the great sovereign himself, the weary Dane was escorted to the party in his nightshirt and slippers. Later again, running afoul of the tsar's perplexing rules, Juel tried a different approach—begging for mercy—to no avail. Pleading on his knees with tears in his eyes, "the Tzar laughingly fell immediately upon his knees, too, saying that he could kneel as long as I, so that we remained in that posture, since neither of us would rise first, until we had emptied six or seven large glasses of wine, and I got up again half drunk."[44] "For the foreign envoy," recounted Juel, "these drinking sessions are a dreadful ordeal: he either participates in them and ruins his health or misses them and earns the tsar's disfavor."[45]

Whether Danish or French, all quickly learned this lesson. In a communique to Paris in March 1721, the French ambassador described Peter's "grande assemblée," where the drinking was led by Zotov, the mock pope, "whose only distinction was to imbibe much wine and vodka and to smoke tobacco." Uncomfortable, the new ambassador rose to leave, only to find the exit blocked by armed guards who ensured that no one left sober. "Never in my life have I undergone such a terrible experience," huffed the ambassador.[46]

Other delegates, such as the high chamberlain from Holstein, Friedrich Wilhelm von Bergholz, were so taken aback by the drunkenness that virtually every page of his memoirs describes the tsar's parties, where Peter forced the duke, foreign dignitaries, and even the ladies of the court to indulge in alcoholic excess. Realizing that escape was not an option, like so many others Bergholz devised familiar strategies to stay sober: drinking slowly and pleading with the servants to water down his portions of wine.[47] While it would be easy to dismiss such playful parties, frequently it was under the influence of alcohol that Peter's cruelty was on display for all to see.

During a dinner following the *streltsy* uprising, the Prussian ambassador M. Printz described how a drunken Peter had twenty prisoners brought into the court and, with each of the twenty rounds of alcohol he drank, happily lopped off the head of a condemned prisoner before proposing to the horrified ambassador that he try to match his feat. When even the tsar's more "civilized" European confidants, such as Franz Lefort, begged not to participate in such brutality, they received a stern reply: there is "no sacrifice more agreeable to the Deity than the blood of a criminal."[48]

Just as Stalin had his Beria, and Ivan had his Skuratov, it was the "prince-caesar" Romodanovsky who stoked Peter's brutality. Between the tsar and his inebriate grand inquisitor, many prisoners—both guilty and innocent—were tortured, hanged, or beheaded without trial. They saved their cruelest devices for nobles and commoners accused of blasphemous utterances against the tsar while stupefied by drink. Many an innocent drunkard was arrested on nothing more than rumor and hearsay. When asked—as often happened—why any particular wretch should be so tortured, Peter answered: "he must needs be guilty, or he would not have been imprisoned."[49]

Perhaps it should come as little surprise that Peter inflicted his greatest cruelty when he was with Romodanovsky—a man who kept a bear in his palace. that he allegedly trained to perform a very interesting trick: the bear would present to any visitor who wanted to meet with his master a large glass of peppered vodka. Those who downed the awful-tasting liquor without flinching were allowed to pass; those who did not were mauled. Such incivility and drunken atrocities have confused generations of historians: "What kind of civilsation could that be which was inaugurated under such auspices as these, and by so brutal a reformer? Truly did Peter once observe, that 'he wished to reform others, yet was unable to reform himself.'"[50]

The list of Peter's modernizing reforms was indeed impressive. He taught the mannerisms of the European nobility and did away with such medieval practices as growing long beards. He outlawed arranged marriages and introduced the Julian calendar. He instituted a new tax code to pay for his new capital of St. Petersburg and to maintain the military that helped to secure it. He abolished the old boyar class, instituted noble ranks based on merit and service, and even instituted compulsory education as necessary for a competent and well-functioning government bureaucracy.[51] Yet for all of his accomplishments, Peter's vivid memories of the *streltsy* uprisings and the almost fatal dynastic rivalries of his childhood kept the issue of succession at the forefront of his thoughts.

In his youth, Peter's mother arranged his marriage to Evdokiya Lopukhina, the daughter of an influential boyar. The marriage was an unhappy one. Of their three children, only one—the tsarevich Alexei Petrovich—survived infancy. Banished to a monastery so that Peter could marry his mistress Catherine, Evdokiya raised Alexei to loathe both Peter and his reforms, which made the pair a natural rallying point for the reactionary opposition. Alexei evaded his father, often pretending to be sick or hungover, thereby stoking the tsar's suspicions.[52] Swirling rumors of discord and conspiracy seemed all the more valid when the tsarevich suddenly fled his father's court for the safety of European exile.

Amid such familial tension, in 1715 Peter and his second wife, Catherine, celebrated the birth of "junior"—Peter Petrovich. The announcement of another potential heir to the throne was met in classic Petrine fashion: military garrisons were given gifts and vodka as they saluted the news with cannon salvos. Peter, Menshikov, and Apraksin set out casks of free vodka and beer for their subjects, who got "inhumanly drunk." In Peter's raucous court, great pies were presented, out of which jumped naked dwarfs who danced for the courtesans' pleasure: a female dwarf for the men's table, a male for the ladies'. According to Otto Pleyer, the consul from the Holy Roman Empire, "the joy at this birth among the great and persons of the lesser or low estate is indescribable, they just sleep it off to drink again and drink to sleep it off. Anyone who is sober pretends to be drunk among the drunk and in all houses the tables are always covered full of food. The tsar calls this prince his real crown prince."[53]

When the prodigal tsarevich Alexei returned from self-imposed exile in 1718, an enraged Peter conducted an official "inquiry" into his son's scandalous flight. Tortured by his father's own order, Alexei implicated his closest friends—ensuring that the tsar would impale or break them on the wheel—before publicly renouncing the throne in favor of Peter's "real" crown prince, Peter Petrovich. Alexei was condemned to death for treason and died in the island fortress of Saints Peter and Paul from repeated lashes by the knout. His son's death weighed heavily on the great tsar, but at least the imperial succession was secure. That is, until the three-year-old heir to the throne Peter Petrovich, died unexpectedly, threatening another Time of Troubles.[54]

With the end of the Romanov bloodline in sight, the increasingly frail Peter instituted a new law on succession that allowed royal power to be appointed rather than inherited. Following bladder infections that left him bedridden in the summer of 1724, the ailing tsar had his beloved wife—a former Latvian peasant—officially crowned Empress Catherine I. As a fitting bookend to his early reign as co-tsar with his brother Ivan, Peter, now at the end of his life, would rule with Catherine. Improving somewhat, Peter even returned for one last conclave of his Drunken Synod—imbibing massive quantities of alcohol that almost certainly aggravated his gangrenous bladder and hastened his demise.[55] On the evening of February 6, 1725, the bedridden emperor finally decided who would inherit his empire and throne. Calling for his slate, he scrawled only "I give all..." before the quill pen dropped from his hand. The great tsar slipped into a coma, never to awaken.

With the death of Peter the Great, Russia came full circle. Just as fifty years earlier the death of his father, Tsar Alexei, set off years of uncertainty, courtly intrigues, and dynastic struggles, so too the death of Peter without a son meant that the leadership of Russia would depend on the competing loyalties of courtiers. Just like Ivan the Terrible a hundred years earlier, Peter the Great was complicit in the death of his son, the sole heir to the throne. Also, in both cases, Russia again seemed poised for another Time of Troubles.

5

Russia's Empresses: Power, Conspiracy, and Vodka

Perhaps Peter the Great's proudest legacy was the founding of his European capital of St. Petersburg among the low swamps of the Neva River delta. Thanks in part to his wrenching reforms and the firm financial footing provided by alcohol, Russia and its capital flourished. By the late eighteenth century, the city unveiled a new tribute to its founder in the shape of the massive statue of the Bronze Horseman: Peter seated heroically on a magnificent steed, his right hand leading Russia majestically forward. The base of this iconic symbol of St. Petersburg is inscribed in Russian and Latin: "To Peter the Great from Catherine II, 1782"—a gift from one "great" to another.

Catherine the Great led Russia's encroachments into Europe: in the south seizing Moldova, Ukraine, Crimea, and the shores of the Black Sea; in the north absorbing the Baltic states and partitioning Poland. At home, her reforms modernized Russia's administrative bureaucracy. She was an enlightened despot who patronized the arts and education. Catherine corresponded personally with European scholars and philosophers from Voltaire to Diderot. With them she articulated such enlightenment values of liberty and democracy yet refused to permit them in her own dominions. For all of her accomplishments, Catherine nonetheless needed grandiose symbols, such as the Bronze Horseman, to secure her place in the line of "great" Romanov leaders, perhaps because the woman who was crowned Catherine II, "Empress and Autocrat of All the Russias," had not an ounce of Russian blood and—assuming power through a palace coup— no legitimate claim to the Russian throne. As was the case with every empress crowned during the eighteenth century, Russia's heavily paternal society and patrilineal dynasty stacked the cards heavily against the young tsarina. Also like her female predecessors, Catherine relied heavily on vodka politics to solidify her rule.

Elizabeth's Disappointment

Two of the most influential figures in eighteenth-century Russia were not Russian at all. From Stettin in the Baltic arose Sophia Augusta Frederica, the French-educated daughter of a Prussian prince who, through cunning and good fortune, led Russia as Catherine the Great. Meanwhile, in the German port city of Kiel was born Peter of Holstein-Gottorp. On his father's side, Peter was grand-nephew of Swedish king Charles XII; on his mother's side, he was grandson of Charles's adversary in the Northern War—Peter the Great of Russia. With this lineage, the young Holstinean was a potential heir to both thrones.

The dunderheaded Peter compensated for his high pedigree by lacking woe-fully in virtually every other characteristic imaginable. Orphaned young, his education was left to a drunk and ignorant courtier who beat and humiliated the cowed lad. At the age of fourteen, in 1742, Peter's aunt—the recently crowned Tsarina Elizabeth Petrovna—summoned her young nephew to St. Petersburg and named him heir to the Russian throne. Expecting the arrival of an astute and refined aristocrat, Elizabeth was horrified to learn that she had instead anointed a drunken, ignorant, immature, irritable, royal pain in her backside. According to the Russian historian Vasily Klyuchevsky, Peter "viewed serious things child-ishly and approached childish enterprises with the seriousness of a grown man. He resembled a child who imagined himself an adult; in fact, he was an adult who always remained a child."[1]

Hoping to solidify an alliance with Prussia, Tsarina Elizabeth arranged for Peter to marry the prominent Pomeranian princess Sophia Augusta Frederica. In 1744, the princess arrived in Russia. Well-mannered and well-educated, Sophia was everything Peter wasn't. She ingratiated herself with the empress—fastidi-ously mastering the Russian language and (unlike Peter) eagerly converting from Lutheranism to Russian Orthodoxy. Sophia even chose to be baptized with the Russian name Ekaterina Alekseyevna—Catherine—in honor of Elizabeth's mother and wife of Peter the Great: Catherine I.

The brooding Peter did not share the empress's enthusiasm for his new bride. While the festivities following their wedding on August 21, 1745, lasted ten days—with free meats roasted in the public squares and fountains running with wine so that even the common folk could join in the celebration—the two were soon conjoined in a cold, distant, and loveless marriage. It was nine full years before Peter and Catherine finally consummated their marriage—but even that was more the result of pressures to produce a royal heir than any expression of mutual fondness. In the meantime, they both carried on love affairs—encour-aged by the tsarina, who hoped the two would eventually warm to each other.[2]

Catherine's memoirs paint an unflattering picture of the young Peter: writ-ing that from the age of ten Peter was prone to drink. Even years before arriving in Russia, the young princess met him at a family gathering (they were second cousins, after all), where she heard that Peter was restive, hot-headed, and that not even his attendants could keep him from getting drunk.[3]

After their wedding Peter's alcoholic antics continued, now on display before the entire court. Obsessed with all things Prussian, Peter smoked and drank beer to excess, believing it would make him "a real manly officer." According to Catherine, he got so drunk at royal feasts that he "no longer knew what he was saying or doing, slurred his words, and made for such an unpleasant sight that tears came to my eyes, for I hid or disguised as much as possible what was reprehensible in him."[4]

When he tired of the world of grown-ups, Peter retired to the couple's imperial residence at Oranienbaum to take refuge in games and alcohol. Oftentimes Peter would drink through the night with his besotted lackeys who plied him with wine and liquor. Other times he retreated to his room to drink and play with his toys. In her memoirs, Catherine recalled once finding Peter in the middle of a military-style execution of a rat that had eaten two of his papier-mâché toy soldiers. Thinking it was all a joke, Catherine burst into laughter. Peter's gaze turned cold. This was deathly serious—she just couldn't understand.[5]

Scornful of his haughty wife, Peter turned his gaze toward someone who appreciated his crudeness instead of being embarrassed by it—Countess Elizabeth Vorontsova. Sallow and shallow, Elizabeth was dirty, rude, squint-eyed, and covered with smallpox scars. Her ability to drink, curse, and sprawl on the bed for his pleasure fascinated Peter—and in turn perplexed the entire royal court. One night, Catherine recalled

> I had only just fallen asleep when the Grand Duke came to bed as well. As he was drunk and did not know what he was doing, he tried to strike up a conversation with me about the eminent qualities of his belle. I pretended to be in a deep sleep so as to make him shut up more quickly, but after having spoken even more loudly to wake me up and seeing that I gave no sign of being awakened, he gave me two or three rather hard punches in the side, cursing the depth of my slumber, then turned, and fell asleep. I cried a great deal that night over the affair and the blows he had given me, and over my situation, which was in every way as disagreeable as it was tedious.[6]

Catherine detested the tsar-to-be, but her long-term fate was tied to his. In the short-term, however, her future was in the hands of the current empress, Elizabeth, and Catherine did her best to balance the two. At the culmination of her pregnancy with their first child in December 1758, Catherine summoned both Peter and Elizabeth. Peter arrived first and—true to his adoration for all things German—was exquisitely clad in the uniform of a Holstein officer, replete with spurs, sash, and sword. He pronounced his intention to aid the distressed Catherine by fastidiously defending her against her enemies. "One might have thought that he was joking, but not at all," Catherine wrote; "what he said was very serious. I easily understood that he was drunk and I advised him to go to bed so that the Empress, when she came, would not have the double displeasure of seeing him drunk and armed from head to toe in his Holstein uniform, which I knew she detested."[7] Indeed, Elizabeth could hardly stand Peter any more than Catherine could. The empress rarely spent more than fifteen minutes with him and was repulsed that detestable Peter was destined to lead Russia, often weeping that "my nephew is a monster, the devil take him!"[8]

It was not easy to stay in Elizabeth's good graces, since the tsarina was as much of a disagreeable, vengeful lout as her nephew. One nineteenth-century chronicler even refused to describe her "unblushing excesses," as they would "stain the page of history."[9] Exhausted by a lifetime of drunken affairs to curry favor with one court faction or another, Elizabeth suffered hallucinations, convulsions, and fits of terror from which she only found escape in wine and sex. Indeed, the Chevalier d'Éon—the transgender spy of French King Louis XV who gained access to the court by disguising himself as one of the empress's maids—noted Elizabeth's "pronounced taste for strong liquors." Returning to her chambers from another night of drinking, she often passed out in her regalia and had to be cut out of her corsets by her oft-abused servants before they carried her to bed.[10]

The fading tsarina occasionally awoke in the morning with the sight of Peter and Catherine attending her bedside. In her paranoia, she feared they were in cahoots with her enemies at court to plot her overthrow. On her deathbed rumors circulated throughout St. Petersburg over who would take the throne. The detestable Peter? The German Catherine? Catherine's infant son Paul? Finally, in 1762, at the age of fifty two—the same age as her father Peter the Great—the empress finally succumbed to her demons.

> Elizabeth rallied slightly; but any hopes of her recovery were always dispelled by her persistent demand for spiritous liquors. Such was her eagerness for them, that any attempt to keep the stimulating beverage, as she thought it, from her lips threw her into a frenzy that brought on agonizing pains. The fatal cup was then handed to her, and she drank, and drank, continually, gradually sinking into lethargy, insensibility, and death.[11]

Mocking the solemnity of the funeral services for the deceased tsarina, Peter played the drunken fool—interrupting the priests with outbursts of laughter and sticking out his tongue—further stoking the hatred of his subjects-to-be.

From that moment forth, "every word he uttered, every gesture he made, contributed to his ruin."[12]

Despite hopes that his behavior would become more regal once he was ensconced on the throne, Tsar Peter III only further alienated himself from his court and other people. Under Elizabeth, the Russian army—along with its Austrian, Swedish, and French allies—were trouncing Prussia in the Seven Years' War. With the Russian capture of the last Prussian port of Kolberg, victory was all but assured. Thoroughly defeated, Frederick II, the distraught king of Prussia, planned to renounce his throne and even contemplated suicide. Yet by some miracle, the tsarina had passed, leaving Russia in the hands of the Prussophile Peter. The fist command of the young tsar was unthinkable: Russia would switch sides in the war—give back the prize of Kolberg and all occupied territories and defend the Prussian king he so adored against Austria, which had been Russia's ally just days before.[13] Back in St. Petersburg, the new tsar redecorated his walls with the Prussian order of the Black Eagle and even wore a ring with the visage of Prussian king Frederick II, which Peter would kiss fervently. When the Prussian ambassador came to visit he found the tsar almost unable to stand he was so drunk. "Let us drink to the health of your King, our master. . . . I hope he will not dismiss me. You can assure him that, if he gives the order, I will make war on hell with my whole empire!"[14] According to the nobles at court who witnessed Peter's continued drunken and treasonous conduct, "the hearts of his subjects bled with shame."[15]

As for his personal life, Peter mocked Catherine by openly cavorting with his mistress, the detestable Elizabeth Vorontsova, who "swore like a trooper, squinted, stank and spat as she spoke." He humiliated Catherine further by exiling her to an apartment at the far end of the Winter Palace. Ironically, this banishment gave Catherine the freedom of movement and secrecy that were necessary for an eventual palace coup. Even before the death of Elizabeth, some of her closest friends and lovers—all of whom held positions of power in the government and the military—urged her to seek power. Now that the new tsar was seemingly intent on selling Russia out to its foreign enemies, the intrigues kicked into high gear. With every nobleman whom Peter offended Catherine gained another ally. On the eve of her coup, Catherine could count on more than forty officers and over ten thousand guardsmen. "The Empress is in the most cruel situation and is treated with the most marked contempt," wrote French ambassador Baron de Bretuil. "Knowing as I do the courage and violence of this Princess, I cannot imagine that she will not sooner or later be moved to some extreme. I know that she has certain friends who are trying to calm her but who would risk everything for her, if she required it."[16] The actors were in place and the stage was set for a dramatic power struggle, but how would the script play out?

The Princesses' Path To Power

When time came for Catherine's revolution, events happened swiftly. Yet there was surprisingly little need for advanced coordination, propagandizing, or even a detailed plan of action. In fact, the plotters simply recycled the time-tested Russian script for placing a princess on the throne: a popular figure to rally the troops and plenty of vodka.[17] Even back in 1682, the rebellious Moscow *streltsy* who invaded the Kremlin—hacking to death prominent nobles and relatives of a terrified ten-year-old Peter the Great—were treated to feasts and limitless wines and vodka poured from the hand of princess Sophia herself. (This was itself an echo of the Moscow Uprising of 1648, when outrage over corruption and increases in the salt and vodka taxes prompted a drunken, *streltsy*-led mob to set the city aflame, beheading and dismembering prominent nobles, before being pacified by a three-day vodka- and mead-drenched feast in the Kremlin.)[18] The military rewarded Sophia's hospitality by supporting her regency, making her the first woman to hold the reins of the great Russian state. Other women would emerge from similar succession struggles to claim the throne. All did so by using vodka to curry favor with elites, generals, and troops.

This was especially true in 1725, when Peter the Great died seconds before anointing a successor. Within hours of his death, Peter's favorite Menshikov rallied the Preobrazhensky guard with alcohol to support the candidacy of Peter's wife Catherine, whom the troops admired for her many qualities, not the least of which was her capacity to down glass after glass of vodka "like a real man." With the troops behind her, Catherine I was triumphantly proclaimed sovereign of all the Russias. The widow Catherine took a bevy of lovers from competing noble families, and in regaling them, she drank like a sailor, often passing out drunk in her lovers' arms.[19] Unsurprisingly, given the hardcore binges of drinking and lovemaking, Catherine passed two short years later in 1727, leaving the throne to Peter II, who quickly succumbed to smallpox on his wedding day at the age of fourteen.

With the death of Peter II in 1730, the scheming nobles of the Russian Supreme Privy Council crowned Peter the Great's little-known niece, Anna Ivanovna, as a pliable figurehead empress. They underestimated the mannish, roughhousing, gun-toting Anna, who continued the empresses' tradition of solidifying their popularity with the lesser nobility and imperial guards by offering them copious amounts of vodka.[20] Once secure in her position through liquor and loyalty, Anna quickly shrugged off any limits to her autocratic power and engaged in all manner of drinking and debauchery. Occasionally, during her decade-long reign, Anna invoked bizarre spectacles that were highly reminiscent of her "great" uncle Peter: when the esteemed, elderly nobleman Mikhail Golitsyn crossed the empress, she forced him to marry a hideous Kalmyk woman and "honeymoon" naked together on a bed made of ice within a specially constructed ice palace on the frozen Neva River. But that's another story.[21]

Even the Empress Elizabeth Pretrovna learned this lesson. When Anna died in 1740, leaving the throne to the three-month-old Ivan VI, Elizabeth courted the Preobrazhensky Regiment. She regaled the generals with stories of her father, Peter the Great, and flirted with them over round after round of drinks. Wine was plentiful on the night of November 21, 1741, when Elizabeth visited the regiment wearing a silver breastplate and wielding a silver cross. Leading the drunken troops, she marched on the Winter Palace and had the infant tsar Ivan VI, his parents, and their supporters imprisoned, placing herself on the throne in a bloodless coup. During her reign, she continued the grand Russian tradition of plying potential adversaries with liquor in order to worm compromising information from them.[22]

To be sure, vodka was a central ingredient in any Russian putsch. The only question was—would the German-born Catherine follow this recipe?

From German Princess To Russian Empress

If Peter III's decision to give up Russia's hard-fought gains in Prussia had not already made him enemies at court, his plan to wage war on Denmark to simply aggrandize his native Holstein certainly did. All of St. Petersburg seethed with discontent—especially the military. Word of open denunciations reached the tsar at his suburban residence of Oranienbaum but was simply ignored.[23] Meanwhile, from the seclusion of her Winter Palace apartment, Catherine's well-placed sympathizers multiplied, including Grand Chancellor Alexei Bestuzhev-Ryumin, Princess Ekaterina Dashkova (who had strong connections to the guards through her husband), the generous Cossack Hetman Kirill Razumovsky (whose father helped put Elizabeth Petrovna on the throne a generation earlier) as well as a host of young officers of the Preobrazhensky and other guard regiments. At the center was the dashing and brave artillery officer Grigory Orlov—Catherine's secret lover—and his brother Alexei. The Orlov brothers were the soul of the regiments: idolized by the young guardsmen, they organized drinking bouts and bare-knuckled boxing competitions on the outskirts of St. Petersburg.[24] The stage was set for a coup d'etat.

If vodka was the Russian conspirators' instrument of choice, in this instance it also provided the pretext for revolution. On the night of June 27 in one of the capital's taverns, an inebriated conspirator—guard captain Peter Passek— openly derided the tsar and hinted of a possible overthrow. He was promptly arrested. Word spread quickly, and the conspirators feared that Passek would give them away under torture.[25]

It was Alexei Orlov who collected Catherine in the middle of the night. Barging into her chambers, he announced purposefully: "Passek has been arrested. We must go."

By seven in the morning, Catherine stood hesitantly before the Preobrazhensky regiment. According to historians, "She need not have been afraid: the soldiers were fired with enthusiasm. Besides, they had been promised a distribution of vodka." Within a matter of moments, Razumovsky and the Orlov brothers proclaimed Empress Catherine to be the sole and absolute sovereign of Russia, and the regiment joyously proclaimed their allegiance to her. Amid the tumult, Catherine gave hushed orders: close the gates of the capital, watch the taverns, and allow no one to travel the road to Oranienbaum, so that word of the coup does not reach the tsar.[26]

That afternoon, Peter, his mistress Elizabeth Vorontsova, and his German entourage left Oranienbaum for the summer palace at Peterhof. It was there, at Peter the Great's seaside estate, that a secret messenger informed the tsar that Catherine was in the capital and had been proclaimed empress. His ministers urged Peter to heroically march on Petersburg. Instead, the tsar broke into tears, which he tried to drown in glass after glass of burgundy wine. Alternating between panic and resignation, Peter drew up manifestos condemning Catherine before heeding his ministers' advice to sail to the naval base at Kronstadt to rally the sailors and mount a counteroffensive. Drunk, staggering, and sobbing uncontrollably, the tsar had to be helped aboard a schooner with Elizabeth Vorontsova and her cackling ladies in tow.[27]

At one in the morning, the tsar, his ladies and ministers arrived at Kronstadt, only to find that the garrison had already sworn allegiance to Empress Catherine. If the tsar's ship did not immediately depart, the sailors brusquely announced, they would open fire, sending the schooner to the sea floor. As they set sail, Peter's own field marshal, Burchard Münnich, could hardly stifle his laughter at the pathetic spectacle of the tsar cowering in the hold of the boat, drinking and weeping alongside his ladies. The group retreated to Oranienbaum, where the childlike Peter threw himself on the bed and cried over the loss of his empire.[28]

Meanwhile, the conspirators prepared for what they expected to be an imminent attack from the vindictive tsar. On the run, Catherine and her weary general staff holed up overnight at a wretched inn at Krasny Kabak (red tavern) to await their fate. A number of the tired and thirsty guardsmen broke into a wine cellar and quickly downed gallons of Hungarian wine. In the ensuing drunken commotion, a rumor spread that the Prussians were coming to kidnap Catherine. In order to prevent a riot, Captain Passek (who was only imprisoned for twelve hours and did not give anything away) awakened Catherine in the middle of the night. Only when the weary, disheveled empress made a personal appearance did the troops calm down. Understanding the need for vigilance, Princess

Dashkova persuaded the troops to roll the barrels back into the cellar and sent for spring water instead: "I gave them whatever money I had left, then turned my pockets inside out to show I had no more to give, and promised that on our arrival in town all the taverns would be open to them and they would be able to drink at the expense of the Crown. My arguments were appreciated and had the desired effect."[29]

When the dawn broke, it became clear that no attack was coming. Tsar Peter's collapse was total, the empress's victory secure. All of St. Petersburg rejoiced, as Catherine's triumph hailed a return to sanity. What's more, Princess Dashkova made good on her promises to both her vigilant guardsmen and the joyous throngs in the capital. In the words of the Russian historian Vasily Klyuchevsky:

> So ended this revolution, the most lighthearted and delicate of all those known to us, which cost not a single drop of blood—a real ladies' revolution. It did cost a great deal of wine, however: on the day of Catherine's entry into the capital, June 30, all the drinking establishments were opened to the troops. In a mad ecstasy, soldiers and their wives hauled out the vodka, beer, mead, and champagne, pouring it into tubs, kegs, or whatever came to hand. Three years later the matter of compensation for the Petersburg wine merchants "for wines pilfered by soldiers and other people during Her Majesty's happy accession to the imperial throne" was still being processed in the Senate.[30]

Recognizing his defeat, Peter abdicated and retired to Ropsha—the residence he owned as grand duke—requesting only that the empress provide him with his favorite burgundy wines, his pipes and tobacco, and his favorite African slave, Narcissus.[31] The inept tsar was hardly a political threat to Catherine, yet so long as Peter lived the empress's reactionary opponents could rally behind his legitimate claim to the throne. Apparently without Catherine's knowledge, then, her conspirators plotted to finish him off.

The Orlov brothers persuaded a court apothecary to poison a bottle Peter's favorite burgundy wine. On July 17, 1762, Alexei Orlov and his men set out to visit the former tsar at Ropsha. They found the half-dressed Peter drawing a fortress with chalk and happily announced that he was soon to be liberated. Celebrating the news, the joyous tsar dined with his assassins over vodka, when Peter himself called for his beloved burgundy. Catherine's accomplices calmly watched as the frail Peter rose and wailed "I am poisoned!" But he did not die. Embarrassed and a bit puzzled, the conspirators then tried smothering Peter with a pillow so that there would be no signs of struggle. But that too did not work. Finally the group bound the screaming prince and, making a noose from a large cloth napkin, violently strangled the grandson of Peter the Great to death.[32]

Upon hearing of the detestable tsar's passing, the Russian people pitied Peter's unfortunate fate. As Walter Kelly suggests: "They forgot his defects and caprices in the recollection of his amiable qualities, and his sad reverse of fortune. The sailors cast it in the teeth of the guards that they had sold their master for brandy and beer."[33]

The following thirty-four years of Catherine the Great's reign marked the resurgence of Russia's military dominance as well as the awakening of Russian cultural life. The enlightened tsarina patronized the arts and manufactures of her adopted homeland. She bestowed gifts of Russian vodka on European monarchs, philosophers, and luminaries from Frederick the Great and Voltaire to Carl Linnaeus, Immanuel Kant, and Johann Wolfgang von Goethe. And while Russia's greatest—and last—empress even drew up new rules for the nobility based on temperance and moderation, quite unlike the drunken bacchanals of Peter the Great, it is hard to dismiss how drunkenness and immoderation were crucial to her ascent to power—just as it had been for every Russian empress who had come before.[34]

In 1796, Catherine died of a stroke, leaving power to her son Paul, who despised his "father" Peter's inglorious end and, in the ultimate spiteful move, had the coffin of Peter III—buried now thirty-five years—exhumed and opened during Catherine's funeral procession. With the remaining conspirators—including Alexei Orlov—charged by imperial decree to be front and center as "chief mourners," the lifeless body of the great empress was laid alongside the decayed flesh of the husband she so loathed. At the end of the three-hour viewing, the vindictive Paul laid the two to rest, side by side, with the inscription: "divided in life—united in death."[35] Ironically, four short years later Paul met the same fate as Peter—he was trampled and strangled to death at the hands of a mob of drunken palace conspirators.[36]

Virtually every coup d'etat in Russia's long history was carried out in a state of inebriation, and often alcohol was used intentionally to win over the troops. This practice was especially pronounced when women were the regents-to-be. In order to overcome questions of legitimacy for not being part of the male bloodline, Russia's ruling ladies, from the regent Sophia to Elizabeth and the two Catherines, all turned to vodka to shore up support for their rule.

This set a dangerous precedent for future palace intrigues, but using alcohol to gin up popular support was quite effective. In addition to the drunken mob of dismissed generals who in 1801 killed Paul and placed Tsar Alexander I on the throne, when Alexander died unexpectedly in 1825, another group of aristocratic conspirators—this time with a regiment of imperial guards—refused to swear allegiance to Nicholas I. These liberal "Decembrists" as they would be known, hoped to effect an overthrow of the imperial order and the adoption of a Western-style constitution. In order to regain control over his new capital from this increasingly drunken mob, Nicholas ordered forces loyal to him to crush the rebellion by force. The Decembrist leaders were arrested, tried, and hung. Although the plot was unsuccessful, the revolutionary potential of alcohol among the rabble was warily recognized. The people of St. Petersburg "are the deadly enemies of the police," claimed one conventional account, "and brandy, liberally distributed among them, will, at any time of danger or uncertainty in the government, render them pliant and desperate tools of revolutionary agitators."[37]

Even within living memory the intrigues of Russian high politics have always been accompanied by the waft of vodka. Indeed, even plotters like Gennady Yanayev and Valentin Pavlov—two of the leaders of the hardline State Emergency Committee that attempted to ouster Mikhail Gorbachev in 1991—stammered through the entire ordeal in a drunken stupor.[38] One might wonder how Russian history—and indeed world history—would have been different had these men followed the putschist playbook of imperial Russia and used vodka to win over the troops rather than further their own ruin. We can only imagine what might have happened during those tense days of August 1991 if instead of being won over to the cause of freedom, the Soviet troops were so drunk that they unhesitatingly trained their guns on their fellow countrymen and opened fire.

6

Murder, Intrigue, and the Mysterious Origins of Vodka

Take a good look at the vodka section of your local liquor store. On the upper shelves you'll find shimmering glass bottles of all shapes and sizes originating from every corner of the world. Vodka today is the world's most popular liquor and a true global commodity. Looking below the so-called top shelf import and boutique vodkas you'll see cheap, domestic products, their plastic bottles usually emblazoned with Russian symbols, often bearing the name of the Russian entrepreneur who fled the Bolshevik Revolution to set up shop in the West.[1]

Without a doubt, vodka is the definitive Russian cultural product. But what *is* vodka? Where does it come from, and why do the Russians seem to have a particular affinity for it?

In 2006 I went to Russia to find answers—and if you go to Russia today with such questions, you'll invariably end up in the same place I did: the Vodka History Museum at Izmailovsky Park in northeast Moscow. In the tumultuous 1990s, Izmailovsky Park was a bustling souvenir bazaar and open-air flea market. Today, the rickety stalls of the souvenir peddlers have been updated with colorful, sturdy veneers, while happily towering over the market is a bright, Disney-fied kremlin housing the Vodka Museum. I had visited the museum years earlier— before it was moved from the somber shadows of the Bronze Horseman statue in St. Petersburg to the Izmailovsky amusement park in Moscow. I highly recommend it: after perusing the museum's artifacts you can knock back complimentary vodka samples in their re-created nineteenth-century tavern with windows festooned with gilded decorations and wooden tables bracketed by long, sturdy benches of dark mahogany.

Upon entering the replica tavern I was welcomed by the museum's pleasant hostess. Declining the obligatory tour, I instead directly asked her two simple questions: "Where did vodka come from?" And "When did it originate?"

Apparently caught off guard by the directness of my questions, she hesitated momentarily before popping behind a counter to pull out a well-thumbed paperback of a book I knew only too well: *Istoriya vodki* (*History of Vodka*) by Vilyam Vasilevich Pokhlebkin—the bible of Russian vodka history. I'll admit that I only feigned interest as the guide proclaimed how the illustrious historian Pokhlebkin unquestionably proved that vodka as we know it was first made inside the Moscow Kremlin, sometime between 1448 and 1478.[2] Though disappointed, I politely thanked the hostess for her time and left without ever getting to the free samples.

The Mysterious Life And Death Of Vilyam Pokhlebkin

Vilyam Pokhlebkin was a unique cultural icon in Russia—beginning with his unusual name. His father, Vasily Mikhailov, was an ardent communist revolutionary, whose nom de guerre in the revolutionary underground—Pokhlebkin— invoked a traditional Russian peasant stew. Instead of the usual Ivans, Vladimirs, and Borises, when the Pokhlebkins had their first boy they instead named him "*Vil*yam" incorporating the initials of the great Bolshevik leader *Vl*adimir *Il*yich Lenin.

After serving in the Red Army in World War II, Vilyam turned to culinary history as a researcher in the Institute of History of the Soviet Academy of Sciences, writing a popular history of tea, which became a literary sensation in tea-drinking nations. With his meager resources, he amassed a sizable library of rare manuscripts in his nondescript apartment in Podolsk—a sleepy industrial suburb due south of Moscow.

In the repressive 1960s and 1970s under Leonid Brezhnev, Pokhlebkin's culinary histories ostracized him from Soviet academia. His magnum opus— a collection of thousands of global recipes and their origins—was censored by the authorities: since even the most basic ingredients were widely unavailable, such recipes would shine an unwelcome spotlight on the inherent shortcomings of the Soviet system itself. Branded a dissident, he was effectively unemployed (and unemployable) in a country that boasted a job for everyone.[3]

According to the foreword of his *Istoriya vodki*, events then took a strange turn for Pokhlebkin. Perhaps borne of the same anti-Soviet sentiment that launched the Solidarity movement in the shipyards of Gdansk, in 1978 the communist government of Poland apparently sued the Soviet Union for exclusive commercial rights to the word *vodka*, claiming that it originated in Poland, not Russia. Perhaps the Poles had not read the single-paragraph entry on "vodka" in their standard issue *Big Soviet Encyclopedia*, which clearly states that vodka "was first produced in Russia in the late 14th century."[4] What more debate could there be?

For the Russians, this was a stab in the back—their socialist allies in the Warsaw Pact were not only threatening the Soviets' lucrative international trade; they were also inflicting an emasculating blow to Russia's cultural heritage.

Pokhlebkin claimed that definitively "proving" the origins of vodka with any degree of reliability was next to impossible due to a lack of surviving documents. Neither side could point to a page from their respective archives— such as the Scottish Exchequer Roll of 1494–95 that established the origins of whiskey or the famous German Beer Purity Law, the *Reinheitsgebot* of 1516— to settle the dispute.[5] As his story goes, the Soviet export ministry, known as Soyuzplodoimport, first turned to the organization known (in typically bureaucratic parlance) as the Higher Scientific Research Institute of the Fermentation Products Division of the Central Department of Distilling of the ministry of the food industry of the Union of Soviet Socialist Republics, which could not pin down the origins of vodka. In a move that has been immortalized as a pivotal scene in a recent Russian novel, the dismayed government authorities turned to Pokhlebkin: the only man who could establish the Soviet Union's legal claims before the international court and in the process defend Russia's national pride.[6]

According to Pokhlebkin, his work was a success! In 1982 the tribunal found on behalf of the Soviets, based primarily on Vilyam's research that "proved" the Poles began making vodka several decades after the Russians. This finding allowed Soviet products such as Stolichnaya—which had been sold in American stores since 1972 through a barter deal with Pepsi Cola—to trade under the proud (yet slightly redundant) motto: "Only vodka from Russia is genuine Russian vodka."[7]

Pokhlebkin's landmark victory was all the more impressive—as subsequent Russian writers noted—because "he *alone* performed the work, and built the entire system of circumstantial evidence ultimately recognized by the international legal experts."[8] This research—which Pokhlebkin claimed was never meant for public consumption—was not published until 1991, just as the Soviet Union was collapsing. *Istoriya vodki* only added to Pokhlebkin's celebrity as dispenser of folk wisdom on Russia's favorite vice, including claims that if one does not drink before 3p.m. or after midnight it is impossible to become what he called "a professional alcoholic."[9]

In private, Pokhlebkin was eccentric and ascetic: though amassing an impressive collection of historical manuscripts and exotic teas, he nonetheless denied himself a simple television or telephone, relying instead on written correspondence and telegrams. In his later years, Pokhlebkin became a paranoid recluse— seldom emerging from behind the numerous locks on his Podolsk apartment door for fear of being followed... or worse. Thirty years in the same three-room apartment, he never opened the door to strangers—including all manner of inspectors, repairmen, and plumbers.

Vilyam Vasilyevich Pokhlebkin was last seen alive on March 26, 2000: the same day that a man with the same monogram—Vladimir Vladimirovich Putin—was first elected president of Russia.

After returning on the suburban commuter train from a meeting with his publisher in Moscow, Pokhlebkin was apparently followed from the train station, set upon by thugs, and brutally murdered in his own home. Pokhlebkin's body—stabbed eleven times with a long-handled screwdriver—was found weeks later by his chief editor, Boris Pasternak (grandson of the world-famous author of *Dr. Zhivago*), who demanded that the police smash in the door to Pokhlebkin's apartment after his dependably punctual writer suddenly stopped returning his letters.[10]

According to the police investigation, none of Pokhlebkin's most valuable possessions—his vast collection of rare manuscripts—were taken from the apartment. Moreover, according to the autopsy, Pokhlebkin had the equivalent of an entire bottle's worth of vodka in his bloodstream—very suspicious, since despite his subject of expertise, Pokhlebkin never drank alcohol.[11]

The brutal murder of Vilyam Pokhlebkin remains unsolved. Speculation continues to swirl over culprits and motives: some even alleging that he was murdered by a vengeful Pole in retaliation for securing "vodka" for the Soviets.[12] As claimed by the producer of the 2005 investigative documentary *Death of a Culinarian: Vilyam Pokhlebkin*—which aired nationwide on Rossiya channel 1—"Pokhlebkin has reserved for himself a place in Russian history by saving Russia millions of dollars, perhaps tens of millions of dollars" by conquering Poland in this so-called vodka war. As the tragic stories of Pokhlebkin have grown, so has his legend.[13]

Pokhlebkin Reconsidered

"His name was magical. Legendary," claimed an article in the newspaper *Vechernyaya Moskva* (Evening Moscow) on the third anniversary of Pokhlebkin's death. "Many believed it to be a pseudonym for an entire research institute, since one man could not know so much." Moreover, the eulogy continued, if a debate ever erupted about Russian food or drink, "if one simply says to another 'Pokhlebkin wrote it'—that was enough to end any dispute."[14]

Clearly, Vilyam Pokhlebkin is the unquestioned authority on vodka history. Over the past twenty years dozens of popular books and hundreds of articles and webpages—in Russian, English, and other world languages—have recounted his research and findings, his stories and anecdotes from the pages of *Istoriya vodki*, almost verbatim.[15]

The problem is that Pokhlebkin is dead wrong, and much of his heralded *Istoriya vodki* is a complete fabrication.

HISTORIAN VILYAM POKHLEBKIN (1923–2000). October 2, 1984.
Source: RIA-Novosti/Prihodko

"If you read this book," wrote alcohol historian David Christian, "keep a bottle of strong vodka by your side to stun the more thoughtful parts of your brain." His scathing 1994 review of Pokhlebkin in the flagship academic journal *Slavic Review* certainly pulled no punches. "The parts that are left should enjoy this eccentric collection of curious facts, crackpot hypotheses, phony statistics, anticapitalist polemics and stalinist snobberies without worrying if it all fits together."[16]

Christian soberly chronicles Pokhlebkin's many inaccuracies and misleading conclusions, from his claims that no etymological dictionaries mention the word *vodka* to suggesting that unlike vodka, beers and mead were never subject to taxation. Beyond these, I have uncovered even more factual errors, from the sloppy—dating Ivan the Terrible's establishment of taverns from 1533 instead of 1553—to the substantive, such as discussing the reign of Vasily III Temnyi ("the Blind") in the 1420s, even though such a leader never existed. Perhaps he was referring to Muscovite grand prince Vasily III—but as we saw in Chapter 3, that Vasily reigned in the early 1500s, making Pokhlebkin's timeline off by one hundred years! Whether from sloppy research or (in some cases) mistakes in translation, the sheer quantity of obvious historical inaccuracies casts serious doubt on Pokhlebkin's authority and legend: a problem multiplied as his mistakes are renowned as unquestionable truths and reproduced far and wide.[17]

David Christian's manhandling of Russia's culinary icon suddenly seems warranted, especially since Pokhlebkin's "definitive" conclusion that vodka was discovered in Moscow in 1478 is far more precise than the sparse, murky evidence permits. "Most frustrating of all," Christian writes, "Pokhlebkin often does not bother to offer evidence for his sometimes fascinating claims. How can we know if he is writing fiction or fact?"[18]

Indeed, Pokhlebkin asks that his arguments be taken on trust—and for whatever reason, most Russians continue to extend him that trust. Many popular vodka books are composed not by trained historians, but rather by uncritical writers, journalists, and the culinary curious, like Pokhlebkin himself. Moreover, just as the front and back covers of Pokhlebkin's *Istoriya vodki* are adorned with alluring bottles of Moskovskaya brand vodka, many such trade publications include page after page of nostalgic, full-page product placements for all manner of vodka brands—and often are printed by the publishing wing of Russia's most famous distilleries. So perhaps the producers of such pop histories aren't particularly interested in investigating the matter further.

The biggest hoax of all is the so-called Soviet–Polish vodka war that allegedly prompted Pokhlebkin's investigation. Against the backdrop of the international Peace Palace in the Hague, the nationally televised *Death of a Culinarian* documentary boldly proclaims: "The 1982 decision of the international arbitration in favor of the USSR indisputably secured the precedence of the creation of vodka as a uniquely Russian alcoholic drink, giving them the exclusive right to advertise under that name on international markets, with the Soviet export-advertisement slogan recognizing the founding: 'Only vodka from Russia is genuine Russian vodka.'"[19]

However, neither of the international courts of the Peace Palace—the International Court of Justice (ICJ) and the Permanent Court of Arbitration (PCA)—ever heard such a case between the Soviets and their fraternal counterparts in communist Poland.[20] According to Peter Maggs, a foremost expert on Russian trademark law and international commercial arbitration, "the USSR as a matter of principle did not submit to international state-versus-state arbitration, because it regarded—with considerable justification—the major international arbitration institutions as dominated by the capitalist West."[21]

This is not to suggest that there was no sparring over the geography of alcohol. As in previous battles over geographically specific alcoholic products, such as French champagne, cognac, and Bordeaux, it follows that similar disputes could arise over vodka. Throughout the 1970s, the Poles claimed that vodka had been drunk in Poland since the early fourteenth century and that by the sixteenth century distillation was taxed.[22] But such a definitive, internationally recognized legal ruling "proving" beyond doubt that vodka originated in Russia simply never happened.

Following the anti-Soviet rumblings of the Solidarity movement, one would expect that such a symbolic "victory" for the Soviets over their restless subordinates in Poland would make headlines globally—or at the very least in the Soviet Union. But even researchers at the Library of Congress could find no mention of it in the global press. Scouring the archives of the main Soviet newspapers, *Pravda* and *Izvestiya*, likewise uncovered nothing. In fact, no Russian periodical or academic journal ever mentions this alleged "case" until *after* the release of Pokhlebkin's book in 1991.[23]

Only recently have Russian writers stopped taking Pokhlebkin's claims on faith and started to aggressively fact-check them. In his 2011 book *Bolshoi obman* (*Grand Deception: Truth and Lies about Russian Vodka*), Boris Rodionov concludes that virtually everything Pokhlebkin wrote about vodka was "a grandiose mystification." Too many questions remained: If this dispute with Poland was so crucial to both Soviet finances and national pride, why wasn't Pokhlebkin immediately given unfettered access to the Soviets' vast archives? Why wasn't this lone, outcast academic given an army of research assistants? And how could such a herculean research task be completed by one man in just a few short months?

Interviews with Yuri Zhizhin, the director of Soyuzplodoimport from 1974 to 1987, and Boris Seglin, the head of the firm's legal department, confirmed that no one commissioned Pokhlebkin to undertake such research. Moreover, they claimed that the Poles had never taken the Soviet Union to any international court over vodka's origins…ever.[24] In a little-known 2002 interview, Zhizhin stated that Soviet relations with fraternal Poland had actually been quite amicable. The vodka question "was never even raised at the Coordination Council of Comecon": the organization that oversaw trade among East European satellite states. "The volume of vodka traded between our countries was so small that such a dispute didn't make sense," claimed Zhizhin. "Since most of the world's population already associates vodka with Russia, proving that we alone have the rights to the word 'vodka' is like trying to stake our claim to a perpetual motion machine. It'd be a waste of effort and money."[25]

As it turns out, not only *wasn't* there such a legal dispute—there *couldn't* have been, claims Peter Maggs, who has litigated international cases concerning iconic trademarks like "Smirnoff," "Stolichnaya," and even the likeness of the Hotel Moskva on the labels of Stoli.[26] "It is a very clear principle of international trademark law that a generic term cannot be protected," he argues. "And if there ever was a generic term, it is 'vodka.'"[27]

If the question was not raised within the Comecon, the only other international legal institution that could have adjudicated such a dispute between these two communist countries was the World Intellectual Property Organization (WIPO), which administers the main international laws regarding patents and intellectual property rights, including the Paris Convention for the Protection of Industrial Property that protects well-known trademarks. But "vodka" is not a valid trademark associated with a particular producer, such as "Levi's," "Toyota," or "Coca-Cola." The Paris Convention also lacks mechanisms to arbitrate intellectual property disputes between countries, which helped prompt the creation of the modern World Trade Organization. "Furthermore," Maggs continues, "almost all international commercial arbitration is over contract disputes, and a trademark dispute is not a contract dispute."[28]

Taken together, these accounts finally explain why, in this "high stakes" diplomatic tiff, Poland never actually put forth a legal defense of their position (which probably would be based on the appearance of "wodka" in Polish court documents in 1405 and their taxing of distilled spirits the following century) and indeed why most Polish authorities have no knowledge of this "case" that Pokhlebkin alone claims they lost.[29]

Perhaps most remarkable about Pokhlebkin's fabrications is how they have been elevated to the status of legend: standing above serious scrutiny for two decades. While we may devise all manner of hypothetical intrigues about why the eccentric Pokhlebkin felt compelled to weave such intricate lies—both about the substantive origins of vodka and the reasons for undertaking his investigation—unfortunately such questions are doomed to lie forever unsolved, alongside the mysterious murder of Pokhlebkin himself.

Back To Square One

If the unquestionable Pokhlebkin is now to be questioned, we are back to where we were before we entered the Vodka Museum at Izmailovsky Park, asking again: "where does vodka come from?" Fortunately, there are other theories.

Polish-American historian Richard Pipes has suggested Russians first learned distillation techniques from the Tatars of Asia in the sixteenth century. Whether by "pot distillation" where the alcohol was driven-out of fermented beverages in pots placed in a stove, or a "Mongolian still"—where they were left out to freeze so that ice could be removed from concentrated liquid alcohol—such indigenous experiments were crude. They were often fatal, too: producing highly concentrated "fusel oils"—poisonous liquids produced by incomplete distillation that are today used in industrial solvents and explosives. So it seems unlikely that vodka immigrated to Russia from the east.[30]

Not all Russian historians agree with Pokhlebkin's designated birthdate of vodka as 1478 or its birth place in Moscow. Some go back even further, dating vodka's origins from the year 1250 in the ancient Russian city of Veliky Novgorod—the ancient trading outpost between the Hanseatic League and Byzantium. How did they come by this claim?

In the early 1950s, Artemy Artsikhovsky—head of the archeology department of the prestigious Moscow State University—excavated the soil around ancient

Novgorod. Deep in the waterlogged clay archeologists unearthed more than 950 well-preserved letters—written not on paper (as papermaking was not yet widely known), but etched into the bark of local birch trees. These resulting birchbark documents give a unique snapshot of everyday life in medieval northern Europe. Among these fragments of bark are numerous texts dating from the late 1300s (such as no. 3 and no. 689) that refer to the brewing of barley. While fermented beers, meads, and wines were known throughout northern Europe, distillation is an entirely different technology and constituted a historic technological achievement.

It is tricky to interpret these documents, since they are not in Russian but, rather, an Ancient Novgorodian dialect of early Slavic and Finnish/Karelian languages. That issue notwithstanding, historian A. P. Smirnov (no relation to the vodka of the same name), focused particular attention on birchbark document no. 65, which clearly includes the letters that spell the word ВОДА, pronounced *vodja*.

Linguists agree that the word *vodka* is the diminutive form of the Slavic word for water: *voda*. Certainly *vodja* sounds a lot like the Russians' dear "little water," *vodka*. Since letter no. 65 dates from the mid-thirteenth century, therefore—according to Smirnov—this supposedly "most important document in the history of the production of vodka" dates its birth to 1250.[31]

If this sounds like an even bigger stretch than Pokhlebkin's fabrication, that's because it is. First of all, Russian archaeologists determined that the stratum in which this document was found dates from the early fourteenth century at the earliest. Besides, any archeologist knows that fieldwork is never so precise as to pin down any specific year. As with Pokhlebkin, these scientists' claims are far more precise than the evidence warrants. Second, Smirnov does not explain how or from whom the early Novgorodans learned the science of distillation, since 1250 predates the technique's arrival even in Europe.

![Novgorod birchbark document with ruler showing 0 to 38]

0 1 2 3 4 5 6 7 8 9 10 11 12 13 14 15 16 17 18 19 20 21 22 23 24 25 26 27 28 29 30 31 32 33 34 35 36 37 38

NOVGOROD BIRCHBARK DOCUMENT NO. 3, CIRCA 1360–1380 C.E.
Source: Birchbark Literacy from Medieval Rus, http://gramoty.ru/index.php
Birchbark Literacy from Medieval Rus, http://gramoty.ru/index.php?

№ 3

NOVGOROD BIRCHBARK DOCUMENT NO. 3, CIRCA 1360–1380 C.E.
Source: Birchbark Literacy from Medieval Rus, http://gramoty.ru/index.php
Birchbark Literacy from Medieval Rus, http://gramoty.ru/index.php?

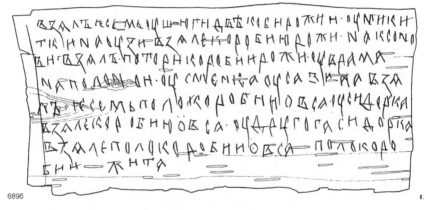

Novgorod Birchbark Document No. 689, circa 1360–1380 c.e. (part a). Source: Birchbark Literacy from Medieval Rus, http://gramoty.ru/index.php
Birchbark Literacy from Medieval Rus, http://gramoty.ru/index.php?

Novgorod Birchbark Document No. 689, circa 1360–1380 c.e. (part b). Source: Birchbark Literacy from Medieval Rus, http://gramoty.ru/index.php
Birchbark Literacy from Medieval Rus, http://gramoty.ru/index.php?

Novgorod Birchbark Document No. 65, circa 1300–1320 c.e. The letters spelling ВОДА can twice be seen in the bottom section, no. 65 b. Source: Birchbark Literacy from Medieval Rus, http://gramoty.ru/index.php
Birchbark Literacy from Medieval Rus, http://gramoty.ru/index.php?

Finally, Smirnov's interpretation rests on a complete distortion of the word *vodja* that is inconsistent with all linguistic scholarship. While Russian etymologists debate whether *vodja* ("he leads") in the document has something to do with marriage, there is near-universal acknowledgment that the word is in fact a verb participle, not a noun. "Birchbark documents don't give information about the early days of vodka," insists Jos Schaeken, accomplished Slavic linguist and head of the international Russian Birchbark Literacy Project. "The idea of vodja = vodka should be rejected by every serious scholar."[32]

So it seems we are back to square one, yet again.

Tracing Vodka's International Roots

Debunking false histories is fun in its own right, but it doesn't get us any closer to vodka's true origins … or if there is such a truth at all. What *do* we know? Perhaps we need to delve deeper into the global history of alcohol.

The first alcoholic beverages were relatively light fare: wines, meads, and beer. The natural process of fermentation, whereby yeasts interact with sugars in grape or other juices to create wine, was first observed in the Stone Age. Winemaking facilities recently unearthed in Armenia date from 4000 B.C.E. The Chinese fermented rice, honey, and fruit around 5000 B.C. Wines and beers have even been found in the tombs of Egyptian pharaohs.[33] Yet for all the pleasure and anguish they bring, fermented beverages are relatively weak—a maximum of 15 percent alcohol by volume—when compared to the standard eighty-proof (40% alcohol) vodka that we find in liquor stores today.[34] Reaching these higher concentrations can be done only through *distillation*—heating a fermented liquid mash above alcohol's relatively low boiling point of 78°C. At that point the alcohol evaporates, leaving the water, mash, and impurities behind, which is then cooled and condensed in a separate container.

Vodka—along with all modern spirits like gin, brandy, rum, and whiskey—can be traced back to the distillation by European alchemists of the twelfth century. While today we think of them as quixotic mystics forever seeking to turn metal into gold, medieval alchemists mined the scholarship of ancient Greeks, Romans, and Arabs for practical remedies for the body and mind, founding modern chemistry and medicine in the process. While ancient Arabs and Greeks had distilled fermented grapes, this process was only rediscovered by the alchemists in their attempts to create an elixir of longevity—a youth potion.[35]

Unlike today's recreational liquors, beginning in the thirteenth century medicinal spirits were distilled from fermented grape wine lees, most likely originating in the medical school of Salerno, in the south of Italy.[36] There, as throughout medieval Europe, the search for scientific knowledge was a spiritual endeavor closely tied to the Church of Rome. Accordingly, both the development and spread of distillation depended on schools and monasteries with abiding interests in philosophy and religion.

So how did distillation emigrate from pre-Renaissance Italy to the imperial court of Moscow? That's where the Poles and the Russians can't seem to agree. Historians credit—or blame—the colorful troubadour-turned-missionary Ramon Llull for spreading the technique to much of Europe. Before aspiring to convert Jews and Muslims to Catholicism, Llull taught Arabic and philosophy in the Franciscan convent on the Mediterranean island of Majorca off the coast of Spain. In 1290, after his missionary endeavors to North Africa ended in violent expulsion, he arrived in the north Italian city-state of Genoa, where he wrote extensively on distillation and rectification. Based perhaps on their shared interests in alchemy and Arabic, Llull teamed with physician Arnaldus de Villa Nova (Arnold of Villanova—not to be confused with the American university), who drew on his experiences treating popes, nobles, and kings to write *Liber de vinis*, the first medicinal book on viniculture.[37] Most likely, it was Arnold of Villanova who first introduced the Arabic word *al-kuhul* (alcohol) into the European nomenclature through his investigation of fermented grape wines and these new distilled or "burnt" wines. In his treatise *De conservanda juventute*, he writes:

> Burnt water also known as *aqua vitae*, is obtained by the distillation of wine or wine yeast. It is the subtlest portion of the wine. Some say that it is "the everlasting water", also that, because of its sublime method of preparation, it is the "gold water" of the alchemists. Its advantages are well known. It cures many diseases, prolongs life and hence deserves to be known as *aqua vitae*.[38]

Through Arnold of Villanova this *aqua vitae*, or "water of life," became known to Genoese merchants, who were intent on profiting from this mysterious new medicine. The Genoese discovered that spirits could be distilled not only from expensive wine lees but also from cheaper fermented fruits and grains. By this time the small Italian fishing village had grown into a powerhouse of naval commerce and exploration: even Christopher Columbus hailed from Genoa. By the fourteenth century *aqua vitae* was one of the most prized wares of apothecaries throughout Europe.[39]

When it came to commerce in the Mediterranean, the Genoese vied for control with their nautical rivals in Venice. Outmaneuvering the Venetians, Genoa established an alliance with the Byzantine Empire, which granted Genoese

Liber de arte Diftil
landi de Compofitis.
Das buch der waren kunft zu diftilieren die
Compofita vñ fimplicia/vnd dz Bůch thefauruo pauperũ/Ein fchatz d armẽ ge)
nãt (Dicarũ/die bzôfamlũ gefallen võ dẽ blichern d Artzny/vnd durch Experimẽt
võ mir Ißeronimo brũfchwick vff geclubt vñ geoffenbart zu troft denẽ die eo begerẽ.

getruckt un gendigt in die keisserliche frye statt Strassburg
uff sanct Mathis abent in dem jar 1507.

EARLY GERMAN WOODCUT PORTRAYING THE DISTILLATION OF *AQUA VITAE*

merchants the right to duty-free trade throughout Byzantium and a monopoly on commerce in the Black Sea.[40]

The science of distillation most likely came to the Slavic peoples through the bustling Genoese-controlled port city of Caffa—present-day Feodosia—on the Crimean Peninsula. In the colorful, multiethnic and multi-confessional bazaars, early Russians did a bustling trade in metals, furs, and slaves.[41] Spanish explorer Pero Tafur described the "bestial" natives of Caffa, where young virgins could be—and were—bought for a measure of wine in the taverns run by the Genoese. Perhaps, then, it should come as little surprise that Russians were first introduced not only to *aqua vitae* in the Genoese ports but also to liquor's close cousin—venereal disease.[42]

In the fourteenth century distillation could have made its way north from the Crimea across the vast grasslands, fields, and forests to Muscovy by a variety of means. *Aqua vitae* was the most popular potion of the alchemists and physicians who accompanied diplomats on their international missions. In his seminal work on Russian cultural history *The Icon and the Axe* (1966), Librarian of Congress James Billington underscores the "fact that vodka apparently came into Russia by way of the medical profession points to the importance of Western-educated court doctors as channels for the early influx of Western ideas and techniques."[43] Even Pokhlebkin suggested that the Genoese ambassador from Caffa occasionally visited Moscow en route to and from Lithuania in the late fourteenth and early fifteenth centuries—each time bringing medicinal *aqua vitae*.[44]

Beyond such sporadic visits, the practice and product of distillation likely came north to Moscow for good accompanying refugees fleeing the Mongol invasion of the Crimea, as Caffa was sacked by the Mongol khan Tamerlane in 1395.[45] The monasteries of Muscovy in general, and of the Kremlin in particular, were fertile grounds for this new practice, as monks quickly transformed the imported Genoese practice of distilling *aqua vitae* into a mass-produceable domestic product—vodka—that could be distilled from local grains (primarily rye and wheat) and soft spring water.[46] It is this combination that gives both Russian and Polish vodkas their "genuine" characteristics, if you believe the advertising slogans.

Beyond a general consensus that distillation reached Moscow by the fifteenth century, like so many things, the details are a little … fuzzy. According to a legend retold by Pokhlebkin, a Greek monk named Isidore—who learned distillation as part of a Russian church legation to Italy in the 1430s—was suspected of having divided loyalties and upon returning to Moscow was imprisoned in the Chudov Monastery of the Kremlin. Having no other raw materials than local grains, the crafty Greek created the first batch of "genuine" Russian vodka, which he then slipped to his captors, fleeing to Kiev after they passed out.

Like most of Pokhlebkin's claims, there is absolutely no factual basis or documentation for this whimsical tale. Think: why would a suspected traitor be imprisoned in a monastery with the tools of chemistry instead of (the more conventional) punishment of being tossed in a dungeon and tortured ruthlessly? What's more, the entire story oozes with Russian nationalist symbolism: vodka was allegedly born in the Chudov Monastery—the Monastery "of the Miracle," which was completed in 1365 and razed by Stalin in 1929 to make way for the stolid, concrete Palace of Congresses. Although the legend cannot be taken seriously, many in Russia continue to date vodka's origins from the 1440s based primarily on this tale.[47]

Another, more plausible alternative is that distillation came to Moscow not from the south, but from central and Western Europe via long-established Hanseatic trade routes to Russia's Baltic outposts of Pskov and Novgorod. The importation of wine along this trade route has been regularly documented as far back as 1436. Forty years later, the archbishop of Novgorod presented lavish gifts to Ivan the Terrible's grandfather—Grand Prince Ivan the Great of Moscow— including barrels of both red and white wines. While these wines were prized as fantastic luxuries, there is no mention of *aqua vitae*, much less vodka.[48]

So, where and when did vodka originate? Who was the first person to distill local grains into a potent alcoholic beverage—and was he Russian or Polish?

We may never know for sure. Anything I claim here would be speculation based on inference and conjecture, and probably no more definitive than the efforts of the "luminary" culinary Pokhlebkin, whose testament still stands as the well-thumbed reference at the Vodka Museum at Izmailovsky Park.[49]

Ultimately, though, it does not matter. Beyond nationalist sparring between Russians and Poles, the questions of who, where, and when aren't nearly as important as the question of *why* vodka?

What we do know is that by whatever route or as a result of whoever's handiwork, by the early sixteenth century the medicinal *aqua vitae* of the alchemists had already taken root as "burnt wine" or what we might recognize as beverage vodka.[50]

Russia would never be the same.

Why Vodka? Russian Statecraft and the Origins of Addiction

Pointing out that Russia has a serious alcohol problem may be impolite, but it isn't particularly controversial. What outsiders see as a crude stereotype, Russians have long understood as a persistent social challenge—one that has endured through the tsarist, Soviet, and post-Soviet eras. Still, while few histories even acknowledge Russia's vodka problem, even fewer actually attempt to address its sources.[1]

Of all substances, why do Russians drink vodka? Why do they drink so much of it? And why do they drink it in such a destructive manner? Conventional answers revert to long-standing practices, the enigmatic "Russian soul," or some other eternal, immutable, and inalienable cultural trait. And culture cannot be questioned. Still, there are very powerful political and economic forces behind the development and maintenance of such self-destructive cultural practices.

A popular belief is that Russians, Scandinavians, and others living in Nordic climes are drawn to spiritous liquors because supposedly they give motion to the blood in extreme cold. Anyone who's been warmed by a swig of vodka on a frigid night can relate. Even Montesquieu, in his *Spirit of Laws* (1748), pontificated on the stark cultural differences between the spirits-drinking peoples of northern Europe and their beer- or wine-drinking counterparts to the south, arguing that "the climate seems to force them into a kind of national intemperance, very different from personal sobriety," leading him to conclude: "Drunkenness predominates throughout the world in proportion to the coldness and humidity of the climate."[2] Accordingly, throughout the historical record we find descriptions of Russian men who spurn wine but "will toss off his glass of whisky like a genuine child of the north."[3]

An unscientific "geoalcoholics" literature has built on such climatological determinism to map the dominant alcohol-consumption cultures of Europe. Climate indeed explains some of the map: the wine-drinking regions are mostly southern, Mediterranean climes where viniculture thrives. The so-called beer

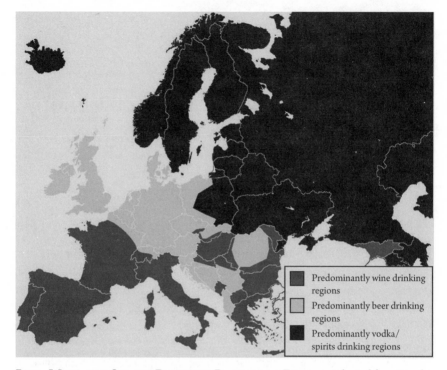

BEER, WINE, AND SPIRITS-DRINKING REGIONS OF EUROPE. Adapted from Frank
Jacobs, "442—Distilled Geography: Europe's Alcohol Belts," Strange Maps (blog),
January 30, 2010, http://bigthink.com/ideas/21495.

belt includes the grain-growing regions of central Europe, whereas a vodka belt
encompasses what's left: the Nordic and Baltic states, Russia, Ukraine, Belarus,
and central and eastern Poland.[4]

Yet if we set aside the vineyards of the Mediterranean and look north, the climatological map looks eerily like a political map of nineteenth-century Europe.
The differences in climate between Berlin and Tallinn, for instance, are not particularly stark—yet in the nineteenth century, while Berlin was the capital of the
German Empire, Tallinn was ruled by Russian tsars. Tellingly, the westernmost
frontier of the vodka belt that splits modern-day Poland is the exact border of
the old Russian empire, suggesting that politics may be as important as climate
in shaping drinking cultures.

Five hundred years ago there was no vodka belt. Back then, Russians brewed
beers and fermented mead from honey. The well-to-do imported wines from
more temperate climes. Tales of early Muscovite politics are steeped in inebriety,
but it wasn't vodka they were drinking.[5]

Consider, for instance, the founding of Nizhny Novgorod (literally
"Lower New-town"—now the fourth-largest city in Russia) on the banks

of the Volga River in 1222. Back then the middle Volga was populated by pagan Mordvinian tribes who, on hearing that Grand Prince Yury II of Vladimir-Suzdal was approaching down the Volga, dispatched a delegation with cooked meats and vessels of "delicious beer" to welcome the prince. Unfortunately, the young Mordva men of the delegation instead got drunk on the beer and devoured the meat, leaving nothing for the prince except earth and water. Interpreting this as a sign of submission—that all the tribes had to offer was their land and water—the prince rejoiced at his apparent conquest. And thus, as the story goes, "the Mordvan land was conquered by the Russians."[6]

Yet perhaps the most curious tale of alcohol in ancient Russia comes from the very birth of the Russian nation itself. Along with their eastern Slavic brethren the Ukrainians and Belarusians, Russians trace their lineage to Kievan Rus'. Kiev was the intellectual capital of Slavdom as well as the dominant power of Eastern Europe from the ninth through thirteenth centuries. It was there that legends of Russia's origin were compiled into the *Povest' vremennykh let* (*Primary Chronicle*), including descriptions of Russia's conversion from paganism to Christianity.[7]

At its height, the Kievan state stretched from the Baltic Sea to the Black Sea, covering present-day Ukraine, Moldova, Belarus, and the heartland of western Russia. Much of that territory was conquered by Grand Prince Vladimir the Great, who was renowned for his heathen debauches with his many wives. In a political calculation, neighboring princes and kings urged Vladimir to put away petty superstitions and adopt their modern faiths.

Vladimir agreed, sending forth fact-finding delegations to learn of different religious beliefs. Before long, Kiev was soon visited by ambassadors of the major monotheistic denominations to pitch to the great prince why he—and by extension his people—should convert to their faith. In the year 986 Vladimir hosted Jewish Khazars from the lower Volga, followed by papal emissaries from Germany who regaled the prince with tales of the power and grandeur of the Church of Rome. Greek scholars representing Byzantine Orthodox traditions took issue with the primacy of the pope before "Bulgars of the Mohammedan faith" arrived from the steppeland of the lower Don River and told the prince of the wondrous fulfillment of all carnal desires in the Islamic afterlife. "Vladimir listened to them," according to the *Chronicle*, "for he was fond of women and indulgence, regarding which he heard with pleasure." The Muslim Bulgars then described the rite of circumcision and the necessary abstinence from pork and wine. Furrowing his brow, Vladimir uttered a rhyme destined to be retold through the ages: "*Rusi est' vesel'e piti, ne mozhem bez togo byti.*"[8] "Drinking," said he, "is the joy of the Russes. We cannot exist without it."

The following year, in the water of the Dnieper River, Vladimir and the subjects of Kievan Rus' were baptized into the church of Constantinople, and the Russians have been Orthodox Christians ever since.

The point is that while Russia has a long history of inebriety, much of it did not include vodka. Moreover, even Russia's long history of drunkenness isn't unusual: Europeans of every region had been drinking nearly as long as the Russians, since before pasteurization alcoholic beverages were considered safer than milk, juices, and even water, which often transmitted disease-carrying microbes. (Incidentally, Louis Pasteur originally developed the pasteurization process to keep fermented beer and wine from spoiling.)[9] One could just as easily chronicle English history from the Roman introduction of beer brewing to the pagan Britons, perhaps recounting the murder of legendary fifth-century chieftain Vortigern at a drunken feast, or the death of King Henry I's only son in 1120 when the *White Ship* was run aground by drunken sailors, or the legendary intemperance of Richard the Lionheart, James I, Charles II, and straight through to Winston Churchill.[10] Russia is hardly "oriental" in this regard: since the middle ages, all European nations drank heavily.

So if early Russians had so much in common with their beer- and wine-drinking European neighbors, what made them switch to vodka? Think about it objectively: colorless, odorless, and tasteless—it makes as much sense to drink vodka as rubbing alcohol. In recent years, the fastest-growing segment of the global alcohol market has been flavored vodkas.[11] From raspberry and huckleberry to chocolate and cookie dough, from waffles and doughnuts to bacon and smoked salmon, manufacturers are in a rush to make their products taste like anything *but* vodka. "The Frenchman will praise the aroma of cognac, and the Scotsman will laud the flavor of whiskey," explains Russian writer Viktor Erofeyev. By contrast, "the Russian gulps his vodka down, grimacing and swearing, and immediately reaches for something else to 'smooth it out.' The result, not the process, is what's important. You might as well inject vodka into your bloodstream as drink it."[12]

Why, then, would an entire nation come to prefer such a torturous drink over the more palatable beers, wines, and meads that predominated in Russia until the fifteenth and sixteenth centuries?[13] This is not a trivial question. Geoalcoholic maps of European vodka, beer, and wine belts make it seem like the difference is simply a matter of taste—chalk it up to culture—but nothing could be further from the truth. Compared to traditional fermented beers and wines, distilled liquors were latecomers to the alcohol scene, but their arrival embodied a dramatic technological leap. As historian David Christian suggests, if beer and wine were like bows and arrows, vodka was like a cannon—an innovation with a potency unimaginable to traditional societies that would revolutionize both economy and culture.[14]

The Political Foundations Of Cultural Practices

Rarely do we scrutinize the origins of cultural practices—it is far easier to just assume that they have always been that way or simply embody some inherent national trait. Why do Russians seem to have a weakness for vodka? The conventional explanation is that it is just part of being Russian—overconsumption is hardwired into their DNA. That's wrong: what we assume today are essential cultural traits can often be traced to political and economic sources. Accordingly, I argue that the widespread, problematic drinking habits of today are actually the product of *political* decisions made during the formation of the modern Russian state over four centuries ago.

Going back, feudal Russia was starkly divided between the handful of local lords and the masses of impoverished peasants. Even before their formal enserfment by the *Sobornoye Ulozhenie*, or Law Code of 1649, most peasants were so indebted to the local landlords that they were already slaves in everything but name. Tied to their masters' estates, few serfs ever ventured beyond their village. Each village had at least one tavern, or *korchma*, through which the feudal lords extracted the earnings of the peasants. Tellingly, the Ulozhenie also outlined the gruesome tortures for those caught bootlegging or otherwise undermining alcohol revenues.[15]

Until the mid 1500s, village taverns were retail outlets for breweries located on the lords' estate or in a nearby monastery. These *korchma*s offered traditional fermented drinks like beer, mead, and *kvas*—a low-alcohol drink made from black or rye bread. By the early sixteenth century, many taverns began adding vodka to their menus as just another drink option. This early vodka production was primitive and small-scale—distilling just enough for the local estate or tavern.[16]

It quickly became clear that this early "burnt wine" (*goryachee vino*) or "bread wine" (*khlebnoe vino*) was a very lucrative business. The technology to distill vodka was basic and cheap.[17] All that was needed was a simple still: a stove to heat a fermented mash and buckets to collect the concentrated alcohol as it condensed. The ingredients were plentiful: water from a local river or spring and rye or wheat from the local fields—which would be harvested at little cost to the landlord by his indentured peasants. And at the end of the day, the final product could be sold back to the peasants at a price that was tens or hundreds of times the cost of the raw materials. Advances in industrial rectification from the nineteenth century through today has made contemporary vodka, in the words of alcohol historian Boris Rodionov, "the most primitive and the cheapest (in terms of production costs) drink in the world"—certainly something to remember the next time you consider buying any bottle of top-shelf vodka for more than $10.[18]

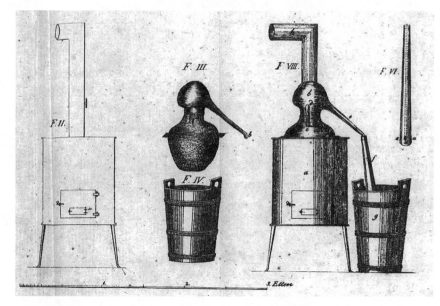

TRADITIONAL RUSSIAN STILL. It had a stove for heating the fermented mash (on left) and a funnel for the cooling and condensing of the alcohol, which was collected in a bucket (right). Riga, Neures Œkonomisches Repertorium für Liesland: 1814. Author's personal collection.

Back in the sixteenth century, Muscovy was undergoing an agricultural revolution, adopting a three-field system of crop rotation that dramatically raised yields. What was a landowner to do with all that excess grain? He could send it to market—but with so much supply, prices were low, and the cost of transporting wagonloads of grain to market was high. A better option was to distill it into vodka, the price of which was high while the cost of transporting it was low: one horse-drawn cart could easily transport the vodka distilled from mountains of grain. Plus, unlike fermented beer or mead, vodka never spoils, so it is a constant store of value—a value that can be easily measured, divided, and sold by volume. For all of these reasons, vodka was the perfect mechanism for both commerce and extracting resources. For all of the doubt cast on Vilyam Pokhlebkin's efforts to date vodka's origins from this period, his resulting interpretation is astute, claiming that "if vodka had never existed, it would have been necessary to invent it, not from any need for a new drink but as the ideal vehicle for indirect taxation."[19] And indeed it didn't take long for the young Russian state to also appreciate vodka's tremendous revenue potential.

If vodka does not immediately pop to mind as the quintessential symbol of Russia, the iconic visage of St. Basil's Cathedral on Red Square probably does. With its many colorful onion domes, the cathedral was ordered built by Ivan the Terrible to commemorate the 1552 conquest of the rival Khanate of Kazan on the Volga River. During the siege, which ended with the wanton slaughter of the population of Kazan, Ivan was impressed by the government-run taverns the Tatars called *kabak*. Upon his return to Moscow, he decreed that Russia too should have a system of government-run *kabaks*, outlawing the privately run *korchmas* so that all profits from the liquor trade were funneled directly into Ivan's treasury.[20]

These *kabaks* were described by English ambassador Giles Fletcher the Elder, who was dispatched to Russia in 1588 by Queen Elizabeth I. His resulting treatise, *Of the Russe Common Wealth* (1591), underscored the growing importance of the liquor trade to the tsar's finances and the burdens it placed on the peasantry.

> In every great towne of his Realme he hath a *Caback* or drinking house, where is sold *aquavitæ* (which they cal *Russewine*) *mead, beere, &c.* Out of these hee receiveth rent that amounteth to a great summe of money. Some yeeld 800, some 900, some a 1000 some 2000 or 3000. rubbels a yere. Wherein besides the base, and dishononourable means to encrease his treasurie, many foule faultes are committed. The poore labouring man, and artificer, manie times spendeth all from his wife and children. Some use to lay in twentie, thirtie, fourtie rubbels, or more into the *Caback*, and vowe themselves to the pot, till all that be spent. And this (as he will say) for the honour of *Hospodare*, or the Emperour. You shall have manie there that have drunk all away to the verie skinne, and so walk naked (whom they call *Naga*.) While they are in the *Caback*, none may call them foorth whatsoever cause there be, because he hindereth the Emperours revenue.[21]

Over the following century, the might of the autocratic Russian state was built upon a pillar of vodka. In order to maintain a steady flow of revenues, the government waged a clandestine war to root out illegal stills and taverns. The same Law Code of 1649 that codified serfdom also outlawed the purchase and sale of vodka outside of the *kabak* under penalty of torture—which could include lashings with the knout, singeing by fire, or the strappado: tying the victim's hands behind their backs and hoisting them in the air by a rope attached to the wrists, dislocating the arms and causing excruciating pain.[22] Three years later, the government imposed a total monopoly by outlawing all private commercial distillation. When the German scholar-ambassador Adam Olearius visited Russia in the 1630s, he claimed that there were more than a thousand government-run taverns throughout the land and that these taverns brought the government "an extraordinary amount of money, since the Russians know no restraint in drinking vodka." Consequently, Olearius concluded that the Russians "are more

addicted to drunkenness than any nation in the world."[23] His firsthand run-ins
with Russian peasants at the tsar's taverns are particularly illuminating.

> While we were there, taverns and pothouses were everywhere, and any-
> one who cared to could go in and sit and drink his fill. The common
> people would bring all their earnings into the tavern and sit there until,
> having emptied their purses, they gave away their clothing, and even
> their nightshirts, to the keeper, and then went home as naked as they
> had come into the world. When, in 1643, I stopped at the Lübeck house
> in Novgorod, I saw such besotted and naked brethren come out of the
> nearby tavern, some bareheaded, some barefooted, and others only in
> their nightshirts. One of them had drunk away his cloak and emerged
> from the tavern in his nightshirt; when he met a friend who was on his
> way to the same tavern, he went in again. Several hours later he came
> out without his nightshirt, wearing only a pair of under-drawers. I had
> him called to ask what had become of his nightshirt, who had stolen it?
> He answered with the customary "Fuck your mother," that it was the
> tavern keeper, and that the drawers might as well go where the cloak
> and nightshirt had gone. With that, he returned to the tavern, and later
> came out entirely naked. Taking a handful of dog fennel that grew near
> the tavern, he held it over his private parts, and went home singing
> gaily.[24]

This hardly sounds like the popular image of the kindly, hospitable bartender,
always happy to lend a sympathetic ear to his customers. No. If anything, the tavern owner was the villain of the traditional Russian village: the cold and unscrupulous defender of state finance above all else.

Tavern keepers were the main interface between the state and Russian society, and it was clear which side they were on. In fact, they were not known as
tavern keepers but, rather, as *tselovalniki*—"kissers." They swore allegiance to the
tsar by kissing the Orthodox cross—vowing to honestly serve the emperor by
keeping the liquor flowing into the peasants' mouths and money flowing out of
their pockets. The Russian *tselovalnik* was the shameless instrument of a predatory state. He would never tell a customer to leave unless the peasant had no
more money and nothing of value left to pawn. Even according to government
regulations in 1659, the tavern keeper could not so much as refuse a habitual
drunkard—lest the revenue stream be diminished.[25]

Since their highly lucrative positions depended on delivering more and more
money to the provincial government and national ministries, the entire tavern
administration deliberately pushed the more potent distilled vodka over traditional fermented beers and meads because the profit margins were so much

greater. While other feudal institutions like serfdom and direct taxation funneled the productive capacity of the peasantry into wealth for the state, they
could not match the sheer revenue-generating capacity of vodka. Vodka had to
be paid for in cash, which required the peasants to earn the money necessary to
drink. Even when the tavern keeper let their customers pawn their belongings
or drink on credit, the money paid to the government still had to be in cash. In
this way, the tavern became the primary mechanism through which the Russian
state exploited its own society. Within a generation of the introduction of vodka
and the tsar's *kabaks*, the traditionally self-sufficient Russian village was gone,
replaced by a system dominated by the state, gentry, and merchants that both
propagated and profited from the misery of the peasantry and that integrated
even isolated, far-flung communities into the autocratic system.[26]

While over the *longue durée* the system's promotion of drunkenness and corruption proved detrimental, the more immediate consequences were positive
for the imperial state. As the treasury filled, the state's capacity for both extraction and defense grew. It permitted Russia to not only accumulate the largest
territory on earth but also to effectively broadcast its power over even the most
sparsely populated territories without a massive government bureaucracy. And
as both the state's boundaries and its capacity grew—as we shall see in later
chapters—so to did its ability to raise, finance, and control the largest army in
the world.

The Old Style Of Russian Drinking

Once vodka became ensconced as the cornerstone of Russian statecraft, untold
generations of Russians would pay the cost—not just the retail cost of billions
of bottles of liquor, but also the staggering social, health, and demographic consequences of an autocracy that promotes dependence on alcohol. One consequence of this fundamental tenet of vodka politics is that even today Russian
drinking culture is marked by dangerous binges and overconsumption of vodka.
To come to terms with the effects of this deadly binge-drinking culture, it is not
enough simply to ask why Russians die from drinking; in the words of leading
health researcher Martin McKee, we need to ask: "Why do they drink? What do
they drink? Why, when they drink to the extent that they do, do they fall down,
and why does no one pick them up?"[27]

So, how do Russians drink today, and how have those drinking patterns
evolved over time? Returning to the imperial era, we may envision a lowly
drunken peasant, daily stumbling to the village tavern to drink up his last
kopeck, neglecting his family who live in squalor in some dilapidated, dimly lit
hut. This stereotype may resonate with anyone who has spent time drinking in

bars in Russia today, but we cannot simply project Russia's modern drinking culture backward in time. As it turns out, before vodka, the location, timing, quantity, and even ceremonies associated with drinking were dramatically different.
The subsequent transformation of even the *style* of alcohol consumption can be
attributed to vodka politics.

Before vodka, the lightly alcoholic "liquid bread" *kvas* was the day-to-day
drink for most Russians, while mead and imported wine were reserved for
wealthy lords and boyars. By the fourteenth century, beer had made inroads
as the most common alcoholic beverage, as the Russian word *pivo*—originally
meaning "drink" in general—came to apply to beer in particular. These early
hopped brews were so strong that even fifteenth-century Venetian explorer
Iosaphat Barbaro described the native Russian drinks "as stupefying and intoxicating as wine."[28]

Beer and mead were primarily for special occasions: celebrating births and
deaths, marriages and christenings, church festivals and feasts. In addition to
paying duties on the hops and grains, brewing also required the permission of
the grand prince for an exemption from government restrictions aimed at limiting widespread drunkenness.

"They are great drunkards and are exceedingly boastful of it, disdaining those
who do not drink," wrote Venetian diplomat Ambrogio Contarini, who was
received by Grand Prince Ivan III ("the Great") in 1476. "They have no wines,
but use a drink from honey which they make from hop leaves. This drink is not at
all bad, particularly if it is old. However, their sovereign does not allow everyone
to prepare it freely, because, if they were free to do so, they would be drunk every
day and would kill one another like beasts."[29]

On such occasions Russian peasants did drink to excess, but the number of
calendar days when drinking was possible were very few. On most days, peasants
were preoccupied with the draining work of tilling, plowing, or harvesting the
fields. Drunkenness was a luxury most subsistence farmers could not regularly
afford.[30]

Overindulgence was especially problematic during the Christmas–Epiphany
season. Such drunken, and even pagan, debauchery was denounced by an
Orthodox Church Council of 1551—the same assembly charged with providing moral guidance to Ivan the Terrible and his boyars. The council's *Stoglav*—
or *Hundred Chapters*—repeatedly condemns celebrations that promote "deeds
loathsome to God, [where] there is defilement of young men and debauchery
of the girls": ironic in that the council's proclamations were actually overseen by
the head defiler and debaucher, Ivan the Terrible. The church elders denounced
both the peasants' alcohol-fueled bacchanals that "do anger the Lord God" and
the lack of concern, guidance, and punishment from local priests and judges.

"*Piti podobaet ne vo p'ianstvo, no v veselie*" concluded the council: it is proper to drink to the point of gladness, but not of drunkenness. The *Stoglav* counseled the tsar to end such pagan practices and to punish those priests implicit in them.[31] Yet the traditions continued.

Long before there even were tsars, the traditional Muscovite drinking culture was characterized by long periods of sobriety punctuated by occasional drunkenness. Drinking was a social ritual and often a religious one as well. Alcohol historian Boris Segal even suggests that the Orthodox Church deliberately incorporated alcohol into their religious celebrations in order to wean the peasantry from their heathen traditions, in which alcohol likewise played a communal role.[32] Whether pagan or Christian, drinking was not done alone, but rather in groups—either in the home, among friends, or with the entire community—in sharp contrast to the drinking houses that came later.

Even before there were taverns, attempts were made to control drinking through moral suasion and economic regulation. The quasi-official sixteenth-century moral codex known as the *Domostroi,* or *Domestic Order,* outlined the elites' household, familial, moral, and civil obligations regarding alcohol. "When you are invited to a wedding," it says,

> do not drink yourself to the point of inebriation and do not remain seated until late, because in inebriation and lengthy sitting are quarrels, brawls and shedding of blood. I do not say that you should not drink at all! No. I do say that you should not get drunk. I do not disparage God's gifts, but I do berate those who drink without self-control.[33]

The *Domostroi* also offered practical advice about the new science of distilling, suggesting that its aristocratic readers "Distill vodka yourself" and "Never leave it unguarded. If you are otherwise occupied, have someone trustworthy take your place."[34] Even early on both vodka's potency and profitability were evident. In confronting this new technology, the grand princes' regulations on gentry brewing were extended to the more potent distillates. The Mogilev statute of 1561 stipulates that "every burgher is free to keep mead and beer for his own use, but not for sale. With the knowledge of the tax collector he can distill spirits for his son's or daughter's wedding and for caroling. In addition to this the burghers can distill spirits five times a year: at Christmas, in Cheesefare week, on Easter, Trinity Sunday and autumnal St. Nicholas Day [December 6]; they cannot, however, use more than four chetverts of malt each time for the spirits."[35]

Such regulations reinforced the traditional overconsumption on festivals and holidays, often with tragic consequences. "In the *Carnaval* before...*Lent,* they give themselves over to all manner of debauchery and luxury, and in the last week they drink as if they were never to drink more," wrote Englishman Samuel

Collins, personal physician to Tsar Alexei Mikhailovich Romanov, in 1671. Beyond being the source of drunken quarrels, fistfights and murders, Collins explains how

> Some of these going home drunk, if not attended with a sober com-
> panion, fall asleep upon the Snow (a sad cold bed) and there they are
> frozen to death. If any of their acquaintance chance to pass by, though
> they see them like to perish, yet will they not assist them, to avoid the
> trouble of examination if they should die in their hands: For those of
> the *zemsky precaus* [department of urban and police matters] will extort
> something out of every bodies purse, who comes to their Office. 'Tis
> a sad sight to see a dozen people brought upright in a Sledge frozen to
> death, some have their arms eaten off by Dogs, others their faces, and
> others have nothing left but Bones: Two or three hundred have been
> brought after this manner in the time of Lent. By this you may see the
> sad consequence of drunkenness, the Epidemick distemper not only of
> *Russia,* but of *England* also."[36]

Unfortunately, this traditional drinking culture has proven to be quite durable. The Dutch diplomat Balthazar Coyet, who visited Moscow in 1676 wrote: "We saw only the scandalous behavior of debauchees, glorified by the thronging crowd for their proficiency in drunkenness."[37] Two hundred years later the future editor of *the Times* of London, Sir D. Mackenzie Wallace, simi- larly observed: "As a whole, a village fête in Russia is one of the most saddening spectacles I have ever witnessed. It affords a new proof—where, alas! no new proof was required—that . . . the people do not know how to enjoy themselves in a harmless, rational way, and seek a refuge in intoxication, so that the sight of a popular holiday may make us regret that life has any holidays at all."[38]

While drinking was largely a male activity, the traditional drinking culture also ensnared women and children, who often drank alongside their men. Describing a typical village celebration, Adam Olearius wrote: "After they got drunk, the men struck their wives for the pleasure of it, and then proceeded to tipple with them again. Finally the women, sitting astride their sleeping husbands, drank to each other until they toppled over alongside them and slept. One may easily imagine the peril to honor and modesty, and its frequent ruin, under such condi- tions of life."[39]

Vodka was even central to the "circling dances" of young peasant girls during village festivals. Children sang folk songs ranging from the fantastic to the satiri- cal: some spun stories of witches and vampires while others (disturbingly) glori- fied the infidelity of particular villagers, wife-beating, and the vodka that helped perpetuate it all. Envision a band of pre-teen girls—dressed in their Sunday best—entering the traditional drunken banquet as Olearius described and performing an homage to vodka. They stumble about—imitating the drunken women of the village—singing gaily as they dance.

> Vodka delicious I drank, I drank
> Not in a cup or a glass, but a bucketful I drank.. .
> I cling to the posts of the door.
> Oh, doorpost, hold me up, the drunken woman, the tipsy rogue.[40]

Shocking as this may seem to our modern sensibilities, children were not spared from alcohol within the communal drinking culture. "One can hardly fail to be surprised when a child who cannot yet walk or talk reaches out for vodka, asks for some with gestures, is given some, and then drinks it with pleasure," describes a Yaroslavl parish priest in the nineteenth century. "A four- or five-year old will already drink a full glass....And even a young unmarried girl does not find it shameful on occasion, for example during work parties [*pomoch'*], to drink a good glass of vodka and another of beer."[41] Socialized from such a young age into a community that not only tolerates, but actively encourages, drunkenness—is it any wonder that such practices endure for generations?

Touring Russia's rural provinces, nineteenth-century agrarian reformer Andrei Zablotsky-Desyatovsky recalled the lamentable—but typical—use of religious holidays as a pretext for getting inebriated. Upon entering a village, he found nothing but drinking and debauchery.

"What are you celebrating, and why are you so drunk?" he asked one of the peasants.

"What do you mean? Today is the Assumption of the Mother of God," one drunk replied, adding wryly: "perhaps you have heard of her?"

"But the day of the Assumption was yesterday!"

"So? You've got to drink for three days," claimed the peasant.

"Why three days?" Zablotsky-Desyatovsky shot back. "Did the Mother of God command that?"

"Of course she did. Our Holy Mother knows how we peasants love to drink!"[42]

While the ritual-based traditional drinking culture led to bouts of extreme intoxication, the oversight of a tight-knit community helped prevent chronic, day-in, day-out alcoholism. "It must also be said," as one nineteenth-century parish priest from Yaroslavl suggested, "that in spite of their inclination towards drunkenness, there are extremely few or even no drunkards. Even the most hardened drinker will return home at midnight, or early in the morning, sleep, sober himself up with *kvas*, and work as hard as ever until the next Sunday."[43]

The traditional drinking culture can be seen even today throughout Russia, especially around holidays. During the thirteen days between Christmas

(December 25) and Orthodox Christmas (January 7), many Russians engage in a two-week bender. Consequently, the first week of January in Russia is always marked by a dramatic spike in alcohol poisonings, crimes, highway accidents, murders, and all manner of alcohol-related mortality.[44] According to Russia's foremost alcohol researcher, Aleksandr Nemtsov, Russia's annual vodka "marathon" is a more dire threat than terrorism—annually killing over two thousand inhabitants of Moscow alone. Some have even suggested that a modern "cult of Bacchus" has supplanted traditional Orthodox Christianity as the basis for religion and social interaction. "Once, when people wished each other well, they prayed for you—now, they drink to you." One's friendships are measured by how much you've drunk together, and even when you die, your friends will carry you to the grave, drinking on your behalf.[45]

These are the roots of the uniquely Russian tradition of *zapoi*—a period lasting days or even weeks dedicated to continuous overintoxication, which may

EARLY SOVIET PROPAGANDA POSTER. "Away with Church Celebrations!" depicts two drunken workers leaving a church festival. Side panels show the disastrous consequences of holiday drinking, from fights and hooliganism to family destitution and getting run over by public transportation. Source: Hoover Institution Archives, Stanford University

or may not correspond with a religious holiday. During a visit to Russia in the 1850s, Baron von Haxthausen described it in the following terms: "The Great Russians do not drink constantly, nor daily, and many of them not at all for months, nor will they take brandy even when offered to them; but times and temptations occur when, if they taste a drop, a perfect rage for it seizes them [*zapoi*]: they will then drink continuously for days, nay weeks, and squander all they possess, to their last farthing. On these occasions arises the great profit of the *kabak*."[46]

New Drinks, New Drinking Patterns

These destructive elements are deeply rooted in a Russian traditional drinking culture that predated vodka. The arrival of vodka and the tsar's taverns not only wedded those practices to a drink of unmatched potency but also introduced "modern" social relations, economic conflicts, and individual drinking customs that proved to be even more destructive.

As in other countries, once introduced, the tavern quickly became the center of village life, with traditional, communal celebrations even taking place within its walls. But the tavern was open every day, not just on holidays and feast days. It was an especially powerful temptation for village artisans and workers: paid in cash, they could more easily pay for booze than could peasants reaping grains in kind. These, then, became Russia's first "modern" alcoholics: men who drank regularly and individually rather than strictly according to the communal calendar.

For those accustomed to traditional patterns, finding dozens of inebriates holed up in a dank village tavern in the middle of a workday was difficult to comprehend. In the 1850s, the Russian traveler Protasyev was so struck by it that he barged into taverns and bluntly asked the drunkards there why they drank.

"The temptation is huge. I myself am not glad that I drink, but what can I do?" answered one man, who professed that life would be better without taverns. "The vodka seems to beg me to drink it. Sometimes, I do not want to go into the tavern, but I go onto my front steps and it's there, right there, as if beckoning to me. I go in, and once I am in no good can come of it."[47]

The combination of these two distinct drinking cultures—one ancient, one modern—was even reflected in different characterizations of the drinkers themselves. Adjectives like *temperate* or *sober* normally denote someone who does not drink at all. "But in Russia," as nineteenth-century observers noted, the "sober" label applies to "one who only gets drunk upon the festivals of the Church," in other words, to one who adhered to the traditional drinking culture, not the modern.[48]

In economists' terms, the demand for alcohol in the traditional drinking culture was inelastic—limited only by regular communal rituals. In the modern culture, demand was elastic—limited only by the peasant's ability to pay. Consequently, the state stood to profit far more from the modern, individualistic drinking culture, which in turn worsened the negative social and health consequences of widespread intoxication.[49] Vodka, the tavern, and the individualistic drinking culture also created the modern alcoholic. While close-knit communal drinking resulted its share of embarrassing, alcohol-fueled escapades, oversight by the community at least discouraged the type of chronic alcoholism engendered by the modern drinking culture. "At a single blow vodka destroyed social, cultural, moral and ideological taboos," even our old friend Pokhlebkin claimed. "In this respect it acted like an atomic explosion in the stagnant calm of patriarchal feudalism."[50] Indeed.

The arrival of vodka, the tsar's *kabak,* and the tavern keeper changed everything. Instead of weaker fermented beverages, people now drank the more potent vodka. Instead of drinking within the community, now peasants escaped whenever to the tavern to drink away their last dime, often leading their families to destitution. What's more, the welding of the new, individualistic drinking culture to the traditional, communal one irreversibly changed the relationship between state and society: tearing peasants away from their communities and tethering them to the state with a bond of alcohol that proved to be more durable than even serfdom. In this way, it broke the economic self-sufficiency of the traditional Russian village.[51]

At the same time, the tavern also exacerbated feudal class divisions. For one, it wasn't the peasantry, but the local gentry, landowners who had the resources (raw materials, labor, and imperial permission), to conduct large-scale distillation on their estates. So, it was the regional landlords who provided the vodka to the local tax farmers and village taverns. Meanwhile, these wealthy elites could afford to drink at home—enjoying more expensive, higher quality imported wines stored in their well-apportioned wine cellars—rather than patronize the village tavern and mingle with artisans, tradesmen, and peasants who dwelt in the taverns—the veritable drug dens of imperial Russia. The culture of tavern drinking thus accentuated class distinctions between rich and poor in Russia, while the liquor trade itself made the rich richer and the poor poorer.[52]

The modern drinking house effectively loosened the community's hold on a would-be alcoholic, drawing him away from the oversight of village elders and into the solitary recesses of the tavern, where he could better serve the financial interests of the state. At this time, even the issue of drunkenness was recast from a moral conflict between the individual and his religious community into a social and political conflict over state finances. In addition to new social conflicts, the arrival of vodka also created early industry in the form of distillation (as distinct from the traditional trades and handicrafts); it sharpened feudal class conflicts between the gentry and the peasantry; it established new political institutions, such as the highly corrupt tax farm; and firmly entrenched the tavern as the primary interface between Russian society and the state.

From its first introduction, then, vodka fundamentally transformed both Russia's society and politics. Its potency ensured a steady demand; its advanced manufacturing and laws outlawing distillation except by the nobility meant that the uneducated peasants had to pay cash for this new commercial product; and its monopolization transformed vodka into the primary mechanism by which the government—in concert with feudal lords—simultaneously dominated and exploited the lower classes. Once vodka became entrenched as a key mechanism of autocratic statecraft, the subsequent history of vodka politics in Russia revolved entirely around the inherent contradiction of minimizing the social harms caused by this powerful drug, of which the state was the sole dealer and most eager pusher.[53]

The conclusions, then, are unavoidable: if one is looking to explain why Russians drink what they do and how they do it, the answer isn't culture; it's politics. The financial needs of the early Russian state dictated pushing the more potent and more profitable distilled vodka over less lucrative beers and meads. To maximize revenues, the state actively encouraged its subjects to become alcoholics. Consequently, Russia's long-standing addiction to vodka is not some eternal, immutable cultural trait, but the result of political decisions intended to enrich the state.

Finally, the introduction of vodka fundamentally altered cultural drinking patterns—augmenting the episodic drunkenness of community celebrations with an even more damaging culture of individual alcoholism. While this perversion of the noble, medicinal ends of the "water of life" would have surely appalled earlier generations of medieval doctors, mystics, priests, and ambassadors who helped introduce distilled spirits into Russia, even those medieval alchemists—to quote historian David Christian—"would have envied a process that transmuted grain so readily into gold."[54]

8

Vodka and the Origins of Corruption in Russia

"You can't change this system from within. Its founding principles are corruption, hypocrisy, and cynicism," claimed Russia's prominent anti-corruption blogger, Alexei Navalny. If you join this system, your main instruments become corruption, hypocrisy, and cynicism, and it's impossible to build anything with such instruments."[1]

Fed up with Russia's systemic bribery and corruption—which undermine the ideal of a state bureaucracy, staffed by professionals implementing rules evenly and impersonally, and whose salary is their means of income rather than money culled from their station—this tenacious Moscow lawyer began tracing countless cases of embezzlement, kickbacks, and graft often leading to the highest levels of power. In the frigid winter of 2011–12, massive protests erupted in Moscow against allegations of widespread fraud in the series of elections that heralded Vladimir Putin's return for a third term as Russia's president. Before gradually retreating unfulfilled, this predominantly young, predominantly urban, predominantly middle-class protest movement shook Russia's stagnant political scene and rallied against Putin's corrupt United Russia party, which Navalny forever branded as "the party of crooks and thieves."

According to Transparency International, in 2012 Russia was far and away the most corrupt of the world's twenty largest economies, ranking 133rd of 176 countries—placing it squarely behind such paragons of clean and effective governance as Sierra Leone, Vietnam, and Ethiopia. As a percentage of overall economic activity, the shadow economy in Russia is larger than in Chad or Senegal. And as cost projections for the 2014 Winter Olympic games in Sochi ballooned over 400 percent to $50 billion—eclipsing even China's world-record $40 billion tab for the 2008 Beijing Summer Olympics—many cited pervasive corruption, with businesses paying kickbacks in excess of fifty percent. The Russian edition of *Esquire* even estimated the construction cost of one notorious stretch of Sochi roadway as the equivalent of paving its entire length in Louis Vuitton handbags.[2]

Russians are well aware of corruption, regularly ranking it just behind alcoholism as one of the country's most pressing problems. Patients pay off doctors for their "free" healthcare, students grease teachers for better grades, families bribe draft boards to keep their sons out of the army, and police officers spend more time on shakedowns than stakeouts. According to the government's own statistics, Russians shell out more than $300 *billion* in bribes every year. While the economic costs are staggering, so too are the political impacts: Russia is saddled with an enormous, outmoded, and notoriously corrupt *sistema*, throughout which bureaucrats exploit their public positions for private gain.[3]

Yet while Navalny and throngs of shivering protesters were quick to blame Vladimir Putin and his United Russia party for this state of affairs, systemic corruption in Russia predates both Putin and the oft-cited weak post-Soviet institutions he inherited from his predecessor, Boris Yeltsin.[4] Its roots go far deeper.

Even in the 1970s, Soviet leader Leonid Brezhnev championed a "decisive struggle against greed, bribe-taking, parasitism, and drunkenness"—those vestiges of Russia's capitalist past—words that parroted his predecessor, Nikita Khrushchev a decade earlier.[5] Yet bribes and favors were often the only way to get scarce goods necessary to fulfill the state's economic plans. "Corruption may be as integral to Soviet life as vodka and kasha," concluded one Cold War study—it was the secret oil that lubricated the communist system. Not surprisingly, *every* Soviet leader waged a half-hearted war on corruption, and they lost every single time.[6]

Corruption likewise plagued the tsars' feudal economy. In the 1850s, Nicholas I commissioned an anti-corruption investigation, which exposed graft and bribery even among the tsar's highest officials. When asked how many of Russia's forty-five governors would not take bribes, the commission could only find *two* honest men—no more. "To live in the middle of such conscious corruption was horrible," explained Nicholas's biographer, "yet to remove it was impossible. In despair, the czar threw the report of the commission into the fire." Privately Nicholas lamented that he was the only honest man in Russia.[7]

Corruption and alcoholism are the twin systemic afflictions that have "debilitated Russia as long as anyone can remember."[8] These diseases are symbiotic: each is perpetuated by the other. Like so many of Russia's social ills, one major source of corruption in Russia can be found at the bottom of the bottle.

Blat, Bribery, And Corruption

Any discussion of corruption begins with *blat*—a word so quintessentially Russian that it defies literal translation. Unlike "bribery"—so cold and impersonal—*blat* embodies the warmth and friendship of mutual assistance as friends

struggle to cope with both hardship and red tape through favors and connections. Bribery demands cash for action. *Blat* can be a favor that needn't be repaid
immediately or in cash. Even incorruptibles who would never take a bribe would
happily use their connections to help family and friends.[9]

Bribery is an exchange—corruption is an attribute. The socio-political system becomes corrupted when bribery, nepotism, and the use of public office for
private advantage are widespread.[10] Corruption blurs the line not only between
public station and private interest—between formal duties and informal obligations—but more fundamentally between the legal and the illegal. So it makes
sense that the roots of corruption extend back to when public and private were
indistinguishable and law itself was imprecise.

Rooted in peasant hospitality and traditions of provincial officials living off
the land they administered, petty bribery was a sporadic feature of early Russian
society. Only with the harnessing of vodka's extreme revenue-generating potential did a pervasive system of obligatory corruption come into full bloom.

While autocrats back to Ivan the Terrible knew of the great potential of vodka,
the Muscovite state had no way to administer the nationwide liquor trade. Even
Ivan's system of state-run taverns, or *kabaks*, was crude: tavern keepers, or *tselovalniki*, swore to protect the tsar's revenue, which led to pushing the more lucrative vodka over beer and mead. "As the Emperours Territories are great, so is
his Revenue," the tsar's English physician Samuel Collins noted in 1671. "The
Cabacks (or places where in are sold *Aqua-vitae* and strong Beer) are his Royalty,
and farms out some for 10000 Rubbles *per annum*, and some again for 20000
Rubbles."[11]

To further maximize revenues, by the seventeenth century the state leased
out individual taverns to entrepreneurs eager to tap into the lucrative trade.
Without an effective state bureaucracy it was only a matter of time before the
entire administration of the vodka trade would be outsourced to private entrepreneurs, in what was known as the vodka tax farm.

Like a traditional tenant farmer harvesting crops in the field, a tax farmer harvests tax revenue. And just as a tenant farmer pays the landlord to cultivate a
parcel of land, the tax farmer pays the state to cultivate the vodka trade over a
particular territory. Every four years the state auctioned off the exclusive right to
collect liquor taxes, licenses, and fees for a given district. For the winning bidder,
any income beyond his administrative costs and what he owed to the state was
pure profit, and the tax farmer had every incentive to maximize that profit by any
means possible.

Dating back to the sprawling Roman Empire, tax farms were the earliest form
of outsourcing. Given the expansive, sparsely populated terrain and the shortage
of qualified administrators and bookkeepers, the tax farm system was well-suited
to the early Russian empire too. Passing both the administrative burdens and

commercial risks onto the private tax farmer, it guaranteed the government a reliable, consistently growing source of revenues that was immune from market peaks and troughs, since the annual rent had already been set at auction. "No other major source of revenue enters the Treasury so regularly, punctually, and easily as the revenue from the liquor tax farm," the finance ministry reported in 1816: "indeed its regular receipt on a fixed date each month greatly eases the task of finding case for other expenditures."[12] The primary expenditure of the empire was its growing military, which—thanks to the tax farm—could be effectively financed even without a large government tax-collection bureaucracy.

Tax farm systems were common across renaissance Europe, but as the extractive capacity of states increased, they were increasingly replaced with direct taxes overseen by a professional bureaucracy. Compared to such modern institutions, the tax farm seems downright medieval: a hallmark of weak central government, it gives free license to unscrupulous individuals to exploit the peasantry for their own gain. Since the system fused together public tax revenues and private commercial profits—and since the essence of corruption is the confusion between public and private—it makes sense that the origins of systemic Russian corruption can be traced precisely here.[13]

Even before vodka, tax farming shaped early imperial history: the rising power of Moscow over rival principalities like Tver resulted in part from it being a more loyal and efficient tax farmer for the fourteenth-century Mongolian overlords. Tax farming outlasted the Mongolian yoke through the system of *kormlenie* (literally "feeding") whereby officials were expected to support themselves from their administrative territory, so long as they collected taxes for the state. And although *kormlenie* was outlawed in 1555, tax farming endured for customs duties, salt taxes, and, most importantly, vodka.[14]

The vodka trade became the bread and butter of the Russian autocracy. In 1680, income from the tax farms on salt and vodka accounted for 53 percent of all state revenues. By the 1830s, the "indirect" vodka taxes outpaced even direct taxes.[15] In an investigation of the tax farm in his *Provincial Sketches*, famed writer and onetime deputy governor Mikhail Saltykov-Shchedrin lamented that up to two-thirds of government revenue came from the vodka farm.[16]

To maximize their take from the vodka trade, the state imposed ever stricter regulations on the tax farmer. So as not to flood the market, the treasury allocated each *otkupshchik* (tax farmer) only a set quota of vodka from the government's warehouses and stipulated that it be sold at a fixed price, leaving the farmer only a razor-thin margin for *legitimate* profit.[17] Since the vodka farmers were still reaping outlandish profits through various abusive practices, the treasury squeezed them even more, demanding that even the paltry amounts that the tax farmers were to gain legitimately would also go to the state—implicitly acknowledging and sanctioning the *otkupshchik's* corrupt practices.

"Who can buy from the government a given quantity of vodka at a fixed price, sell it to the people without raising its price, and from it pay the government ten times as much?" queried a scathing exposé in Aleksandr Herzen's influential independent newspaper *Kolokol* (*The Bell*).[18] This riddle underscored the inherent contradiction of corruption: on the one hand, the government demanded strict adherence to the letter of the law while, on the other hand, it could only maximize its take by implicitly (and in some cases, actively) *encouraging* its administrators to break those laws. It was the state's willingness to look upon the tax farmers' transgressions with a wink and a nod that transformed traditional *blat* and petty bribery into a political system permeated with obligatory corruption from top to bottom. "What is really sold at the tax farm auctions is an exemption from the rules," even admitted Russia's most infamous *otkupshchik*, Vasily Kokorev.[19] He personally benefited from such exemptions countless times.

"In Russia in the early nineteenth century, it was tax farming that accounted for almost all forms of 'obligatory corruption,'" stresses David Christian, the foremost historian of Russian tax farms. "Corruption was not a mere side-effect of the tax farm's operations, it was its very life blood."[20] Once entrenched, such systemic corruption becomes incredibly difficult to dislodge, as even contemporary anti-corruption crusaders like Alexei Navalny can attest.

Corruption Entrenched

Almost single-handedly the vodka farm transformed sporadic bribes and gratuities into a system of routine, semi-formal payments to all levels of government officials. At the height of the vodka farm in the nineteenth century, observers noted that "Every person having any degree of influence receives regular cash payments from the tax farmers, according to their influence, as well as a monthly gift of vodka." Every year, the typical *otkupshchik* doled out tens of thousands of rubles to district government officials, jurists, and law enforcement in order to ply his trade.[21]

The biggest bribes went to local politicians—the governor, his chancery, and mayors—to buy powerful political cover for his schemes. These payoffs often exceeded the officials' annual salaries. Penza governor A. A. Panchulidze annually received 24,000 rubles—or three times his official salary—from the local tax farmer, allowing the *otkupshchik* to rule Penza province "in the style of a medieval turkish pasha."[22] As contemporaries noted: "The receipt of a payment from the tax farmers means that the official must, at the very least, look through his fingers at all the abuses of the tax farm, and that no complaints or denunciations against the tax farm or its employees can be proceeded with."[23]

Then (as today) Russian corruption also permeated law enforcement: officers, commissioners, captains, and everyone in between became complicit in the vodka trade. Today, as then, they engaged in the same extortive schemes. Nowadays in Russia one common scheme is for the notoriously corrupt State Automobile Inspectorate (GAI) to deliberately place obstacles in the road and lie in wait to catch anyone who then (illegally) swerves across the double-yellow line to avoid them.[24] Any driver who's slipped an officer $20 in order to avoid trumped-up charges can relate to nineteenth-century stories of the Kharkov cordon guards—the tax farmer's private police charged with stopping liquor smuggling between tax farm districts—who would hide vodka bottles inside sacks of oats left along the roadside on market day:

> As the [peasant] came along, with a cart containing several sacks of rye, he saw the sack lying on the ground. Crossing himself, he picked it up, untied it and, seeing that it contained oats, put it on his cart and went on his way, supposing that it had been dropped by someone passing along the road before him. He approached the cordon. The guards were ready, for they knew that he picked up the vodka. They stopped the peasant and began to inspect the load carefully. They left one bag to the end and in it, to his horror, they found the smuggled vodka. The peasant swore he was innocent, tried to prove it, wept—but they had no mercy. They bound him, placed him amongst the sacks and carted him to the police. The affair ended with the peasant losing everything he was taking to the market for sale, as well as a good part of his modest means.[25]

The police also targeted businesses, like the respectable inns that relied on vodka sales to stay in business. Innkeepers who refused to pay the exorbitant kickbacks demanded by the tax farmer would be raided by the police, during which "illegal" vodka would surely be discovered.

Oftentimes village constables simply ignored the disorderly conduct of a drunken peasant or serf until they thought it possible to extort a few rubles from the man or his master, which would buy their indifference for a few more months. It wasn't much of an exaggeration for contemporaries to claim that "nowadays, the police officials are themselves farmed out to the tax farmers."[26]

Like any kingpin worth his salt, the vodka tax farmer was above the law. Even if charged with a crime, the *otkupshchik* could not be brought to court until after his farm had expired and all accounts had been settled—a process that could take years. Even then, allegations could only be tried in the capital—further straining relations between the central government and its far-flung regions.[27]

Even with the politicians and law enforcement in his pocket, there was still enough to buy off the judiciary, too: hundreds of rubles annually for the circuit court judge, assessor, secretaries of the rural police courts, and presidents of the exchequer court who supervised liquor tax revenues. As the *Kolokol* exposé pointed out: "Having made such deals with the tax farmers, the government of course not only cannot prosecute the tax farmers for the abuses, but is actually obliged to protect them; otherwise they'd be wishing for a miracle requiring the tax farmers to do the impossible! Therefore, by tolerating and enabling the tax farmer, the government is consciously robbing the people—dividing up the spoils with the tax farmers and others who have participated in the crime."[28]

From the bottom to the top, government officials often relied more on the tax farmer's bribes than their meager state salaries. Not surprisingly, their loyalties were divided between their official legal duties and breaking those laws to keep the "gifts" flowing from the tax farmer.[29]

Of course not *everyone* was complicit in the systemic corruption. Some officials were too insignificant to deserve a bribe, while an admirable few refused to soil their hands on moral or ethical grounds. Such "untouchables" did not last long in Russia: rather than being rewarded for their honesty, the fastidious were looked at with suspicion and mockery. According to a nineteenth-century French account:

> Most officials show little respect for an honest subordinate, but will view him as a Utopian, a restless "frondeur." Further, to refuse a bribe is to ensure the enmity of the rich and influential caste of tax farmers, who will always work for the removal of an honest official. And sooner or later they will succeed....As the laws are complicated and the formalities insurmountable, an official is bound to have broken some, and that is enough....As a result, once an honest official has earned the enmity of the tax farmers, his superior will leave him to their mercy, public opinion will not shield him, and he will be left with nothing but his conscience.[30]

In such a permissive environment corruption always wins. Accepting a bribe is not only profitable, but safe and socially acceptable—like picking up money found lying on the ground.[31] To refuse was to raise the scorn of powerful people within the system. Yet the corruption of the entire governance system was a natural consequence. According to one report from 1853: "For the tax farm to exist without corruption is now impossible. The whole atmosphere of the tax farm is such that no one even thinks of abiding by the legal conditions. They think of only one thing—how to get around the regulations, and to extract the maximum advantage from their obscurity and imprecision."[32]

Most troubling: such chicanery was done with the implicit (and often explicit) support of the monarchy. In a 1767 decree, even Catherine the Great pronounced: "We assure the future tax farmers of Our Imperial protection, ordering that the sale of drinks be described and treated as government business, and the tax farmers, during their period of office, be regarded as trusted agents for the crown, and entitled to carry swords."[33] Or, as *Kolokol* bluntly put it: "Under the vodka tax-farm system, the state pillages itself, but then has neither the right nor the opportunity to prosecute the robbers!"[34]

Such divergence between how the political *sistema* should operate and the corrupt way it actually worked not only subverted the law's legitimacy; it also bred a corrosive culture of tacit acceptance of illegal activity. This helps us understand how historical accounts could, for example, describe an Arkhangelsk governor as absolutely "not a bribe taker," adding "though he did receive from the tax farmers an annual gift of 3 or 4,000 silver rubles." Likewise in the 1830s, it was reported that the governor of Kazan, General-Lieutenant Strekalov "didn't take bribes"...once again with the proviso "though he did receive an annual tribute form the tax farmers. At that time, this was reckoned a quite acceptable [*bezgreshnyi*—"sinless"] form of income. For several tens of thousands of rubles, Strekalov allowed the tax farmers...to rob local households at their pleasure."[35]

The natural result was a state thoroughly corrupted from bottom to top. In some cases it was unclear who controlled whom. Consider, for instance, the absolute autocrat Nicholas I: in 1848, a wave of nationalist, democratic revolutions swept across Europe, threatening its established monarchies. Responding to an invitation from the imperiled royal House of Habsburg, Russia's conservative "gendarme of Europe" flexed Russia's international muscle by crushing the restive Hungarians, subordinating them once again to Habsburg control. Two years later the omnipotent Nicholas was enraged to discover no vodka for sale at the low, government-mandated price anywhere in his own capital. Incensed, the all-powerful autocrat launched an immediate inquiry into this obvious violation of the tax farm regulations. Within days, the St. Petersburg tax farmers met with the finance minister and made clear that following the law by providing such cheap drinks would threaten their ability to pay the taxes on which Nicholas' government relied. Ten days after ordering the inquiry, Russia's supreme autocrat quietly rescinded his own order.

With the corrupting influence of the tax farmer reaching all the way to the emperor, it is hard to disagree with the sad assessment of observers of the time that "the government has no officials—they all serve the tax farm; some by cooperation, others through connivance or silence."[36]

Where Does The Money Come From?

On paper, the tavern keeper was regulated just as heavily as the tax farmer. He had to keep order both in the tavern and the street outside, sell vodka according to legal measures, and prevent dilution, adulteration, and undermeasuring by allowing the customer himself pour the liquor. The tavern keeper was strictly forbidden to drink on the job, sell drinks on credit, or even befriend agents of the tax farm.

However, as today's Russians are fond of saying: "the rigidity of our laws is compensated for by their nonobservance."[37] Indeed, *all* of the following shenanigans, and more, were found in the local tavern:

> In the tavern, the tavern-keeper is dictator. He knows only one authority—the authority of the tax farmer; one law, that of the tax farmer; one goal, to rob the people, to rob and rob again, using any method available. In his tavern one can fund undermeasuring, short change, theft of the clothes of drunkards, pick-pockets, water served with a whiff of vodka in it and a mixture of something spicy to deceive the taste, side dishes designed to sharpen the thirst, together with all the various temptations to which animal life is subject, music, women, and gatherings of various kinds, of thieves and robbers, slanderers, and planners of criminal deeds. And from all this, gathered together by the art of the tavern-keeper, a river of gold flows into the pockets of the tax farmers. On these dregs [*podadonkakh*] of Russian life are constructed immeasurable fortunes.[38]

Beyond extortion, the most common deception was simple price inflation: while the state mandated that ordinary vodka—or *polugar*—was to be sold at a set price of 3 rubles per bucket (*vedro*), tax farmers and their tavern keepers could sell "special" or "improved" vodkas for higher prices. If a thirsty peasant waded into a bar looking for the cheap *polugar*, he'd be told they were out, but there was always plenty of "improved" vodkas—flavored with berries, honey or molasses, or cheaply filtered through charcoal or sand—which could be marked up by the tax farmer or watered down by the tavern keeper. None of this was a mystery to the customer—as one wrote in 1859: "Everyone knows that the retail price laid down in the regulations has not been observed since 1839."[39]

Even the imperial ministry of finance was complicit. In 1859 it ordered governors to turn a blind eye to such abuses in the interest of squeezing every kopeck for the treasury: "A certain increase in the sale of imported beverages at higher prices does not breach the tax farm regulations and should not be regarded as an abuse on the part of the farmers, but is rather the consequence of the calculations necessary for the successful transfer to the Treasury of 366,745,056 silver rubles, which the farmers are obliged to surrender over the present four-year period."[40]

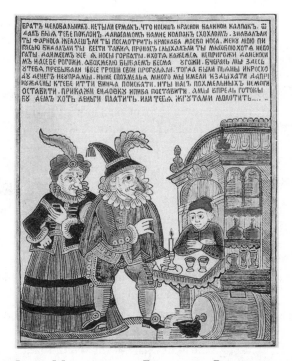

TRADITIONAL *LUBOK* WOODCARVING: FARNOS AND PIGASYA IN THE TAVERN. Mid-eighteenth century. The red-nosed drunkard Farnos and his wife Pigasya address the local tavern keeper in verse, part of which translates as: "Yesterday when we were here, we went broke on drinking beer. When we drank till we got dizzy, spending money was quite easy. Now, with headaches, we do whine, and we've come to get some wine. Bring us then, don't torment more, beer and vodka like before. And later we'll be glad to pay or maybe thresh you like the grain." Translation by Alexander Boguslawski, http://tars.rollins.edu/Foreign_Lang/Russian/Lubok/lubfools.html.

Another scheme to stretch one's vodka allotment was to simply water it down. An unscrupulous tavern keeper (as most of them were) could easily dilute one bucket of 40-proof vodka into two buckets of 20-proof vodka. Even selling the drinks at the low, government-mandated price, the proceeds from one bucket would go to the tax farmer and on to the state; the rest would go into the bartender's pocket. While drinkers expected some watering down, there were limits, as customers paid for round after round without ever getting drunk. During Russia's notoriously frigid winters, one recourse was for the customer to simply set his vodka outside. Since standard 40-proof alcohol only freezes at -27°C (-17°F), if the customers found that their drinks had turned to ice, the busted tavern keeper could potentially have a riot on his hands![41] More often, however, the deception was begrudgingly accepted: "Moses may have worked a miracle when he drew water from a rock," mused one nineteenth-century drinker, "but to turn water into gold requires no miraculous powers at all."[42]

Under-measuring shots was another tried-and-true tactic, which could bolster the tavern keeper's profits another ten percent. Once bartenders introduced progressively smaller glasses, the state imposed strict controls on the size of containers, but even then undermeasuring was the norm. If—for whatever reason—a customer actually received a full measure of vodka, he often poured some back into a special container kept by the barman as an in-kind gratuity.

In rural Russia, where money was scarce, such in-kind, barter, and credit transactions were common. But since the tavern keeper could not pay the tax farmer in IOUs, pawned clothing, livestock, or stolen goods, the networks of rural credit further entrenched the tavern keeper as the corrupt linchpin in the local economy:

> They sell on credit, and in autumn they are paid back in cattle, grain, hay, and other products, not at commercial prices, but at values fixed by the traders, who miss no opportunity to make huge profits. Quite often a peasant will pay 1½ puds [54 pounds] of flax for a bucket of vodka, allowing it to be weighed, usually when not in a sober condition, on the trader's scales.... Often, the tavernkeepers travel, under the cover of the autumn nights, around the local villages with casks to gather the fruits of their work. In such cases, they get the householders, their workers and their women and even children drunk, and make themselves masters of the house.[43]

Corruption Creeps Everywhere

While perhaps the most odious, the tavern keeper was hardly the sole source of corruption in the villages. Tax collectors, conscription officers, and gentry land agents all conducted their daily business in the tavern over rounds of vodka. Even the parish doctor received kickbacks for prescribing vodka as a cure for every imaginable ailment. Recounting his impressions of Russia in 1843, German agriculturalist Baron August von Haxthausen described how "in the Crown villages the officials conspired with the brandy farmers, who bribed them for their connivance. Every communal and cantonal meeting was held before the brandy-shop, and all business transacted glass in hand."[44]

In this way, the corrupting influence of the vodka trade permeated even the most enduring institutions of Russian village life: the self-governing village commune (*obshchina*). Rather than individual farmsteads, most peasant land was held collectively in a system of mutual dependence against the threat of famine or crop failure. The village was governed by an assembly, or *mir*, which managed the commune's affairs by adjudicating disputes, allocating the parcels of tillable land, and doling out the burdens of taxation and conscription imposed by the state. Such collective responsibility for taxes encouraged idleness and drunkenness over industry, as the hardworking peasant had to make up for his inebriated neighbor's slack.[45]

The peasant commune was no less corruptible than the rest of the autocratic system. Communal affairs were often decided in the tavern by a noisy majority, and almost any communal decision "may be obtained by 'treating the Mir'—that is to say, by supplying a certain amount of *vódka*."[46] As one nineteenth-century commentator noted: "Of vodki there is always enough in the Mir, for it is a means of government. It circulates by the pailful at election time; it is plentiful on saints' days, when if not drunk, the men might muster and grumble about their hardships; it comes forth again in mysterious abundance whenever, from some cause or other, the mayor gets into evil odour and wants to regain his popularity."[47]

The village court was likewise not above reproach: litigants often treated judges to drinks at the tavern or dropped off half-buckets of vodka at their homes as a "gift." Peasants had good reason for claiming that any elder "takes a sin on his soul" upon becoming a village judge—corruption was so entrenched that one report from Smolensk explained that offering vodka as a "fee" for hearing a court case is itself "considered a law."[48] Many village taverns even had an open tab for township judges, to be paid by litigants. Often the bill would be paid twice, once by the plaintiff and once by the accused.[49] If that were not enough to achieve the desired judgement, witnesses could be persuaded to alter, retract, or even invent their testimonials. "There are persons who, for a bottle of vodka, will serve as a witness in any kind of case," claimed one nineteenth-century account in the Russian state archives. "Bribing witnesses or getting them drunk takes place everywhere, and [peasants] are so used to this that it is considered natural."[50]

Peasants risked financial ruin with a losing court judgement, as village elders usually confiscated the culprit's tools, livestock, and even clothing to sell at auction or at the tavern in exchange for vodka.[51] Nineteenth-century Russian revolutionary Sergei Stepniak explained how even a sober, honest peasant—so confident of his innocence that he needn't stoop to bribery—succumbed to the tavern after the corrupt village judges regardless found against him in a civil dispute:

> I promised the inn-keeper to sell him my hay, at two copecks a stone, provided he would give me [vodka]; and I drank and drank till I lost my senses...from that time forth I was a lost man. Lost—absolutely lost! The tavern grew to be my only consolation. I began even to steal! Everything went from bad to worse....I shall end in the galleys, take my word for it.[52]

While vodka was often the source of a peasant's damnation, it occasionally was also his redemption. Once the community's punishments were levied, the accused was obliged to buy rounds of drinks at the tavern, symbolizing acceptance of the punishment and legitimacy of the customary institutions of village self-governance. By treating the village to drinks, a thief won both forgiveness and re-admittance to the community. One story from Oryol province tells of a peasant, Mikhail, who was found guilty of stealing sheep and was required to buy the village elder and his friends a half-bucket (about six liters) of vodka at the tavern. Quickly downing the offering, they promised Mikhail clemency in exchange for another half-bucket, which he reluctantly bought. Now thoroughly sauced, the judge and his friends berated Mikhail, until he snuck back home, which enraged the elders. After finishing their drinks, they went to Mikhail's home, angrily rejected his pleas for forgiveness, and demanded more vodka. When Mikhail cursed them as drunks and thieves, they requisitioned a wheel from his wagon to be sold for vodka. They then tethered a heavy sack of oats to his back and leading the humiliated Mikhail through the village streets back to the tavern, where he was forced to pawn his clothes for another three liters. With this last offering, the village leaders finally let him off with a stern reprimand—things would end much worse if he ever so insulted the community by stealing again.[53]

Holy Riot: Vodka And The Church

Speaking of redemption, you might think that if any institution was above corruption and inebriety, it would be the Orthodox Church. You'd be wrong. "The drunkenness in all classes strikes Russian statesmen with dismay," wrote Lady Frances Parthenope Verney—influential writer and elder sister of Florence Nightingale, "and the priests and the popes, are among the worst delinquents. They are fast losing the authority they once had over the serfs, when they formed part of the great political system, of which the Tsar was the religious and political head. A Russian official report says that 'the churches are now mostly attended by women and children, while the men are spending their last kopeck, or getting deeper into debt, at the village dram shop.'"[54]

As the ecclesiastical wing of the Russian political system, it makes sense that even the local clergy came to worship vodka almighty. Whether from the tax farmers or gentry distillers, local priests at first got a small cut of all of the drink sold in their parish, later replaced by lump-sum payments "nominally as an Easter gift, but on the tacit understanding that they are to push the sale of vodki by every means in their power. The pious men do not go the length of urging their parishioners to get drunk," claimed one account, "but they multiply the church feasts whereon revelry is the custom; they affirm that stimulants are good for the health because of the cold climate, and they never reprove a peasant whose habitual intemperance is notorious."[55]

In his *Provincial Sketches*, Mikhail Saltykov-Shchedrin claimed that even the contracts the vodka farmers negotiated with the imperial senate expressly commanded all parish priests to strictly observe every saint's day, fête, and royal birthday. Heeding the call of the church bells, the pious peasants abandoned the field for the festival or sanctuary, after which they received their benediction in drunkenness and debauchery at the nearby tavern, leaving the harvest to rot in the fields.[56]

Even communal hospitality undermined the authority of the Orthodox priests. One traditional practice was that of *pomoch'*, or, quite literally, "help." Ideally, *pomoch'* entailed the voluntary collaboration of the community for the benefit of the local parish priest, whose only income came from meager fees for blessings and administering sacraments.[57] From basic maintenance of the sanctuary and residence to raising crops to support his family, there simply was too much work for the priest alone.

The problem is that Russian peasants were not predisposed toward the degree of voluntarism we might associate with an Amish barn-raising. The priest often begged for help, which was only forthcoming if booze was involved. As nineteenth-century Russian parish priest Ivan Bellyustin explained:

> *Pomoch'* is inconceivable without vodka. The work begins with vodka; it continues with vodka; it ends with vodka. In this case the misfortune is twofold: if you do not give the peasant plenty to drink, he will work poorly out of annoyance; if you do, he will work poorly because he is so inebriated that he cannot work well.... Thus cultivation of the land through *pomoch'* provides the priest with the worst possible support. Grain that he obtained from the soil costs him as much as it would if he bought it. Thus all his pains, toil, anxieties go virtually unrewarded. That is why most priests would have abandoned the soil long ago if only it were possible.[58]

Compounding the problem, the moral authority of the priest—along with any entreaties to temperance—was undercut by the fact that on *pomoch'* Sundays he himself poured the liquor until his parishioners were drunk. If the priest ever browbeat his flock for their drunkenness, he would surely never get their "help" again. So in order to get the fields plowed and repairs done, the priest would take a drink—then another, and another—until he became just as sodden as his sinful flock. Meanwhile, the drunken handiwork was often so shoddy that it had to be redone almost immediately, beginning the whole sad process anew. In the end, the priest spent an unforgivable amount of money on vodka and materials and got nothing but headaches and hangovers.[59]

The Orthodox Church's multitude of holidays presented further opportunities for the priest's undoing. During Easter, for instance, the village priest
proceeded from house to house with his holy icons. At each peasant hut the
distinguished guest was offered food and drink. Lest he offend the master of
the house and ensure never receiving his help in the future, the priest dared
not refuse the gift of vodka. "By the time he has gone through the whole village even the most cautious, sturdiest soul hardly has the strength to perform his
duty," Bellyustin reported. "A priest who is less cautious or whose constitution
is weaker simply passes out. And what scandals do not occur when the priest is
in such a condition!"[60]

How could the clergy ever escape such omnipresent intemperance? As early
as the 1630s Adam Olearius described inebriated priests who stumbled through
the streets dispensing blessings in their underwear, having pawned their cloaks.
"Since such spectacles may be seen daily," he claimed, "none of the Russians are
astonished by them."[61] Two and a half centuries later, Bellyustin painted a similar
picture of the typical village priest as the ever-present, unwanted, and drunken
guest who long ago surrendered his piety to drunkenness, bribery, and thiev-
ery. These pervasive, corrupting influences provide insight into the infamous
Russian proverb: "All steal except Christ" (and its blasphemous addendum: "and
He would too, if his hands weren't nailed to the cross.")[62]

Virtually the only group beyond reproach was the sect of so-called "Old
Believers," who were persecuted as heretics for resisting the seventeenth-
century ecumenical reforms of the Russian church. These most conservative
"schismatics" (*raskolniki*) of the Orthodox faith fiercely rejected the alterations to sacred texts and traditional rites that followed the great church schism
(*raskol*) of the mid-seventeenth century as well as such modern social innovations as tobacco and distilled liquors. As a result, while the Russian authorities
openly oppressed—exiled, imprisoned, even tortured—the Old Believers as a
threat to both church and state, in their seclusion they established a reputation
for incorruptibility, industriousness, temperance, and integrity. It is a blunt,
yet telling illustration that the imperial Russian state would for so long and
so vociferously condemn those dedicated to honesty, purity, and sobriety as a
threat to the corrupt system of autocratic governance, which promoted thrift-
lessness, indolence, and inebriety.[63]

Since feudal Russia was so vast, so poor in capital, and so lacking in effective administration, such coercion-intensive measures like vodka tax farming
made sense. Unfortunately, continuing to rely on the unscrupulous tax farmers
to quench the insatiable thirst of the imperial treasury only entrenched Russia's
twin miseries of alcohol and corruption. "Upon closer inspection," concludes
the influential *Kolokol* exposé that placed tax reform on the political agenda, "the
treasury receives so little benefit in proportion to the losses of the people, that

all would likely say with revulsion—was all of this worth the soiling of our conscience and honor?"[64]

A Tenacious Legacy

Corruption is a weed that grows in the cracks between the public and the private, between the political and the economic. So it makes sense that the roots of this weed go down all the way to the feudal origins of the Russian state, where these distinctions were blurred: when the interests of the state reflected those of the ruling classes and private profits were interlaced with public taxes in the name of the state.[65]

But what does this history lesson tell us about Russia's corrupt governance *sistema* today and the prospects for Navalny and the anti-corruption movement? Today, as back then, the divisions between politics and business in Russia are horribly blurred. Kremlin politics has taken on a distinctly feudal character—a ruling caste dominating a system of vassals in which political loyalty and profitable public positions are bought and sold. Then, as now, corrupt practices among the political leadership provide a model for the rest of society—which in turn casts doubt on who is actually in control: the government or the agents of corruption? Then, as now, the state is saddled with an inefficient, corrupt, and ever-growing bureaucracy that nobody designed and nobody seems to control.[66] Now, as then, the resulting economic incentive is to invest in bribes rather than legitimate business practices to spare harassment by the authorities, which only further entrenches these practices. Now, as then, this systemic corruption hinders economic development by obstructing investment and inhibiting trade.[67]

Intriguingly, there is implicit acknowledgment by contemporary Kremlin opponents that now, as then, vodka politics is part of the problem. In his closing defense of a politically motivated embezzlement trial in July 2013—allegedly orchestrated to discredit him and prevent him from holding future office—Alexei Navalny declared he would "do everything possible to defeat this feudal regime...under which 83 percent of national wealth belongs to 0.5 percent of the population." Navalny challenged the judge, those assembled in the courtroom, and those watching the live online broadcast to consider what benefits they've seen from skyrocketing oil and gas revenues over the past decade.

> Has anyone received access to a better medical care, education? To new apartments? What have we got?...We have only got one thing. You all know the one product that since Soviet time has become more

affordable: vodka. This is why the only thing that is guaranteed to all of us, citizens of this country, is the degradation and the chance of drinking ourselves to death. [68]

Popular apathy "only helps this disgusting feudal regime, which, like a spider, is sitting in the Kremlin." In concluding, Navalny declared that indifference toward the corrupt *sistema* only benefits the state and the well-connected few, while putting the rest of "the Russian people on the path of degradation and drinking to death, and to take away all of the national wealth from the country," just as in imperial Russia.[69] Well then—if the parallels are so stark, what does history suggest in terms of the prospects for genuine reform? Here too, the outlook is gloomy.

Following its embarrassing military defeat in the Crimean War in 1855, the great reformer, Tsar Alexander II, enacted sweeping reforms: revamping the military, judiciary, bureaucracy, and financial system and abolishing both serfdom and the tax farm. But corruption has a cockroach-like tenacity in systems of personalized power: even though the cause of obligatory corruption was gone, the corrupt officials remained, finding other dubious paths to riches. For instance, the notorious, aforementioned tax farmer Vasily Kokorev simply moved into distilling while using his government contacts to snag upwards of eight million rubles.[70] What's more, these reforms did nothing to stop the petty corruption of the tavern keepers, who still watered down and undermeasured drinks while maintaining a lucrative pawn-and-credit trade on the side. It did nothing to remedy the infiltration of vodka, money, and influence into Russia's traditional institutions of local self-government and the Orthodox Church.

Simply changing the method of tax collection could not undo generations of systemic corruption. Even approaching the dawn of the twentieth century, German author Hermann von Samson-Himmelstjerna explained that the highest civil servants appointed by Emperor Alexander III were "the most hopeless mediocrites, bigots or mere seekers of wealth and position" and explained how below this ruling mediocracy toils

> an innumerable army of minor officials, of whom many are good, intelligent, honest men, who, however are compelled by the acting *system* of government to act mostly in the capacity of tyrants, of stiflers of every token of personal independence and intellectual life, and agents for pressing taxes out of the economically exhausted population. The better part of these officials try to avoid doing, so far as they possibly can, what the system forces them to do; the worse part try to turn their power into a means for personal profit; and this creates a most unnatural position of things in the country: both parts practically (though silently) teach the population that laws are created in order not to be observed.[71]

For Samson-Himmelstjerna, the disconnect between the corrupt, out-of-touch leadership and the suffering of the Russian people was most vividly illustrated in 1892, as the government debated resurrecting the reviled vodka tax farm amid a devastating famine along the Volga that claimed nearly a half-million lives. To the horrors of typhus, scurvy, and cholera the imperial ministry of finance sought to add the burden of a salt tax and the vodka tax farm—"those two scourges of the unfortunate nation, that contributed so much to its impoverishment and demoralisation—speak for themselves of what is the present Tsar's government from the economic point of view."[72]

Since corrupt individuals and practices outlast the reasons for their formation, generations of imperial, Soviet and post-Soviet leaders have had to grapple with these consequences. Indeed, placing debates over present-day anti-corruption measures in this deep historical context underscores corruption's intractability and the inadequacy of proposed remedies.

On the one hand, many of the practical policy suggestions for grappling with corruption in present day Russia—like empowering autonomous business organizations, redrawing legal districts, or rotating judges to reduce the potential for patronage—are simply not enough to meaningfully overcome the problem. Even the monumental reforms enacted by Alexander II—which fundamentally attacked the roots of systemic corruption—hardly made a dent. Why should we expect greater results from smaller, more easily circumvented initiatives like rotating judges?

On the other hand, academic accounts claiming that—theoretically—corruption can be restrained by "strengthening the rule of law" or by empowering "accountable local self-government" may well be true, but these suggestions are vague and impractical.[73] Virtually every Russian leader over the past hundred years—including some of the world's most powerful autocrats—has vowed a war on corruption, and each one has failed. "*Blat* is higher than Stalin," as the old Soviet saying goes—and it isn't far from the truth.[74] Patronage, bribery, and corruption are the legacies of Russian state building. Along with the corrupt officials who secured positions of economic and political power through such means—they are also the intractable foundations of the autocratic state itself. They serve the needs of the autocracy, which in turn relies on them.[75]

The only conclusions for true reform, then, are the most pessimistic ones. Some suggest that real change will come with only a complete overhaul of the social and political systems that make corrupt behavior in people's economic interest. Not only are such wholesale structural changes in contemporary Russia unrealistic, but history suggests that they are not adequate.[76] To root out corruption, Russia would need to completely demolish its political, economic, and social structures, develop a vibrant economy that makes bribery and graft less vital to a household's bottom line, *and* adjust to cultural norms that no longer tolerate the rewards of position.[77] As with drinking cultures, cultures of corruption change only glacially over generations—and this says nothing about how such mass socio-cultural re-education could ever be done.

The sad prognosis is that Putin and every Russian autocrat who follows will continue the eternal battle with corruption.[78] And whether genuine or half-hearted, every such attempt is likewise doomed to fail until they meaningfully confront the nexus of alcohol, corruption, and autocracy that constitutes Russian vodka politics.

9

Vodka Domination, Vodka Resistance…Vodka Emancipation?

From Peter the Great onward, the history of modern Russia is often told in terms of its imperial conquests: an expansive empire searching for warm-water ports from the Baltic Sea to the Black Sea and eastward to the Pacific Ocean. These geopolitical ambitions brought Russia in conflict with Swedes and Turks, Poles and Persians, and the empires of Japan and Britain. While *realpolitik* characterized imperial Russian foreign policy, the domestic foundations for these conquests were provided by *vodkapolitik*. Russia's great power status was built not only by her massive military but also by the Russian peasantry who paid dearly to support it.

From Peter's twenty-year Great Northern War against Sweden, to Alexander I's triumphant showdown with Napoleon, and to Nicholas' fiasco in the Crimea, wars are costly—not only for the peasant conscripts who paid with their lives but also for the society that endured ever greater requisitions, impositions, and taxes. Even in peacetime the costs of repaying war debts and maintaining a standing army brought little respite for the people and ensured that vodka revenues would remain crucial to the state's ambitions.[1]

Yet by the mid-nineteenth century it was obvious that Russia's outmoded political system—built on medieval serfdom and a corruption-generating tax farm—could no longer keep up with the industrializing and modernizing powers of Europe. The autocracy was besieged by reform pressures from European liberals, abolitionists, and temperance advocates, while Russia's embarrassing military defeat in the Crimea finally triggered sweeping political reform. Yet even the death of serfdom and the tax farm could not kill the political dynamics of Russian vodka politics: the state's thirst for revenue was unquenchable, and once again it would be society that paid the tab with its misery.

The Drunken Budget

Figuring out exactly how much vodka contributed to the imperial treasury sounds simple: just leaf through the archives of the finance ministry. The problem is that—like most European states—until 1802 Russia did not actually have a finance ministry or even a unified state budget. Instead, a hodgepodge of different institutions was empowered to both raise and spend revenues in the name of the tsar. Add to that the generations of monarchs who considered the land and people as their personal possessions, and suddenly untangling public (government) from private (royal) funds becomes difficult, and retroactively constructing a modern-looking "budget" becomes almost impossible. Of course it was the same entanglement of public and private through the vodka tax farm that bred Russia's systemic corruption in the first place, as the state encouraged private tax farmers to profit handsomely from the collection of public taxes.[2]

For the sake of simplicity, let's consider just the two main revenue sources: direct and indirect taxes. The link between specific expenses and specific revenues was far more explicit then it is today, especially between military expenditures and direct taxes. To pay for war debts and maintain the army, after the Great Northern War with Sweden (1700–1721), Peter the Great replaced a tax on households with a poll tax—or "soul tax"—levied on every man (except the clergy and gentry) from the youngest baby to the village elder. Peter reasoned that the tax from 35.5 "souls" paid for each infantryman, 50.25 for each cavalryman, and so forth. The army itself collected the tax before later outsourcing tax collection to the same landowners who were already responsible for rounding up conscripts from among their serfs. But the poll tax was not reliable for the state: it was tough to collect across Russia's vast territory, and its collection—often requiring military backup—was highly unpopular. Since any tax increase threatened to ignite a peasant rebellion, revenues from the poll tax were historically stagnant, since the size of the taxable population also was stagnant.[3]

For the state at least, indirect taxes—including the *gabelle* on salt and the tax on vodka—were far easier to collect thanks to the tax farmers. They had the appearance of being voluntary rather than forced, and the amount of the tax was not visible: it was just simply hidden within the retail price. Peter's salt tax was incredibly lucrative, but by the early 1800s, rising fuel and labor costs had turned the salt trade into a loss-making venture.[4]

Vodka, by contrast, was easy money. Whether for religious, medicinal, or recreational purposes, liquor was always in high demand. Unlike the stagnant poll tax or the declining *gabelle*, the vodka trade was incredibly lucrative, and vodka revenues could be increased by simply raising the tax rate, encouraging greater consumption, or both. This inherent contradiction—that the financial power of the autocratic state rested on the debauching of its own people through drink—was the ultimate deal with the devil. As historian John P. LeDonne argued, once the treasury was hooked on vodka, the government "could not escape the dilemma that in encouraging the nobility to produce and the masses to consume liquor, it contributed to the spread of drunkenness and moral turpitude in town and countryside alike. This dilemma remained with the Imperial government until its demise in 1917."[5] Indeed, this is the essence of Russia's autocratic vodka politics: this fundamental dilemma outlasted the tsarist empire to bedevil the Soviet empire and the present-day Russian Federation as well.

The state's "big three" revenue sources were always the poll tax, the salt tax, and the vodka tax. From the few historical re-creations of eighteenth-century Russian finances that we have, already by 1724 the 900,000 silver rubles gained from the liquor trade constituted 11 percent of all government receipts, eclipsing the *gabelle's* 600,000 rubles (7 percent) to be the biggest indirect tax source. By 1795 vodka's contribution had grown to 17.5 million rubles, or fully 30 percent of the budget, while the salt trade *lost* 1.2 million rubles. In 1819 receipts from the vodka trade eclipsed even direct taxes, and from 1839 until the empire's death throes in the Great War, vodka consistently provided the single greatest source of revenue to the imperial treasury.[6]

Yet, even in light of these staggering statistics, is it fair to characterize this as subjugation of the Russian lower classes? After all, the peasantry seemed all too willing to drink up and endure not just the vodka tax farm, but also the systemic corruption it created.

"To be under the will of a lord is a good thing for subjects [*muzhiki*]," claimed godfather of the *kabak*, Ivan the Terrible, "for where there is no will of the lord set above them, they get drunk and do nothing." But it was not just the tyrannical Ivan who saw slavery as preferable to alcohol: an early-seventeenth-century Dutch visitor found the penchant for drunkenness as proof that the Russians "better support slavery than freedom, for in freedom they would give themselves over to license, whereas in slavery they spend their time in work and labor." Ultimately, in Ivan's era, alcohol and slavery were two sides of the same coin: when it came to amassing laborers, some were indentured by force, "others were merely asked to drink some wine, and after three or four cups they found themselves slaves in captivity against their will."[7]

But that was medieval Russia, well before the codification of serfdom in the Ulozhenie of 1649. What then? As it turns out, even foreign visitors from the eighteenth century found the same subservience of the enserfed classes through alcohol.

"The vice of drunkenness is prevalent among this people in all classes, both secular and ecclesiastical, high and low, men and women, young and old. To see them lying here and there in the streets, wallowing in filth, is so common that no notice is taken of it," wrote Adam Olearius in the 1630s. Highlighting the class

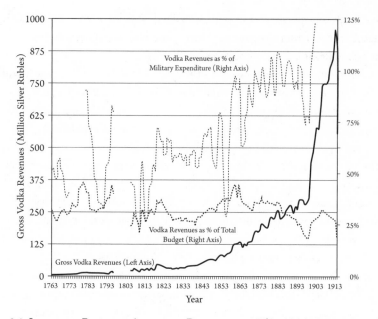

Figure 9.1 IMPERIAL RUSSIAN ALCOHOL REVENUES, 1763–1914 *Sources*: Arcadius
Kahan, *The Plow, the Hammer, and the Knout* (Chicago: University of Chicago Press,
1985), 329, 337; David Christian, *Living Water: Vodka and Russian Society on the Eve of
Emancipation* (Oxford: Clarendon, 1990), 382–91.

distinctions, he noted: "The common people, slaves, and peasants are so faithful
to the custom [of drinking elites' vodka] that if one of them receives a third cup
and a fourth, or even more, from the hand of a gentleman, he continues to drink
up, believing that he dare not refuse, until he falls to the ground—and sometimes the soul is given up with the draught."[8]

Similar accounts of the people's submissiveness to vodka litter the eighteenth
century, too. In 1778 Englishman William Coxe described how a "benevolent"
tax farmer—who had enriched himself by foisting vodka upon the peasantry—
threw a liquor-infused public feast for his inebriate flock, who "crowded around
the casks and hogsheads; and with great wooden ladles lapped incessantly wine,
beer, and spirits. The confusion and riot, which soon succeeded, is better con-
ceived than described; and we thought it expedient to retire. But the consequences of this feast were indeed dreadful." He continued: "Many intoxicated
persons were frozen to death; not a few fell a sacrifice to drunken quarrels; and
others were robbed and murdered in the more retired parts of the city, as they
were returning late to their homes. From a comparison of various reports, we
had reason to conclude that at least 400 persons lost their lives upon this melancholy occasion. (The following day I counted myself no less than forty bodies,
collected in two sheds near the place of entertainment.)"[9]

By the early nineteenth century this system had long been entrenched—its human costs ever more apparent. "During the chilling blasts of winter," begins Englishman Robert Ker Porter,

> it is then that we see the intoxicated native stagger forth from some open door, reel from side to side, and meet that fate which in the course of one season freezes thousands to death.... After spending perhaps his last copeck in a dirty, hot *kaback* or public house, he is thrust out by the keeper as an object no longer worthy of his attention. Away the impetus carries him, till he is brought up by the opposite wall. Heedless of any injury he may have sustained by the shock, he rapidly pursues the weight of his head, by the assistance of his treacherous heels, howling discordant sounds from some incoherent Russian song; a religious fit will frequently interrupt his harmony, when crossing himself several times, and as often muttering his *gospodi pomilui*, 'Lord have mercy upon us!', he reels forward...and then he tears at the air again with his loud and national ditties: staggering and stumbling till his foot slips, and that earth receives him, whence a thousand chances are, that he will never again arise. He lies just as he fell; and sings himself gradually to that sleep from which he awakes no more.[10]

In the early 1800s, foreign visitors moved beyond simply describing the drunken misery of the peasantry; they wanted to explain it, too. "The masses of the nation, the genuine Russians, still bears, in a very great degree, the stamp of northern barbarism," wrote Hannibal Evans Lloyd in 1826. "They are a vigorous race, but rude, slavishly governed by the knout, almost *contented* with their melancholy degradation, grossly superstitious, and even without a notion of a better condition. The word of their priests, the images of their saints, and the brandy bottle are their idols."[11] The irony was just as apparent as it was tragic: the more the serfs turned to vodka as an escape from their forced bondage, the more they became slaves to it.

Lest we be accused of patronizing orientalism in pointing out the pervasive drunkenness of the serf populations of Russia, it is worth mentioning that their additional enslavement to the bottle permeated Western countries as well. Consider American activist and orator Frederick Douglass: born into slavery in antebellum Maryland, the self-taught Douglass escaped to freedom in New York City in 1838 and quickly dedicated himself to the abolitionist cause. Published in 1845, his influential autobiographical *Narrative of the Life of Frederick Douglass: American Slave*—a riveting firsthand account of man's inhumanity toward man—became a bestseller and a galvanizing call for emancipation.

In it, Douglass describes how the only respite from the backbreaking labor, whippings, and the master's general cruelty came—as with their enserfed counterparts in Russia—during the holidays. "It was deemed a disgrace not to get drunk at Christmas," Douglass explained, as it was "the most effective means in the hands of the slaveholder in keeping down the spirit of insurrection." He continues:

> Their object seems to be, to disgust their slaves with freedom, by plunging them into the lowest depths of dissipation. For instance, the slaveholders not only like to see the slave drink of his own accord, but will adopt various plans to make him drunk. One plan is, to make bets on their slaves, as to who can drink the most whisky without getting drunk; and in this way they succeed in getting whole multitudes to drink to excess. Thus, when the slave asks for virtuous freedom, the cunning slaveholder, knowing his ignorance, cheats him with a dose of vicious dissipation, artfully labelled with the name of liberty. The most of us used to drink it down, and the result was just what might be supposed; many of us were led to think that there was little to choose between liberty and slavery. We felt, and very properly too, that we had almost as well be slaves to man as to rum. So, when the holidays ended, we staggered up from the filth of our wallowing, took a long breath, and marched to the field,—feeling, upon the whole, rather glad to go, from what our master had deceived us into a belief was freedom, back to the arms of slavery. I have said that this mode of treatment is a part of the whole system of fraud and inhumanity of slavery. It is so.[12]

Alcohol was even more a part of Russia's system of fraud and inhumanity of serfdom. At the same time as Frederick Douglass was escaping his bondage in "democratic" America, in 1839 the reactionary French aristocrat Marquis de Custine was touring Russia, searching for arguments against the "mob rule" of democracy. When he got there he was put off by the Russian system of autocracy and the people's complicity in their bondage through drink. "The greatest pleasure of the people is drunkenness; in other words, forgetfulness," he wrote. "Unfortunate beings! they must dream if they would be happy." Custine empathized with the brutalized serfs, whose virtue shone through their happy and affectionate intoxication, so unlike the mean drunks back in France. "Curious and interesting nation! it would be delightful to make them happy. But the task is hard, if not impossible," he concluded. "Show me how to satisfy the vague desires of a giant,—young, idle, ignorant, ambitious, and so shackled that he can scarcely stir hand of foot. Never do I pity this people without equally pitying the all-powerful man who is their governor."[13]

Yet by mid-century the inherent contradictions in this antiquated system of dual slavery—physical subjugation under the knout and economic subjugation to the bottle—were becoming evident. "The consumption of brandy is one of the greatest evils, the true plague of the Russian empire," wrote German agriculturalist August von Haxthausen in his detailed 1843 study of rural Russia. His conclusions—widely debated both in Russia and abroad—placed the blame squarely on the system of vodka politics, through which "the peasants were tempted to drink," if not actively "forced to do so." When it came to solutions, he argued: "The Government could adopt no more salutary measure than to put it down, but there are great difficulties in the way of effecting this: the farming of the trade in spirits yields an immense revenue, which cannot be relinquished, and could not be easily raised in any other way."[14]

Studies like these make it clear that—instead of blaming the victim—it was the system of autocratic vodka politics that created the peasants' subjugation and misery and that the inherent tensions of slavery to both master and bottle were growing.

Resistance And Rebellion

If the peasantry were truly held captive by vodka, shouldn't we expect there to have been popular resistance to it? Indeed, by the nineteenth century, the onward march of Enlightenment ideals and the Industrial Revolution were leaving Russia's feudal culture and economy in the dust while an expanding transnational network of temperance activism championed greater sobriety, which threatened the very foundations of Russia's autocratic vodka politics.

The temperance contagion entered Russia by way of its European conquests: the third and final partition of Poland in 1795 brought much of the once-great Polish–Lithuanian Commonwealth under Russian control. These "new" subjects were more attuned to the political and ideational fashions of Europe, while their link to the Catholic Church in Rome only accentuated their cosmopolitanism. These ecumenical links provided a vital conduit for transmitting new—and potentially subversive—ideas into the Russian empire. While enlightenment liberalism and later socialism loomed as the most obvious foreign threats to the conservative Russian autocracy, the seemingly innocuous temperance cause may have been even more dangerous. "The temperance movement," in the words of one historian, was "the most important social movement aimed at combating the political and socio-economic policy of tsarist Russia."[15]

The international temperance movement can be traced to the American Temperance Society (ATS), which had dazzled the French liberal Alexis de Tocqueville during his travels in the United States in the 1830s. "I at last understood that these hundred thousand Americans, alarmed by the progress of drunkenness around them, had made up their minds to patronize temperance." Tocqueville concluded: "Nothing, in my opinion, is more deserving of our attention than these intellectual and moral associations of America."[16]

Tocqueville was hardly alone in introducing American-style temperance to Europe: Protestant activists like the American missionary Robert Baird and the scotsman John Dunlop reported not just the successes of the ATS, but also their mechanics: local self-help communities organized into lodges with members signing a pledge of abstinence from liquor. Ideas begot action: in 1836, an article about the successes of the ATS was published in Riga. Within days the Russian government was flooded with petitions to establish ATS-inspired temperance lodges. Rather than encourage the sobriety of their subjects (and threatening the foundations of state finance), the government resolutely banned all temperance societies, "lest they should be mistaken for separate religious sects." After an audience with Tsar Nicholas I in 1840, Baird privately lamented that "it will not be possible to form temperance societies here for years," adding that still "much may be done at once by diffusing information."[17]

Yet perhaps the most fertile areas for temperance activism in the tsarist empire lay along its newly incorporated western borderlands. Just as the Catholic Church provided a bulwark against cultural Russification by the Russian Orthodox Church, the temperance cause provided a defense against Russian political colonization. By 1858, the Catholic clergy of Poland and Lithuania had developed a "Brotherhood of Sobriety," which infused ATS structures with ecclesiastical elements of the Father Mathew and Rechabite temperance societies of Ireland. Father Mathew was a Catholic crusader not just against alcohol, but also against imperial subjugation to the hated English and their Anglican Church. The parallels with the plight of the Catholics under the Orthodox Russian empire were lost on no one.[18]

The movement spread with breakneck speed (by nineteenth-century standards, at least). From one town to another, priests encouraged their parishioners to take a temperance pledge—not to give up *all* alcohol, just vodka. Beer, wine, and mead were okay as long as you didn't get drunk, but vodka—and the Russian imperial domination that it represented—was clearly off limits. Within a year, 83 percent of Catholic parishioners in Kaunas *guberniya* had taken the oath. In the neighboring provinces of Vilnius and Grodno temperance membership quickly topped one million, accounting for fully three quarters of the population.[19]

The unexpected outbreak of sobriety threatened financial ruin for the tax farmers and the imperial treasury. Annual liquor sales fell by 40 percent in Vilnius, 33 percent in Grodno, and 70 percent in Kaunas province. Glowing reports described empty taverns, shuttered distilleries, improved health, and more affordable prices for grains, given their greater supply. Tax farmers went bankrupt. Finally, the imperial government stepped in to directly administer the trade and deal with the temperance "emergency." The lessons of the liquor boycott were painfully clear: if at any point the majority of Russians suddenly decided to sober up, the government would face immediate bankruptcy.[20]

This was the embarrassing dilemma of vodka politics: if the state promoted the health and well-being of its citizens it faced financial ruin—yet the only alternative was to double down and support the drunkenness and corruption of the tax farm system. Time and again generations of Russian autocrats chose the latter. Defending the tax farmers from Lithuania's dangerous sobriety, the ministry of internal affairs confiscated abstinence petitions and reprimanded censors for publishing temperance manuals. Yet they stopped short of enforcing the finance ministry's demand that the Catholic clergy publicly renounce their heresy and preach the gospel of vodka as a "harmless," even "necessary," indulgence.[21]

By the spring of 1859, news of the sobriety movement in the Catholic provinces had spread to the hard-drinking heartland of Russia, from Moscow to the Volga. Among the rural peasants and urban poor, the vodka boycotts were largely peaceful. By that summer, temperance societies had sprung up in thirty-two Russian provinces, with peasants vowing abstinence pledges and village assemblies drafting new fines and corporal punishments for drinkers.[22]

Yet in migrating to the Orthodox heartland, the temperance movement lost the anti-colonial character of the Catholic provinces of Poland and Lithuania and the Protestant regions of Estonia, Latvia, and Finland. Temperance forces could not coalesce around the Orthodox Church, which had long been complicit in the vodka trade. As Ivan Pryzhov, author of the earliest history of the Russian *kabak*, noted in the 1860s: the Orthodox monasteries not only introduced and developed distilling in Russia; they also benefited handsomely from kickbacks from the tax farmer. Plus, the village priest's chronic inebriation meant he could not preach abstinence without being ridiculed at as a hypocrite.[23] "If the Church would direct her maternal solicitude to the peasant's drinking," wrote nineteenth-century *Times* correspondent D. Mackenzie Wallace, "she might exercise a beneficial influence on his material and moral welfare. Unfortunately she has a great deal too much inherent immobility to do anything of the kind."[24]

By contrast, the corrupt agents of the tax farm were extremely mobile when mass sobriety threatened their lucrative incomes. In one recorded instance from February 1859, the vodka tax farmer from Balashov district enlisted the local police captain (to whom he routinely paid bribes) to help defend his economic "rights." The police chief tapped the local prosecutor, who opened a formal investigation into the "conspiracy not to drink tax farm vodka." The *otkupshchik* himself accompanied the prosecutor to the estate of a local noble to ask his serfs why they were not drinking.

"We've seen the error of our ways," they replied. "This vodka is ruining us! It is a joke—8 rubles a bucket! How many carts of grain would you need to buy a single bucket?"

"In any case," pressed one of the peasants, wearing the medals of a former soldier, "the vodka is terrible; it's worse than river water."

The insulted tax farmer flew at the peasant: "what do you mean, 'terrible'?"

"Just that. It's bad. All it does is bloat your stomach."

"How dare you say that!" raged the tax farmer, who then proceeded to beat the peasant, as they say, "in the customary manner." The scandal caused a huge backlash in the village. Rumors flew that the tax farmer paid to hush up the entire incident, without success. As a last-ditch effort, the authorities persuaded the landowner to assemble his serfs and present each of them with a free bucket of vodka. "But to their credit," the report notes, "not one of them would touch it."[25]

As time went on, confrontations between the sober peasantry and the alcohol-pushing agents of state finance became more frequent, contentious, and even violent. Occasionally peasants torched taverns, prompting the dispatch of the armed forces to suppress the rebellion. Upwards of 780 "instigators" were tried before military tribunals, whipped and beaten with rods before being exiled to Siberia. Aghast, one British journalist described how "the teetotalers were flogged into drinking; some who doggedly held out had liquor poured into their mouths through funnels, and were afterward hauled off to prison as rebels; at the same time the clergy were ordered to preach in their churches against the new form of sedation, and the press-censorship thenceforth laid its veto upon all publications in which the immorality of the liquor traffic was denounced. These things sound incredible," he added, "but they are true."[26]

It wasn't just foreigners who shook their heads at such absurdity—liberal Russian critics also were appalled. "Is it true that the crime of sobriety has become so common in Tambov province that governor Danzas has sent army units to suppress non-drinkers?" asked abolitionist Aleksandr Herzen, whose influential magazine, *Kolokol* (*The Bell*) avoided Russian censorship by being published from exile in London:

> Poor troops! Poor officers! Is it not enough to have to defend the throne and the altar, the whips of the serfowners and the depredations of officials; but now you have to defend the *kabak*, with its sales by the bottle and glass? Perhaps they will start giving out knighthoods of the tax farm with a vodka bucket for the epaulettes, half-*shtof* [bottle] crosses for the buttonhole, and, for the lower ranks, medals showing a dove descending towards an open *shtof* bottle, with the inscription: "*Spiritus sanctus—spiriti vini!*"[27]

This was getting out of control. It didn't take an outspoken critic like Herzen to see that something was very wrong here.

Freedom From Chains And Bottles?

"The Liquor Tax Rebellion," according to the *Big Soviet Encyclopedia*, "was a spontaneous protest not only against the tax farmers and the responsible government agencies, but also against the system of serfdom."[28] As we've seen, serfdom and vodka politics were cut from the same cloth of feudal servitude—and by the mid-nineteenth century, all it took was a westward glance across Europe to see how outmoded this medieval system was.

The inadequacies of the system were painfully obvious during the Crimean War (1853–1856), when the mighty Russian empire was decimated by the Turks, British, French, and Sardinians *on their own territory* around the Black Sea. Greatest among the casualties of the war may have been Tsar Nicholas I himself: obsessing over military planning day and night, the ultraconservative gendarme of Europe succumbed to pneumonia on March 2, 1855.

It was up to his successor, Alexander II, to wind down the humiliating and exhausting debacle, and confront the shortcomings it had laid bare. The practical initiatives of Russia's "great reformer" included reorganizing and modernizing the military, judiciary, and bureaucracy, and also loosening press censorship— for the first time permitting discussion about social and political challenges, including the alcohol problem. While historians commonly point to defeat in the Crimea as prompting Russia's emancipatory reforms, the protests and riots that pitted entire swaths of Russian society against the state's antiquated system of dual servitude through serfdom and vodka were arguably a more proximate cause. Serfdom was certainly the most obvious relic of a bygone era, but the state's reliance on the antiquated tax farm was arguably just as important. So intertwined were the two, it was difficult to consider getting rid one fossil without the other—which is just what Alexander did.[29]

Sometime between 1858 and 1860, the tsar decided that the vodka farm had to go. Beyond the perverse impact on public health and morality and the specter of an ever-widening vodka rebellion—corruption was running rampant, tax farmers were getting more brazen with their wealth, and neither the treasury nor the gentry distillers were profiting. In 1860, a report by the Department of Political Economy to the State Council openly admitted the fundamental contradiction of vodka politics:

> The government cannot and must not lose sight of the effects of this system on the moral and economic welfare of the people. Everyone

knows that tax farming ruins and corrupts the people; keeps the local administration itself under a sort of "farm," which nullifies all efforts to introduce honesty and justice to the administration; and slowly leads the government into the painful situation of having not only to cover up the flagrant breaches of the law engendered by the system, and without which it cannot operate, but even to resist the people's own impulses to moral improvement through abstention. In this way, the government itself offers a model of disrespect for the law, support for abuse and the spreading of vice.[30]

On October 26, 1860, Tsar Alexander II assented to the report and its recommendation not to renew the tax farms set to expire in 1863, at which time they would be replaced with modern system of excise taxes. Not only did this signal the end of the ancien régime in Russian finance, it also nominally removed the source of the systemic corruption (though not the deeply ingrained practices it produced) that was the lifeblood of the vodka farm and finally separated the public from the private—taxes and profits—when it came to the vodka trade. Nevertheless, the systemic corruption and dynamics of vodka politics proved to be far more resilient.

The liquor question likewise had a palpable influence on Alexander II's other monumental reform: the abolition of serfdom in 1861. "If there have been riots for a bottle of *polugar* [cheap vodka]," asked Yakov Rostovtsev—one of the major figures in drafting the emancipation—"what will happen if we cut off a *dessiatin* [hectare] of land?"[31] While the fate of serfdom may have been determined well before the roiling liquor riots, the logistics were not. The gentry slaveholders were pressuring the Crown to protect their power by granting the serfs their release without land. The specter of a massive peasant population that was both restive *and* dispossessed spooked the "Tsar Liberator" Alexander II into a compromise arrangement that made Russia's newly landed citizens nominally self-sufficient but still retained significant power for the landowners. In this way, then, as historian David Christian suggests, "it is reasonable to maintain that the liquor protests did play a significant role in the shaping of the emancipation settlement."[32]

Laissez Faire, Laissez Boire

In 1861, Alexander II liberated the peasants from serfdom and by ending the tax farm in 1863 liberated them from their slavery to vodka too...right? Unfortunately, no. Just as Abraham Lincoln's 1863 Emancipation Proclamation was an important symbolic break with America's feudal past that did not translate into immediate freedom from domination, the same could be said about Russia's emancipation. For one, the land the newly liberated peasants received was rarely enough for their own survival, while the crushing weight of the redemption tax—meant to compensate the landowner for the sudden loss of his work-force—effectively kept the village dependent on the landowner. Likewise, the dumping of the tax farm for a free market system that collected only an excise of four rubles per bucket (or *vedro*—3.25 gallons) of 100-proof spirits only masked the continued subservience of Russian society to the state through the bottle.[33]

The new system effectively strengthened Russia's state capacity by expand-ing its bureaucracy to take over functions that had been outsourced to the tax farmers. Regulating the liquor trade and collecting vodka revenues required recruiting over two thousand honest and competent civil servants—no small task. To reduce the incentives for bribery, the new administrators had to have no ties to the former system and had to be paid well—to the tune of over three million rubles per year in combined salaries. The system aspired to meritoc-racy: well-performing regulators received bonuses while incompetence, nep-otism, and corruption would be punished. Still, elements of the old system endured. For one, the tavern remained untouched as the central exchange point between the village and the state, and the tyranny of the unscrupulous *tselovalnik*, or tavern keeper, continued unabated. Also, many of the tax farm-ers who had long profited handsomely from the drink trade simply moved into the lucrative practice of distilling—since it was effectively no longer monopo-lized by the nobility—and colluded to hide much of their actual production to avoid paying the excise tax.[34]

The greatest continuity, however, was the state's reliance on vodka revenues. As figure 9.1 demonstrates, from the introduction of the excise system in 1863, government revenues crept upward steadily before being replaced by a state vodka monopoly in 1894 (at which time they increased even more dramatically).

Did the demise of the tax farm lead to cheaper vodka prices, and an "orgy of drunkenness," as the defenders of the old system warned? At first, perhaps: with their tax farms expiring and with warehouses of vodka to dispose of before the introduction of new taxes and market competition, the years around 1863 saw a spike in alcohol consumption. Overall, though, the years of imperial Russia's excise tax experiment generally saw a gradual decrease in alcohol consumption (see figure 9.2).

The slight decline of consumption and simultaneous increase in alcohol revenues in the late nineteenth century hints at the autocratic state's steady retreat from laissez faire principles to reestablish a greater presence in the vodka market. Liquor licenses in 1865, for instance, cost all of 10 rubles—twenty years later, they had risen to 1,100 rubles, leading to fewer outlets. In another effort to squeeze out every kopeck, the government increased the excise tax in

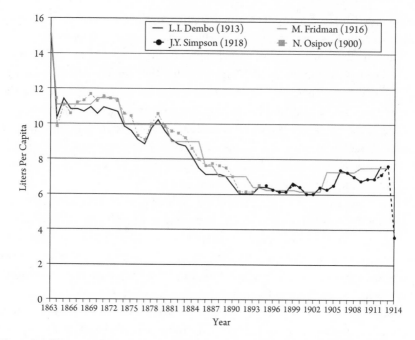

Figure 9.2 ESTIMATES OF RUSSIAN PER CAPITA CONSUMPTION OF 40-PROOF
VODKA, 1863–1914 Sources: L. I. Dembo, *Ocherk deyatel'nosti komissii po voprosu
ob alkogolizmeza 15 let: 1898–1913* (St. Petersburg, Tip. P. P. Soikina, 1913),
163; Mikhail Fridman, *Vinnaya monopoliya, tom 2: Vinnaya monopoliya v Rossii.*
(Petrograd: Pravda, 1916), 66, 265, 444; Nikolai Osipov, *Kazennaya prodazha vina*
(St. Petersburg: E. Evdokimov, 1900), 77; J. Y. Simpson, *Some Notes on the State Sale
Monopoly and Subsequent Prohibition of Vodka in Russia* (London: P. S. King & Son,
1918), 32.

1864, 1869, 1873, 1881, 1885, 1887, and 1892, leading to gradual decreases in
consumption.[35]

Many countries of Europe and North America achieved similar decreases
in alcohol consumption but by different means: political reform coupled with
grass-roots temperance activism.[36] Yet while the vodka market was heavily
regulated, it was at least nominally free—unlike the tsar's subjects. With civic
activism still outlawed, ordinary Russians could scarcely hope to stand up to the
imperial alco-state. For all of the modernizing reforms of Alexander II, the state
still largely relied on alcohol revenues (figure 9.1) and would not tolerate any
threat to the state's finances, no matter how well intentioned. If temperance were
to succeed, the Russian state would fail—it was as simple as that.

"In 1865 the people fancied that because they were no longer serfs they could
not be treated so unceremoniously as of yore," wrote British journalist Eustace
Clare Grenville Murray about Russia's temperance aspirations, "but they found
out their mistake. They were simply dealt with as insurgents, and though not

beaten, were fined, bullied, and preached at till there was no spirit of resistance left in them." Written in 1878, Murray's *Russians of To-Day* explained:

> A person may also be severely punished for not getting drunk, as a certain Polish [!] schoolmaster whom we met one day disconsolately wielding a besom on the quays in company of a dozen kopeckless rogues who are being made examples of because they have no friends. The crime of our schoolmaster was that he lifted up his voice in his school and in tea-shops against "King Vodki," and tried to inveigle some university students into taking a temperance pledge. He was privately warned that he had better hold his peace, but he went on, and the result was that one evening as he was walking home somebody bumped against him; he protested; two policemen forthwith started up, hauled him off, charged him with being drunk and disorderly, and the next day he was sentenced to sweep the streets for three days—a sentence, which fortunately does not involve the social annihilation which it would in other countries.
>
> The fact is that in Russia you must not advocate temperance principles; the vested interests in the drink trade are too many and strong. Nobody forces you to drink yourself; the Raskolniks, or dissenters, who are the most respectable class of the Russian community and number 10,000,000 souls, are in general abstainers, but they, like others, must not overtly try to make proselytes. There are many most enlightened men who hate and deplore the national vice, who try to check it among their own servants, who would support any rational measure of legislation by which it could be diminished; but if one of them bestirred himself too actively in the matter he would find all his affairs in some mysterious fashion grow out of joint. Authors and journalists are still less in a position to cope with the evil, for the press censors systematically refuse to pass writings in which the prevalency of drunkenness is taken for granted.[37]

Even after winning their emancipation, the peasantry of late-imperial Russia knew little more of freedom than that of their forefathers. Instruments of mass servility can take many forms—so even when it came time to put away the whips and chains, vodka remained. Indeed, the bottle proved to be an even more durable and effective means of maintaining dominance and control. Not only did it mollify the people; it made a tremendous profit in the process.

"It must be remembered that the policy of the Russian Government has always been to keep the State wealthy at the expense of the population. Ever since Ivan the Terrible the Tzars have been fabulously rich princes of a very poor country." Writing in 1905, Italian diplomat and historian Luigi Villari explained that "it enables the Government to undertake great schemes of territorial expansion while keeping the people in a state of economic subjugation and rendering them incapable of rising against their rulers. Of course the final object is to increase the wealth and the importance of the whole Empire, but everything is done from a narrow bureaucratic point of view, so that the end is apt to be forgotten in the elaboration of the means."[38]

The macabre beauty of building such a system on a foundation of vodka was that the peasant did not see vodka as the source of his bondage but, rather, as an escape to freedom.[39] The bottom of the bottle promised sweet annihilation from life's boundless disappointments and hardships. For the drinker, there was no escape: the only escape from slavery was a different slavery—one disguised as freedom. For the state, it was an almost perfect system—so long as the state need not concern itself with the well-being of its society. Of course, only autocracies can completely disregard the interests of their peoples, which is why it is necessary to understand vodka politics as an intractable and enduring element of Russia's autocratic system, from its very beginning to the present.

10

The Pen, the Sword, and the Bottle

The sapient reader, to this point, has likely already discerned a particular affinity between the thesis that Russia's feudal autocracy used vodka to both suppress and exploit the poor for the benefit of the state and the brash, anti-capitalist polemics of later generations of socialist revolutionaries. This begs the question: if vodka truly *was* how the imperial Russian state exploited its society, wouldn't Karl Marx or some of his Russian followers have something to say about it? As it turns out, they did. In fact, just as it is difficult to discuss feudalism without Marxism, it is also tough to discuss both communism and the anti-tsarist literature of Russia's "golden era" without the vodka that served as an unmistakable symbol of the corrupt autocracy itself.

"The history of all hitherto existing society is the history of class struggles," began German philosopher Karl Marx and his coauthor Friedrich Engels in their *Communist Manifesto* (1848).[1] In its most basic form, Marxism argues that history can best be understood as conflict between the rich (bourgeoise) and the poor (proletariat), with the former exploiting the latter. In feudal societies— where the economic and legal power of a noble derived from the subjugation of his peasants—the links between exploiter and exploited were obvious. Marx argued that this exploitation continues into capitalist societies, where bourgeois landlords and factory owners owed their riches to the sweat and toil of the peasants and shop floor workers. As Marx's theory of historical development metamorphosed into the political ideology of communism—promoting the overthrow of the bourgeois minority by the more numerous proletariat—the working classes would cast off those institutions that have long kept them under the boot of the rich capitalists.

Those institutions are many. Marx considered the state itself as merely a "committee for managing the common affairs of the whole bourgeoisie." Even religion was an instrument of bourgeois domination: "Religion is the sigh of the oppressed creature, the heart of a heartless world, and the soul of soulless conditions," Marx said. "It is the opium of the people."[2] The people had other opiates too, and alcohol was foremost among them. "Drink is the curse of the working classes" was a common rallying cry for both Marxists and temperance advocates, who both preached abstinence as a cure for poverty. Others took a more tongue-in-cheek approach, instead siding with Oscar Wilde's 1893 proclamation that "work is the curse of the drinking classes."[3]

Karl Marx never wrote much about Russia. Why would he? In his time, Eastern Europe was largely untouched by the Industrial Revolution and its inherent hardships and exploitations. Better to focus on places where capitalism and its abuses were most perverse—Britain, France, and Marx's native Germany—where a working-class revolution seemed far more likely. Still, Marx did consider alcohol as one mechanism of subjugation. "The specific economic form in which unpaid labour is pumped out of the direct producers determines the relationship of domination and servitude," he wrote in *Das Kapital*, "as this grows directly out of production itself and reacts back on it in turn as a determinant. On this is based the entire configuration of the economic community arising from the actual relations of production and hence all of its specific forms."[4]

Engels went further in *The Condition of the Working Class in England in 1844*. His vivid, firsthand study describes the putrid residences and deplorable working conditions of Manchester and Liverpool and the resulting disease, decay, and immorality of urban capitalism. That the workers "drink heavily is to be expected," Engels explained:

> On Saturday evenings, especially when wages are paid and work stops somewhat earlier than usual, when the whole working-class pours from its own poor quarters into the main thoroughfares, intemperance may be seen in all its brutality. I have rarely come out of Manchester on such an evening without meeting numbers of people staggering and seeing others lying in the gutter....And when their money is spent, the drunkards go the the nearest pawnshop [to] pawn whatever they possess....When one has seen the extent of intemperance among the workers in England, one readily believes Lord Ashley's statement that this class annually expends something like twenty-five million pounds sterling upon intoxicating liquor; and the deterioration in external conditions, the frightful shattering of mental and physical health, the ruin of all domestic relations which follow may readily be imagined.[5]

Not surprisingly, Engels lays the blame for drunken destitution solely with the system of capitalist exploitation that cares nothing for the enlightenment and happiness of the average worker. Along with Marx, Engels also highlighted the bourgeois state's monopolization of the means of production—vodka production, in our case—as driving the dominance of the proletariat by the bourgeois state.[6] So even though Marx never wrote much specifically about Russia, many educated eighteenth-century Russians read his general critiques of capitalism as describing the tsarist system to a tee.

In fact, an entire spectrum of opponents to absolute monarchy—from moderate liberals wishing for representative democracy to radical nihilists—all drew on Marx's condemnation of capitalist domination. As opponents of tsarism, they likewise all suffered the heavy-handed wrath of Russia's conservative autocracy. To sneak past government censors and avoid the suspicions of the *okhrana*—the tsar's secret police—all manner of critics were forced to bury their anti-autocratic messages deep in their writing. Why do we still pour over Fyodor Dostoevsky's classic novel about a double murder, *Crime and Punishment*? Partly because it is about much more than just a double murder! Literature could speak truth to power without the power necessarily hearing. This is why early revolutionaries—from Aleksandr Herzen to Nikolai Chernyshevsky—wrote both fiction and literary criticism. The "thick" literary journals in which social commentaries were published alongside fiction became conduits of revolutionary ideas. Indeed, Herzen's journal *Kolokol* (*The Bell*) was the first to publish the *Communist Manifesto* in Russian, which unleashed a firestorm of debate in educated circles throughout the empire.[7]

Just as literature provided a veil to criticize tsarism, highlighting lower-class drunkenness and exposing the corruption of the vodka administration constituted a frontal attack on the entire autocratic system. Not surprisingly, vodka politics was a popular theme in the "greats" of Russian literature.

In 1847, pro-Western Russian liberal Aleksandr Herzen emigrated from Russia, never to return. From self-imposed exile in London he became immensely influential as the first independent Russian political publisher. Believing political legitimacy lay with the people and that all oppression originated with the tsarist state, Herzen called for a genuinely democratic social revolution. Clandestinely smuggled and circulated in Russia, his journal *Kolokol* bashed the corruption of the tsarist system in general and the vodka tax bureaucracy in particular.[8]

As was noted back in chapter 8, it was a series of scathing 1858–59 *Kolokol* articles on the corruption radiating from the the vodka tax farm that made abolishing it a hot political topic. Just a few short years after the *Communist Manifesto*, the denunciation was unabashedly Marxist: "By tolerating and enabling the tax farmer, the government is consciously robbing the people—dividing up the spoils with the tax farmers and others who have participated in the crime."[9]

To be clear: it wasn't just that the system bred corruption, but that the state actively promoted the poverty, drunkenness, and backwardness of its own people. "Upon closer inspection," concluded the *Kolokol* exposé, "the treasury receives so little benefit in proportion to the losses of the people, that all would likely say with revulsion—was all of this worth the soiling of our conscience and honor?"[10] Even after such broadsides prompted the abolition of the medieval tax farm system, writers of all political persuasions continued to use vodka as a call to reform the autocracy ... or even overthrow it.

The Best, Worst Novel Ever

If Russians truly looked to literature for political cues, which writer was most influential? Leo Tolstoy? Dostoevsky? Ivan Turgenev? Surprisingly, none of the above; arguably it was Nikolai Chernyshevsky and his novel *What Is to Be Done?*—"a book few Western readers have ever heard of and fewer still have read," according to Stanford professor Joseph Frank. "No work in modern literature, with the possible exception of *Uncle Tom's Cabin*, can compete with *What Is to Be Done?* in its effect on human lives and the power to make history. For Chernyshevsky's novel, far more than Marx's *Capital*, supplied the emotional dynamic that eventually went to make the Russian Revolution."[11]

An erudite revolutionary, Chernyshevsky coined the phrase "the worse, the better"—the worse the hardships and grinding poverty of the peasantry, the better were the prospects for socialist revolution. When it came to the serf question, for instance, Chernyshevsky advocated emancipation *without* land, resulting in "an immediate catastrophe" for the peasants and an instant crisis for the state.[12]

Like Herzen, Chernyshevsky railed against the tsarist autocracy through his influential journal, *Sovremennik* (*The Contemporary*), which was read widely among Russia's intelligentsia. Instead of writing from the safety of London, though, he worked in the Russian capital, within easy reach of the tsarist authorities. In 1862, Chernyshevsky was arrested on suspicions of subversion and tossed into solitary confinement in St. Petersburg's island bastille—the famous Peter and Paul Fortress in the middle of the Neva River. The prison authorities saw no problem in granting his seemingly innocuous request for pen and paper to write a novel, and in four months, Chernyshevsky's *What Is to Be Done?* was done.[13]

Perhaps "the worse, the better" described not only Chernyshevsky's political philosophy but his literary merits as well, for the book has been universally panned—there is no real plotline or tension, and the environment and characters are stagnant. It has been called the worst novel ever written. Chernyshevsky himself even admitted that his novel contains neither talent nor art, but only "truth."[14] Even Alexander Herzen, reading it years later, described it as an artistic failure: "What a worthless generation whose aesthetics are satisfied by this," he wrote. "The ideas are beautiful, even the situations—and all this is poured from a seminarian-Petersburg-bourgeois urinal."[15]

On the surface, *What Is to Be Done?* is a stumbling narrative of a group of young Russians: the sympathetic Vera Pavlovna defies an arranged marriage to a man of wealth and power to elope with a young medical student, Dmitry Lopukhov. Once freed from the patriarchal "tyranny" of the traditional Russian family, they adhere to strict equality between the sexes. Vera then falls for Lopukhov's best friend, Kirsanov. True to his egalitarian principles, Lopukhov does not object and even fakes his own suicide so that Vera can marry Kirsanov, start a sewing commune, and secretly yearn for an even more bizarrely ascetic revolutionary, Rakhmetov. The end. That's it.

The prison censor—apparently a less-than-sapient reader—leafed through the pages of Chernyshevsky's dime-store romance, deemed it publishable, and turned it over to *Sovremennik*'s interim editor, who promptly lost the manuscript on a cab ride through the capital. Panicked, the editor took out an advertisement in St. Petersburg's police newspaper pleading for its return, and in what must be the most incredible case of authoritarian-bureaucratic bungling, it was the detested tsarist police that not only found but also returned the most subversive, anti-government novel in Russian history.[16]

The first installment of *What Is to Be Done?* appeared in *Sovremennik* in 1863 and was a smash hit. One revolutionary fan claimed there had been "only three great men in history: Jesus Christ, St. Paul and Chernyshevsky." Georgy Plekhanov—founder of the social-democratic movement in Russia—asked "Who has not read and reread this famous work?" From his exile in London, the German Karl Marx taught himself Russian just to read the works of this "great Russian scholar and critic."[17] High praise indeed.

"It had become the kind of book people who had given up all their other possession kept strapped to the inside of their peasant tunic," explained one literary historian. Literary critics of Chernyshevsky's day were baffled by the overwhelming popularity of such an awful book. They simply didn't understand: "it wasn't that the Chernyshevsky fans had bad taste in writing; it was that they didn't care about writing. What they cared about was thinking, and thinking was what Vera Pavlovna and Chernyshevsky gave them."[18]

The novel passed the censor only because these subversive ideas were tucked away between the lines and gobbled up by an audience only too willing to crack the Chernyshevsky code. The "rational" relations between Vera Pavlovna and her husbands—as well as the agitation for female education—has been read as a women's-rights attack on the traditional order. Yet that attack is doubly reinforced by Chernyshevsky's frequent reference to the role of alcohol in that old order.

Frankly, Chernyshevsky took less time to address Russian drunkenness in *What Is to Be Done?* than I do in this book—which is saying something. Piecing together a mysterious shooting in the opening scene, the police's first hypotheses are either a drunken murder or a drunken suicide—alcohol naturally being the most likely culprit for any violent crime. Later, futilely trying to come to terms with a woman as progressive and assertive as Vera, many characters representing the "old" traditional order simply dismissed her as a drunk.[19]

Strangely, generations of literary critics hardly notice that the entire story is swimming in vodka. From the auspicious decanter of vodka in the cupboard of Vera Pavlovna's childhood home to her parents' chronic alcoholism, every mention of liquor is shorthand for the degeneracy of the old order. "You should never believe anything I say when I'm drunk," Vera's mother stammers, revealing her true colors. "Do you hear? Don't believe a word of it!"[20] Her "boorish" father offers all manner of alcohol to his guests, even lauding vodka's medicinal benefits. Of course, Vera's father was not simply a bureaucrat, but one who "was in the habit of loaning money on pawn of personal property," just as the despised tavern keepers.[21]

All of the novel's heroes come to terms with their own alcoholism as part of their ascetic preparations for the coming revolution. When it comes to Lopukhov, we learn "there's rarely been a man who has abstained for so long," not only from alcohol but also sexual promiscuity. Earlier, though, he was an alcoholic who drank even "when he had no money for tea and sometimes none for boots." Even here, the blame clearly lies with the system. "His drinking came about as a consequence of depression over his intolerable poverty," wrote Chernyshevsky, "and nothing more."[22]

"In my day we used to drink a good deal," Lopukhov himself replies to his host's hospitality. "I drank enough to last a long time. When I had no luck and no money, I used to get drunk; but now I have enough to do, and enough money,

SOVIET-ERA STAMP COMMEMORATING NIKOLAI CHERNYSHEVSKY
(1828–1889)

I don't need wine. I feel gay enough without it."[23] In unassuming exchanges such as these, Chernyshevsky conveys his fundamental position on the liquor question, which he fully articulated in a series of penetrating articles on the Russian vodka trade in *Sovremennik* in 1858–59.

Writing as L. Pankratev—his well-known nom de plume for economic issues—Chernyshevsky loudly proclaimed that the peasantry's slavery to the bottle would end only after they could afford food, clothing, and adequate housing. The outmoded tax farm was the focus of his most stinging criticism. "From the tax farm comes all of life's miseries: both poverty and debauchery have taken hold of a great part of the population, and the consequences of poverty and debauchery are our ignorance, our moral impotence, and our inability to comprehend our own human dignity." Never one to mince words, Chernyshevsky blasted: "the vodka tax farm is the single greatest evil in our lives, and only with the elimination of this evil will we thrive and prosper."[24]

Ever the sapient observer, Chernyshevsky made the now-familiar argument that the state's harnessing of vodka's tremendous profitability not only debauched the Russian people but also sacrificed Russia's rich brewing and wine-making trades. Abolishing the vodka tax farm would benefit not only the peoples' health and morality but Russian agriculture, viniculture, and brewing as well.[25]

Chernyshevsky fingered everyone in the vodka administration. The tax farmer?—more like a savage Chechen warlord: mercilessly raiding the Russian people. The tavern keeper? "Not even the great American showman P. T. Barnum can match the ingenuity of the tavern-keeper when it comes to luring-in visitors"—and once inside, the *tselovalnik* would take everything.[26]

According to Chernyshevsky, even "the most simple, uneducated person" understood that the entire system was antithetical to the proper, moral relationship between the government and society. Indeed, he may have provided the most succinct summary of Russia's vodka politics.

> For the government, money is not the ultimate goal, it is only a means to achieve other goals, such as increasing its might among foreign powers, achieving glory, consolidating its notorious political system, and developing public institutions to maintain the legal and administrative system. The state's cash needs come from these goals, and is subordinate to them. But by its very nature, the state's interest extends beyond simple financial conditions: in its operations there is always another, more moral side, promoting national honor, the moral welfare of the nation, justice and fairness. The tax farm is by its nature completely alien to all such considerations. The only reason for its existence is monetary; its sole purpose and concern is money, money, money.[27]

Chernyshevsky used international comparisons to underscore Russia's drinking problems. Nowhere else in Europe, he argues, do doctors have to confront *zapoi*—the multiday benders stemming from the traditional Muscovite drinking culture (see chapter 7), which often culminate in alcohol poisoning.[28] The closest European parallel, he claims, is Father Mathew's hard-drinking Irish: exploited and impoverished by a corrupt system of foreign British domination. Yet once the "ignorant, dirty, and lazy Patrick" leaves the British yoke and immigrates to New York, he finds an impartial and just system where his hard-earned money is no longer appropriated by a shiftless landlord. Within years, Chernyshevsky argues, Patrick is reborn as hardworking, sober, and thrifty, "proving" that only by improving social conditions—along with abolishing the state's oppressive vodka farm—will the Russian nation flourish.[29]

Perhaps Chernyshevsky's characterization of Irish-Americans may have *slightly* missed the mark. Still, he effectively and consistently used vodka to highlight the shortcomings in Russia's autocracy. Back in Chernyshevsky's awful *What Is to Be Done?* Anastasia Borisovna describes how she was a drunken floozie before being "reborn" as a good socialist thanks to the virtuous Kirsanov.

> I stretched out on his sofa, and said: "*Nu*, where is your wine?" "No," says he, "I shall give you no wine; but you can have tea, if you want." "With whiskey," I said. "No, without whiskey." I began to do all sorts of foolish things, to be utterly shameless. He sat down and looked at me; but he did not show any interest, so offensive was it to him. Nowadays you can find such young men, Vera Pavlovna; since that time young men have been growing morally better, but then it was a very rare thing.[30]

The distinction between the mindless inebriety of old Russia and the ideal of an enlightened, abstinent generation could hardly be more stark. But in case it is not, Anastasia continues to tell how the young medical student diagnosed her condition.

"You must not drink at all; you have very weak [chest]."

"*A kak zhe nam ne pit'?*—How could we not drink? Anastasia asks. "*nam bez etogo nel'zya*—We cannot exist without it."

"Then you must give up the life that you are leading," prescribes Kirsanov.

"Why should I give it up? *Ved' ona veselaya!*—It's such a joyous life."

"No," replies Kirsanov, "*malo vesel'ya*—there's little joy in it."[31]

Here Chernyshevsky explicitly invokes the legend of Prince Vladimir of Kiev who—as described in chapter 7—allegedly chose Orthodox Christianity for the Russian people over the abstinence of Islam with his pronouncement that "drinking is the joy [*vesel'e*] of the Rus', we cannot exist without it."[32] Why else would Anastasia twice answer in the plural "we" to such a question about her personal drinking habits? Against this well-known adage, the lesson is crystal clear: it is not simply Anastasia who must give up the drunkard's lifestyle—it is the entire Russian nation.

Thus when it comes to vodka politics, if there was indeed an answer to the not-so-rhetorical titular question *What Is to Be Done?* Chernyshevsky surely suggested abolishing the vodka tax farm as the the only way to liberate the Russian people from drunkenness and corruption. This, of course, would require nothing less than the overthrow of the entire feudal structure of Russian autocracy.

And to think that the poor imperial censor missed all of that.

Such embarrassing public unmasking of vodka politics could—and did—get you thrown in jail on vague charges of sedition. After two years of solitary confinement while the authorities sought in vain for damning evidence against him, in 1864, a secret senate tribunal found Chernyshevsky guilty and sentenced him to civil execution, "for criminal intent to overthrow the existing order."[33] Chernyshevsky knelt in a cold downpour as a wooden sword was broken over his head, symbolizing his civil degradation, before being sent to a Siberian penal colony in leg irons. Twenty-five years later, broken physically and mentally, Chernyshevsky was finally allowed to return home to Saratov, to die. His martyrdom at the hands of the tsarist autocracy enshrined Chernyshevsky as a veritable saint of the Russian intelligentsia. Yet perhaps the crowning irony is that generations of his disciples sang his praises in—of all things—a popular drinking song:

> Let's drink to the author of
> *What Is to Be Done?*
> To his heroes and his ideals.[34]

Decoding The Classics

While it would be a stretch to count Chernyshevsky among Russia's greatest novelists, in the wake of *What Is to Be Done?* many world-famous works of Russian literature shared a common theme—using alcoholism to slam the autocracy itself.

Consider Chernyshevsky's better-remembered contemporary, Dostoevsky. Although the two writers ran in the same St. Petersburg circles, their politics could not have been more distant. In the spring of 1862 aspiring young Marxists rocked the capital in a wave of revolutionary agitation, arson, and violence. The police arrested and accused Chernyshevsky as their ideological ringleader, but days before facing the authorities, he confronted an irate Dostoevsky, who had found a leaflet calling for "bloody and pitiless revolution." In their meeting,

Dostoevsky implored Chernyshevsky to halt such "abominations." Satisfied, Dostoevsky later wrote that he had "never met a kinder and more cordial person" than Chernyshevsky. Meanwhile, Chernyshevsky described Dostoevsky as a deranged lunatic and would say anything simply to appease him.[35]

Either in person or in print, the two never saw eye-to-eye, as almost everything Dostoevsky subsequently wrote lampooned Chernyshevsky's ideas.[36] Yet while generations of experts debate whether Dostoevsky's existentialism and anti-nihilistic symbolism directly refute Chernyshevsky's enlightened rational materialism and economic determinism, *both* consistently used alcohol as a symbol of the decrepit autocratic system.

Take, for instance, Dostoevsky's famed *Crime and Punishment*, written in 1865, one year after Chernyshevsky's mock execution and banishment. It tells of Raskolnikov, an impoverished intellectual who, in the name of the greater social good, butchers the crusty old pawnbroker to whom he is indebted with a hatchet before being betrayed by his own conscience. We're told that Raskolnikov was hardly a drunk, but as soon as the thought enters his mind to murder the old woman he staggers "like a drunken man" into a nearby tavern for a few rounds of beer to clear his head. There he meets Marmeladov, a hopelessly irredeemable drunkard, whose inebriety caused him to sell his own daughter into prostitution.[37]

Indeed, as critics have noted, alcoholism "runs like a red thread throughout the novel." Marmeladov is only the first noteworthy drunkard. Both the rural village setting of Raskolnikov's horse-beating dream and the dingy urban thoroughfares of St. Petersburg are littered with drunkards, young and old, male and female. Raskolnikov is often mistaken for a drunk, and he frequently meets friends in taverns, where they get him "to drink like a pig." By contrast, the diligent police investigator Porfiry Petrovich makes a point of noting that he does not drink at all. Even the most positive male character in the story, Razumikhin (whose name in Russian connotes level-headed reason), is a heavy drinker: stumbling drunk when he meets his friend's family and downing bottles of beer even while caring for his sick friend, Raskolnikov. To repeat a now-familiar theme, Dostoevsky stresses how Razumikhin was "extremely worried by the fact that . . . while drunk, he let out to Raskolnikov that he was suspected of the murder."[38]

As in *What Is to Be Done?* Dostoevsky's allusions to drunkenness are understandable against not only the backdrop of mass inebriation but also the ongoing public debates in the "thick journals" over alcohol, poverty, and disease. Herzen's *Kolokol*, Chernyshevsky's *Soveremmenik*, and even Dostoevsky's *Vremya* (*Time*) sparred over various proposals to address the liquor problem, the appropriateness of the state's involvement in the liquor trade, and the morality of basing the economic well-being of the state on the degradation of its people.[39]

While millions have been engrossed by Dostoevsky's morose exposition on murder and human psychology, most might be surprised that this was not the original intent behind *Crime and Punishment*—nor was that the original title. With his gambling debts piling up, in June 1865, Dostoevsky wrote to the editor Andrei Krayevsky asking for an advance of three thousand rubles for this proposed work. His letter reads: "My novel is called 'The Drunkards' and it will be connected with the current problem of drunkenness. Not only is the problem examined, but all of its ramifications are represented, most of all depictions of families, the bringing up of children under these circumstances, and so on."[40] Apparently, this idea didn't fly, so Dostoevsky folded *The Drunkards* into *Crime and Punishment* by way of the tragedies of Marmeladov and his family.

Dostoevsky's diaries contain fragments from early drafts of *The Drunkards*, including the following exchange, which sounds downright Chernyshevskian:

—We drink because there is nothing to do.
—You lie!
—It's because there is no morality.
—Yes, and there is no morality…
—Because for a long time there has been nothing to do.[41]

Were that not enough to make his position clear, Dostoevsky privately confided: "The consumption of alcoholic beverages brutalizes and makes a man savage, hardens him, distracts him from bright thoughts, blunts all good propaganda and above all weakens the will, and in general uproots any kind of humanity."[42] A close reading of *Crime and Punishment* clearly reveals Dostoevsky's denunciation of alcohol as an impediment to the blossoming of Russian society.

Contemporaries read it that way, too—including the great Tolstoy, author of such classics as *Anna Karenina* and *War and Peace*. Tolstoy admired *Crime and Punishment* more as a temperance parable than psycho-thriller. Tolstoy demanded that it was alcohol that clouded Raskolnikov's judgment and led to his inhuman axe murders: "The greatest possible lucidity of thought is particularly important for the correct solution of the question which arises," wrote Tolstoy, "and it is then that one glass of beer, one smoked cigarette can impair the solution of the problem, hinder its solution, deafen the voice of the conscience, and cause the question to be decided in favor of one's lower animal nature, as it was with Raskolnikov."[43]

In his famous 1890 essay, "Why Do Men Stupefy Themselves?" Tolstoy invoked Raskolnikov to argue that humans have both a physical and a spiritual existence and that they turn to alcohol and drugs to suffocate their higher spirituality, concluding that the entire purpose of drinking was to blind one's own conscience and put oneself in the state of mind to rape, murder, and rob.[44] Like his predecessors, Tolstoy was a literary realist who exposed social and political inadequacies, and as with Chernyshevsky and Dostoevsky, vodka topped that list. Since his international celebrity status afforded him greater leeway with the censors, Tolstoy wrote straightforward nonfiction essays in which he need not cloak his words.

While Tolstoy admitted hating the "bedbug-stinking" Chernyshevsky and his dangerous radicalism, when in 1886 he composed his foremost political treatise he gave it a familiar-sounding title: *What Is to Be Done?* Even given their profound personal and political disagreements, both similarly condemned the tsarist autocracy and capitalist order for profiting from the misery of the lower classes.[45]

While conventional Marxists highlighted the plight of urban factory workers as the oppressed proletariat, Tolstoy looked to the rural peasantry: "freed" from serfdom, but still burdened by the local landlord, the state, the village commune, and above all, by vodka. "Observe toward autumn how much wealth is gathered together in villages," Tolstoy began.

> Then come the demands of taxes, rents, recruiting; then the temptations of vodka, marriages, feasts, peddlers, and all sorts of other snares; so that in one way or other, this property, in all its various forms, passes into the hands of strangers, and is taken first to provincial towns and from them to the capitals. A villager is compelled to dispose of all these in order to satisfy the demands made upon him, and the temptations offered him, and, having this dispensed his goods, he is left in want, and must follow [to the cities] where his wealth has been taken.[46]

Once there, the peasant is tempted by sin and alcohol, leading even the most temperate to succumb to drunkenness, poverty, and ruin.

"Let us not deceive ourselves," Tolstoy wrote in laying bare the motivations of the capitalist bourgeoisie,

> all that [the worker] makes and devises he makes and devises for the purposes of the government or of the capitalist and the rich people. The most cunning of his inventions are directly aimed either at injuring the people—as with cannon, torpedoes, solitary confinement cells, apparatus for the spirit monopoly, telegraphs, and so forth, or . . . for things by which people can be corrupted and induced to part with the last of their money—that is, their last labour—such as, first of all vodka, spirits, beer, opium, and tobacco.[47]

Tolstoy went to great lengths to underscore how vodka was both the source of the peasant's poverty and the autocracy's wealth.

Count Tolstoy's inward dedication to the common people was matched by an outward one. Born into affluence and plenty, Tolstoy chose to till the land by hand with a simple scythe in a simple tunic, as peasants had done for ages. In the peasant's blind faith he sought salvation from his own spiritual restlessness and doubt. "Was it reason that helped them to bear the burden of their existence?" asked Tolstoy biographer Henri Troyat. No—it was their unquestioning Christianity. "They drew their courage from the most simple blind faith, as taught by the pope in the little country church with the tarnished gilt cupola. God, like vodka, was to be swallowed at a gulp, without thinking."[48]

Tolstoy emulated everything about the peasant except their reliance on alcohol, which clouded their spiritual endeavors. To that end, in 1887, Tolstoy built his own temperance society, the Union against Drunkenness (*Soglasie protiv p'yanstva*), consisting of adherents who pledged not only abstinence from alcohol but also to publicize its harmful effects. As with previous grass-roots temperance activities, the tsarist autocracy refused to officially recognize the organization.

Tolstoy's temperance was both a moral statement and a political one, as he chastised the Russian Orthodox Church for relations with the tsarist state that hindered the spiritual and material advancement of the people. True Christian dedication—Tolstoy maintained—was based on universal love rather than dogmatism. His resulting pacifism would inspire world leaders from Mahatma Gandhi to Martin Luther King Jr., and since the state was the sole instrument of warfare, this necessitated also that Tolstoy take an anarchist position against the autocracy. In 1901, the Orthodox Church officially excommunicated the great writer for such blasphemy.[49]

Blackballed by both church and state, Tolstoy's authority only grew. One popular joke held that Russia had two tsars: Nicholas II and Leo Tolstoy.[50] His Christian-anarchist philosophy drew followers both at home and abroad, and his church was built on a foundation of temperance. "Intoxication," he wrote, "no matter of what kind, is the sin, abandonment to which makes struggle with any other sin impossible; the intoxicated person will not struggle with idleness, nor with list, nor with fornication, nor with the love of power. And so in order to struggle with the other sins, a man must first of all free himself from the sin of intoxication."[51]

It is impossible to understand Tolstoy without his opposition to alcohol: it was not just the cornerstone of his religion; it was also the basis for his fearless opposition to the Russian autocracy. In November 1896 Tolstoy angrily rebuffed a request to meet with the powerful finance minister, Sergei Witte. Instead Tolstoy wrote Witte—the architect of Russia's newly reestablished vodka monopoly—arguing that "the chief evil from which mankind suffers and the disorders of life come from the activities of the government.... The government not only permits but encourages the manufacture and distribution of the poisonous evil of liquor, from the sale of which comes one-third of the budget. In my opinion, if the government really was making every effort for the good of the people, then the first step should be the complete prohibition of the poison which destroys both the physical and the spiritual well-being of millions of people."[52]

It seems we have now come full circle. Despite Tolstoy's deep loathing for Chernyshevsky and the radicalism he inspired, their critiques of autocracy through vodka are virtually indistinguishable. But instead of facing banishment to Siberia for their opposition, many Tolstoyans within the government—and even the royal family—welcomed the old man's wisdom, imploring him to advise Tsar Nicholas II to "help save Russia." Tolstoy replied in the starkest possible terms, writing directly to the tsar that both His state and His alcohol monopoly were guilty of shackling the people. This tension between the autocracy and the people's progress and well-being could not continue. "That is why it is impossible to maintain this form of government, and the orthodoxy that is attached to it, except by violence," he concluded.[53]

Tolstoy never received a reply from the tsar, though the number of plain-clothes secret police observers around his Yasnaya Polyana estate outside Tula increased markedly. Despite the similarity of their denunciations, the state could hardly send the famed Tolstoy to the same Siberian exile that left Chernyshevsky a broken man—leaving him instead to wander the countryside as a monkish and tormented sage in a threadbare peasant's sheath.[54]

Taking It To The People

Tolstoy wasn't alone in seeing Russia's peasantry as victims of autocracy, capitalism, and vodka. While the count embarked on a lifelong spiritual journey to the countryside, other educated city folk made sporadic—and ultimately unsuccessful—excursions to "the people" in hopes of inciting them to topple the tsar.

Many of these would-be revolutionaries were less inspired by Tolstoy's pacifism and other-serving Christian asceticism than by the single-minded revolutionary abstinence of Chernyshevsky's heroes in *What Is to Be Done?* They gave up alcohol, sex, and worldly pleasure as distractions not from spiritual enlightenment (as per Tolstoy) but, rather, from the cause of proletarian revolution. Leaving their comfortable urban dormitories, many so-called *narodniki* (populists) went to the countryside—not to learn from the simple peasant as Tolstoy did—but to overcome their simplicity and ignorance that caused their oppression and misery. All the peasants needed, the *narodniki* thought, was a vanguard of Chernyshevskian "great men" to lead them to revolt. Eventually scuttled by the imperial authorities, the movement ended in complete failure, partly because its valorization of the rural poor was misplaced. Once in the countryside, the *narodniki* came face to face with the obstacles of autocracy: namely, a population hopelessly mired in superstition and vodka.[55]

In the tradition of literature-as-political-commentary, another great Russian writer, Ivan Turgenev, published his last novel, *Virgin Soil* (1877), on this very theme. Early on Turgenev describes the reality of the village that confronted the *narodniki* newcomers.

> It was Saturday evening; there were few passing in the street; but, on the other hand, the taverns were crammed. They could hear hoarse voices, drunken singing, mingling with the nasal sound of an accordion.... At times, a peasant, with his shirt and waistcoat open, his belt loosened, on his head a winter cap, of which the top hung down over his back like a bag, would be seen staggering out of the tavern, resting his chest against one of the shafts and standing there still, groping about with his hands, as if seeking for something; or else it was some puny, feeble factory hand, his cap all awry, his feet bare—his boots being left in pawn at the tavern—who, after staggering a little, would stop, scratch his neck, and, with a sudden exclamation, retrace his steps.

"That's what's killing the Russian peasant," gloomily professed Turgenev's hero Markelov—"vodka." As they pass tavern upon tavern, his coachman morosely notes "It's to drown sorrow."[56]

Reminiscent of Chernyshevsky's implication of alcohol as the primary affliction of the old order, Turgenev's *narodniki* likewise diagnose the condition of Russia in prose.

> Sleep.
>   It was long since I had seen the place of my birth, but I found there no change. Deathlike torpor, absence of thought, roofless houses, ruined walls, filth, and vileness, and poverty, and misery, the insolent or sullen looks of slaves, all is as before.... the peasants are sleeping the sleep of death; the gather in the harvest, they toil in the fields—they sleep; they thresh the corn, still sleeping; father, mother, and children all asleep. He who beats and he who is beaten, both sleep. The tavern alone is awake, its eye always open. And clasping between its five fingers a jug of brandy, its head toward the North Pole, its feet at the Caucasus, sleeps in an eternal sleep—
>   Russia, the holy country![57]

Turgenev was no fan of the socialists' "to the people" campaign, portraying them as fish out of water, especially in the village tavern. "I went into six taverns," complains Alexei Nezhdanov, the main *narodniki* protagonist. "I can't bear that drug vodka! How can our peasants drink it as they do? It is inconceivable! If it is necessary to drink vodka in order to simplify ourselves, then no, thank you!" Underscoring the culture clash the revolutionaries encountered, Turgenev concludes: "What hard work it is for an ascetic to bring himself into contact with real life!"[58]

In many ways, the culmination of the story comes when the revolutionary Nezhdanov gets uproariously drunk in the tavern, invoking the "slumber" of the peasantry as he incites them to riot:

"Hulloh!" he shouted, "are you asleep? Get up! the hour has come. Down with taxation; down with the proprietors!"[59]

Ironically, the peasants initially mistook Nezhdanov's ravings for drunkenness. Yet as his words gained traction, he was welcomed by a burly, approving peasant into the tavern, where—unsurprisingly—things went awry for the young intellectual. To prove his allegiance with his peasant comrades, the firebrand lightweight accepted round after round of their vodka-laced hospitality.

> Ugh! He swallowed it with the resolution of despair, as he would have marched up to a battery or to a line of bayonets. But, heavens, what has happened? Something struck him down his back and legs, burned his throat, and chest, and stomach, and brought tears to his eyes—a qualm of nausea, which he could hardly conquer, ran over his whole body. He shouted as loud as he could the first thing that came into his head, to dull that terrible feeling....
>
> A voice shouted again, "Drink!" and Nezhdanov swallowed another draught of the vile poison. It was as if iron hooks were tearing him inside, his head began to spin, green circles were turning before his eyes. There was a ringing in his ear—a roar. Horror—a third glass! Is it possible that he swallowed it? Red noses flew toward him; dusty heads of hair, sunburned necks, furrowed, scarred throats. Hairy hands took hold of him. "Come, finish your speech!" shouted wild voices. "Come, speak! Day before yesterday a stranger, like you, told us lots of things. Go on! You four-legged son of a sea cook!"
>
> The earth waved beneath Nezhdanov's feet. His voice sounded strange to him, as if some one else was speaking. Could he be dead?[60]

He wasn't dead, of course, but he well could have been had the naive *narodnik* not been carried away from the frenzied crowd by his more level-headed comrade, Paul. As the peasants pressed for his views as Paul hauled away the drunken revolutionary we get perhaps the best taste of Tugenev's disdain for the *narodniki*: "It would be perfect, if there were no masters and if the whole world belonged to us, of course," he replied. "But, up to the present time, there has been no *ukase* [government decree] ordering that."[61]

Like the works of Dostoevsky and Tolstoy, Turgenev's *Virgin Soil* spurned Chernyshevsky's revolutionary ideology, all the while sharing the same language of all of Russia's great writers—the language of vodka.

The Brothers Ulyanov

Historian Orlando Figes argues that letting Chernyshevsky's brilliantly awful novel slip through their fingers was one of the tsarist state's greatest mistakes, "for it converted more people to the cause of the revolution than all of the Marx and Engels put together."[62] And that gets it just about right, as the educated Russian youth of the 1870s and 1880s became increasingly restive and the universities churned out revolutionaries who made the "populist" *narodniki* look amateurish by comparison.

The most infamous group inspired by Chernyshevsky came to be known as *Narodnaya volya* or the People's Will. This faction of perhaps five hundred revolutionary radicals sought to replace the "propaganda of ideas" condemning the autocratic system with the "propaganda by deed"—in the process becoming the first modern terrorist organization. For them, Alexander II's emancipatory reforms did not go far enough: the people could never be truly free until the tsarist system was destroyed, which could best be achieved by assassinating key government officials, members of the royal family, and the tsar himself.[63]

On a cold Sunday in St. Petersburg in March of 1881, the tsar-liberator Alexander II fell victim to the People's Will. That Sunday, as on every Sunday, the tsar's motorcade was riding along the Griboedov (literally, mushroom-eater) Canal when a revolutionary chucked a bomb at the bulletproof horse-drawn carriage of the tsar, killing one of the tsar's Cossack guards and injuring nearby civilians. Stepping out to survey the damage, Alexander was easy prey for a second revolutionary, whose bomb killed both tsar and assassin. The magnificent Church of the Savior on the Spilt Blood was erected in the middle of the street to commemorate the very spot where the tsar met his gruesome end.

The assassination prompted a police clampdown, domestic espionage, and the infiltration of radical student groups. Since explicit meetings of revolutionary groups could land them in jail or Siberia, radical students held innocent-looking parties—replete with music, dancing, and gratuitous amounts of vodka—as a front for serious back-room plotting. And in a now-familiar pattern, the revelers served their guests "enough strong drink to soften their vigilance": and occasionally potential collaborators revealed themselves as stool pigeons for the police.[64]

One extreme, Chernyshevsky-inspired group was the Terrorists' Faction of the People's Will. Its leader was a young biology student at the University of St. Petersburg named Aleksandr Ilyich Ulyanov, older brother of Vladimir Ilyich Ulyanov, better known later by his nom de guerre, Lenin. Inspired to revolution, Aleksandr set aside his study of sea spiders to learn bomb making. On the sixth anniversary of the assassination of Alexander II, the elder Ulyanov was arrested with a larger circle of comrades-in-arms as they planned to hurl bombs at the new tsar, Alexander III, as he rode down the Nevsky Prospekt after paying tribute to his slain father at the Church on the Spilt Blood. Despite the radicals' best efforts, the secret police had infiltrated the organization and found sufficient reason to arrest everyone.

While all of the conspirators were sentenced to death, the tsar pardoned all but five: one whose bragging about the effectiveness of terrorism tipped off the authorities, the three bomb throwers, and Ulyanov—their chief ideologue and bomb maker. Unrepentant to the end, in May 1887 the 21-year-old revolutionary hung from the gallows at the tsar's island prison of Schlüsselburg—executed by the autocracy he so vehemently opposed.[65]

News of his brother's martyrdom only hardened the revolutionary resolve of the younger Ulyanov, then a mere seventeen. The young Lenin took up his brother's cause of Marxist revolution with unmatched vigor, beginning by picking up his brother's copy of *What Is to Be Done?* Lenin later reminisced over his inspirations, most notably Chernyshevsky:

> He fascinated my brother and he fascinated me. He plowed me up more profoundly than anyone else. When did you read *What Is to Be Done?*...I myself tried to read it when I was about fourteen. It was no use, a superficial reading. And then, after my brother's execution, knowing that Chernyshevsky's novel was one of his favorite books, I really undertook to read it, and I sat over it not for several days but for several weeks. Only then did I understand its depth....It's a thing that supplies energy for a whole lifetime. An ungifted work could not have that kind of influence.[66]

Lenin fondly kept a number of photos of Chernyshevsky and frequently lauded him in print. And when he later penned his manifesto calling for a professional, Marxist vanguard party to push forward with revolution by all means necessary he gave it a now familiar title: *Chto delat'?*—In English: *What Is to Be Done?*[67]

To be sure, Lenin did not go to absurd lengths to emulate the heroes in Chernyshevsky's *What Is to Be Done?*—such as the enigmatic Rakhmetov who slept on bare boards and denied himself both drink and women in the name of revolution.[68] The radicalism of Lenin's public politics stood in stark contrast to the modesty and temperance of his private life. Whether conspiring in underground circles in St. Petersburg, enduring the epic brutality of Siberia, or writing in European exile, both Lenin and his wife Nadezhda Krupskaya only occasionally drank wine or beer, and never to excess. For them, vodka was completely off limits, not as a matter of taste, but as an extension of their revolutionary philosophy and lifestyle. "Religion is opium for the people," Lenin wrote, invoking Marx's famous maxim. But he continued in terms that would do Tolstoy proud: "Religion is a sort of spiritual booze, in which the slaves of capital drown their human image."[69]

And while religion may be the opiate of the masses, as American satirist Stephen Colbert (or, more likely, one of his writers) reminds us, "vodka . . . is the vodka of the masses."[70]

Lenin would have wholeheartedly agreed—though it is hard to say whether the trite turn of phrase would have elicited a chuckle from the generally humorless revolutionary, whose cold and businesslike reputation preceded him. The widow Krupskaya reminisced that even before she first met Lenin, she was told that he read only "serious" books and never read a novel in his life, a caricature she was surprised to debunk during their shared Siberian exile. "Vladimir Ilyich had not only read Turgenev, Tolstoy, Chernyshevsky's *What Is to Be Done?* but reread them many times and was generally fond of the classics which he knew intimately."[71]

Of course, these were hardly just works of fiction. As we have seen, each of these classics conveyed important social and political commentary. Does it come as any surprise, then, that both Lenin's personal temperament and political philosophy greatly resembled Chernyshevsky, Dostoevsky, Turgenev and Tolstoy—at least in terms of vodka politics?

Echoing these great writers, Lenin often lambasted the tsarist government for systemically debauching and repressing the impoverished Russian masses whose lives were often cut short by alcoholism and domestic violence. While in Siberian exile in 1899 Lenin completed his first academic critique of capitalism and tsarist autocracy in *The Development of Capitalism in Russia*, which devoted an entire section to the importance of distilling to capitalist development and strengthening the local landlords and nobility at the expense of the peasantry.[72] In particular, he railed against the state liquor monopoly as one lever "of that organized robbery, that systematic, unconscionable plunder of national property by a handful of *pomeshchiki*, bureaucrats, and all sorts of parasites, plunder which is called the 'state economy of Russia.'"[73]

Lenin's general understanding of the role of alcohol in tsarist statecraft informed his journalistic critiques of imperial policies in the pages of revolutionary periodicals like *Iskra* (*Spark*), *Zvezda* (*Star*) and *Pravda* (*Truth*). For instance, beginning in 1901, Lenin blasted the tax on vodka—an indirect and therefore regressive tax—as "*the most unfair* form of taxation," tantamount to a tax on the poor.[74] Responding to the resurrection of the imperial vodka monopoly under Finance Minister Sergei Witte, Lenin argued that the move would enrich the noble aristocratic exploiters while "dooming millions of peasants and workers to permanent bondage."[75]

"There is nothing patriotic in the liquor trade," Lenin railed on the pages of *Zarya* (*Dawn*) in 1901 in perhaps his most scathing critique of the "notorious" imperial liquor monopoly:

> What benefits our official and semi-official press expected from it! Increased revenues, improved quality, and less drunkenness! But instead of increased revenues, all we actually have so far is an increase in the price of spirits, confusion in the budget, and the impossibility of determining the exact financial results of the whole operation. Instead of improvement in quality, we have deterioration; and the government is hardly likely to impress the public with its reports, displayed in the entire press, of the successful results of the "degustation" of the new "government vodka." Instead of less drunkenness, we have more illicit trading in spirits, augmented police incomes from this trading, the opening of liquor shops over the protests of the population, which is petitioning against their being opened, and increased drunkenness in the streets. But above all, what a new and gigantic field is opened for official arbitrariness, tyranny, favor-currying and embezzlement by the creation of this new state enterprise, with a turnover off many millions of rubles, and the creation of a whole army of new officials! It is the invasion of a locust-swarm of officials, boot-licking, intriguing, plundering, wasting seas of ink and reams upon reams of paper. [It] is nothing but an attempt to cloak in legal forms the striving to grab the fattest possible slices of the state pie, a desire which is so prevalent in our provinces, and which, in view of the unrestrained power of the officials and the gagging of the people, threatens to intensify the reign of tyranny and plunder.[76]

Lenin's condemnations, often written in exile, continued throughout the end of the tsarist regime. In 1908, when the imperial government effectively increased the price of vodka by 42 kopecks per pail to generate an additional 185 million rubles in needed revenue, Lenin blasted it as a foremost "specimen" of the autocracy's "predatory economy."[77]

He also blasted the government's use of alcohol as a mechanism of social control. For instance, in response to the 1905 Revolution—generally considered a dress rehearsal for 1917—Tsar Nicholas II conceded to create a representative parliament and constitution in order to keep his tenuous hold on power. Much of the revolt took place in St. Petersburg, but there were uprisings in cities throughout the empire. Regiments had to be called in from St. Petersburg to suppress the uprising in Moscow, as the imperial authorities admitted that only perhaps one-third of the 15,000-strong Moscow garrison was "reliable." For those who were wavering toward the cause of socialist revolution, Lenin described how the government bribed and "doped them with vodka," thus removing the least reliable "through treachery and violence. And we must have the courage to confess," Lenin declared, "openly and unreservedly, that in this respect we lagged behind the government."[78]

Beyond such revolutionary polemics and abstract economic critiques, Lenin—much like his idol Chernyshevsky—occasionally delivered his message of revolutionary struggle through vignettes of everyday life in the tsarist system. In one such case, Lenin recounted the trial in the murder of Nizhny-Novgorod peasant Timofei Vozdukhov, who was arrested, hatless, while lodging a complaint with the regional governor that earlier he had been mistreated and assaulted by the local police. Determining that he was "drinking but was not drunk," the governor's superintendent turned the man back over to the police, who took the quiet, not-drunk Vozdukhov to the drunk tank, where (according to witness testimonial) he was beaten to death by—ironically—three policemen "who had been continuously drinking in the police-station since the first day of Easter week" three days earlier. Intent on "teaching the peasant a lesson," the drunken officers bloodied his face and body and broke ten of his ribs before hauling the passive and repentant Vozdukhov to the infirmary, where he soon died of a brain hemorrhage. Lenin replayed the courtroom drama to highlight the everyday brutality of the imperial police as well as shortcomings in the autocratic judicial system that let the officers off with a minor slap on the wrist.[79] Like Chernyshevsky, here too Lenin's portrayal of alcohol, corruption, and brutality were a none-too-subtle avatar of the entire autocratic system. Of course, despite such creativity, Lenin's direct language won him about as much adulation as a writer among literature critics as Chernyshevsky's overwrought prose in *What Is to Be Done?* . . . which is to say, none at all.

Lenin was resolute when it came to dealing with vodka. Like all manner of Marxists, liberals, nihilists, and other critics of the tsarist autocracy in the late nineteenth century, Lenin agreed that alcohol was a scourge on Russian society—the parasitic means by which the state and the capitalist elites at once both subordinated and leached off the impoverished workers and peasants. "The proletariat as a rising class does not need drunkenness that would deafen or provoke them," Lenin proclaimed. "They need only clarity, clarity, and again clarity. The communist upbringing of the working class requires the rooting-out of all vestiges of the capitalist past, especially such a dangerous vestige as drunkenness."[80]

As it turns out, Lenin's vodka politics were not unusual in this regard. Using alcohol to speak out against the excesses of the Russian autocratic system was not a tactic reserved for communist extremists. The ubiquity of alcoholism and degeneracy in imperial Russia, and the extent to which it was promoted for the benefit of the government, was evident to sapient observers from across the political spectrum. Liberals, Marxists, democrats, nihilists, and others—anyone who felt that the people were being held back by the autocratic system, or anyone who had a personal axe to grind with the tsar, were quick to point out the unseemly contradiction of making the prosperity of the Russian state dependent on the misery of its people.

11

Drunk at the Front: Alcohol and the Imperial Russian Army

For all of the derision heaped upon the autocratic state for exploiting and encouraging the drunkenness of the lower classes, even stalwart opponents of tsarism like Chernyshevsky acknowledged that vodka revenues were not an end in themselves but rather a means to provide for defense, military expansion, and the greater glory of the Russian empire.[1] And many Russian soldiers fought for that glory with ice in their veins... and vodka in their bloodstream.

Who could blame them? In the barracks, trenches, or at sea, drinking boosts camaraderie and morale. It numbs the senses of soldiers ordered to kill their fellow man while surrounded by carnage and bloodshed. Unfortunately, drunkenness also undercuts military preparedness, leads to bad strategic decisions, and undermines the effectiveness of the military as a fighting force—in some cases, with disastrous results. By the mid-nineteenth century, the autocratic vodka politics that had long enriched the state while wedding the people to the bottle started backfiring on the Russian state by corroding its military might.

Russia's long military history is filled with alcohol-laced turning-points. One could begin with the 1506 Trojan Horse–style ambush of Muscovite Grand Prince Vasily III's army during a siege of the Khanate of Kazan. Outgunned and outmanned, the cunning Kazanites built an encampment outside their city walls and sent their bravest fighters to hide in the hills. When the Muscovites approached, the people fled as though in panic, leaving the Russians to pillage the camp, eating and drinking their fill. Once their guests were sufficiently drunk, the khan's army hacked the Muscovites to pieces. Only a handful staggered back to the boats on the Volga to take news of the complete destruction of the Russian army back to the Kremlin.[2] Six years later Vasily III led his reconstituted army into battle against the grand duchy of Lithuania. After six weeks laying siege to the imposing Smolensk kremlin, Vasily "strengthened the heart of his army with beer and mead" before his decisive midnight assault, which ended with the decimation of the drunken Muscovites by Lithuanian cannon fire.[3]

Of course a few hundred soldiers assaulting a medieval fortress is a far cry from modern European warfare. By the nineteenth century, military tactics and technology had improved dramatically. The armaments and artillery borne of the Industrial Revolution made killing at a distance ever easier. Wars got bloodier. They also got bigger and more expensive, as the mercenaries and professional warriors of yesteryear gave way to mass armies of peasant conscripts. In Russia this meant that the empire's awesome military might increasingly relied on the very alcoholic peasantry it had for ages been plying with vodka.[4]

By the eighteenth century, mass conscription was essential to nationalism and the modern nation-state as we know them. Before the American and French revolutions, *volunteering* to fight and die for your country was almost unheard of. Before then, most military recruits were desperate for work or were fleeing an even worse fate elsewhere. Others were forced or tricked into service. "Throughout the eighteenth century," Margaret Levi explains, "a single shilling pressed into the hand of a drunken man in a public house by a recruiting sergeant constituted enlistment of a soldier in the British army."[5]

Throughout Europe liquor was the recruiter's favorite tool. While attending the University of Marburg in Germany, the luminary Russian scientist, writer, poet, and philosopher Mikhail Lomonosov—for whom the prestigious Moscow State University would later be named—similarly fell in with a Prussian recruiter in 1740. The morning after a night of heavy drinking, Lomonosov found himself in the uniform of a Prussian cavalry soldier. His protests that he wasn't even German did not matter to the officer.[6]

Universal conscription was first introduced in France in 1793, and within a decade it provided Napoleon's Grande Armée with more than a half-million fighters. Armed with the most formidable military the world had ever seen, Napoleon was intent on subduing virtually all of Europe.[7] The army of Russian Tsar Alexander I was pretty much the only fighting force standing in his way.

Russia still used Peter the Great's system of conscription: divide the country into blocks of peasant households from which either serf owners or the village councils chose which unfortunate boys would be drafted to fulfill the villages' communal obligations. As Russia's territory and population grew, so too did its pool of available recruits, with an incredible 1.5 million men serving in the army in the twenty-five years of Tsar Alexander I's reign.[8]

"Conscription," writes Russian military historian William C. Fuller Jr., "was a species of death." So much so that women sang funeral dirges outside assembly points for the young call-ups who—torn from families and friends—were likely never to return. The Russian conscript faced not only the enemy's bayonets and bullets but also epidemic diseases, supply shortages, and his superiors' brutal discipline. Then there's the military's machismo culture of heavy drinking that—through hazing and ridicule—forced even the most temperate recruit to the bottle.[9]

Even in modern-day Russia, the military seems stuck in the distant past. Rather than a volunteer army, today's Russian armed forces continue to rely on military conscripts, and the brutality, corruption, and alcoholism in the ranks have only gotten worse. "Even if you are not an alcoholic when you go into the Army," a Soviet soldier claimed in the 1970s, "you are when you come out."[10]

But certainly, when the troops left the barracks for the front they dropped the bottle to pick up a rifle, right? Alcohol itself could not be a decisive factor on battlefield… could it?

Did Vodka Beat Napoleon?

Certainly there are any number of factors that contribute to the success or failure of a military campaign: from training, equipment, and strategy to topography, weather, and even disease. Yet could it be that the insatiable ambitions of the great Napoleon Bonaparte and his unstoppable army were ultimately subdued not so much by the heroism of the Russian people as by their liquor?

Having vanquished most continental powers, Napoleon first confronted the formidable Russian army in 1805 on the fields outside Austerlitz (now Slavkov u Brna in the present-day Czech Republic). The French heard of the Russian soldier's fearsome reputation for "blind obedience," "savage valor," and ability to hold his liquor.[11] Yet that reputation was earned defeating "mere" Turks and Persians—the Grande Armée would be another matter. According to Napoleon's spies, the heretofore menacing Russian army "was marked by riot and intemperance" and spent the eve of battle "in drunkenness, noise and revelry." Later writers suggested that Napoleon chose to commence the battle at dawn, when "the fumes of brandy had not yet evaporated from the heads of the soldiers, [which] may have assisted to produce, or at least to heighten the disasters of that fatal day."[12] Despite being vastly outnumbered, the French dealt the Russians and their Austrian allies a quick, humiliating, and total defeat. The resulting Peace of Pressburg marked the pinnacle of Napoleon's power: not only did it knock Austria out of the war; it also dissolved the Third Coalition against France and effectively ended the Holy Roman Empire.

In defeat, Tsar Alexander I retreated to Russia with his armies. Following another French rout at Friedland two years later, Napoleon and Alexander concluded an uneasy armistice. Hearing rumors that Alexander was making contingency war plans, on June 23, 1812, Napoleon crossed the Nieman River and invaded the vast Russian heartland. Against his generals' advice, he intended to force Alexander's capitulation by capturing Moscow, a thousand kilometers to the East. It was a fateful decision, colored perhaps by Napoleon's impressions of the weakness—and drunkenness—of the Russian army at Austerlitz.

Early encounters confirmed Napoleon's hunches: instead of risking direct confrontation, Alexander's armies retreated ever further across the vast, sparsely populated terrain. The Russians scorched the earth—destroying crops, livestock, and shelter, thereby preventing the French troops from living off the land—but also straining their supply lines and morale.In the smoldering ruins of Vyazma, still 100 miles from Moscow, Napoleon grew frustrated. Finding his troops, half mad with hunger, looting the vodka and wine stores, he flew into a rage, beating and whipping them for their lack of discipline.[13]

On September 7, in the fields of Borodino, Napoleon finally got his long-awaited showdown. By day's end, over sixty-five thousand men lay dead or dying on the battlefield in one of the bloodiest battles in human history. Borodino was a pyrrhic victory for the French, who were too exhausted to pursue the withdrawing Russian army. A week later, Napoleon confidently approached Moscow, fully expecting the vanquished tsar to formally surrender and bestow upon the victorious emperor the keys to the city. Much to his disappointment, Alexander did not ride out to meet him. No one did. Incensed that the Russians had denied him his greatest triumph, Napoleon occupied the historic Kremlin while his famished troops pillaged the abandoned city.[14]

But the worst lay ahead. Moscow governor Fyodor Rostopchin had vowed that were he forced to abandon the city, the French would find nothing but ashes. He made good on his promise. Rostopchin ordered the withdrawal of all of Moscow's fire pumps and the emptying of the prisons before turning the highly flammable taverns and vodka storehouses into firebombs and igniting boats loaded with alcohol that burned three-quarters of the city to the ground.[15]

At first, the French ignored the thick clouds of smoke in the distance: they had seen it in every town they occupied. But as Napoleon explored the majestic imperial palaces, burning embers began falling within the walled courtyard of the Kremlin itself. Fearing the explosion of the gunpowder in the Kremlin armory, Napoleon and his entourage fled the firestorm. Narrowly escaping the chaotic, smoke-filled streets toward the Petrovsky Palace on the northeastern outskirts of the city, Napoleon watched his coveted prize reduced to rubble.[16]

In his memoirs, Napoleon blamed the city and its officials for the catastrophe.

A great part of [Moscow was] built of wood, contained warehouses of brandy, oil, and other combustible materials. All the fire-engines had been carried off; the city kept several hundred, the service being carefully organized, but only one could be found. For some days the army struggled in vain against the fire; everything was burnt. The inhabitants who had remained in the town escaped to the wood or country-houses; none remained but the lowest rabble, who stayed for the sake of pillage. This great and superb city became a desert and sink of desolation and crime.[17]

"Moscow was burned by its citizens—that is true," Tolstoy wrote in *War and Peace*, "not, however, by the citizens who remained, but by those who went away."[18] Those who remained confronted an orgy of drunken chaos virtually identical to the uprisings in Moscow in 1648 and 1682 (see chapter 5). Fleeing the flames, the French command lost all control of the city. Desperate French soldiers wandered the streets alongside disoriented Russians—all simply foraging for food. An eclectic mix of the few remaining well-to-do Muscovites, occupying French troops, and Russian criminals sought to save/loot anything of value, including "wine and brandy in abundance" that only fueled the drunken disorder.[19]

"The army had dissolved completely," wrote French major Pion des Loches, "everywhere one could see drunken soldiers and officers loaded with booty and provisions seized from houses which had fallen prey to the flames."[20] Muscovites—regardless of age, sex, or stature—who dared safeguard their valuables were bludgeoned to death by the French while any drunken French looter who stumbled away from his battalion mates met the same fate at the hands of the locals. The encroaching din of fire was punctuated only by screams of people and animals being burned alive, the howls of men being beaten and women raped in the streets. "The troops, no longer restrained by the fear of their superiors, indulged in every excess imaginable," officer Eugène Labaume wrote in his memoirs. "No retreat was safe, no sanctuary sufficiently sacred to protect against their rapacity." Soldiers even violated the tombs of the Muscovite grand princes—including Ivan the Terrible—interred in the Cathedral of the Archangel in the Kremlin.[21]

To their credit, a French battalion succeeded in saving the Kremlin, to which Napoleon returned after the fires subsided. To protect against more fires and disorder he commanded that remaining vodka warehouses be defended by French guards. The miserable Grande Armée and their equally miserable emperor lived among the smoldering ruins for another full month. The remaining livestock died of starvation, and leaving the city to seize cattle risked further demoralizing skirmishes with Russian Cossacks. Starving French soldiers sifted through charred ruins hoping to find leftover wine and vodka, which they would drink from exquisite looted crystal, even though they had no food to eat.[22]

Napoleon waited in vain for the tsar's surrender, even writing Alexander to describe his commission of inquiry into the arson. The French captured and executed over four hundred Russians, whose "patriotic" acts were, according to Napoleon, "founded on the casks of brandy which had been given them."[23] The entire fiasco, Napoleon wrote Alexander, could have been avoided with a friendly letter of capitulation either before or after Borodino. He never received an answer. Winter was drawing near.[24]

Thoroughly humiliated, on October 19, 1812, the French abandoned Moscow with only one hundred twenty thousand of the original half-million-man army, and most of them would perish thanks to Russia's brutal winter and the epidemic of typhus that had infested the Grande Armée.[25] Endlessly harassed by military attacks from the rear, the retreating French fought westward for hundreds of miles against fierce winds, sub-zero temperatures, and drifting snow along the same Smolensk road that had been stripped of all supplies just months before. As their horses fell from exhaustion, the starving, diseased, and demoralized troops devoured the carcasses raw. Some even resorted to cannibalism. Absent any shelter, thousands of frozen corpses littered the roadsides.

When the starving French re-entered Vilnius, they looted the city. They "broke open the magazines, and fell, overcome with brandy and a full meal, after long exhaustion, in all parts of the city, their frozen corpses lying unheeded, while the rest hastily fled from it at the sound of the Cossacks."[26] Only forty thousand lived to see home. Within two years, Tsar Alexander I triumphantly led his troops into Paris, forcing Napoleon's abdication before his final defeat at Waterloo a year later.

Russia's tremendous size and brutal climate usually are credited for Napoleon's downfall, with estimates of French deaths from fatigue, cold, hunger, and typhus (132,000) exceeding even those slain on the battlefield (125,000).[27] Compared to the toll of hardship and disease, vodka was only a minor contributing factor. Still, had the decision not been made to set Moscow's vodka warehouses ablaze and the city with it, Russia's biggest, richest city would have been an ideal bivouac for the Grande Armée. The soldiers could have waited out the frigid winter cloistered in Moscow's warm residences, in (relatively) more sanitary conditions, thereby reducing the spread of typhus so that the army could emerge in the spring rejuvenated and ready to finish off the beleaguered Russians. One can only speculate as to the outcome of such a scenario—but it would likely have been dramatically different from the humiliating expulsion from Russia that sealed Napoleon's political fate.

So, did Tsar Alexander I defeat the French—or was it vodka? Even beyond the battlefield, the climate and typhus certainly ensured Napoleon's doom. Still, the role alcohol played in making Moscow uninhabitable and hastening the drunken, diseased, and demoralized retreat cannot be overlooked. In this way, it might be argued that—at this time of its greatest crisis—vodka helped save Russia. Even so, such alco-triumphs would be short-lived.

War And Drink In Crimea

Modern impressions of Russia's war against Napoleon are colored by the vivid descriptions of Tolstoy's epic novel *War and Peace*. Yet given that the great writer was not yet born, those riveting tales were not firsthand accounts. Tolstoy's literary realism actually drew from his experiences in the Crimean War, and his "dissipated military life" of booze, gambling, and women in the Russian army.[28] During this disastrous war Tolstoy first appreciated the difficulty of finding "truth" amid the fog of war, since everyone is "too busy staggering about in smoke, squelching through wounded bodies, drunk with vodka, fear or courage, to have any clear sense of what is going on."[29]

Russia's road to war was confused and muddled. When Tsar Nicholas I ascended the throne in December 1825, an inebriated Petersburg mob of liberal-minded "Decembrists" dared challenge his legitimacy. Without hesitation the young tsar violently dispatched the rebels with cannons and bayonets. Still, the threat of European liberalism weighed heavily on Nicholas, who hardened into an ardent defender of conservative autocracy, even sending Russian troops to Hungary in 1848 to crush the liberal uprisings there. His own geopolitical ambitions focused on the the Ottoman Empire to the south. In 1853 Nicholas's forces pushed into the Ottoman principalities of Moldavia and Wallachia in present-day Romania. Fearing what an Ottoman collapse would do to the European balance of power, Britain, France, and Sardinia sided with the Turks, dealing Russia an embarrassing defeat in their own backyard.

The combined forces soon beat back the Russian incursion before turning their attention to the Crimean citadel of Sevastopol to destroy Russia's Black Sea Fleet, which would continue to threaten the Ottoman Empire, the Dardanelles, and the Mediterranean beyond. So, in 1854, the allies landed their forces well north of the city and marched southward to take Sevastopol.

The war in Crimea is remembered for many things: the suicidal "charge of the light brigade" immortalized by Alfred Lord Tennyson, Florence Nightingale's pioneering work as a battlefield nurse, and the first ever war correspondents covering the human tragedies of wartime.

One such chronicler on the Russian side was an enlisted Pole, Robert Adolf Chodasiewicz. A decade before volunteering his services to the Union army in the American Civil War, Chodasiewicz wrote a gripping firsthand account of the Russians' first clash with the allies at the Battle of the Alma River. There, the cocksure commander Prince Aleksandr Sergeyevich Menshikov—great grandson of Peter the Great's confidant of the same name (see chapter 4)—even invited the ladies of Sevastopol to join him in watching Russia's certain victory from a nearby hilltop. Meanwhile, his troops sensed impending disaster:

"Why?" asked Chodasiewicz.

"As if you don't know as well as I do!" One veteran explained: "we are to have no vodka, and how can we fight without it?" The others all agreed.[30]

Why were the men denied their daily combat ration of bread, meat, a garnet of beer, and two *charkas*—good-sized cupfuls—of vodka? "Our worthy Colonel thought it advisable to put the money in his own pocket, remarking that half these fellows will be killed, so it will be only a waste to give them vodka."[31]

Such corruption in the ranks was not unusual, but it dealt a devastating blow to Russian morale.

On the battlefield, this despair turned to panic—and panic mixed with alcohol is a recipe for a rout. Even without their *charkas* soldiers could still get liquor from merchants in nearby towns, corrupt officers, and even by happenstance. Chodasiewicz's regiment, for instance, was "saved" from sobriety when the canteen man fled the field after bullets started flying. While the allies besieged the Russian positions, the Russian soldiers—"in high spirits"—besieged vodka.[32] The officers offered no tactical leadership: they were often just as drunk and confused as the troops. For Chodasiewicz, it was the demoralization and lack of leadership that spelled defeat. "During the five hours that the battle went on we neither saw nor heard of our general of division, or brigadier, or colonel: we did not during the whole time receive any orders from them either to advance or to retire; and when we retired, nobody knew whether we ought to go to the right or left."[33]

Not even the army high command was sober. Rather than direct the left flank of the Russian defenses, Lt. Gen. Vasily Kiryakov instead threw a champagne party. Generally described as "utterly ignorant, totally devoid of any military ability and rarely in a completely sober state," on this day Kiryakov stumbled to his feet and—bottle of champagne in hand—ordered his Minsk regiment to open fire on what he thought was the French cavalry. It was actually his own Kiev Hussars, who were decimated by the barrage. Enraged, the Hussar commander had to be physically restrained from running Kiryakov through with his sword. With no confidence in their drunken commander, the Minsk regiment also retired—in some cases without ever firing a shot at the enemy. In the disorder Lt. Gen. Kiryakov mysteriously disappeared, only to be found hours later cowering in a hollow in the ground. Nearby, British forces discovered a Russian artillery captain sprawled dead drunk in a wagon. The jovial sot offered his captors a swig from his bottle of champagne, which turned out to be empty.[34]

The battlefield fiasco rudely upset commander Menshikov's viewing party, which was abandoned so hastily that the parasols, field glasses, and even the picnic spread were left behind. In Menshikov's carriage the French found "letters from the Tsar, 50,000 francs, pornographic French novels, the general's boots, and some ladies' underwear."[35] After the disastrous battle of Alma, Menshikov withdrew his army to the interior of the Crimea, leaving the sailors and civilians of Sevastopol to their fate. When riders brought news of the catastrophe to Tsar Nicholas in St. Petersburg, he brooded in bed for days, "convinced that his beloved troops were cowards led by idiots."[36]

Things were just as bad in the imperial navy in Sevastopol. Consider for instance the heart of the naval citadel, Malakhov Hill: towering over Sevastopol

Bay and its nearby estuaries where the mighty Russian fleet was anchored, it was the linchpin to the city's defenses. Today, Malakhov Hill is a popular city attraction: a serene, wooded park and open-air memorial complex replete with an eternal flame. Given the hill's strategic and historic importance, surely this Malakhov fellow after whom it is named was some legendary military hero, no?

Actually... no.

Mikhail Malakhov was a lowly ship's purser in the tsarist navy in charge of bookkeeping and buying provisions. His position allowed him to acquire great quantities of *charka* liquor on the navy's tab, which he then sold for immense personal profit. Even after being court-martialed for such corrupt abuses, Malakhov used his connections with shifty procurement officers and bootleggers to open an illegal, ramshackle (but extremely popular and lucrative) vodka shop, built into the side of the hill that now bears his name.[37]

Following the defeat at the Alma River, Malakhov Hill was the city's last defense against the allied invaders. With the Russian army in flight, the entire population of Sevastopol—military and civilian, men and women, police and prostitutes—dug trenches, built barricades, and prepared for the imminent attack. To slow the allies' seaward advance, Russian warships were scuttled in the harbor, many fully stocked with armaments and provisions. Demoralization, insubordination, and despair swept the city. To make matters worse, the discovery of a large storehouse of liquor wharfside resulted in a three-day drunken rampage.

"A perfect chaos reigned throughout the town," Chodasiewicz recalled. "Drunken sailors wandered riotously about the streets, and in some instance shouted that Menshikov had sold the place to the English, and that he had purposely been beaten at the Alma."[38] In a quixotic effort to restore sobriety and confidence, Vice Adm. Vladimir Kornilov—the fleet's chief of staff—instituted emergency anti-alcohol measures by closing vodka stores, taverns, hotels, and restaurants, actions ultimately having "little or no effect in restraining the populace from drunkenness."[39] On October 17, 1854, the artillery barrage began. In that initial battle a British round detonated a Russian magazine, killing Adm. Kornilov, ironically, atop Malakhov Hill. Today, a monument to Kornilov's sober heroism crowns the hill named after the city's corrupt vodka dealer.

The siege of Sevastopol continued for months—the tense stalemate occasionally interrupted by salvos of artillery or an occasional ground attack—while conditions in the city deteriorated. Most residents drank a tumbler of vodka with breakfast and dinner and even more in-between. In his *Sevastopol Sketches*, a young Count Tolstoy described how officers spent their off-duty hours drinking, gambling, singing, and carousing with what few prostitutes remained in the city. The heavy drinking was always ramped up just before an attack in order

LITHOGRAPH DEPICTING THE FINAL FRENCH ATTACK ON THE MALAKHOFF HILL, 1855 Library of Congress Prints and Photographs Division/William Simpson.

to bolster the soldiers' courage. Stammering into battle, the unsteady soldiers made easy targets. "The army that came out of Sevastopol to attack the other day…were all drunk," recalled one British regimental paymaster. "The hospitals smelt so bad with them that you could not remain more than a minute in the place and we were told by an officer who they took prisoner that they had been giving them wine till they had got them to the proper pitch and asked who would go out and drive the English Dogs into the sea, instead of which we drove them back into the town."[40]

Still, over the ensuring months the heroic defenders of Sevastopol repulsed five separate allied assaults on Russian positions, inflicting heavy losses on both sides. Finally, on their sixth assault, the French successfully overran the city's last defenses and captured Malakhov Hill on September 8, 1855. The city of Sevastopol surrendered the following day.

The Crimean War was an embarrassing defeat: Russian battle casualties topped one hundred thousand, with another three hundred thousand succumbing to disease, malnourishment, and exposure.[41] Among those casualties might be listed Tsar Nicholas I himself, whose military fixation and despair took a dramatic toll on his health. In the spring of 1855, while reviewing troops departing for Crimean battlefields, the tsar contracted pneumonia and died shortly thereafter.

Soon diplomats mingled in Paris while negotiating peace terms, as did former belligerents on the battlefield. A diary entry of British soldier Henry Tyrrell dated Sunday, April 6, 1856, paints a vivid picture:

> The great objects of attraction to-day were the Russians, who...wandered into every part of our camp, where they soon made out the canteens. By one o'clock there were a good many of them "as soldiers wish to be who love their grog." A navvy [British manual laborer] of the most stolid kind, much bemused with beer, is a jolly, lively, and intelligent being compared to an intoxicated "Ruski."...Their drunken salute to passing officers is very ludicrous; and one could laugh, only he is disgusted at the abject cringe with which they remove their caps, and bow, bareheaded, with horrid gravity in their bleary leaden eyes and wooden faces, at the sight of a piece of gold lace. Some of them seemed very much annoyed at the behavior of their comrades, and endeavoured to drag them off from the canteens; and others remained perfectly sober. Our soldiers ran after them in crowds, and fraternised very willingly with their late enemies.[42]

Indeed, the French, British, and even the Turkish soldiers happily drank with their newfound Russian friends. At the end of each night's revelry the Russians returned to their encampments across the deep Chernaya River, which could be crossed only by means of fallen trees—quite a challenge even when sober! Cossack patrols used ropes to pull drunks half-dead (and occasionally fully so) from the water. "Down they came, staggering and roaring through the bones of their countrymen (which in common decency I hope they will bury as soon as possible), and then, after elaborate leave-taking, passed the fatal stream," Tyrrell wrote. "General Codrington was down at the ford, and did not seem to know whether to be amused or scandalized at the scene."

The British posted guards along the roads to keep "all the drunken Ruskies out of the town" and sentries along the cliffs and harbors "to prevent them coming in after their jollification at the bazaar." And still they came—especially the more affluent Russian officers who bought huge quantities of champagne and liquor that cost half as much in the allied camps as in the Russian ones.[43]

Clearly the embarrassment of pervasive drunkenness contributed to humiliating military defeat in Crimea. Alexander II's consequent political reforms—abolishing serfdom and the corrupt tax farm—did not stop the state from profiting from the drunkenness of its people, including the lowly peasant conscripts. Only in 1874 did Russia finally scrap Peter the Great's village quota system for universal conscription, requiring six years of military service for all men. Unfortunately, this reform also universally conscripted Russians to the bottle: even peasants who never touched vodka before enlisting often returned home as drunkards. Later studies found that some 11.7 percent of St. Petersburg workers began drinking vodka only in the military.[44] Ultimately, universal conscription became just another tool in the alcoholization of Russian society.

Even in peacetime alcoholism in the ranks was epidemic. Expressly blaming the vodka ration, one military physician estimated that seventy-five percent of the soldiers in infirmaries were there due to alcohol poisoning and that between ten and forty-four percent of all military deaths were attributable to alcohol. "Was he drunk?" became the medic's standard first question for treating any accident or ailment. But the military brass wasn't listening. At the dawn of the twentieth century, the imperial ministry of war flatly denied that there was any alcohol problem at all, much less one caused by the troops' vodka rations.[45]

The insobriety and ineptitude of the tsarist military was a disaster waiting to happen. And if Crimea suggested that alcohol was a major problem, Japan proved it.

Stumbling Toward Defeat In The Far East

Just as the imperial double-headed eagle peered both west toward Europe and east toward Asia, by the early twentieth century Russia's imperial ambitions brought it into conflict not only with European powers but increasingly with Asian ones as well. Following combined efforts to suppress the Chinese Boxer Rebellion of 1900, the empire of Japan held much of Korea while Russia occupied Chinese Manchuria, including Port Arthur (today, Lüshunkou) on the Liaodong Peninsula—Russia's coveted ice-free port on the Pacific. Previously occupied by Japan before an eight-nation European alliance forced its concession to Russia,[46] Port Arthur was crucial to propagating influence in the Far East. The opening salvo in the Russo-Japanese War was a surprise nighttime torpedo attack on the Russian fleet anchored at Port Arthur on February 8, 1904. Japan hoped to strike quickly before Russian reinforcements could arrive from Europe across the still-incomplete Trans-Siberian Railway.

Reinforcements were slow in coming and not simply due to Russia's anemic infrastructure. Mobilizing hundreds of thousands of unwilling sons, husbands, and fathers to fight and die in the Far East unleashed drunken pandemonium at assembly points. Torn from their villages and families, some committed suicide rather than enlist. Officers shot themselves with rifles, slit their own throats with knives, hung themselves, or worse: in his memoirs, military physician Vinkenty Veresayev described how a widower with three dependent children broke down before the military council.

" 'What shall I do with my children? Instruct me what to do! They will all die from starvation without me!' "

"He acted like a madman," Veresayev recalled: "shouted and shook his fists in the air. Then he suddenly grew silent, went home, killed his children with an axe, and came back.

" 'Now take me' " said the recruit. " 'I've attended to my business.'

He was arrested."[47]

Beyond such extreme cases, the tearful send-offs at assembly points often turned into orgies of mayhem, as recruitment officers corralled drunken conscripts with bayonets. With surprising frequency commanders were overwhelmed by the drunken masses, as vodka-fueled mobs ransacked local taverns and businesses and murdered recruitment officers.[48]

Even when recruits were corralled into the trains the drinking did not stop. From the luxury of the officers' car Veresayev reported that in the cramped, musty cars of the common soldiers, drinking went on day and night. "Nobody knew how or where the soldiers got the vodka. But they had all they wanted." Not surprisingly, easy access to alcohol and weapons was a recipe for tragedy.

" 'Have you heard this story?' " Veresayev's traveling companion asked. " 'Officers just told me at the station that soldiers yesterday killed Colonel Lukashóv. They were drunk and started shooting from the cars at a herd that was passing by. He tried to stop them, and so they killed him.'

" 'I heard it differently,' " Veresayev calmly replied. " 'He treated the soldiers very brutally and they promised before departing that they would kill him on the way.' "[49] In either case, the long trip across the vast Siberian landmass was marred with drunken misfortune—and more would be waiting on Far Eastern battlefields.

Even more than in the Crimea, coverage by embedded journalists was unflattering for the Russian side. On his first visit to Port Arthur, Associated Press war correspondent Frederick McCormick first noted the grandeur of the Russian ships in the small, crowded port; and second, the "pile of perhaps ten thousand cases of vodka" by the train station. Journalists found alcohol in the barracks, in the officers' quarters, and on the battlefield. In the ensuing battle of Port Arthur, Russian troops stumbled into battle drunk. Correspondents described the entire Manchurian campaign between Russia and Japan as a "scuffle between a drunken guardsman and a sober policeman."[50]

The chief engineer of the Pacific fleet at Port Arthur, Evgeny Politovsky, would not survive the Russian war in the Far East, but his diaries did. On October 7, 1904, he wrote of how many were more willing to follow vodka than follow their commanders.

The crews of the ships at Port Arthur asked leave to go to the advanced positions, and returned under the influence of liquor. No one could understand how they became drunk. In the town liquors were not sold, and yet men went to the advanced positions and returned intoxicated. At last it was discovered, and how do you suppose? It appears that the sailors went to the front in order to kill one of the enemy and take away his brandy-flask. Just imagine such a thing. They risked their lives to get drunk! They did all this without thinking anything of it, and contrived to conceal it from the authorities.[51]

As in Crimea, it was not just the common foot soldier who got tipsy, but their commanders as well. As a guest of the Russian military command, McCormick described his encounter with a drunken Cossack colonel who threatened to shoot him for refusing to drink vodka and wine.[52] As an outsider, McCormick was appalled—both at the unimaginable quantity of alcohol the commanders consumed and their complete nonchalance about Russia's staggering battlefield losses.

Up to this time, although the troops had been continually beaten, the army seemed outwardly, at least to the casual observer, as care-free as possible. In the back court in the International Hotel captains, colonels and generals could be found any day, and occasionally from late morning breakfast to late at night, repeatedly greeting each other with kisses through their heavy beards and making merry over liquor, champagne and beer. It reminded one of Port Arthur just before the opening of the war. Every night had its orgy, and out of these grew many troubles for the commander-in-chief. It seemed to be a natural characteristic to begin breakfast with champagne. A young officer...would begin in the morning on a bottle of liquor, and at night was always certain of being carried out to his room by the Chinese waiters. It took a fortnight by military process to transfer him from the army base to the rear. A staff officer and three companions, who mixed their champagne with beer and vodka, and among them could not raise fifty rubles with which to pay their bill, would monopolize the hotel.[53]

Unsurprisingly, perhaps, Port Arthur was a repeat of the disaster at Sevastopol—both in terms of the drunkenness and corruption. "The Russian appears to devote himself to champagne as to the very elixir of life," McCormick reported. "The thirst for this liquor was the cause of the very gravest charges of corruption against the Red Cross department and the quartermaster's department, both of which handled quantities of it. Such a demand was created for this drink that the price advanced to nearly ten times the normal, and the opportunities for profit were irresistible to those officials who had control of the champagne supplies."[54]

Some drunken havoc was to be expected, McCormick surmised, from a system of universal conscription that had could not weed out those unfit for service.[55] As in the Crimea, this inebriated, incompetent, and corrupt military force was dealt one embarrassing blow after another. By mid-1904, the Japanese had blockaded the Russian fleet, and besieged the port, while scoring land victories at the Yalu River.

Something dramatic had to be done. And odds were, it wouldn't be good.

What Do You Do With A Drunken Sailor?

The young Tsar Nicholas II and his top brass grew frustrated. Reinforcements were slow in coming. In addition to the mobilization fiasco, supplying the war effort had clogged Russia's frail infrastructure—including the still-incomplete, single-rail Trans-Siberian Railway—bringing commerce to a standstill.[56] If the front could not be reinforced by land, perhaps it could by sea! Nicholas turned to his uncle, Grand Duke Alexei Aleksandrovich—who commanded the entire navy despite spending "less time on the fleet than he did on drinking bouts and various love affairs."[57] In 1904, Nicholas and Alexei authorized the most harebrained military scheme ever: sending forty-five ships from the Baltic Fleet to the Pacific to take on the Japanese. To get there, these ships had to circumnavigate the entire Eastern Hemisphere—from their home ports in the Baltic Sea, around the Iberian Peninsula, the Horn of Africa, Madagascar, across the Indian Ocean, through the Dutch East Indies, and up the Chinese coast. This epic eighteen thousand mile journey was the longest voyage of a coal-powered battleship fleet in history.

Under the command of Adm. Zinovy Rozhestvensky, the voyage was a microcosm of the hubris and misfortune of Nicholas' entire reign (see chapter 12): beginning with drunken tragedy and ending in epic disaster. Upon setting sail from Libau in October 1904, Rozhestvensky's newly commissioned flagship the *Knyaz Suvorov,* with its largely inexperienced crew, immediately ran aground, while one of its escorts lost its anchor. After the anchor was retrieved and the flagship re-floated, a destroyer rammed the battleship *Oslyaba,* which had to return for repairs.[58]

Incredibly, things got even worse in open water. Rumors circulated that the Baltic and North seas were teeming with Japanese torpedo boats that, despite all evidence or logic (torpedo boat squadrons have an extremely limited range), had allegedly completed the improbable eighteen-thousand-mile voyage from the Far East, around Siam, Ceylon, India, and Africa to mine the waters of Northern Europe.

Upon approaching the coast of Denmark, a local fishing vessel was dispatched to relay consular communications from Tsar Nicholas II. Mistaking the vessel for a Japanese fighter, the fleet opened fire, though due to the appalling standards of Russian gunnery, the two fishermen made it through unharmed to deliver the imperial communique: Admiral Rozhestvensky—Congratulations! Your exemplary performance has earned you a well-deserved promotion.

Before continuing on from Denmark, the heavily inebriated captain of the repair ship *Kamchatka* hysterically claimed to have been attacked "from all directions" by up to eight Japanese torpedo boats that no one on the other ships ever saw.[59]

Yet the fleet saved its greatest embarrassment for the Dogger Banks—a rich fishing area between Denmark and England. On the evening of October 21, the captain of the *Kamchatka*—again drunk by all accounts—mistook a nearby Swedish ship for a Japanese torpedo boat and radioed that his ship was under attack. Nearby were a number of British fishing trawlers, which through the fog of alcohol were mistook for Japanese warships, which (again) somehow made the unfathomable eighteen-thousand-mile journey to engage the Russians in the North Sea. These unfortunate and unarmed vessels were met by the full fury of the fleet's thunderous guns. As Russian spotlights panned across the British trawlers, the fishermen hurriedly splayed their catch across their bows to show they were no threat. Despite the all-out barrage, only one British ship was sunk and three fishermen killed.[60] In the confusion, several Russian ships signaled that they had been hit by Japanese torpedos while sailors on others scurried about hysterically, claiming they were being boarded by Japanese raiders.

Belatedly realizing their mistake, the fleet's battleships then trained their heavy-calibre fire on the *real* enemy—an approaching formation of actual warships. Unfortunately, it turned out that these were in fact Russian cruisers from their own formation including the *Dmitry Donskoi* and the *Aurora*.

As an aside: the *Aurora* later gained fame for her catalyzing role in the October Revolution of 1917. Her sailors defied orders to put to sea, and a blank shot from its forecastle gun signaled the assault on the Winter Palace. Some *Aurora* sailors joined in the storming of the Winter Palace, while most stormed a nearby tavern.[61] Today, the *Aurora* is moored in the Neva River in St. Petersburg as a museum ship—but on that October night in the Dogger Banks she saw her first military action . . . against her own drunken fleet.

Both the *Aurora* and the *Dmitry Donskoi* sustained modest damage in the attack. Further damage was saved only by the incompetence and incapacitation of the artillerymen themselves: the battleship *Orel*, for one, fired more than five hundred artillery shells in the incident without ever landing a single hit.[62]

The British were understandably livid. Relations were already strained by Russians seizing neutral British commercial steamers in the Pacific theater. This was the the last straw: an unprovoked attack against unarmed civilians was an act of war. Admiral Rozhestvensky's reaction did not help: rather than assess injuries or assist the victims, Rozhestvensky simply sailed on, acknowledging the incident only days later while off the coast of Spain. As news of the event spread, so did international outrage. According to one reporter, "In the United States, in France, and even in Germany, unsparing reprobation of a deed so unjustifiable was freely uttered, and the belief was confidently expressed that the only possible explanation was to be found in the undiscipline and probable drunken frenzy of the Russian naval officers."[63]

It was vodka that pushed Russia to the brink of war. Amid the public outcry, the government of Arthur Balfour delivered an ultimatum and prepared the British Mediterranean fleet to sink the Russian squadron en route to the Pacific. Russia was already stretched thin both on land and at sea; a war against the mighty British navy would have been disastrous. Ultimately, the British were satisfied only after repeated public apologies by the Russian government, the payment of indemnities to the fishermen, and the promise of an official inquiry.[64]

Having narrowly averted war with the Brits, Russia still had the Japanese to contend with. But unfortunately, more embarrassments would follow.

RUNNING AMUCK. November 16, 1904, cover of the satirical magazine *Puck* depicting Russia—clutching a jug of vodka—stumbling into war against a Japanese hornet. Note the injured John Bull character in the background. Library of Congress Prints and Photographs Division.

Massacre At Mukden, Tragedy In Tsushima

While the fleet was re-coaling in Madagascar, news reached the Russians that Port Arthur had surrendered to the Japanese on January 2, 1905. But that was not the end of the war. On land, the Japanese continued to beat Russian forces back north along the Russian Manchurian Railway, some two hundred and fifty miles inland to the city of Mukden—destined to be the site of the decisive battle of the war and one of the largest military conflicts in world history to that point.[65]

Although the Russians outnumbered the Japanese and had secured defensive positions, a series of tactical mistakes and a drunken, demoralized army proved disastrous in a two-week battle involving up to a million combatants. Once the frontline troops faltered, it was all over. Medical encampments filled with the wounded and dying—once at the rear—were overrun by Russian regiments retreating in disarray. The collapse was so quick that the commissary stores could not be evacuated. Rather than setting them aflame to keep the goods out of the hands of the enemy, officials simply gave away the food and vodka, pouring it into the canteens and fur caps of the retreating troops. The results were predictable—the tottering, "beastly-drunk soldiers lost their rifles, shouted songs, and fell down and rolled in the dust. The bushes were filled with motionless bodies."[66]

Attempting to render medical assistance in such conditions was pointless. The medic Veresayev described the scene as follows:

> Drunken men were wallowing at each side of the road. A soldier would be sitting on a mound, his rifle between his knees, his head drooping. If you touched him on his shoulder, he would roll down like a bag. Was he dead? Was he sleeping a deep sleep from fatigue? His pulse was beating, his face was red, and he exhaled an odor of liquor.[67]

In their retreat, Cossacks raided local distilleries and artillerymen grabbed as much liquor as they could carry. The more entrepreneurial troops charged fifty kopeks for a bottle of stolen cognac, rum, or port wine. In a moment of reflection, Veresayev pondered,

> Who were these commissary officials? Traitors, who had been bought by the Japanese? Scoundrels who wished to enjoy the complete disgrace of the Russian Army? Oh, no! They were only good-natured Russians, who could not comprehend the idea of personally putting fire to such a precious thing as liquor. All the subsequent days, during the period of the grievous retreat, our Army swarmed with drunken men. It was as though they were celebrating a joyous, universal holiday. It was rumored that in Mukden and in the villages Chinamen who had been bought by

Japanese emissaries had been filling our war-worn, retreating soldiers with the devilish Chinese liquor, han-shin. Maybe that was so. But all the drunken soldiers whom I asked told me that they had received brandy, liquor, or cognac from all kinds of Russian stores which had been ordered to be burned. What was the use for the Japanese to waste money on the Chinamen? They had a more faithful and more disinterested confederate, and one that was more terrible to us.[68]

Back in St. Petersburg, Russian papers broke the tragic news by describing how "the Japanese found several thousand Russian soldiers so dead drunk that they were able to bayonet them like so many pigs."[69]

The stunning defeat was one thing; the quiet resignation of the military commanders, another. As the troops fell back from Mukden, foreign correspondents rode in the luxurious train of the Russian high command, where officers ordered rounds of champagne. "Through the windows could be watched the scene of headlong flight of the soldiers up the railway," Frederick McCormick wrote. "The foreigners were plunged into a state of confused and sympathetic embarrassment, for in no country which any one of them represented was it possible to drink to such a state of affairs. But all thoughts of chagrin and mortification as far as the Russian officers were concerned seemed to vanish under the spell of the opportunity to drink."[70]

Mukden was yet another painful humiliation; it was not the last. Russia still had hope that—after eight months at sea—the Baltic Fleet would turn the tide of war. With Port Arthur in enemy hands, the fleet sailed for Vladivostok—Russia's port on the Pacific—through the narrow Tsushima Straits between Korea and the Japanese mainland. On May 27, 1905, Admiral Rozhestvensky's fleet was intercepted by Japanese admiral Togo Heihachiro. Less than twenty-four hours later, Togo was accepting the Russian surrender as all Russian battleships and most cruisers and destroyers lay on the sea floor.

Inebriety was as pervasive in the navy as the army. On the Baltic Fleet's long circumnavigation, drunkenness led to countless fights, thefts, insubordination, and more than a few drunken officers being lost overboard.[71] In addition to the daily double *charka* rations, vodka celebrated victories and holidays, rewarded hard work, and prepared for battle. At Tsushima, a number of officials were drunk. Even in defeat, the demoralized sailors aboard the surrendered vessels that were fortunate enough to not be sunk defied orders and raided the ships' wine cellars and alcohol stores.[72]

Faced with a roiling revolution at home, and the demoralizing defeats at Mukden and Tsushima, Nicholas II sued for peace with Japan. In the resulting Treaty of Portsmouth mediated by American president Teddy Roosevelt, Russia ceded its lease to Port Arthur as well as the south half of Sakhalin Island to the Japanese.

After the ratification of the peace, the Russian prisoners of war—including Admiral Rozhestvensky himself—were released from their internment at Kobe to proceed on to Vladivostok on the steamer *Voronezh*. But even before they could depart, trouble was brewing. Echoing revolutionary sentiments being expressed throughout Russia in 1905 (to be explored in the next chapter), the twenty-five hundred underfed soldiers and sailors "were agitated, singing revolutionary songs, swearing by the red banner hidden in a dark corner of the hold, and drinking vodka by the mugful." Riots ensued, threatening the fifty-six officers with a full-fledged mutiny that required the intervention of the Japanese police. With order restored, the Russians finally set sail for Vladivostok.

The scene that met them upon returning to Russia was even more surprising: as in many cities throughout Russia, Vladivostok was grasped by the "revolutionary spirit"—which is to say drunken mobs had been rioting for days, burning and looting much of the port city. Indeed, as McCormick explained: "The first cargo to arrive in Vladivostok after the ratification of peace was a shipload of alcoholic liquors. There was no other merchandise on board."[73]

In the end, the Russians were decisively beaten by a better organized, better equipped, and better prepared foe in the Pacific. Yet many observers focused far less on the triumphs of the rising Japanese empire than on the struggles of their waning imperial counterparts in Russia. "The chief enemy of an army is the nation's moral diseases," McCormick concluded from his experiences being embedded with the Russian military. "A great people with a great army, who could not defeat the Japanese in one single battle, must first have been the victim not of the enemy, but of themselves."[74] Indeed, this was the first occasion that a major European power had been defeated—and convincingly—by a non-European one. For many in Europe and America it was unthinkable that the great Russian war machine could be beaten so soundly by such an "inconsequential foe" as Japan.[75] And while the Japanese force was far more formidable than their contemporaries gave them credit for, mass drunkenness was clearly debilitating to Russia's military machine.

In what would become the international conventional wisdom before the Great War, the correspondent of the *Neue freie Presse* was even more blunt: "The Japanese did not conquer, but alcohol triumphed, alcohol, alcohol."[76] The unpleasant, but unavoidable lesson for Russia was that not only had the military become an agent in the alcoholization of society, but Russia's system of autocratic vodka politics was severely hampering the geopolitical ambitions of its leaders.

12

Nicholas the Drunk, Nicholas the Sober

Virtually every soldier in the imperial Russian military—uneducated peasant conscripts and aristocratic officers alike—drank with little regard for the consequences. As one observer noted, "the main occupation of the Hussar regiment is getting drunk." Based at Tsarskoe Selo—the suburban residence of the royal family located south of St. Petersburg—he described the ridiculous behavior of the elite regiment's leadership: "They would frequently drink all day and into the evening, to the point of hallucination," believing themselves no longer humans, but wolves. The officers all "stripped naked and ran out into the streets of Tsarskoe Selo, which are usually deserted at night. They crouched on their hands and knees, raised their drunken heads to the sky and began to howl loudly."

Apparently such lupine behavior by the young commander was so common that it was not at all surprising to the old commissariat waiter, who understood his place in this routine. "He would carry a big tub out onto the porch and fill it full of vodka or champagne. The whole pack of officers would then rush on all fours to the tub and lap up the wine with their tongues as they yelped and bit one another. Occasionally, an intoxicated commander would have to be pulled down—naked—from the roof of his home, where he was howling at the moon or drunkenly serenading the merchant's wife."[1]

Such behavior would be unbecoming for any regiment in a modern army. But this was no ordinary regiment: it was the elite Cossack cavalry of Russian Hussars. And the young leader who regularly drank to the point of believing himself a werewolf was no ordinary commander: he was Nikolai Aleksandrovich Romanov—the future Tsar Nicholas II.

Nicholas is one of the most scrutinized and romanticized figures in Russian history: less for his accomplishments than for his tragic end. His reign was marred by one high-profile debacle after another: his constitutional concessions in the 1905 Revolution prompted by Russia's embarrassing defeat to Japan temporarily forestalled the overthrow of the monarchy, but no concessions could

169

save the tsarist system from the drubbing of World War I and the flames of revolution in 1917; neither could they save the deposed emperor and his family
from being ruthlessly slaughtered at the hands of Bolshevik revolutionaries the
following year.

Generations of historians have recounted the misguided political and military decisions of Russia's "tragically ignorant and weak" ruler who seemed predestined to lead his people to ruin.[2] Yet few—if any—have sought the reasons
for perhaps the most momentous political gaffe of them all: on September 28,
1914, Nicholas II did the unthinkable and declared that Russia would forever
be sober, the first country to adopt prohibition. With one fell swoop Nicholas
undid hundreds of years of vodka politics in Russia by knocking down the central pillar of autocratic statecraft—with disastrous consequences for the empire's
finances—and ultimately transforming one of the mightiest empires in Europe
into a failed state.

So, what prompted this young boozer—who dutifully confided to his diary
how he would get so rip-roaring drunk that he needed to be carried home[3] —
to become such a devout temperance convert that he forced abstinence on his
people and in the process destroyed the most fundamental dynamic of Russian
vodka politics? To answer that question we need to go inside the intimate world
of Russia's last royal family as they struggled with the challenges of a fast-chang-
ing political order.

All In The Family—Sergei And Alexei

Tracing the logic of any policy decision means parsing out the diverse social,
political, and familial influences on the tsar himself. Sometimes this means delv-
ing into the complex dynamics of the royal family. Although they ruled one-
sixth of the earth's territory for over three hundred years, the Romanovs were
still a just a family. Like any family, it was full of love and respect, petty rivalries
and suspicions, honored elders and jealous children, favorite uncles and outcast
cousins. Since by virtue of their birth many relatives held powerful military and
governmental offices, the never-ending family drama often had political consequences. The few competent civilian ministers who rose through the imperial
bureaucracy were often regarded with deep suspicion by the narcissistic royals.

The tsarevich Nikolai Aleksandrovich was the eldest son of Tsar Alexander
III—the gruff reactionary who surrounded himself with inebriate bootlicks and
favor seekers as drinking companions. A bear of a man, Alexander would delight
these friends with feats of great strength. His only weakness, it seemed, was his
debilitating alcoholism. When he first fell ill with kidney disease and the tsarina
forbade him to drink, he took to hiding his cognac in secret flasks sewn into his

boots. Unexpectedly—though not surprisingly—Alexander succumbed to kidney nephritis and died while on vacation in the Crimea on November 1, 1894. He was four months short of his fiftieth birthday.[4]

Expecting to rule another thirty years, Alexander III did little to prepare the young Nicholas II to lead. Consequently, the tsarevich led a sheltered life, had a shallow education, and preferred hunting, high society soirees, and the theater over the boring affairs of state. As a junior officer in his late teens Nicholas picked up the vices of the officer corps. "No one could fail to notice," one contemporary noted, "that Nicholas Alexandrovich's body was being poisoned by alcohol, and his face was becoming yellow, his eyes glistened unhealthily, and bags were beginning to form beneath his eyes, as is customary with alcoholics."[5]

The sudden death of his father forced the uninspiring twenty-six-year-old tsarevich to take the reins of power, however reluctantly. Over the intelligentsia's calls for liberal reforms, Nicholas instead reaffirmed his dedication to absolute monarchy. Politically tone-deaf, Nicholas's unwavering belief that he was empowered by God to lead Russia only accentuated his indifference to the plight of his own people. Appearing resolute in public, the "all-powerful" Nicholas was weak and indecisive in political matters, ceding great power and influence to his grand duke uncles—brothers of his father, Alexander III. Already in places of great authority by virtue of their birth, they were unafraid to bully the timid tsar in order to get their way.[6]

Uncle Sergei Aleksandrovich was one of the four grand dukes. When the junior officer Nicholas was drinking himself into thinking he was a werewolf, Sergei was his major general and "actively encouraged the depraved debauchery" of the regiment.[7] At Sergei's urging, Nicholas married princess Alix of Hesse—younger sister of Sergei's wife—becoming the tsarina Alexandra Fyodorovna. Sergei was the "favorite uncle and brother-in-law of the tsar," and used his leverage over the tsar to great effect.[8]

When Alexander III died in 1894, Grand Duke Sergei was the powerful governor general of Moscow, a position that put him in charge of planning a grand celebration for all Muscovites following the coronation of their new tsar, Nicholas II. This attempt to foster popular goodwill backfired spectacularly. Following the solemn coronation in the Kremlin's Uspensky Cathedral in May 1896, a lavish, free banquet was to be held on the Khodynskoe Pole (Khodynka Fields) northwest of Moscow. Today, the fields have been overrun by drab Soviet-era apartment blocks, Dinamo Stadium, and the Khodynka Megasport Ice Arena, but in 1896 the Khodynka Fields, replete with trenches and gullies, served as training grounds for the imperial Moscow garrison. Nevertheless, it was thought that the fields were the only place that could reasonably accommodate the hundreds of thousands of Muscovites expected to celebrate the newly crowned tsar.

A massive royal pavilion was erected, along with twenty pubs to dispense hundreds of barrels of free beer and souvenirs.

From Moscow and villages throughout central Russia, thousands of peasants—many already drunk—showed up the night before the festivities. By morning, their numbers had swelled to almost *a half million*. Among the boisterous crowds a rumor spread that there was not enough alcohol for everyone, prompting a massive stampede across the uneven ground. Men, women, and children were knocked over and trampled underfoot. Thousands of injured people clogged the city's few hospitals, but they were the lucky ones: 1,389 people were trampled to death at Khodynka Fields, which more closely resembled a European battlefield strewn with casualties than a celebration of the "mystical bond of mutual devotion and love uniting tsar and 'people.'"[9]

The new tsar was understandably distraught. Nicholas planned to cancel the remaining activities, call for national mourning, and retire to a monastery to pray for the victims. Yet the callous grand dukes urged him not to offend Russia's sole European ally, France, by spurning the lavish ball already planned by their ambassador, the Marquis de Montebello. While Nicholas and the Tsarina Alexandra later visited survivors at area hospitals, doling-out a thousand rubles to each, the Grand Duke Sergei—Moscow's Governor General and orchestrator of the event—neither visited the victims, nor the scene of the calamity, and denied any responsibility for the outcome. The superstitious peasantry saw this drunken tragedy an omen of an unhappy reign. For revolutionaries, the sight of the young emperor and his "German woman" celebrating amidst such a disaster underscored the shallowness of the tsar, and the glaring disconnect between the heartless autocracy and the needs of the people. Even at the very beginning of his reign, Russians referred to the tsar as "Bloody Nicholas" and Sergei as the "Duke of Khodynka."[10]

Ironically, if Sergei had one redeeming feature it was his patronage of temperance. In addition to holding figurehead positions with the state-sponsored Guardianship for Public Sobriety, the grand duke and duchess actively promoted temperance through generous donations, public appearances, and even establishing clinics to treat alcoholics. Yet many—even within the royal family—found Sergei obstinate, arrogant, an antisemitic "reactionary chauvinist," and "a complete ignoramus in administrative affairs."[11] In that regard, at least, Sergei was hardly unique among grand dukes who combined incompetence and inebriety to unwittingly undercut the legitimacy of the tsarist government itself.

Consider another of the tsar's uncles, Grand Duke Alexei Aleksandrovich Romanov. With a lifelong interest in maritime affairs, Alexei was made commander-in-chief of the Russian navy even though he preferred the life of a drunken playboy. "Fast women and slow ships" aptly summarized his military career.[12]

Of all the grand dukes, Alexei Aleksandrovich was certainly the best known to Americans of the day, thanks in large part to his raucous visit to the United States in the 1870s. The highest ranking Russian royal to ever visit the United States, Alexei was wined and dined by the cream of East Coast society, including President Ulysses S. Grant. The grand duke declared his desire to participate in an authentic "Wild West" buffalo hunt. His American host—former Civil War general Philip Sheridan, famous for carrying out a scorched-earth policy similar to that of William Tecumseh Sherman's march to the sea—graciously obliged, going so far as to create "Camp Alexis," a veritable Potemkin village on the Nebraska plain. The "authentic" frontier conditions at the sumptuous camp included a brass band, the finest foods and wines, and crate upon crate of champagne. The once-fearsome chief Spotted Tail and his Lakota tribesmen were paid to act as stereotypical Indian savages, and Alexei was taught how to hunt on the open prairie by none other than Gen. George Armstrong Custer and "Buffalo Bill" Cody. Their "genuine" Wild West hunts were interrupted promptly at lunchtime by caterers with wagonloads of sandwiches and champagne.

American newsmen followed Custer and Cody as they taught their royal guest to hunt buffalo on his twenty-second birthday. (Apparently nursing a hangover from the previous day, General Sheridan couldn't keep pace with the others.) Upon bagging his first buffalo, the grand duke cut off its tail and whirled it around his head with joy. "Within moments, champagne corks were popping again," described one journalist in tow. "The fun continued with displays of Indian dancing, feasting and drinking copious amounts of liquor," which strengthened the camaraderie between the Americans and their guest but also threatened to tear them apart: completely wasted, Alexei and Custer openly competed for the affections of Spotted Tail's daughter—much to the anger of the proud Lakota chief.[13]

After a week of drunken hunting, the grand duke continued westward to Denver, the camp was dismantled, and the Sioux went home. But Alexei had so much fun that he demanded another hunt and even shot at buffalo from the window of his train car. Custer spared no time in telegraphing Fort Wallace for horses, wagons, food, provisions, and most importantly, "every kind of liquor and champagne" they could find, as the Russian delegation was running low on booze. At their camp near Kit Carson, Colorado, even the servants, soldiers, and cooks joined the hunters in their revelry. In a scene reminiscent of Russian defeats in Crimea and Manchuria, reporters noted that "Champagne bottles, liquor bottles, and every other kind of bottle littered the ground. That battlefield showed more 'dead ones' than the hunting-ground did buffaloes."[14]

Happier to raid a brothel than an armada, Alexei somehow became commander of the entire Russian navy. Like the other grand duke, he wasn't afraid to use his leverage over his tsar-nephew, who was scared that even mentioning the need for military reforms would upset his favorite uncle.[15] Together with the tsar, Alexei welcomed the war with Japan as a cakewalk in which he'd surely bask in his navy's glorious victory. It was Alexei who authorized the quixotic mission of the Baltic Sea Fleet that ended at the bottom of the Tsushima Straits. Drunk and indisposed at key moments in the Japanese War, Alexei was a commander in no sense of the word—forever blaming anyone but himself for the drunken and inept performance of his sailors.[16] Following the destruction of his entire fleet at Tsushima, Alexei resigned in disgrace in June 1905 and spent his remaining years living the playboy lifestyle in Paris.

The unresponsiveness of the monarchy and the demoralizing defeat to the Japanese prompted the workers' strikes, peasant riots, and military mutinies that led to the full-blown Revolution of 1905. Ironically, it was Nicholas' temperance-minded uncle, the Grand Duke Sergei, who caught the full fury of the uprising. As the powerful governor general of Moscow, Sergei felt himself to be a high-profile target for terrorist revolutionaries who had already claimed scores of high-ranking military and government officials. He resigned the governorship and fled to the security of the Kremlin under the cover of night. On the afternoon of February 17, 1905, his worst fears were realized when Sergei's carriage entered the Kremlin and passed by the Chudov Monastery (yes, the same "Miraculous" Monastery where vodka was alleged to have been born), when a member of the so-called Combat Detachment of the Socialist Revolutionary Party lobbed a nitroglycerin bomb into his lap, blowing the grand duke to bits. His wife, the grand duchess, was one of the first arrivals to the horrific scene of blood-soaked snow littered with shrapnel, flesh, and "a ghastly crimson mess where the torso had been." Still adorned with his royal rings, the grand duke's fingers were later found on the roof of a nearby building.[17]

The Hangover Of 1905

The assassination of Grand Duke Sergei was only part of the roiling Revolution of 1905 that threatened to overthrow the entire autocratic order. The tsar and tsarina dared not even leave their residence at Tsarskoe Selo to attend the funeral, so real was the threat that they too would be cut down. All Russia was in disorder following the events of "Bloody Sunday," January 22, 1905—when the Imperial Guard opened fire on thousands of peaceful protesters outside the Winter Palace as they delivered a petition for better pay, better working conditions, and an end to the disastrous war with Japan.

Nicholas could not understand why his meager concessions and unfulfilled promises were not enough to quiet the strikes, rebellions, insubordination, and assassinations. In May, the Baltic Fleet was mauled by the Japanese at Tsushima.

Just as Grand Duke Alexei resigned his naval command in disgrace in June, insurrections rocked the naval bases of Sevastopol, Kronstadt, and Vladivostok before culminating in the famous mutiny aboard the battleship *Potemkin* in Odessa harbor. The slain Grand Duke Sergei's replacement as governor general of Moscow was likewise assassinated by the combat detachment. Things were getting out of hand, and fast.

The last line of defense for the royal family was the St. Petersburg military district and its commander, the Grand Duke (yes, *another* grand duke) Nikolai Nikolaevich Romanov (the younger), first cousin of the tsar. Growing up, cousin Nikolai was given the affectionate diminutive "Nikolasha" to differentiate him from little "Niki"—the future tsar. "Microcephalitic in figure, a hunter by inclination, a fool and incorrigible alcoholic," Nikolasha was colonel of the Hussar regiment where werewolf Niki also learned to drink. Older than the tsar by twelve years, like the other grand dukes the conservative, military-schooled Nikolasha wielded tremendous influence over the young tsar as a trusted confidant and advisor, and their relationship bred jealous intrigues among the royal family. Rightly or wrongly, Grand Duke Nikolai Nikolaevich was blamed for much of the misfortune under the reign of the last tsar.[18]

With riotous (and frequently drunken) mobs threatening outright revolution, Nicholas II faced a stark choice: accede to popular demands for a legislature and constitution or violently crack down on his own people. With the military on the verge of complete mutiny, Nicholas implored Grand Duke Nikolasha—the only figure who commanded the soldiers' respect—to assume the role of military dictator. Refusing, Nikolasha drew his service revolver to his temple and threatened to shoot himself on the spot if the tsar did not acquiesce to a constitutional monarchy to end the unrest. This dramatic display was instrumental to adopting the historic October Manifesto, which granted Russia a weak representative parliament (the Duma) based on universal suffrage and a bill of rights protecting basic civil liberties. The concessions staved off the demise of tsarism…at least for the time being.[19]

Inching back from the brink of disaster, educated segments of Russian society and government took stock of what had just happened. When it came to laying blame, many faulted alcohol: military experts focused on the drunken mobilization, the ineptitude and intoxication of the armed forces, and the vodka-fueled pogroms that targeted state liquor stores at the outset of the Revolution of 1905. Financiers looked at the sporadic liquor boycotts of 1905–6, where socialist-minded workers swore off vodka and picketed taverns to strike at the government's purse. Across the board tsarist officials agreed that alcohol was enemy number one.[20] Grand Duke Nikolasha obsessively set about remedying these deficiencies—abolishing the traditional vodka ration (*charka*), forbidding alcohol sales in military stores, and limiting the hours of restaurants near military encampments. Should the need arise, the military was prepared to take even more drastic actions to prevent the drunken disorder of the past.[21]

It was not just the Russians who had learned the lesson. In what I have elsewhere described as "the cult of military sobriety," the high command of virtually every army on earth viewed alcohol as public enemy number one. Even the tsar's cousin—Kaiser Wilhelm II of Germany—boldly proclaimed in 1910 that victory in the next European war would go to the army that was most sober.[22]

Beyond the military, the civil rights enshrined in the October Manifesto unleashed the pent-up temperance activism that had been building since the boycotts of the 1850s. "Words were straining to be free but were held back in vices," wrote Dr. Aleksandr Korovin in October 1905. "We spoke earlier of drunkenness but not in connection with the circumstances that generated it." No longer muzzled by censorship, writers who once masked their criticism of the government with allusions to alcohol now freely joined their foreign counterparts in laying blame for the poverty, ignorance, and drunkenness of the Russian people squarely on their government.[23]

Shortly before his untimely death in 1894, Tsar Alexander III charged his young Minister of Finance Sergei Witte with reforming the system of excise taxes that had been levied on vodka since the abolition of the tax farm in the 1860s. Gradually replacing the excise tax system with a crown monopoly on the retail sale of vodka, Witte declared that his system "must be directed first of all toward increasing popular sobriety, and only then can it concern itself with the treasury."[24]

While the gentry reclaimed their right to distill alcohol, it could only be sold to the state, which controlled the entire retail market—ostensibly in the interest of temperance—while simultaneously making a hefty profit. In a now-familiar pattern, the allure of easy money was too great, and the cause of temperance was sacrificed to the interests of the treasury. The tsar's "drunken budget" became a favorite target of critics and revolutionaries, including Vladimir Lenin. In 1913, even Sergei Witte—the architect of the vodka monopoly—condemned his own creation, claiming it had been corrupted by his replacement as minister of finance, Vladimir Kokovtsov.[25]

Also under fire after 1905 was the handmaiden of the imperial vodka monopoly—the Guardianship of Public Sobriety (*Popechitel'stvo o narodnoi trezvosti*). This sole nationwide temperance organization was an appendage of the ministry of finance and as such never promoted abstinence from vodka, only "moderation."[26] For true advocates of temperance like Tolstoy, the Guardianship was an abomination: its activities were dictated from on high, making it unable to tap into whatever zeal for temperance existed at the local level. Ever mistrustful of grass-roots activism, the Guardianship and its leaders refused to cooperate with the smattering of small, independent, genuine temperance societies emerging from elite intelligentsia circles concerned with peasant health and welfare, the concerned medical community, or even the church.[27] When the powerful Witte went to meet with Tolstoy, who made temperance the cornerstone of his civic religion (see chapter 10), Tolstoy angrily refused to even meet him. "Temperance societies established by a government that is not ashamed that it itself sells the poison ruining the people through its own officials seem to me to be either hypocritical, silly, or misguided—or perhaps all three—something with which I can no way sympathize," Tolstoy wrote. "In my opinion, if the government really was making every effort for the good of the people, then the first step should be the complete prohibition of the poison which destroys both the physical and spiritual well-being of millions of people."[28] Tolstoy was hardly alone: both liberal and conservative parliamentarians, such as representative Mikhail Chelyshev of Samara, openly derided the Guardianship and the "drunken budget" on the floor of the new Duma itself.[29]

The politicization of the alcohol question was on full display at the First All-Russian Congress on the Struggle against Drunkenness held in St. Petersburg during the winter of 1909–10. Officially convened by President of the Council of Ministers Pyotr Stolypin, thousands of delegates representing all manner of interests were invited to discuss the alcohol problem. Representatives of the church, physicians' groups, women's groups, trade unions, village *zemstva* and city *dumas* confronted officials from the ministry of finance, the Guardianship of Public Sobriety, ministers, and members of the state Duma. Alongside other workers' representatives, Lenin sent a Bolshevik delegation to the congress. As you might expect, conflict was inevitable. The scene devolved into angry confrontations between supporters of the system and their radical opponents. The clergy angrily stormed out, rabble-rousing workers' delegates were arrested, and scholars who linked alcoholism to poverty were barred by the police from presenting their research. The Congress's final report on the liquor monopoly was unequivocal: "Down with the whole system."[30] Reported widely, the debates drew considerable interest throughout the empire—especially the workers' condemnations of the Guardianship and vodka monopoly for enriching the state and the landlords at the expense of the people. Before 1905, Russia's autocratic vodka politics could only be alluded to; after 1905 the system was laid bare for all to see.

Many in the tsar's inner circle were steadily pushing the tsar toward temperance. Nicholas held fond memories of his uncle Sergei, who actively patronized temperance before his untimely detonation. His widow was still active in the cause, as were Aleksandr, Prince of Oldenburg, Prince Meshchersky, and the Grand Duke Konstantin, all of whom pleaded with the tsar to wean the treasury from its unhealthy reliance on vodka revenues while weaning his subjects from their unhealthy reliance on alcohol.

No consideration of palace intrigues under the last tsar would be complete without the "Mad Monk," Grigory Rasputin. The story of how this dubious Siberian mystic won influence with the royal family for his "miraculous" ability to heal the hemophilia of the tsarevich Alexei is well known. Equally well known are Rasputin's infamous debauches: his tremendous clout won him many female admirers within the aristocracy, who willingly partook in the drunken orgies of this "holy man" who preached grace through sin.[31] So it is quite ironic that the strongest admonishments to temperance and prohibition came from Russia's most infamous drunken and lustful debaucher. "It is unbefitting for a Tsar to deal in vodka and make drunkards out of honest people," Rasputin bluntly said. "The time has come to lock up the Tsar's saloons."[32]

It seems that, over time, such entreaties—both public and private—persuaded Tsar Nicholas II that the vodka monopoly was the root of Russia's economic, social, and political problems. After the upheavals of 1905, the tsar's excessive drinking moderated greatly. To his ministers, the normally hands-off tsar expressed dissatisfaction over efforts to combat drunkenness and demanded research on the liquor question. By the 1910s, Nicholas was a full convert: on an extensive tour of his domain in 1913, he claimed to be moved by "the painful pictures of public distress, the desolation of homes, the dissipation of economies, the inevitable consequences of drunkenness."[33]

In January 1914 Nicholas fired the man synonymous with the loathsome monopoly—Finance Minister Vladimir Kokovtsov—for ruthlessly squeezing every last ruble from the vodka trade. In his stead Nicholas appointed Pyotr Lvovich Bark, with the charge of no longer making "the treasury dependent on the ruination of the spiritual and economic forces of the majority of My faithful subjects." Bark's mission to reform the very foundations of Russia's autocratic vodka politics would be preempted by the outbreak of World War I later that year, which led to the demise of the entire tsarist system itself.[34]

Great War And The Royal Family

On June 28, 1914, the presumptive heir to the Austrian throne, Archduke Franz Ferdinand, was assassinated in Sarajevo by Gavrilo Princip—a nineteen-year-old nationalist dedicated to the liberation of the south Slavic (Yugoslav) peoples from Austrian rule. The entanglement of military alliances in the Balkans quickly drew all of the major European powers into a conflagration that would claim sixteen million lives, devastate an entire continent, and see the Romanov dynasty sacrificed to the flames of revolution.

Exactly one month after the assassination Austria declared war on Russia's ally, Serbia. When Russia mobilized for war, Austria and Germany declared war on Russia, too. While Britain, France, and later the United States joined with Russia in fighting the so-called Central Powers on the Western Front, Russia stood alone in confronting the Germans and Austro-Hungarians in the east.

Suddenly facing the challenges of war, Nicholas II turned (as usual) to the royal family—quickly appointing his cousin Nikolasha as supreme commander of the entire Russian military despite his never having commanded armies in the field. With Kaiser Wilhelm's temperance proclamation ringing in his ears and the drunken debacle with Japan on his mind, Nikolasha requested an emergency prohibition on the sale of alcohol in areas actively being mobilized for war. His petition was granted by the temperance-minded tsar, marking Russia's first steps down the disastrous road toward prohibition and revolution.[35]

Nicholas romanticized the discipline and honor of the military. For him, "orderliness was a cardinal virtue." So it makes sense that arguments about prohibition promoting discipline and virtue in the ranks resonated with the tsar.[36] Events of the next few weeks seemingly confirmed the wisdom of the decision. The high command received nothing but glowing news about the mobilization measures. Field reports assured the leadership that prohibition facilitated the deployment of troops to the front in half the time expected, well before their German and Austrian enemies were prepared to meet them. Accolades from domestic and foreign temperance advocates flooded the tsar, lauding his benevolence in adopting prohibition. Witnessing the benefits to their once-alcoholic

Tsar Nicholas II disembarks His Automobile on a Visit to the Front, circa 1914–15. Commander of the Armed Forces, Grand Duke Nikolai Nikolaevich Romanov ("Nikolasha," right) stands in the car with Count Dobrinsky. Library of Congress Prints and Photographs Division/ Bain News Service.

fathers, sons, and husbands, women across Russia urged his highness to make prohibition permanent.[37]

"With the closing of the vodka-shops Russia has become sober," wrote one British observer. "True, it is a sobriety enforced, and drunkenness is too inherent a trait of the Russian for this temporary abstinence to be taken as anything but a break in the usual pastime, yet even if it is regarded as nothing better, it is certainly a sign of miraculous times."[38]

Still, the prohibition was both temporary and partial: it did not apply to the aristocracy's well-to-do restaurants, and it applied only in militarized districts. Plus, so long as vodka still provided between one-quarter to one-third of the empire's budget (figure 9.1), swearing off liquor revenues would be financial suicide. What's more, a complete prohibition would infuriate both powerful nobles and Romanov family members who, like Grand Duke Nikolasha, owed much of their wealth to their private distilleries.[39]

Bolstered by the apparent good news from all sides, in August 1914 the tsar decreed that the partial, emergency prohibition be extended for the duration of the war, again prompting adulation from bootlicks throughout the government. Foremost among them was Finance Minister Bark, who was charged with the utterly impossible task of weaning the empire from its primary source of revenue at its time of greatest crisis. Telling the tsar exactly what he wanted to hear, Bark informed Nicholas that "the difficulties of the Treasury are only temporary and that a judicious financial policy will enable us to overcome them."[40] Quickly convening a high-level government commission that included Bark, the tsar's trusted former Prime Minister Sergei Witte, economists, academics, and Duma representatives, Bark presented his sovereign with a most audacious plan.

By early September, the commission devised an alternative budget without vodka. Assuming that prohibition would miraculously unleash the long pent-up industriousness of the entire country, it forecast tremendous economic growth, even as millions of able-bodied men abandoned their jobs for the front lines. With such growth, they assumed that the hole in the budget left by the loss of vodka revenues could easily be patched with a slapdash mix of foreign loans, war bonds, and taxes on income, textiles, transport and tobacco. "Well, we have stopped the gap without difficulty or effort," Bark later reassured foreign journalists. Even with the cost of supporting the largest army ever put in the field, Bark explained how easily "the problem was solved. I increased some few taxes during the remaining months of last year [1914], and I found that the solvency of the peasants had been raised very considerably by the law prohibiting the consumption of alcohol."[41] Bark's arrogance was matched only by his obliviousness. It was a fantastic proposal—in that it was pure fantasy.

Still—satisfied that the empire's finances were in order, Nicholas made the most disastrous decision in the history of Russian vodka politics: on September

28, 1914, the tsar announced that Russia would forever go dry by decree. But strangely, instead of a traditional imperial proclamation, prohibition was declared in the form of a widely reprinted telegram from Tsar Nicholas II to his uncle, the temperance advocate Grand Duke Konstantin Konstantinovich Romanov, which simply read:

> Petrograd. To the Grand Duke Constantine Constantinovich. I thank the Russian Christian Labor Temperance Organization. I have already decided to abolish forever the government sale of vodka in Russia.
>
> NICHOLAS[42]

Not only would there be no state trade in vodka; there would be no private commercial trade in vodka either. Russia's all-powerful temperance convert assumed that his sovereign command was all that it would take to banish all vodka from Russia forever.

Swearing off vodka—and the lucrative vodka revenues—flew in the face of centuries of autocratic tradition. Now, at the hour of Russia's greatest military crisis, the tsar effectively sawed the legs off his own empire. But to get the complete picture of this monumental decision it is necessary to decipher the intentions behind the tsar's telegram.

Dearest Uncle Kostya

"It can be said without exaggeration," wrote Russian historian Pyotr Zaionchkovsky, "that the members of the imperial family were for the most part rather stupid individuals who divided their lives between the barracks and the restaurant," where the elite went to get drunk. This book, even to this point, seems to confirm as much. Yet the one outlier Zaionchkovsky found was the truly "exceptional" Grand Duke Konstantin Konstantinovich Romanov, to whom the tsar's fateful prohibition telegram was addressed.[43]

Lamentably, for all his talents, Konstantin took little interest in politics. Perhaps on account of this disinterest (which he and Nicholas II had long shared), little Niki forged an especially close bond with his "dearest uncle Kostya"—his favorite of all his uncles.[44] (Yes, for anyone keeping track, that makes him the third different "favorite uncle" of the tsar mentioned in this chapter.)

Something of a bohemian, Konstantin Konstantinovich spurned the military training expected of male Romanovs in favor of the arts. A gifted pianist, he was a close friend of Pyotr Ilyich Tchaikovsky. He wrote poetry of exceptional quality and even performed as a stage actor, portraying the role of Joseph of Arimathea in the play *King of Judea*, which he himself wrote. He translated the works of Shakespeare into Russian for a number of literary societies he founded and was appointed president of the Russian Academy of Sciences. Notably, he sponsored the All-Russian Labor Union of Christian Teetotalers (Vserossiiskii trudovoi soyuz khristian trezvennikov or VTSKhT), which made mild, though frequent, temperance admonishments to Nicholas II and other prominent leaders.[45] Practicing what he preached, the town of Pavlovsk that housed his royal palace (a quick five miles south of the tsar's palace at Tsarskoe Selo) was an island of prohibition in a vast, drunken Russian sea.[46]

Konstantin's candid diaries contrast a high-profile royal lifestyle with a private turmoil over his bisexuality.[47] By night, Konstantin frequented St. Petersburg's male brothels, but by day he was a loving husband and dedicated father to his eight children. The apple of his eye was unquestionably his fourth son, Prince Oleg. Nurturing his natural curiosity and intellectual gifts, Konstantin enrolled Oleg in the Alexander Lyceum—a prestigious school of high culture—instead of the conventional royal military academies. Yet with the outbreak of war, the twenty-two-year-old Oleg voluntarily enlisted, ultimately commanding an entire cavalry platoon. Seeing active duty on the front west of Vilnius in the early days of the war, Oleg valiantly pursued a battalion of German cavalry when he was wounded by the shot of the retreating German horsemen. Entering through his right hip and lodging in his gut (kishka), the bullet left a wound that quickly became infected. Unfortunately, the combined efforts of military doctors could do nothing to save the doomed prince. Even on his deathbed Oleg proclaimed that his passing would benefit the war effort—conveying to the troops that the Imperial House was not afraid to shed its own blood.[48] On September 27, 1914, succumbing to his injuries, Prince Oleg Konstantinovich became the first—and ultimately the only—Romanov to die in battle during World War I.

The news took a devastating toll on the doting father, Grand Duke Konstantin, who was already in ill health. The outbreak of war caught Konstantin and the grand duchess at a health spa in Germany, where their entire entourage was arrested as political prisoners. Only entreaties by the Russian court to their cousins in the German royal family secured their release. But with all borders between east and west closed amid total war, Konstantin, his wife, and their entire retinue were forced to cross the front lines into Russia on foot, which further weakened the ailing grand duke.

Upon hearing that his son had been wounded, on September 28, Kostya hastily wrote to inform his nephew the tsar of the tragedy before rushing from Pavlovsk to be by his son's bedside. It was all for naught. By the time they reached Vilnius, death had already claimed the young prince.[49]

The now-famous prohibition telegram from Tsar Nicholas II to Grand Duke Konstantin Konstantinovich was sent as a response on that very day— September 28, 1914—and was confirmed by the tsar's Council of Ministers on the following day. While the tsar never penned a memoir shedding light

GRAND DUKE KONSTANTIN KONSTANTINOVICH ROMANOV (1858–1915)

on these events, it would seem that the momentous decision to wean Russia from vodka was in part a sympathetic gesture from a doting nephew to his much-loved prohibitionist uncle in his time of greatest sorrow. The death of Prince Oleg allowed the tsar to attach even greater personal significance in executing a vital decision of public policy—one that would have devastating consequences.

Coda

The State Archives of the Russian Federation—a drab, concrete monolith in downtown Moscow chiseled with figures of Soviet heroism—contains many holdings related to the last years of the royal family. Yet the files of Tsar "Niki" and his dearest uncle Kostya are mute on the prohibition telegram. It was only on the following day, September 29, that the tsar wrote in his diary how moved he had been by the sad news of Oleg's passing. Four days later Niki was at his uncle's side at the state funeral for the young prince.[50] It would be the first of many devastating tragedies for the royal family.

Grieving to the end for the loss of his beloved son, Konstantin Konstantinovich died less than a year later. His other sons—Ivan, Igor, and Konstantin (the

PRINCE OLEG KONSTANTINOVICH ROMANOV (1892–1914)

younger)—were arrested shortly following the Bolshevik Revolution in 1917 and exiled to Alapaevsk—a small Ural town north of Ekaterinburg. On the night of July 17–18, 1918, Bolshevik forces marched the grand duke's family into the woods, where they were beaten, shot, and their bodies tossed into a mineshaft—a mere one hundred miles away from the Ipatiev House in Ekaterinburg where, just the night before, Tsar Nicholas II, the tsarina, their daughters, and the ruling House of Romanov had met a similarly grisly fate.[51]

13

Did Prohibition Cause the Russian Revolution?

Pyotr Pavlovich Bukhov had a problem.

To be sure, in 1916, with Russia embroiled in a disastrous military fiasco that was decimating the conscripts on the front line, creating bread shortages and social unrest on the home front and runaway inflation threatening national economic collapse, the troubles of this provincial gentleman from Voronezh may have seemed insignificant by comparison: he had a tax bill from the imperial ministry of finance that he could not pay. As a member of the privileged Russian gentry, Bukhov was in the business of providing alcoholic beverages—mostly fruit and berry wines—to the imperial alcohol monopoly, but since Tsar Nicholas II made Russia dry by decree at the outset of the Great War, Bukhov had a warehouse full of alcohol that he could not legally sell and an enormous burden of overdue taxes that he could no longer pay—and he was not alone.[1]

Some of Bukhov's colleagues probably found his circumstances enviable—or at least coveted his location far from the thunder of war that was daily growing louder and closer. Not only were the gentry alcohol producers in the empire's western borderlands prohibited from selling their liquor, but they were also faced with an imperial decree that all alcohol warehouses located in militarized districts near the battlefields be summarily destroyed, lest they entice the weak-willed peasant-soldiers into drunken insubordination. Every day the front was inching uncomfortably closer. While the travails of well-to-do aristocratic distillers may seem inconsequential against the backdrop of global war and revolutionary upheavals in Russia, their activities highlight the variety of ways that vodka politics—and the decision to enact a general prohibition—actually helped destroy the old imperial order.

Bark's Dilemma

Sir Pyotr Bark is a largely forgotten figure in the sunset of imperial Russia. His extensive, unpublished memoirs—written in English as an émigré fleeing bol-shevism—gather dust in the archives in Leeds. Yet it is hard to understand this critical moment in world history without him. The onset of total war in 1914 required tremendous dexterity and sleight of hand from this newly appointed finance minister to pay the tremendous costs of putting the world's largest army in the field. Bark was hamstrung in this titanic endeavor by the decision of the tsar to institute prohibition—with a single stroke wiping out between one-quarter and one-third of all government revenues, blowing a massive hole in the treasury that was impossible to fill, even without the added burden of total war. Expected to reassure his tsar, foreign creditors, and the Russian people, Bark became the ultimate spinmeister: everywhere promoting an image of a stable, functioning, and even prospering Russia while the entire economy and the state crumbled around him. Bark's public proclamations, interviews, and reports based on them led many to believe that prohibition was having an overwhelm-ingly positive impact on Russia.[2] But it was all a lie.

Having learned the painful lessons of the drunken debacle of the Russo-Japanese War, at the outset of the Great War in 1914, the newly minted supreme commander, Grand Duke "Nikolasha" (Nikolai Nikolaevich Romanov), imme-diately ordered the lockdown of all liquor stores in districts being actively mobi-lized for war. Military experts believed it necessary to maintain tranquility, which allowed Russia to mobilize nearly four million men in *half* the usual timespan—a resounding success.[3]

Sir Alfred Knox, the British military attaché in the patriotically rechristened capital of Petrograd, dutifully reported the orderliness of the mobilization: "The spirit of the people appeared excellent. All the wine shops were closed and there was no drunkenness—a striking contrast to the scenes witnessed in 1904. Wives and mothers with children accompanied the reservists from point to point, but the women cried silently and there was no hysterics."[4] In his memoirs, Bark confirmed it: "With a few trifling exceptions, the mobilization had been carried out everywhere with great precision and order and His Majesty attributed this happy state of affairs largely to the fact that the young men who were joining their regiments had been unable to obtain drink."[5]

In late 1915, War Minister Vladimir Sukhomlinov's newly appointed suc-cessor Alexei Polivanov corroborated prohibition's benefits to American tem-perance advocate William E. "Pussyfoot" Johnson: "Thanks to temperance, the results of the war are scarcely noticeable at all." He recounted a dramatic fall in crime and arson, a prompt and orderly mobilization, and an upsurge in labor productivity, religious and patriotic sentiment—all part of prohibition's moral and economic rejuvenation of the countryside. Reflecting their better treatment at home, Polivanov claimed "the women are happy and pray God that the sale of alcohol may never again be allowed. In their joy, they are almost ready to bless the war." Ever confident of Russia's dry and shining future, Polivanov concluded: "if there will be no more liquor, Russia will be the richest country in the world."[6]

At best, Russian officials just saw what they wanted to see; at worst, it was part of a grand deception. The archives of the imperial ministry of internal affairs and the main administration of the general staff is filled with hundreds of reports on mobilization riots from virtually every *guberniia* across Russia. That the tsar locked down all liquor stores apparently meant little to the marauding hordes of conscripts who stormed the padlocked stores, saloons, and warehouses in search of vodka. Indeed, the first order for military commanders in mobilizing districts was to place armed guards outside of alcohol stores and warehouses—and even that was often not enough.[7]

In the city of Ekaterinoslav rioters smashed the windows of those first-class hotels that were still permitted to sell alcohol. In the Igumensky district drunken mobs looted liquor stores before setting upon the local distillery.[8] In Barnaul the mobs seized control of the city, torching houses, stores, and a liquor warehouse, forcing the residents to flee for their lives. More than one hundred died in the battle between the conscripts and local police.[9] According to reports of the internal affairs ministry, in the last weeks of July 1914 alone, drunken mobilization riots left 51 state officials wounded and 9 dead, while 136 rioters were injured and 216 killed.[10] The tsar's dry decree was hardly as effective as it was made out to be. In some cases the drunken disorder was even worse than a decade before: the police captain of the second-largest city in the region of Bashkiria urgently telegrammed his superiors in St. Petersburg:

> In Sterlitamak, over 10,000 reservists began a disturbance that is threatening devastation of the entire city. The havoc began at the liquor warehouse that was ransacked. The assistant superintendent has been wounded when the police guards opened fire. The stores and shops are all closed on account of the devastation of the property of the residents....We never had this sort of disturbance during the war with Japan.[11]

Why were the tsar and his military leaders so blissfully unaware of this epidemic of drunken riots? Perhaps they simply chose not to acknowledge the severity of the problem. More likely, the leadership simply never found out.

"In Russia, ministers have no right to say what they really think," Russia's foreign minister candidly acknowledged to an audience of foreign dignitaries at the outbreak of the war. Since all of Russian officialdom owed their offices, entitlements, and salaries to the benevolence of the tsar, there was little incentive to deliver bad news or otherwise rock the boat.[12]

Perhaps this explains why, despite reams of evidence to the contrary in the archives of each respective ministry, Tsar Nicholas received nothing but glowing reports of prohibition's benefits from the minister of war, Gen. Vladimir Sukhomlinov, Assistant Interior Minister Vasily Gurko, and Finance Minister Bark, among others.[13] Widespread reports claimed that the tsar's prohibition was "universally approved by all his official representatives and Russia's best people."[14] Such glowing statements accompanied a mass of letters and petitions to the tsar from his grateful subjects imploring that he make the temporary measures into a permanent prohibition decree.[15]

Despite his growing temperance inclinations, Nicholas could not simply order an eternal prohibition, since almost one-third of the revenues of the entire Russian government came from the vodka monopoly. So in August 1914 Nicholas commissioned his most trusted and experienced ministers to study the feasibility of prohibition by identifying replacements for the lost vodka revenues—a truly herculean task given the wartime circumstances. The commission was chaired by State Comptroller Pyotr Kharitonov and included Finance Minister Bark, trusted former Prime Minister Sergei Witte, and the ministers of agriculture, transportation, and commerce as well as prominent professors and experts on state finance, who together quickly drafted a plan to patch the gaping hole in the budget with a hodgepodge mix of taxes on income, transport, tobacco, textiles, and government bonds and foreign loans.[16]

Read in hindsight, the report is equal parts comedy, tragedy, and horror. The top civilian and royal leaders of the Romanov empire gambled on the blind faith that prohibition would somehow unleash the long-dormant economic capacity of Russian society, just as millions of its most productive members put down their scythes and marched off to the front. Finance Minister Bark wagered the stability of the empire itself on a miracle—one that never came. In late August 1914, Bark personally delivered to an approving tsar the report confirming exactly what Nicholas wanted to hear: vodka's budgetary contributions were apparently quite minor, and their loss through a permanent prohibition could be easily overcome with a few painless reforms.[17]

With the revenue matter supposedly resolved by his most trusted ministers and the mobilization benefits of prohibition being hailed throughout the empire and by temperance advocates abroad, there was little stopping the tsar from enacting his most benevolent decree—forever banishing the liquor evil that had long tormented his dearest subjects. The tragic death of Prince Oleg provided the opportunity to attach greater symbolic meaning to prohibition, but it was still a decision based on bad information and even worse calculations.[18]

From Prohibition To Revolution

Ultimately the strains of total war were too great for the tsarist regime: the mobilization of fifteen million men disrupted industrial and agricultural production just when both were needed more than ever. Russia's fragile railway infrastructure collapsed from the strain of war, hampering the delivery of food and fuel to beleaguered cities like Moscow and Petrograd. A string of demoralizing military defeats at the front unleashed a wave of deserters, who only added to the widespread hostility with the incompetent tsar and his regime. Nicholas's actions did not help: his inept handling of the war effort at the front and the rapid turnover of key ministerial positions made governance uncertain, unstable, and ineffective.

Frustrations boiled over in February 1917, as striking factory workers and hungry citizens staged mass demonstrations in the capital, Petrograd. The military garrison called on to suppress the rioters refused to fire on their own people and defected to the demonstrators. Boldly defying the tsar, liberal Duma deputies held session to hastily form a so-called Provisional Government. Drawing on the experiences of the 1905 Revolution, workers in the capital created a separate representative body—the Petrograd *Soviet*, or Council—representing the city's disgruntled workers and soldiers. The train on which Nicholas was returning from the front to reclaim his lost capital was blockaded by striking railroad workers and mutinous soldiers. Informed that he no longer had the support of his military commanders, the tsar sheepishly abdicated his throne (ironically, from the train's saloon car), ending three centuries of imperial Romanov rule.[19]

Beyond simply mapping the empire's road to ruin, historians and social scientists have long tried to explain what causes social revolutions in general and the Bolshevik Revolution in particular.[20] Explanations for the demise of the imperial Russian regime usually come from one of two camps—one focusing on proximate causes associated with the strains of Great War, the other faulting long-term structural weaknesses and contradictions of Russia's autocratic statecraft that made systemic collapse virtually unavoidable.[21]

Remarkably, vodka politics contributes to arguments on both sides. Much of this book has highlighted the fundamental dilemma of utilizing vodka as a tool of autocratic statecraft, yet no historical study has explicitly considered the role of vodka politics in felling the once mighty Romanov empire. This consistent omission is even more baffling when one realizes how thoroughly vodka politics permeated even the most often cited proximate causes for the collapse of the empire: widespread and systemic discontent with the tsarist system, the collapse of the economy amid wartime hyperinflation, and the breakdown of Russia's infrastructure under the burdens of total war.

Distillation And Its Discontents

Accurately measuring a leader's popularity is difficult even in modern dictatorships and becomes ever tougher looking back in time. Without modern opinion polls, figuring out whether prohibition enamored or alienated Russia's citizenry is a daunting task. Ever since his coronation disaster on the Khodynka Fields, Nicholas II was long viewed as indifferent to the plight of his people; one would assume that commanding his subjects to go cold turkey would not be popular. "There is no evidence to suggest that prohibition, tsarist or early Soviet, received popular support from working-class Russians, for whom alcohol remained central to their social, cultural, and economic lives," suggested historian Kate Transchel: "the strength of custom and tradition ensured that the *narod* would find ways to evade prohibition."[22]

While ministers touted open letters and women's petitions to continue prohibition, citing fantastic improvements in the health and disposition of their chronically drunken husbands, fathers, and sons,[23] the actual record is...hazy. Contemporaries noted that "the population could not stand forced abstinence," which not only promoted discontent with the imperial leadership but also led to the drinking of dangerous homebrews and liquor surrogates, such as eau-de-cologne, shoe polish, industrial lacquers and varnishes. Within months of prohibition, "dry" Russia was inundated by a nationwide wave of alcohol poisonings.[24]

While the tsar's wartime patriotic support was eroding thanks to debilitating and humiliating losses on the front, prohibition did not help bolster his legitimacy. Foreign observers lamented that the tsar's prohibition policy "did not enhance his popularity."[25] Many Russians approached the question with a dark sense of foreboding. "Our sobriety was forced upon us, and at a time when every good person, even without prohibition, cannot enjoy life," explained one Russian survey respondent in late 1914. "Therefore such a change in the life of the people is due not only to temperance but to the expectation of something terrible and indefinite that is going to happen."[26]

The sobering reality of war bred widespread distrust of the tsar, as many viewed any government restriction—however "benevolent" its intentions—as a fiendish attempt to increase the autocrat's control over his peasant subjects while the moneyed elites were given free license to indulge as they pleased. The fact that first-class restaurants were allowed to continue serving alcohol during the first months of prohibition while the taverns and liquor stores frequented by the lower classes were locked down only entrenched the cynicism. Just as in the war itself, it was clear that the masses, rather than the elites, would sacrifice the most for the tsar's poor decisions. Such widely held sentiments have led historians to argue explicitly that "prohibition led to the decline of the czar's popularity and, increasingly, political radicalization."[27]

Vodka In The Trenches

While long-simmering discontent with the tsar and his regime provided the backdrop for the revolution, academics point to the constant series of demoralizing losses at the front as a more proximate cause. Here, too, vodka played a dubious role: knowing full well their enemy's traditional "weakness" for alcohol, both the Germans and Austrians allegedly enlisted alcohol as a valuable, anti-Russian weapon. In an effort to incapacitate the army and stymie Russian advances, they deliberately left bottles of vodka in the trenches and stocked houses near the battlefields with liquor to encourage drunkenness and insubordination in the ranks of the enemy.[28]

Surviving accounts of life in the Russian trenches are drenched in alcohol. Soldiers looked to the bottle not only to build camaraderie but also to cope with the inhuman misery of modern trench warfare. In his *Notes of a Soldier,* Dmitry Oskin wrote how Russian soldiers focused their attacks on Austrian troops who carried flasks of rum. Oskin even admitted that he was seriously wounded after stumbling drunk out of the trenches to find more rum.[29]

Holidays and occasional breaks in the hostilities allowed for battlefield "fraternizations"—the relaxed mingling of opposing troops who had been fighting tooth and nail for months. During such temporary ceasefires, alcohol was openly distributed to the Russian troops by their enemies. The quantity of liquor was on such a scale that front-line Russian regiments could occasionally create their own regimental liquor stocks.[30] Military discipline eroded in step with morale as the Russian army suffered one crushing defeat after another.

With declining morale, Russian soldiers deserted en masse. The Germans crept further into the motherland as the clock ticked closer to the fateful year of 1917. In a futile effort to maintain discipline, army officers up and down the line smashed any liquor warehouse near the front, but all for naught.[31] By the time of the February Revolution, officers no longer controlled the enlisted men, many of whom actively pillaged and looted liquor stores, wine cellars, and wealthy estates. Sociologist Dmitry Shlapentokh has written of the Russian Fifth Platoon stationed near Oryol, where twenty thousand soldiers looted the wine cellars of a local nobleman, in the process destroying various Italian masterpieces, antiques, pianos, and an extensive library. When the wine ran out, the horde besieged the local distillery, which they quickly drained of alcohol and burned to the ground. A detachment sent to quell the riot disobeyed orders and instead joined in the revelry.[32]

In Moscow, the police battled to surpress drunken rioters who torched every German-named business while also looting the idle liquor stores. As one Englishman's diary notes: "Whilst the wine-shops were being looted the police came along and had them closed and sealed up, leaving in many cases a large number of the rioters dead drunk inside, who at the end of the war will be found like brandy-cherries!"[33]

To add insult to injury, the tsar's prohibition threatened to undermine Russia's wartime industry. Beyond its use as a beverage, alcohol is crucial to the manufacture of gunpowder and other war materiel. At the outset of hostilities the state had plenty of alcohol for industrial purposes, but by 1916 the closing of distilleries further disrupted Russia's already strained defense industry.[34]

Certainly many factors contributed to the utter collapse and dissolution of the Russian army in World War I. Yet vodka's role can no longer be ignored, as it facilitated the disorganization long credited with dooming the Romanov dynasty.[35]

Farewell, Drunken Budget

"From time immemorial countries waging war have been in want of funds," wrote Andrei Shingarev, official *rapporteur* of the imperial Duma's budget and finance committees, in a 1915 report on the financial effects of the tsar's prohibition, "but never since the dawn of human history has a single country, in a time of war, renounced the principal source of its revenue."[36]

Indeed, the tsar's vodka monopoly brought in an average of four hundred million rubles a year, or between a quarter to a third of all revenues, to the imperial treasury. This vital stream of funding dried up almost immediately following Nicholas's fateful prohibition telegram to his dear uncle Kostya. Even with the supplementary taxes, bonds, and loans cobbled together by Finance Minister Bark, state revenues decreased by over five hundred million rubles in the second half of 1914 alone and by nine hundred million rubles per year thereafter—just as Russia stumbled into the greatest military conflagration in world history.[37]

There are good reasons why countries typically do not renounce their principal revenue source in wartime. Wars are expensive, and countries that can't pay for them usually meet with an unfortunate end. Despite frantic warnings from outside of government, Russia would not avoid this fate. "Government indebtedness exacerbated wartime inflation," as prominent historians have pointed out, "which aggravated the social and economic crises that eventually toppled the tsarist government."[38]

So it seems all the more ironic that, instead of sounding the alarm about the obvious financial disaster awaiting the country, *rapporteur* Shingarev's claim that Russia would be the first country to renounce its principal source of revenue was, if anything, *boastful*. In fact his report claims that "the government's repudiation of the fiscal taxation of spiritous liquors and the discontinuation of their sale will provide the greatest economic, social and moral benefaction for the population."[39] While difficult to comprehend in hindsight, Shingarev was not alone in disastrously misreading the state's finances. Similar unbridled optimism was shared by temperance advocates in Russia, Europe, and North America who believed that the people's natural industriousness would be miraculously unleashed once liberated from the yoke of alcohol. According to this logic, any lost vodka revenues would be more than made up for by the overall growth of economic activity.[40] Unfortunately for prohibitionists the world over—and for the fate of Russia in particular—prohibition's much-anticipated productivity boost never happened. Compounded by the astronomical costs of war, the hole in the budget grew ever larger.

Trying to patch the hole, the imperial government simply printed more rubles, without regard for the hyperinflationary consequences. "What if we do lose eight hundred million rubles in revenue?" asked the dismissive Premier Ivan Goremykin. "We shall print that much paper money; it's all the same to the people."[41] Even embattled Finance Minister Bark seemed oblivious to the consequences of uncontrolled inflation: in submitting his 1917 budget estimates to Tsar Nicholas II (against the backdrop of escalating war costs, growing social resentment, and the worthlessness of paper rubles), Bark forecast an astounding increase in government revenue that "enables us also to increase our expenditure on the Church, Education, Public Health, Agriculture, Trade and Industry, Postal and Telegraphic Service, and the construction of railway lines, thus providing for the spiritual and practical needs of the nation."[42] With the economy and state crumbling around him, it seemed as though Russia's finance minister was living on some distant planet.

Russia's hyperinflationary spiral has always been considered a primary cause of dethroning both the tsar (in the revolution of February 1917) and his successor—the Provisional Government—in the Bolshevik Revolution that October.[43] Yet the destruction that prohibition wrought on imperial finances was not simply the result of the sudden lack of alcohol sales. The old vodka monopoly was a retail and distribution monopoly—a compromise arrangement that not only allowed the treasury to reap tremendous revenues from the sale of alcohol (and manipulate the retail price of alcohol as it saw fit) but also left the lucrative production of alcoholic beverages in the hands of gentry distillers and brewers who had long enjoyed the exclusive right to production.[44] Prohibition not only left the imperial government with huge stores of unsold alcohol; it also left politically influential gentry distillers with massive liquor stockpiles they could not legally sell, depriving many of their primary source of wealth—and they were not happy. As part of existing long-term contracts, many distillers had already paid taxes on future alcohol deliveries. If that alcohol was not to be delivered, the producers wanted their money back, draining even more rubles from the treasury.[45]

For every distiller who effectively served as a creditor to the ministry of finance by paying their taxes in advance there were debtors, like Pyotr Pavlovich Bukhov mentioned earlier, who owed back taxes to the treasury. Thanks to prohibition, Bukhov and many like him had built tremendous debts to the treasury only to suddenly find themselves without a stream of income with which to repay them. While the finance ministry later allowed debtors to renegotiate contracts, in the short term the treasury was starved of badly needed funds, causing the financial hole to grow ever deeper.[46]

Meanwhile, the costs of enforcing prohibition rose dramatically. Think of the murderous reign of the gangster Al Capone in Prohibition-era Chicago: the conventional wisdom among historians is that Russian prohibition also begot rampant moonshining and smuggling but it actually took years for it to become pervasive.[47] A stack of letters and telegrams in the archives of the ministry of finance tells a much different story: already by the first months of 1915, Finance Minister Bark was buried under an avalanche of reports describing an explosion of illegal activities: alarms of a "broad increase in the clandestine trade in alcohol" from neighboring Manchurian territories were sounded from Russia's Far East. Reports from the taiga proclaimed that "secret distilling is increasing completely unimpeded," while memos from every region of Russia chronicled a disturbing increase in underground distilling. In the last half of 1914 alone, the ministry of agriculture uncovered some 1,825 illegal distilleries, while the following year, the excise department discovered 5,707 cases of illicit distilling[48] —all underscoring the authorities' need for dramatic reinforcements to keep Russia dry.

Then came the military fallout. Whether sacked by marauding recruits in mobilization riots or by deserters looting stores, distilleries, and private residences, the imperial government was liable for the destructive actions of their officers and conscripts, and the gentry class demanded compensation for their losses. Given their political influence, they often got it. Most straightforward were the instances when military commanders destroyed alcohol warehouses, stores, and production facilities near the front so as not to tempt insubordination. In perhaps history's biggest example of "you break it, you bought it," gentry alcohol producers presented the treasury with the bill for their lost alcohol stocks. With the Russian army backpedaling furiously, and the zone of mandatory destruction of alcohol marching steadily eastward across Russia's populous western territories—the expected remuneration ran into the millions, if not tens of millions, of rubles.[49]

Thus, far beyond simply starving the imperial treasury of its single greatest source of revenue in the midst of Russia's grandest military engagement, prohibition bled the treasury dry by paying for alcohol the government was destroying. The combined effect was predictably tragic: by deepening the government's debts, prohibition exacerbated wartime inflation, which compounded the political, economic, and social crises that ultimately doomed the entire regime. Vodka politics may not have single-handedly caused the downfall of the tsarist government, but it certainly hastened its fall.

Alcohol And Infrastructural Paralysis

A final alleged cause of revolution was the infrastructural paralysis that accompanied the total war raging on Russian territory. Russia's infamously cold winters discouraged travel while the spring thaw and rains turned the country's dirt roads into impassable bogs, increasing the reliance on Russia's anemic railway network to both supply the war effort and maintain the traditional exchange of food and grain from Russia's rural provinces for manufactured goods produced in its cities. As it turns out, Russia's overburdened railroads failed spectacularly on both counts: woefully undersupplying the forces at the front and preventing grains from being delivered to cities from the countryside, leading to food shortages and even starvation.[50] Certainly, alcohol could not have contributed to this problem too...or could it?

As it turns out, many enterprising gentry distillers did not complacently let their investments—their alcohol stocks—fall victim to roving hordes, or worse: sit idle until the cessation of hostilities. The tsar's prohibition barred distillers from selling their wares at home, but that did not prevent them from selling their alcohol to foreign markets. Some distillers even secured promises from the imperial government to open new markets in foreign countries to compensate for prohibition at home.[51] Many well-connected Russian elites inked deals to ship their alcohol to Russia's primary ally, France. The only problem was the front: from the Gulf of Riga in the north to the mouth of the Danube in the south (and later from the outskirts of Petrograd to the mouth of the Don), the war zone and trade embargo halted all east-west commerce in Europe, while Entente warships shut down all maritime commercial traffic in the Baltic, Black, and Mediterranean seas.

Embattled distillers planned to load their massive stores of alcohol into railway cars—chronically in short supply—from threatened territories near the front (Petrograd, Vilnius, Poltava, and Kuban districts), first to safer locations away from the hostilities and then north to the White Sea ports of Arkhangelsk and Murmansk for the long sea voyage to markets in France.[52] Foreign observers remarked that "enormous quantities have been exported to France" in such a manner.[53] Emboldened by Russia's initial and ephemeral victories against the Austro-Hungarian Empire in Galicia in 1915, a convention of potato growers and alcohol manufacturers in Minsk gleefully noted that these newly "liberated" territories were technically outside the purview of the prohibition decree. Subsequently, "The representatives of the Russian Government promised to pave the way for the Russian alcohol industry and trade toward the Galician territories," and "The assembly decided to take up at once the necessary steps for an extensive export trade of Russian alcohol to Galicia."[54]

This is how Russia's groaning railway infrastructure—rather than adequately supply front-line combatants or provide sustenance to its beleaguered cities—became clogged with trainloads of vodka. Most mind-boggling of all were plans by distillers in the Kharkov and Poltava regions—today in east-central Ukraine—to load their wares onto scarce rail cars for a 7,000 km trip across the Trans-Siberian Railway to the Pacific port city of Vladivostok and from there by sea to markets in Japan and coastal China.[55] Amid nationwide suffering and total war, such schemes to save alcohol at all costs defied all rational comprehension and only exacerbated the infrastructural paralysis.

Finally, the elimination of the vodka trade disrupted the traditional urban-rural trade cycle: Russian peasants traditionally exchanged their agricultural surpluses for manufactured goods, vodka foremost among them. With vodka illegal and other commodities in short supply due to the war, the village had little incentive to trade with the city, as the peasant either hoarded grain, distilled it himself (*samogon*), or sold it to the few private distilleries that operated through 1916 in hopes of capturing a greater market share following a swift conclusion to the war.[56] According to historian David Christian, the subsequent "failure of peasant producers to market their surpluses was, of course, a major cause of the grain shortages in major towns which helped provoke the urban insurrections which brought down the Tsarist government in February 1917."[57]

In retrospect, Tsar Nicholas' biographer, Sergei Oldenburg, summed up the bizarre and unprecedented decision to adopt prohibition by autocratic decree.

> During the first days of the war, the most difficult domestic problems seemed amenable to easy solutions. The Emperor, therefore, seized the opportunity to carry through a bold reform which in past years had been especially dear to His heart, namely the prohibition of the sale of alcoholic beverages.... Only wartime conditions, which upset all normal budgetary considerations, made it possible to adopt a measure that amounted to a renunciation of the state's largest source of income. Before 1914 no other nation had adopted such a radical measure in the struggle against alcoholism. It was a grandiose scheme, quite unheard of.[58]

It goes without saying that Nicholas was tragically unaware of the myriad of different ways that this fateful decision would hasten his downfall. By exacerbating grain shortages, further stressing the transportation system, and irreparably debilitating the treasury, the tsar's prohibition decision stoked the already red-hot embers of revolution—to say nothing of the increased resentment for the tsar among the working classes, who did not appreciate being forced to quit "cold turkey" from what was, in many cases, their sole solace.[59]

Historians may never fully agree about which factor—social discontent, military pathologies, economic and financial problems, or infrastructural breakdown—was most important in bringing about the end of the Russian empire. Yet a good case can be made for vodka politics—the pervasiveness of alcohol in late-imperial Russian society and its abrupt prohibition—in catalyzing the overthrow of the centuries-old Romanov dynasty. Indeed, astute observers of the day noted as much, bluntly concluding that the "chief contributory cause to the revolution was the prohibition in 1914 of the sale of spiritous liquors."[60]

14

Vodka Communism

"The very nearest future will be a period of a heroic struggle with alcohol," proclaimed Leon Trotsky—the firebrand Bolshevik ideologue and founder of the Red Army. Shortly after the communists seized power he warned: "If we don't stamp out alcoholism, then we will drink up socialism and drink up the October Revolution."[1]

Of course, Marxists of all stripes had long criticized alcohol as the means by which the bourgeois capitalists leached their wealth from the oppressed working class, especially in tsarist Russia (chapter 10). When Vladimir Lenin and the Bolsheviks replaced Europe's most conservative monarchy with the world's first communist state, everything was bound to change: all political, economic, social, and even cultural relations were to be re-cast—including Russia's relationship to the bottle.

Yet before the Bolsheviks could take on Russia's deeply rooted alcohol dependence, there were more pressing concerns—namely, taking and holding political power in an environment of unimaginable chaos, suffering, and despair.

The Two Revolutions

While certainly not the sole factor, Nicholas II's disastrous alcohol prohibition unquestionably hastened the empire's undoing. Following the tsar's famed prohibition telegram of September 1914, the imperial parliament—or Duma—began to codify the declaration into law. With deaths and desertions mounting on the war front and discontent brewing at home, in 1916 the Duma passed a bill making Russian prohibition permanent and absolute. Yet by the time it could be officially submitted to the emperor for ratification there was no tsar left to send it to.[2]

By the bitterly cold January of 1917, Russian war casualties topped six million. Thousands of exhausted soldiers deserted monthly, joining civilian refugees from war-torn areas into a disaffected and disgruntled mass of millions flowing steadily eastward. Even without the stench, death, and misery of trench warfare, things weren't much better away from the front lines: food shortages threatened both famine and rebellion.[3]

On International Women's Day—February 23—women textile workers went on strike in Petrograd. Their simple demands for bread and an end to the war resonated with a war-weary population. Within days, hundreds of thousands of protesters clogged the thoroughfares of the capital, clashing with the police— culminating in a massacre on Nevsky Prospect when a training detachment of nervous, young recruits opened fire into the crowd. As the emboldened mobs grew larger, and potentially more dangerous, the military defied orders to fire on unarmed civilians. The government was paralyzed. Meanwhile, a council of soldiers and leaders of labor unions were organized by socialists into the so-called Petrograd *Soviet* (Council) that quickly gained legitimacy as an alternative political authority. En route to the capital from the front, the tsar's train was stopped by rebellious soldiers and railway workers. With his people and military against him, and Grand Duke Nikolasha "on his knees" beseeching him to abdicate his throne, Nicholas II did so, bringing the Romanov dynasty to its end.[4]

With the police in hiding or defying orders, mobs laid siege to police stations, government ministries, and the tsar's prisons. There was little opposition to the hundreds of thousands of workers, mutinous soldiers, and recently liberated criminals roaming the streets of Petrograd. Armed gangs looted homes, shops, and liquor stores. Some commandeered motor cars—which they promptly crashed, since few knew how to drive, especially through a haze of pilfered vodka.[5] Hundreds died, and thousands more were injured in the February Revolution, yet there was a sense that things could have been much worse. With the monarchy gone, the mood in the capital was largely festive—even euphoric—a state that foreign observers chalked up to prohibition and the relative paucity of alcohol: "If vodka could have been found in plenty, the revolution could easily have had a terrible ending."[6]

The tsar's abdication decapitated the old political order. With the royal family gone, who was in charge of the country? Actually, the imperial institutions and bureaucracy were still in place, and—even before the official abdication—members of the imperial Duma had already hastily organized a new "temporary" or Provisional Government. Yet while foreign powers enthusiastically recognized the liberal, self-appointed Provisional Government as the Russian power de jure, the de facto political power lay with the socialist Petrograd Soviet, which both represented and directed the soldiers and workers—first in the capital and then throughout the country.

At the center of this system of dual power was Aleksandr Kerensky—a moderate, Socialist Revolutionary Duma deputy who had a foot in both camps: being elected as vice-chairman of the Petrograd Soviet and as minister of justice (and later minister of war) in the Provisional Government. Trying to guide this unwieldy arrangement was like skiing with each ski pointed in a different direction—and Kerensky was going downhill fast. Socialists in the Petrograd Soviet demanded an immediate end to the disastrous war, land reform, and giving control of factories to the workers. Meanwhile, the Provisional Government continued many of the tsar's unpopular policies, including fighting the war (so as not to disappoint Russia's wartime allies) and the alcohol prohibition.[7]

The mostly sober and orderly spring of 1917 gave way to a summer of increasingly drunken disorder as more drubbings at the front, mutinies in Petrograd, and government gridlock eroded Kerensky's support. By the fall, the Provisional Government—holed up in the immaculate Winter Palace of the tsars—had no supporters left to defend it.[8]

As Kerensky's legitimacy waned, the power of the Bolsheviks was on the rise. Lenin and a group of exiled Bolsheviks arrived at Petrograd's Finland Station from their European exile in April. By summer, they had secured control of the Petrograd Soviet and set about overthrowing the Provisional Government in the name of the workers and peasants.[9]

Relative to its importance in changing the course of world history, the October Revolution itself was rather mundane. The night of October 24–25 was just like any other in the strife-weary city. Restaurants and theaters in the capital were open and conducting a brisk business, even as the Bolsheviks quietly seized control of strategic assets: government offices, train stations, and major newspapers. The popular image of a dramatic communist advance on the Winter Palace putting Kerensky to flight is more a product of Sergei Eisenstein's epic film adaption *October* than a reflection of actual events. In fact, the Winter Palace was stormed by a relatively small and disorganized group of revolutionaries—many of whom bypassed the priceless works of art and other royal treasures to instead loot the imperial wine cellars. Were it not for the Bolsheviks ability to *maintain* power, the events of that night would have been just another episode of instability among many in wartime Russia.[10]

Once the Provisional Government fled, jubilant soldiers and sailors drank themselves into oblivion. "In the wine cellars of the Winter Palace, which were the first to be smashed, many unfortunate souls have already died from overdrinking," wrote Lenin's confidant Vladimir Bonch-Bruevich. "Crates of wine were thrown into holes in the river ice, but crazed people dove in after it, and drowned in the Neva trying to catch that cursed potion. From there a drunken pogrom erupted, as with furious and rabid joy the crazed and drunken crowd stormed private apartments throughout the city."[11]

War correspondent for the *San Francisco Bulletin* Bessie Beatty described how the night the Winter Palace cellars were looted, "we thought the whole populace was going to be killed; but it later developed that the sounds we had taken for shots were nothing more fatal than popping corks, and the soldiers who lay on the white snow were not dead, but merely dead drunk."[12]

At a national conference of workers' and soldiers' soviets held the following day, Lenin triumphantly proclaimed the beginning of a new socialist order—vowing to withdraw Russia from the war and nationalize land in the name of the peasants. The new era had begun.

But the old system would not go so quietly into the "dustbin of history." While the Bolsheviks had a tenuous hold on the capital, the same could not be said throughout the vast Russian landmass, where communist "red" forces confronted royalists, conservatives, and others intent on defending the old imperial "white" order. Ever mindful of the relative ease with which both the weak tsarist and provisional governments were overthrown, Lenin was determined not to meet the same fate through counterrevolution. What the Bolsheviks had that their opponents lacked was discipline—and they knew that the biggest threat to discipline was vodka. Therefore, the first order of business in communist Russia was to affirm the prohibition inherited from their bourgeois predecessors.

This anti-alcohol paranoia was well founded, as throughout November and December Petrograd was rocked by liquor riots—mostly among the soldiers—that threatened the stability of the new regime. The new communist leadership quickly discovered that Petrograd was "mined" with over eight hundred wine cellars: one alone held 1.2 million bottles. In desperate need of foreign credits, the Bolsheviks first thought to sell these collections—including vintage wines and champagnes aged hundreds of years—to English and American customers. But events were moving too fast. A detachment of the liberal Constitutional Democrats sowed insubordination among the revolutionary guard by telephoning barracks with rumors of free alcohol at various locations throughout the city, which predictably degenerated into drunken chaos.[13]

Meriel Buchanan, the daughter of the British ambassador in Petrograd described the fearful chaos in the snows of December.

> Even as far down the Quay as the Embassy the air was infected with the reek of spirits, and everywhere drunken soldiers lay about, broken bottles littered the streets, the snow was stained rose red and yellow in many places where the wine had been spilt. All through the town the drunken hordes spread themselves, firing indiscriminately at each other or anybody who molested them. Scenes of indescribable horror and disgust took place, the crowds in some instances scooping up the dirty, wine-stained snow, drinking it out of their hands, fighting with each other over the remains....A drunken soldier stood before one of the huge fires that burned at the corners of all the streets, a broken bottle held in one hand, a pistol in the other, while a Red Guard leaning

on his gun watched him with an indulgent smile. Singing and laughing the soldier swayed, perilously near to the leaping flames, now and then pointing his pistol at the passers-by, cursing them, or laughing at them as they drew nervously away. Still a little farther along another soldier lay face down in the snow, an empty bottle still clutched in one hand, while two little boys stood nervously at a distance, and a third, more courageous, tried to loosen the fast-clasped fingers from the bottle, to see perhaps whether there were a few drops left.[14]

Before his newspaper *Novaya zhizn'* (*New Life*) fell prey to Bolshevik censorship (and before he himself became a Bolshevik apologist), in 1917 the liberal writer and critic Maxim Gorky reported how the communist mob looted alcohol stores nightly, falling into the mire "like pigs," covered in blood from smashed liquor bottles. As for the official claim that "bourgeois provocation" was to blame for the drunken disorder? "It is a blatant lie." Gorky argued it was the product of the socialist revolution itself—devoid as it was of social consciousness.[15]

Whatever their source, the constant threat of drunken pogroms was perhaps the new government's most immediate challenge. "What would you have?" the exasperated People's Commissar of Enlightenment, Anatoly Lunacharsky, told a reporter, throwing up his hands. "The whole of Petrograd is drunk."[16]

The new communist government—the Military Revolutionary Committee—took quick and drastic action by forming a new internal security organization to confront the drunken disorder: the All-Russian Extraordinary Commission for Combatting Counter revolution and Sabotage—often referred to simply as the Extraordinary Commission or by its Russian initials "Ch" and "K": the "CheKa." Later reorganized as the People's Commissariat for Internal Affairs (NKVD) and then as the Committee for State Security (KGB)—the Soviet secret police was associated with the darkest horrors of totalitarian terror. The most fearful symbol of Soviet repression and intimidation was a massive, fifteen-ton "Iron Felix" statue erected in 1958 in front of Stalin's NKVD headquarters at the notorious Lubyanka Prison in downtown Moscow. This despised monument to the founder of the Cheka, Felix Dzerzhinsky, was among the first statues toppled when communism collapsed in 1991.

Long before his likeness was immortalized in iron, Dzerzhinsky was charged with mercilessly suppressing the counterrevolutionary vodka threat. "The bourgeoisie perpetuates the most evil crimes," Lenin wrote Dzerzhinsky in December 1917, "bribing the cast-offs and dregs of society, getting them drunk for pogroms."[17] In Petrograd, all alcohol producers were to immediately disclose the whereabouts of their liquor stores or stand trial before the Military Revolutionary Court. Bootleggers were to be shot on sight. The mammoth collection of liquors and vintage wines in the Winter Palace wine cellars—valued at

$5 million ($91 million in 2013 dollars)—was flooded by an emergency fire battalion, drowning those soldiers too drunk to escape. The frigid waters did little to deter would-be thieves, so the entire collection was later removed to the Baltic island fortress of Kronstadt that defended the approaches to the capital and dutifully smashed by Red sailors there.[18]

"The men who wanted that wine were so mad for it that even machine guns would not keep them back. So the comrade in charge turned the machine guns on the bottles and destroyed them," described American journalist Anna Louise Strong. "The wine rose to the tops of his hip-boots so that he was wading in it. He used to be a drinker himself before he became a Communist and it hurt him to see that good wine destroyed. But it was necessary to preserve order in Petrograd."[19]

The seriousness of vodka's counterrevolutionary threat was also chronicled in American socialist John Reed's famous firsthand account, *Ten Days that Shook the World*. Reed even reproduced a Bolshevik order posted throughout the neighborhoods of Vasily Island, just across the Neva River due west of the Winter Palace.

> The bourgeoisie has chosen a very sinister method of fighting against the proletariat; it has established in various parts of the city huge wine depots, and distributes liquor among the soldiers, in this manner attempting to sow dissatisfaction in the ranks of the Revolutionary army.
>
> It is herewith ordered to all house committees, that at 3 o'clock, the time set for posting this order, they shall in person and secretly notify the President of the Committee of the Finland Guard Regiment, concerning the amount of wine in their premises.
>
> Those who violate this order will be arrested and given trial before a merciless court, and their property will be confiscated, and the stock of wine discovered will be
>
> BLOWN UP WITH DYNAMITE
> 2 hours after this warning,
>
> because more lenient measures, as experience has shown, do not bring the desired results.
>
> REMEMBER, THERE WILL BE NO OTHER
> WARNINGBEFORE THE EXPLOSIONS.
> —*Regimental Committee of the Finland Guard Regiment*[20]

With the city under martial law, Lenin appointed both a commissar to combat drunkenness and pogroms and an official anti-riot committee to aid Dzerzhinsky and his chekists' fight against alcohol. Together, their confrontations with drunken instigators often escalated into pitched street battles involving machine guns and armored cars. Outside the Petrov Vodka Factory, for instance, Red Guard detachments sworn to be "sober and loyal to the revolution" clashed with unruly and drunken elements of the Semenovsky Guards Regiment, leaving eleven dead.[21] The normally reliable Preobrazhensky Regiment assigned to guard the liquor warehouses "got completely drunk." The Pavlovsky Regiment also "did not withstand temptation." Other assigned guards likewise "succumbed." Armored brigades ordered to disperse inebriated crowds "paraded a little to and fro, and then began to sway suspiciously on their feet."[22] Scenes like these were repeated in Moscow, Saratov, Tomsk, Nizhny Novgorod, and throughout Russia in the tumultuous months following the October Revolution, forcing authorities to use only their most loyal and untouchable Red Guards to quell the counterrevolutionary alco-disorder. "The duty of the Red Guard," according to its own pledge, "includes the struggle with drunkenness so as not to allow liberty and revolution to drown in wine."[23]

Such extreme countermeasures against vodka were hardly new. A decade earlier, during the so-called dress rehearsal Revolution of 1905, socialist battalions were often infiltrated by royalists and extremists, including the ultra-nationalist "Black Hundreds," which terrorized would-be revolutionaries by inciting violent pogroms with vodka. Even then, Lenin preached vigilance: "Prepare for the decisive struggle, citizens! We will not allow the Black-Hundred government to use violence against Russia," he declared. "We shall order our army units to arrest the Black-Hundred heroes who fuddle ignorant people with vodka and corrupt them; we shall commit all those monsters…for public, revolutionary trial by the whole people."[24]

Whether aspiring for power in 1905 or maintaining power in 1917, such "practical" defenses only hardened Lenin's intellectual disdain for alcohol. Like many early socialists, he derided alcohol as a tool of capitalist domination of the working classes, especially in Russia (chapter 10). For Lenin, the imperial liquor trade was an "unparalleled and shameless exploitation of the peasantry"; the noble landlord was "a usurer and robber, a beast of prey," and "village bloodsucker" for promoting the booze trade.[25]

"Death is preferable to selling vodka!" Lenin declared prior to the revolution. True to his prohibitionist principles, he held fast to that conviction after seizing power.[26] Even with vodka's counterrevolutionary threat subsiding, Lenin's ruling Sovnarkom, or Council of People's Commissars ("commissar" being proletarian-speak for the bourgeois title of "minister"), nationalized all alcohol production facilities and existing alcohol stocks. In 1919, the Sovnarkom forbid distilling "by any means, in any quantity and at any strength"—punishable by confiscation of all property and a minimum of five years in Siberian labor camps.[27]

Such draconian penalties were necessary for a Bolshevik government in a fight for survival. The Treaty of Brest-Litovsk (1918) freed Russia from the nightmare of World War I—and all it cost them was control of Finland, Estonia, Latvia, Lithuania, Poland, and most of present-day Belarus, Moldova, and Ukraine. But the horrors of the Great War were replaced by the tragedy of civil war: of Russia's vast territories, the Bolsheviks effectively controlled only those areas from Petrograd on the Baltic southeast to Astrakhan on the Caspian. In the Urals to the east, the "reds" fought against the "white" royalist forces of Adm. Aleksandr Kolchak and a legion of Czech volunteers. In the Caucasus and Central Asia to the south, they faced British and Turkish forces, white Cossacks, and an indigenous Basmachi rebellion. To the southwest were the white armies of Anton Denikin, Cossacks, Ukrainian separatists, and a well-armed anarchist movement. In the west, they confronted Poles, Germans, and the white armies of Nikolai Yudenich. From the northwest, the Finns advanced on Petrograd. American and British forces occupied the arctic ports of Murmansk and Arkhangelsk in the north.

From 1917 through 1923 the Bolsheviks had their hands full. Lenin's right-hand man Leon Trotsky hastily assembled a Red Army of five million men: mostly peasants and former imperial soldiers who often joined only out of fear that they or their families would be taken hostage or shot—a common terror tactic on both sides.

In this light, the Bolsheviks' anti-alcohol measures seem only slightly less draconian. This was "War Communism": everything in their control was mobilized for victory. Trade was abolished. All industries were nationalized. To feed the urban workers, food was requisitioned from the rural peasantry at gunpoint. Bootleggers who distilled grains into vodka were declared enemies of the revolution for sabotaging the state's food supply and often were imprisoned or shot. Even so, hundreds of thousands of tons of grain were annually made into alcohol, often with the connivance of corrupt local Bolshevik officials. In one town in south-central Russia alone, authorities discovered that the peasants had distilled vodka from grain that could have fed a city of ten thousand people.[28] This system may have delivered Red victory in the civil war, but it also produced unthinkable desperation and hardship.

Misery

As the civil war wound down, the human misery left in its wake is difficult to fathom, much less quantify. Four disastrous years of world war killed upwards of three million Russians. The ensuing civil war, red terror, white terror, and Cheka executions claimed at least as many. Another two million fled the country. Then came epidemics of typhus, typhoid, dysentery, cholera, and Spanish flu claiming millions more. Years of total war destroyed both infrastructure and authority: people did not know who might come the next day to take their food, forcibly conscript them, or senselessly terrorize them. There were no schools, no transportation. Struggling to survive, hungry orphans roamed the rubble-strewn streets of deserted cities. Moscow lost over half its population—Petrograd lost two-thirds. Most fled to the countryside, but even there they had no incentive to farm or produce, as anything they reaped would likely be torn from them. In the early 1920s, Russia's agricultural output was less than half of what it was before the Great War—with its factories in ruins, industrial output was less than twenty percent. Within a decade, the national income of Russia—one of the world's greatest powers—was only forty percent of what it was in 1913, "a fall of the productive forces," as one economic historian describes it, that "is unexampled in the history of mankind."[29] And to this laundry list of horrors, we now add famine.

As the Bolsheviks consolidated control in the spring of 1921, the Volga basin grappled with a crippling drought. In normal times a peasant family held a small surplus of grain to get through a bad harvest: they might go hungry, but they wouldn't starve. But with the terror of War Communism, all grain that wasn't forcibly seized by "collection squads" was distilled into vodka, leaving desperate millions to face starvation.

Lenin and the Bolshevik leadership admitted that "we actually took from the peasant his entire surplus, and, sometimes we took not only the surplus but part of his necessary supply in order to meet the expenses of the army and to support the workers." With the news of drought in the Volga region, Lenin concerned himself not so much with the threat it posed to the peoples' welfare but to the government itself—announcing to the Tenth Party Congress in March 1921: "If there is a crop failure, it will be impossible to appropriate any surplus, because there will be no surplus." He added, "since we cannot take anything from people who do not have the means of satisfying their own hunger, the government will perish."[30]

As a part of his NEP, or New Economic Policy, Lenin relented: strategically retreating from the bayonet-point requisitions of War Communism to in-kind taxation, NEP left some surplus for the peasants to sell at market, providing a "breathing space" for Russian agriculture to recover. But for the starving millions along the Volga, it was already too late. Within months Russia would be rocked by the deadliest famine in modern European history. Diseased and dying livestock was set upon by children with distended bellies; the weathered, gaunt-faced men who piled corpses like cordwood into mass graves ate grass, tree bark, or worse. In the city of Samara alone, ten butcher shops were closed for peddling in human flesh.[31]

This was not the first devastating famine in Russia, and it would not be the last. A generation earlier in tsarist Russia a hard freeze followed by extended drought created a famine that claimed a half-million souls in 1891–92. Yet it was the famine's all-too-human causes and the callous indifference of the tsarist government that galvanized many critics—including Lenin—into steadfast opponents of the old regime. That fall, peasants rushed to sell their meager harvest to pay their taxes, debts, and liquor bills—glutting the market and driving down grain prices, forcing the peasants to sell even their precious reserves to get by. By mid-winter, their food stocks were gone. In a vicious cycle, the only means of survival was by going deeper in debt to the local pawnbroker or landlord, but that only increased the peasant's burden and narrowed next year's margin of survival.

The tone-deaf government response, which included resurrecting the imperial spirits monopoly that "contributed so much to its impoverishment and demoralisation" at the hour of the peasantry's greatest need, drew the ire of many both in Russia and abroad.[32] Even the relief efforts were exacerbated by alcohol: both the food to tide the needy over until the next harvest and the seed grain needed to grow it was often "either drunk up in the taverns or sold to speculators at an unusually low price."[33]

The situation in 1921 was an eerie echo to the famine thirty years earlier, especially concerning alcohol. In both cases—despite the widespread food shortage—vodka was everywhere. While providing a temporary psychological respite for both the victims and aid providers, vodka—and the clandestine distillation of grain to prevent its requisition—was partially to blame for the misery. As before—even amid widespread hunger—both the relief provisions and the seed grain necessary for future crops were often distilled by bootleggers into vodka. In the heart of the famine zone, one aid worker explained: "The principal distraction of the villages (grown wild as they are) is generally drink, which fills up all the hours of all the holidays and festivals. No idea can be formed of the huge extension of secret vodka-distilling; it has pervaded Russian life throughout and is a calamity both for the national morals and the national health."[34]

Famine politics are fascinating in their own right. Amartya Sen, who won the 1998 Nobel Prize in Economics for his research into the causes of poverty, has argued that famines are never caused by crop failures alone but rather are symptomatic of autocratic political systems that can easily ignore the needs of their citizens.[35] This resonates with the thesis of this book: Russia's society-wide addiction to alcohol is not only a social and cultural problem in its own right but is also symptomatic of a deeper political illness—an autocratic state that benefits from alcoholic excess and is consequently hostile to grass-roots activism that promotes the interests and welfare of society.

There is perhaps no clearer illustration of these dynamics than the American Relief Administration (ARA) expedition to alleviate the Russian famine of 1921–22. A quasi-governmental aid agency directed by future U.S. president Herbert Hoover, the ARA delivered food and relief supplies to war-ravaged Europe during and after the Great War. Along with the International Committee of the Red Cross and Britain's Save the Children Fund, Hoover and the ARA answered an appeal by famed writer Maxim Gorky (who by now had become reluctantly allied with the communist leadership), pleading that millions were at risk of starvation.[36] Following delicate, high-level negotiations with the new Bolshevik government, the ARA was permitted to extend its reach into the famine-ravaged Volga area, where they had to tread a thin line: if they were seen as strengthening Lenin's communist regime, they would run afoul of American public opinion and lose their logistical support. But if the Russians viewed the Americans as using aid to destabilize the Bolshevik government, they would be evicted, leaving millions more to die. Still, by 1922, ARA kitchens were feeding nearly eleven million Russians a day.[37]

Between communists and capitalists, "vodka was the supreme test of good government relations," writes Bertrand Patenaude in his history of the ARA, *The Big Show in Bololand*—the Americans' name for the exotic land of the Bolsheviks. The letters, diaries, and memoirs of the cowboys, college students, and former doughboys of the ARA repeatedly tell of the jarring discord between the needs of the starving population and the ostentatious local Bolshevik authorities on whom they relied to deliver their much-needed relief. Whether well-intentioned displays of traditional hospitality (as the Russians thought) or efforts to get the Americans drunk in order to rob them of their "dignified reserve" (as the Americans thought), throughout the famine zone the ARA was welcomed with festive banquets and copious amounts of liquor. Some were treated to 85-year-old port requisitioned from old imperial cellars; others were given bootleg kerosene seasoned with ammonia. In either case, ARA workers were struck by the "curious contradiction" that such prolific indulgence could take place in the shadows of the apocalyptical scenes of famine just beyond the commissars' doors. "Just as incongruous," Patenaude wrote, "was the fact that the sponsors of these events were representatives of the dictatorship of the proletariat, who it might have been thought would have banished banqueting to the irretrievable past. Instead, the proletariat's parvenu vanguard seemed intent upon outdoing the defeated class enemy even in the social sphere, as if to demonstrate its suitability to rule the country."[38]

The letters of ARA officer William Kelley describe life as the government's guest in the Bashkir city of Sterlitamak. In one instance, a surreal banquet of Bolshevik leaders and four ladies began over a gallon of "the vilest" bootleg vodka.

With the first toast the fight was on, they fighting to get me drunk, and I determined to stay on deck....Midnight found the bottle empty. The Commissar of Transport was oozing vodka at every port, but still cheerful and peaceful. [The government host] Bishoff was sick and very quiet. Churnishev was unperturbed. Lady No. 4 had been led away to bed. Nos. 2 and 3 were plainly drunk. The hostess, I must say, was well mannered and well poised throughout. I caught her eye once and we toasted each other quietly across the table.[39]

The next morning, with his head still pounding from the (alleged) beverages as he returned to the ARA offices, Kelley prided himself on at least not drunkenly blabbing something undiplomatic. "Along the road he passed the body of a soldier who had been killed during the night," describes Patenaude, "through the crowd of onlookers he could see a 'mass of human brains in the mud.' Half a block down the road he came upon a group of children playing hopscotch at a place where the entire previous day had lain the corpse of a child, its clothing and flesh chewed up by dogs. It had been removed, but nearby lay an apparent successor, a woman lying on a doorstep."[40]

Just as the socialists of 1891 were horrified at the tsarist regime's callous indifference to its famine-stricken people, the new "Bolo" government was no different, even though their famine claimed ten times as many victims: capitalist or communist, both regimes were autocracies that transformed the hardship of drought into the tragedy of famine. "The difference between democracy and autocracy," claimed relief-administrator Hoover, "is a question of whether people can be organized from the bottom up or from the top down."[41] Whether private agencies marshaling food relief to famine victims or grass-roots temperance organizations grappling with insobriety, that autocracies actively stifle bottom-up welfare initiatives goes far toward explaining why liberal democracies generally allay mass suffering while autocracies perpetuate it.

Vodka And NEP

The white forces having been vanquished on all fronts in the Civil War, the biggest threat to the new Bolshevik government came from the eternally suffering peasants themselves. Even in areas not decimated by war and famine, bands of peasants (and in the case of the Kronstadt garrison in 1921, even soldiers) rose up against the authorities. But since the landlords of old were gone, these became revolts against the state itself. Compounding the problem was the peasants' hoarding and distilling of grain. Between the insurrections and hoarding,

Lenin concluded that that the only way to save the communist revolution was to pacify the disgruntled peasantry.

Even as a counterrevolutionary mutiny among the Kronstadt sailors was being violently repressed, at the Tenth Congress of the Russian Communist Party (Bolsheviks), Lenin announced what would become known as the New Economic Policy: while the "commanding heights" of the economy—foreign trade, banks, and heavy industry—would stay in state hands, private commercial enterprises were legalized, and the forced grain requisitions were replaced with an in-kind tax, giving the peasantry the incentive to cultivate and sell surplus yields for profit. This strategic retreat from War Communism opened an economic "breathing space" that allowed both manufacturing and agriculture to rebound. To critics, it was a return to capitalism.[42]

Before an audience of hundreds of Communist Party delegates, Lenin argued that along with the "commanding heights," vodka production should also not be ceded to the people. In this way, Lenin claimed alcohol was fundamentally different from other consumer goods like, say, toiletries: "I think that we should not follow the example of the capitalist countries and put vodka and other intoxicants on the market, because, profitable though they are, they will lead us back to capitalism and not forward to communism." His sarcastic addendum that "there is no such danger in pomade" was met with laughter throughout the hall.[43]

In reality, the joke may have been on Lenin: beyond the congress hall in Moscow, very few Russians heeded the proclamation. Indeed, the ARA accounts of widespread illegal alcohol consumption even amid the horrors of famine testified to the indifference to Lenin's prohibition throughout Russia. From outside the famine zone in Smolensk, the *Pravda* correspondent reported "an ocean of home brew," as entire villages had essentially become spirit-distilling cooperatives, shipping liquor as far as Gomel and Bryansk provinces. From Ivanovo came reports of moonshiners popping up "like mushrooms after a rain." "Everywhere you look, stills" was the word from Kursk. The writer, Anton Bolshakov, reported from Tver that virtually every household in the district was engaged in making *samogon* or home-brew. So prevalent was the practice in Tomsk that state prosecutors simply gave up. Illegal alcohol could even be found in Moscow's kiosks, cafés, and restaurants—usually sold as "lemonade in an unsealed bottle." Even in the shadow of the Kremlin anyone could buy *samogon* by simply "requesting 'lemonade' and winking at the salesman meaningfully."[44]

Much of that liquor was never meant for human consumption. In Petrograd, the workers' committee at the Atlas Metal Works complained that employees "drink methylated spirits, varnish and all kinds of other substitutes. They come to work drunk, speak at meetings, bawl inappropriate exclamations, prevent their more class-conscious comrades from speaking, paralyze organisational work, and the result is chaos in the workshops."[45] In Moscow, many warmed to "Eau-de-cologne No. 3." According to the accounts of soldiers,

> It was nothing but 100-proof alcohol, lightly scented. This eau-de-cologne is sold in flasks of 200 or 400 grams, or in other words: by the half-bottle or bottle.... Soldiers, artisans, clerks and officials stock up on this eau-de-cologne, go into the tea-houses, ask for a bottle of lemonade for the sake of appearances, pour some lemonade into a glass before filling it with cologne. Two flasks of it, and you're drunk.[46]

When vodka—either genuine or bootleg—could not be found, Russians increasingly turned to surrogates. During the revolutionary struggle in Samara, a riotous mob got drunk on printers' ink. Others quaffed shoe polish, rectified varnish, or medical and industrial alcohols. The preferred "drink for intellectuals" in Rostov-on-Don was the local eau-de-cologne.[47] Foreigners frequently noted the lengths to which Russians would go for a drink. As part of his mission in the famine zone, Harold Fleming—a Harvard graduate and Rhodes Scholar—wrote home describing a Russian wedding where the host handed out drinks in cups refashioned from ARA milk cans. "May I never have a disease such as will call for such a combination of fuel-oil, benzine, and kerosine, as that liquor was."[48] Most common was what the Americans called the "k-v cocktail"—a mix of kerosene and vodka, which they occasionally used to replace the gasoline in their supply trucks. There are good reasons that we generally don't drink the same industrial alcohols we use to fuel our trucks, light our lamps or polish our shoes: they are poisonous. Not surprisingly, many Russian revelers fatally succumbed to these deadly surrogates.

The Bolsheviks knew full well about their growing problem with illegal alcohol and about their inability to do anything meaningful to stop it. Nevertheless, the new government continued to heave one rhetorical salvo after another against the evils of alcohol because—practical realities aside—prohibition was an issue of pivotal ideological importance. Often it was left to the founder and commander of the Red Army, Leon Trotsky, to launch such ideological broadsides against vodka.

Before the Revolution, Trotsky was an outspoken critic of the tsar's "drunken budget" that provided up to one-third of state income. Not only did vodka exploit the workers financially, it also distracted the workers from political activism and perpetuated the moral and financial bankruptcy that forever binds them to their capitalist oppressors. "The propertied classes and the state bear responsibility for that culture which cannot exist without the constant lubricant of alcohol," the loquacious Trotsky argued. "But their historical guilt is still incomparably more terrible. Through fiscal means they turn alcohol, that physical, moral and social poison, into the main source of nourishment for the state. Vodka not only makes the people incompetent to manage their own destiny, it also covers the expenditures of the privileged. What a real devil's system!"[49]

The Bolsheviks planned to turn the prohibition they inherited from their imperial predecessors as a weapon against that same system of capitalist alco-oppression. As Trotsky wrote in *Pravda*—the official mouthpiece of the Communist Party—prohibition was "one of the iron assets of the revolution."[50] Without alcohol, Russians could turn to more productive tasks, express their real interests through communist political activism, and bring the state budget in line with the real needs of the people. For it was not simply a change in leadership that the communists had long desired but, rather, a dramatic change in all manner of social relationships. Years of war, revolution, chaos, and disorder destroyed the old capitalist structure of oppressor versus oppressed; the task that remained was to form the culture of a new species—*Homo Sovieticus*—with a culture that glorified modesty, honesty, and sobriety. In this world of reborn labor, the state would tutor society and wean the worker from the vices of old. When it came to alcohol, the bland sermonizing of temperance activism would be replaced with modern amusements promoted by the state—cinema, theater, education, and sports—to enlighten and satisfy the working class and to convince them that they no longer needed vodka to cure their boredom.[51]

So even as the Bolsheviks confronted piles of evidence that their prohibition was ineffective and practical voices called for reinstating the traditional vodka monopoly, temperance was such a crucial tenet of the new ruling ideology that it was difficult to imagine any capitulation to alcohol so long as chief ideologues like Lenin and Trotsky were in charge.[52]

The communists' ironclad commitment to prohibition is even more striking when compared to their ideological concessions to capitalist markets as part of the New Economic Policy, which only exacerbated the problem of black market hooch. Under War Communism, to avoid having their harvests forcibly requisitioned, many peasants turned to distilling. Now given control over their own (after-tax) surpluses, even more of the peasant's grain went to the still.[53] But why would so many risk hard labor or even death if they got caught? Were they just *that* hard-up for a drink?

Surely—to paraphrase Humphrey Bogart's character in *The Roaring Twenties*—there will always be guys wanting a drink, whether in Russia, America, or elsewhere. Basic economic theory suggests (and global experiences confirm) that restricting the supply only drives prices higher and brings the insatiable allure of ever-greater profits along with it. But neither simple economics, nor the inability of the new government to exercise their authority, nor even allusions to the allegedly "eternal" Russian penchant for drink, can explain the widespread proliferation of illegal distillation.

We must consider the role of official corruption—borne of the tsarist vodka trade—which remained entrenched in the early Soviet era.[54] As in the past, most moonshiners knew they had little to fear from the local authorities other than pressure for a periodic bribe. Plus those bribes were repaid with tip-offs about upcoming raids. In many cases, the authorities were themselves complicit in the local alcohol trade, just as in the imperial past. In the first half of 1918, for example, the Commissariat of State Control discovered over thirty places where the local communist governments legalized vodka sales in contravention to the official law. Regional soviets occasionally even fixed local prices for *samogon*.[55]

The collapse of the economy from years of war and devastation also contributed to the illegal practice. For many, their traditional trades—centered on flax, cloth, and grain—had been destroyed, leaving *samogon* as the only viable source of income.[56] What's more, vodka was often not just the source of income and a primary household expenditure; frequently it was the medium of exchange, too. Thanks to hyperinflation, the ruble was worthless. As in earlier centuries when money meant nothing, the value-holding, nonspoiling, easily divisible, and even

In the Fight against *Samogon* (circa 1920s). "Homebrewing ruins peasant farming, destroys a man's health, harms his offspring and leads to crime." The bottle contains statistics on the health of alcoholics, as well as birth defects, while practical equivalents of the 200 million pud (3.3 million metric tons) and 140 million rubles are tabulated at right. Note the priest (holding the icon) and *kulak* atop the still, reveling in the peasant's misery and bondage to the bottle. David M. Rubenstein Rare Book and Manuscript Library, Duke University.

more easily consumable vodka stepped in as a surrogate currency. And as in the past when the economy faltered, Russians turned to unofficial exchanges—barter, *blat*, and *pomoch'* (chapter 8)—just to survive.

In order get a complete picture of conditions in the countryside, in 1923 the high-ranking Central Committee sent an official delegation to interview typical peasants in Kursk province. Their report affirmed the centrality of vodka in village life. "A peasant needs *samogon* or vodka, it does not matter which. For example, if one needs to build a house, one can never find workers; but if there is vodka or *samogon*, you treat the neighbors to it, and the house is soon ready."[57]

That the countryside was swimming in alcohol despite the draconian dry law was hardly surprising to the investigators, nor was vodka's durability as a medium of exchange. If there was one surprise for Moscow, it was how unreceptive the peasantry was of the new Soviets' high-minded cultural revolution. "Do not rely on the peasants in your battle with *samogon*," one interviewee bluntly told the commissars: "Do it yourselves." Such ungrateful—and clearly capitalist—sentiments only confirmed the leadership's suspicions that the conservative peasantry remained ignorant, backward, and a dangerous source of potential counterrevolution.[58]

With the economy finally showing signs of life, in March 1922 Lenin rose before the Eleventh Congress of the Russian Communist Party to defend NEP against critics who saw it as selling out their hard-won communist revolution to the principles of capitalism. With famine raging, Lenin remained resolute that—ideologically unpalatable as it was—NEP's pragmatic concessions were the only way forward. Yet he remained steadfast that there would be no compromise with vodka: "If under present conditions the peasant must have freedom to trade within certain limits, we must give it to him, but this does not mean that we are permitting trade in raw brandy. We shall punish people for that sort of trade."[59]

Lenin's threats were only a prelude: the relatively lax attitude toward distillation in the countryside was soon met by a systemic clampdown. The new 1922 criminal code categorically outlawed private distillation. Anti-alcohol propaganda was ratcheted up. Particularly during the high tide of drunkenness around Christmas and Easter, the Soviets stepped up "shock campaigns" against home brewing. Police conducted more than forty thousand searches in fifty-two provinces during the winter of 1922, busting over twenty-three thousand private distilling and confiscating over sixteen thousand stills. The seventy-eight thousand Easter-time searches the following spring produced similar yields. "Wanted" signs advertised rewards for information leading to uncovering secret operations, and both police and informants were paid handsomely. Statistics from the Commissariat of Internal Affairs recorded 904,078 cases of illicit brewing in 1922–23 alone. Yet moonshining was so widespread that these shock campaigns were—as one observer described it—like "shooting a cannon at sparrows."[60]

Despite the difficulties of enforcement, Lenin held firm to his revolutionary prohibition until the end—which was not long in coming. Less than a month after his rousing defense of NEP and prohibition, in April 1922, a surgeon finally succeeded in removing the bullet that had been lodged in Lenin's neck since an assassination attempt four years earlier. A month after the surgery, Lenin suffered the first in a series of debilitating strokes that threw the country's leadership into disarray. A second stroke in December 1922 paralyzed his right side, at which time Lenin—the illustrious revolutionary leader and unquestioned ruler—withdrew from politics. A third stroke in March 1923 left him mute and bedridden until his death from complications from a final, massive stroke on January 21, 1924, at the age of fifty-three.

The Russian people's worst misfortune was Lenin's birth, later claimed Winston Churchill. "Their next worst—his death."[61] A cult-like veneration of the hero Lenin quickly ensued: the old imperial capital of Petrograd (née St. Petersburg) was quickly renamed Leningrad in his honor. Back in Moscow, Lenin's body was embalmed and put on display in a mausoleum on Red Square, where he has lain—part revered icon and part macabre tourist attraction—ever since.

Lenin's gradual fade from politics cast the future of NEP, prohibition, and the leadership of the country into doubt. With no clear line of succession and no one individual able to fill Lenin's shoes, the party's collective Politburo leadership confronted a decade-long succession struggle from the very first stroke. By the end of the 1920s, the Georgian-born Joseph Vissarionovich Dzhugashvili—better known to the world as Stalin—had outmaneuvered Trotsky and his other rivals to become the unquestioned leader of this newly proclaimed Union of Soviet Socialist Republics (USSR). Many of Stalin's policies were a dramatic break from Lenin's—perhaps none more so than his decision to repeal the prohibition on alcohol and resurrect Russia's centuries-old system of autocratic vodka politics.

15

Industrialization, Collectivization, Alcoholization

"The Russian Peasant may be Illiterate, but he is not what you would call Dumb," noted American satirist Will Rogers in the late 1920s. Equal parts cowboy, actor, comedian, and philosopher, the Oklahoma-born Rogers was the foremost social commentator of the age. Writing in his telltale easygoing, folksy style, Rogers clearly identified the new Soviet regime's most pressing challenge: the peasant.

"He knows what's the use raising anything if you can't trade it or sell it for what you want," Rogers wrote. "Sometimes he hides it; but, anyhow, he is not selling it, and that has got the whole Communistic Party about cuckoo right at this minute." While NEP freed the peasantry to live off the land they cultivated, the problem—as Rogers astutely noted—was that "the old Boys in town has got to get enough nourishment from whatever the farmer raises to make those brotherhood-of-man speeches on. The old farmer just grinds his extra up into Vodka, lays in a lot of wood and hibernates for the winter."[1]

Within the Communistic Party leadership, opinions differed on the vodka problem, which was now inextricably intertwined with other pressing challenges: promoting industrial development and subduing the independence of the peasantry. Even though the Bolsheviks outlawed opposition parties and factionalism within the party itself, policy debates, proclamations, and even rumors were routinely printed in the party's official newspaper, *Pravda*. In September 1922 *Pravda* reported that the government was considering reintroducing the old vodka monopoly in the interest of financial solvency. In the closed-door meetings, Mikhail Kalinin—the nominal head of state—reportedly declared that "we have no choice" about building the new Soviet state on the same *vodkapolitik* principles as the imperial system they worked so hard to overthrow: "we've got to do it!"[2] Yet even while recovering from his first stroke, Lenin was resolutely opposed: vodka would never return so long as he had anything to say about it. But in December 1922 Lenin suffered his second stroke, forcing his withdrawal from politics and intensifying the behind-the-scenes rivalries in the Politburo.

As it turns out, of all the political challenges, the vodka question perhaps most starkly divided his potential successors, Leon Trotsky and Joseph Stalin.

Vodka And The Politics Of Succession

From his deathbed, Lenin dictated a political testament to his wife, Nadezhda Krupskaya, which painted unflattering characterizations of the very Politburo members he had entrusted to rule collectively after his passing. Chief propagandist Nikolai Bukharin: too young. Red Army leader and heir-apparent Leon Trotsky: capable but arrogant. Recently appointed Secretary General Joseph Stalin: too rude. Being in charge of personnel and administration, "Comrade Stalin," Lenin noted, "has unlimited authority concentrated in his hands, and I am not sure whether he will always be capable of using that authority with sufficient caution." As a postscript, Lenin even suggested "that the comrades think about a way of removing Stalin from the post and appointing another man in his stead."[3]

Stalin, however, was a master of interpersonal intrigue, as later scenes around his dinner table would attest. Despite a public facade of unity, throughout the late 1920s Stalin deftly outmaneuvered first Trotsky and then all other Politburo rivals to emerge as the unquestioned leader. As Stalin consolidated power his own policies—especially toward vodka, the peasantry, and industrialization—eclipsed those championed by Lenin and Trotsky.

When it came to liquor, Lenin's apparent successor Trotsky sought to continue his prohibition with unmatched zeal. In a 1923 Central Committee meeting Trotsky condemned building socialism on a drunken budget before declaring: "to develop, strengthen, organize and complete the anti-alcohol regime in the country of reborn labor—that is our task. Our cultural and economic success will increase as alcohol consumption falls. There can be no concessions."[4] Yet behind the scenes, concessions to alcohol were already being made by Stalin, who was busy unseating Trotsky from any position of authority. Light wines had already been legalized in 1921, beer in 1922, and all drinks of less than twenty percent alcohol in early 1923. Still, the legalization of weaker, fermented wines and beers did little to stop the flood of distilled vodka and *samogon* inundating in the countryside.

In chronicling the difficulties of NEP, American journalist Anna Louise Strong dedicated an entire chapter of her *First Time in History* to the Bolshevik war on alcohol. She even interviewed Nikolai Semashko—the diminutive, stubbly bearded Commissar of Health—about the apparent retreat on alcohol:

> We are not bothering with wine and beer yet, because our worst enemy is samagonka, this vile illicit drink that is being made so widely now in Russia. It is against samagonka that our main attack is at present. Wine

is not a worker's or peasant's drink; it is too expensive. It makes a show in the cafés of Moscow and it brings in money to the government. But only the profiteers and the rich can buy it. It is not undermining the health of the masses of the people. So it is not so dangerous as sama-gonka.... But wine also must be stopped eventually.[5]

When, in late 1922, an influential economist suggested reintroducing the vodka monopoly, he was publicly dressed down on the pages of *Pravda* as a dangerous counterrevolutionary. "He proposes to get rid of the bankruptcy in our budget. But he would drive that bankruptcy into the bodies and minds and souls of our people," so spoke the Party. "We have made many concessions because of our poverty, but such a concession as the surrender of our national soberness you will not get. *This shall not pass.*"[6]

In both word and deed, Trotsky led the charge for maintaining and even expanding prohibition, despite its glaring shortcomings. When word came to Military Commissar Trotsky that officers of a distant regiment celebrated the fifth anniversary of the revolution with a wine banquet, he court-martialed not only the regimental commander but also his direct superiors for permitting such lenient attitudes toward alcohol in their ranks. News of every crackdown was broadcast widely as part of the Party's anti-alcohol propaganda. "It is no longer sufficient merely to prohibit; we must organise both repressive and educational measures," Trotsky declared in an interview. In his usual firebrand style he defended the necessity of continuing the fight.

> In the scattered villages, where the peasants are making it at home, it is impossible to use repressive measures on every house. But this industry develops like other [capitalist] industries. Very soon some man, richer and shrewder than the others, begins to make it for sale. He becomes a petty exploiter of vice, a corrupter of his village. The children and the women hate him for taking their food by debauching their men folk. Men like this we can arrest and punish.... As our strength in organisation grows, we can carry our repressions farther. *But no repressions will solve the problem at the root. The basic cause is the emptiness of the peasant's life and this must be filled by higher standards of culture, by education and recreation and wholesome social life.*[7]

It is ironic that within two years the "richer and shrewder" man who would become the corrupter and "petty exploiter of vice" was Trotsky's principal rival, Joseph Stalin. In October 1924, just months after Lenin's death, a meeting of the Central Committee of the Communist Party again took up the liquor question. Even as the corpse of Russia's great revolutionary was being embalmed for display on Red Square, his successors were resurrecting the vodka monopoly Lenin so loathed and the principles of vodka politics he had fought so resolutely against.

"Some members of the Central Committee objected to the introduction of vodka," Stalin later wrote of the debate—most likely referring to Trotsky—"without, however, indicating alternate sources of revenues needed for industry."[8] Twelve months later, on October 1, 1925, the Soviets officially repealed the failed, decade-long experiment with prohibition and returned legal vodka to its historic position as the central pillar of Russian statecraft.

Actually, the new government vodka went on sale four days late, on October 5: since the military draft took place during the first days of the month, the Soviets wisely delayed in the hopes of a more orderly call-up.[9] Yet what ensued was anything but orderly. "It seems that Moscow took the restoration of vodka of pre-war strength as a huge holiday, which had to be properly celebrated," chronicled American communist-turned-dissident William Henry Chamberlin.

> The recent resumption of the sale of vodka at the pre-war alcoholic strength of 40 per cent was the signal for a wild orgy of a considerable part of the Muscovite population. Long waiting lines have been forming outside the shops where the fiery liquor is sold, and it is no uncommon sight to see a customer pull the cork out of his bottle and gulp down the entire contents amid a circle of envious and enthusiastic onlookers. There has been an enormous increase in public drunkenness during the two weeks since the *sorokgradusni* (40 per cent) went on sale. Excessive use of the new stimulant has caused a number of deaths, and the police have had their hands full attending to cases of drunkenness and disorderly conduct. In some cases parties of boisterous merrymakers have boarded street cars and created so much disturbance that they had to be removed by force.[10]

Officially, the vodka monopoly was reinstated in the interests of public health, the same reason as its late-imperial predecessor: with thousands of deaths annually from potent *samogon* and poisonous surrogates, a nationwide monopoly was supposedly the only way to ensure safer, high-quality alcoholic beverages.[11] Naturally, that argument was a red herring: it was not simply *that* the people were drinking, or even *what* they were drinking, that concerned the government but, more importantly, *who* was selling them the liquor and deriving the profits. In the Politburo, Stalin proposed getting the profits out of the pockets of the moonshiners and into the treasury.

Repeal put Stalin in a tenuous ideological position—with the veneration of Lenin at a fever pitch it seemed that his successors were undoing the great revolutionary's work, even as he lay in state in a temporary wooden mausoleum just beyond the Kremlin walls. At a time when every decision had to be justified in terms of Lenin's unquestionable wisdom, Stalin had to argue that Lenin would have supported this most un-Leninist repeal ... somehow.

In a March 1927 letter to a communist named Shinkevich, Stalin claimed that Lenin had actually favored the vodka monopoly. Even in public, storyteller Stalin later explained how, when the government failed to secure badly needed foreign loans at the Genoa Conference in 1922, "Comrade Lenin said several times to each of us that ... it would be necessary to introduce a vodka monopoly, which was particularly necessary to stabilize the currency and maintain industry."[12]

None of the other members of the Bolshevik leadership ever mentioned such conversations with Lenin. It would have been a most memorable discussion, since Lenin was uncompromising when it came to vodka. "Whatever the peasant wants in the way of material things we will give him, as long as they do not imperil the health or morals of the nation," Lenin famously declared late in life. "But if he asks for ikons or booze—these things we will not make for him. For that is definitely retreat; that is definitely degeneration that leads him backward. Concessions of this sort we will not make; we shall rather sacrifice any temporary advantage that might be gained from such concessions."[13]

Although Lenin's words were crystal clear, Stalin stuck to his story—repeatedly claiming that, in private, Lenin secretly told him that it was okay to sell out the moral achievements of the revolution in the interest of state finance. "Which is better: enslavement to foreign capital or the introduction of vodka?" Stalin pronounced. "Naturally, we decided on vodka, because we figured that if we have to dirty our hands a little for the cause of the victory of the proletariat and the peasantry, we would resort even to this extreme in the interest of our cause."[14]

Just one week before formally expelling his rivals Trotsky and Grigory Zinoviev from the Communist Party on November 12, 1927, Stalin gave his final, emphatic argument to an audience of European workers' delegations. When a French representative questioned how the monopoly could be reconciled with the fight against drunkenness Stalin explained:

> In general, I think that it is difficult to reconcile them. There is undoubtedly a contradiction here. The Party is aware of this contradiction, and deliberately created it, fully cognizant that this contradiction is itself the lesser evil. ... Of course, in general, it would be better to do without vodka, because vodka is evil. But that would mean temporarily going into bondage to the capitalists, which is an even greater evil. Therefore, we chose the lesser evil. Today, the state revenue from vodka is over 500 million rubles. Giving up vodka now would mean giving up that income, and there is no evidence to suggest that this would reduce

drunkenness, since the peasants would produce their own vodka, and poison themselves with *samogon*.[15]

Strangely, Stalin concluded his widely reprinted statements to the delegates by blaming *them* for the vodka monopoly, since it was an emergency response to the Soviets' inability to secure Western loans. "I think that we would probably not have to deal with the vodka question or many other unpleasant things, if the West-European proletariat took power into their hands and gave us the necessary assistance. But what is to be done?" Stalin mused. "Our West-European brothers apparently do not want to take power yet, so we are forced to do the best we can with what we have. But that is not our fault, it is fate. So as you can see, some of the responsibility for the vodka monopoly lies with our West-European friends."[16] His playful foreign scapegoating was reportedly met with laughter and applause.

It was a much different situation for Stalin's domestic scapegoats: his previous Politburo rivals and their followers. Old Bolsheviks Lev Kamenev and Grigory Zinoviev were expelled from the party alongside Trotsky in 1927, only to be put on show trial as foreign spies plotting a "Trotskyist" conspiracy to overthrow the government. Their executions in 1936 marked the beginning of the Great Purge, as thousands of loyal communists were arrested and killed on trumped-up charges in order to stamp out dissent within the Communist Party. Meanwhile, while in exile in Mexico, Trotsky remained a prolific writer and scathing critic of Stalin's totalitarianism as selling out the true principles of communism...that is, until an undercover Stalinist agent smashed his skull with an alpine climbing axe in 1940.

Seemingly, Winston Churchill aptly compared Soviet power struggles to bulldogs fighting under the carpet: "An outsider only hears the growling, and when he sees the bones fly out from beneath, it is obvious who won."[17]

Vodka And Industrialization

Once firmly ensconced in power, Stalin radically and fundamentally recast virtually every aspect of Soviet life. All elements of this extreme social makeover—including crash industrialization, a revolution in culture, war on the peasantry, totalitarian terror, and Stalin's personality cult—reinforced each other.[18] Yet historians have largely overlooked how vodka politics helped hold together such disparate cultural, social, economic, and political transformations.

According to Karl Marx, communist revolution was the inevitable response to the hardships of industrial capitalism. So the only socialist civilization ever envisioned was an industrial one. The Bolsheviks were well aware that their Russia

was overwhelmingly rural and understood the need to industrialize rapidly—
the bigger and heavier the industry, the better. Even as the Soviets recovered
from war and famine, ambitious plans were devised to accelerate productivity
and make the young state militarily self-sufficient, culminating in the First Five-
Year Plan in 1928. To meet such goals (a year early!) by 1932, the economic
planning agency Gosplan dictated a ludicrous expansion of iron, steel, coal, and
oil output—necessary to build armaments, tanks, tractors, railways, and heavy
machinery.

Rapid industrialization required two things that Stalin lacked: money and
men. More to the point, it necessitated a source of investment revenue and a
competent, disciplined urban workforce. Vodka was crucial to both—and Stalin
knew it.[19]

A communist pariah in a still-capitalist world, the Soviet Union could not get
investments or loans from abroad, so they turned instead back to the vodka trade
that had provided inexhaustible revenues to their imperial predecessors. If Stalin
is to be believed, the move was done primarily for industrialization. "When we
introduced the vodka monopoly, we were facing the alternatives: either go into
bondage to the capitalists, having ceded to them a number of our most important plants and factories, getting in return the necessary funds to allow us to carry
on; or to introduce the vodka monopoly in order to get the necessary working
capital for developing our own industry with our own resources, and avoid going
into foreign bondage."

By the end of 1927, it was already paying dividends: "The fact is, immediately
abandoning the vodka monopoly would deprive our industry of over 500 million rubles, which could not be replaced from any other source," Stalin then
claimed. That translated to ten percent of all state revenues. To hear him explain
it, the monopoly was only a temporary improvisation, and "it must be abolished
as soon as we find new sources of revenue in our national economy for the further development of industry."[20]

Apparently Stalin never found those new sources of revenue. As vodka
production rapidly increased, so too did alcohol's contributions to the
state budget: rising from a mere 2 percent of Union revenues in 1923–24
to 8.4 percent in 1925–26 and fully 12 percent of all income by 1927–28.[21]
These increases resulted in quite a problem of national drunkenness. In
a letter to the liquor monopoly Gosspirt, the finance ministry admitted
that vodka revenues could barely cover the harm it was causing the country. From 675 million rubles in 1927–28, by 1928–29, the letter projected,
"we should net 913.7 million rubles and 1,070 million by 1929/30. Yet the
demands of common sobriety require minimum budgetary revenues from
vodka. Herein lies our present trouble and future problems."[22] Herein, again,
lies vodka politics.

The finance ministry was right to focus on sobriety. Drunkenness bedeviled efforts to build the disciplined, urban workforce needed to man the new assembly lines, iron works, railways, and hydroelectric stations—all built on a gigantic scale. Certainly forced labor provided one answer, as the greatest engineering accomplishments of the Stalin era—from the White Sea Canal to the towering spires of Moscow State University—were largely built by the slave labor of those condemned to the gulags. But the incredible growth of the urban working population—from 26 million in 1926 to 38.7 million in 1932—primarily reflected the forced migration of peasants from the countryside: the same conservative peasantry the communists long suspected of potential counterrevolution; the same rural peasantry that long persisted in distilling their grain into *samogon* rather than giving it to the state; the same illiterate and unskilled peasantry that had a long tradition of insobriety.[23]

By the late 1920s—with Stalin becoming the unscrupulous tavern keeper for all of Soviet society—the People's Commissariat of Labor, or Narkomtrud, suffered the biggest hangover. With the flood of uneducated and intoxicated peasants into the workforce Narkomtrud charted a staggering drop in workplace discipline. Few workers showed up on time, and when (or if) they did, they were often hungover. They could not work the machinery and did not care to learn, a situation leading to waste, broken equipment, and shoddy products. Narkomtrud was inundated with reports of absences, drinking on the job, drunken fistfights, and assaults on factory managers and party representatives.[24] Rank-and-file communists hardly set the example of the honest, sober new "Soviet man" the ideologues had envisioned. As the recruitments of the 1920s transformed the Communist Party from a small vanguard of intellectuals and activists to a mass party of millions, rampant alcoholism became a major problem for the party itself. Since drunkenness was considered a petit bourgeois remnant of the past, the party regularly purged itself of "drunks, hooligans, and other class enemies" in the interest of party discipline.[25]

To promote workplace discipline, the Soviets turned to propaganda. In 1928, Gosplan co-founder Yury Larin and famed theorist Nikolai Bukharin spearheaded a diverse group of politicians, war heroes, writers, poets, and academics in creating the Soviet Union's first temperance organization, the Society for the Struggle against Alcoholism (OBSA).[26] The OBSA focused on improving the dismal conditions in the sprawling urban slums, which were eerily reminiscent of the grinding poverty and desperation of capitalist Europe's industrial working classes that Marx and Engels decried a century earlier. Temperance admonishments peppered the pages of *Pravda*, *Izvestiya*, and a new monthly journal, *Trezvost i kultura* (*Sobriety and Culture*).[27]

Yet temperance was never an end in itself—it was only a means to greater discipline necessary for industrialization. Such well-meaning temperance activism

DOWN WITH DRUNKARDS! (1930). "Down with drunkards we say loudly: from drunkards come only hooliganism and breakage." I. Yang and A. Cernomordik.

was tolerated only so long as it did not interfere with Stalin's greater aspirations. In this respect, Soviet temperance was doubly doomed.

Kate Transchel—the leading historian of the OBSA—noted "it is significant that Bukharin, who is generally accepted as the party's leading theorist after Lenin's death, chose the anti-alcohol movement through which to attack the problems of Soviet society."[28] It is also significant that within a few months of founding the OBSA, Bukharin (who was Stalin's last rival within the Politburo) was disgraced as part of the "Right Opposition." A decade later—suffering the same fate as Kamenev and Zinoviev's "Left Opposition"—Bukharin was put on show trial on trumped-up sedition charges, tortured into confession, and executed.

With Bukharin gone, the OBSA stood little chance against Stalin's unquenchable need for more vodka revenues. In 1930, the society was scuttled, and the problem of alcoholism in the Soviet Union quietly disappeared from official discourse. *Trezvost i kultura* abruptly explained to its readers that there was no longer a need to combat alcoholism since "the socialist way of life would destroy drunkenness." Beginning with the very next issue, the magazine would be known as *Kultura i byt—Culture and Lifestyle*—which vocally denounced OBSA founders Larin and Bukharin as antigovernment demagogues.[29]

Just like Stalin brushed aside Bukharin as an impediment to his single-minded quest for absolute power, he also brushed aside the OBSA as an impediment to his all-out expansion of the industrial and military might of the Soviet state. In complete opposition to his publicly professed desire to "completely abolish the vodka monopoly," on September 1, 1930, Stalin wrote in a letter to Vyacheslav Molotov, then the loyal first secretary of the Moscow Communist Party, that

> I think vodka production should be expanded (*to the extent possible*). We need to get rid of a false sense of shame and directly and openly promote the greatest expansion of vodka production possible for the sake of a real and serious defense of our country. Consequently, this matter has to be taken into account *immediately*. The relevant raw material for vodka production should be formally included in the national budget for 1930–1931. Keep in mind that a serious upgrade of civil aviation will also require a lot of money, and for that purpose we'll have to resort again to vodka.[30]

Two weeks later, the question of maximizing the liquor output was taken up by the Politburo. Strangely, archival records of the Politburo's discussions and decisions of that day were submitted to the so-called special file—reserved for the most secret documents in the Soviet Union. Now housed in the Presidential Archive of the Russian Federation, these documents remain highly classified and strictly off limits to historical researchers.[31]

Vodka And Collectivization

If industrialization was the foremost ideological challenge of the late 1920s, the primary practical challenge was the peasantry. Here too the issue turned on vodka. During the reconstruction from war and famine, agricultural productivity rebounded more quickly than industrial productivity. This makes sense, since you don't have to rebuild a field like you do a factory: simply plant the seeds, till the soil, and come fall you've got crops. In the past, there was an urban-rural trade cycle: the peasants sold their grains to buy goods manufactured in the cities. Only now there was nothing to buy because the factories were still in ruins. By 1923, the Soviet Union was in the middle of what Trotsky dubbed the "scissors crisis": the prices of scarce industrial goods were rising while the cost of the now-plentiful agricultural goods was plummeting—when plotted on a graph, the diverging prices looked like the two blades of an open pair of scissors.

According to most historians, rather than get next to nothing for their crops, the peasants simply hoarded them. That is a half-truth. Since piles of grain easily rot and are difficult to conceal from the authorities, most peasants didn't just hoard their grain; they distilled it. Bottles of *samogon* did not spoil, they were more easily concealed, and they could be consumed or used to bribe local authorities. Plus, since home-brewed vodka could be sold at a black market price that was far higher than the abysmally low price of grain, the terms of trade became more even. Consequently, every time agricultural and industrial prices diverged, the Russian countryside was flooded with illegal alcohol, even as food-stuffs disappeared from store shelves in the cities.[32]

In the early 1920s, the government first tried to crack down on bootleggers throughout the countryside. When it became apparent that the crackdown did not work, they threw up their hands and reimplemented the vodka monopoly, which also generated the resources needed for industrialization. As Chamberlain described it:

> The official justification for the legal return of vodka is that all efforts to prohibit it broke down as a result of the widespread drinking of *samogon*, or home-brewed vodka, which sometimes attained an alcoholic strength of 70 per cent and was considered more harmful than vodka, both in its physical effects and in its waste of grain. The euphemistic explanation for the return of vodka is that it is a "means of fighting *samogon*." While this consideration doubtless carried weight, the action of the government was also influenced by the fact that the Russian peasant is reluctant to part with his grain until he sees something which he may buy with the money which is paid him. It is expected that vodka will help to full up the void which is created by the shortage of manufactured goods.[33]

Even with a functioning—and lucrative—vodka monopoly, the artificially low price of grain produced another so-called scissors crisis in 1927. Although grain production had almost recovered to prewar levels, less than half was being brought to market, leading to food shortages in the cities and *samogon* surpluses in the countryside. A 1927 official study estimated that the rural Russian population annually consumed an average of 7.5 liters of *samogon* per capita—four times their consumption of legal state vodka.[34] This was the dilemma that American satirist Will Rogers described as driving the Soviet government cuckoo. "If you got that Vodka for a companion you got a mighty ally on your side when it comes to forgetting your troubles," Rodgers said of the Russian peasantry. "They can live on what the raise, and drink the surplus and enjoy it."[35] By the Soviet government's own account, illegal distillation was consuming no less than thirty million *pud* (491 million kilograms) of grain every year.[36] Something had to be done.

The response to this scissors crisis would be different from the last—much different. Rather than concede to the peasantry, as Lenin did with NEP, Stalin used this crisis as a pretext for all-out class warfare against the peasantry through a brutal collectivization campaign which—by the estimates that Stalin later confided to Winston Churchill at Potsdam—cost over ten million lives. For Stalin, forcing peasants into modern agricultural communes—oversized, mechanized, and rationalized—was the only way to forever smash the power of the conservative peasantry, eliminate the threat they posed to the food supply by moonshining, and drive out the ideological threat of agricultural capitalism in the countryside.[37]

"The struggle for bread is the struggle for socialism," Stalin declared. The opponent in this struggle was the *kulak*—the class of "rich" peasants that Stalin slated for complete and ruthless liquidation. The line between a (bad) *kulak* and a (good) poor peasant was blurry, leaving the regime tremendous leeway in eliminating suspected opponents. Meanwhile, locals settled private scores by ratting out neighbors as an alleged *kulak* and, thus, an enemy of the people.[38]

Viewed through the lens of vodka politics, strangely, this blurry distinction actually comes into crisper view. Being a *kulak* was not just about having marginally more land, livestock, or "surpluses" than other peasants—it was also about debauching poorer peasants with *samogon*. Indeed, going back to the earliest days of the revolution, *kulak* was virtually synonymous with bootlegger, since bootlegging was the primary means of peasant enrichment. Even in May 1918, when the Russian Republic's government passed its decree on the "Granting of Emergency Power to the People's Commissar of Produce for the Struggle against the Rural Bourgeoisie, Which Conceals Grain Supplies and Speculates with Them," moonshiners and *kulaks* were indistinguishable as counterrevolutionary enemies of the people.[39]

"In many places," explained Committee Chairman Yakov Sverdlov, "the *kulak* elements lure the poorest peasants to their side by inviting them to share in the profits from moonshine. The entire countryside, entire villages, entire rural districts are captured by the spirit of drunkenness; so in order to destroy the corrosive influence of the *kulak* elements by any means, we are sending punishment expeditions and death squads from the cities to these districts to destroy the bootleggers by force."[40]

This association of *kulak* with profiteer and bootlegger continued under NEP, as the path to wealth in the countryside was paved with vodka bottles. The most prosperous *kulaks* did not hoard grain but distilled it into more profitable *samogon.* This association was even apparent in Soviet propaganda movies of the 1920s, in which "the *kulak* and the priest are never portrayed without a bottle of vodka in their hands." (Even according to the cinematic journal of the day, *Sovetsky ekran,* this portrayal was ineffective even as propaganda "because the peasant knows that it is not only the *kulak* who drinks home brew."[41])

The food shortage of 1927 prompted a return to forcible grain requisitions a la War Communism—only more brutal. When the grain deliveries to the state fell short by two million tons in 1928, Stalin was incensed that the harvests were being "hoarded" by *kulaks.* The demands for 1929 would be even greater.

Local Communists Party delegates—aided by the Red Army, NKVD secret police, and self-appointed committees of resentful, poorer peasants—infiltrated the countryside, arresting *kulak* hoarders and looting their wares. Many alleged *kulaks* were deported to Siberia; others were summarily executed. The enforcers were hardly the principled communist idealists state propaganda made them out to be: they were terrorist bands of cynical opportunists, addicts, and drunks— not unlike the *oprichniki* of Ivan the Terrible. At mass execution sites, including the infamous KGB firing range at Butovo (on the road to Podolsk just south of Moscow)—where today more than twenty thousand victims of the terror of the 1930s are thought to lie in mass graves—barrels of free vodka numbed the senses of the secret police. Execution brigades drank as much as they pleased. Others sought vodka from the victims themselves—either through appropriation or extortion. Untold millions of *kulaks* were imprisoned or executed as part of what Stalin heralded as a "great break" with the imperial past.[42]

For the marauding hordes, "for a glass of vodka or a bottle of *samogon,* a kulak could be transformed into a poor peasant or, in the absence of a glass of vodka or a bottle of *samogon,* a poor peasant could be transformed into a kulak," so subjective was the distinction, and so pervasive the corruption amid the murderous chaos.[43]

According to economic historian Alec Nove (born Alexander Novakovsky),

> Those engaged in the process of dekulakization were known to requisition and drink any vodka found in the kulak house. Orders were issued to stop such behaviour. But what could the government expect? There were few reliable party members in the villages and they had to utilize and encourage any ragged ruffians who could be prevailed upon to expropriate and chase out their better-off neighbours (in the name of the class struggle, of course).[44]

In some cases, having collected whatever *kulak* crops could be found in a particular district, some requisition brigades themselves distilled the grain into *samogon* instead of turning it over to the state.[45]

WHAT MOONSHINE CONSUMES IN ONE YEAR (1930). Train transporting annual quantities of grain, potatoes, and flour either to the grain factory or a moonshine distillery. Hoover Institution Archives, Stanford University.

By way of resistance many *kulaks* reverted to a scorched-earth policy, destroying everything they owned rather than hand it over to the state: in 1928 there were 70.5 million head of cattle in the Soviet Union; by 1933 there were only 38.4 million. The number of pigs dropped from 26 million to only 12 million. "Farmsteads were burned down, machinery wrecked in Luddite fashion, rail and truck transports taking peasant grain away were sabotaged, home brewed vodka was consumed to the point of stupor, and livestock was slaughtered en masse."[46] Soviet agriculture would not fully recover until the 1950s—to say nothing of the incalculable human toll. Forewarned, some *kulaks* opted instead for suicide, entire families at a time.[47]

By 1930, collectivization had taken on a life all its own. With unimaginable speed, over sixty percent of peasant households had been forcibly uprooted and swept into the massive collective farms. Afraid the rampage of terror in the heartland might threaten the spring planting—possibly producing another famine—on March 2 Stalin called for a temporary halt, blaming local authorities for the bloody excesses of collectivization: "Some of our comrades have become dizzy with success," Stalin famously wrote, "and for the moment have lost clearness of mind and sobriety of vision."[48]

This pause allowed the Soviets to consolidate their gains before later resuming a less chaotic collectivization offensive. The entire peasantry was collectivized in four years, with private agriculture completely abolished by 1937. Even after being transformed into state farms akin to massive rural factories, collectivized agriculture suffered the same labor discipline problems of drunkenness, absenteeism, and "wrecking" that bedeviled the urban factories.

The Soviet Union paid a tremendous toll for Stalin's twin campaigns of industrialization and collectivization. Between the terror, purges, collectivization, and a devastating terror-famine in the agricultural heartland stretching from Ukraine to northern Kazakhstan (which Stalin naturally blamed on *kulaks* hoarding and distilling grain), the long-suffering Soviet people endured an unrivaled demographic nightmare. With the power of the peasantry broken and collectivization completed, in 1937 the state conducted a nationwide census. Surprisingly, there were roughly fifteen million fewer people in the country than the government originally estimated. Stalin reacted as only a totalitarian despot can: the secret police suppressed the figures and had the census statisticians arrested as "Trotskyist-Bukharinist spies" and shot.[49]

The Great Patriotic War

It is impossible, within the space of a few of pages, to do justice to the unfathomable hardships endured by the Soviet people during the Second World War. In the United States, famed television journalist Tom Brokaw praised American wartime sacrifices by dubbing those who came of age during the Great Depression and the Second World War as "the greatest generation any society has ever produced."[50] Not to disparage their hardships and tribulations—much less the loss of four hundred thousand Americans and another four hundred thousand British soldiers (comprising less than one percent of the population) who did not return from the global battles against fascism—these sacrifices pale in comparison to the horrors on the Eastern Front, where Adolf Hitler was ultimately defeated. More than twenty-four million Soviets—or fourteen percent of the entire population—were sacrificed there. In other words, for every American or British wartime death, more than fifty Soviets paid the ultimate price. Having built a world superpower from scratch while sacrificing millions more to Stalin's totalitarian terror, crash industrialization, gunpoint collectivization, famine, civil war, and revolution, the Soviet people have a legitimate claim to being an even greater generation. Such heroic sacrifice and endurance makes a discussion about alcohol seem almost trivial.[51]

Yet even in a time of unimaginable sorrow and loss, there was vodka.

We have already heard the tale of the liquor-soaked 1939 Kremlin meetings with the Nazis that produced the Molotov–Ribbentrop nonaggression pact, which secretly divided most of Central and Eastern Europe between the two totalitarian titans (chapter 1). As international tensions increased, so too did alcohol consumption in the Kremlin. While observing an uneasy peace with the German fascists to the west, Stalin mended fences with the fascist Japanese foe to the east as well. When Japanese foreign minister Yosuke Matsuoka visited Moscow in April 1941 to meet with Stalin, according to contemporary accounts, "They both got most gloriously drunk and a Pact of Non-Aggression and Neutrality was signed between them."[52]

Indeed. The weekly Trans-Siberian Express that would carry the Japanese delegation home had to wait for an hour and a half at Moscow's Yaroslavsky station before the foreign minister stammered in with an inebriated entourage...including Stalin himself. Stalin was rarely seen in public, and certainly never drunk. Yet according to one journalist, "Stalin went up to the aged and diminutive Japanese Ambassador-General, punched him on the shoulder rather hard, with a grin and an 'ah...ah', so that the General, who has a bald and freckled pate, and is not more than four feet ten in height, staggered back three or four steps, which caused Matsuoka to laugh in glee."[53]

According to the astonished Bulgarian ambassador, the "least drunk" of the participants at the send-off was Molotov—stammering a few feet behind Stalin, "saluting all the time, shouting: I am a pioneer, I am ready!" in the manner of the Soviet youth league.[54]

Yet the Soviet leadership was anything but ready when two months later, on June 22, 1941, Hitler unleashed Operation Barbarossa—the largest and most deadly military operation in human history. As part of the Nazi *blitzkrieg*, over three million Axis troops spilled into Soviet-held territories from the Baltic to the Black Sea. Decimated by endless purges, the Soviet high command was in disarray and incapable of mounting a meaningful defense. On the first day of the invasion twelve hundred Soviet planes—most of the Soviet air force—were destroyed; most were still on the tarmac, having never engaged in combat.[55]

For eleven days Stalin—who had received ample and reliable intelligence about the imminent Nazi attack—was nowhere to be seen. The great leader's conspicuous absence prompted widespread rumors that he was in shock, demoralized, and drunk. Why else would it be left to the uninspiring Molotov to rally the people to war?[56]

Even after Stalin's return, mayhem reigned at the front. Panicked Soviet troops fled east before the German advance. Cities like Kiev witnessed scenes of wild drunkenness, as mobs set upon state liquor stores and looted the houses of evacuees.[57] Within weeks Nazi forces occupied all of present-day Moldova, Ukraine, Belarus, and the Baltic states and were rapidly advancing across the vast Russian heartland: encircling Leningrad in the north, encroaching toward Moscow, and pushing toward an epic confrontation at Stalingrad on the Volga. Stalin dealt with insubordination in the army with characteristic brutality—dispatching

NKVD forces to shoot any soldier who fell back from the line and executing any commander who ordered retreat.

Today, as then, the epic battle to defeat Hitler is not known in Russia as World War II but, rather, as the Great Patriotic War: a surprising title since the communist tenets of Marx and Lenin were antithetical to nationalism. Appeals to patriotism were only one reversion to the traditions of Russia's imperial past. Soviet wartime propaganda valorized epic heroes from Russian history, including Sergei Eisenstein's cinematic depictions of Alexander Nevsky and Ivan the Terrible. Moreover, within the Red Army the traditional daily vodka ration—gone since Nicholas's ill-fated prohibition in the previous world war—was reintroduced. "At Stalin's personal order," wrote historian Constantine Pleshakov, "28 million men were given a glass of vodka a day for four years, thus ensuring that the next generation would be fully trained to function in an inebriated nation."[58] One hundred grams of vodka per day equated to roughly fifteen liters of pure alcohol per year for every soldier. To provide upwards of a billion liters of vodka annually, Soviet vodka factories ran full tilt day and night, much like the armaments factories—both producing badly needed war materiel.[59]

"When a person gets drunk, he feels more determined, more courageous," claimed World War II historian Fyodor Sverdlov. "He doesn't think about being killed in a minute. He marches on, trying to kill the enemy. Being quite frank, I have to say that in the course of the whole war both Germans and Russians were always drunk at decisive moments because a human mind cannot otherwise bear the horrors of modern war."[60] Now certainly, as members of modern, well-regimented armies, the belligerents weren't *always* drunk in battle. Still, such accounts are a useful counterweight to the popular image of the rational, resolved, and clear-headed war hero.

By August 1941 the overextended Nazi advance stalled, as Soviet defenses and resolve hardened, due to both the harsh discipline and vodka. Soviet soldiers—often loaded up with more alcohol than munitions—displayed reckless bravery: desperately charging German lines, inflicting massive casualties on both sides.[61]

Justified or not, the obvious consequence was an upsurge of drunkenness in the trenches. According to Russian vodka historian Boris Segal:

> Soldiers in the Soviet army would offer their last piece of bread to their comrades in order to get vodka, but it was impossible to find men who were willing to give up their own daily vodka ration. When Russian servicemen captured German medical supplies, they drank everything, just as during the Civil War: aftershave lotion, medicines, and even liquids containing poisons.[62]

While the troops drank their courage in the trenches, Stalin's drunken Kremlin debauches continued unabated. But rather than regale German and Japanese delegations, the new guests were British, French, and American. Western missions to the Kremlin hoped to size up their newfound Soviet allies, to whom they were providing military, economic, and humanitarian support instead of opening a western front against Hitler. As the Nazi bombardment encroached ever closer to the Russian capital in December 1941, *Life* magazine told of the Kremlin banquet for visiting American and British military delegates, with "Uncle Joe" Stalin as toastmaster. The reporter's scoop was that the atheist dictator of a godless Soviet juggernaut actually raised his glass in praise of President Franklin D. Roosevelt, with the words "May God help him in his task." Only in passing did the reporter mention that somewhere between thirty and thirty-six other rounds were drunk before Stalin brusquely concluded the festivities by announcing to his foreign guests: "The lavatory is on the left." Then, in English, "Good night."[63]

When Winston Churchill's representative Anthony Eden conducted high-level negotiations with Stalin in December 1941 that helped pave the way for Churchill's visit to the Kremlin the following year (chapter 1), he was surprised by the Kremlin's lavish spread. While the people suffered and battled the German onslaught outside the delegates drank round after round of vodka, wine, and champagne toasts—including Eden's toast to Stalin's health on his sixty-second birthday. According to his accounts, longtime defense minister Kliment Voroshilov "got so drunk that he fell across Stalin's knees," while Marshall Semyon Timoshenko—the man in charge of defense of the central front—had been drunk for much of the day. "Stalin seemed rather embarrassed at the signs of this," Eden noted, "and said quietly to me: 'Do your generals ever get drunk?' to which I replied, I hope diplomatically, 'They don't often get the chance.' "[64]

Fourteen hundred miles overland from Berlin, Hitler's eastward advance was finally stopped at Stalingrad in 1942. Beyond the city's obvious symbolic significance, situated on the Volga, Stalingrad was the last major barrier to the vast oil wealth of the Caspian. Stalin declared that it must be defended at all costs. On July 28, 1942, he issued Order 227 declaring *Ni shagu nazad!*—not one step back. "It is necessary to defend to the last drop of blood every position, every meter of Soviet territory, to cling on to every shred of Soviet earth and to defend it to the utmost."[65] By the bitter-cold February of 1943, some two million combined Soviets and Nazis lay dead, as Hitler's war machine was dealt a decisive blow from which it would never recover.

Ni shagu nazad! became the rallying slogan of ultimate patriotic sacrifice—putting the interests of state and motherland above all else. Perhaps not surprisingly, then, it was also used as the name of one of the best-selling Soviet vodkas.

After Stalingrad, Soviet forces gradually reconquered Nazi-occupied territories, where the Germans had ruthlessly executed Jews, communists, partisans, and other undesirables. The Nazis had little patience for drunkenness, so occupied cities were mostly dry—in stark contrast with the rural areas, which continued the tried-and-true practice of distilling grain into *samogon* instead of handing it over to the authorities. The fields and forests provided protection for "partisans"—remnants of destroyed Red Army units, communist activists, underground resistance movements, and even regular army detachments sent behind enemy lines—all engaging in guerrilla warfare to disrupt Nazi communication, transportation, and occupation. Even amid the Nazi brutality and wintertime food shortages, alcohol was everywhere. "It was amazing how [the partisans] could get *samogon* from their relatives and friends in the villages," recalled A. Lewenberg. "With each trip they took a chance of being arrested, tortured, and killed; but they did it regularly; and each time we had a great celebration, everybody, including me, an 11-year-old Jewish boy, had to drink this terrible liquid."[66]

Even once these Soviet saboteurs were reined in by the Kremlin their drunkenness remained a pressing security issue. On January 23, 1943, NKVD kingpin Lavrenty Beria wrote to Stalin and Molotov with reports that the partisan brigade in Volhynia (northwestern Ukraine) was "on the rampage; they get drunk, terrorize and rob friendly civilians, among them those whose families are our fighters. After I intervened, the battalion commander and commissar promised me these anti-Soviet activities would stop, but they take only hesitant action and try to shield those acting like thugs."[67]

By 1944–45, the Red Army liberated Eastern Europe on their way to toppling Hitler himself. Once in Germany, Soviet officers and soldiers looted houses and liquor stores; avenging German atrocities in Russia with arson, rape, and murder. The Soviet occupiers were confused as to why the German population did not join them in the drinking and looting. Initially, the high command looked the other way when confronted with complaints of Soviet revelry before gradually tightening discipline.[68]

On April 30, 1945, the Soviet flag was unfurled over the German Reichstag— the same day Hitler shot himself in a Berlin bunker—effectively concluding the war in Europe. This was the Soviet peoples' crowning achievement. Over the space of twenty years the Soviet Union had been transformed from a famine-ravaged failed state to a global superpower. But for this, the people endured incalculable human suffering. In addition to the twenty-four million souls lost to the Great Patriotic War, nine million were executed or died in Siberian gulags, and another six million died from collectivization, dekulakization, and famine.[69]

At a well-lubricated, postwar banquet for his Red Army commanders, Stalin drank the last of many toasts...to the health of the Russian people. Close to an apology for his incapacity at the outbreak of the war, Stalin admitted that his regime had made tremendous mistakes. "Any other people would have told their government 'you have failed to live-up to our expectations. So go away and we will install another;" he said. The "confidence of the Russian people in the Soviet government was decisive in securing the historic victory over that enemy of humanity—fascism." And with that, Stalin—both penitent and grateful to his people—sealed his dedication with vodka.[70]

Early on, Stalin recognized the necessity of building Soviet power upon the traditional foundation of autocratic statecraft in Russia: vodka. This was a central tenet not only of his power struggle with political rivals like Trotsky but also of his dramatic economic reforms. Resurrecting the vodka monopoly both smashed the power of the peasantry and facilitated their forcible collectivization; it also provided the revenue necessary for the massive industrialization campaign. Alongside fear, vodka was a useful instrument of totalitarian terror: just as Stalin used fear mixed with alcohol to keep potential opponents in his inner circle inebriated, suspicious, divided, and unable to mount a challenge to his authority, he likewise kept the Soviet people scared and drunk, creating the docile and prostrate civil society characteristic of a totalitarian system. In all of these ways vodka politics contributed not only to the Soviet Union's greatest triumphs but also its most unspeakable tragedies.

Perhaps at no other time in Russian history did these diverse dynamics associated with vodka politics intersect so readily as they did under Stalin; yet Soviet alcoholization is rarely mentioned alongside its better known counterparts—industrialization and collectivization—even though arguably its economic, political, social, and demographic legacies are just as enduring.

16

Vodka and Dissent in the Soviet Union

After World War II, Soviet power effectively stretched from the Elbe River in Germany to the Pacific Ocean. With Mao Zedong's victory over the Chinese nationalists, communism was on the march globally. In 1949, the Soviets detonated their first atomic weapon to join only the United States in the elite club of nuclear powers, as the rift between the capitalist West and socialist East solidified into Cold War standoff.

Behind the scenes of Stalin's seemingly unstoppable juggernaut, the Soviet economic system was in tatters. The people were exhausted from years of total war, terror, collectivization, and famine. Some twenty-five million souls were lost to the war against fascism; another twenty-five million were left homeless. Grain production was only half what it was before the Nazi invasion, and a series of postwar droughts produced yet another famine. Unlike the United States—where the 1940s and 1950s ushered in a golden era of prosperity and a "baby boom" fathered by victorious G.I.s returning from foreign battlefields, the Soviet Union experienced just the opposite: a "baby bust." Of the millions lost to war, famines, and purges, most were men of working age. Women could not find husbands. Children were raised without fathers. An entire generation virtually vanished.[1]

In the postwar Soviet Union image rarely corresponded to reality: military might was built atop ruined socioeconomic foundations; the public's adulation of Stalin masked the all-pervasive private fear of his totalitarian regime; high-profile technological accomplishments overshadowed an economic system that could not meet basic social needs. Here again, the lens of vodka politics helps distinguish fact from fiction in the communist colossus. From the 1940s through the 1980s, not only was alcohol just as essential to autocratic statecraft as it had been under the tsars, but so too did pointing out the pervasiveness of vodka become a central tactic for dissidents and critics of Soviet autocracy.

Liquor And The Thaw

In February 1956—three years after the death of Stalin—his successor Nikita Khrushchev took the first step in confronting Stalin's totalitarian legacies by delivering the so-called "Secret Speech" to the Twentieth Congress of the Communist Party. Before a closed session of party elites, for four hours past midnight, a sullen and tempered Khrushchev criticized Stalin's personality cult, the wholesale deportation of national minorities, and his ruthless purges of the party and military. The speech began a decade-long thaw in Soviet society, culture, and even foreign policy. Censorship was eased, consumer-based economic reforms were enacted, and millions of political prisoners returned from Siberian gulags.

One exonerated former prisoner was an aspiring writer, Aleksandr Solzhenitsyn. A twice-decorated military commander, Solzhenitsyn was arrested in 1945 during the Red Army's German offensive for making derogatory comments about comrade Stalin. After being beaten and interrogated by the NKVD at the Lubyanka Prison, he was convicted for counterrevolutionary activity under the infamous Article 58 of the penal code and sentenced to eight years hard labor—the brutality and senselessness of which he would describe in a string of scathing, historically based novels. His first—*One Day in the Life of Ivan Denisovich*—was published in 1962 with the personal blessing of Khrushchev, who defended it before the Politburo as social catharsis: "There is a Stalinist in each of you," Khrushchev railed, "there's even some of the Stalinist in me. We must root out this evil."[2]

Ivan Denisovich was a hit—not only in the West, where it highlighted the severity of Soviet human rights violations, but in the Soviet Union, too. Just as during Russia's literary golden age of the nineteenth century, government censorship still prevented direct criticism of the state and its leaders, but literature still provided a veil for political discussions. And just as under the tsars, critics seized upon vodka politics as a way to confront the Soviet autocracy.

If the 1960s were the new 1870s, then certainly Solzhenitsyn was the new Tolstoy: beyond their similar physical stature, both were war heroes-turned-historical dramatists, both were prolific writers, both wrote biting condemnations of the ruling autocracy that made them influential moral authorities, and—notably—both were teetotalers whose rejection of alcohol fundamentally conflicted with the autocratic political system. Even battling Nazis in the trenches, where "vodka consumption was second only to battlefield courage as a mark of valor," Solzhenitsyn still refused to drink.[3]

Like Tolstoy, Solzhenitsyn's social criticisms are drenched in vodka. One of his earliest novellas, *Matryona's House*, describes Soviet rural life in the 1950s but is strikingly reminiscent of imperial days. The hero, Matryona, reluctantly

consents to give up part of her tiny hut to her relatives, who want to use the wood
for their house in a village twenty miles away. While the men tear down part
of the house, the women distill *samogon*—as women traditionally did—as payment for the ten men hauling the wood on a borrowed tractor. After a boisterous
evening of drinking, even Matryona joined the men on their ill-fated, drunken
escapade. In the middle of the night, the narrator staying in Matryona's humble
cottage is visited by police, demanding to know whether the group had been
drinking. Knowing "Matryona could get a heavy sentence for dispensing illicitly
distilled vodka," the narrator lies to the officers at the door, even while the foul
stench of half-drunken bottles of moonshine wafted in from the kitchen. As the
police leave, they let it out that Matryona and the drunken men were killed by a
train as the tractor got stuck on a railroad crossing.[4]

Beyond the usual array of drunken characters and drinking parties,
Solzhenitsyn's *Cancer Ward* (1968) also highlights the use of poisonous alcoholic surrogates—as intoxicant or folk medication—for inmates facing termi-
nal cancer.[5] He also uses vodka to take jabs at the systemic corruption. While
lamenting that officials always expected bribes simply to perform their assigned
duties, one worker worried that if they did not " 'come across' with a bottle of

DON'T DRINK METHYL ALCOHOL! (1946). "Methyl alcohol (wood spirits) is a
dangerous poison."

vodka," the bureaucrats "were sure to get even, to do something wrong, to make her regret it afterwards."[6] (Solzhenitsyn wasn't alone in linking vodka and Soviet corruption: when referring to *khrushchoby*—the shoddy four- or five-story tenements hastily built during the Khrushchev years—the popular joke was that some only have four stories because the fifth was stolen and sold for vodka.)[7] All the same, like those of Tolstoy, virtually all of Solzhenitsyn's works use drunken tragedy to both expose the autocracy and share the author's disdain for drinking.

Unfortunately the cultural, political, and social openness of the Khrushchev era was doomed by the bombastic premier's domestic gaffes and foreign policy fiascoes. To Mao Zedong in China, Khrushchev's "Secret Speech" was a sell out, and his de-Stalinization was misguided, and this disagreement drove a wedge between the two communist giants. *Détente* with the Americans was sidetracked by one crisis after another: the downing of an American U-2 spy plane in 1960, the construction of the Berlin Wall in 1961, and finally the 1962 Cuban Missile Crisis, which pushed the world to the brink of thermonuclear war. Meanwhile, Khrushchev's domestic reforms went nowhere. His vaunted campaign to transform the arid Kazakh steppe into rich farmland turned to dust. All this, when added to his brash and erratic behavior, such as his embarrassing shoe-banging incident at the UN, culminated in Khrushchev's forced retirement in October 1964. His replacement, Leonid Brezhnev, put a quick end to the "thaw"—clamping down on expression and opposition. The eighteen years of Brezhnev's rule, from 1964 until his death in 1982, was an era of *zastoi*, or stagnation, in the economy, arts, and society.

Brezhnev embodied the corruption, decay, and drunkenness that mushroomed in Soviet society under his tutelage. Dour and stodgy, he had none of the in-your-face exuberance of Khrushchev. Some of his closest associates depict Brezhnev as an unstable and increasingly senile alcoholic who, in failing health, stumbled into such disastrous decisions as the Soviet invasion of Afghanistan in 1979.

Anatoly Dobrynin—the Soviet ambassador to the United States—seemed particularly irked by Brezhnev's incessant drinking, especially since he was usually on the receiving end of the general secretary's drunken, late-night, prank calls on the Kremlin's hotline to the Soviet embassy in Washington. After Brezhnev's death, his longtime foreign minister Andrei Gromyko was asked whether Brezhnev had a serious drinking problem. "The answer," he replied after a reflective pause, "is Yes, Yes, Yes." Gromyko admitted "It was perfectly obvious that the last person willing to look at this problem was the general secretary himself."[8]

Brezhnev's alcoholism was a product of his rise through the military under Stalin. The morning after Brezhnev's extremely well-lubricated seventieth birthday celebration in 1976, advisor Anatoly Chernyaev remembered how—still visibly intoxicated—Brezhnev waxed nostalgic for getting drunk during the Stalin years. Brezhnev reminisced how, as a Red Army hero, he got so hammered at Stalin's World War II victory banquet that he stopped in the Kremlin courtyard and carried on a meaningful conversation with the *tsar-kolokol*—the world's largest brass bell, which was cast in the eighteenth century but dropped and broken before it could ever be rung.[9]

For dissident writers like Solzhenitsyn, tightening censorship under Brezhnev not only forced their writings underground; it also sharpened their criticisms. The KGB kept him under close surveillance and routinely seized his manuscripts, and the world-famous writer could no longer find a willing publisher. In 1969 Solzhenitsyn was expelled from the Union of Writers. The following year he was awarded the Nobel Prize in Literature, which he could not accept for fear of not being allowed to return home to the USSR. Sheltered by a secretive circle of underground friends, Solzhenitsyn secretly worked on his magnum opus, the three-volume *Gulag Archipelago.* Completed in 1968, *Gulag* was a bombshell—chronicling not only the unimaginable hardships in the camps but also the entire system of political repression from arrest, detention, and interrogation to transportation and incarceration. Smuggled out of the country to be published abroad (*tamizdat*—literally "publishing over there") in late 1973, it was hailed by America's foremost Kremlinologist-diplomat George F. Kennan as "the greatest and most powerful single indictment of a political regime in modern times."[10]

On September 5, 1973, Solzhenitsyn candidly wrote to Brezhnev, articulating what he saw as the most pressing challenges for the Soviet leadership both at home and abroad. With surprising audacity, Solzhenitsyn described the malaise in the economy, dilapidated collective agriculture, outdated military conscription, the exploitation of women, the lack of societal morality, and a destructive corruption that pervaded the entire Soviet system. "But even more destructive is vodka," continued Solzhenitsyn's Tolstoyan indictment of the state's complicity in the alcohol trade.

> So long as vodka is an important item of state revenue nothing will change, and we shall simply go on ravaging people's vitals (when I was in exile, I worked in a consumers' cooperative and I distinctly remember that vodka amounted to 60 to 70 percent of our turnover). Bearing in mind the state of people's morals, their spiritual condition and their relations with one another and with society, all the *material* achievements we trumpet so proudly are petty and worthless.[11]

Solzhenitsyn was a nationalist and Slavophile who viewed the alien, European ideology of Marxism–Leninism as the root cause of all of Russia's ills—corrupting the spirituality and the morals of the people through "that same old vodka."[12]

Brezhnev never wrote back, but the Kremlin responded in other ways. In February 1974—five months after penning his letter—Solzhenitsyn was arrested, stripped of his citizenship, and deported. He ultimately settled in the secluded hills of Cavendish, Vermont. Though Solzhenitsyn was persona non grata in the Soviet Union, his works were published to greater acclaim abroad and were often smuggled back in to the Soviet Union where his—and other dissidents'—banned works were circulated and reproduced by hand through underground networks in a process known as *samizdat*—or self-publishing.

With Solzhenitsyn in exile, the main dissident voice in the USSR belonged to Andrei Sakharov—nuclear physicist and father of the Soviet hydrogen bomb. Sakharov's early warnings of the dangers of nuclear holocaust gave way to a broader criticism of the oppressive Soviet system itself. Like Solzhenitsyn, he was denounced as a traitor by his government. Like Solzhenitsyn, Sakharov wrote brazen letters to the Kremlin leadership—and also like Solzhenitsyn, Sakharov took particular issue with Soviet vodka politics. "Our society is infected by apathy, hypocrisy, petit bourgeois egoism, and hidden cruelty," Sakharov wrote in a second letter to Brezhnev in 1972. "Drunkenness has assumed the dimensions of a national calamity. It is one of the symptoms of the moral degradation of a society that is sinking ever deeper into a state of chronic alcohol poisoning."[13]

Increasingly famous for advocating democracy and human rights, Sakharov understood alcohol's centrality to the system of repression: trapped in fear, unable to emigrate, and deprived of a voice in politics, the dissatisfied Soviet people turned to "internal protest" that takes on "asocial forms": drunkenness and crime. "The most important and decisive role in maintaining this atmosphere of internal and external submission is played by the powers of the state, which manipulates all economic and social control levers. This, more than anything else, keeps the body and soul of the majority of people in a state of dependence."[14] That the state itself profits from this dependence, while the people grapple with the social, health, and criminal consequences only compounds the tragedy. Accordingly, in his letters and statements, Sakharov railed not only against the death penalty and torture but also for education and healthcare reform and remedying the alcohol problem.

Sakharov was long aware of the pervasive liquor problem. His *Memoirs* describe working at a munitions factory during World War II, recalling "with horror the day a roommate of mine came back from his shift after drinking a cupful of the methyl alcohol used in the plant. He became delirious and went berserk. Half an hour later, he was taken away in an ambulance, and we never saw him again."[15]

In addition to the more-or-less conventional stories about rewarding workmen with drink or drunken hotel brawls, he also explained how the prodigious academics involved in the Soviet atomic bomb project gave the straight-laced

Sakharov lessons in drinking pure 100 percent alcohol. He described how in
the 1960s government procurement officers flew in helicopter loads of vodka
to swindle Siberian trappers hunting in the rugged north. "After a few days the
trappers and their parents, wives, and children would all be drunk, and the helicopter would fly off with furs for export."[16]

Following the 1982 death of Leonid Brezhnev, Sakharov straightforwardly
condemned Soviet vodka politics.

> Drunkenness is our great national tragedy; it makes family life a hell,
> turns skilled workers into goldbricks, and is at the root of a multi-
> tude of crimes. The rise in drunkenness is a reflection of social crisis
> and evidence of our government's unwillingness and inability to take
> on the problem of alcoholism. More recently, cheap fortified wines
> have become the favored means of turning people into drunkards and
> siphoning off surplus rubles.[17]

It is worth stepping back for a moment to appreciate the bigger picture here.
Despite deep philosophical differences between Sakharov and Solzhenitsyn,
these two greatest dissidents of the age were both teetotalers.[18] Neither feared
confrontation with General Secretary Brezhnev, who—like all the heirs of
Stalin—was a drop-dead alcoholic. In a country where few abstained from
drink, both understood and condemned Russia's vodka addiction as central to
an autocratic system that denied individuals their basic human rights and hindered their personal fulfillment.

A Surreal Ride

While Solzhenitsyn and Sakharov were the reluctant celebrities of the Soviet dissident movement, many poignant social criticisms were written under assumed
names and disseminated through the *samizdat* underground. My all-time favorite is a short 1968 novel by Venedikt Erofeyev called *Moskva-Petushki*, sometimes translated as *Moscow to the End of the Line*. David Remnick, editor of the
New Yorker, called it "the comic high-water mark of the Brezhnev era" and picked
it as his favorite obscure book.[19] It is easy to see why.

Moscow to the End of the Line may well be the first work of gonzo journalism. A satirical firsthand account steeped in humor, sarcasm, and copious pro-
fanity, it is a Soviet *Fear and Loathing in Las Vegas* written three years before
Hunter S. Thompson's descent into drug-addled hallucinations while searching
for the American dream in the desert southwest. In Erofeyev's counterpart we

follow the vodka-, sherry-, wine-, vermouth-, and eau-de-cologne-swilling alco-holic Venya, who has just spent his last kopecks on a suitcase full of liquor "and a couple of sandwiches so as not to puke" for the train ride from Moscow to his much-embellished childhood home of Petushki some eighty miles distant.[20] Did Venya ever find what he was seeking? We may never know. As reality melts into drunken hallucination, only his blackouts seem definite.

Even before the alcoholic haze sets in, Venya describes getting canned as fore-man of a cable-laying crew for playfully charting his comrades' alcohol consump-tion. "We pretend to work, they pretend to pay us," was the unofficial motto of the *zastoi* era, which Venya took to the extreme.

> In the morning we'd sit down and play blackjack for money. Then we'd get up and unwind a drum of cable and put the cable underground. And then we'd sit down and everyone would take his leisure in his own way. Everyone, after all, has his own dream and temperament. One of us drank vermouth, somebody else—a simpler soul—some Freshen-Up eau de cologne, and somebody else more pretentious would drink cognac.... Then we'd go to sleep.
>
> First thing next morning, we'd sit around drinking vermouth. Then we'd get up and pull yesterday's cable out of the ground and throw it away, since, naturally, it had gotten all wet. And then what? Then we'd sit down to blackjack for money. And we'd go to sleep without finishing the game.
>
> In the morning, we'd wake each other up early. "Lekha, get up. Time to play blackjack." "Stasik, get up and let's finish the game." We'd get up and finish the game. And then, before light, before sunrise, before drinking Freshen-Up or vermouth, we'd grab a drum of cable and start to reel it out, so that by the next day it would get wet and become use-less. And, so, then, each to each his own, for each has his own ideals. And so everything would start over again.

Erofeyev's satire wasn't much of an exaggeration. In a fitting epitaph to the entire era of Brezhnevite stagnation, a loaded Venya utters his sodden trib-ute: "Oh, freedom and equality! Oh, brotherhood, oh, life on the dole! Oh, the sweetness of unaccountability, Oh, that most blessed of times in the life of my people, the time from the opening until the closing of the liquor stores."[21]

The *samizdat* underground didn't just disseminate trenchant works of fic-tion—much nonconformist literature was academic: historical, economic, social, and political critiques of the autocratic system in which alcohol played a major role.

Lies, Damned Lies, And Soviet Statistics

The official position of the Communist Party on any question of significance was articulated in the *Big Soviet Encyclopedia*. When it came to its drinking problem, the official line was that the Soviet Union was a largely temperate nation, steadily working to eliminate the alcoholism that was a remnant of the capitalist past: "In Soviet society alcoholism is considered an evil, and the fight against it is carried on by the state, Party, Trade-Union, and Komsomol (Communist Youth League) organizations and health agencies. Great importance is attached to measures of social influence, to raising the cultural level of the population, and to overcoming the the so-called alcoholic traditions which exert an influence on the youth." Apparently they were making great strides: the official Stalin-era consumption figure of 1.85 liters of pure alcohol per person annually was far below the 5.1 liters in the United States or the 21.5 liters in France.[22]

When it came to the central paradox of vodka politics, namely, the state's profiting from the alcohol trade: "vodka prices are fixed by the Soviet state at a level which facilitates the struggle against alcoholism," if we are to believe the official line. "In the USSR the production of vodka is not governed by fiscal purposes and the income obtained from selling it accounts for an insignificant proportion of the state's revenue."[23]

Well, if the first step in Khrushchev's thaw was his "Secret Speech" of February 1956, perhaps the second came three months later with the publication of the Soviet annual statistical handbook, *The National Economy of the USSR*. This statistical digest stood on the reference shelf of virtually every research library in the Soviet Union and abroad. They were flawed and incomplete, but for those who knew where to look, these figures told a dramatically different tale from the official narrative.[24] *Samizdat* researchers in the Soviet Union and a small cadre of foreign specialists used these government data to highlight the gaping chasm between image and reality in social well-being.

The most detailed study was undertaken by a shadowy academic known only as A. Krasikov, who wrote a series of underground articles declaring vodka "Commodity Number One" in the Soviet Union. As it turns out, A. Krasikov was a pseudonym of former *Izvestiya* reporter Mikhail D. Baitalsky—whose true identity was only revealed after his death in 1978. "The late M. D. Baitalsky may rightly be considered one of the most talented publicists of contemporary, nonconformist, native literature," declared his *samizdat* obituary.[25] A Trotsky devotee, he secretly chronicled efforts to oppose Stalin's rise in the 1920s. In the Great Purge of the 1930s Baitalsky was fired from *Izvestiya*, denounced by his wife, and sent to the notorious forced-labor camp at Vorkuta. Following a brief "respite" to the Eastern Front in World War II, he was sentenced to work in the scientific institute described in Solzhenitsyn's *First Circle* before being released in 1956 during Khrushchev's thaw.

Like Solzhenitsyn and Sakharov, Baitalsky was a teetotaler who was alarmed that instead of combating alcohol as state propaganda claimed, the Kremlin was ramping up production to unprecedented levels. By 1960 vodka output was already double prewar levels, while beer production had quadrupled—and this according to the government's own statistics![26] The official State Statistical Commission (Goskomstat) abstracts showed the upward march not only of alcohol production but also of a whole raft of related social indicators that did not bode well for the Soviet public—crimes, suicides, abortions, and even infant mortality numbers were actually increasing rather than decreasing.

When Khrushchev was ousted in 1964, the thaw in Soviet statistics ended as well. With vodka factories running full tilt, and Goskomstat chronicling the consequences, Brezhnev simply halted the publication of such embarrassing statistics. But that did not deter Baitalsky.

Unlike the unflattering statistics on infant mortality that simply vanished without a trace, Baitalsky noted that as soon as the statistical column on "alcoholic and non-alcoholic beverages" disappeared, a separate column for "other foodstuffs"—which typically included spices, soybeans, mushrooms, and vitamins—suddenly expanded tenfold. If the state statistical handbooks are to be believed, by 1970 Soviets were spending 27 billion rubles every year on these "other foodstuffs," of which he estimated that 23.2 billion was spent on vodka.[27]

Baitalsky also noted a staggering rate of growth in this miscellaneous category in contrast to the usually stable expenditures on spices, soybeans, and the like. Comparing these estimates with the other consumer expenditures—from household furniture to printed publications—he deduced that, at some twenty-three billion rubles spent per year, "Alcohol is, indeed, the leading commodity among all those purchased by our people. It has become Commodity Number One, with Number Two ('clothing and underwear') and Number Three ('meat and sausages') lagging behind not by half a length, not by half a billion rubles, but by 9 and 12 billion respectively."[28]

Somehow, Baitalsky got his hands on an in-house report from Glavspirt, the chief administration of the alcohol industry. Even omitting beer, wine, illicit home brew and poisonous surrogates, these government figures on per capita vodka consumption (figure 16.1) show a dramatic—and damning—expansion of state alcohol production interrupted only by the horrors of total war. Against the Kremlin's data blackout, even such fragmentary figures demonstrate both the staggering increase of alcohol consumption and the government's role in promoting it. Back in the tsarist era in 1913, Russians drank an average of 7.75 liters of pure alcohol per year. While the Soviets claimed that alcoholism—as a remnant of the capitalist past—would wither away under communism, even

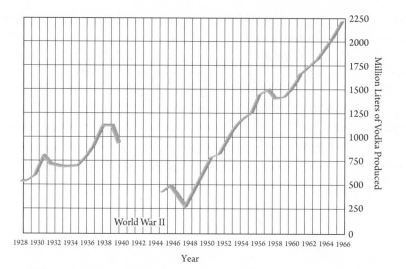

Figure 16.1 LEGAL VODKA PRODUCTION IN THE SOVIET UNION, 1928–1966.
Source: Mikhail Baitalsky [A. Krasikov], "Tovar nomer odin," in Roy A. Medvedev, ed.,
Dvadtsatyi vek: Obshchestvenno-politicheskii i literaturnyi al'manakh, vol. 2 (London: TCD
Publications, 1977), 118.

after fifty years of "withering," in 1967 the Russians were quaffing up to 9.1 liters
of pure alcohol per person annually from state vodka factories alone.[29]

Baitalsky further underscored vodka's centrality to the autocratic state, esti-
mating that more than ninety kopecks from every ruble spent on vodka went
directly into the treasury, making vodka both the single largest and most lucrative sector of the entire Soviet economy.[30] For the government, vodka is the perfect commodity.

> Alcohol does not go bad, as meat and butter do, does not turn sour,
> like milk, does not go out of fashion, like clothes and footwear, does
> not require such elaborate packaging as china and porcelain. It has no
> need of refrigerators. It can be transported easily.... Alcohol does not
> demand much shop space: a single counter served by one shop-assistant
> will bring a food store a larger trade turnover than ten other counters
> with ten other shop-assistants. And, finally, stock-taking—that opera-
> tion which testifies to the degree of trust which our state has learned
> to place in its trading apparatus—is incomparably easier to carry out
> where alcohol is concerned.[31]

While Russian autocrats and their motivating ideologies changed dramatically
over the centuries, vodka politics has remained the fundamental pillar of the

Russian state. Even while communist ideologues denounced the feudal roots of tsarist/capitalist oppression of the masses, the Soviets hypocritically embraced this core mechanism of psychological subjugation and financial exploitation through vodka. Of the entire 156-billion-ruble annual budget of the Soviet superpower, some eighteen billion—or twelve percent—was the net profit from the sale of vodka, wine, and beer. This amount could cover all expenditures on universal healthcare (9.3 billion) and their vaunted programs in science and technology (6.6 billion) with two billion to spare. Moreover, given the inelastic demand for alcohol, if the government felt a budget crunch it simply increased the price. "A bottle which yesterday cost 2 rubles today costs 2 rubles 10 kopecks—and by then end of the year, a billion more rubles are lying on the little saucer with the blue border," as Baitalsky put it.[32] No wonder a famous Russian allegory depicts Soviet finances as an island—*terra alcoholica*—defended by three whales: the ministry of trade (Mintorg), the State Planning Commission (Gosplan) and the ministry of finance (Minfin).[33]

Hard data were crucial because they were so rarely reported. Soviet journalists rarely made up stats, but they were masters of spin. As a former journalist, Baitalsky was well-versed in such trickery. When it came to potentially embarrassing statistics the Soviets relied on misdirection: reporting absolute statistics for foreign foes but only relative figures for the USSR. For example, Soviet reporters eagerly seized on "imperialist" Britain's annual police reports of over a million crimes annually as evidence of Western decadence. They would compare that to a glowing report claiming that in the glorious USSR—as a percentage of all violent crime—murder plunged twenty percentage points (from, say, thirty percent to ten percent) from last year.

Catch the trick?

It *sounds* like the Soviets are doing better than their British rivals in tackling crime—but they aren't. Think about it: if murders went from thirty percent of violent crimes to ten percent of violent crimes, all that means is that violent crimes that *weren't* murders increased from seventy percent to ninety percent—which is to say it doesn't tell us anything meaningful at all. While such stories were meant to ridicule British criminality, the real lesson was that—unlike in the Soviet bloc—in the West, the police were accountable to the people and that even embarrassing information was being reported openly for all to see.[34]

This was why nonconformist researchers combed statistical abstracts and arcane periodicals, pouncing on any statistics that weren't couched as percentages of something else—especially concerning alcohol. "The significance of these figures is confirmed most convincingly by the very fact that they are concealed," Baitalsky explained. "Unimportant facts are not hidden so carefully. On the other hand, the concealment of factual material concerning the question of drink hinders from the outset any attempt to fight against the increase in the consumption of alcohol, for society cannot combat an evil without knowing its locations and its dimensions."[35]

Like most Soviet- and imperial-era critics, Baitalsky saw societal drunkenness as a symptom of a deeper, political disease: autocracy. Whether discussing crime or falling labor productivity, he claimed that vodka alone was not

> the soil from which these phenomena grow. That soil is something different, which we are not allowed to name, and I shall not touch upon it. Alcohol serves as a sort of fertiliser. It is spread over and dug into the soil from which these phenomena grow. We sow the seed, and we produce this fertiliser on a generous scale and sell it at a big profit in the hundreds of millions of bottles, accompanying our trade with unctuous newspaper articles about the harmfulness of alcohol.[36]

Compounding the usual health and criminal consequences were the willingness of the state to lie through misinformation and a prostrate civil society's complacency in accepting this state of affairs as somehow normal.[37] This was not a product of the ruling ideology—capitalist or communist—but rather came from an unresponsive autocratic system, which had long used vodka to keep the people disoriented while profiting handsomely from their misery. And if sunshine is the best disinfectant—as the old cliché goes—then where better to start than by confronting such secrecy? That is exactly what Baitalsky had in mind. In his memoir, *Notebooks for the Children*, he writes:

> Who is helped by keeping statistics a secret? The most unpleasant figures (honest figures, and not a percentage as compared with last year!) mobilize society. Hiding the scope of evil is the major reason for indifference to it. For all the savagery of the censors, truth cannot always be concealed.... The snow on a city sidewalk melts slowly from the sun all by itself. But scrape a bit of the sidewalk down to the asphalt and the black surface will begin to warm from the sun, and the snow—inch by inch—will begin to disappear. It is important that a thirst for knowledge be awakened in our youth; and the snow will not last for long.[38]

In a harbinger of things to come, he argued that revealing the truth about Soviet social and economic statistics in general—and those that concern alcohol in particular—would beget systemic reform of the autocracy itself. It is unfortunate that he died just a few short years before his prophecy came true.

Mirrors From Abroad

Dissidents weren't the only ones frustrated by the lack of meaningful political information. At a time when foreign Kremlinologists—and Soviet citizens— sought clues about Politburo struggles by scrutinizing their seating arrangements for May Day parades atop the Red Square rostrum (which allegedly hid spreads of vodka and hors d'oeuvres), dedicated researchers in Washington sifted through mountains of reports for reliable statistical information.[39]

One such scholar was Murray Feshbach—an unassuming, owl-eyed researcher toiling for the U.S. Bureau of the Census—who had logged, tagged, and cross-referenced every tidbit of data on Soviet social problems since the 1950s. Little known beyond an "invisible college of specialists," as an in-depth 1983 *Atlantic Monthly* article described him, Feshbach stood out as "one of the more unusual and, in his way, indispensable students of the Soviet Union."[40]

Daily pouring over every bit of new social and health information published in dozens of Soviet newspapers, professional magazines, obscure health and economic journals, and hundreds of books annually, no other American matched Feshbach's encyclopedic knowledge of the Soviet Union. His biggest frustration was the same numerical sleight of hand that infuriated Baitalsky: "I used to admire the Soviets," Feshbach said with a chuckle. "They could write a book of 500 pages and not say a single thing, not *one thing*. It was beautifully done; you really had to admire it. How could they do it? Lo and behold, they did."[41]

Feshbach was a master of confronting Soviet deceptions with their own data. Sure, some indicators were no longer published for the Soviet Union as a whole—but in many cases they could still be found at regional and local levels, reported in distant media reports or arcane Soviet academic journals. First at the census department and later at Georgetown University (where your humble author had the distinct pleasure of working as his research assistant), Feshbach's offices famously overflowed with piles of clippings from Russian newspapers, research bulletins, subscriptions to little-known Soviet trade journals, and even a mimeographed copy of Baitalsky's original *samizat* manuscript of "Commodity Number One," written under the pseudonym A. Krasikov.[42]

For more than half a century the boisterous and self-effacing Feshbach was the unofficial chronicler of the afflictions of Soviet, and then post-Soviet, society. In addition to a raft of insightful publications, Murray's enthusiasm and investigations inspired a multitude of scholars writing about Russia, including the one you are currently reading. "Guys like this are diamonds," explained author and *New York Times* journalist Hedrick Smith, who won a Pulitzer Prize in 1974 for his reports on the Soviet Union. "Reporters have learned that his feeling for the place is accurate, so they go back to him."[43]

<u>Russkaia mysl'</u>(Paris) Dec.27,1984,p.1-2

СССР

80 МИЛЛИОНОВ
АЛКОГОЛИКОВ
к 2000 году?

Московское бюро Агентства Франс-Пресс получило текст доклада об алкоголизме в Советском Союзе, составленный, как сообщает АФР, социологами Сибирского отделения АН СССР (Новосибирск) для высшего партийного руководства. Подлинность данных, приводимых в тексте, к сожалению, не вызывает сомнений. Резкие эмоциональные оценки, цитируемые в депеше АФП, тоже впечатляюще подлинны — единственно, что смущает, так это вопрос, способны ли советские исследователи, даже глубоко и остро переживающие национальное бедствие, пойти на риск откровенного высказывания своих взглядов (а не только представления сухих, но красноречивых цифр) в докладе, имена авторов которого, безусловно, известны там, куда этот доклад подан (или где он был заказан). Тем не менее, никак не следует исключать возможность и такого рода гражданской отваги.

Окончание на стр. 2

Начало на стр. 1

По данным доклада, в 1980 г. Советский Союз насчитывал 40 миллионов алкоголиков и хронических пьяниц, состоящих на официальном учете. Число «клинических алкоголиков» составляет 17 миллионов, остальные считаются просто «сильно пьющими».

Каждый год, говорится в докладе, водка убивает миллион человек. Потребление водки возросло с 5 л на человека в год в 1952 г. до 30 литров в 1983-м. Если эта нарастающая тенденция сохранится — в 2000 году на каждого советского человека, без различия пола и возраста, придется 50 л водки в год, и страна будет насчитывать 80 миллионов алкоголиков и горьких пьяниц.

Впрочем, пьют и так «без различия пола и возраста». Новосибирские ученые ссылаются на результаты обследования, проведенного в 1979 году: регулярно пьют 99,4% мужчин и 97,6% женщин, притом 95% девушек младше 18 лет. АФП сообщает, что газета «Сельская жизнь» опубликовала заметку, в которой указывается, что девять десятых тех, кто проходит первый в своей жизни курс антиалкогольного лечения, не достигли 15 лет, а треть — десяти.

Рост алкоголизма резко повышает как детскую смертность, так и число рождений умственно неполноценных детей. Детская смертность за двадцать лет возросла на 47%: 7,1 на тысячу человек населения — в 1960 г., 10,4 — в 1980-м. Детская смертность в СССР на 50% выше, чем

TYPICAL DOCUMENT FROM THE MURRAY FESHBACH COLLECTION. This 1984 *Russkaia mysl'* article discusses a report from the Soviet Academy of Sciences in Novosibirsk claiming that—if present trends continued—the average Soviet citizens in the year 2000 would drink fifty liters of vodka per year and that the USSR would have eighty million alcoholics. The handwriting at the top, declaring "Murray, have you seen this? Very interesting!" and "agrees with my estimates" on alcohol consumption, belongs to Vladimir Treml. Feshbach's pencil highlights the link between the rise in alcoholism and infant mortality, the 1979 Siberian report that 99.4% of men and 97.6% of women drink regularly, including 95% of girls under the age of 18, and that of those receiving anti-alcohol treatment for the first time, 90% were not yet 15, and one-third were not yet ten years of age. Author's personal collection.

Despite his appearances on *60 Minutes* and C-Span and in *People* magazine, Feshbach's name is not widely known, perhaps because his most provocative claims were as technical and modest as he was.[44] In September of 1980 the Census Bureau in Washington released an unassuming report titled "Rising Infant Mortality in the USSR in the 1970s," co-authored by Christopher Davis and Murray Feshbach. The level of infant mortality is a primary barometer of national health in any country. In the 1950s and 1960s the Soviets proudly touted their falling rates as evidence of tremendous social progress. But when the numbers started trending in the opposite direction in the 1970s—like with alcohol data—the government did their best to hide them.

Cobbled together from a myriad of sources, the finding that the rate of infant deaths was not only rising but rising *dramatically* (up thirty-six percent from the beginning of the decade to 31 deaths per 1,000 live births) was a sensational— but well-reasoned—claim. The sudden reversal was attributed to a combination of social, economic, health, and medical factors, with maternal alcohol abuse foremost among them. Drawing from his vast archive of evidence, Feshbach even quoted Soviet health experts who linked rising infant mortality to rising alcoholism and the growing reliance on abortions (the average Soviet woman had six during her lifetime) in lieu of birth control. One Russian study concluded that the mortality rate of infants born prematurely to drinking mothers with previous abortions was thirty times higher than that of full-term infants.[45]

The unassuming report caused an uproar. Back in Moscow, the Soviet planning agency Gosplan convened a rare press conference to dismiss the findings while state news broadcasts denounced the "lurid reports" from abroad. Yet without any fanfare, the Soviet Union's longtime health minister, Dr. Boris V. Petrovsky, was suddenly relieved of his position. In subsequent C-Span television appearances, Feshbach dug up and cited Petrovsky's own research that bluntly labeled alcoholism as "Illness Number Three" among Soviet women— just behind cancer and heart disease.[46]

Despite the bluster of Cold War politics, Russian scholars were keenly interested in such research. In the wake of the report, Duke University economist Vladimir Treml was cordially introduced—and warmly received—in Moscow as a "collaborator of Murray Feshbach" before the Institute of Economics of the Academy of Sciences of the USSR.[47] With a shared interest in alcohol's economic impacts, Treml and Feshbach were longtime colleagues—sharing evidence, arguments, and manuscripts. Throughout the seventies and eighties Treml sought the truth about Soviet alcohol: What was being drunk? How much? And what were the consequences for the treasury and the people?

The first problem was simply determining how much people drank—combining both state vodka and illegal home brews (*samogon*). Treml developed models of Soviet *samogon* consumption—accounting for urban-rural

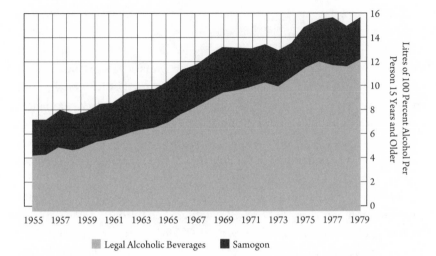

Figure 16.2 VLADIMIR TREML'S PER-CAPITA ESTIMATES OF LEGAL VODKA AND SAMOGON CONSUMPTION IN THE SOVIET UNION, 1955–79. Source: Vladimir Treml, *Alcohol in the U.S.S.R.: A Statistical Study.* Duke Press Policy Studies. (Durham, N.C.: Duke University Press, 1982, 68.

population indexes (since home distilling was primarily done in rural areas), slicing-up the "other foodstuffs" statistics a la Baitalsky, and double-checking against regional consumption of sugar, flour, potatoes, and sugar-beets—the usual ingredients in illicit moonshine. His results—suggesting that the average drinking-age Soviet citizen imbibed thirty percent more than official production figures—is presented in figure 16.2. Such rigorous estimates were corroborated by Soviet statisticians, anecdotal evidence, interviews with Russian experts, and even defectors from Soviet officialdom. Even today Treml's estimations are cited widely in Russia as more accurate than Soviet government statistics: Treml captured not only the true scope of the alcohol problem but also the magnitude of the black market that the Soviets had been battling since the very first hours of communist rule.[48]

These findings were even more damning than the brouhaha over Davis and Feshbach's report. Based on the greater harmfulness of the potent, low-quality *samogon* and the culture of drinking to stupefaction, Treml boldly announced to the Soviet academy that the upsurge of alcohol consumption was accompanied by a spike of alcohol poisonings to the tune of fifty thousand fatalities per year or over one hundred times higher than the rate in the United States.[49]

These revelations were damning... or they would have been had they been acknowledged. Instead, foreign studies of Russian drinking were held in only a few Soviet libraries—and even in those, books like Treml's *Alcohol in the U.S.S.R.*

were kept under lock and key in *spetskhran*—the secure section—officially off limits to all but the most well-connected researchers.[50]

Why was the government going to such lengths to cover up this epidemic? Having met privately with Soviet academics, Treml later recalled their callous explanation: "the authorities are aware of the problem, but they want these alcoholics to die" in order to relieve the state's burden in caring for those beyond rehabilitation.[51]

Outlandish? Perhaps. Yet with vodka contributing nearly one-quarter of all government revenue—or enough to cover the entire defense budget of the Soviet superpower—the state's budget needs were always paramount. So much so, Treml claimed, that "no anti-alcohol measure can be contemplated without considering its impact on tax earnings."[52]

"This is what Vlad Treml has called the 'fiscal dilemma,'" Feshbach replied to a question on Soviet alcoholism during a 1985 C-Span call-in television show. "The average per capita consumption of alcohol between 1952 and about 1980 has increased by about six times in the Soviet Union, and again, most of it being hard liquor." Murray was on a roll—a seemingly endless twelve-minute ramble of facts, figures, and anecdotes without pause or punctuation. "The dilemma is do you supply alcohol or vodka or whatever, or do you stop that and then make people complain about other things—and they might complain even more than they are. And here it seems to be that it just is increasing dramatically."[53]

Despite the official line of a sober and prosperous socialist future, nobody was buying it—at home or abroad.

Is Anybody Listening?

From the victory over Hitler in 1945 through the stagnation of the early 1980s, Soviet alcohol sales increased eightfold. Social, health, economic, and criminal statistics deteriorated accordingly—to say nothing of the unquantifiable misery of broken lives and families left in vodka's wake. Today, Russia's foremost alcohol researcher Dr. Aleksandr Nemtsov argues that "the very high level of drinking, the predominance of strong drinks, the significant quantity of illegal alcohol, the low quality of liquor, its use in socially unacceptable circumstances—is all a product of the post-war Soviet epoch, not having been previously seen at such levels before in Russia."[54]

No amount of propaganda could comb over such blemishes: they were just as apparent to researchers in far-off America as to dissidents and common citizens across the Soviet Union. Were the Soviet leaders just so out of touch that they did not realize the incredible toll their vodka politics was taking on their people? Didn't they care? Or had they become stupefied victims of vodka themselves?

Back in 1958, Nikita Khrushchev characteristically responded in autocratic fashion: ramping up anti-alcohol propaganda and education, curtailing hours of alcohol sales, and immediately hiking retail prices by twenty-one percent. The measures failed: state production dipped slightly (figure 16.1), but drinkers simply turned to black market *samogon*. In those scratchy tapes recorded after his ouster, Khrushchev admitted as much: "I, too, thought that by raising the price of vodka we could bring the level of consumption down. But it did not work. The only result was that family budgets were hit harder than before, and people had even less money to spend on necessary goods. Besides, it makes people angry when the government arbitrarily raises prices."[55]

At the very least, the leadership was aware of the problem and the yawning distance between the official image and alcoholic reality. "I shall not conceal the fact that we receive letters in which workers, collective farmers and engineers propose an intensified struggle against loafers, drunkards, and dodgers," declared Brezhnev before the workers at the Kharkov Tractor Factory in 1970, responding to complaints about about the type of workplace alcoholism satirized by Erofeyev. "I believe this is a very proper demand."[56] Yet when the Central Committee finally instituted reforms two years later they too contained little beyond the usual calls to "eradicate drunkenness" through education and propaganda campaigns and by increasing expenditures on cultural and sports alternatives. As Treml's statistics suggest (figure 16.2), even Brezhnev's 1972 command to reduce vodka production in favor of safer, lower-alcohol beers and wines only survived one year before getting ramped up once again.[57]

"One cannot affirm the norms and principles of communist morality," proclaimed an aging Brezhnev in 1978 to the Komsomol, Communist Youth League, "without waging a continuous hard struggle against anti-social behavior and spiritual poverty, and its inevitable concomitants—drunkenness, hooliganism and breaches of labor discipline." Yet such pronouncements rang hollow, as the hard-drinking general secretary (and his equally inebriate Politburo) had as little interest in confronting society's debilitating alcoholism as in confronting his own.[58]

For the twenty-eight years from 1957 to 1985, Andrei Gromyko served as the Soviet Union's stalwart foreign minister. Late one night in the 1970s he found himself driving back to Moscow from the country residence at Zavidovo with General Secretary Brezhnev himself. Gromyko seized this rare opportunity—alone with the powerful Soviet leader—to broach a subject that had been troubling him for some time.

"Leonid Ilich," he said, "something has to be done about vodka. The people are becoming alcoholics. Why is the Politburo silent on this?"

Gazing at the road in front of them, Brezhnev was silent. For five minutes, the two drove on in awkward silence, while Gromyko increasingly regretted having said anything.

"Andrei," Brezhnev finally replied, "the Russian people have always enjoyed drinking. They can't get by without it."

"He wouldn't agree to any further discussion," Gromyko later recalled. "He particularly emphasized the words: 'They can't get by without it.'"[59]

If these words sound familiar—they should. This was the legendary utterance of Prince Vladimir of Kiev in the year 986 in justifying his choice of Orthodox Christianity for his people.[60] And while Brezhnev's proclamation was not nearly as bold, it did make clear that there would be no dethroning of king vodka so long as he was in power.

17

Gorbachev and the (Vodka) Politics of Reform

With the aid of hindsight, most histories of the Soviet Union refer to the three years from 1982 through 1985 as an interregnum—a relatively unimportant discontinuity between the death of Leonid Brezhnev and the rise of Mikhail Gorbachev. Yet doing so misses a number of important tensions and developments, especially as they relate to vodka politics. If the post-Stalin era highlighted the key division between "dry" dissenters against the "wet" Soviet leadership and their alcohol policies, the transition from Brezhnev to Gorbachev shows how the wet/dry distinction—both in policy and personal temperament—became among the most important political cleavages within the Soviet leadership itself.

By the beginning of the 1980s both the aspirations and ills of the Soviet system were incarnate in its leader, Leonid Brezhnev—his suit jackets overflowing with medals proclaiming the heroism of past glories, all pinned to an aging and decrepit chest. Like its political leadership, Soviet society was increasingly corrupt, drunk, and in deteriorating health. Brezhnev valued order and predictability through the so-called stability of cadres: once ensconced in powerful positions, Communist Party leaders were difficult to remove. The result was gerontocracy—rule by the elderly. In the early 1980s the combined age of Brezhnev's thirteen-member Politburo was 909, for an average age of 70.[1] No new faces or ideas meant greater stagnation, corruption, and political decay. As the temperate Foreign Minister Andrei Gromyko learned, Brezhnev met serious confrontations about drunkenness, stagnation, and corruption with resigned indifference: "You don't know life," Brezhnev said when discussing the scale of the shadow economy, "Nobody lives just on his wages."[2]

Since keeping your position and perks depended on not rocking the boat, most in Brezhnev's graying cadre shared his dismissiveness. One exception was KGB head Yury Andropov—a man with a great deal of blood on his hands. As Soviet ambassador to Hungary, he helped crush the 1956 liberalization movement there. After his promotion to head of state security, Andropov believed only military force could safeguard faltering communist regimes: accordingly, he rolled in the tanks to squash the Prague Spring in 1968, invaded Afghanistan in 1979, and supported martial law in Poland in 1981. The KGB chief's "Hungarian complex" also meant squashing opposition at home, including oppression of dissidents like Solzhenitsyn and Sakharov.[3]

So it is ironic that the ruthless head of the KGB actually shared these dissenters' understanding of the threat posed by alcoholism, shysterism, and corruption. A relatively dry ascetic who preferred sipping Johnnie Walker scotch to quaffing bottles of vodka, Andropov was appalled at the privilege, drunkenness, and corruption among the party elite.[4] He dedicated himself to streamlining the KGB into a regimented, efficient, anti-corruption force.

As Brezhnev disappeared from view due to his failing health, in 1982 Andropov's KGB investigated a high-profile ring of embezzlement, money laundering, and international diamond smuggling that included the suspiciously affluent, notoriously depraved, and rabid drunk Galina Brezhneva—daughter of the ailing general secretary himself. This was an unmistakable signal to the party elite that when Brezhnev finally passed it would be anything but politics as usual.

Brezhnev died peacefully at his state dacha outside Moscow in November 1982. Gathering at his bedside, Brezhnev's elderly Politburo comrades agreed that Andropov would be his successor. At the nationally televised funeral, few Soviets missed how Andropov solemnly embraced Brezhnev's grieving widow but turned his back on Brezhnev's daughter, who was conspicuously flanked by two burly guards. KGB investigations concluded that the hedonistic Galina and her many lovers and ex-husbands were smuggling diamonds on such a scale that they threatened to undermine the DeBeers cartel. Under Andropov, the alcoholic Brezhneva quietly disappeared before being committed to a psychiatric hospital, where she died in 1998.[5]

Andropov used his very first policy address to launch a wide-ranging labor-discipline campaign patterned on his KGB reforms—including a sweeping anti-vodka initiative—which was carried out with all the subtlety one might expect from a former KGB chief. In a move completely unthinkable during Brezhnev's two decades in power, the new secretary general checked in on workplace drunkenness through widely publicized surprise visits to factories. He launched "Operation Trawl," a nationwide dragnet of restaurants, movie theaters, saunas, metro stations, and parks for anyone getting drunk and playing hooky from work.[6]

Andropov was serious. The Presidium also made drunkenness on the job grounds for immediate termination—a dramatic move in the land of full employment. Even if the terminated worker found another job, the stigma of alcoholism followed him, as a disciplined drunkard could receive only half the usual bonuses. Drunks were now liable for damage—including defective output—caused in an intoxicated state. Managers who did not root out shop floor drunkenness lost their coveted bonuses.[7]

Since it only addressed the symptom of labor indiscipline, rather than the disease of vodka politics, Andropov's approach was doomed to fail. Indeed, stiff penalties for drunkenness remained the same as in the past—as did their lax enforcement. There were no attempts to improve education, living standards, or healthcare or to limit state vodka sales.

In fact, Andropov's other break from traditional practices—*reducing* rather than raising the price of vodka—seriously hampered his labor-discipline campaign. Cheap bottles of "Andropovka" (as drinkers affectionately dubbed them) were meant to draw customers away from dangerous *samogon*. Still, despite the stepped-up penalties, home brewing endured, especially in rural areas.[8]

Historians are left to debate whether Andropov's reforms would have succeeded had he not succumbed to his failing kidneys. At least he shook up the drunken, aging "cadres" of the Brezhnev era by promoting young, like-minded, and mostly "dry" reformers like Yegor Ligachev and Mikhail Gorbachev. By the summer of 1983 Andropov was conspicuously absent from official meetings, leaving the day-to-day operations to the elderly second secretary, Konstantin Chernenko. From his bed Andropov wrote that since he was unable to chair Committee meetings, "I would therefore request members of the Central Committee to examine the question of entrusting the leadership of the Politburo and Secretariat to Mikhail Sergeyevich Gorbachev," as his anointed successor rather than the corrupt and stodgy old Chernenko. Yet when the Brezhnevite old guard disseminated his letter to the Politburo, this final paragraph was conveniently redacted.[9]

On February 9, 1984, Yury Andropov died of kidney failure. At his state funeral on Red Square a virtually unintelligible eulogy was delivered by his successor—Konstantin Chernenko—who was already dying from chronic lung, heart, and liver diseases. The 72-year-old "new" secretary general was perhaps the most ineffectual leader of any state at any time. Despite expressing "serious concern" about pervasive alcohol abuse that "destroys people's health and brings misfortune to the home" and preaching a desire to "free society from this great evil," Chernenko's words were not matched with deeds.[10] His inability to continue the labor-discipline campaign can be chalked up to his failing health while his unwillingness to do so was rooted in his loyalties to his former drinking buddy, Brezhnev. Indeed, if there was anything at all remarkable about Chernenko it may have been that he could drink even Brezhnev under the table. Ever boastful of his "amazing capacity to consume alcohol"—a trait he ascribed to his upbringing in the harsh Siberian climate—"Chernenko never got drunk, no matter how much he consumed."[11]

His prodigious alcoholism no doubt compounded the liver cirrhosis and lung and heart aliments that killed him on March 10, 1985. "Whatever the cause of Mr. Chernenko's cirrhosis," diplomatically concluded the official Kremlin autopsy, "the disease reduced his liver function and disrupted the complicated biochemical reactions necessary to sustain life."[12]

The Soviet superpower was now poised to get its fourth leader in as many years—a political embarrassment both at home and abroad. "How am I supposed to get anyplace with the Russians if they keep dying on me?" recalled a frustrated American President Ronald Reagan in his memoirs.[13]

The Choice Of A Dry Generation

Reagan wasn't the only one fed up with the gerontocracy. As the usual story goes: with the demise of Chernenko the Soviet elders reluctantly agreed that a new generation must lead. And so the Politburo chose its youngest, most promising member—the 54-year-old Mikhail Gorbachev—as his successor. Yet this conventional wisdom is overdetermined.

The choice was not simply whether the next general secretary would be old or young but also whether he would be drunk or sober. This was no trivial matter, since the leader's personal relationship with the bottle seemed to be a reliable bellwether for reform. As we have seen, aside from Lenin most Soviet leaders were heavy drinkers with little interest in weaning society (or themselves) off the bottle. The relatively more sober leaders, including Khrushchev and Andropov, weren't content with the drunken stagnation and initiated reform. It is worth bearing this distinction in mind when considering the two top contenders for secretary general in 1985: Mikhail Gorbachev and Grigory Romanov.

Born in the southern region of Stavropol in 1931, Gorbachev—like Andropov—was not a complete abstainer but leaned toward the "dry" side. In his *Memoirs*, he traced his distaste for distilled spirits to a rite of passage in 1946, when he was fifteen years old. After a hard day working in the fields alongside his father, the harvesting team leader declared, "It's time you became a real man" and forced the boy to down a full mug of what he thought was vodka. It turned out to be one hundred percent pure medical alcohol. "After that experience I have never felt any pleasure in drinking vodka or spirits."[14]

Gorbachev left Stavropol to attend the prestigious Moscow State University, where he met his future wife, Raisa. The two wed in 1953. Following graduation, they returned to Stavropol, where Mikhail rose through the ranks as an able reformer of the notoriously inefficient collective farms. When in 1978 his mentor and patron—Politburo member Fyodor Kulakov—died of a sudden heart attack after a night of heavy drinking, Gorbachev succeeded him as secretary of agriculture, where he enjoyed the support of his like-minded, fellow Stavropol-native Yury Andropov. As a regional party secretary in the 1970s, Gorbachev pioneered the fight against indiscipline, corruption, and drunkenness in agriculture, which Andropov drew from once in power.[15]

Gorbachev did not rock the boat when Chernenko succeeded Andropov, but he made waves by highlighting the need for thoroughgoing economic, political, and legal reform. Hidden between the usual invocations of Marxism-Leninism in his landmark December 1984 speech on ideology, Gorbachev suggested wide-ranging reforms—from market-like incentives and greater enterprise autonomy to greater openness and self-government throughout the party—to remedy the economic slowdown. In candid discussions with his future foreign minister Eduard Shevardnadze, Gorbachev went further: agreeing that "Everything had gone rotten" in the Soviet system. "It has to be changed."[16]

Gorbachev's main contender for the top post was Grigory Romanov (no relation to the old royal family, though conservative British Prime Minister Margaret Thatcher confessed she would have loved to have seen a Romanov return to rule Russia). At sixty-two, Romanov was the second-youngest Politburo member and—had he been selected—would also have been the first general secretary born after the Revolution. Like Gorbachev, the long-time first secretary of the powerful Leningrad region was a smart, competent organizer empowered by Andropov. Responsible for the military and defense industry, he had a portfolio that overshadowed Gorbachev's base in agriculture. And while Gorbachev assumed a greater role under the ailing Chernenko, it was Romanov who was nominally the second secretary.

In terms of age, competence, and ability there was little separating Gorbachev and Romanov. Indeed, Romanov had more power and responsibility within the party, and his amicable links to Brezhnev's retinue arguably made him an even more desirable alternative for the remaining old guard.[17]

The primary difference between the two—and potentially the deciding factor—was personal temperament. Unlike Gorbachev, Romanov was a raging alcoholic. Beyond his daily drunkenness were damaging rumors that he abused his power as Leningrad party chief by commandeering Catherine the Great's priceless dinner service for his daughter's wedding, where in the ensuing bacchanal it was smashed by the revelers. Romanov denied such rumors—blaming his opponents for trying to discredit him. Yet Thatcher had heard it even in London and admitted that the rumor colored her opinion of his candidacy.[18]

Politburo members were more aware than anyone of Romanov's temperament and indiscretions, which were heavily reminiscent of the Brezhnevite past. Andropov was "perfectly aware that Grigory Vasilievich Romanov was a narrow-minded and insidious man, with dictatorial ways, and he recognized that at Politburo meetings Romanov rarely came up with a sound proposal or idea," at least according to Gorbachev's account.[19] Others in the Politburo affirmed that "he proved to be incompetent" and that "his style showed traces of *vozhdizm* [authoritarianism]."[20]

"We were different kinds of people, and we had different outlooks," wrote the teetotaling junior Politburo member Yegor Ligachev, describing his strained relations with Romanov and his Brezhnevite drinking buddies.[21] Such divisions grew deeper with reports from Leningrad that a drunken Romanov—with a pop singer girlfriend thirty years his junior—was apprehended by a Finnish patrol vessel as their boat somehow strayed into Finnish waters in the Baltic. On Romanov's last official visit to Helsinki just weeks before Chernenko's death, he got so drunk that "the Soviet embassy doctor had been required to restore him to a condition suitable for making a speech."[22]

This was a far cry from Gorbachev's temperate temperament: even during the well-lubricated banquets of the Brezhnev era, Gorbachev limited himself to two glasses of wine—never more—before diplomatically deflecting pressures to drink.[23] How much Romanov's alcoholism and dictatorial personality harmed his candidacy is difficult to tell, but his vices certainly accentuated Gorbachev's virtues.

Firsthand accounts largely agree that the weighty endorsement of longtime Foreign Minister Andrei Gromyko was the determining factor in the selection of Gorbachev as general secretary. Known in the West as "Mr. Nyet," the hard-nosed diplomat seemed an unlikely ally from the old guard, but as it turned out, Gromyko was even more "dry" than Gorbachev. In circumstances eerily similar to Gorbachev's, Gromyko gave up drinking at a very young age after his boyhood friend nearly died from sneaking bootleg *samogon*.[24] Gromyko shared not only Gorbachev's disdain for liquor but also his conviction that the Soviet system desperately needed fundamental reform—starting with vodka politics.

In his *Memoirs*, Gromyko described working closely with Gorbachev and having "intensive discussions on the most varied aspects of domestic and foreign policy" with the experienced and capable reformer.[25] And so when Gromyko rose to sing Gorbachev's praises, not a voice was raised in opposition. Gorbachev was selected unanimously.

Historians widely assume that that the Soviet economy was such a mess that whoever came to power in 1985 would face the same need for a major overhaul, and that the only thing that prevented it was the older generation. Accordingly, the subsequent reform program "was not a personal whim of Gorbachev" but, rather, "a natural result of the emergence of a new generation of leaders."[26]

But there was nothing "natural," "inevitable," or "inescapable" about reform just because there was demand for it.[27] There also needed to be a supply: a leader willing to initiate reforms. Otherwise the stagnant Soviet system could have continued to limp along, just as it had under the three previous leaders. Suggesting that the younger generation was united in demanding reform—and that the older generation was uniformly against it—is not just misleading; it is wrong. There were influential members of the older generation—like Andropov and Gromyko—who understood the need for change. Likewise there were those in the younger generation, including Romanov, who were more content with the stability, corruption, and alcoholism of the Brezhnevite past.

From Stalin's First Five-Year Plan in 1928 through the Twelfth Five-Year Plan in 1986, the most consistent predictor of the willingness to undertake meaningful reforms of the Soviet administrative-command economy was not age or generation, but rather the leader's relation to the bottle. It follows, then, that the more important impetus to reform was not that Gorbachev was young but that he was dry.

Why I'm Glad I'm Not Gorbachev

Another Western misconception about Gorbachev is that *Time* magazine's "Man of the Decade" was somehow a closet democrat—a "mole" who rose to the heights of the Communist Party only to institute political reforms like *perestroika* (economic restructuring), *glasnost* (openness), and *demokratizatsiya* (democratization) for the sake of liberty and freedom.

Gorbachev was indeed an ambitious reformer, but his primary focus was economic rather than political. He did not want to destroy communism; he wanted it to work better. Appreciating his reign in terms of vodka politics clarifies these momentous changes and suggests that even the commonly accepted timeline for reform needs to be reappraised accordingly.

The conventional wisdom is that Gorbachev unveiled his radical *perestroika* reforms at the Twenty-Seventh Party Congress in the spring of 1986—one short year after coming to power. The openness of *glasnost*—with greater freedom of speech and the relaxation of censorship—followed shortly thereafter. Then in 1987 came the multi-candidate elections and liberalization of *demokratizatsiya*, which weakened the coercive capacity of the state and eased the Soviet Union into Trotsky's famed "dustbin of history."

Rushing to dissect these momentous undertakings, most accounts mention only in passing that—just like his mentor, Andropov—Gorbachev's very first initiative was an all-out war on alcohol. Given the centrality of vodka to Russian statecraft, Gorbachev's wide-ranging (and ultimately disastrous) anti-alcohol campaign was more than a footnote to history: it was a dramatic and fundamental break with the legacies of the past that had a huge impact on subsequent political reforms the fate of the Soviet Union itself.

May 17, 1985: six short weeks after Gorbachev assumed power, the front page of *Pravda* announced a sweeping campaign against alcohol. "The population is not being instilled with a spirit of sobriety and is insufficiently informed about the harm the use of alcoholic beverages causes to the health of the present, and especially future generations,"[28] the mouthpiece of the party boldly declared. The ensuing Measures to Overcome Drunkenness and Alcoholism began by ramping up anti-alcohol propaganda. As in the past, these conventional tactics addressed only the symptoms of societal alcoholism rather than the disease. In admitting the failure of previous campaigns under Khrushchev, Brezhnev, and Andropov, it was clear that Gorbachev would go further... much further. A national temperance society was created. Recreational outlets and medical treatment facilities—both voluntary and compulsory—were expanded. Alcohol sales were dramatically restricted and production slashed. "This is one problem that I will get the better of," the energetic new general secretary privately declared.[29]

This was the most comprehensive anti-alcohol movement since the Society for the Struggle against Alcoholism (OBSA) of Nikolai Bukharin and Yury Larin in the 1920s (chapter 15). Like the OBSA of old, the Kremlin decreed a new All-Union Voluntary Society for the Struggle for Temperance. Even the OBSA's monthly journal, *Trezvost i kultura* (*Sobriety and Culture*) was dusted off and published under the exact same name. Within months it had over six hundred thousand subscribers, and the Temperance Society magically enrolled over fourteen million "voluntary" members in four hundred and fifty thousand branches in factories, collective farms, schools, and other facilities. The Society's charge of promoting workplace sobriety, rooting out home brewing, and ensuring compliance with anti-alcohol regulations were likewise reminiscent of the OBSA of the 1920s.[30]

At the time, Swedish economist Anders Åslund noted a certain neo-Stalinism in Gorbachev's battles, describing the war against alcohol as "a full-fledged disciplinary campaign of the old style, staged with impressive stamina."[31] But it was not just the state-sanctioned organizations, the swelling of their ranks through "cattle-drive techniques of recruitment,"[32] or even the ubiquitous propaganda that were reminiscent of the past—it was demanding sobriety by dramatically restricting vodka itself.

Under no circumstances could vodka be sold to minors under age twenty-one. Alcohol was prohibited near schools, hospitals, public transport, sports arenas, and rehabilitation centers. The number of retail alcohol outlets was slashed, as were their hours. To reduce workplace alcoholism, liquor could be bought only after 2:00 p.m. Liquor stores closed at 7:00 p.m. and all weekend, leading to long lines and disgruntled customers.

The state manufacture of vodkas, liqueurs, and wines was dramatically reduced. Prices were jacked up too. To sop up the rubles not spent on vodka and encourage healthier lifestyles, fruits, juices, jams—as well as sporting goods, athletic facilities, and artist supplies—were expanded. Laws against home brewing were strengthened: the manufacture or possession of *samogon* or distilling equipment could earn a three hundred ruble fine or two years in a labor camp.[33]

In a final throwback to the 1920s movement to create a "new Soviet man," Communist Party members were expected to be paragons of sobriety. Alcoholism became grounds for many—especially older—communists to be purged from the ranks. "The demands of the the Party are unequivocal," stated *Pravda* in no uncertain terms. "The calling of a Communist, and all the more so of an executive, is incompatible with this vice."[34] As in the 1920s, Party members who fell victim to vodka were shamed publicly, as the details of their drunken offenses were published for all to see.[35]

The most famous victim of the anti-alcohol housecleaning was Gorbachev's heavy-drinking former rival, Grigory Romanov. Just weeks after losing the top job, Romanov again disgraced himself publicly—this time getting sauced at the March 1985 Hungarian Party Congress. During the first week of the anti-alcohol campaign Romanov was dismissed while away on vacation. "I let him know quite bluntly that there was no place for him in the leadership," Gorbachev recalled. "He did not like this, but there was nothing he could say to change things." With his career effectively over, Romanov quietly wept.[36]

While using alcoholism as a pretext for purging undesirables harkened back to the Stalinist past, other moves were far more novel: official receptions at local and regional governments, Soviet embassies abroad, and even in the Kremlin itself were bone dry, much to the dismay of communist officials and visiting dignitaries. Still, the temperate Gorbachev led his anti-alcohol crusade by example—for the first time suggesting that not even the party elite was above the law.

Perhaps the most dramatic break with the autocratic past was through *glasnost*. Rather than a synonym for Western-style freedoms of speech, thought, or conscience, *glasnost* simply denotes "openness" or "frankness" in discussing public affairs. It wasn't freedom for freedom's sake but rather constructive criticism to supplement economic reforms. The thinking was: How could we fix the economy if people are too afraid to talk about what ails it?

Historians generally date *glasnost* from Gorbachev's symbolic telephone call to dissident Andrei Sakharov in 1986. Sakharov, the famous (and dry) dissident, and his wife Elena Bonner, had been under close KGB surveillance in the closed city of Nizhny Novgorod—then known as Gorky—on the Volga following their public protests against the Soviet invasion of Afghanistan in 1979. By telling the famed dissidents that they were permitted to return to Moscow, Gorbachev "conveyed to reformers and liberals not only that this regime would deal with opponents differently than had previous regimes, but also that the great physicist had been right all along."[37]

Yet even before such symbolic gestures, *glasnost* had already begun in earnest with the open publication of long-suppressed social statistics—a move that dissident Mikhail Baitalsky would certainly have applauded, were he still alive. In January 1986 the reports on the previous year's progress toward fulfilling the five-year plan acknowledged—for the first time—that alcoholic beverages were indeed sold in the Soviet Union. The official economic forecasts followed suit.[38]

More importantly, the first Gorbachev-era issue of the Goskomstat statistical abstract for 1985 (released in August 1986) saw the return of thirty pages of long-suppressed social and economic data, including those that reflected poorly on Soviet progress. Figures on life expectancy at birth—64 for men and 73 for women—meant that Soviets were still dying on average ten years younger than their counterparts in the industrialized West. The controversial infant mortality figures also also published—26 per 1,000 was slightly less than the estimates provided by Western demographers like Murray Feshbach and Christopher Davis but still confirmed the Soviets' deteriorating health and welfare. Later volumes not only acknowledged the existence of a "second economy" in the Soviet Union; they attempted to measure it. Subsequent publications released hard figures on crime, abortions, suicides, and executions that had not been seen since the 1920s.[39] Openly publishing such troubling statistical data was an open admission of the difficult reality that Gorbachev and his reformers faced.

Perhaps most shockingly, the 1985 abstract finally revealed alcohol sales figures, which showed that alcoholic beverages constituted a full quarter of all retail trade in the Soviet Union. "The figures made it clear," wrote Stephen White in his comprehensive history of Gorbachev's anti-alcohol campaign, "for the first time so far as official statistics were concerned, that the output of vodka and other hard liquors had more than trebled between 1940 and 1980."[40] Between 1962 and 1982, alcohol consumption increased 5.6 percent per person *per year*.[41] This was a bombshell wrapped in numbers. Not only did the official figures confirm worst-case estimates by Soviet dissidents like Mikhail Baitalsky and Western economists like Vladimir Treml—it exceeded them.

This statistical *glasnost* was a boon to anyone looking to understand Soviet social challenges—and it was painting an ugly picture of vodka and the decline of the Soviet economy. The costs of alcohol to Soviet productivity reached fifteen to twenty percent of all economic output. With new public surveys suggesting that twenty-five percent of Soviet factory workers regularly came to work already having a drink or two of vodka, it is clear why Gorbachev's first reform to jumpstart the moribund economy was to confront alcohol.[42]

Most historians consider the economic restructuring of *perestroika* and the openness of *glasnost* as two sides of the same coin. But if we are to really appreciate Gorbachev's reforms, we need a different metaphor. His approach can better be thought of as a three-legged stool of *perestroika, glasnost,* and the anti-alcohol campaign. Each element was reinforced by the others and strengthened by them in turn.

Indeed, if *glasnost* was the frank and constructive dialogue about confronting the ills of the Soviet system, *glasnost* did not begin with the symbolic phone call to Sakharov—it began with the earlier truth telling about alcohol and public health. The open acknowledgment of these problems distinguished the Gorbachev regime from all predecessors. For Gorbachev, *glasnost* was necessary to show his fellow countrymen—and indeed the rest of the world—the scope of the problems to be confronted through *perestroika*. And since releasing such information was necessary to bolster support for his anti-alcohol policy, vodka and *glasnost* were inexorably intertwined.

It did not end there. When it comes to *glasnost* about state finances, historians point to the importance of Gorbachev's speech at the June 1987 Plenum of the Central Committee. "Take for instance the state budget," Gorbachev argued. "From the outside, everything looks in order—incomes cover expenses. But how is that achieved?"

Gorbachev then enumerated the "sick elements" in the Soviet budget that began with commodity number one: vodka. "Of course, nothing can justify increasing the production and sale of wine and vodka. But while state income from the sale of alcoholic beverages in the eighth five-year plan comprised only 67 billion rubles, by the eleventh five-year plan, it exceeded 169 billion."[43] *Glasnost* was vital in coming clean about the Soviet Union's problems—and that meant first coming clean about vodka politics.

Who Is To Blame?

"Tell us about the most furious row you witnessed at the Politburo."

Before the KGB inexplicably expelled him from Russia in 1989, this was *Sunday Times* correspondent Angus Roxburgh's standard question as he interviewed over one hundred of the most senior Soviet elites. The typical reply was a lighthearted chuckle followed by, "Oh, there were so many of them, so many...."

"Most Politburo members were willing to part with only one or two of their secrets," Roxburgh wrote, "though almost all of them jumped at the chance to expose what appears to have been the most divisive issue in the early years of *perestroika*, the ill-fated attempt to stamp out alcoholism."[44] The decision to begin such historic reforms by confronting Russia's autocratic vodka politics says a lot about the dynamics of political reform as well as the crucial wet/dry divisions within the Soviet elite.

As Gorbachev's first major initiative, the anti-alcohol campaign took most observers by surprise. That, combined with its recognition as a dismal failure—both by critics and supporters—has led to rampant speculation: *why* was it instituted, and *who* was to blame?[45]

Based on an oversimplified, what-the-leader-says-goes caricature of Soviet policy making, most mistakenly blame General Secretary Gorbachev alone. Maybe his roots in the milder, moderate, and wine-drinking south meant that Gorby did not understand the importance of vodka in colder climates? Or perhaps Raisa Gorbacheva—moved by her brother's tragic alcoholism—persuaded her husband to confront vodka.[46] Maybe this is what Mikhail meant when, on the eve of his inauguration, he confided in Raisa that "we simply cannot go on living like this."[47] But this was no conspiracy or a secret: it was widely understood that alcohol had long dragged down economic productivity and undermined the well-being of its citizens. Since the Soviet leadership was privy to classified social and economic data, they knew the magnitude of the problem. With Gorbachev at the helm, it seemed that they were finally willing to do something about it.

"The statistics were appalling," Gorbachev later told writer Viktor Erofeyev when asked the "why" question about the anti-alcohol campaign.

> Injuries in the workplace, falling productivity, diminishing life expectancy, accidents on the roads and railways. In 1972, they discussed the problem in the Politburo, but deferred it. It was impossible to solve, because the state budget itself was "drunk"—it relied on the income from vodka sales. Stalin set it up that way—temporarily, but there's nothing as permanent as a temporary decision. In Brezhnev's time, the "drunken" component of the budget increased from a hundred billion rubles to a hundred and seventy billion—that was how much profit vodka brought to the state.[48]

To hear the Soviet leader candidly acknowledge the central paradox of Russia's vodka politics—not just the importance of alcohol revenues to the treasury, but also the state's consistent efforts to hush up the embarrassing social consequences—is truly revolutionary. Indeed, when it came to this historically central pillar of Russia's autocracy, the dry Gorbachev was more aligned with the dry Soviet dissidents than with the wet Brezhnevite party line. "Long ago Gorbachev internally rebelled against the native System" that had "created, nursed and formed him," recalled Gorbachev's onetime Politburo ally Nikolai Ryzhkov.[49] Both in policy and in temperament, his position on alcohol seems to best illustrate that.

"There were many causes for the widespread drunkenness: poor living conditions, the difficulty of everyday life, cultural backwardness," Gorbachev wrote in his *Memoirs*. "Many drank because of the impossibility of realizing their potential, of saying what they thought. The oppressive social atmosphere pushed weak natures to use alcohol to drown their feelings of inferiority and their fear of harsh reality. The example of the leaders, who paid lavish tribute to the 'green snake' of alcohol, also had a bad effect."

From blaming the state for the alcoholization of society, like Solzhenitsyn and Sakharov, to sharing Baitalsky's lament that the only worse thing was the acquiescence and indifference toward vodka, it sounded as though the dissidents were in charge. "Perhaps the saddest thing," Gorbachev recalled of his Brezhnevite inheritance, "was that although there was a severe shortage of consumer goods the authorities could not think of any way to maintain monetary circulations other than by selling alcohol to make people drunk. This sounds crazy, but it is the pure truth. The gap between the enormous money supply and the wretched supply of goods was filled with alcohol."[50]

Certainly, something had to be done, but it would be wrong to lay all of the blame on Secretary General Gorbachev alone. The one-man totalitarian dictatorship had been cast off along with Stalin's fetid corpse—most political decisions in the late Soviet era were made collectively, with the general secretary first among equals. Indeed, while Gorbachev ultimately bears (and according to his *Memoirs*, accepts) ultimate responsibility for the anti-alcohol policy and its failure, he was not the driving force behind it. The architect was actually Mikhail Solomentsev. A zealous dry, the reformed-alcoholic Solomentsev was promoted to full Politburo member just before Andropov's death and was in charge of party discipline as chair of the powerful Party Control Committee. Since the Brezhnev era Solomentsev had floated policies—like strengthening anti-alcohol propaganda and expanding nonalcoholic entertainment, sports, and recreation—that become the basis of the anti-alcohol campaign.

If you are searching for a smoking gun, look no further than Solomentsev's 1984 speech before the Party Control Committee—delivered when acknowledging alcoholism was still taboo. Never before mentioned in historical accounts, Solomentsev's words embody both the spirit and content of the anti-alcohol campaign:

> I would especially like to focus on the question of strengthening the fight against drunkenness and alcoholism. As you know, in 1972 and subsequent years appropriate decisions were taken in this regard. But they were not supported by the necessary degree of organizational work or the strengthening of anti-alcohol propaganda. Consequently, in recent years, drunkenness has become widespread, penetrating all layers of society—among communists, *Komsomol* members, and managers.
>
> The reasons for the growth of drunkenness, of course, include the weak monitoring of the implementation of party decisions.

Consequently, some managers even create "cognac" and "banquet" funds from employee requisitions to organize collective boozing. Such drunken banquets are often used to celebrate the completion of socialist competition and community service, the arrival of official delegations, holidays, employee birthdays, and so on. Sometimes they are even held within the very walls of the enterprises and institutions themselves.

Systematic inspections carried-out by the Party Control Committee show that many places continue to underestimate the dangers of drunkenness. Some party committees and commissions have not taken a principled position, and exhibit insufficient toughness toward those who abuse alcohol. For example, in the Sverdlovsk region the drunken, indecent behavior of a number of communists was not even discussed among the party. In the Chernigov region, communists who were convicted for moonshining were not even expelled from the party.

We need to make it absolutely clear that appeasement of or forgiveness towards those who abuse alcohol or violate the anti-alcohol laws will no longer be tolerated. Every case that arises in relation to alcohol should be viewed through the prism of the social danger of this evil. Many of the most heinous crimes, including bribe-taking, are often committed in a state of intoxication. Drunkenness is causing enormous material and moral damage to our society, harming not only the health of the current generation, but future generations as well.

Following the obligatory references to Lenin's opposition to alcohol, and the token acknowledgment to Secretary Chernenko, Solomentsev boldly declared: "Comrades! Our party's commitment—to rooting-out the theft of socialist property, malfeasance, bribery, profiteering, drunkenness, and other vices—is strong and uncompromising."[51]

Such audacious declarations under the wet Konstantin Chernenko are especially noteworthy, since the ascension of a dry secretary general was hardly a given. With the rise of Gorbachev—whose dry worldview was broadly congruent with his own—Solomentsev's opportunity had finally arrived.

And so, during the first week of April 1985—just after his appointment—Gorbachev chaired a two-hour, closed-door meeting of the Politburo on the liquor question, which the abstentionist Minister of Foreign Affairs Andrei Gromyko later described as "an important turning-point in our party's history."[52]

In addition to listing the report of comrade Grigory Romanov's visit to Hungary (the one where he got rip-roaringly drunk), the front page of *Pravda* blithely announced that, "considering the numerous suggestions of working people submitted to central and regional authorities, the Politburo discussed in depth the question of fighting drunkenness and alcoholism." The typically gray announcement of "a complex of stringent social-political, economic, administrative, medical and other anti-alcohol measures"[53] belied what many participants recalled as being an especially raucous affair—an intervention, as it were—about the viability of Soviet vodka politics itself.

The meeting began with Solomentsev's report on the alcohol question, which was commissioned under Andropov. His colleagues recalled how Solomentsev regularly came to Politburo meetings armed with "great tomes" of research on combatting alcoholism and delivered lengthly lectures based on official studies and long-hidden social and economic statistics, which "all contained truly horrifying data."[54]

Upon reading these "devastating reports," as well as heartfelt letters from the people about alcoholism, an outraged Gromyko—whose support weeks earlier had secured Gorbachev's leadership—boldly expressed his frustrations with comrade Brezhnev for dismissing his concerns about vodka. "Imagine, in this country people drink everywhere—at work and at home, in political and artists' organizations, in laboratories, school and universities, even kindergartens!"[55]

Gorbachev agreed: they weren't "just talking about a major social problem of the present, but about the biological condition of our nation, about its genetic future," according to Anatoly Chernyaev's account. The new secretary general threw down the gauntlet: "If we don't solve this problem, we can forget about communism."[56]

The strongest advocate for dramatic action—and the one most associated with the anti-alcohol campaign—was Yegor Ligachev. An effective reformer who championed public sobriety as first party secretary in Tomsk from 1965 to 1983, Ligachev was a staunch Gorbachev ally until their relationship soured. A puritanical teetotaler, he denounced alcoholics within the party and shut down forty-five of the forty-seven liquor stores in Tomsk. "My official responsibilities and my personal refusal to tolerate drunkenness coincided in this case," he later said of his dedication to the anti-alcohol campaign.[57]

Ligachev was still only a candidate (non-voting) Politburo member and therefore not involved in the drafting of reports or legislation, as were the full (voting) members, but his condemnation of alcohol was virtually identical to the senior Solomentsev. Before the campaign, Ligachev decried the lax attitude within the party, which seemed not to care that two hundred thousand party members and three hundred and seventy thousand Komsomol members had been cited for drunkenness. Like Solomentsev, he wanted hard-drinking members of the party to be relieved of their responsibilities as part of a "general condemnation of drunkards."[58]

Ligachev was particularly moved by the piles of heart-wrenching letters from despondent wives and mothers. "In these letters, women, crushed with grief, cursed the drunkenness that took away the lives of their sons and husbands and crippled their children," Ligachev recalled. "This was a veritable cry for help. Moreover, many scientists were sounding the alarm and forecasting the threat of degeneration of the nation's genetic stock." Unlike the political chasms that later divided Ligachev and Gorbachev, both agreed about the urgency of confronting this national tragedy.[59]

In sum, the reformers' overriding concern was not only (or even primarily) economic revitalization but rather the "moral atmosphere"—in Gorbachev's words.[60] Still, not everyone agreed with the proposed policy solutions. The Politburo still contained a significant "wet" faction that, for economic, social or personal reasons, actively opposed the campaign. The most vocal foe was Nikolai Ryzhkov, a young reformist ally who later became one of Gorbachev's most outspoken critics.

"I was in favor of taking measures against alcoholism, and agreed that the nation was going to ruin," Ryzhkov said in his interview with British journalist Angus Roxburgh, "but I was categorically against the methods being proposed. At first I thought they were joking when they said that 'drunkenness would continue so long as there was vodka on the shelves.' Then I realized they were dead serious."[61]

Repeatedly referring to the ineffectiveness of past measures, and the failures of draconian prohibitions in other countries, Ryzhkov pleaded for moderation—calling for conventional band-aid approaches of increasing prices and clamping down on workplace indiscipline. Protesting the proposed extreme measures, he pointed out the necessity of rationing sugar—the primary ingredient in what he (correctly) foresaw as driving a dramatic upsurge in illegal moonshining. Yet despite the support of some half-dozen senior officials, Ryzhkov's opposition was steamrolled.

"And what was their response?" Ryzhkov wrote in his scathing *Perestroika: History of Betrayal*. The anti-alcohol forces berated him.

> Ryzhkov does not understand the importance of the moment. Ryzhkov does not feel that this is a time of actions, not words. Ryzhkov is not aware that the moral atmosphere of the country needs to be saved by any means. Ryzhkov cares more about the economy than morality. I cannot remember all of the accusations they heaped on. Gorbachev actively supported these fighters against alcoholism, in his concern for the country's "moral atmosphere."[62]

For centuries, alcohol revenues were the central economic pillar of the Russian autocratic state, so it is no surprise that the most vocal opposition came from those most aware of the economic consequences. When the deputy director of the state economic planning agency Gosplan warned that there was no conceivable way to cover the gap of five billion rubles that would result from the campaign, Gorbachev gave him a dressing down: "You want to build communism on vodka?"[63]

After refusing to sign off on the plan three different times, the Gosplan director was threatened with expulsion from the Communist Party. He was joined in his dissent by Vasily Garbuzov. Promoted to minister of finance under Khrushchev in 1960, Garbuzov oversaw and promoted vodka as "Commodity Number One" for the Soviet treasury over the following twenty-five years. As architect of late-Soviet vodka politics he understood more than anyone the economic implications of the proposed measures, so it was Garbuzov whom Gorbachev first summoned to discuss the issue. His protests notwithstanding, Garbuzov also refused to sign the anti-alcohol resolution. Within weeks the elderly finance minister followed Gorbachev's rival Romanov into forced retirement.[64]

Gorbachev's threat of dismissal sufficiently intimidated those on-the-fence Politburo members, including Eduard Shevardnadze—who soon replaced Gromyko as Soviet foreign minister and later became president of an independent Georgia. Reflecting the moderate traditions of the predominantly wine-drinking Caucasus, Shevardnadze says he was "horrified" over the anti-alcohol plans but admitted that he voted for them, "although inwardly I disagreed."[65]

Others were not so easily cowed, including Heydar Aliyev, who later became president of post-Soviet Azerbaijan, next door to Shevardnadze's Georgia. The Politburo's only Muslim member, the cultured Aliyev drank only the cognac of his native Caucasus and preferred the company of composers, actors, and artists over the usual "alcoholics, foul-mouthed swearers and womanizers" of the Kremlin.[66] Yet the powerful deputy prime minister embodied the corruption and nepotism of the old Brezhnev era—transforming Soviet Azerbaijan into a personal fiefdom of oil, cotton, and caviar.

In protecting his own interests, Aliyev also refused to sign the anti-alcohol resolution. He continued even after the campaign was in full swing: protesting—ultimately in vain—the closure of a champagne factory he recently had set up in Azerbaijan with high-end equipment imported from West Germany. This continued opposition brought him toe to toe with the drys: Gorbachev, Ligachev, and Solomentsev. When he later protested the closing of breweries on the grounds that beer was "not really alcohol," Solomentsev threatened to produce a report "proving that people got more drunk from beer than vodka." When he argued that drunkenness was not a big problem in traditionally Muslim, wine-producing Azerbaijan and that ninety-five percent of their wine was exported to other regions, "Ligachev went to Azerbaijan and carpeted the republic's leaders, accusing them of poisoning the rest of Russia with their drink."[67]

Aliyev's opposition to the anti-alcohol campaign only hardened the reformers' view that he exemplified the nepotism, privilege, and corruption of the

Brezhnev era. In 1987 "Gorbachev unleashed a full-blown, Stalin-style denunciation of Aliyev," dismissing him for corruption and cronyism.[68] Just like that— as with Romanov and Garbuzov—another powerful critic of the anti-alcohol campaign was gone.

Ultimately, when it came to launching Gorbachev's historic reforms with an all-out war against vodka politics—the very foundations of the Russian autocracy itself—there is plenty of blame (or credit) to go around. As Ligachev and Gorbachev both acknowledged, the decision was made collectively—which is not to say that it was unanimous. What's more, the personal rivalries that emerged from the heated debates over the anti-alcohol campaign shaped the course of future reforms, while the mismanagement of the campaign itself hastened the unraveling of the entire Soviet autocracy.

18

Did Alcohol Make the Soviets Collapse?

Q: What is a Soviet historian?
A: Someone who can accurately predict the past.[1]

Even in Soviet dissident circles the above was perhaps not the funniest political joke. Still, that did not stop American president Ronald Reagan from delivering it—and others like it—to great political effect with domestic audiences. As a former actor, Reagan understood the power of wit, and he had aides collect wisecracks told in the Soviet Union that captured the Russians' wry sense of humor. Dropped into the middle of a speech, a well-delivered Soviet pun could not only win over a crowd but also convey that beyond the bombastic rhetoric of "evil empire" there were human beings on the other side of the Iron Curtain: regular, cynical people who well understood the substance of their system's shortcomings. Plus, Reagan loved to tell audiences jokes they had never heard.

> *Two fellas are walking down the street in the Soviet Union, and one of them says "Have we really achieved full communism? Is this it?" Then the other one says, "Oh hell no—things are going to get a lot worse."*[2]

Beyond just his comedy stylings, Russians might be shocked to hear just how many present-day Americans believe that it was actually Reagan's oratorical skill that singlehandedly ended the Cold War and fell the mighty Soviet Union. Consider this: according to historian Garry Wills, Reagan said " 'Tear down this wall,' and it was done." And today "we see no Soviet Union. He called it an Evil Empire, and it evaporated overnight."[3]

That guy won a Pulitzer Prize.

Overstated? Certainly—but such arguments are increasingly common in an ever-growing Reaganology literature dedicated to valorizing "the Gipper." As the standard line goes: Reagan's steadfast moral resolve against a "godless" enemy and the dramatic increase in American defense spending overextended the Soviet Union and exposed the bankruptcy of communism, leading to Soviet capitulation, democratization of Eastern Europe, and liberalization throughout the socialist world. That is how Reagan alone "freed a billion slaves from their Communist masters."[4] And no, that wasn't meant to get a laugh.

There are (at least) two fatal flaws that plague this literature. The first is that most Reaganology writers lack even the slightest familiarity with Soviet politics or history, focusing instead on the bountiful charisma of the American president. The other is sloppy reasoning. Pundits who credited Barack Obama for the Arab Spring beginning in late 2010 made the same error: there is little causal connection between a foreign leader's rhetoric on one side of the globe and domestic political developments on the other.[5]

Reagan's oratory was far less important to the future of the Soviet Union than the actual ills of the autocratic system itself. Many of those problems—from public dissatisfaction with the leadership, rising inflation amid a shortage economy, and even the exacerbation of nationalist tensions—were linked to vodka politics. Upon coming to power, Gorbachev was particularly horrified by the appalling social statistics, which showed that by the late 1970s the Soviet Union had begun a process of "demodernization." Rather than expanding, economic productivity was on the decline; instead of blossoming, Soviet society was becoming more corrupt and stagnant. Instead of living longer, healthier lives, Soviets were becoming more sickly and dying earlier. The raw health statistics, shown for the first time under Gorbachev, confirmed that not only was infant mortality on the rise—as Western demographers like Murray Feshbach had suggested—but also that "life expectancies began to fall, a development without precedent in the industrial world in peacetime."[6]

Indeed, the statistics that were made available thanks to Gorbachev's alco-*glasnost* were horrific. The following is just a taste:

In 1985, Russians consumed on average of 14.9 liters of pure alcohol per person per year: according to the World Health Organization, anything over 8 liters is damaging to the overall health of the population. In other words, the *average* Russian man consumed 130 of the conventional half-liter bottles of vodka per year—or a bottle of vodka every three days for every man in the Soviet Union.[7]

While life expectancy for Soviet women was 72.6 years at the end of the 1970s, for men it had dropped to 62.5 years—lower than in any other European country. Not only did alcohol poisoning claim twenty thousand lives annually, but vodka also killed working-age Soviets through accidents, traumas, and cardiovascular and respiratory diseases. Together, it was estimated that between 1960 and 1987 thirty to thirty-five million Soviets had been sacrificed to vodka—ten million more than were lost to Adolph Hitler in World War II.[8]

Once a mostly male activity, by the early 1980s more than ninety percent of Soviet women drank regularly. Even without including Fetal Alcohol Syndrome, drinking mothers were prone to dramatically higher rates of infant mortality, underweight and premature deliveries, and children born with physical and

mental disabilities. Drinking often led to unwanted sex and unwanted pregnancies. The dramatic upsurge in abortions rendered more women barren
at a younger age. Vodka invaded Russian universities, high schools, and even
elementary schools: 84 percent of Soviet kids began drinking before the age of
sixteen. According to a controversial report by the Soviet Academy of Sciences
in Novosibirsk—headed by Gorbachev's future chief economic adviser, Abel
Aganbegyan—of those receiving anti-alcoholism treatments for the first time,
ninety percent were under the age of fifteen, and a third were under the age of
ten.[9] This was devastating.

Vodka also tore apart Soviet families. Alcoholism was a major factor in up
to eighty percent of divorces and eighty percent of traffic deaths. Alcohol was
the single largest cause of suicides, drownings, and new cases of syphilis and
gonorrhea. Statistics on crime were even more stark: in the Russian Republic,
seventy-four percent of all murders were committed in a state of intoxication
and sixty percent of all thefts, two-third of all fires, seventy-four percent of rapes,
eighty-four percent of robberies, and ninety percent of all cases of hooliganism
were attributable to alcohol. As one Soviet study concluded, "if there was no
drunkenness and alcoholism, there would be no more of the crimes that make
up most of the elements of the criminal statistics, above all violent, domestic and
mercenary crime."[10]

The costs to the Soviet economy were equally astonishing. The economic
costs of illness and early death, workplace accidents, absenteeism, and the lack of
labor discipline—so vividly described in Venedikt Erofeyev's *Moscow to the End
of the Line*—leeched billions of rubles from the economy every year. According
to exhaustive studies, alcohol abuse cost the Soviet economy more than a third
(36.9%) of national income—or more than five times what the state was reaping in vodka profits. Aganbegyan's Academy of Sciences claimed that drunkenness contributed more than any other factor to the failure of the Eleventh Five
Year Plan (1981–85) before concluding that alcoholism constituted the "most
appalling tragedy in Russia's thousand-year history."[11]

If you were the new leader confronted with unending statistics like these, what
would you do? It is clear why Gorbachev began his reforms with an anti-alcohol
campaign aimed at improving the health, morality, and economic productivity
of the Soviet people.[12] Although we tend to focus on the campaign's failures, it
did have some demonstrable early successes: in its first year vodka production
and sales dropped by a third; within two-and-a-half years it was down by two-
thirds.[13] By 1989 per capita alcohol consumption dropped from 14.9 to 12.5
liters. In the first year alone, overall crime dropped by a quarter. There were far
fewer divorces, automobile accidents were down twenty percent, and absenteeism fell by a third.[14] Early on, the draconian restrictions on sales and availability
seemed to deliver results.

Twenty- to thirty-year-olds saw an instant twenty percent drop in mortality. In the Russian Republic, alcohol-related mortality plummeted from 26.4 per 100,000 in 1980 to 9.1 in 1987. Deaths from accidents at work dropped by a third; deaths from alcohol poisoning were cut in half. Happily, just as the death rate was dropping, the number of births was rising, and the babies were statistically far healthier than in the past. Perhaps most astonishing was the dramatic rise in life expectancy. From 1984 to 1987 average female life expectancy increased by a full year while Soviet men could expect to live fully three years longer.[15] Indeed, before the policy was quietly withdrawn in 1988, the campaign was credited with saving up to a million Soviet lives.[16]

"It would be wrong to say that the anti-alcohol measures were absolutely useless," Gorbachev later claimed in defense of the policy. "There were decreases in accidents, fatalities, lost working time, hooliganism and divorces due to drunkenness and alcoholism.... For the first time information was available on the manufacture and use of alcoholic beverages, along with statistical data that had previously been kept secret. However, the negative consequences of the anti-alcohol campaign greatly exceeded its positive aspects."[17]

Gorbachev certainly had a good appreciation for the benefits of the campaign, but he also kept his sense of humor about the frustration his policies caused the average Soviet drinker. Even before the breakup of the Soviet Union, a jolly, self-effacing Gorbachev himself told foreign audiences this well-known joke:

> *Fed-up at a mile-long line for vodka at the liquor store, one guy finally snaps:*
>   *"That's it. I'm going to the Kremlin to kill Gorbachev!"*
>   *An hour later, he came back to the same line.*
>   *"Well?" Everyone asked. "Did you kill him?"*
>   *"Kill him?" the man replied. "That line's even longer than this one!"*[18]

So, what went wrong? Despite the social and demographic achievements, the campaign's political and economic losses were too great to ignore, beginning with the growing dissatisfaction with the Kremlin and a cynicism toward *perestroika* that proved difficult to overcome.

"The state, in effect, created two hundred million criminals," explained Russian journalist Leonid Ionin, by forcing thirsty customers turn to illegal *samogon*. "The *perestroika* rhetoric was discredited. The authorities showed their stupidity and powerlessness. The people's belief that the new leaders knew what they were doing, and could do it, was undermined."[19]

The unpopular policies caused prime minister of the Russian Republic Vitaly Vorotnikov some uncomfortable public encounters. "The people were outraged," he told the Politburo. "You couldn't visit a factory without being shoved into a corner and shouted at, 'What are you doing? You can't do this to us!'" Fellow opponent of the anti-alcohol measures, candidate Politburo member Vladimir Dolgikh explained to his colleagues not only how the ubiquitous liquor store lines were caused by an undiversified economy that failed to deliver anything else to spend their rubles on but also how he was personally shouted down every time he passed one in his black Zil limousine.[20]

It wasn't just irredeemable drunks who were inconvenienced—even casual drinkers waited in long lines to get drinks for family celebrations and holidays. At the height of the campaign, the *average* Muscovite spent over ninety hours— or almost four full days—in line waiting for alcohol. Simply to maintain order in the capital's vodka queues required four hundred police officers and dozens of additional patrol cars every day.[21]

Even the well-meaning propaganda about the harms of alcohol was met with cynicism and scorn. Beyond the constant temperance entreaties in magazines and newspapers, drinking and party scenes were expunged from theaters, cinema, radio, and television programs. And still, when friends gathered to drink the very first toast often was raised "to the struggle against drunkenness."[22]

"People became more and more frustrated by hours of queuing and the impossibility of buying a bottle of vodka or wine for some special occasion," Gorbachev recognized in his *Memoirs*. "They cursed the leadership, most of all the General Secretary, who was traditionally held responsible for everything. It was then that I got the nickname 'Mineral Water Secretary,'" or *mineralny sekretar* as a snide take on the title of *generalny sekretar*, or General Secretary.[23]

Yet while Soviets naturally vented their angst toward Gorbachev the man, the real source of frustration lay with the autocratic system itself. From their perch atop a closed, autocratic hierarchy, the insulated leadership often bolstered their legitimacy with bold proclamations. But policy implementation was always complicated by Russia's traditionally obsequious bureaucracy. As it was before communism, and just as it is today, bootlick bureaucrats dutifully advance even the most misguided policies so long as it keeps them in good standing with their immediate superiors. Consequently, even the most unrealistic directives are amplified to the point of absurdity. As with Stalin's collectivization campaign, it seemed as though the Soviet bureaucracy was again "dizzy with success" in persecuting alcohol. The overfulfillment mentality led local officials to exaggerate their successes and downplay their failures. Gorbachev admitted as much: "As is often the case [in the traditional Russian autocracy at least], the idea and its implementation were miles apart. I would say that we were both realistic and responsible during the discussion and decision-making, but when the time came to carry out our decisions we began to do things helter-skelter and to allow excesses, and thus we ruined a useful and good initiative."[24]

In the name of socialist competition village leaders went far beyond the original decree, forcing "dry months" upon their jurisdictions. Local and regional bureaucrats across the USSR proclaimed their results were so encouraging that there was a real prospect of eliminating *all* alcohol consumption within five years or at least by the year 2000. "The leadership, for its part, left no room for doubt about what it wanted to hear," claimed historian Stephen White, "calling (as Ligachev did in late 1985) for sobriety zones to be established and 'the sooner, the better,' or even for total prohibition."[25]

If Solomentsev was the program's architect, and Gorbachev its enabler, it was Yegor Ligachev who kicked the policy into hyperdrive. Ligachev encouraged regional leaders to overfulfill the plan: close down even more retail outlets and encourage greater competition between vodka producers to see who could slash output the most. Those who hesitated were given a public dressing down or booted straight out of the Party. Before he retired in 1988, Mikhail Solomentsev did the same. They "punished so many people," recalled Vorotnikov, "ruined so many people with terror if they dared to decline to carry out the decisions."[26]

"Ligachev and Solomentsev...began with irrepressible zeal, but eventually they took everything to the point of absurdity," Gorbachev later recalled. "Well, I must admit that I bear a great share of the responsibility for this failure. I should not have entrusted the implementation of the policy entirely to others."[27]

The rift between Gorbachev and the conservative Ligachev over the botched anti-alcohol campaign widened when Ligachev openly derided Gorbachev and his reforms as going to far. His hard-line economic criticisms first won Ligachev a demotion to agriculture secretary in 1988 and then dismissal from Gorbachev's Politburo in 1990. "I am not dodging responsibility for the fact that these measures initially turned out to be excessively harsh and bureaucratic," Ligachev responded to those blaming him for the anti-alcohol mess. "As a nondrinker, I was psychologically unprepared to accept the fact that someone would not be able to 'kick' drinking if the possibility of obtaining alcohol were sharply curtailed. This was undoubtedly a mistake on my part, [but it] seemed to be that if you went at it with a will, drunkenness could be eliminated quickly."[28] Only later did he realize that undoing the alcoholization of an entire society would be a gradual, long-term undertaking, not something that could be solved with shock tactics.

Q: *What is Soviet business?*
A: *Soviet business is when you steal a wagonload of vodka, sell it, and spend the money on vodka.*[29]

As we learned in chapter 13 about prohibition's role in the demise of the Romanov dynasty, it takes more than just discontent to topple an autocracy. There is usually a precipitating crisis: a disastrous war or economic collapse that weighs heavily on the people. In the case of Nicholas II those crises were only exacerbated by the tsar's ill-fated prohibition, which blew a massive hole in the treasury at the worst possible time. Patching the hole with paper rubles accelerated the hyperinflation that pushed the empire toward revolution. Unfortunately for Gorbachev, his reform followed the exact same script, leading to the demise of the Soviet superpower itself.

Let's begin with another unfortunate parallel with the ill-fated imperial prohibition: unrealistic expectations. Dusting-off imperial Finance Minister Peter Bark's script from some seventy years earlier, defenders of the Soviet anti-alcohol campaign declared that any loss of revenue from decreased vodka sales would be more than compensated by a miraculous economic growth from casting off the yoke of vodka that had long stifled the peoples' productive capacity.[30] The treasury's prayers would again go unanswered.

Gorbachev inherited an absolute mess of Soviet state finances. While, on paper, state income neatly covered expenditures, the two largest contributors were the domestic vodka sales and international oil and natural gas exports. Just as Finance Minister Garbuzov continuously ratcheted up vodka production, the Soviet Union also increased its petrochemical production eightfold from 1971 to 1980.[31] So long as international oil prices hovered between thirty to forty dollars per barrel, the Soviet treasury was assured a constant stream of hard-currency revenues. But just as Gorbachev assumed power, the global price of oil collapsed to less than ten dollars a barrel. The Kremlin suddenly lost the foreign-currency reserves that funded the Brezhnev-era illusion of growth. By slashing supply in a futile attempt to drive global prices higher, they lost even more.[32]

On its own, the falling price of oil wasn't a fatal blow to Soviet finance. Unfortunately, there were more budgetary hardships to come. On April 26, 1986, the electro-energy station at Chernobyl—north of Kiev in present-day Ukraine—suffered a full meltdown, causing the worst civilian nuclear disaster in history. In addition to the widespread radioactive contamination and the incalculable human costs, the cleanup and relocation cost the government billions of rubles. Two years later, in December 1988, the Soviet republic of Armenia was rocked by a magnitude 6.9 earthquake. More than twenty-five thousand perished, mostly in shoddily constructed Brezhnev-era buildings. The reconstruction costs further strained the government, so much so that "the leadership included losses of alcohol revenues alongside the cost of the Chernobyl disaster and the earthquake in Armenia as the major disruptions threatening the success of *perestroika*.'"[33]

While economic historians are quick to fault the oil glut for the Soviet Union's woes, few likewise consider the financial impact of the anti-alcohol campaign. Ed Hewett—President George H. W. Bush's economic advisor on the Soviet Union—calculated that the declining oil prices had cost the Soviets thirty billion rubles. Based on numbers provided by Gorbachev's outspoken prime minister Nikolai Ryzhkov, Hewett added another eight billion rubles for Chernobyl, unspecified expenditures for Armenian earthquake relief, and twenty-one bil-lion in unanticipated expenditures for reforming healthcare, education, and other social initiatives tangentially related to the anti-alcohol campaign. For comparison, Ryzhkov estimated that lost tax receipts from vodka amounted to fifteen billion rubles in 1988 *alone*.[34]

In sum, after three years of the anti-alcohol campaign, Soviets spent thirty-seven billion fewer rubles on government alcohol, creating a loss of tax reve-nues of at least twenty-eight billion rubles—which is to say, a loss similar to the collapse of world oil prices. Gorbachev admitted as much in a public speech in 1988: "Now that the world business cycle has changed and energy prices have fallen and we have been compelled to cut down the production and sale of wine and vodka to safeguard the social health of our population, the economy of our country is faced with a most serious financial problem."[35]

Since the communist Soviet Union did not have the tradable financial instru-ments of the capitalist world, the only ways to finance their budget deficit were either through foreign loans or monetary emission—simply printing more rubles to cover the difference. Like their ill-fated tsarist predecessors, the Soviets chose the latter.

"I disagree with those who believe that we did not plan how to compensate for the loss to the state budget resulting from reduced alcohol sales," claims Gorbachev in his *Memoirs*. "Special economic calculations took into account the losses to industry due to drunkenness. The plan was to reduce alcohol sales gradually (I emphasize—gradually), as it was replaced by other goods in cir-culation and sources of budget revenue."[36] Yet as we know, alcohol sales were reduced rapidly rather than gradually, and there were no alternative products to sop up the excess rubles.

So, where did all of that money go? Where it always goes in times of drastic alcohol restrictions: underground.

Signs of a home-brewing epidemic popped up quickly. As Ryzhkov had fore-seen in his debates with the Politburo, Cuban sugar—a primary ingredient in home brewing—disappeared from store shelves. This "sugar panic" of 1988 prompted the imposition of strict rations the following year. The satirical maga-zine *Krokodil* even ran a political cartoon of a man with a gin-blossomed nose in an upscale restaurant ordering "300 glasses of tea. The sugar—on the side"![37] Better yet, a popular Soviet ditty invoked the bootleggers' practice of igniting their drink to test its proof strength:

> *O thank you, thank you, Cuba*
> *Every Russian does proclaim.*
> *A pint from every pound of sugar*
> *And it burns with bright blue flame.*[38]

According to Gorbachev's lead economic advisor, Abel Aganbegyan, the straw that broke the camel's back was not the original 1985 regulations, but a second round of retail restrictions and a further twenty-five percent price hike in July 1986, which unleashed the illegal production that eventually doomed the campaign. The state's retreat from the market created a huge opportunity for entrepreneurs to meet the demand with low-quality, black market *samogon*.[39] It was the fulfillment of a popular, drunken shanty of the Brezhnevite past:

> *Vodka now costs us five rubles*
> *Yet we ain't gonna stop drinking.*
> *Give Brezhnev this message from us:*
> *We will even pay ten rubles a bottle—*
> *But if it goes up to twenty rubles—*
> *Well, then we'll march on the Winter Palace*
> *And seize it once more.*[40]

Thanks to Gorbachev's *glasnost*, the Soviets could no longer hide the resulting bad news in statistics. After two years of improving demographic numbers, the home-brewing epidemic hit with unmatched ferocity. In 1987 alone over forty thousand Russians were poisoned with illicit *samogon*, and another eleven thousand died from acute alcohol poisoning.[41]

The most hard up drinkers turned to alcohol surrogates: from mouthwash, eau-de-cologne and perfume to gasoline, cockroach poison, brake fluid, medical adhesives, and even shoe polish on a slice of bread. In the city of Volgodonsk five died from drinking ethylene glycol, which is used in antifreeze. In the military, some set their thirsty sights on the Soviet MiG-25, which—due to the large quantities of alcohol in its hydraulic systems and fuel stores—was affectionately dubbed "the flying restaurant." The measures also may have led to an upsurge in the use of illegal narcotics.[42]

Before 1987 it could be argued that the tax losses and the people's grumbling discontent was offset by palpable improvements in social health and morale. But with the explosion of home brew destroying even those gains, there was little reason to continue the restrictions. "In a country where vodka had become a currency more reliable than the ruble, and where drunkenness was a factor in over 70 percent of murders, vodka proved more powerful than Gorbachev," writer Viktor Erofeyev commented after interviewing the former Soviet leader. "When he saw the poisoning statistics, he said he simply gave up."[43]

Tacitly admitting defeat, by 1989, the Politburo quietly rolled back the restrictions on alcohol sales. The dreary alcohol consumption stats quickly rebounded to pre-reform levels, as did the social indices: mortality was again on the rise, along with drunk driving deaths, suicides, homicides, and other crimes.[44]

Unfortunately, the policy reversal was too late to save the Soviet budget, which had already entered a hyperinflationary death spiral. Gorbachev advisor Aganbegyan estimated that the effective loss of the state monopoly to the bootleggers cost the treasury some eight to ten billion rubles. Famed economist Nikolai Shmelev put it even more bluntly:

> According to my calculations, the government took two-thirds of the revenue from alcohol in the early 1980s and the moonshine producers one-third. Today, with the same level of per capita consumption, we have reversed these proportions. But by giving away its revenue to the bootlegger, the government in the last two years has sharply increased its budgetary imbalance and incurred a deficit which is today being covered in a most dangerous and unhealthy way, by the printing press.[45]

Chechen economist and Speaker of the Russian Supreme Soviet Ruslan Khasbulatov claimed it was only when the losses from the anti-alcohol campaign mounted "that useless money began to be printed, the source of the present inflation."[46]

In a tragic replay of how the treasury's shortfalls contributed to the hyperinflation, shortages, and general discontent that claimed the Romanov dynasty, the irreparable hole blown in the budget by Gorbachev's anti-alcohol restrictions prompted the Soviets to turn to the printing press—exacerbating the hyperinflation, shortages, and general discontent that doomed the Soviet autocracy. But there was another dimension to the demise of the Soviet Union: the national question.

Q: What do you call the middle stage between socialism and communism?
A: Alcoholism.[47]

While Marxism–Leninism predicted the withering away of national identities, the Soviets actively institutionalized and promoted national identity as the foundation of the federative union itself, creating an air of imperialism between Moscow and the non-Russian union republics. Residents of what would become the non-Russian former Soviet states—especially the Baltics and Caucasus that had a previous history of independent statehood—viewed the Soviet era as a period of forced bondage within a multinational empire. Every issue from the dangerous, Chernobyl-type nuclear installations to the alcoholization of society was decried as a "foreign" intrusion and quickly became surrogates for anti-Soviet, anti-Russian nationalism.[48] Consequently, Gorbachev's particular brand of vodka politics even hastened the decay of the tenuous center-periphery relations of the late Soviet era.

In January 1988 the first inter-ethnic disorders erupted in the Caucasus over the status of Nargorno-Karabakh: a mountainous, predominantly Armenian enclave completely within the neighboring Azerbaijan Soviet Socialist Republic (SSR). Skirmishes in the Karabakh capital of Stepanakert over ethnic-Armenian demands to return to "the mother country" of the Armenian Soviet Socialist Republic fueled anti-Armenian pogroms in Azerbaijan and escalating tensions that followed the Christian Armenians and Muslim Azeris into their independent statehood. Shortly after the collapse of the Soviet empire these tensions erupted into a devastating, all-out war and a "frozen conflict" in which Armenians won de facto—but not de jure—control over Karabakh.

Yet before even the first blood was spilt in 1988, vodka was there. In 1986 Armenian Igor Muradian led a delegation to Moscow with a draft letter proposing to transfer Karabakh from the Azerbaijan SSR to the Armenian SSR. It was a delicate proposition, since it would open the pandora's box of renegotiating many of the contentious, Soviet-drawn borders. Still, he persuaded nine high-ranking Armenians to sign. The most prized signature was that of Abel Aganbegyan, Gorbachev's lead economic advisor, whose Academy of Sciences in Novosibirsk produced copious amounts of research in support of the anti-alcohol campaign. Yet when Aganbegyan entered the room to sign the petition for the Karabakh transfer "he didn't know where he was going and why they were taking him there, and before he signed he spent four hours there. During those four hours he drank approximately two liters of vodka."[49]

Even more important were the impacts that the anti-alcohol campaign had back in the Caucasus. With their Mediterranean climate, the Caucasus in general and Georgia in particular are known for their history of viniculture—even the serpentine curves of the Georgian alphabet are said to invoke the vine. Accordingly, the culture of alcohol consumption in the Caucasus more resembles the wine-drinking nations of southern Europe than the vodka-quaffing practices of Russia to the north. Still, wine was just as integral to daily life in the Soviet south, where the draconian anti-alcohol restrictions were met with even greater hostility.

The autocracy's "bureaucratic excesses" in the Caucasus resulted in the forcible uprooting of historic, centuries-old vineyards, even over the howls of local protestors. On the other side of the Black Sea in wine-drinking Moldova, sixty thousand hectares—or twenty four percent the republic's vineyards—were destroyed. From Moldova and Crimea to Georgia and beyond, the anti-alcohol campaign was yet another callous imperial diktat that ravaged local customs and economies and sharpened nationalist sentiment.[50] As throughout the Soviet periphery, the mismanagement from the center "led to nationalist calls for radical decentralization of economic authority and control, giving the nationalities control over their own economic destinies, and ultimately independence."[51]

In sum: just as vodka politics contributed to every widely acknowledged factor in destroying the tsarist empire of old, it likewise hastened the demise of the Soviet Union itself. From exacerbating nationalist tensions in the non-Russian republics and stoking discontent within the Soviet leadership to destroying the central financial pillar of the state, Gorbachev's anti-alcohol campaign was another important factor in the collapse of the Soviet regime. As Gorbachev himself lamented: "In our society people are more used to 'revolutionary leaps' than to diligent work over a long period of time. Alas, the anti-alcohol campaign became one more sad example of how faith in the omnipotence of command methods, extremism and administrative zeal can ruin a good idea."[52]

It is no joke to suggest that the Soviet autocracy's vodka politics sowed the seeds of its own demise. Or, at the very least, it makes more sense than claiming that it was all the handiwork of American president Ronald Reagan. But for those who remain unconvinced, and hold fast to the dictum that the words of "the great communicator" somehow slew the Soviet monster from half a world away, consider the following:

In the summer of 2011, professor Paul Kengor—arguably the dean of the school of Reaganology and author of *The Crusader: Ronald Reagan and the Fall of Communism*—penned an article titled "Predicting the Soviet Collapse" for the conservative magazine *National Review*. The article describes a long-classified 1983 CIA memorandum written by Reagan's vice-chairman of the National Intelligence, Herbert E. Meyer. Recently released through the Freedom of Information Act, the eight-page, Andropov-era memo won Meyer the prestigious National Intelligence Distinguished Service Medal and "ought to rank among the most remarkable documents of the Cold War," according to Kengor.[53] I am inclined to agree.

Based on "highly credible research" by "Soviet specialists and generally well informed individuals I know, whose political views and affiliations range across the spectrum," Meyer concludes in his once-secret memo that "time is not on the Soviet Union's side." Strangely, he never mentions the arms race Reaganologists usually cite in vanquishing the Soviet juggernaut. Instead he points to the Soviet Union's debilitating vodka-driven health and demographic problems and the challenges they posed for future Soviet economic growth in a complex, multinational empire.

Reagan was apparently moved by the "demographic nightmare" of falling birthrates and skyrocketing abortions. Meanwhile, Meyer's forecast that "the Soviet economy is heading toward economic calamity" reinforced Reagan's bold claim that Soviet communism would soon be dismissed "as some bizarre chapter in human history whose last pages are even now being written."[54]

In corroborating Reagan, Kengor proudly concludes that "Herb Meyer deduced from solid research what Ronald Reagan had deduced by intuition."[55]

I contacted Herb Meyer about this solid, highly credible research that formed the backbone of his influential memorandum. Where did this inspired analysis come from?

"My source was, indeed, Murray Feshbach," Meyer kindly replied. This was the same Census Bureau researcher and Georgetown professor whose Soviet infant-mortality studies and worrisome predictions about alcohol's demographic toll were being vindicated by the newly released statistical information under *glasnost*.

"I got the information from Murray himself," Meyer wrote. "I made it a point to chat with him from time to time, since he knew more about this issue than anyone at the CIA."[56]

So as it turns out, Reagan's visionary condemnations about the weakness of the Soviet Union were informed less by abstract moral principles than by information from those who understood the very real consequences of Soviet vodka politics. And that's no joke.

19

The Bottle and Boris Yeltsin

The collapse of communism and the peaceful end to the Cold War were transformative events in world history. En masse the former satellite countries of Eastern Europe rejected their communist autocracies for democracy. By 1989 a global wave of liberalization crested with the euphoric toppling of the Berlin Wall and the defiant heroism of student protestors in Tiananmen Square. Between Beijing and Berlin stood the vast Soviet Union, where Mikhail Gorbachev's reforms effectively devolved power down to the fifteen republics that together made up the USSR, including the largest and most vital: the Russian Soviet Federated Socialist Republic (RSFSR). Meanwhile, the Russian people joined the chorus of nationalist voices in the Baltic republics calling for greater autonomy within—and then outright independence from—the Soviet Union. As the old Soviet empire imploded there was optimism that—for the first time—Russia would join the global wave of democracy and self-determination. While the challenges would be monumental, for the first time in generations Russia had the opportunity to make a clean break with the autocratic—and alcoholic—political traditions of the past.

Instead, Russia suffered a grueling economic and social collapse that became the most drunken period in all of Russian history—no mean feat. While the causes of Russia's post-independence catastrophes are many and complex, they were only exacerbated by democratic Russia's first president. Dubbed "a revolutionary who preserved tradition," he both repudiated and restored Russia's autocratic traditions at the same time.[1] While espousing freedom and democracy, Russia's first elected president was a product of the Soviet autocratic system of vodka politics through and through. So before the very real devastation of Russia in the 1990s can be addressed, we must first confront the man whose very name has become an international synonym for drunken excess: President Boris Nikolaevich Yeltsin.

Stumbling Toward The Exits

By 1991 the Soviet Union was in its death throes. The massive hole in the budget, of which lost vodka revenues was a significant cause, was papered over with reams of new rubles, stoking inflation. With money losing its value as they held it in their hands, citizens scrambled to buy essentials and even food, most already gone from store shelves. Fistfights and skirmishes in the lengthening queues highlighted that the half-measures of *perestroika* weren't wreaking just economic chaos, but social instability as well.

Meanwhile, the openness of *glasnost* and the self-liberation of the Eastern European satellite states emboldened nationalists in the Soviet Baltic Republics, Georgia, and even the Russian Republic itself. The fissures of nationalism threatened to shatter the Soviet Union as one republic after another pressed for autonomy, then independence. Hoping to peaceably accommodate pressures for self-determination, Gorbachev proposed a new treaty that would reorganize the Union of Soviet Socialist Republics into the Union of Sovereign States—a confederation of independent countries that would maintain a common executive as well as a shared military and foreign policy.

This was a bitter pill for many Soviet patriots to swallow—especially for a group of high-level conspirators in Gorbachev's own cabinet who decided that they could no longer sit idly by and watch the dismemberment of the only motherland they had ever known. On August 19, 1991—one day before the signing of the new union treaty—they acted. At dawn, citizens awoke to news that Gorbachev—then vacationing at the presidential retreat in Crimea—had suddenly fallen ill and was unable to perform his duties. Gorbachev's vice president, Gennady Yanayev, assumed the role of acting president and head of the so-called State Committee on the State of Emergency (GKChP), which vowed to solve the crippling shortages and restore the "honor and dignity" of the Soviet people. Following the announcement, the media came under emergency control. All meetings and street demonstrations were strictly outlawed. Martial law was imposed, and tanks rolled through the streets of Moscow.

This was a coup d'etat. And like every coup in Russia's imperial past, this too was drenched in vodka.

According to witnesses, on the afternoon of Sunday August 18, both Vice President Yanayev and Prime Minister Valentin Pavlov had been out drinking with friends when they were summoned to the Kremlin by KGB chairman Vladimir Kryuchkov, who set the plan in motion. "Yanayev wavered and reached out for the bottle," Gorbachev wrote in his *Memoirs*. Along with the other conspirators, it is doubtful that Yanayev was sober at any time during the bungled three-day coup.[2]

Co-conspirator Defense Minister Dmitry Yazov later confirmed that not only was Yanayev "quite drunk," but so too were other plotters: KGB head Kryuchkov, Interior Minister Boris Pugo, and even Marshal Yazov himself. According to Yazov's trial testimony, Pavlov was incapacitated by headaches and unspecified illnesses from the very beginning. After chasing his blood pressure medications with alcohol, Pavlov had to be pulled unconscious from the bathroom. After that, "I saw him two or three times, and each time he was dead drunk," Yazov testified. "I think he was doing this purposefully, to get out of the game."[3]

Whether or not the failure can be chalked up to the liquor, the conspirators forgot rule number one of any takeover: neutralize your rivals. Their main opponent was Boris Yeltsin, who just the year before had been popularly elected president of the Russian Republic—the largest and most important of the fifteen republics that constituted the USSR. Yeltsin was a champion of liberalization, democratization, and devolution of power from the Kremlin to the republics. Yet while the plotters in the Kremlin dispatched KGB troops to his dacha, somehow they never ordered his arrest.

On Sunday, August 18, Yeltsin was in Almaty, concluding a weekend trip to shore up relations with the Kazakh republic and its president, Nursultan Nazarbayev. After a long Saturday of forging friendship treaties, Sunday began with vodka. "Yeltsin was well and truly drunk," Nazarbayev remembered, as the tipsy Russian president tried to ride the magnificent black stallion Nazarbayev had just given him. "He kept rolling out of the saddle first one way, then the other, while his security men did their best to keep him from falling as the stallion kicked out and reared up. It was quite dangerous." Escaping unharmed, the delegates relocated to the scenic mountain rivers of the Talgar Gorge above Almaty, where to the horror of his handlers the sauced Yeltsin tried to dive into in the frigid, fast-moving waters that masked jagged rocks. Reluctantly diverted to a calmer backwater, Yeltsin then called for shots to warm up. And then more vodka at the farewell lunch. Knowing his guest's propensity for drink, Nazarbayev ordered the erecting of a *yurt*—the traditional tent of steppe nomads—for a post-celebration nap. When the bearish Yeltsin emerged, he called for even more toasts, further postponing his flight home. "I had to order the police to keep everyone away from the airport so that nobody could see the President of Russia in such a condition. We had to push him up the aircraft steps to get him on his plane," recalled Nazarbayev—unaware of the momentous events awaiting Yeltsin back in Moscow.[4]

At his dacha outside Moscow, Yeltsin was rudely awoken not only by a splitting headache, but also by news of the State Committee on the State of Emergency's takeover. Top aides and panicked opposition figures soon arrived, including Yeltsin's confidant and bodyguard Aleksandr Korzhakov, speaker of the Russian legislature Ruslan Khasbulatov, the popular deputy mayor of

Moscow Yury Luzhkov, and even Anatoly Sobchak, mayor of the recently re-christened St. Petersburg.

Amazed to find his fax and phone lines still working, the hungover Yeltsin started making phone calls: first to Nazarbayev, his Kazakh host from the evening before.

"What is happening there, Boris Nikolayevich?"

"I don't know," slurred Yeltsin, "But I think this is a real coup and we must prepare ourselves for the worst."[5] The president planned to denounce the takeover, call for nonviolent opposition, and stage a protest in downtown Moscow. During the Soviet era Moscow was not only capital of the Soviet Union—whose government ruled from the Kremlin—but also of the Russian Republic of the USSR, whose government was located at the "White House," the towering parliament building on the Moscow River some three kilometers due west of the Kremlin. The White House was the symbol of Russian self-determination against Soviet power—he would go there.

To arrange safe passage, Yeltsin phoned paratrooper commander Pavel Grachev, whom Yeltsin had befriended months earlier over a vodka-fueled banquet. Describing their encounter, airborne commander Aleksandr Lebed (who also rose to prominence for supporting Yeltsin) simply invoked the famed words of Vladimir of Kiev a thousand years earlier: "'drinking is the joy of the Russes'—and that centuries old tradition was not broken, as the entire cavalcade set upon the open bar [*brazhnyi stol*]."[6]

Supported by Grachev and Lebed, Yeltsin's entourage made their way with surprising ease to the White House, where scores of protesters were already erecting protective barricades. Nonviolent protestors convinced the tank troops dispatched to the White House to defect and instead defend Yeltsin and the leadership of the Russian Republic. In an iconic moment captured by the global news media, Yeltsin—defying threats of sniper fire—courageously climbed atop a tank turret to address the crowd, denouncing the coup and calling for a general strike. Assuming command of the resistance, witnesses recalled how Yeltsin sternly declined offers of vodka at the White House, claiming "there was no time for a drink" at this moment of supreme crisis.[7]

The exuberance and tension—serious and sober—at Yeltsin's White House stood in stark contrast to the coup plotters just blocks away. That evening, the gray-clad Yanayev and the hard-liners of the State Committee on the State of Emergency held a press conference that was televised internationally as well as nationally. With the legitimacy of the coup unexpectedly challenged by stubbornly noncompliant reporters, the country and the world focused on the trembling hands of the befuddled Gennady Yanayev as evidence of the bankruptcy and irresolution of the plotters. This "stunning spectacle exposed these mediocrities to public scrutiny," recalled Russian history professor Donald J. Raleigh. "A sniffling Gennady Yanayev, his face swollen by fatigue and alcohol, had a tough time fielding the combative questions. His trembling hands and quivering voice conveyed an image of impotence, mediocrity, and falsehood; he appeared a caricature of the quintessential, boozed-up Party functionary from the Brezhnev era."[8] That's precisely who he was.

In the face of growing opposition and a military unwilling to follow orders, the coup collapsed on August 21. The police were dispatched to arrest the plotters. With the authorities banging down his apartment door, Interior Minister Pugo chose to shoot his wife before turning the gun on himself. Others sought refuge in the bottle: Pavlov was drunk when the authorities came to arrest him, "but this was no simple intoxication," said Kremlin physician Dmitry Sakharov, "He was at the point of hysteria." When the incoherent Vice President Yanayev was carried out of his Kremlin office—its floor strewn with empty bottles—he was too drunk to even recognize his one-time comrades who had come to arrest him.[9]

In his subsequent interrogation, Defense Minister Dmitry Yazov was asked how he lost command of his own military. He faulted the battalion commanded by "Yeltsin's personal friend," an allusion to Grachev. "And when the second day began, I saw a whole busload of vodka being brought to them," Yazov claimed. "That's how they tried to encourage the soldiers to betray their duty. Just imagine drunks in the armored personnel carriers! That's a whole different sort of danger."[10] Although Yazov's audacious claims bear a shocking similarity to the way that Empress Elizabeth won over the imperial regiments who placed her on the throne in 1741 (and again with the ascension of Catherine the Great in 1762), there is little evidence to substantiate them.

While Yazov was being interrogated on August 22, a relieved Mikhail Gorbachev landed safely back at Moscow's Vnukovo airport alongside his visibly shaken family. Moscow looked the same as before, but in his brief absence the country had been transformed: while he nominally held on to authority, Yeltsin's sober defiance bolstered his political legitimacy, especially when juxtaposed against those drunken members of the State Committee on the State of Emergency whom Gorbachev himself had appointed.

In the following months the Communist Party was outlawed. Gorbachev and his outmoded USSR were further marginalized as one union republic after another declared its independence. As devastating as it was, the coup was not the end of the Soviet Union. That began in December 1991, when representatives of the Russian, Ukrainian, and Belarussian Soviet Socialist Republics—the three republics responsible for creating the original USSR—met at a Belarussian hunting lodge and signed the Belovezh Accords, legally undoing that union and leaving Mikhail Gorbachev as a president without a country.

A jubilant Russian president Boris Yeltsin was joined by Ukrainian Republic president Leonid Kravchuk and Belarussian chairman Stanislau Shushkevich to negotiate the final dissolution. Yet unlike his sober resolve atop the tank, Yeltsin's final political triumph over his rival Gorbachev was "lubricated in traditional fashion." Indeed, witnesses recalled how Yeltsin got so drunk that he fell out of his chair just as the doors were opened for the ceremony. According to one witness:

> Everyone began to come into the room and found this spectacular scene of Shushkevich and Kravchuk dragging this enormous body to the couch. The Russian delegation took it all very calmly. They took him to the next room to let him sleep. Yeltsin's chair stayed empty. Finally, Kravchuk took his chair and assumed the responsibility of chairman. When Kravchuk finished his short speech to everyone about what had been decided, he said, "There is one problem that we have to decide right away because the very existence of the commonwealth depends on it: don't pour him too much." Everyone nodded. They understood Kravchuk perfectly.[11]

The Soviet Union was finished two weeks later, on December 21, 1991, back in Almaty, Kazakhstan, where the leaders of eleven soon-to-be post-Soviet republics (not including the Baltics or Georgia, which had already left the Union) signed into existence the Commonwealth of Independent States (CIS) as a confederal alternative to Gorbachev's USSR. As the assembled presidents discussed a retirement package for Gorbachev, Yeltsin was drunk again—only occasionally raising his head to mutter a slurred "What you say is right," before passing out. Yeltsin again had to be carried from the room.

"This is terrible! Who's ruling Russia?" growled a scornful Armenian president Levon Ter-Petrossian to one of Yeltsin's aides. "How are you Russians going to live? We don't envy you."[12]

And so independent Russia was born.

Role Reversal

The end of the Cold War and the collapse of the Soviet Union were largely peaceful, yet the political chaos, economic collapse, and demographic crisis that Russia suffered thereafter were similar to what happens in countries vanquished in war. Amid the disorder, Boris Yeltsin confronted the virtually insurmountable tasks of simultaneously transitioning not only from dictatorship to democracy, and from a command economy to the market, but also from an antiquated empire to a modern nation-state, complete with new borders and fourteen brand new international neighbors. Yet perhaps the greatest Soviet legacy that Yeltsin had to confront was vodka politics.

Democratic theatrics aside, Boris Nikolaevich Yeltsin was a product of the Soviet autocratic system, and it showed through his temperament. Raised in the austere Urals countryside, young Boris was an adventurer—he lost his left thumb and index finger cracking open a hand grenade stolen from a local army depot. Still, his adventurism was tempered by parents and teachers who sternly condemned alcohol. Even as a teen, Yeltsin had no patience for drunkards: he was known to snatch vodka from the hands of classmates and dump it on the ground.[13]

Yeltsin's steadfast temperance weakened as he rose through the Communist Party, where no banquet, celebration, or transaction was complete without liquor. By 1976 he had been promoted to first secretary of the Sverdlovsk (Ekaterinburg) district—effectively the governor of one of the country's most important regions. The following year the Kremlin entrusted Yeltsin with the midnight demolition of a persistent symbol of anti-Soviet activism: the Ipatiev House in Sverdlovsk, where Tsar Nicholas II and his family met their gruesome ends at the hands of a Bolshevik firing squad back in 1918.[14] Within the party Yeltsin became an acclaimed toastmaster. He would take guests and subordinates on vodka-fueled hunting trips in the Siberian wilderness. A small-scale carbon copy of the courtly dynamics of Stalin, Ivan the Terrible, or (Yeltsin's professed hero) Peter the Great, these drunken escapades had the usual ulterior benefits. "Keeping everyone under control at work, during vacation, and even during their spare time allowed Boris Nikolaevich to know even the most intimate things about all his colleagues," recalled one of those colleagues, Viktor Manyukhin. "Most importantly, it allowed him to see with his own eyes that there were no groupings against him. On the contrary—everyone was giving him their full support on everything."[15]

Yeltsin's drinking rarely interfered with his work, and he had little patience for those who let vodka inhibit theirs—even firing factory directors for drunkenness.[16] His energetic party work was noticed by Yegor Ligachev, the teetotaler from nearby Tomsk, who became Yeltsin's political patron. Ligachev visited Sverdlovsk in 1984 and later noted that Yeltsin did not touch a drop of liquor. If he had, it is questionable whether the notoriously dry Ligachev and Gorbachev would have brought Yeltsin to Moscow, entrusted him as first secretary (de facto mayor) of Moscow, or promoted him as candidate member of the Politburo.[17]

It wasn't long before the outspoken Yeltsin ran afoul of Gorbachev. At a 1987 party plenum Yeltsin scathingly criticized the slow pace of *perestroika* reforms, warning that a destructive cult of personality was forming around Gorbachev, before requesting that he be able to resign his Politburo post. This was sensational: no one had voluntarily stepped down from the Politburo—*ever*. Such audacity galvanized Yeltsin's popularity as a hero among Russian liberals, who attributed his stand to his unwavering principles. "Unwavering" was just the opposite adjective used by those Communist Party leaders who were present in the hall that day. They described Yeltsin as "not in total control of his thoughts"; his speech, "incoherent." One Yeltsin supporter claimed "I could smell the alcohol on his breath. He was probably drinking all night."[18]

Yeltsin was ritually denounced by Gorbachev and the communist leadership. The barrage of beratements sent Yeltsin—complaining of chest pains—to the hospital, where later it was revealed that he had suffered a nervous breakdown. Physical and psychological withdrawal would become a defining pattern of Yeltsin's political career.[19]

The general secretary had effectively ended Yeltsin's career, just as Gorbachev's democratization reforms began to offer the possibility of political redemption. In 1989, competitive, multi-candidate elections were held for a new nationwide parliament: the Congress of People's Deputies (CPD). Yeltsin was elected as a representative from Moscow with a decisive ninety-two percent of the vote, and soon assumed a leadership role. In March 1990 Yeltsin was again elected, this time to the parliament of the Russian Republic, which quickly appointed him to its highest post: chairman of the Presidium. In June 1991—two months before the August coup—Yeltsin won another landslide election to become the first democratically elected president of the Russian Soviet Federative Socialist Republic of the USSR. With fifty-seven percent of the vote, he defeated the Gorbachev-backed Nikolai Ryzhkov, who garnered only sixteen percent. Yeltsin's dramatic political rise, then fall, then rise again were accompanied by moderation in alcohol. The accounts of foreign dignitaries, close associates, and even fierce political opponents affirm that during these years he rarely drank to excess like he did in later years.[20] Yeltsin's steady hand in the roisterous August putsch can be seen as part of that.

But everything changed once the Soviet Union dissolved and Yeltsin replaced Gorbachev in the Kremlin. Yeltsin's loyal drinking buddy/bodyguard Aleksandr Korzhakov—who stood alongside Yeltsin atop the tank—became Yeltsin's closest confidant. As gatekeeper to Yeltsin's inner circle where major political decisions were made, Korzhakov became a powerful political player in his own right. Equally important, Korzhakov also became the keymaster of Yeltsin's alcoholism. He was an enabler—ensuring that the trunk of the presidential limousine was stocked with Yeltsin's favorite vodkas, champagne laced with cognac, shot glasses, and appetizers. However, Korzhakov was the only one "who could put his hand over Boris Nikolayevich's glass and say, 'Enough,'" according to Kremlin sources. There is little evidence that he did this very often. The two were inseparable—whether on the tennis court, the sauna, or late night at the dacha, Korzhakov and Yeltsin were almost always drinking. Yeltsin's wife Naina and their daughters repeatedly tried to intervene, but in vain. They openly derided Korzhakov for plying Yeltsin with alcohol just to maintain his own political status. Meanwhile, Yeltsin's alcohol intake skyrocketed through the first half of the 1990s.[21]

There could not have been a worse time for the president to hit the bottle: guiding Russia from the Soviet administrative-command system to a functioning market economy would take a steady hand. On January 2, 1992, Yeltsin announced a "shock therapy" program of macroeconomic stabilization that included the immediate liberalization of prices, currency, and trade. It was thought that, like ripping off a band-aid, the suffering caused by this dramatic leap to the market would be short-lived. It wasn't. Ending price restrictions meant that hoarded goods soon reappeared on store shelves—but reflecting their demand, the prices were too high for many to afford. The credit crunch made it impossible for old, uncompetitive Soviet firms to stay in business, which led to a spike in unemployment. Hyperinflation wiped out people's life savings, forcing tens of millions into abject poverty while sending Russia into a decade-long economic depression. The economic disaster was reflected in social and demographic statistics: alcoholism skyrocketed, as did suicides. Average life expectancy for men—sixty-five at the height of the anti-alcohol campaign in 1987—plummeted to sixty-two in 1992. Two years later it dipped below fifty-eight: indicative of a demographic catastrophe without parallel in peacetime human history, so dramatic was Russia's fall.[22]

The most vocal opponents of Yeltsin's painful economic reforms included his closest allies just months before: his nationalist running mate, Vice President Aleksandr Rutskoi, denounced them as "economic genocide."[23] Head of the Russian legislature Ruslan Khasbulatov, who once stood with Yeltsin against the coup, now called for his impeachment. According to the constitution, Khasbulatov's legislature—the CPD—held more power than the presidency, but recognizing the need to be able to make quick decisions in a time of crisis, the legislators had allowed the president to temporarily rule by decree. Now the Congress wanted their power back from Yeltsin, whom they saw as increasingly drunk with power . . . and vodka.

In March 1993 Yeltsin "created a strange impression" with legislators at the CPD as he slurred through a rambling defense of his policies. His opponents loudly denounced their president as a drunk. As Yeltsin left the chamber a *Kuranty* journalist asked him point-blank whether he had been drinking. Yeltsin stopped.

"Smell my breath!" Yeltsin proclaimed.

"And with that," as David Remnick described it, "the leader of the largest landmass on the globe exhaled into the face of the Fourth Estate."

"Well?"

The reporter admitted that he did not noticeably reek of alcohol.[24]

By the early 1990s Yeltsin's inebriety had become the stuff of legend. While all legends are fed by exaggeration, they also rely on the willingness of the audience to believe it. Certainly Yeltsin did little to dispel the image, as his drinking and the enormous burdens of leadership took a noticeable toll on his health. His CPD opponents seized every opportunity to make Yeltsin the butt of political jokes, highlighting his resemblance to the drunken dinosaurs of the old Brezhnevite gerontocracy. Khasbulatov himself "regularly told reporters that the president was nothing more than an erratic drunk who could not be trusted with the nuclear button."[25]

At loggerheads with the president, the Congress let the people decide: a nationwide referendum of April 1993 would ask the disillusioned electorate whether they still had confidence in Yeltsin and his policies. Just three days before the critical vote Yeltsin appeared at a massive rally behind St. Basil's Cathedral, alongside famed human rights advocate Elena Bonner, widow of the fastidiously dry Soviet dissident Andrei Sakharov. Horrified by Yeltsin's drunken state, Bonner snatched the microphone away from the Russian president.[26] Yeltsin was lucky to escape the referendum with only fifty-three percent of voters supporting his reforms.

Accusations, proclamations, and legal investigations flew furiously as both sides vied for political power while economic reforms ground to a halt. His ally just months before, Khasbulatov now scoffed at every Yeltsin move, claiming that "after he's had a few" drinks, Yeltsin would sign anything.[27]

On September 21, 1993, Yeltsin took to the airwaves to cut the gordian knot. While the constitution empowered the parliament, Yeltsin believed that his narrow victory in the referendum gave him greater legitimacy. He would violate his constitutional authority and dissolve the Congress—effectively overthrowing his own government. With the cameras rolling and his message beaming across the country and around the globe, Yeltsin noticeably reached off camera to his right and calmly sipped from a white cup of tea. The signal was loud and clear: no, Yeltsin was not drunk. He was deadly serious.[28]

Ironically, Khasbulatov, Vice President Rutskoi, and their supporters did what Yeltsin himself had done just two years earlier: barricaded themselves in the White House to denounce the Kremlin's coup. Despite having their electricity, hot water, and phones cut, the Congress voted to impeach Yeltsin, replacing him with Rutskoi. The threat of civil war loomed, as Russia had two men both claiming to be president. Asked whether he thought Yeltsin would dare storm the building, Rutskoi said only half in jest: "That depends on how much the president drinks."[29]

After days of tense standoff—including the deadly attempt to storm the national media center at the Ostankino TV tower by White House paramilitaries—on October 4 Yeltsin did what the State Committee on the State of Emergency could not do two years before: he opened fire on his own parliament. Relying on the begrudging support of his drinking buddy and now Minister of

Defense Pavel Grachev, Yeltsin ordered tanks to shell the upper floors of the White House, setting it ablaze; at the same time, an intense firefight raged outside, catching civilians in the crossfire.

Rutskoi's mocking insinuations turned prophetic: high-level figures within Yeltsin's Kremlin later told how the decision to attack was made at Grachev's defense ministry, where Yeltsin was "in an incapacitated state." According to these sources, "His drunken retinue...propped him up against a wall in one of the ministry's lounges and gave practically no one access to him." While his top officials planned the operation, Yeltsin was kept in seclusion, with only Korzhakov acting as go-between.[30]

In the end, Korzhakov and Defense Minister Grachev cobbled together the necessary equipment and reluctant personnel to storm the White House, jail the parliamentary leaders, and stop the descent into civil war. Korzhakov recalled that in apprehending the conspirators at the White House, "Not one of the Deputies reeked of alcohol, and their outward appearance struck me as quite orderly [*akkuratnyi*]." The same could not be said of Yeltsin: upon returning from his historic mission, Korzhakov found him drinking in the banquet hall. "I was astonished to discover that the victory celebrations had been going on long before the victory had been won." When the latecomers presented the president with a trophy of sorts—the rebel Khasbulatov's personal smoking pipe—a drunken Yeltsin smashed it in the corner of the room and laughed. More rounds were poured.[31]

Hundreds of Muscovites died during the so-called October Events. The White House—the recent symbol of Russia's independence aspirations—was now pocked by artillery rounds and charred black by fire. While Yeltsin's Kremlin was quick to repaint and repair the building, Russia's deep political rifts would not be as easy reconciled. The Congress of People's Deputies was disbanded, and Yeltsin continued to rule by decree until a nationwide referendum provided for a new, more pliable legislature and a new constitution that vested most political authority in the office of the president—a president whose drinking was increasingly out of control.

Insobriety Goes International

By 1994, Yeltsin's alcoholism had blossomed from an open secret to a national embarrassment. In August Yeltsin was the honored guest of German chancellor Helmut Kohl to commemorate the departure of the last Russian forces from the former East Germany. The Russian delegation landed in Berlin at sunset. That evening Yeltsin suffered one of his periodic bouts of insomnia. Late at night, Yeltsin summoned Korzhakov and Defense Minister Grachev, who reportedly considered "every shot of vodka he took with Yeltsin to be another star on his general's epaulettes."[32]

Apparently Grachev won many decorations that night, as the drinking went through the night and into his public appearances the next day. Throughout the morning ceremony Chancellor Kohl had to repeatedly support the unsteady Russian president, who grew even less steady at the lunch banquet: Yeltsin ordered a coffee to help sober up, which he promptly dumped down the front of his shirt. Fortunately his staffers always carried a spare. Meanwhile, in the square outside the local Rathaus, a police brass band assembled to serenade the departing troops. Before an ensemble of astonished leaders, diplomats, and journalists, the inebriated Yeltsin grabbed the conductor's baton and "woozily stabbed the air with it for several minutes as the band played on."[33] He then grabbed a microphone and slurred his way through the Russian folk song *Kalinka* before blowing kisses to a tittering crowd of onlookers.

The media soon broadcast Yeltsin's buffoonery around the globe. Western audiences were amused, Russians were mortified. This was a public relations disaster for a proud country still stinging from its loss of empire and superpower status. Russia endured unfathomable suffering, the Red Army battled so heroically into Berlin to depose Adolph Hitler a half-century before... and *this* is how they leave?

A visibly intoxicated Russian president Boris Yeltsin (left) accepts the report of Col.-Gen. Matvei Burlakov on the official withdrawal of Russian troops from Germany as German chancellor Helmut Kohl looks on. August, 31, 1994. Corbis Images/ Wolfgang Kumm.

The president's top advisors considered resigning en masse. Instead, they attempted an intervention. The next month, on a flight to the resort city of Sochi, Korzhakov hand delivered what the press later dubbed "The Letter of the Aides to Their Sultan." In perhaps the most shocking communique in Russian history, the candid document laid out the enormous challenges ahead of the fast-approaching 1996 elections alongside Yeltsin's shortcomings displayed at Berlin.

> Above all else is the neglect of your health—which has been sacrificed to Russia's well-known vice. It exacerbates a certain complacency and self-assurance, together creating arrogance, intolerance, an unwillingness to listen to unpleasant information, moodiness and occasionally abusive behavior towards people.
>
> We speak of this sharply and openly not only because we believe in you as a strong individual, but also because your personal fate and your example are intimately tied to the fate of Russia's transformation. A degraded President would significantly degrade Russia itself. We cannot allow that to happen.[34]

No diplomatic language could soften such a blunt diagnosis. Yet their practical suggestions were even more galling. Item number one was the "decisive reevaluation of your attitude toward your health and your harmful habits." To that, they urged Yeltsin to put an end to the "unexpected disappearances and rehabilitations"; set a better example as an open and democratic president; forego the pomp, seclusion, and other "tsarist habits"; and find more cultured ways to relax that do not end at the banquet table.

"So?" the aides in the Kremlin asked those who were with Yeltsin on the airplane: "how'd he take it?"

"Snarling."

After taking it all in, Yeltsin raged at his advisors and even Korzhakov: "How could you allow this?!" While he later admitted the letter was a wake-up call, it apparently took some time for it to sink in. The brooding president refused to shake hands with his advisors and in some cases refused to even speak with them for upwards of six months.[35] Driving the point home, Yeltsin excluded the offending aides from his high-profile visit to North America and Europe the following month—a trip that would end in even greater embarrassment.

Bill And Boris

You could not blame Richard Nixon for being gruff. In January 1993, not only did the Republican former president observe his eightieth birthday; he also had to watch the inauguration of Bill Clinton—a Democrat—over Nixon's close friend, George H. W. Bush. Now here he was just days later offering advice to Clinton's team on engaging Russia. Dismissing Yeltsin's competitors as "crazy communists and fascists," Nixon encouraged the new administration to support him. "He may be a drunk, but he's also the best we're likely to get in that screwed-up country over there."[36] Having squared off with the bombastic Nikita Khrushchev in the so-called Kitchen Debate in the 1950s and experienced his own liquor-filled encounters with Leonid Brezhnev in the 1970s, Nixon was in a unique position to evaluate the Russian leaders and their peculiarities.

"He's preaching to the converted," laughed Clinton upon hearing Nixon's advice. "In fact, he's preaching to the preacher!" Clinton had called Yeltsin just days earlier, saying a solid relationship with Russia was America's top foreign policy priority. Yeltsin hardly listened, and his responses were slurred and incoherent. "A candidate for tough love, if ever I heard one," Clinton later chuckled to his advisor Strobe Talbott. Just to be on the safe side, of the fifty phone conversations between the two presidents over the following eight years, Clinton's aides were sure to schedule all of them before dinnertime in Moscow.[37]

Within months the two presidents hit it off in Vancouver at the first of a series of high-level summits. Clinton aide George Stephanopoulos recalled the Americans' astonishment at how much alcohol the Russian president dared to hold: three scotches on the boat ride followed by a straight wine lunch—ignoring the food and going straight for round after round of alcohol. While some thought it undiplomatic to keep score, little did they know that this was part of a centuries-old tradition: foreign envoys from von Herberstein to Ribbentrop and de Gaulle, and even Nixon and Kissinger, had all tallied the drinks of the Russian leaders, and all with equal amazement.[38]

Writing his last article before his death in 1994, Nixon offered a cold rebuke to Clinton's Russia policy: "Most important, the U.S. should be candid with Russia when our views do not coincide. We are great world powers and our interests will inevitably clash, but the greatest mistake we can make is to try to drown down differences in champagne and vodka toasts at 'feel-good' summit meetings."[39] Yet such warnings were roundly ignored, both in Washington and European capitals.

Many European leaders joined in Clinton's anthem: "Yeltsin drunk is better than most of the alternatives sober." If that meant Yeltsin showed up to a summit meeting with a hangover, so be it. When he shelled his own parliament? "I guess we've just got to pull up our socks and back Ol' Boris again." The separatists in Chechnya? Clinton likened them to the Confederate south in the U.S. Civil War, by extension casting Yeltsin as a modern-day Abraham Lincoln.

"I want this guy to win so bad it hurts,"[40] said Clinton. It showed.

In this context, Clinton was willing to overlook all sorts of indiscretions, even the outrageous events of Yeltsin's September 1994 visit to Washington. On the first night, Clinton was roused by reports of a major predawn security breach at Blair House—the presidential guest house. Secret Service agents had found a drunken Yeltsin alone on Pennsylvania Avenue in his underwear, apparently trying to hail a cab to get some pizza. The next night guards apprehended a drunken intruder trying to sneak into the Blair House basement. A tense standoff between Russian and American agents ensued. After everyone's credentials were sorted out, it became clear that it was just Yeltsin, again. Asked whether Clinton ever saw fit to speak to Yeltsin about his alcoholism, Clinton demurred—unsure of his place or the political consequences.[41]

Thankfully, there were no journalists or cameras…this time. That wasn't the case on the return trip, which included a brief two-hour stopover with the prime minister of Ireland, Albert Reynolds, to ink economic agreements at the famed Dromoland Castle near Shannon. Around 12:30 p.m. on a cold and drizzly autumn afternoon, the plane carrying the Russian advance team approached the Shannon airport. But after half an hour, Yeltsin's plane still had not descended through the low clouds.

Nikolai Kozyrev, Russia's first ambassador to Ireland, was understandably worried. He rushed to find the senior Aeroflot representative, who explained that "aircraft No. 1 bearing the Russian president had long come into view, but for some reason it was not landing, it was circling over the airport" in an inexplicable delaying tactic. After an hour the plane finally broke through clouds and landed safely.

Once their hosts quite literally rolled out the red carpets for the Russian president, Ambassador Kozyrev dashed past the color guard, the international press corps, and a crowd of flag-waving onlookers, and boarded the plane to invite Yeltsin to meet the waiting Irish delegation. Instead he was intercepted by Yeltsin's burly bodyguard Korzhakov outside the president's compartment. "You can't go in there, the president is very tired," Korzhakov insisted. Deputy Prime Minister Oleg Soskovets—disheveled, distressed, and being hastily prepared in the back of the plane—would conduct the negotiations instead.[42]

"There was no point in trying to bargain further," thought Kozyrev, after being repeatedly rebuffed: "all I could do was descend the ramp under the lights and flashing of journalists' cameras, in anticipation of Boris Yeltsin's appearance, and explain the whole situation to the Irish premier. What is more, I had to think up words of apology as I went along (naturally Korzhakov did not supply anything on this account), as well as the version that the president was not feeling well due to supposedly high blood pressure."

Kozyrev exchanged meaningful glances with the disappointed Irish Taoiseach. "Well now, if he is sick, there is nothing we can do about it," concluded the visibly disappointed Reynolds, "but Mr. Yeltsin, my guest, is on Irish soil, and I cannot miss this opportunity to go on board the airplane for five minutes, shake the president's hand and wish him a speedy recovery." Yet that too was impossible. No one could see the Russian president.

And so the Irish summit failed before it began, producing enmity and indignation rather than trust and cooperation. "We Irish, like you Russians, also like to drink, and all kinds of things happen here," a high-ranking Irish official later confided. "So if your president had come out to see us, we wouldn't have paid any attention to his state and would have forgiven him, but his refusal to come out of the airplane insulted us to the depth of our souls and showed us that a small country like Ireland wasn't worth reckoning with."[43]

When Yeltsin finally did emerge—at Moscow's Vnukovo airport—he was peppered with questions. His reply was artless at best: "Well, you see I was sleeping and no one woke me up. But they're not going to get away with it. And I am well, who said I was sick?" Yeltsin later apologized personally to Reynolds, again claiming that he had overslept.

The truth about what really happened at Shannon remains a mystery. The Aeroflot representative recalled seeing Yeltsin emerge from his compartment in suit and tie eager to go to the talks and was agitated that his handlers, "fearing for the state he was in," would not allow it. Korzhakov's muckraking biography claimed that Yeltsin was having chest pains. Yeltsin's daughter and advisor, Tatyana Yumasheva, later revealed it was a mild heart attack. Still, these conflicting accounts at least agree that the party Yeltsin began in Washington continued on the transatlantic flight.[44]

Whether he was drunk, sleeping, or ill, the Shannon snub provided even more ammunition for Yeltsin's opponents to depict him as unfit for leadership. The press had a field day, with one headline more scathing than the next. One front-page political cartoon depicted the waiting Irish delegation watching as an empty vodka bottle tumbled down the plane's staircase with the inscription "Hello from Yeltsin." Back in Russia, former vice president turned critic Aleksandr Rutskoi joked that Yeltsin was in a "permanent state of visiting Ireland."[45]

While such high-profile diplomatic gaffes tarnished Yeltsin's once-heroic image, other alcoholic episodes would have much more tangible—and tragic—results.

Chechnya

At the time of the failed August 1991 coup Boris Yeltsin encouraged the various republics across the Soviet Union to "take as much sovereignty as you can swallow" to weaken the authority of Mikhail Gorbachev. Former Soviet air force general Dzhokhar Dudayev—the recently elected president of the tiny republic of Chechnya in Russia's rugged northern Caucasus mountains—did just that. On November 1, 1991, Dudayev expelled Kremlin operatives from the predominantly Muslim Chechnya and declared its independence from both from Gorbachev's Soviet Union and Yeltsin's Russian Republic, to which it was nominally subordinate. The tiny, breakaway republic maintained de facto sovereignty even after the Russian Federation's independence, until the unsteady Yeltsin took decisive action to reassert Kremlin control after a series of bus hijackings in November 1994.[46]

Emotions ran high at a November meeting at Yeltsin's dacha attended by more drinking buddies than government ministers (including those like Defense Minister Pavel Grachev, who conveniently filled both roles). Yeltsin suddenly gave the order: "Reestablish control of Chechnya!" Unsurprisingly, according to those present, Yeltsin was "drunk" and "out of control." Russia's dilapidated military had neither the plans nor the troops in place to carry out such a brash order. Nevertheless, within days, a ragtag collection of ill-equipped units pressed into Chechnya, where they were quickly pinned down by rocket-propelled grenades and sniper fire.[47]

The focus of the Russian advance was the Chechen capital, Grozny. With a population of four hundred forty thousand, it was a vibrant, multi-ethnic city larger than Omaha, Nebraska. The decision to besiege the city—the first indiscriminate aerial bombardment of a European city since World War II—was ordered in such haste that it was not even assigned an official code name. The newspaper *Izvestiya* reported that the decision to attack on New Year's Eve—which caught tens of thousands of innocent and unsuspecting ethnic-Russian and Chechen civilians in the crosshairs—was made by Defense Minister Grachev and other high-ranking officials in the middle of a vodka binge. "The front-line units then received the command—whoever took the [Chechen] presidential palace would receive three Hero of Russia awards."[48]

It would be easy to simply portray the first war in Chechnya as a series of awful tactical decisions that were implemented disastrously, but that would trivialize the tragedy of some thirty thousand killed in Chechnya between 1994 and 1996 and perhaps another seventy thousand killed following the resumption of hostilities in 1999—to say nothing of the hundreds of thousands of refugees, the indiscriminate attacks on innocent civilians, a litany of torture, forcible disappearances, terrorist attacks, and human rights atrocities committed by belligerents on all sides.[49] And as with the more epic military engagements of Russia's storied past (chapter 11), this war was also drenched in alcohol. Interior ministry generals and Cossack volunteers were notorious for their brutality and open drunkenness. Chechen civilians also feared the underpaid Russian foot soldiers, who "were extremely savage—hysterical, terrified, drunken—they would kill for no reason at all."[50] Eyewitnesses told of rogue Russian troops menacing civilians for food, cash, and vodka or bartering their weapons to obtain them.

"We were all going absolutely nuts, what with the racket and the corpses and the blood and the lice," explained a Russian unit commander.

> Street fighting is hell. We were all drunk and high. Otherwise we couldn't have stood it. There was no other way. But I smile sometimes when I speak, because it seemed funny to us at the time. It was so much fun when a house filled with civilians was hit with depth charges, the kind you use against submarines. What it does is, it smashes through nine stories and after a while it explodes. When the dust all settles, there's nothing left but the outside framework, the four walls.[51]

Yet it wasn't just the Russian side that was drunk: one of the most frequently reported ironies of the Chechen separatists were tales of "true Muslim" fighters preparing to take on the Russian enemy after quaffing bottles of Russian vodka.[52]

Chechnya is one of the great humanitarian tragedies in post-Soviet Eurasia as well as an enormous political challenge for the Kremlin. For some, laying at least partial blame with vodka could be construed as absolving politicians, commanders, and troops of responsibility. That is not my intent. Instead Chechnya underscores the persistence of the autocratic traditions of Russian vodka politics. For all the rhetoric of liberty and democracy in the immediate post-Soviet years—when Russia was arguably its most democratic—under Yeltsin, political decision making was still insular and autocratic. In well-functioning, responsive governments, big decisions about issues like war and peace are rarely entered into lightly: usually after extensive coordination within the government and in dialogue with the public rather than on a whim over rounds of drinks. Indeed, one need not focus on Yeltsin's drinking to see the continuities with the Soviet autocracy from which he emerged; you need only consider Chechnya and the drunken callousness with which Yeltsin and his inner circle unnecessarily imperiled hundreds of thousands of their own, voting citizens.

Political Death, Political Resurrection

To say that Yeltsin was in trouble with Russian voters was an understatement. Chechnya was just another failure laid at his feet, alongside the implosion of the Russian economy and his high-profile drunken gaffes. Even worse, between July and December 1995 Yeltsin's heavy drinking culminated in three separate life-threatening heart attacks. His sudden disappearance in the run-up to the 1995 legislative elections to the Duma entrenched perceptions that Yeltsin was unfit to lead. His most vocal opponents made significant gains through populist, anti-Yeltsin positions. Ironically, the ultranationalist Vladimir Zhirinovsky— subsequently better known for his bombastic rhetoric and for starting fistfights on the floor of the Duma—scored points with the everyday Ivan-in-the-street by demanding even lower vodka prices. Many snickered when he launched his own brand of vodka with his face on the label. But when Zhirinovsky's Liberal Democratic Party of Russia, along with the Communist Party of the Russian Federation, became the two largest factions in the legislature, nobody was laughing.[53] Indeed, Richard Nixon's warnings sounded ever more prophetic.

The real prize was the presidency, which was due to be contested in the summer of 1996. While the communists and the nationalists surged ahead, Yeltsin's approval numbers were in the single digits—in some cases even less than the poll's margin of error. Many whispered that it might be necessary to cancel the elections in order to save "democracy" from itself. The economic stability of the Soviet past promised by Yeltsin's principal rival, Communist Party leader Gennady Zyuganov, sounded increasingly alluring amid the hardships of transition. With a seemingly insurmountable lead, Zyuganov accentuated Yeltsin's personal and political shortcomings. "I'm not against a good glass of wine or a little shot of vodka," Zyuganov reminded voters. "But I drink quite modestly. I can't handle more than three vodkas. Someone has to be sober among today's politicians."[54]

At his hospital bed, Yeltsin received a blunt ultimatum from his Kremlin doctors: either stop drinking or die—plain and simple. From that point on, Yeltsin vowed to shape up and compete. Facing his own mortality, however, may have been easier than facing the hostile electorate. When pollsters asked what adjectives best described Yeltsin, "drunk," "ill," and "out of touch with the common person" made the top five. A rededicated Yeltsin tried to resurrect the image of a dynamic leader. Traveling the country, famously dancing onstage at concert rallies, a reinvigorated Yeltsin lost twenty pounds and stopped drinking. Days before the first round of voting he even fired his longtime enabler/gatekeeper Alexander Korzhakov. On the campaign trail, when he was bluntly asked whether he was an alcoholic, he answered,

> To say yes would be untrue. To say no would not be convincing. Here people will not believe it unless they check it themselves. They would even say: "What kind of Russian man are you if you can't drink?" So I will only say that I can drink, but that I don't abuse alcohol![55]

While many remained skeptical that he had turned over a new leaf, kicking the bottle was just part of the formula that brought Yeltsin back from near death—both politically and physiologically—to achieve ultimate victory over the communist Zyuganov with fifty-four percent of the vote in a runoff election. He ended the disastrous war in Chechnya. His campaign re-framed the election as a referendum on the communist past represented by Zyuganov. Against the memory of Soviet rule, Yeltsin's alcoholism did not seem nearly as bad.[56] Yet his message could not resonate if no one heard it. To bankroll his campaign, Yeltsin turned to a group of "oligarchs," the super-rich winners of Russia's new capitalist game, who had everything to lose should the communists return. In the ensuing "loans-for-shares scandal," these oligarchs not only bankrolled Yeltsin's campaign, but they also had their media holdings shower Yeltsin with positive coverage—in exchange for some of the remaining yet-to-be-privatized jewels of the old Soviet economy. When, as expected, the government failed to repay the loans, the oligarchs walked away with the commanding heights of the Russian economy, having paid only kopecks on the ruble for them.

From day one of his second term Yeltsin was seen as a lame duck president. His newfound sobriety could have been a bigger story, had Yeltsin not again disappeared shortly after his victory—this time for a quintuple heart bypass that landed him in the hospital for months—again inviting comparisons with the infirm Brezhnevite gerontocracy. Upon his return, Yeltsin seemed politically beholden to the oligarchs as the Russian economy lurched from one crisis to another, culminating in the government's default and economic collapse amid the 1998 financial crisis.

On December 31, 1999—while the rest of the world waited anxiously to see whether the Y2K bug would crash the global computer grid—Yeltsin appeared on Russian TV to give his annual new year's address. He tearfully pleaded for forgiveness for promises unfulfilled before announcing his immediate resignation. The recently appointed prime minister, Vladimir Putin, would serve as interim president until new elections could be held.

When Yeltsin left office, his approval rating was around three percent in polls with a margin of error of plus or minus four percent. He had very few friends left—save perhaps for Bill Clinton, who had suffered his own political disgraces. Though Yeltsin withdrew from public view, those who met him in private said that his continued sobriety had done wonders for his health. Friends claimed he looked ten years younger and was at peace, enjoying family, reading, and following tennis. Nevertheless, Boris Yeltsin finally succumbed to congestive heart failure on April 23, 2007.[57]

Three years later, Yeltsin's normally reclusive daughter and former advisor Tatyana Yumasheva tried to dispel the misperceptions. "Many in the West have a caricatured image of Yeltsin, a larger-than-life character for whom drinking was a way of life," she said. "That's absolutely untrue." While she admitted that he often drank to excess, it was only to cope with the monumental political challenges he faced. In his exhaustive and engaging biography of Yeltsin, Harvard political scientist Timothy Colton argued that Boris Yeltsin became the butt of so many jokes not because he drank more than his Soviet predecessors, but rather because his torments played out in public, thanks to a media that was freer and livelier than in any other period in Russian history. Yumasheva would concur: "They do so because it's a cliché which sells."[58] This is most certainly true. Yeltsin was hardly the most drunk leader in Russian history. He wasn't even among the most drunk leaders of the previous fifty years—arguably consuming less than Brezhnev, Chernenko, and perhaps even Stalin—all of whom drank far from the peering eyes of the public.

Nevertheless, to the extent that alcoholism was part of the Yeltsin story, the legacy of his heavy drinking is intimately connected to the fate of modern Russia itself. Ironically, Russia's first post-independence president was perhaps the purest product of Soviet vodka politics, which nurtured both his debilitating alcoholism and his closed system of autocratic decision making under the veneer of democracy. His public temperament set an awful example for Russian citizens to follow and fostered ever-greater cynicism toward Yeltsin the man as well as his economic and social reforms that culminated in a decade of misery and despair.

‖ 20 ‖

Alcohol and the Demodernization
of Russia

From the outset, Russia's reformers were in uncharted waters and sinking fast. The received wisdom going back to Karl Marx was that the great challenge of history would be the transition from capitalism to communism, not the other way around. Right up to the collapse of the Berlin Wall, few people thought a reversion to capitalism was even possible. Even fewer thought about *how* to do it. Reformers in the communist satellites of Eastern Europe and the Soviet homeland thought they knew what hardships it would entail—unemployment, dislocation, and economic contraction—but they could only guess how deep the pain would be or how long it would last.

To right the ship, Boris Yeltsin—fresh from victory over the August 1991 hardline coup—pushed for radical reforms. "The time has come to act decisively, firmly, without hesitation," he declared. Top experts drafted a "500 Days" program that denationalized land and housing, freed fixed prices, abolished subsidies for inefficient firms, and implemented austere fiscal and monetary reforms. "The period of movement with small steps is over."[1] Yet he too was uncertain about the suffering it would entail.

"I have to tell you frankly: today in the severest crisis we cannot carry out reform painlessly. The first step will be most difficult. A certain decline in the standard of living will take place," Yeltsin said. In preparing the country for the shock therapy of rapid liberalization he claimed, "It will be worse for everybody for about half a year. Then, the prices will fall and the consumer market will be filled with goods. And toward the fall of 1992...the economy will stabilize and lives will gradually improve."[2]

But things did not improve. Into 1993 Russia was still stuck in a hyperinflationary spiral, which wiped out most Russians' entire life savings. With consumer prices rising over two thousand percent per year, the ruble became worthless, eroding the real wages of those who still had jobs and plunging millions into abject poverty. The average Russian schoolteacher's monthly salary during the

1990s was just $34, well below their counterparts in Thailand, and often below the government's official "minimum subsistence" (i.e., poverty) level. Even after the economy stabilized at the end of the millennium, one study concluded that the minimum monthly income in Novgorod region was barely enough to feed five live cats.[3]

Economic indicators were equally frightening: Russia produced two hundred and fourteen thousand tractors in 1990. By 1994 it was fewer than twenty-nine thousand—a collapse of eighty-seven percent. The production of all foodstuffs in 1994 was half what it was under Gorbachev and had still farther to fall. By the late 1990s, Russia's annual grain harvests were smaller than they were under the tsars before World War I. The Red Cross even mobilized food aid to avert a potential famine.[4]

The economic hardships helped unleash a tidal wave of drunkenness larger than anything seen before in Russia's long, inebriated history. Russia's heavy-drinking men were dying off at an alarming rate, with deaths from alcohol poisonings, liver and cardiovascular diseases, drunken homicides and suicides all skyrocketing. Russian male life expectancy dropped from sixty-four to fifty-eight—worse even than under Stalin's tyranny.[5]

In many ways it seemed that Russia was not simply in the throes of economic depression but was somehow regressing backward in time—undoing all of the economic and social progress that had been achieved through such tremendous human sacrifice under the Soviets. From the most remote regions to the capitals Russia experienced a "steady retreat of civilization": citizens were forced into premodern survival strategies as the Soviet-era industrial, commercial, healthcare, and law enforcement systems corrupted, decayed, and collapsed around them.[6]

"It's difficult to talk about the twenty-first century when you're sitting here reading by candlelight," confided one teen in Russia's desolate Kamchatka Peninsula on the eve of the new millennium. "The twenty-first century does not matter. It's the nineteenth century here."[7] This was no ordinary economic recession.

From "Transition" To Demodernization

To read the economic literature on Russia's "lost decade" of the 1990s is to get lost in the technocratic language of "-ions": stagnation, transition, recession, depression, contraction, liberalization, inflation, stabilization, deregulation, denationalization, privatization, commercialization. Examining developments through such high-altitude, macroeconomic "-ions" conveniently—and perhaps deliberately—blinds us to the true cost of a decade-long turmoil that by some estimates reduced economic output by over fifty percent—far worse even than the Great Depression.[8] Economists' estimates of diminishing GDP—even on a per capita basis—tell only one side of the story.

In the wake of Russia's 1998 default, NYU professor Stephen F. Cohen described the horrific scope of the realities on the ground: "When the infrastructures of production, technology, science, transportation, heating and sewage disposal disintegrate; when tens of millions of people do not receive earned salaries, some 75 percent of society lives below or barely above the subsistence level, and millions of them are actually starving; when male life expectancy has plunged as low as fifty-eight years, malnutrition has become the norm among schoolchildren, once-eradicated diseases are again becoming epidemics, and basic welfare provisions are disappearing; when even highly educated professionals must grow their own food in order to survive and well over half the nation's economic transactions are barter—all this, and more, is indisputable evidence of a tragic 'transition' backward to a premodern era." Cohen concludes that "so great is Russia's economic and thus social catastrophe that we must now speak of another unprecedented development: *the literal demodernization of a twentieth-century country*".[9]

Although neither Cohen nor any other scholar have elaborated on "demodernization" as a concept, his underlying claim is most assuredly true: adding social indicators to economic ones, we find that not only was Russia's "lost decade" worse than either Japan's "lost decade" or America's Great Depression in degree, but it was also fundamentally different in kind—a process of destruction and deindustrialization without parallel in the peacetime history of the world.[10]

Perhaps the best way to illustrate this difference is to fold social indicators into the conventional economic comparisons. Recently, sword-swallowing Swedish statistician Hans Rosling and his Gapminder Foundation have developed just such an approach. Bridging the "gap" between inaccessible social-scientific data and a broader public utilization, Gapminder is a user-friendly clearinghouse of official health, economic, and social statistics compiled by national and international agencies around the globe, which facilitates comparisons across countries and over time. For instance, by plotting a standard indicator of prosperity (income per capita) on the horizontal axis and social well-being (average life expectancy) on the vertical, Rosling animates over two hundred years of data for two hundred countries to show how, due to industrialization and modernization, all countries have generally moved toward the upper-right quadrant—his so-called "healthy, wealthy corner"—where all modern states aspire to be.[11]

Following Rosling, figure 20.1 presents twenty-year sections of data: Russia and Japan from 1980 to 2000 and the United States from 1920 to 1940. The results are telling: Japan's "lost decade" was a prolonged recession: economic growth may have slowed, but Japan was still progressing toward the healthy–wealthy corner. By contrast, America's experience in the Great Depression was

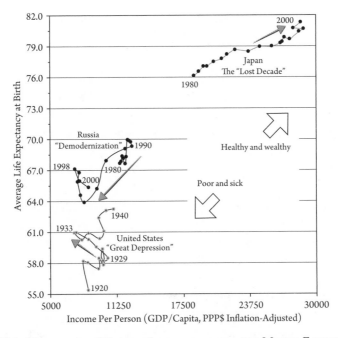

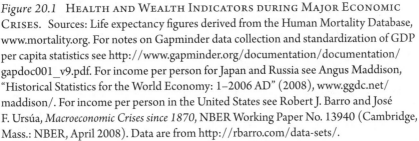

Figure 20.1 HEALTH AND WEALTH INDICATORS DURING MAJOR ECONOMIC CRISES. Sources: Life expectancy figures derived from the Human Mortality Database, www.mortality.org. For notes on Gapminder data collection and standardization of GDP per capita statistics see http://www.gapminder.org/documentation/documentation/gapdoc001_v9.pdf. For income per person for Japan and Russia see Angus Maddison, "Historical Statistics for the World Economy: 1–2006 AD" (2008), www.ggdc.net/maddison/. For income per person in the United States see Robert J. Barro and José F. Ursúa, *Macroeconomic Crises since 1870*, NBER Working Paper No. 13940 (Cambridge, Mass.: NBER, April 2008). Data are from http://rbarro.com/data-sets/.

movement toward the upper-left quadrant: the economy was contracting, yet the overall health of the population actually improved.

These experiences were fundamentally different—not only in degree but also in kind—from what Russia endured: moving dramatically away from the healthy–wealthy corner for the duration of the 1990s, becoming both far poorer and more sickly. The only other examples of such dramatic retrograde motion come from countries devastated by war: World War I and the 1918 flu pandemic, Germany in World War II, Bosnia in the Yugoslav wars of the 1990s. To have such dramatic backsliding in peacetime is unheard of.

What happened?

My argument here is straightforward: economic crisis plus the legacies of vodka politics lead to demodernization, which undercut Russia's long-term potential for both economic growth and successful democratization.

The End Of Autocracy, The End Of Vodka Politics?

Vodka politics has been the central pillar of Russian statecraft since the earliest tsars. Yet so radical was the break with the Soviet past that even the mighty state vodka monopoly fell to liberalization, marketization, and democratization.

In January 1992 the old Soviet vodka monopoly was abolished. The once-fixed price of alcohol would now be set by supply and demand, capped with an eighty percent excise tax. The state maintained some control by monopolizing the necessary raw materials for distillation—ethyl alcohol—which could only be *legally* procured from one of the 162 state-run rectification facilities at a price that reflected the additional taxes levied on it.[12] The old Soviet alcohol producers and importers were reorganized and privatized while private distilleries and *samogon* moonshiners flourished. To evade government taxes and regulations most alcohol production shifted off the books and into the black market. Untaxed imports flooded in from the West, and illegal shipments arrived by the trainload from Belarus and Ukraine. Vodka was everywhere. A half-liter bottle of questionable origins and ingredients could be had for a dollar. Whereas vodka contributed almost a third of the Soviet superpower's budget, by 1996 that share had plummeted to three percent—with the money that once would have gone to the treasury ending up in the hands of black market producers and bootleggers.[13]

"The tradition of drinking oneself under the table," once quipped Soviet dissident Mikhail Baitalsky, is "the popular tradition most profitable to the state."[14] Yet just because the state was no longer profiting as it used to did not mean that Russians instantly sobered up. Government policies change quickly; cultures change glacially. So although the Soviet autocracy and monopoly were suddenly gone, they left behind an entire population that for generations had relied on vodka as "the Russian god"—omnipotent and omnipresent, in good times and bad.[15]

And times were getting very, very bad.

With their life savings gone, jobs evaporating, the uncertainty of economic calamity, and the lack of steady leadership, is it any wonder that more and more Russians turned to vodka, practically the only product that was both cheaper and more available than under the Soviets?[16] By the time of Yeltsin's 1996 re-election bid, per capita alcohol consumption approached fourteen liters of pure alcohol per year—returning to the astronomical levels of the Brezhnev era and erasing what little benefits remained of Gorbachev's well-intentioned anti-alcohol program.[17]

Gorbachev's campaign was a vivid reminder that clamping down on legal vodka breeds a thriving underground of moonshiners and bootleggers who

skirt government regulations through bribes and graft. The growth of dangerous *samogon* home brew and mushrooming corruption undercut Gorbachev's
initiatives just as they had done to every previous, dramatic anti-alcohol measure, including the ill-fated prohibition during World War I. Economic logic
suggested, then, that once restrictions were lifted and the alcohol market was
liberalized, the black market in alcohol would emerge from the shadows and
become a legitimate contributor to Russia's new capitalist economy. As it turns-
out—due to vodka's complex role in Russian culture—something quite different happened.

When times are tough, vodka has always been there—not just as a product to
be bought to drown one's sorrows, but also as the currency used in the exchange.
Indeed, just as Russia's economy was demodernizing, so too was its monetary
system. With the ruble rendered practically worthless by hyperinflation, more
and more transactions were conducted through the primitive commodity
money of vodka rather than modern paper currency.[18]

Back under the tsars, Orthodox priests gave villagers vodka in exchange for
working for the parish (chapter 8). Set against the Bolshevik Revolution and
civil war, Boris Pasternak's Nobel Prize–winning novel *Doctor Zhivago* described
vodka as Russia's "favorite black-market currency."[19] Alcohol even greased the
wheels of the modern administrative-command economy itself: most Soviet
enterprises employed supply officers, or *tolkachi*, well-connected black market
hustlers who, equipped with a few cases of vodka, could find the scarce materials
necessary to help the factory fulfill their production quotas. The ministry of foreign trade even got Pepsi Cola from the United States by bartering Stolichnaya
vodka.[20]

Whenever cash was unavailable or unreliable, vodka was there. *Butylka za
uslugu*—a bottle for a favor—was how things got done: whether it was getting a leaky faucet fixed or expediting bureaucratic paperwork, vodka delivered
results.[21] But what of those, like rural pensioners, who could not afford vodka?
From necessity rather than thirst, many turned to home brewing. "We have to
harvest potatoes, mow hay and lay in firewood," explained one elderly *babushka*
in a 1984 Soviet investigation, "and for every favor the collective farm workers
do, you give them two or three bottles of vodka. We don't have the money to
do this, so we have to brew the liquor ourselves." After compiling many similar
complaints from the countryside, the Soviet journalist simply lamented, "It's as
if money itself is too inconvenient."[22] To make matters worse, even elderly home
brewers were often fined forty rubles for violating laws against moonshining—a
penalty that rose during Gorbachev's anti-alcohol campaign.[23]

Understanding vodka as a medium of barter, and home brewing as a means
of coping with personal economic hardship, helps explain why—when the
post-communist transition rendered the ruble worthless and pushed millions

into poverty—Russia saw a dramatic increase in moonshining by those on fixed incomes: not just pensioners, but teachers, nurses, engineers, scientists, and soldiers.[24] So although the old state monopoly was gone, the illegal vodka trade did not wither away—it exploded.

Yet vodka from homemade stills was just a drop in the bucket compared to the tsunami of illegal alcohol flooding into Russia from abroad. By early 1994—unfathomably—as much as sixty percent of all of the vodka sold in Russia was imported.[25] Rather than the top-shelf European liquors like Absolut or Finlandia, these were cheap, and often poisonous, knockoffs smuggled in from other post-Soviet republics. A quick bribe to a hard-up border guard or inspector was often enough to sneak an entire shipment through Russia's porous borders, which could undercut the price of legally produced, regulated, and taxed Russian hooch by as much as fifty percent.[26]

In the West, those concerned about Russian border security normally feared Russia's "loose nukes" sneaking into the hands of international terrorists. In Russia, the bigger challenge was preventing trucks and even trainloads of illegal, unregulated, and therefore often poisonous alcohol from entering the country, especially in the volatile Caucasus. Forty percent of the vodka consumed in Russia was produced—most of it illegally—in the small province of North Ossetia, where fully one-third of the entire adult population was employed in vodka production. In addition to distilling a large, subsidized quota of ethyl alcohol from the ministry of agriculture, cheap raw-material spirits were imported from Ukraine, with false documents listing Russia as a transit country and therefore exempt from Russian customs duties.[27]

When the government-subsidized supply of ethyl alcohol dried up thanks to market reforms, and stepped-up customs regulations put a kink in the "Great Vodka Route" from Ukraine to Russia, North Ossetian producers turned to smuggling cheap foreign spirits through the Georgian port of Poti, from where it was trucked over the mountains and smuggled into Russia through the Roki Tunnel. In July 1997, with the backing of President Yeltsin, General Andrei Nikolayev of the Federal Border Service closed the Russian border to Georgian alcohol trucks that did not pay full import duties.

The tense standoff quickly escalated into a small-scale "vodka war" when a caravan of over three thousand metric tons of pure ethyl alcohol destined for North Ossetia was denied entry to Russia. When the border guards were unswayed by bribes in excess of $1 million, the heavily armed rum-runners opened fire, attempting to fight their way into Russia before being pushed back by military reinforcements. One Georgian truck driver was killed in the crossfire. In the face of pressure from the Georgian foreign ministry and President Eduard Shevardnadze, Yeltsin relented: Nikolayev was dismissed, and the flow of alcohol resumed.[28]

Hundreds of trucks laden with illegal alcohol imports are stranded on the Russian–Georgian border, September, 19, 1997. Associated Press/Shakh Aivazov.

Armed standoffs illustrated just how high the stakes—and the payoffs—were for anyone who could sidestep government regulations and meet the demand for cheap booze. Corrupt entrepreneurs set up shell companies to import a single shipment before vanishing without paying duties. Others forged foreign documents for Russian products to sidestep regulations on domestic production.

Shockingly, in 1993, President Yeltsin decreed that particular charitable organizations that had earned his favor—including the Afghan War Veterans' Union, the Hockey Federation of Russia, the National Sports Foundation, and the Moscow Patriarchate of the Russian Orthodox Church—were exempt from paying customs duties on imports. Consequently, these charities suddenly found themselves knee-deep in the corrupt world of the international vodka trade. The Department of External Relations of the Russian Orthodox Church became a major importer of vodka and cigarettes. The National Sports Foundation—nominally charged with promoting healthy lifestyles—imported thirty-one railroad cars containing nine hundred and seventy-five thousand bottles of vodka in one transaction alone, never paying the 43.5 billion rubles in import duties. Heads of both the Hockey Federation and the Veterans' Union were assassinated in bloody contract killings in the settling of accounts. When the import loopholes were finally rescinded in the late 1990s, the government estimated that these charities left the woefully indebted Yeltsin regime on the hook for another thirty-seven trillion rubles or some nine *billion* dollars.[29]

How much black market vodka actually came from abroad is impossible to know. However, Russian law enforcement estimated that, during the 1990s, a mere two percent of Russia's thriving shadow market came from homemade *samogon*. The other ninety-eight percent was either imported illegally or man-ufactured off the books in regular distilleries.[30] The reason was simple: it was more cost effective to pay bribes than the heavy eighty percent excise tax levied on alcohol. With corruption as historically entrenched as alcohol (and, as we've seen, actually a consequence of it), and with a population that had little experi-ence in paying taxes under the Soviets, it was apparent why so much of the vodka market remained underground.[31]

As if out of a Hollywood prohibition drama, the savvy Russian bootleg-ger directed a complex operation with creative bookkeeping: one set of books recording a distillery's official production—and hence the quantity of alcohol he pays taxes on—which is entirely different from the factory's actual output. Since taxes were so high and the competition for cheap booze so intense, profit margins on legal vodka were a razor-thin four or five percent.[32] It was much more lucrative to move production off the books all together—oftentimes leasing out their facilities during off-hours to third parties who had little concern for tax or safely regulations. So prevalent was this "third shift" vodka that many distilleries in the 1990s—especially in the North Caucasus—reported operating at only five percent of their known capacity.

"It is hard to believe that any sound-thinking businessman would want to launch a business that would work at 4% to 5% of its real capacity," acknowl-edged mayor general of the tax police, Viktor Khvorostyan. "This means that the bulk of the work is being done at nighttime, when no one should be work-ing. Can you imagine how huge a potential for illegal production of alcohol this creates?"[33]

The sheer size of the black market in vodka was impossible to mask. Official Russian statistical data (figure 20.2) showed a dramatic—and growing—dif-ference between the amount of vodka officially sold and the amount that was officially produced and taxed. By 1996, upwards of two-thirds of sales were untaxed, constituting around $8 billion in potential tax revenue that the treasury lost in those five years alone—on top of the $9 billion from Yeltsin's "charitable" exemptions.

This potentially dangerous black market vodka was everywhere. By 1997—according to Russian ministry of trade statistics—forty-six percent of all vodka sold was of "unacceptable" quality.[34] When combined with the astronomical consumption of vodka, this diminishing quality had horrific consequences. In the United States—with a population double that of Russia—roughly three hun-dred people die per year from alcohol poisoning. In 1994, in Russia there were fifty-five thousand such deaths, prompting Russia's foremost alcohol researcher,

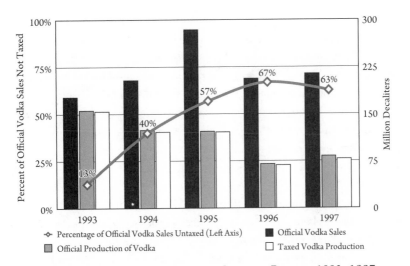

Figure 20.2 Taxed and Untaxed Vodka Sales in Russia, 1993–1997.
Sources: Goskomstat Rossii, *Russia in Numbers: Concise Statistical Handbook*
(Moscow: Goskomstat, 1999), 197, 272. Taxed production statistics are from
T. Kosmarskaya, "Problemy gosudarstvennogo regulirovaniya rynka alkogol'noi
produktsii," *Voprosi ekonomiki* (1998): 141. See also "Shadow of a Doubt," *Business in
Russia/Deolvye lyudi* no. 82 (1997): 34.

Dr. Aleksandr Nemtsov, to claim that "history's gift of freedom was partly paid
for with death at the vodka stall."[35]

Against the backdrop of economic suffering and widespread drunkenness,
such horrific statistics were difficult to ignore—as was the traditional temptation for the state to rein in the alcohol trade and again make it the centerpiece
of Russian statecraft. "The government should use all means to prevent people
from poisoning themselves," Yeltsin himself declared in a special radio address
in September 1997. "But if people spend money on vodka, their money should
go to the budget, rather than the pockets of all sorts of crooks. Then we will be
able to use it to pay pensions to the elderly and wages to servicemen, doctors
and teachers, and to heal our economy."[36] Yet it was the oligarchic "winners" of
the transition to capitalism who benefited most from continued economic dis-
tortions and used their political clout to undercut further market reforms that
threatened their fortunes.[37]

It wasn't just the Kremlin that was tempted by vodka revenues—resource-
starved governors across Russia's regions also were also stalking the cash cow,
since legally alcohol excises were to be split fifty-fifty between the federal government and the region of origin.[38] Consider the Pskov region—which borders
on Estonia, Latvia, and Belarus. There, governor Evgeny Mikhailov decreed a
regional distribution monopoly (*Pskovalko*) to control the retail market—giving him control over prices and the lucrative excises while keeping illicit and

foreign products out. While such protections allowed legitimate start-ups to flourish, it was not to last. The governor used his political muscle (what Russians call "administrative resources") to seize a hopelessly indebted food-processing facility and retool it as a distillery. The regional government subsidized the raw materials for its new vodka factory, lowering their production costs and allowing them to sell at below-market prices. Unable to compete, all legitimate manufacturers went under, leaving the governor with a veritable production monopoly that generated even more revenue. In this way, by the end of the 1990s more than thirty of Russia's regional governments had built their own local vodka monopolies.[39]

"In all sensible regions the authorities fight fiercely for their producer," governor Mikhailov explained after leaving office, "especially when the producer pays a lot of taxes."[40] His replacement as governor was a businessman and advocate of greater market liberalization in Pskov—but once in office, he confronted the unpleasant reality that Mikhailov's vodka system was the largest contributor to the region's budget, and replacements were virtually nonexistent. Economists call this outcome a "revenue trap," but really it is the reproduction of Russia's traditional vodka politics at the regional level: politicians rely on vodka for tax revenue while vodka producers rely on their political patrons to maintain market dominance. As throughout Russia's autocratic past (and as in other lucrative sectors in the post-Soviet economy), there is little incentive to upset this "trap" that benefits both the government and the well-connected producer and sacrifices market competition and social welfare: even as the local Pskov economy suffered through the 1990s, the region's alcohol production skyrocketed, to the obvious detriment of drinker health.[41]

Repeated time and again across Russia's eleven time zones, "each region in the Russian Federation currently maintains what can effectively be described as a regional vodka monopoly," claimed economist and pro-market politician Grigory Yavlinsky. "In many cases, the interests of those monopolies are vested with regional governments and protected by informal enforcing agencies, including criminal gangs." In such a situation, Yeltsin's Kremlin was "powerless to break such monopolies, with the result that high prices and inefficiencies persist in many regions, even if adjacent regions offer better-quality products at lower prices."[42]

The siphoning off of tax revenues—vodka and otherwise—from the federal government to regional governors and corrupt oligarchs was a primary cause of Russia's most debilitating economic problem: the massive deficit that forced the country into bankruptcy in 1998. Ironically, the leaching of the state's coffers was facilitated by an expansion in barter transactions: just as Russian citizens switched their economic transactions from the worthless ruble to the more "liquid" alternative of vodka (both fiscally and physically), so too did Russian manufacturers.[43]

According to economists, *theoretically*, free market competition would push the inefficient and outmoded "dinosaurs" of the old Soviet system into bankruptcy, leaving their employees out on the street. Instead, such abstract economic predictions (once again) failed miserably in the context of Russia: many uncompetitive, loss-making firms continued to produce shoddy products—not to be sold for cash but to be exchanged in massive barter networks constituting Russia's so-called virtual economy.

This may be hard to visualize without an example, so consider the case of the NIIRP rubber products factory in Sergeyev Posad, northeast of Moscow. Located near the spiritual capital of the Russian Orthodox Church, NIIRP was half owned by the state and maintained a large workforce. The rubber transmission belts they produced were of decent quality but were so overpriced that few Russian companies would spend cash on them. Even so, NIIRP was expected to pay both its tax bill and its employees' wages in cash, leaving little money for its suppliers. In such a catch-22, the managers instructed their supply department to never use money to buy the necessary raw materials but instead barter those raw materials for the belts they produced. This was a tall order, even for the most well-connected *tolkach*...that is, until NIIRP found a way to sweeten the pot: "the factory has started up a new vodka sector, which makes the Roma (Gypsy) Brand. To get industrial soot used in making rubber from a factory in Komi province, it has to pay in vodka as well as belts."[44] Yet it wasn't just suppliers that had to be bought off with vodka; the government did, too. To soothe relations with high-level officials, many firms employed "government relations" specialists who became known as *pechenochniki*—literally "those with liver problems"—based on the copious amounts of vodka they had to drink to secure favorable relations with the bureaucracy.[45]

If the *pechenochniki* were successful, they could even persuade the government to accept vodka as payment for their tax bill. The Russian ministry of agriculture even used vodka received as in-kind tax payments to pay its subsidies to collective farms in Buryatia, on the eastern shore of Lake Baikal. Initially this delighted the farmers—until unregulated, poisonous concoctions began appearing, so the experiment was ended.[46] In 1998 teachers in the mountainous Altai Republic were given fifteen bottles of vodka in lieu of pay. Since they had not seen a paycheck in half a year, "teachers reckon it is better to get the vodka— which can be sold in local markets—than nothing at all." According to a BBC report, the "attempt to pay them in toilet paper and funeral accessories provoked indignation."[47]

Thanks to the unquenchable demand for their products, alcohol producers became the hubs of vast webs of barter transactions—and therefore crucial to Russia's virtual economy. If a clothing manufacturer needed wool, they simply went to a distiller or wholesaler willing to trade vodka for coats and then traded that vodka to the wool supplier.[48] Directors of state farms—who traditionally had organized banquets, weddings, wakes, and other rites of passage—traded grain for the celebratory vodka, which strengthened the solidarity between workers and managers.[49] Even Mikhail Khodorkovsky—the Yeltsin-era multi-billionaire oligarch-turned-dissident—got his start by using alcohol to simplify the unwieldy barter chains for his upstart computer-importation business. During the free-for-all of the 1990s, Khodorkovsky branched out into importing stonewashed jeans, fake Napoleon brandy, and counterfeit Swiss vodka bottled in Poland. "Okay," one of Khodorkovsky's partners later admitted. "We financed the cognac. No one, ultimately, was poisoned by it."[50]

In these ways, the same vodka that was the lifeblood of the tsarist and Soviet empires became a primary lubricant of a bizarre virtual economy of premodern barter transactions. Such widespread barter further weakened the federal government while strengthening and integrating firms and governments at the regional level. The apparent irrationality of this system has perplexed economists, who usually focus on the long barter chains and offsets used by Russia's influential oil and natural gas companies.[51] Yet if they really want to understand Russia's post-Soviet demodernization, they should instead look at the vodka sector.

In 1996 the government commissioned Pyotr A. Karpov to examine the books of Russia's top companies to find out why taxes weren't being paid in cash. Karpov found that only twenty-seven percent of all enterprise earnings in Russia were in cash. Strangely, the *only* ones flush with cash were Russia's alcohol producers, with sixty-three percent of transactions in cash.[52] This is just further evidence of alcohol's unique role in Russia's post-Soviet demodernization. On the one hand, the de facto regional vodka monopolies dramatically expanded output under the political cover of their governors, earning "outstanding taxpayer" awards along the way.[53] On the other hand, the alcohol sector—both legal and illicit—helped a half-reformed economy stagger along until finally crashing in 1998. Even that crash was largely a consequence of the way this bizarre system starved the Kremlin of tax revenue, coupled with the tremendous debts Yeltsin's government had to cover just so corrupt traders and favored "charities" could maintain their lucrative alcohol-import loopholes. All the while, the sheer quantity of vodka needed to lubricate this economic Rube Goldberg machine utterly decimated the Russian population, thoroughly demodernizing a once-mighty superpower.

For generations, Russia's autocratic vodka politics encouraged the alcoholization of society to keep the treasury flush and the people unsteady. Yet although Russia was now nominally a democracy, the alcoholic traditions endured by using vodka as a medium of exchange and stalling the economic "transition."

Indeed, it was such legacies of vodka politics that transformed an arduous economic depression into full-scale societal demodernization.

From One Swede To Another

If there is one singular authority on post-communist transitions it is the Swedish economist Anders Åslund. In the late 1980s, Åslund highlighted the economic contradictions of *perestroika*; in the 1990s, as an advisor to the Russian government, he advocated rapid "shock therapy" measures. Even today he is a thoughtful commentator on developments throughout the former Soviet space. A general theme of his work holds that Russia's transition to capitalism has not been as dire as many accounts (likely including this one) suggest: not that there weren't hardships but, rather, that Soviet statistics that provided the point of departure were so wildly inflated that the resulting "fall" was not as dramatic as it might seem.[54]

The social consequences, according to Åslund, have been similarly exaggerated. Sure, "poverty soared shockingly in the early transition," but thankfully, "most of it is relatively shallow, with many people living just below the poverty line." The healthcare system may have deteriorated, but as a share of the shrinking GDP, health expenditures actually increased.[55] For all of his optimism, Åslund's international survey of post-communist transitions still had to confront the "shocking" decline in male life expectancy, especially in Russia, Ukraine, Belarus, Moldova, and the Baltic republics: "Russia experienced the greatest decline—seven years—from 1989 to 1994, when male life expectancy at birth reached the deplorable nadir of 57.6 years, 14 years less than for Russian women, the greatest gender disparity in the world. Disturbingly, it has stayed very low, around 59 years."[56]

As Åslund wades through the morass of macroeconomic and macrosocial indicators for all of the post-communist countries, from the Czech Republic to Kyrgyzstan, you can almost sense his frustration over being unable to explain why some economic depressions were coupled with social demodernization while others were not: "In Central Europe, male life expectancy rose by 3.6 years from 1989 to 2004, and in Southeast Europe by one year. Strangely, the war-ridden countries in the Caucasus did not suffer; neither did the destitute Central Asian states." It couldn't just be about poverty: the poorest former Soviet Republics— like Kyrgyzstan or Armenia—did not regress in terms of health. Neither did the poorest regions of Russia, like Ingushetia or Dagestan. Throwing up his hands, Åslund is forced to conclude: "The countries concerned do not form any clear economic pattern."[57]

With no clear economic pattern, and hence no rationale for the health collapse, Åslund trades his economic rigor for vague cultural explanations: "The problem was not starvation or abject poverty. Nor was it deteriorating health care," he declares. "Instead the dilemma was that East Slavic and Baltic men were typical company men with little ability to handle change. Their cultural response to transition was to start drinking even more heavily than usual, which reduced their life expectancy."[58]

Yet when viewed through the lens of vodka politics, the pattern of demodernization could not be more clear. Returning to the two-dimensional, health-and-wealth diagrams of Åslund's Swedish compatriot Hans Rosling, we can quickly identify distinct patterns of post-communist transitions from 1980 to 2000 (figure 20.3). Poland and the Czech Republic represent the primarily beer- and wine-drinking Visegrad countries of Eastern Europe, which paused only briefly before continuing toward the healthy-wealthy corner. Other countries from the war-ridden Caucasus

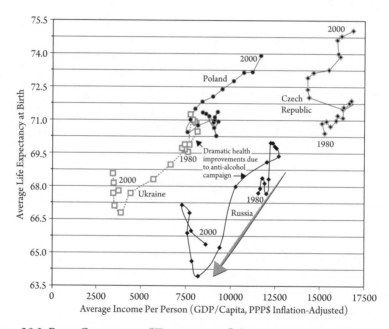

Figure 20.3 Post-Communist "Transitions" Compared, 1980–2000.
Sources: Life expectancy figures derived from the Human Mortality Database, mortality.org. For notes on Gapminder data collection and standardization of GDP per capita statistics see http://www.gapminder.org/documentation/documentation/gapdoc001_v9.pdf. For income per person for Poland, the Russian Federation, and Ukraine see Angus Maddison, "Historical Statistics for the World Economy: 1–2006 AD" (2008), www.ggdc.net/maddison/. For income per person for the Czech Republic see Maddison (2008) supplemented by UNSTAT II (2008 adjusted), http://unstats.un.org/unsd/snaama/dnllist.asp.

to the economically isolated and unreformed autocracies of Central Asia suffered economic contraction but little corresponding deterioration in health—due partly to the lack of a strong vodka-drinking culture in those states. The only countries that show a similar "demodernization" trajectory toward the lower left are Russia and Ukraine (shown), as well as Moldova, Belarus, and the Baltics.

What explains this demodernization? First, these are all countries with a well-entrenched vodka-drinking culture, cultivated through years of subservience not only within the Soviet empire but also the Russian empire that preceded it—both of which encouraged vodka consumption as the cornerstone of autocratic statecraft.[59] Second, with the exception of the Baltic states, the economic reforms in these "demoderinizing" countries were similarly haphazard and halting. As a consequence, when researchers investigated barter transactions and the Russian-style "virtual economy" of the 1990s, they found the practice most prevalent in the same region: from Moldova and Ukraine to Russia, Belarus, and (to a lesser extent) the Baltics.[60] Since the Baltic states made a cleaner break with the economics and the politics of the past in their effort to gain entry to the European Union, the duration of their demodernization was dramatically shorter than their similarly heavy-drinking neighbors to the south and east.

Åslund's explanation for the social demodernization is based on unseen ethnic traits: "East Slavic and Baltic men are company men who found it exceedingly hard to adapt to the transition and instead fell for the temptation of heavy drinking, causing many to die young."[61] This misses the point—it is not ethnicity or genetics at work; it is a complex, centuries-old historical legacy of vodka-politics statecraft, which has been embedded into cultural and economic patterns.

When the Soviet Union collapsed in 1991 it left some twenty-five million ethnic Russians—many of whom had lived their entire lives in cosmopolitan cities like Odessa, Baku, or Almaty—beached in the so-called "near abroad"—the other newly independent post-Soviet republics. Some chose to "return" to a Russian homeland they had never visited and were often shocked at what they found. "They drink, as a norm," marveled an ethnic Russian from Kyrgyzstan after settling in the Oryol region. "You can buy anything for a bottle, they don't know any other price...here women living on their own, when they ask for help with the cattle or the allotment, they must have a bottle, nobody ever takes money...so you learn to make *samogon*."[62]

Jarring experiences like this—even between members of the same ethnic group—suggest that ethnicity is not what causes social demodernization, but vodka: not just how much people drink, but the ways in which it has been entrenched into both people's accepted day-to-day coping strategies and the economic life of the country itself.

In simplest terms: economic crisis plus vodka politics equals demodernization.

Demodernizing Values

Russia's vodka-fueled demodernization also impacted its political prospects. Just as Hans Rosling has mapped the movement of nations toward the healthy-wealthy corner over the past two centuries, political sociologists have charted a similar evolution of cultural traits supportive of democracy and effective governance. For them, "modernization" is in the triumph of rationalism over tradition, secularism over religion, tolerance over xenophobia, gender equality over patriarchy, and liberalism, happiness, life satisfaction, individualism, and self-expression over basic survival needs. The relationship between economic modernization and the cultural changes that support democracy has proven quite robust, since it is not the elites, but the orientations of the citizenry that motivate them to push for liberty and effective governance. "Genuine democracy is not simply a machine that, once set up, will function effectively by itself," concludes University of Michigan political scientist Ronald Inglehart. "It depends on the people."[63]

Yet his own work, which tracks the global progress of such values, bodes poorly for Russia in the 1990s. Based on his exhaustive World Values Survey—conducted regularly by a network of social scientists in over eighty countries—Inglehart scores each country in terms of simple survival values versus modern self-expression values and traditional values versus modern secular/rational ones. Happily, from the 1980s through the 1990s every country surveyed improved on at least one of these dimensions, and most improved on both... except two. Russia and Belarus slid backwards: instead of becoming more secular and modern, they were becoming more religious and more traditional than under the Soviets. Russians were also becoming more suspicious, insular, distrustful, and dissatisfied: over half of Russian respondents said they were "not happy" or "not happy at all," placing Russia among the world's most miserable populations, while their trust in public institutions ranked as the world's lowest. Findings like these suggest that the economic and health catastrophes of "transition" were accompanied by a cultural demodernization.[64]

For development sociologists, the conclusion is clear. Inglehart claims that "support for democracy is relatively weak in Russia—indeed, it is weaker than in almost any other country." In some ways this is understandable, since the tumultuous 1990s led many to associate democracy with drunkenness, disorder, and economic insecurity.[65] This societal weakening of pro-democratic values was just another impediment to meaningful political reform demanding more effective governance.

Demodernization, then, is a complex phenomenon encompassing political, economic, social, and cultural attributes—and vodka seems central to understanding it all. Post-communist transition, when mixed with the legacies of vodka politics, produced the thoroughly unprecedented demodernization of a global superpower. In turn, the economic, political, and even cultural consequences of this demodernization have bolstered the durability of Russian autocracy, making democratization far more difficult.

Certainly this was anything but an ordinary economic downturn.

21

The Russian Cross

The television news magazine *60 Minutes* has been a weekly staple for genera-tions of American TV viewers. Since 1968 its poignant brand of investigative journalism has made it the longest-running, highest-rated, and most successful show in television history.

In early 1996—just as Boris Yeltsin began his miraculous political resurrec-tion—a most remarkable *60 Minutes* investigation presented the true costs and human suffering of the post-Soviet "transition" to an otherwise disinterested American public. It painted an alarming picture: while Yeltsin battled to keep the communists from returning to power, "Russia," it declared, "is confronting a humanitarian tragedy of immense proportions."

Cut to CBS journalist Tom Fenton strolling through a snow-covered Moscow courtyard casually discussing Russia's arduous transition to capitalism and democracy with an owlish man with a thick Brooklyn accent. While many Russia watchers were preoccupied with the economic side of demodernization—how many lost their jobs or how much production had contracted—this man was horrified by Russia's deteriorating health statistics, which told of a wholesale social catastrophe that had accompanied Russia's economic collapse. No one was better positioned to sound the alarm: Fenton's interviewee was none other than Murray Feshbach—the same American demographer who had been pub-lishing worrisome health statistics for decades. As we saw in chapter 16, it was Feshbach's coauthored reports on infant mortality in the 1970s that suggested that the Soviet superpower was in dangerously frail health. And as we noted in chapter 18, it was Feshbach's encyclopedic knowledge of the impairments to Russian health—alcohol foremost among them—that was consulted by jour-nalists, academics, and policy makers alike. If his Cold War–era warnings were grim, his new reports about the collapse of Russian healthcare, its skyrocketing mortality, plummeting fertility, and shrinking, sickly population were down-right apocalyptic.[1]

"Is there any parallel with this anywhere?" Fenton asks.

"No. Certainly not in any developed country."

Like the Roman poet Virgil accompanying Dante Alighieri through the nine circles of hell in the *Divine Comedy*, Feshbach then guided the American journalist through the horrors of post-Soviet society: touring decrepit healthcare facilities, underfunded orphanages, polluted swimming holes, smog-filled cities, drug dens, vodka kiosks, and cigarette stores before winding up where Russians were arriving at an unprecedented rate: the cemetery. All the while, Feshbach spouted devastating statistics, explaining with his dark humor (no doubt a necessary defense against the depressing subject matter) how the decidedly unsexy issue of population health was quickly becoming a massive political challenge. "It puts in danger their economic and political reforms if everybody is dead. Of course, not *everybody* is dead, but their conditions are not very good," Feshbach explained.[2]

Skeptics have challenged such dire assessments: Were things really that bad? How could the nation's health really impact the future of Russian politics? And what role did vodka play in this?[3]

In 2006, academics Andrei Korotayev and Daria Khaltourina explained that the demographic crisis was generated by the "Russian cross." They weren't referring to the Russian Orthodox Church but rather to the dramatic upsurge in the Russian death rate in the 1990s just as the birth rate plummeted, statistics that formed the shape of a cross when plotted on a graph. With far more people dying than being born, the size of the Russian population has shrunken dramatically since the collapse of communism and will likely continue to do so.[4]

Certainly, some argue, other countries also have higher death rates than birth rates—and not just Russia's neighbors in post-Soviet demodernization. The "graying" of Western Europe also has produced more deaths than births and a gradual population decline. But as figure 21.1 shows, when compared to wine-drinking Italy or the post-communist tribulations of the beer-swilling Czechs, the suddenness of the change combined with the sheer scale of lives lost makes the Russian cross categorically unlike anything seen before. According to Russia's state statistical agency, in the twenty years from 1992 to 2012 some 12.5 million more Russians were buried than were born.[5] Outside of the horrors of total war, the only comparisons to such depopulation are the 1918 flu pandemic, China's catastrophic Great Leap Forward, and the AIDS epidemic in sub-Saharan Africa.[6] Yet since this devastation appears almost self-inflicted, Russia's suffering has been passed over in relative silence.

Dead Drunk

What caused this horrific state of affairs? As it turns out, Khaltourina and Korotayev's list of culprits is virtually identical to what Murray Feshbach

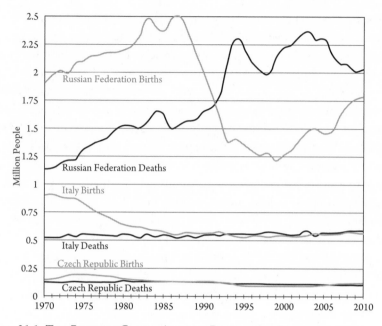

Figure 21.1 THE RUSSIAN CROSS: ANNUAL BIRTHS AND DEATHS IN THE
RUSSIAN FEDERATION, ITALY AND THE CZECH REPUBLIC, 1970–2010.
Sources: Goskomstat Rossii, http://www.gks.ru/dbscripts/Cbsd/DBInet.
cgi?pl=2403012; Istat, http://demo.istat.it/index_e.html; Czech Statistical Office,
http://www.czso.cz/eng/redakce.nsf/i/population/.

explained to *60 Minutes* a decade earlier, beginning with a disaster in healthcare. Amid the worst of the crisis in the mid-1990s, Feshbach took the American
viewing audience into a typical Russian hospital, which was struggling just to
operate as ever more government resources were siphoned off to pay for the war
in Chechnya. Proceeding across crumbling floorboards down a dimly lit hallway, viewers saw discarded plastic water bottles reused as drip containers, rubber sheeting used as a mattress, a neonatal unit with only one respirator, and vital
drugs in such short supply that patients are told to buy their own.

"We can't believe what's become of our country. It's worse than the war," said
one elderly woman in the hospital ward, choking back tears. For the past eight
months she had spent her entire pension on prescriptions that should have been
covered under the universal healthcare bequeathed by the Soviets. "Under the
communists we were alive," she says, suggestive of demodernization's undermining of political values. "Now we are dying with this kind of democracy."

Over 75 percent of Russian patients have to resort to bribery, the *60 Minutes*
narrator explains.

"And they call this 'free public health'"—Fenton sarcastically puts it to
his host.

"Well, if *you* want to call it that, fine," Feshbach shoots back. "I don't."[7]

A resource-starved healthcare system alone cannot explain the plummeting statistics. In fact, when compared to Brazil, India, and China (Russia's other BRIC counterparts sharing a similar level of economic development), Russia not only spends more per capita on healthcare, but it also has more medical professionals. More doctors and more money translates into better health the world over—except in Russia, where life expectancy is still a decade less than models would predict based on healthcare availability and expenditure statistics. Russia's nagging ailment isn't so easily "cured," at least in the epidemiological sense.[8]

Russia actually has many ailments beyond its alcoholic affliction. In the 1990s, AIDS entered the former Soviet bloc primarily through drug addicts sharing dirty needles. While an outmoded HIV-screening system has allowed the state to downplay the prevalence of the disease, international organizations warn of a potential AIDS disaster looming just below the surface. Beyond AIDS, there was an explosion in diseases that have been all but wiped out in the West: polio, measles, rubella, and one hundred fifty thousand new cases of tuberculosis annually—half of which are of a mutated TB strain that festers in Russia's crowded prisons and is stubbornly resistant to all known treatments.[9] Add to that the polluted drinking water that spreads bacterial dysentery, malaria, and diphtheria.

"This is a *huge* catalogue of horrors," Fenton notes, as they continue to walk through the gently falling Moscow snow.

"I'm sorry," Feshbach stops, as if to emphasize the point, "that's why people thought that I spoke in hyperbole. That is, I couldn't be right about all of this. But unfortunately I feel I am."

Still, the single greatest cause of this dismal state of affairs is vodka. Soviet medical experts used to call alcohol "Disease #3," as the third leading cause of death, behind only cancer and cardiovascular diseases. By the 1990s vodka had leapfrogged both, officially becoming "the main killer of Russians." Alcohol-related mortality in Russia was the highest in the entire world.[10]

How could it come to this? Against images of staggering homeless drunks, vodka kiosks, and Yeltsin's drunken Berlin embarrassment, Fenton narrates: "To quench its sorrows, the average Russian male now guzzles an incredible half-a-bottle of vodka per day. And remember, that's the *average*." That's roughly 180 bottles of vodka per year.[11] Stop for a minute—let that sink in.

With illicit *samogon* and third-shift vodka permeating the market, calculating alcohol consumption is a tricky matter. The best estimates are that in the 1990s Russians quaffed some fifteen to sixteen liters of pure alcohol annually—doubling the eight-liter maximum the World Health Organization deems safe. Making accommodations for nondrinkers (children and abstainers) and how much men drink relative to women, as well as their drink preference, these abstract numbers mean that the average drinking Russian man downs thirteen bottles of beer and more than two bottles of vodka every week—week in and week out.[12]

Not surprisingly, Russia is either at or near the top of every list of the world's hardest-drinking nations, along with Ukraine, Moldova, the Baltic states, Hungary, and the Czech Republic. Yet even though all of these countries endured post-communist transitions, perhaps only Ukraine has had a collapse in public health indicators similar to that of Russia (see chapter 20). How are we to make sense of this?

The answer is that the destructiveness of alcohol depends not just on how much alcohol is consumed, but on what kind and *how* it is consumed. The Czechs, for instance, have long had a beer-drinking culture, with the average man downing only two-thirds of a bottle of spirits per week but sixteen beers and a bottle of wine. In wine-drinking Hungary, the average man quaffs the same two-thirds of a bottle of liquor along with eleven beers and two and a half bottles of wine per week. Each scenario describes a lot of heavy drinking, but the legacy of vodka politics reflected in Russians' preference for potent, distilled liquors over milder, fermented beer or wine is the difference between a moderate social-health concern and a full-blown demographic crisis.[13]

Consider alcohol poisoning. Four hundred grams of pure ethyl alcohol is usually enough to kill you. If you're a beer drinker, to get that much pure alcohol into your bloodstream, you'd have to down almost an entire keg in one sitting. In the United States, every year there are a few tragic cases—usually college students—who die in such a manner, but a beer drunk usually passes out clutching the toilet bowl long before he approaches a lethal dose. The same thing is true for wine drinkers, who tend to fall asleep well before downing a lethal five and a half bottles at once. Passing out is the body's defense mechanism—shutting down before you completely poison yourself. Due to vodka's higher potency, it takes only two half-liter bottles to deliver a lethal dose: an amount that can be more easily consumed before the body can shut itself down.[14]

"It's not just that consumption is high, although it is," Feshbach explained about Russia's peculiar drinking culture. "It's the way they consume. It's chug-a-lug vodka drinking that starts at the office during the morning coffee break and goes right into the nighttime."[15] Until recently, instead of twist-off lids, vodka bottles in Russia came with tear-off caps that could not be resealed. Why would you want to put the lid back on? A "real man" would finish off the entire bottle rather than let it go to waste. Moreover, in contrast to the communal drinking culture of the imperial past, Russia's modern, individualistic drinking culture means that Russians today often drink alone (and without proper nourishment), only compounding their health problems.[16] A further complication, as we found in chapter 7, is the unique practice of *zapoi*: when an individual withdraws from social life—sometimes for days at a time—to go on an alcohol-fueled bender. This binge drinking leads to higher rates of sudden heart failure from acute stress on cardiovascular muscles.[17]

This is to say nothing about the quality of vodka. With *samogon* moonshine and unregulated third-shift vodka making up more than half of the market, there was little quality control in the 1990s. To cut costs, some unscrupulous alcohol producers even cut their vodka with toxic technical, medical, or industrial alcohols to save a few rubles.[18] Then come the alcohol surrogates: from antifreeze and break fluid to eau-de-cologne and cleaning compounds. Recent fieldwork suggests that one in twelve Russian men—some ten million people or more than the entire population of Hungary—regularly drinks potentially toxic medicinal or technical alcohols.[19] Not surprisingly, those who turn to such alternatives tend to be desperate men from the poorest socioeconomic groups. Also unsurprisingly, the risk of death among those who regularly drink antifreeze and other toxins is six times higher than even clinical alcoholics and a full *thirty times higher* than men who don't drink at all.[20]

In sum, the individualized culture of tossing back huge quantities of hard liquor—often of low quality or outright poisonous—has produced a level of alcohol poisonings in Russia that is up to *200 times* higher than that in the United States, making vodka the single greatest contributor to Russia's unparalleled health disaster. When Dr. Feshbach rather nonchalantly explained to the *60 Minutes* audience that over forty-five thousand Russians died from alcohol poisoning in one year, this is how.[21]

Alcohol kills in other ways, too. Notably, deaths from liver cirrhosis and chronic liver disease have steadily increased since the collapse of communism, adding another sixteen deaths per one hundred thousand throughout the 1990s. Vodka also contributes to coronary heart diseases and strokes, harms that accumulate gradually over a long period.[22] Indeed, more than half of the increase in male mortality is attributable to cardiovascular diseases in which alcohol and tobacco play a lethal role. As a consequence, in 1995 the rate of deaths from cardiovascular diseases in Russia was 1,310 per 100,000. In Spain, by contrast, it was only 268. Demographer Nicholas Eberstadt has translated these numbers with brutal clarity: "the world has never before seen anything like the epidemic of heart disease that rages in Russia today."[23]

But as Eberstadt explains, deaths from heart disease are compounded by fatal injuries for which Russian men "have no peers."[24] This is especially true of men who die suddenly in the prime of life. In a survey of a typical city morgue, fifty-five percent of the corpses had dramatically elevated blood-alcohol levels. The majority of murder victims and half of suicide victims were drunk at the time of death. Statistically speaking, alcohol is complicit in the vast majority of robberies, home invasions, burglaries, car thefts, and hooliganism as well as traffic accidents, drownings, suicides, wife beatings, rapes, and murders.[25] Back in Moscow, CBS journalist Tom Fenton was understandably flabbergasted when a hospital's chief surgeon matter-of-factly told him that ninety-nine percent of all injuries treated at his hospital were caused by alcohol.

"Ninety nine percent?!" Fenton exclaimed—doubling over with shock as though he had been punched in the gut.

Ringed by patients with rudimentary tourniquets, the surgeon nonchalantly replied: "*Da—99 protsentov.*"

It goes without saying that all of these problems are only made worse by the collapse of the public health infrastructure. Take, for instance, the sixteen percent of working-age men who are problem drinkers or the five percent of the able-bodied population considered to be clinical alcoholics. The vast majority of these unwitting victims of Russia's autocratic vodka politics go without treatment. The demodernization of the 1990s ravaged the specialized hospitals and outpatient clinics confronting this epidemic alcoholization of Russian society.[26]

Taken together—directly and indirectly—vodka claims over four hundred and twenty-five thousand Russian souls every year and is the single greatest contributor to the dismal post-Soviet life-expectancy statistics, especially among men.[27]

Consider this: in the nondrinking cultures of the Muslim world, women live on average only four to five years longer than men. In the primarily beer-drinking countries—like those in Western Europe—men die about six years earlier than women. In wine-drinking regions, the difference grows to eight years. But in the liquor-swilling countries of Eastern Europe, men generally die a full decade earlier. Here again Russia tips the scales, with Russian men dying a world-record *fourteen full years* before the average Russian woman.[28] More than any other statistic, the gender gap in life expectancy captures the true scale of Russia's autocratic *vodkapolitik* legacy.

Birth Dearth

The disturbing upshot in mortality is only one-half of the Russian cross; the other is the dramatic collapse in the birth rate. Amid the crisis of economic demodernization, Russian women suddenly stopped having kids.

Demographers like Dr. Feshbach speak in terms of a country's "total fertility rate" (TFR) or how many births a typical woman has during her lifetime. To maintain a stable population, the TFR must stay around the replacement rate of 2.15 children per woman: one to replace the mother, one for the father, and the additional 0.15 covering those who do not reproduce (either due to choice, infertility, or premature death). In the Soviet era, Russia's TFR hovered around 2.0 before jumping temporarily with the liberalization and anti-alcohol campaign of the Gorbachev era. In 1987 the TFR was 2.23 kids per mother. Within eleven years it had fallen to a shocking 1.23—well below the replacement rate. As Feshbach explained to *60 Minutes*, this constitutes the lowest birthrate of any country in the world, the consequence being that, by the late 1990s, more than a million more Russians died every year than were born.[29]

To find out why, Fenton and Feshbach called on Stanley J. Tillinghast, an American cardiologist and director of a healthcare-reform program in Russia. He explained: "Their outlook for the future is very poor, which is part of the reason the birthrate is so low." Turning toward the camera he explained how many of his Russian colleagues had children of the same age: all born during the early days of Gorbachev's *perestroika* a decade earlier. "They were the children of hope: they were born during the early stage when people were still very optimistic."

"And she's had no children since then?" Fenton concludes, rather than questions.

"And she's had none since then, correct."[30]

Russia's dilapidated healthcare system has implications for fertility as well as mortality: according to the World Health Organization, even as recently as 2005 a Russian's risk of death in childbirth was over six times higher than for women in Germany or Switzerland.

Increasingly, couples that want to have children simply cannot: fifteen to twenty percent of all Russian families experience infertility, which is often the result of syphilis or other untreated sexually transmitted diseases. Russian men, hobbled by disease and alcoholism, are also becoming impotent at an alarming rate.[31]

Women can also be rendered barren through botched or repeated abortions. The "abortion culture" that so shocked American President Ronald Reagan back in the 1980s was borne of the lack of reliable contraceptives. Soviet birth control pills had such high levels of hormones that they occasionally caused cardiac arrest. Consequently, Soviet women turned to abortions as a form of contraception, with the number of abortions routinely outnumbering live births even in the best of times. Dr. Archil Khomassuridze was the physician tasked with filing Soviet fertility and abortion data with the World Health Organization in Geneva. In the late 1980s, the WHO mainframe consistently rejected his reports, programmed as it was not to believe that any woman could undergo more than twenty abortions in a lifetime.

In Khomassuridze's Georgian homeland, as in Russia, this trend intensified in the post-Soviet period, when some *two-thirds* of all pregnancies ended in abortion. Yet as he told Pulitzer Prize–winning journalist Laurie Garrett, rather than scorn these women, Khomassuridze felt only sympathy for their plight. They had to live not only with deep financial difficulty but also with "abusive, often drunken men. Not only was sex often involuntary for the women," they told him, "it was rarely pleasurable even when mutually consenting."[32]

Back during the Soviet Union's epic struggle against fascism in World War II, more than twenty million young Russian men bid a tearful farewell to their loved ones and left for the front lines, never to return. Consequently, at the same time that returning American soldiers contributed to a postwar "baby boom" in the late 1940s, postwar Russia experienced a "baby bust": eligible men were few and far between, vastly outnumbered by legions of forlorn widows. A half-century later, the birth-dearth dynamic has returned, though on a smaller scale. With alcohol-related mortality rendering the working-age, childrearing-age Russian man an "endangered species," Russian women have even complained: "there simply aren't any men!"[33] The number of marriages has fallen accordingly. The obvious conclusion is borne out by Russian studies: the absence of a loving partner is the most powerful factor in the decision to not have children.[34]

As if the lack of suitable husbands and the increasing possibility that some sort of (often drunken) tragedy will claim one or both parents before they are able to reproduce weren't daunting enough, divorce discouraged even more women from having children. Of every one hundred marriages in Russia, fifty-eight end in divorce. I'll leave you to guess the most frequently stated reason for separation.[35]

Domestic violence also reached astronomic figures: in the Yeltsin years, between twelve and sixteen thousand Russian women were killed annually by their spouses, with another fifty thousand suffering severe injuries—a rate ten times higher than in the United States. Across Russia's eleven time zones, there were only six domestic violence shelters. "If the country had a functioning network of battered women's shelters," wrote professor Judyth Twigg, "it would be filled with victims of domestic violence perpetrated by drunken boyfriends and husbands. Yet vodka remains cheaper than milk, supported by a state that relies on almost $500 million in annual revenues from alcohol duties."[36]

The American audience of *60 Minutes* learned that the crisis of the Russian family did not end with divorce—as the tragical history tour rolled into a typical orphanage. There, they were introduced to the ever-growing number of children whose parents had either fallen victim to the mortality calamity or were cast off by their parents as too great a burden. Today, the rate of child abandonment in Russia is the highest in the world: over one hundred thousand children have been cast off every year since 1996. One of every thirty-eight children does not live with his or her parents, and one in seventy is sent to Russia's orphanages, where children are isolated from their community and—in another enduring legacy of the Soviet era—are tainted socially as undesirable and unworthy. In cases where the state deems an adult unfit to parent and places the child in orphan care, alco-holism is again by far the most frequently stated reason.[37] The dramatic increase in the orphan population since the 1990s and dwindling numbers of school-age children have led to the sad trend of repurposing many of Russia's elementary schools as orphanages. As my wife and I learned firsthand, working with the city orphanage in Podolsk south of Moscow (just blocks from the apartment where vodka historian Vilyam Pokhlebkin was brutally murdered), this retrofit-ting includes slapping steel bars on the windows and erecting tall concrete walls in order to isolate the orphanage grounds, indicative of the social stigma that Russia's growing army of orphans are forced to endure. According to the govern-ment's own estimates, thirty percent of institutionalized orphans will end up as alcoholics, and forty percent will end up in prison. With limited education or vocational opportunities, upon "graduating" from state custody—usually at the age of sixteen or seventeen—most are unable to live on their own and wind up on the streets, where they join the one to four *million* other homeless children in Russia.[38]

In her best-selling exposé *Betrayal of Trust: The Collapse of Global Public Health*, Laurie Garrett interviews some of Russia's "lost generation" in orphan-ages and shelters across the former USSR. One pattern clearly emerges from the stories: parental alcoholism leading to child abuse and abandonment. She recounts the story of the emotionless, eleven-year-old Vanya whom she found in a Moscow homeless shelter. When Vanya was just nine, his drunken father began to regularly thrash his wife and son. Vanya's mother "drowned her sorrows in moonshine purchased at local kiosks. The bad booze drove her insane, and escalated the violence in the household." After the nightly domestic bloodlet-ting, Vanya and his mother packed their bags and left for the Belorussky station. Just as a train was pulling away from the platform, Vanya's mother dropped her son's hand and jumped aboard, never looking back.

"I lost her at the railway station," Vanya morosely recalled. The entire follow-ing year—his tenth—was spent wandering the streets, begging for food, and sleeping in a telephone booth before he eventually fell into a small children's shelter reliant on charitable donations. Sapar Kulyanov, the shelter's director, tells of "an avalanche" of abandoned and abused children since the collapse of communism, with upwards of ninety percent coming from homes torn apart by drug and alcohol abuse.[39]

If that wasn't enough, the prospects are if anything even more bleak for chil-dren born with physical or mental disabilities. Cast off by their parents, Russia's most vulnerable citizens suffer systemic ostracism, neglect, and abuse. In what one Russian disability advocate calls an "undeclared war," those with mental and physical limitations are denied even the most basic social, educational, and med-ical services.[40] The alcoholization of society borne of vodka politics is making things worse here too: a recent epidemiological investigation into the health of orphans in Murmansk diagnosed fifty-eight percent of the babies with damage to the brain and central nervous system associated with Fetal Alcohol Syndrome.[41] All told, only *one in four* Russian babies is born healthy. Russia's chief pediatrician, Aleksandr Baranov, estimates that perhaps only five to ten percent of all Russian children have a clean bill of health. Meanwhile, seventy percent of the teens of the 1990s—the post Soviet generation expected to transform Russia into a vibrant and prosperous economy—suffer chronic diseases.[42]

Meanwhile, during their televised orphanage tour, excursion guide Murray Feshbach continued to rattle off one disturbing statistic after another to his accidental tourist. For instance, in the worst areas of industrial pollution, upwards of forty percent of children are born with mental impairments.

"That is devastating!" exclaims a flabbergasted Fenton. "That's a *huge* number."

"It's awful," admits Feshbach. "It's much worse than what I even knew. And I must say I've been prepared for many awful things . . . but not that figure."[43]

Russians born in the late 1980s and 1990s are saddled with enormous expectations in the new millennium: charged with transforming Russia into a robust market economy while reclaiming its past political and military glory. Yet this generation is not only far smaller (by half) than previous generations; it is also far sicker. The Russian armed forces rely on a system of obligatory conscription beginning at age eighteen. So in 2002, to get a feel for the incoming recruits, the Kremlin commissioned a detailed health survey of children from age zero through seventeen—everyone born since Gorbachev came to power in 1985. The results of this Child Health Census—intended only for President Vladimir Putin and his cabinet but obtained by (you guessed it) Murray Feshbach— painted a shocking picture of demodernization's toll on Russia's children. Compared with the children surveyed only a decade earlier, the rate of mental disorders had doubled; instances of muscular-skeletal illnesses and cerebral palsy tripled; and the rate of both cancers and tuberculosis among children had quadrupled. When it came to vodka, the rate of alcoholism among Russian children—not kids having a drink occasionally or even regularly, but clinical alcoholism—was increasing by 33 percent *per year.* Indeed, to the extent that vodka is one of the primary engines of Russia's demographic nightmare, more recent statistics suggest that the average age when Russian boys become committed drinkers has dropped from sixteen to thirteen. The number of "tweens" aged ten to fourteen who regularly drink vodka is now over ten million.[44]

At some point statistics like these become almost impossible to comprehend. Could a global superpower truly fall so far, so fast? To be sure, the crisis caused by skyrocketing mortality and sudden infertility is multifaceted: an onslaught of diseases, depression, and societal self-destruction straining a social safety net already shredded by the hardships of "transition." Yet from the kiosks to the hospitals to the orphanages—every place that Fenton and Feshbach explored for *60 Minutes*—one could distinctly see the shadow of alcohol and the looming legacy of Russia's autocratic vodka politics. Finally, at the end of their grueling expedition, like Dante and Virgil having weathered the nine circles of the *Inferno* only to ascend to purgatory, the American journalist and his chaperone take a moment to reflect.

"Is this a country that is dying?" Fenton asks.

"Yes."

"It's almost as if it is committing suicide."

"Well, I think that's one way of reading all the data." Feshbach pauses for only a brief moment. "I don't want to read it that way, but the answer is almost 'yes.' What I do in what I write and in working with my Russian colleagues is to alert people that this is a problem, and you'd better do something about it."

"And if they don't?"

"Well," Feshbach blinks. "Then they'll die. More and more—at younger and younger ages. That's all."

22

The Rise and Fall of Putin's Champion

Samokatnaya ulitsa—Bicycle Street—in eastern Moscow isn't one of the city's biggest or best-known thoroughfares. Compared to the noise of the busy capital, it is relatively serene. A quick ride uphill from the meandering Yauza River below is to be transported back in time one hundred years. Crowning the hill stands a sprawling, imperial-era red-brick industrial complex contrasted against the expressionless Soviet-era buildings that have grown up around it. This is the Kristall Distillery—the largest and most famous vodka manufacturer in Russia. Towering over the dozens of interconnected tin-roofed buildings loom a pair of smokestacks, evoking the mystery of Willy Wonka's chocolate factory from the 1971 Gene Wilder movie.

"Moscow State Wine Warehouse No. 1" was built in 1901 as part of Tsar Nicholas II's vodka monopoly. There was no better location: this was once the German quarter of taverns and whorehouses where the young Peter the Great learned to imbibe unthinkable quantities of alcohol. The grandiose palaces that Peter had built for his mistress Anna Mons and his drinking buddy Franz Lefort lie just across the river (chapter 4).

The Kristall plant has quite a history of its own. Even during Nicholas's disastrous World War I prohibition, Kristall kept producing alcohol for foreign diplomats and for export to allies in far-off France (see chapter 13) before returning to maximum capacity when Joseph Stalin resurrected the state monopoly. It was a prime target of Nazi bombers during World War II, since it supplied both vodka and Molotov cocktails to the front. Like so much of Russia, it was severely damaged in 1941 but kept working anyway (chapter 15). In 1953—the year of Stalin's death—the factory began producing Stolichnaya, which would gain worldwide fame as the quintessential Russian vodka. Only during *perestroika* in 1987 did the factory get the name Kristall. Following the collapse of communism, it was quickly privatized and became embroiled in a contentious legal battle over the rights to the Stolichnaya brand.[1] But none of this compared to the surreal events of the summer of 2000, Russia's first year under Vladimir Putin.

On August 4, 2000, truckloads of heavily armed men in black ski masks rolled up Bicycle Street. In broad daylight they forced their way past plant security and stormed the factory: truncheons and pistols drawn, AK-47 Kalashnikovs at their side. But these weren't gangster thugs or Chechen terrorists—it was the Russian Federal Tax Police Service, and they were there to confiscate evidence of tax evasion.

Tax evasion? How could that be? The plant had *just* been hailed as "Russia's Outstanding Taxpayer of 1999," contributing $89 million in taxes on $142 million in profits. Plus, even after privatization, a controlling fifty-one percent stake in the factory was held by the Moscow city government of longtime mayor Yury Luzhkov.[2]

So—the government was not only charging its most heralded taxpayer with tax evasion but was actually raiding *its own* firm? What was really going on here?

International business reports dismissed it like so many business-related shoot-outs and *mafiya* drive-bys of Russia's wild capitalist frontier under Boris Yeltsin. But Yeltsin was gone now, and his successor, Vladimir Putin, was intent on reining in the political and economic power Yeltsin devolved to others. So instead of cops versus crooks, or right versus wrong (in Russia, such absolute distinctions quickly get hazy), the drama on the Kristall factory floor was part of a larger Kremlin battle to recentralize power. Kristall was Moscow's version of the local vodka monopolies that had become cash cows for struggling governors across Russia (see chapter 20). Thanks to Yeltsin's goodwill toward his loyal mayor Luzhkov, even though the Kremlin retained the controlling fifty-one percent stake in Kristall after privatization, they allowed the mayor's office to manage it and profit by it.[3] That was all about to end.

Return To Center

"How can you govern a country with 246 different types of cheese?" French President Charles de Gaulle famously proclaimed in a moment of French exasperation with French politics. His apt *précis* weighed on later Russian commentators, who wondered how the newly elected President Putin could govern a country with 180 vodka producers from across the country making some five thousand (supposedly) different types of vodka, each of which had become "a business as profitable as diamonds or oil" for *mafiosi* and regional governments alike.[4]

Apparently Putin had a plan.

On the eve of the new millennium—December 31, 1999—a tottering Boris Yeltsin surprised the world by tearfully resigning as Russia's first democratically

The iconic red-brick Kristall vodka factory in Moscow. ITAR-TASS/Vitaly Belousov.

elected president. His recently appointed Prime Minister Vladimir Putin would take his place until new elections could be held in March—elections that Putin would win in a landslide.

On May 7, 2000, Putin strode confidently into the Kremlin's opulent Andreyevsky Hall to take the oath of office. "We must not forget anything," Putin boldly proclaimed in his inauguration speech. "We must know our history, know it as it really is, draw lessons from it and always remember those who created the Russian state, championed its dignity and made it a great, powerful and mighty state."[5]

Of course, vodka politics helped to create the mighty Russian state but was also its Achilles heel. Now, at the depth of Russia's economic despair, it seemed that Putin was eyeing vodka to make Russia great again. The day before his inauguration, Putin's administration created Rosspirtprom (an acronym for "Russian Spirits Industry") to centralize control over the dozens of vodka factories in which the federal government retained a controlling interest, with Kristall as the ultimate prize.[6] Indeed, Rosspirtprom would become Putin's first "national champion company."

As Wellesley emeritus professor Marshall Goldman has explained, "these national champions would most likely be more than 50 percent owned by the Russian government" and "would put promotion of the state's interest over profit maximization."[7] Just as industrial giants like Rosneft and Gazprom served the Kremlin's interests in oil and natural gas (while making their Kremlin-appointed directors money hand over fist), Rosspirtprom came first, consolidating state control over the lucrative vodka market. "Vodka may not be gas or oil," later explained the journal *Ekspert*, "but it too is a strategically important product. So important that to control its production it was necessary to create an alcohol equivalent of Gazprom."[8]

In every case, building a "champion" meant first unseating the existing ownership. In their first attempt, the Kremlin instructed Kristall's director, Yury Yermilov, to quietly buy up shares from employees. But instead of being transferred to the state, these stocks were shuffled to offshore shell accounts. "I admit that 19 percent of the stock belongs to an offshore company in Cyprus," said Yermilov's sweat-browed chief accountant Vladimir Svirsky. "But this is a friendly company, and the stocks never vanished: they are working for the collective."[9]

Perhaps that would appease the feds. In the past, they had certainly looked the other way for worse. It was then revealed that, of the 700 million rubles that Kristall earned on domestic sales in 1999 (to say nothing of its lucrative Stolichnaya exports), the firm only reported earnings of 292 million rubles.

So—what happened to those other millions?

Time after time, the government-controlled board of directors attempted an audit. Time after time Yermilov headed them off—even using armed guards to bar entry to the plant. The board then elected a new director—Aleksandr Romanov (no relation)—to depose the corrupt Yermilov, who was now facing two to seven years in prison for tax fraud. Yermilov did what any upstanding businessman would do: he checked himself into a local hospital and bequeathed the job of factory director to his chief accountant Svirsky, who quickly hired a small army of shaved-head guards to hold off the auditors. But even they had to stand aside when the Federal Tax Police stormed in.[10]

Within minutes of the Tax Service raid of August 4, the state's recently approved director Romanov—with his own personal army of some twenty Kalashnikov-toting officers—announced his arrival to "re-establish the state's control" of the factory's executive offices.[11] While Romanov held the central offices, Svirsky's troops occupied the rest of the factory. In addition to their guns, Svirsky defended himself with a local court ruling that invalidated Romanov's election. And so, a farcical, months-long armed standoff ensued between Kristall's two managers and their personal armies: Romanov's in green fatigues, Svirsky's in blue. Both managers refused to leave the premises. And still, the plant churned out its two million gallons of vodka every month like clockwork.

"I don't know whose orders we're obeying—some director or other. Maybe they'll kick us all out," dismissively lamented one assembly line worker. "We don't talk about it, we don't have time—we do everything manually, as you can see. We don't have time, we have to make a lot of vodka—our job is to work, to work and that's all."[12]

Such indifference was not shared by the combatants. His phone lines having been cut by the blue opposition, Romanov hunkered down in his office day and night, afraid to leave. "I see many men with guns out there."[13]

"I never saw such a situation as this," one guard told a reporter, chuckling and nodding toward his rival down the way. Surrounded by journalists on the factory floor, Svirsky pleaded ignorance: "We're giving the state and the country fuel, in the form of liquid energy (vodka), we pay our taxes—and all of the sudden they decide to change the leadership. We don't understand what happened. There was a court decision and the court said [Romanov's claim] was illegal."[14]

Unaware of the Kremlin's plans for a national-champion vodka company, Svirsky was blindsided. After a monthlong standoff across production lines of rattling vodka bottles, the Moscow court that previously annulled Romanov's appointment suddenly—and suspiciously—reversed its decision and upheld the power of Romanov and the federal government. After weeks of futile appeals, armed with a court mandate and a local police battalion, Romanov swept the entire plant without incident. In one fell swoop, Svirsky was deposed, the plant was wrestled out of Mayor Luzhkov's hands and squarely put in the federal government's pocket.[15]

Tax raids and confrontations soon became the standard operating procedure for Putin's recentralization, often at the expense of the so-called oligarchs— the super-rich power brokers of the Yeltsin era—who would not play ball with the Kremlin. Closed-stock company Soyuzplodimport—the lucrative, former Soviet alcohol export agency held by Yeltsin-era oligarch (and Putin foe) Boris Berezovsky—was likewise investigated for fraud and embezzlement. Investigations into his shady business dealings pushed Berezovsky out of the inner circle of power and into self-imposed exile in London. "It looks as though the Federal Government is making it known that it intends to hold the vodka industry in its own hands and not allow anyone to compete," wrote one Russian commentator: "not Yury Luzhkov, not Boris Berezovsky."[16]

The vodka industry was among the first in line for recentralization, alongside the Media-MOST company of Vladimir Gusinsky. Not only had Gusinsky bankrolled Putin's political opposition, but his independent television network, NTV, was openly critical of Putin's government and the recently resumed Chechen war. Following the storming of NTV headquarters by the tax police, Gusinsky was pressured to sell to another state-controlled national champion, Gazprom. Within months, Russia's main independent media outlet was back under state control, and Gusinsky fled into European exile.[17]

Gusinsky and Berezovsky were the first to violate Putin's so-called "*shashlik* agreement." In May 2000, Putin invited many of the Yeltsin-era oligarchs to his presidential dacha outside Moscow. Over shish-kebabs (*shashlik*), Putin reportedly laid down the rules: he would not mess with their businesses so long as these neo-boyars did not interfere in politics. Political apathy was acceptable—opposition was not.[18]

Moguls who did not fall in line fell victim to raids like those at NTV and Kristall. The interior ministry used chainsaws to break in the doors of Transneft—the state pipeline monopoly—to install its new president. Heavily armed troops forcibly ousted the director of the Kachkanar vanadium mine. In 2004, armed tax police raided the headquarters of oil giant Yukos after arresting its owner, Mikhail Khodorkovsky. At the time, Khodorkovsky was Russia's richest man, and his political ambitions and seething distaste for Putin were hardly a secret. His company was broken up and renationalized while Khodorkovsky was convicted for fraud, embezzlement, and money laundering. The selective application of the law to a political opponent, lack of due process, harassment of his witnesses and lawyers, and the levying of additional, overlapping charges led the European Court of Human Rights to determine that Khodorkovsky's human rights had been violated. Amnesty International named him a "prisoner of conscience."[19]

Likewise, in 2007 tax authorities raided investment fund Hermitage Capital Management, which earlier had exposed instances of high-level government corruption. Hermitage lawyer Sergei Magnitsky was arrested and held for eleven months without trial (or medical treatment) until his death in police custody, prompting an international outcry.[20] In her analysis of power networks and the *sistema* of informal governance in contemporary Russia, Alena Ledeneva describes such leveraging of "administrative resources" as an extreme form of corporate raiding, the primary difference being not only that such *sistema* raiding is the most hostile of hostile takeovers but also that such moves are undertaken for the benefit of well-connected government officials rather than the capitalist raiders themselves.[21]

Say what you will of the tactics, by the end of Putin's second term as president in 2008, he had not only leveraged many Yeltsin-era cronies from power, but he had also recentralized many important sectors of the Russian economy, including vodka—or at least placed them in the hands of "useful friends" deemed to be more trustworthy members of Putin's governing *sistema*.[22]

Who Is Vladimir Putin?

By interesting coincidence, Vladimir Putin's grandfather was once a cook for Vladimir Lenin at the state's country retreat. Spiridon Ivanovich Putin continued to work for Lenin's widow, Nadezhda Krupskaya, after Lenin's death. In the 1930s he cooked for Joseph Stalin at his dacha outside of Moscow, where some of the momentous, vodka-fueled dinners so vividly described by Nikita Khrushchev took place ... and perhaps Putin's "*shashlik* agreement" did, too.[23]

Spiridon's son Vladimir was a hardened veteran of the brutal nine-hundred-day Nazi siege of Leningrad. Throughout the war and beyond, by Vladimir's side was his wife Maria, who gave birth to Vladimir Vladimirovich Putin in 1952. The couple raised the boy with strict discipline. Occasionally rowdy at school, young Vlad was an ordinary kid who took an interest in sports—first boxing (which he quit after having his nose broken) and then judo. In his 2000 biography, *First Person*, Putin explained it was judo's holistic combination of sport and philosophy that saved him from delinquency: "If I hadn't gotten involved in sports, I'm not sure how my life would have turned out."[24]

Putin graduated from Leningrad State University in 1975 with a degree in international law before joining the KGB. He married Lyudmila in 1983, and the couple had two daughters in Dresden, East Germany, where Putin was stationed from 1985 to 1990. In an interview for *First Person*, the family was asked about Putin's temperament. Lyudmila replied that Vladimir wasn't much of a drinker. "He is indifferent to alcohol, really," she said. "In Germany, he loved to drink beer. But usually he'll drink a little vodka or some cognac."[25]

With the reunification of Germany, Putin returned to Russia to work for his former professor, Anatoly Sobchak, who became mayor of St. Petersburg. Confident, responsible, and reliable, Putin quickly rose within the mayor's office. When Sobchak lost reelection in 1996, Putin was summoned to Moscow. In the Kremlin, Putin's star continued to rise: from deputy chief of Yeltsin's presidential staff he became head of the FSB (successor to the KGB) in 1998 and then prime minister on August 9, 1999. At Yeltsin's traditionally well-lubricated official meetings and state banquets, Putin discreetly emptied his drinks into decorative flowerpots.[26] By outward appearances, Putin was just another face card in the constant reshuffling of Yeltsin's lame-duck administration—but in his memoirs, Yeltsin claimed that he had hoped to bequeath his legacy to Putin all along. "After all, I wasn't offering him just any promotion," Yeltsin writes, "I wanted to hand him the crown of Monomakh"—the traditional fur-lined, gem-encrusted crown of the grande princes of Muscovy.[27]

Days before Putin ascended to the ministership, Chechen insurgents besieged the Russian republic of Dagestan. By September, a series of suspicious (and still unsolved) apartment bombings in Moscow killed over three hundred, putting the entire country on edge. The natural reaction was to blame Chechen terrorists.[28] Putin's coarse response that he would "corner the bandits in the shit-house and wipe them out" showed assertive and sober leadership in stark contrast to the incapacitated Yeltsin.[29] Rallying 'round their tricolor flag, the Russian people enthusiastically supported a resumed war in Chechnya as an anti-terror operation.

Putin's star was rising in the economic sphere, too. The ruble devaluation and debt default in August 1998 instantly made Russian products more competitive on international markets. The price of Russia's oil and natural gas exports—now under the control of Putin's national champion companies—climbed uninterrupted for the next decade, buoying the economy with it. After the demodernization of the 1990s, Russia was finally picking up steam. Little by little, life was getting better. Not surprisingly, four months after Yeltsin installed Putin as interim president, he won the job outright with fifty-three percent of the nationwide vote in March of 2000.[30]

How do we understand the system that emerged during Putin's first two terms as president (2000–2008)? Was it democracy with some autocratic traits? Autocracy with a veneer of democracy? Was it a market economy or a reversion to some sort of state socialism or even feudalism? Supporters hailed it as "Putinomics"; critics scorned it as "Putinism."[31] Whatever you call it, the defining characteristics were social *stabilnost* (stability), political centralization, and steady economic growth. Opponents would hasten to add: entrenched cronyism and corruption, a lack of transparency, the eroding of civil liberties, and a continuing disregard for public health. Still, how was this remarkable recentralization possible in such a short period of time?

A decade earlier, still under the Soviet umbrella, president of the Russian Republic Boris Yeltsin famously encouraged regional leaders to "take as much sovereignty as you can swallow" to weaken Soviet president Mikhail Gorbachev.[32] Unfortunately for Yeltsin, this devolution of power from Moscow to the regions would be his inheritance, as governors built mini-fiefdoms—as in Pskov, often funded by vodka—at the expense of the center. While Yeltsin was unable to rein in the newly empowered governors, his successor Putin made it a top priority.

Under Yeltsin's constitution—born of the shelling of the parliament in 1993—each of Russia's eighty-nine regions appointed two delegates to the Federation Council, the flaccid upper house of parliament. Appointees included crooks, cronies, regional vodka producers, and even the governors themselves, who took advantage of their parliamentary immunity to live the high life in the capital.[33] In the summer of 2000, again wielding the threat of criminal investigations, Putin expelled the governors and installed pliant replacements. At the same time as the tax raid on Kristall, Putin grouped all of the regions into seven "federal districts" to strengthen oversight of federal agencies across the country.

Critics quickly raised alarms that these federal representatives were collecting salacious, compromising materials—*kompromat*—on governors and regional power players to be used as blackmail should they deviate from Kremlin expectations. More importantly, the tax ministry set up interregional audit departments in each district—staffed by federal rather than regional appointees—to strictly monitor the governors' compliance with tax laws.[34] As with Kristall, accusations of tax evasion and corruption would be the pretext for raiding and reestablishing federal control.

The heart-wrenching 2004 hostage crisis at Beslan School No. 1—where a firefight and botched attempt to rescue one thousand captives of Chechen terrorists led to the tragic deaths of 334 hostages, mostly children—was pivotal in bringing the regions further under the center. Blaming the tragedy on blundering, disconnected regional authorities, the Kremlin used Beslan to justify eliminating the direct election of governors. Henceforth, governors would be appointed by the president, and serve at his pleasure, allowing Putin to replace potential rivals with loyal disciples and rendering Russia a federation in name only.[35]

What does this have to do with vodka politics? Well, for one, since many regional governments were built atop vodka mini-monopolies, those arrangements and revenues would now be in the hands of trusted Putin loyalists. In this way, the national champion Rosspirtprom was "a cornerstone of Putin's centralization policy," according to Yulia Latynina. "But in order to effect this centralization, the governors must be stripped of their control over state budget cash flows, and no fewer than half of those are generated by vodka sales."[36] Plus—in theory at least—this should have led to greater oversight and coordination of an industry still plagued by counterfeit and third-shift vodkas.

Second, centralization destroyed the ability of the various regions to act as—in Louis Brandeis's famous adage—"laboratories for social experimentation."[37] Any hope for civic activism or policy innovation "from below" were all but snuffed out. As professor Ekaterina Zhuravskaya explained, "federalism combined with the absence of elections at the local level can potentially work only when the policy is designed solely to deliver economic growth and is not aimed at providing public goods, such as quality education, health care, and social protection."[38] Instead of encouraging civic activism that might help alleviate Russia's public health woes, centralization only cemented the dominance of regional authorities and their liquor interests.

With alcohol consumption reaching alarming heights into 2007–2008, researchers from the London School of Hygiene and Tropical Medicine tried to determine why nothing was being done. Wasn't there public concern at the local level? If so, why wasn't it being translated into action? Based on in-depth interviews with a wide variety of stakeholders concerned with alcohol control, the London group found that the widespread concern with problem drinking was stymied by a general powerlessness to influence policies regarding taxation, education, drunk driving, minimum drinking ages, and other restrictions. Health-sector organizations, physicians, psychiatrists, pharmacists, educators, church organizations, labor unions, employers, and even the local health ministry all decried the moral, health, and economic problems caused by alcohol—but all also lamented that they had no way to influence policy. In other words, unlike the civic response of temperance to alcohol problems (of far less severity) in the West, the researchers found "no evidence of an existing or emerging multi-sectoral coalition for developing alcohol policy to improve health."[39]

Caught in their vodka revenue trap, even the regional governments were powerless to undertake meaningful reform. State and municipal authorities "faced a conflict because of the substantial contribution of the alcohol industry to oblast [regional] tax revenues." Given the primacy of alcohol revenues to regional governments, their representatives "acknowledged little opportunity to influence federal alcohol policy, and did little within their own areas of responsibility, such as their power to restrict hours when alcohol can be sold."[40]

So, who could stand up against the flood of alcohol? Who controlled the local policy process? Not surprisingly, the London group found only two key political players: the Kremlin and the local alcohol producers themselves. In their case study region the local distillery generated over $70 million in tax revenue annually. With sixty-four percent of their output sold within the region, they strongly opposed any local restrictions. Despite the facade of federalism, any genuine policy change would have to be handed down from the Kremlin on high. The study concluded that "although ministries and regulatory agencies recognize that there is a problem, they are either conflicted, because of the revenue provided by the alcohol industry, or feel that it is not their responsibility. In part, their unwillingness to assume responsibility reflects a belief that it is up to the federal bodies to act."[41]

In sum, even the centralization of high Putinism was triangulated through vodka politics—strengthening the regions' reliance on alcohol revenues while disempowering civic initiatives to confront vodka in the name of public health. The result was a return to the eternal dynamics of Russia's autocratic vodka politics—only now at a local level, multiplied a hundredfold.

Domesticating The Opposition

Reclaiming power from the regions was only part of Putin's recentralization. *Stabilnost* also required marginalizing partisan opposition and subordinating the legislative and judicial branches to the executive. The result was a system of bureaucratized politics that shared corrupt elements with both Russia's feudal and Soviet past.

Boris Yeltsin—even standing triumphantly atop a tank in the early 1990s—always saw himself as above partisan politics. His decision to be a president without a party was a major mistake. Thanks to the wrenching hardships of post-Soviet demodernization, popularly elected legislators across the political spectrum freely took potshots at a president, who had few defenders.

There were occasional attempts to create a "party of power" to support Yeltsin's government and groom potential heirs. Unfortunately, the president's coattails weren't particularly long when he was lying drunk on the floor. In 1995 Yeltsin backed the centrist "Our Home is Russia" party to support then-prime minister (and founder of the natural gas mega-corporation Gazprom) Viktor Chernomyrdin. The party received only ten percent of the votes in the 1995 Duma elections before fading into oblivion. It did not help that Chernomyrdin shared Yogi Berra's curse of tragicomic malapropisms: "Wine we need for health, and the health we need to drink vodka!" When asked about alcohol and Russian health, he quipped: "Better than vodka there is nothing worse!"[42]

Yeltsin shelled his own parliament in 1993 to constitutionally secure tremendous power for the executive. Even still, his Duma opponents were a constant nuisance. Pro-Western liberals condemned corruption and the brutal war in Chechnya. Nationalists and communists blasted Yeltsin for selling out Soviet greatness and regularly blocked his ministerial appointments.

Even at the close of his lame-duck second term, Yeltsin's Duma opposition wanted to send him out with a black eye. In 1999, shortly after the U.S. Congress finished their impeachment of Bill Clinton for lying about inappropriate sexual relations, the Russian parliament tried impeaching Clinton's buddy Boris. The accusations against Yeltsin were a tad more severe, however. The Duma charged him with treason and murder for unlawfully dissolving the USSR, the shelling the parliament, launching the bloody war in Chechnya, and selling out Russia's military might. The final accusation was the most damning: genocide. In May 1999, chairman of the Commission on Impeachment, Vadim Filomonov, highlighted the 4.2 million lives lost on the president's watch. "Yeltsin consciously accepted the worsening of the living conditions of Russian citizens, with an inevitable rise in the mortality of the population and a decrease in the birthrate. All suggestions that the political course be changed were consistently refused." Filomonov concluded the indictment with the melodramatic proclamation: "The blood of the murdered and crippled, the tears of the dying, degraded, and insulted beat in our hearts!"[43]

"Depopulation proceeds against the background of the worsening health of all age groups in the population," explained Dr. Viktor Benediktov in the proceedings. "There is every reason to believe that the population of the country will be reduced to such a level in the twenty-first century that its preservation and replication will be impossible." Amid allegations of $70,000 bribes for votes against impeachment—which would have forced Yeltsin from power—the motion fell seventeen votes short.[44]

Three months later, Vladimir Putin became prime minister and later president. Putin's recentralization prevented similar humiliation at the hands of the opposition. In 2001 he began raising the requirements for registering political parties. By 2004 all parties required a minimum of fifty thousand members distributed evenly across Russia's regions. New parties could be created only with the consent of the Kremlin. Over-the-top criticism of the government could be construed as "extremism"—and adequate grounds for disqualifying a candidate.[45]

While small parties were swept away, changes ahead of the 2007 Duma elections squeezed out medium-sized opposition parties. Electoral rules were changed from a mixed system to straight proportional representation, with a raised minimum threshold of seven percent of votes cast. Aimed at solidifying the major parties, liberal opposition parties like Yabloko and the Union of Rightist Forces, which received just less than seven percent, were suddenly on the outside looking in. The simultaneous elimination of legislative districts meant that no individual, no matter how charismatic or influential (like Yeltsin), could enter national politics without going through established parties. Consequently, the 2007 election empowered only four parties: Zyuganov's Communist Party, Zhirinovsky's Liberal Democrats (who are neither liberal nor particularly democratic), a small leftist coalition called A Just Russia, and Putin's United Russia party. With seventy percent of the seats in the Duma, United Russia was the main beneficiary of the alleged vote-rigging, ballot-stuffing, voter intimidation, media restrictions, and constriction of civil liberties that only seemed to increase from one election to the next.[46] Such a supermajority made it easy to rubber-stamp Kremlin legislation and amend the constitution itself.

From threatening impeachment and blocking legislation in the 1990s to being effectively left out of the legislative process altogether by 2008, the organized party opposition had been marginalized within a few short years, with Putin and United Russia ruling supreme.[47] But what was this United Russia party? Where did it come from? What did it stand for?

Amid economic turmoil and default in 1998, Moscow's loyal, ambitious, and bald mayor Yury Luzhkov—whose office dominated the lucrative Kristall plant—hoped Yeltsin would appoint him as the new prime minister. He ultimately did not. Jilted, Luzhkov amassed dissatisfied members of Yeltsin's Kremlin into a new party—Fatherland—to act as a powerful, centrist opposition to contest the 1999 Duma elections and the presidential elections the following year. Fatherland added powerful figures—like hawkish former Prime Minister Evgeny Primakov—and the "All Russia" faction of big business leaders and regional governors to create the Fatherland-All Russia coalition.

Suddenly threatened by this powerful centrist rival, the Kremlin hastily threw together a party called Unity to support the new prime minister, Vladimir Putin. Ironically, the hodgepodge of governors and Kremlin lackeys had little actual unity beyond their support for Putin. Also ironically, Putin has never been an actual member of Unity or its successor, United Russia—only "associated" with it. Initially, Unity's only platform was to support the war in Chechnya. It was also endorsed by President Yeltsin, which normally would have been a political kiss of death. Yet partly due to Putin's self-assured leadership, within two months Unity had become the country's second largest political party (23%), well ahead of Fatherland-All Russia (13%), and just behind Gennady Zyuganov's Communist Party (24%). Putin's subsequent torching of Zyuganov in the 2000 presidential election (53% to 29%) extinguished the ambitions of the Fatherland-All Russia leadership, and in 2001 the party merged with Unity into a new party: United Russia.[48]

The rest, as they say, is history: greater *stabilnost*, economic growth driven by rising oil prices, rekindled national pride over the Chechen war effort, and a good deal of electoral shenanigans ensured United Russia's victory in the 2003 Duma elections, with thirty-eight percent of the vote. In the face of Putin's growing popularity and slanted playing field, longtime rivals like Zyuganov, Zhirinovsky, and Yavlinsky decided it was futile to even try to run for president, conceding a landslide seventy-one percent presidential victory for Putin in 2004.[49]

At the end of Vladimir Putin's second presidential term, United Russia decimated the opposition, securing seventy percent of Duma seats in 2007. Shortly thereafter, Putin was crowned *Time* magazine's "Person of the Year." He is no boy scout, democrat, or paragon of free speech, *Time* explained, but "at significant

Russian President Vladimir Putin celebrates the two hundred and fiftieth anniversary of the founding of prestigious Moscow State University by sampling students' traditional *kvas* and mead. Associated Press, ITAR-TASS.

cost to the principles and ideas that free nations prize, he has performed an extraordinary feat of leadership in imposing stability on a nation that has rarely known it and brought Russia back to the table of world power."[50]

Putin's centralizing reforms gradually, yet effectively, reconstituted the traditional Russian autocracy. Increasingly, political power is exercised not through institutional checks and balances, but through a growing number of informal ties and extraconstitutional bureaucratic bodies: the Presidential Administration, the State Council that "advises" on social issues, the Security Council that considers military matters.[51]

Western fearmongers have hastily condemned Putinism as the "Soviet Union 2.0." That is shortsighted. Certainly, neither Putin's Russia nor the Soviet Union was a democracy—but then again, neither was the ultra-conservative tsarist empire that preceded it. The USSR was an expansionist empire driven by communist ideology. Putin has neither global expansionist interests nor an ideology of any kind—much less an anti-capitalist one.[52] Putin's primary goals are maintaining stability and the power of the system—another enduring trait of the traditional Russian autocracy.[53] However, United Russia has filled the hegemonic political functions vacated when the old Communist Party of the Soviet Union (CPSU) crumbled. Like its Soviet predecessor, United Russia is "the guiding and directing force" of Russian politics, with power resting only in the hands an inner core of loyalists. Like in the Soviet days, party membership is the primary means of political advancement. Like the CPSU, the organs of the United Russia party parallel the formal institutions of governance and in many cases supersede them. Likewise, Putin's Russia has an elaborate (though mostly decorative) formal system of representation, which is superseded by the informal ties of a small ruling elite. In the Soviet past those elites were part of the Central Committee of the CPSU—now they are part of the Presidential Administration, which even occupies the same buildings on Staraya Square in Moscow.[54]

More simply—as the unintentionally insightful Viktor Chernomyrdin quipped—"Whatever party we establish, it always turns out to be the Soviet Communist Party."[55]

A Return To Normal?

Particularly among economists, the conventional wisdom about Russia's demographic nightmare of the 1990s was that, since it was caused by economic downturn, once the economy got better so would Russia's health. Logically, if economic uncertainty prevented couples from having children, the return of *stabilnost* should produce more babies. If layoffs, displacement, and poverty drove

Russian men to seek refuge in the vodka bottle, then the expanding wealth and opportunities should lead them back out.[56] Especially under Putin's streamlined flat tax reform, more productivity would mean more government revenues and greater contributions to the cash-starved health system. In sum: Russia's demographic crisis would all but solve itself.

Again, the conventional economic wisdom was dead wrong: while the economy was steaming ahead under Putin, Russia's health did not snap back to the "normal" dynamics of the pre-crisis era. Riding high on oil, economic output finally eclipsed pre-collapse levels in 2004. By the time Putin first left the presidency in 2008, Russian GDP was triple what it was when Putin took office. Yet Russia's health measures did not keep pace. Life expectancy crept slowly up, from 65.3 years in 2000 to 67.9 in 2008. Suicides, murders, and external traumas were all down. In 2008, only twenty-four thousand Russians died from alcohol poisoning—half as many as in 2003 but still *fifty times* higher than in the West. The slight increase in fertility (from 1.2 children per woman to 1.5) wasn't nearly enough to halt the shrinking of the Russian population.[57]

"The country just keeps going down—in numbers, in health, and in its possibilities for the future," demographer Nicholas Eberstadt told *New Yorker* journalist Michael Specter at the time of Putin's 2004 reelection. Putinism was making Russia more wealthy but less healthy. "Russia, like Africa, I am very sorry to say, is taking a detour from the rest of humanity as far as progress is measured by improving general health."[58]

It wasn't just that there were fewer Russians, but those who remained were more sickly—largely due to the epidemic levels of vodka consumption. At the end of Putin's second administration, Dr. Aleksandr Baranov of the Russian Academy of Medical Science reported that Russians had actually become more languid and *shorter* than even during the depths of the Yeltsin-era nightmare. As human societies modernize, they generally get taller, making population height an important health indicator. Baranov's announcement that "Russia is becoming one of the shortest nations"—measuring in a half-inch shorter than during the 1990s—flew in the face of reported macroeconomic progress. (Of course the replacement of the diminutive 5'7" Putin in 2008 by the 5'4" President Dmitry Medvedev did not dispel the image—and actually unleashed a barrage of short jokes, including how the new president was a product of Russia's technological advancements in nanotechnology.) But this was no laughing matter—Russians had gotten more feeble: the average boy had lost eighteen percent of his muscle mass as compared to the Yeltsin years, whereas girls lost twenty-one percent. Average lung capacity was down twenty percent, and one in five children was underweight. Cases of HIV/AIDS, tuberculosis, cancers, hepatitis B and C, all manner of physical and mental disorders—and especially adolescent alcoholism—continued to ravage Russian youth. The ministry of defense raised alarms that the decreased quantity and quality of conscripts would undercut the military's ability to field a healthy standing army—leading to the 2006 establishment of public health as one of four National Priority Projects: to be spearheaded by then-First Deputy Prime Minister Dimitry Medvedev.[59]

To unveil these projects, Putin made a dramatic pause in his 2006 State of the Nation Address from the opulent Marble Hall of the Kremlin.

> And now for the most important matter. What is most important for our country? The Defense Ministry [!] knows what is most important. Indeed, what I want to talk about is love, women, children. I want to talk about the family, about the most acute problem facing our country today—the demographic problem. The economic and social development issues our country faces today are closely interlinked to one simple question: who we are doing this all for? You know that our country's population is declining by an average of almost 700,000 people a year. We have raised this issue on many occasions but have for the most part done very little to address it.[60]

Before detailing new financial incentives to entice mothers to have second and third children, Putin quickly glossed over the most important factor: alcohol—noting only that "we are taking measures to prevent the import and production of bootleg alcohol."[61] Nothing more.

This seemed like a massive oversight. For all of the advances under Putinism, Russia still suffered an epidemic of intoxication, yet Putin never formulated anything resembling an alcohol policy. "As long as a bottle of vodka costs the same as a kilo of apples, milk is more expensive than beer, and a packet of cigarettes is cheaper than chewing gum, you ought not to worry about a demographic crisis," claimed Mikko Vieonen, representative of the World Health Organization in Moscow. "Under such circumstances, any country would have a demographic crisis."[62]

Russian alcohol experts pleaded with the Kremlin to do something: raise the drinking age, limit hours of sales, increase penalties for those selling alcohol to kids, clamp down on drunk drivers, home brewers, and third-shift vodka, increase funding for intensive care units, dispensaries, and alcohol rehabilitation programs, increase educational programs, restrict advertising... *anything*. Yet "not one of these measures was acted upon" under high Putinism. Meanwhile, as we shall see, efforts to consolidate control over the vodka market backfired spectacularly.[63]

How can we account for such inaction? The standard trope, of course, is to fault a lack of political will. But as we have seen, there was extensive political will among those actually coping with the problem at the local level. As in any autocracy—the primary impediment to change is at the top. When his State Council presented him with a draft Concept of State Alcohol Policy, Putin simply laughed: "What? Do you want me to become another Ligachev?" By invoking the scapegoat for Mikhail Gorbachev's disastrous anti-alcohol campaign, Putin ended all discussion.[64] But discussed or not, Russia's alcohol problem raged on.

So we are faced with a paradox: with a treasury flush with oil and gas wealth, and possessing all the instruments of autocratic power, how could the seemingly omnipotent Putin be so powerless to confront his professed top political priority? For commentators like Lilia Shevtsova, the answer boils down to power. "It is not that Putin does not want to realize his pet projects," such as alcohol and the demographic imbalance, but rather that "the interests of the ruling caste force leaders to concentrate only on what is important for its survival."[65] In other words—as it has been for generations of Russian vodka politics—so long as sobriety and health conflict with the economic interests of the autocratic system, they will be kicked to the side.

Meanwhile, Back On Bicycle Street…

At the end of his first presidential term just as at its beginning, the business side of Putin's vodka politics was most evident back at the red-brick Kristall compound. The storied factory was to be the crown jewel of Rosspirtprom—a state-run national champion conglomerate created on the eve of Putin's inauguration. Putin tapped two men to rein in the world's most lucrative vodka market: Sergei Zivenko and Arkady Rotenberg. Who were they, and what qualified them for such important (and incredibly lucrative) positions?

As it turns out, Rotenberg had been Putin's close friend for some forty years, dating from their childhood judo competitions back in Leningrad. In the pre-Putin 1990s Rotenberg was a mildly successful businessman who enjoyed promoting judo. By 1998 he had become director of St. Petersburg's elite judo club, Yawara-Neva, with his buddy Vladimir Putin its honorary president. "I am the CEO, but it's the brainchild of Vladimir Putin," Rotenberg later admitted. "It was his idea."[66] In 1999 Rotenberg started a business relationship with Zivenko—another nondescript thirty-something businessman with an interest in the alcohol trade, despite only ever getting drunk once in high school, while seeing his friend off to the military.[67] Yet within months these inexperienced businessmen were entrusted with controlling Russia's most lucrative market. *How?*

In a recent interview Putin's top advisor Andrei Illarionov described how the Rosspirtprom decision went down. After hearing only secondhand that the "primary and most important stream of federal finances" had been bequeathed to Putin's "clan," Illarionov dialed up Alexei Kudrin—acclaimed austerity hawk and

Putin's decade-long Minister of Finance—to see if he knew anything. He didn't. Minister of Economic Trade and Development German Gref likewise had heard nothing of this huge decision. "I soon realized that for Putin, there are two distinctly separate groups of people," said Illarionov, "let's call them the 'economics group' versus the 'business people.' With the one group—Kudrin, Gref, and me—Putin discussed issues of the general economy; while with the help of the other, he seized control over property and financial flows."[68]

What happened once the trade was in their hands? By the end of Putin's first term Rosspirtprom holdings controlled over forty-five percent of the legal vodka market, worth more than two billion dollars annually, largely through corporate raiding and back-room arm twisting. Trying to get Russians off *samogon* and third-shift vodka and get them back on the state-sanctioned stuff won Zivenko many enemies in the tumultuous vodka underground. They placed a six-million-dollar bounty on his head. Even at his office he retained an armed security detail.[69] Yet, as he confided to Viktor Erofeyev in 2002, he was only a thorn in the side of those who preferred disorder in the alcohol market.

Shortly thereafter he was investigated by the Accounts Chamber and fired. But don't feel sorry for Sergei Zivenko—as the short blurb in his *Forbes* 100 profile explains, he "hit the jackpot" as director of Rosspirtprom. And though he "only stayed in the job two years, he put the experience to good use." In those two short years he went from middling businessman to one of the richest men in Russia, with a net worth of $220 million—not too shabby. Then—along with his other Rosspirtprom managers—Zivenko simply moved down the line: creating the so-called Kristall Trade and Industrial Group, which produces the premium (and potentially copyright infringing) Cristall Black Label, with annual revenues of $400 million.[70] Yet that is nothing compared to Putin's judo partner, Arkady Rotenberg.

Not long ago the Russian business newspaper *Kommersant'* sat down with the reclusive Rotenberg: "In 1998, you led the sports club Yawara-Neva, with Vladimir Putin as its honorary president," began the interview. "And here within a relatively short time, you've become a big businessman with substantial assets across the country and in various sectors of the economy. Is it just a coincidence?"

"I understand the subtext of your question," Rotenberg replied. "Knowing high-level government officials has never been an impediment to business in our country, but it is hardly a guarantee of success. After all, Putin knows far more people than those who have become famous and successful today."[71] Instead, he claimed it was the philosophy of judo that produced his good fortune—first by heading Rosspirtprom and then parlaying that into creating the successful SMP Bank with his brother Boris. By the end of Putin's second term Rotenberg had bought up the companies that built lucrative pipelines for Gazprom. From such humble beginnings in the dojo, through heading the national champions

Rosspirtprom and Gazprom, Rotenberg has a net worth estimated by *Forbes* of $1.1 billion.[72]

Rotenberg seems to embody a core element of Russia's ruling *sistema* whereby useful friends become appointed millionaires—making quick fortunes in the private sector while serving the interests of powerful individuals in the government through their informal ties of trust and loyalty.[73]

Even downplaying direct connections, Putin's indirect effect was unquestionable. Whether as tribute or opportunism, in 2003 a new vodka brand rolled off the production line at Kristall: Putinka. Just like *vodka* is the diminutive for Russia's "little water," *Putinka* is Russia's "little Putin" in a bottle. Adoring Russians drank it up, quickly becoming Russia's second most popular brand. Even in a country with surprisingly little brand loyalty, Putinka maintained its dominance over the next decade—raking in the equivalent of $500 million annually, as the Kristall plant churned out more than eight million bottles monthly. For his part, Putin has repeatedly scoffed at the commercialization of his legacy, but at least when it comes to vodka, he's done surprisingly little to confront it.[74]

Rosspirtprom's privileged position looked to get even better through a series of laws on alcohol production aimed at reducing the "rampant corruption, illegal activity and extremely high rates of alcohol poisonings" and signed by Putin in 2005.[75] Effective January 1, 2006, alcoholic beverages could only be sold with new government excise stamps. All production facilities were required to have new monitoring and accounting equipment and could only be licensed if they were not behind in paying their taxes. Such regulations would clamp down on illicit production, squeeze out small producers, and further consolidate the market for Putin's national champion—all in the name of quality control. Instead, the bungled implementation by a corrupt bureaucracy had the opposite effect— dealing a death blow not only to thousands of Russian consumers but ultimately to Rosspirtprom itself.

"The end result of the laws and resolutions was a farce," claimed Dr. Aleksandr Nemtsov.[76] The new excise stamps hadn't even been printed in time. By the time they were shipped to producers, including Rosspirtprom, their facilities had been idle for weeks or even months. The government scrambled to extend deadlines, but the entire market was in chaos. With liquor stores suddenly empty, thirsty Russians turned to the very illegal producers that the Kremlin had hoped to crush while decimating the company it had planned to strengthen.

The human consequences were the most apparent: many hard-up drinkers reverted to quaffing industrial solvents, antifreeze and the like, while third-shift producers made vodka from similar industrial poisons. With tragic predictability, the spring and summer of 2006 saw a nationwide epidemic of fatal alcohol poisonings. In many countries authorities can declare a state of emergency for widespread civil unrest or acute natural disaster: in Russia, four regions (including the beleaguered governor of Pskov) imposed a state of emergency for bad vodka.[77]

The fiasco gutted state-run Rosspirtprom. An audit by the Federal Accounts Chamber concluded that Rosspirtprom's "financial condition as of 2007 can be characterized as a crisis, in which the company is on the verge of complete bankruptcy."[78] What happened to this once-mighty national champion—the keeper of Kristall and producer of Putinka—that enriched both oligarch and government alike?

For one, much like other national champions, such as Gazprom, Rosspirtprom was overextended and willing to absorb debts by selling its product on credit, especially if it advanced the Kremlin's strategic interests. This would be a problem only if there was a sudden need for cash. Second, the company's production lines stood idle from January through March of 2006 while the government tried to clean up its stamp mess. Rosspirtprom made mostly inexpensive vodkas—which when combined with a healthy amount of government taxes, left little profit margin to recoup those lost revenues.

Third—and perhaps most importantly—new regulations required upfront payment from retailers and distributors rather than credit. Suddenly there was that need for cash, and the company couldn't get it fast enough. When distributors were unable to pay upfront, Rosspirtprom was left holding the bag. With no money on hand they couldn't even pay their tax bills—another no-no according to the new regulations. With its tax arrears mounting, in July 2006 the Federal Tax Service suspended Rosspirtprom's license, crippling the addled giant even further with another $13 million in losses.[79]

Letting Rosspirtprom collapse would have been an embarrassment for Putin: a lucrative national champion suddenly careens into bankruptcy thanks to a disastrously implemented Kremlin policy. Instead, a five-billion-ruble ($165 million) bailout was orchestrated by major state-run bank VTB or Vneshtorgbank. With Finance Minister Kudrin chairing its board of directors, VTB later became a favored target of anti-corruption crusader Alexei Navalny. "VTB is a very good reflection of how business in Russia occurs today," explained one banking insider, "which is on the one hand state ownership and on the other direction by individuals who are much more concerned about their own wealth than about the benefit to the country or the owners of the institution."[80]

In this instance the VTB loan allowed Rosspirtprom to pay its tax bill owed to the government (from which it received the bailout) and enabled it to re-start production. Meanwhile, we can only speculate whether those assembly lines *actually* stood idle all those months or whether the usual third-shift production simply expanded into the first two shifts as well.

While the bailout saved Rosspirtprom from sudden death, it doomed it to a slow, imminent demise. According to the Accounts Chamber, even though the company sold off assets and its most famous trademarks, the thin profit margins led to a "pitiable state of affairs" in which the company could not pay its massive debts, interest on loans, or even its bills. This is how botched government reforms fatally poisoned both scores of Russians and the country's single largest vodka producer. Unfathomably, Rosspirtprom could no longer turn a profit selling vodka to Russians.[81]

With Rosspirtprom unable to meet its loan payments, VTB reluctantly disassembled the company, taking control of the various parcels, including the red-brick Kristall factory.[82] Like a foreclosed home, a bankrupt factory is of little use to a bank. The Kremlin-controlled VTB needed a loyal investor to take one for the team and buy up these toxic assets. They found another well-connected oligarch, Vasily Anisimov.

A battle-tested veteran of the "wild east" of *mafiya* capitalism in the 1990s, Anisimov masterminded the purchase of nonferrous metals at low, state-subsidized prices and sold them at immense profit on world markets. By 1994 he was vice-president of Rossiisky Kredit Bank, where he bought up lucrative metals firms and exported aluminum with the help of Marc Rich—the fugitive Belgian commodities trader infamously pardoned by President Bill Clinton.[83] At the end of Putin's first term in 2004, *Forbes* estimated Anisimov's wealth at $350 million. By the end of his second term, Anisimov had topped $4 *billion*.[84] Certainly he had benefited tremendously from Putinomics.

Anisimov's oldest daughter had been brutally murdered in Ekaterinburg in the 1990s, prompting Vasily to send his family to the "backup airfields" of the United States: "If you're flying high and President Putin decides to confiscate your property, you know you've got somewhere to land," explained one Russian businessman. Living the high life of a billionaire heiress in New York, Anisimov's teenage daughter Anna soon drew comparisons to Paris Hilton. Together the Anisimovs bonded over developing high-end real estate in Manhattan and the Hamptons.[85]

Back in Russia, Vasily continued to diversify his interests...into vodka. In 2009 he purchased from VTB the Rosspirtprom properties languishing in bankruptcy for five billion rubles (the amount of the original bailout loan), which included fifty-one percent control over Kristall. In 2010 he upped his stake in Kristall to eighty-six percent, making him the biggest player in the vodka market alongside Putin's judo partner, Arkady Rotenberg. Of course it is difficult to speculate whether the purchase was informally dictated by the Kremlin, but it is telling that in February 2010 Anisimov got the Putin seal of approval: he was made president of the Russian Judo Federation, even though he never participated in judo or expressed an interest in it.[86]

Equally telling: in his public pronouncements Anisimov seemed indifferent to his new multi-billion-ruble vodka empire, dourly intending, he said, to "bring order to the [alcohol] factories." In a 2010 interview he explained, "We only took them in order to make money." With a shake of his head he added: "troublesome product."[87]

For many factories this meant reorganization. But a different fate awaited the iconic Kristall factory on Samokatnaya ulitsa, a plant that had been integral to centuries of Russian vodka politics. In 2012 Anisimov announced plans to dismantle the factory and relocate the production facilities to a cheaper plot on the outskirts of Moscow. Having spent much time and money investing in properties in the American market, Anisimov apparently determined that the 8.6 hectares occupied by the storied factory on the banks of the Yauza were just too valuable to pass up. And so—that is how the most iconic landmark in the history of Russian vodka is to be transformed into high-end condominiums.[88]

Medvedev against History

We must always remember that today's present was the future for all
those Russian heroes of World War II, who won freedom for all of us.
We are reminded that the same people who won over such a cruel and
relentless Nazi enemy back then should—*no, must!*—conquer corruption and backwardness to establish a modern and livable country.

The nationalist timbre of 2009's *Russia, Forward!* manifesto harnessed the glory
of Russia's historic sacrifices to meet the political challenges of both the present and future. "What will Russia be like for my son, and for all of our children
and grandchildren? What will be the country's international position? How can
we make Russia richer and more free? I have answers to these questions," the
author paused. "But before I formulate them, I would like to assess Russia's current situation."

And that is where the anti-establishment takedown *really* began. Channeling
the spirit of some Soviet-era dissident, the author launched into an exposé of
Putin-era *stabilnost*. Apparently the global financial crisis—which pummeled
Russia far harder than any other G-20 member—prompted some sober political soul searching. Russia, the manifesto claimed, was not living up to expectations: a backward economy reliant on oil, gas, and mineral exports instead of
manufacturing and innovation, and everywhere infested with corruption. The
roots of these problems are in the people's "traditional vices of bribery, larceny,
sloth and drunkenness, that we should be determined to get rid of." The failings
of Putin's Russia were not just economic, but political and demographic as well.

The institutions of democratic governance have been stabilized, but
they are far from ideal. Civil society is weak; grassroots activism and
self-management are too low. Even more problematic: every year there
are fewer and fewer of us left.

Alcoholism, smoking, car accidents, lack of access to modern medicine and environmental pollution cut short the lives of millions. And
the rate of births can't compensate for the population decline.[1]

Finally—someone familiar with the intricacies of Russian politics, economics, demographics, and culture was smashing the Putinist facade. Yet—strangely—the man so keen to speak truth to power *was* the power: Russia's new president, Dmitry Medvedev.

Dmitry Who?

If vodka isn't the quintessential symbol of Russia, then the bear certainly is. From early tsars unleashing trained bears on unsuspecting subjects and nondrinkers (chapters 3 and 4) to Misha, the cuddly bear mascot for the 1980 Moscow Olympics, the bear has grown to symbolize great Russian power. In the political realm, the acronym of Putin's "Interregional Movement 'Unity' " was MeDvEd, the Russian word for "bear."[2] (When it was rebranded "United Russia," they even kept the bear.) And so it was a complete coincidence that when it came time to anoint a successor after his presidential term limit expired in 2008, Vladimir Putin turned to his own bear—Dmitry *Medved*ev. But who was Medvedev? And how could he be so critical of his patron, Vladimir Putin?

Like Putin, Dmitry Medvedev was hardly predestined for Russia's top post—he largely "fell upstairs," as political scientist Daniel Treisman has put it.[3] The only child of college professors, the studious Dmitry earned a law degree from Leningrad State University, where he later taught until 1999. In his youth Medvedev admitted to smoking and drinking but "without fanaticism. I tried it—like everything else, but nothing more." In a campaign interview he explained how "dad and mom always handled vodka responsibly," which shaped his own moderation.[4] In the St. Petersburg city government under mayor Anatoly Sobchak, Medvedev first met Vladimir Putin—and when Putin rose to the Kremlin administration in 1999, he took Medvedev and a handful of others with him.

After becoming president in 2000, Putin installed his campaign manager/chief of staff Medvedev as chairman of the board of Gazprom, the lucrative "national champion" natural gas company. Among Gazprom's many acquisitions under Medvedev was the independent NTV television channel of Yeltsin-era oligarch Vladimir Gusinsky.[5] While still with Gazprom, Medvedev moved into Putin's Presidential Administration (PA) before being appointed first deputy prime minister in 2005. That same year Putin put Medvedev in charge of Russia's four National Priority Projects (NPP): high-profile government initiatives to improve public health, education, housing, and agriculture. When Putin decried Russia's "critical" demographics in his 2006 State of the Nation address, it effectively became a fifth charge for Medvedev's National Projects Council.

Billed as "Russia's New Deal," these National Priority Projects looked like a good-faith effort to use Russia's petrochemical windfall to address key political shortcomings. Medvedev's position gave him firsthand expertise on Russia's debilitating social problems and the state's efforts to address them. His media image was overwhelmingly positive, as Medvedev ensured that popular initiatives, including pay raises for teachers and doctors, were being fulfilled. But beyond the public relations benefits of doling out thirteen billion dollars in government largesse, the National Priority Projects became just another bureaucracy working in parallel to (but not always in concert with) standard government institutions. As economist Leonid Abalkin lamented, the projects were developed "in private, without engaging scholars and specialists," and ignored those who had judged the projects' success—"that is, Russian citizens."[6]

Outside of education, the results were disappointing. Fleets of new school busses and ambulances, computers and medical equipment appeared, but they were still just drops in the ocean. By 2008 half of respondents to a Levada Center opinion poll said the projects had not affected them at all, with a similar number believing that the money was ineffectively spent. Indeed, classified American government cables released through WikiLeaks estimated that "between 10 and 30 percent of NPP funds was diverted to kickbacks in return for program award, and thus not spent as intended." The leaked cables from 2008 concluded that "nearly three years after their launch, and despite Medvedev's personal involvement, most experts agree that the projects have been too small in scope and have failed to reform social systems in need of deep structural changes."[7]

With the storm clouds of global financial crisis looming on the horizon, and an uncertain conclusion to Putin's second presidential term, 2008 was a pivotal time for post-Soviet Russia. With United Russia's legislative supermajority at his back, Putin could easily have amended the constitution to allow him a third consecutive term—but he did not. Instead, in late 2007 Putin tapped Medvedev—trusted friend and head of both Gazprom and the National Priority Projects—for the country's top post. Medvedev immediately announced that he would run for the presidency only if Putin would be his second-in-command prime minister. With two-thirds of the electorate willing to voting for whomever Putin chose, Medvedev easily won the 2008 presidential election with 71.2 percent of the vote.[8]

Hope For Change?

There was a certain amount of déjà vu to Dmitry Medvedev's 2008 inauguration. Just as when Putin took the same long walk through the Kremlin's opulent Andreyevsky Hall eight years earlier, Russia had a new leader whom few people knew much about and whose victory seemed more like the coronation of a system insider than the result of a contentious electoral battle. In 2000 critics scoffed that Putin would be a weak leader—puppet to the Yeltsin-era oligarchs ruling from the shadows. Similarly, in 2008 it was assumed that Medvedev would be a pawn, with the real power moving to the prime minister's office headed by Vladimir Putin—"the former president and current secret president of Russia," as American satirist Stephen Colbert took to calling him.[9]

Although both Putin and Medvedev were previously little-known, little in stature, shared the same hometown, worldview, values, and unshakable trust in each other, there were palpable differences between the two. Whereas Putin was former KGB and product of the security services, Medvedev was a former law professor with a more liberal, Western orientation. While Putin was seemingly guided more by intuition and emotion, Medvedev was cooler—intellectual, reasoned, and reflective.[10] Plus, if his inauguration speech was any indication, Medvedev was more willing both to acknowledge the weakness of civil society and the rule of law and, later, to confront corruption and alcohol in the name of the general good.

Perhaps the biggest difference between the two presidents was the external economic and political environment they confronted. Putin inherited a non-threatening geopolitical situation and stable global economy. Medvedev would not be as fortunate. The investment bank Bear Stearns collapsed two weeks after the "bear" Medvedev secured his electoral victory. The bursting of the U.S. housing bubble decimated securities and pounded global (including Russian) financial institutions, marking the beginning of the Great Recession. With falling demand, the sky-high price of Russia's main exports—oil and metals—plummeted, taking Russian stability with it. On July 11, 2008, global oil prices hit a new record of $147 a barrel—by the end of the year it was only $34.[11]

With Medvedev on vacation and Putin in Beijing for the summer Olympics, tensions between Russia and its southern neighbor, Georgia, exploded into outright warfare. To hear Ronald Asmus's telling, Russia was like the schoolyard bully who had long tormented the neighborhood kids. Little Georgia finally snapped and punched back against the bigger kid, Asmus explained, "and there was little doubt that he would be drubbed in return."[12]

Indeed, the Russian military crushed the Georgian forces as they rolled into the contested regions of Abkhazia, South Ossetia, and beyond. The perception of Russian aggression spooked already jittery foreign investors, who pulled out of the Russian market en masse. Trading on Russian stock markets was halted to prevent complete free fall. Large banks and companies went bankrupt. The economy shrank by eight percent; the stock index lost eighty percent of its peak value; unemployment spiked, and Russia's currency reserves took a major hit. Although Russia wobbled, however, it did not fall down: prudent injections of liquidity and stimulus funds saved a complete collapse of the banking system and supported major companies without renationalization. The Kremlin weathered the storm better than analysts predicted, but the crisis tempered expectations for continuous prosperity while underscoring the dangerous economic consequences of pervasive corruption and overreliance on oil and gas exports.[13]

Medvedev's presidency was marked by well-meaning attempts to increase transparency and confront Russia's "legal nihilism." All government tenders would be published on the Internet to shed light on the bureaucracy's shady back-room deals—yet there was no one to follow up on them. All high-level officials, from the president on down, were required to annually declare their income and wealth. The ease with which these regulations were sidestepped also created tremendous cynicism. Medvedev himself—president and major stakeholder in one of the world's largest lumber companies as well as former chair of the board of Gazprom—declared only eighty-four thousand dollars in savings and one Moscow apartment. Taxpayers soon learned that, from top to bottom, Russia was being run "by the poor husbands of very rich women."[14] But it was a start, at least.

While the anti-corruption efforts grabbed headlines, social issues—including Medvedev's National Priority Projects—were sacrificed to the global economic crisis. "The fate of the national projects is becoming less and less enviable," said Ruslan Grinberg, head of the Economics Institute of the Russian Academy of Sciences, at the end of 2008. "The volume of financing was not significant to begin with. These were little islands of support in a sea of dilapidated infrastructure." Critics who had claimed that the projects were nothing but campaign populism just shrugged as they were de-funded and de-prioritized after the election.[15]

The conventional wisdom is that Medvedev was a pliant stooge who simply kept the seat of presidential power warm for Putin's return in 2012. A closer examination of social and health issues, however, exposes significant rifts within the Kremlin monolith. After a 2010 discussion of social problems by his National Projects Council, the usually cool-headed Medvedev lost his temper and on Twitter criticized officials for delivering thick reports that never offered action plans or solutions. The president even publicly called out finance minister and longtime Putin acolyte Alexei Kudrin, imploring him to increase funding for social projects "for the sake of the country's future."[16] It would not be the last time the two would butt heads.

Overcoming decades of neglect in healthcare would be an especially onerous undertaking. While Russia (at least nominally) still has a system of universal healthcare as part of its Soviet inheritance, the system had only moderately improved since the dreadful Yeltsin years. Band-aid reforms only exacerbated problems and red tape: new requirements of citizens to buy medical insurance contradicted the mandate of universal care; meanwhile, the old system of tying doctors to patients only in specific residential districts prevented many from receiving acceptable treatment. While the well-to-do either pay for high-end services at home or abroad, the most needy and marginalized—pensioners and the handicapped—are effectively denied care if they can't come up with a bribe.

That the healthcare system is increasingly geared toward personal enrichment at the expense of social well-being has made it an appealing target for anti-corruption activists like blogger Alexei Navalny. In 2010 Navalny was tipped off that the ministry of health and social development posted a tender to develop a two-million-dollar computer network connecting doctors and patients to be delivered within sixteen days of winning the bid. "Without a doubt," Navalny claimed the system had already been developed at a far lower cost, leaving plenty of room for kickbacks. More than two thousand of Navalny's readers deluged the Federal Anti-Monopoly Agency with complaints, until the health ministry withdrew the contract. In the meantime, his readers found other egregious tenders for expensive technology projects to be built in an impossibly short time frame. Navalny waged a withering online campaign against the health official in charge of contracts, whom, for obvious reasons, he referred to only as "Mr. Unibrow." Within a week Unibrow was gone. Such rapid and tangible successes inspired Navalny's next project, RosPil.info: a crowd-sourcing website where any reader can upload suspicious government tenders—from the health ministry and beyond—for review by the online community and a team of lawyers. If the suspicions are well-founded, Navalny trumpets the fraud on his blog, leading the agency to be buried in an avalanche of hostile correspondence. As he admits, none of this would have been possible without Medvedev's anti-corruption initiatives. In the end, Navalny's online community is effectively doing what the Anti-Monopoly Agency and the federal prosecutor's office should be doing but aren't.[17]

Suspicious tenders are only part of the problem: bribe-hungry physicians, outmoded equipment, and dilapidated facilities mean that hospitals are more often seen as sources of headaches than as cures for them. Today over half of Russians avoid seeing a doctor to treat their illnesses—meaning that the diseases enumerated in the past two chapters may actually be *more* prevalent since many prefer to suffer in silence rather than seek out medical treatment. "What's most upsetting," says pollster Marina Krassilnikova "is that two-thirds of the population are certain they wouldn't receive good medical care if it were needed."[18]

Despite highly visible upgrades to ambulances and the like, still "people say there's been no improvement whatsoever," according to Aleksandr Saversky, head of the grass-roots Patients' Rights Protection League. Especially when it comes to corruption—just as Murray Feshbach explained to *60 Minutes* some fifteen years earlier—the best way still to get decent medical treatment in Russia is to bribe providers for the services they are legally obligated to provide for free.[19]

If Russia ever hopes to confront its gloomy demographic future it will have to tackle its dysfunctional healthcare system. Promoting a healthy and vibrant citizenry requires more than occasional splurging—it means grappling with the corruption that permeates the system from top to bottom. While the National Priority Projects boosted physician salaries, much of those funds disappeared to graft and kickbacks. Like judges in the equally corrupt legal sphere, the abysmally low pay of doctors forces them to resort to accepting bribes just to make ends meet. Even private clinics have been affected: increasingly employing unqualified staff who bought their medical credentials instead of earning them. "Most clinics are geared toward one thing," one nurse said in a recent exposé, "and that's earning money. State bureaucrats earn good money. All the rest of us real people earn very little. That's what's making the corruption grow."[20] Unless the government overhauls the healthcare system to help confront its continuing demographic struggle, the pervasive corruption will likely increase, in Saversky's words, "until the whole system collapses like a house of cards."[21]

And Then... Unexpectedly... Something Happened

By far the most dramatic split between Putin and Medvedev came over vodka. As president, Putin had occasionally spoken out against Russia's national shame, but like similarly half-hearted admonishments of the imperial, Soviet, and post-Soviet past, words were rarely matched by deeds that would threaten financial interests. For eight years under Putin the world's hardest-drinking country had no semblance of an alcohol policy, and the only political initiatives backfired spectacularly—bankrupting the national champion Rosspirtprom and poisoning thousands of Russians in the process. Reforms meant to reduce dangerous *samogon* and illicit third-shift vodka had the exact opposite effect (chapter 22). Anti-addiction services were nonexistent; measures against drunk driving were half-hearted; and there were no attempts to address the ever-growing wave of drunken children. "Adolescent alcoholization in Russia has an enormous scale," claimed Interior Minister Rashid Nurgaliyev in 2010, citing statistics indicating that eighty percent of teenagers were regular drinkers and that the average age that Russian kids started drinking had dropped from sixteen to thirteen.[22]

"You don't have to read the newspapers, listen to the radio, watch TV, or know anything about high-level intrigues to deduce that the powers-that-be long ago ceased to care about the well-being of the people," explained the dean of Russian alcohol studies, Dr. Aleksandr Nemtsov, in his exhaustive *Contemporary History of Alcohol in Russia.* "You only need to remember these three numbers: 58.5, 13.5, and 16.5": 58.5 years: the depths to which average Russian male life expectancy had dropped; 13.5: how many years earlier Russian men were going to the grave than Russian women—the largest gap in the world—largely thanks to massive vodka consumption; and 16.5: the number of years earlier Russian men were dying than their counterparts in Europe. "With just these three numbers, you can easily infer the seriousness of the consequences of Russian drinking. We are forced to confront the reality that the alcohol situation in the country is catastrophic, and the government has done almost nothing about it."[23]

Though frustrated, President Medvedev seemed content to watch Russian healthcare limp through the global financial crisis with little more than band-aid solutions. But he took a decidedly more aggressive approach to Russia's vodka problem beginning in the summer of 2009. At his seaside retreat outside of Sochi, Medvedev declared that he was "astonished to find out that we now drink more than we did in the 1990s, although those were very tough times." And when it came to assessing Putin's policies: "I believe no changes have taken place, really." The new president concluded simply that "nothing has helped."[24]

Heralding the first concerted effort to address vodka politics since Mikhail Gorbachev's ill-fated anti-alcohol campaign, Medvedev declared: "Alcoholism in our country is a national disaster." Casting vodka as a threat to national security, the president spouted a series of telling statistics, beginning with (an arguably inflated) per capita consumption of eighteen liters of pure alcohol per year: more than double the maximum deemed acceptable by the World Health Organization. "When you convert that into vodka bottles, it is simply mind-boggling," Medvedev said. "This is approximately 50 bottles of vodka, for each resident of the country, including infants. These are monstrous figures." The government's own Public Chamber declared that alcohol was involved in eighty percent of murders and forty percent of suicides and that, directly or indirectly, alcohol abuse was killing a half-million Russians every year. Separately, an extensive study published in the acclaimed British medical journal *The Lancet* that same summer was even more eye-opening: alcohol caused *more than half* of all deaths of working-age Russians (ages 15–54), making it the greatest contributor to Russia's mortality crisis.[25]

Unlike Putin's jokes about not becoming "another Ligachev," Medvedev actually praised the Gorbachev-era anti-alcohol campaign. "It is fact rather than speculation that the period saw unprecedented demographic growth in our country," he told his advisory State Council. "We must think about a system of measures, including restrictive ones"—though he rightfully warned against

Russian President Dmitry Medvedev (right) chairs the first meeting on alcohol abuse and anti-alcohol measures at the Bocharov Ruchei presidential residence in Sochi on August, 12, 2009. Associated Press, RIA-Novosti/ Dmitry Astakhov.

the "idiotic bans and mistakes, which fueled a legitimate indignation among the population."[26]

Gorbachev himself approved of Medvedev's long overdue initiative. "We are destroying ourselves, and then we will look for those who destroyed our country, for those who made us drink," declared the former Soviet president. "The situation is such that we must take control."[27] Yet while polls suggested that sixty-five percent of Russians approved of a renewed anti-liquor push, many dismissed it as quixotic folly. "It's impossible. He doesn't stand a chance," one drinker told the *Los Angeles Times*. As under Gorbachev's campaign, "the Russian man will always be drinking. Russians don't surrender."[28]

Although Medvedev was wary of repeating the disasters of Gorbachev's campaign, many of the goals and tactics in his initiative were strikingly similar. Just as in 1985, the ministry of health and state-run television launched a propaganda campaign against heavy drinking, promoting "a healthy lifestyle among the citizens of Russia." Also as in 1985, the Kremlin instituted stiff penalties for retailers who sold to minors, restricted sales hours, and raised the minimum price of a bottle of vodka—first to three dollars and increasing incrementally thereafter. And as in 1985, Medvedev's initiative was kicked off with wildly ambitious, long-term goals: cutting alcohol consumption in half within ten years and raising life expectancy to age seventy-five by 2025.[29]

Still, this was hardly your father's anti-alcohol campaign. Rather than merely circulating pamphlets and posters, the dangers of drinking were articulated by famous celebrities in well-produced public service announcements. Russia's burgeoning online community was abuzz with humorous viral videos from the health ministry, which quickly racked up millions of views on YouTube. The most famous portrayed a mangy, computer-animated squirrel or *belka*—which is also Russian slang for delirium tremens. The drunken, paranoid squirrel climbs the walls, breaks into song, talks of shooting imaginary *kudyapliks*, and describes how his friend murdered his wife in an alcoholic stupor, believing her to be the devil. "Drinking tonight?" the squirrel asks, the question looming. "Well then maybe I'll be coming to visit you."

(Astonishingly, an entrepreneurial vodka maker quickly capitalized on the Internet buzz by creating a sarcastic new line of vodkas called *Belochka: Ya prishla!* (*The Squirrel: I Have Arrived!*). "Belochka is a truly Russian spirit of self-irony that helps people overcome difficulties by laughter," the product's website claims. "If you have no sense of humor this vodka is not for you.")[30]

Other policies were far less playful: dropping the legal blood alcohol level for drunk driving to 0.0; encouraging healthful, moderate consumption of wine over more potent and destructive vodka; expanding control over sales at kiosks and other retail outlets; limiting the size of canned cocktails, requiring health warnings on alcoholic drinks, including the fruity "alcopops" that entice younger drinkers; and—yes—even "moving the legal drinking age up from zero," as comedian Seth Meyers joked on *Saturday Night Live*.[31] Yet by far the most important break from past campaigns is that each reform has been introduced incrementally, allowing for adjustment and evaluation of the policies. Much to their credit, Medvedev's Kremlin eschewed the autocratic excesses and "shock troop" mentality that popular habits can easily be made to conform to the government's wishes. Unlike the dramatic prohibition of the Great War, or the hastily implemented restrictions of the Gorbachev era, Medvedev apparently understands that changing popular habits could only be done gradually, not instantaneously. Such small steps are unquestionably a good start, but the lack of any effort to treat alcoholism as a disease—which would require expensive investments in the country's creaking medical infrastructure and serious commitment to rehabilitation programs—calls into question whether the Kremlin is genuinely intent on reducing drinking, especially knowing what that means for state revenues and entrenched vodka interests.

Still, by the time Medvedev handed the presidency back to Putin in 2012, the anti-alcohol campaign had quietly produced marked improvements in Russian health. Per capita consumption of all types of alcohol had dropped from eighteen liters per capita to fifteen. Suicides, homicides, and—most tellingly—alcohol-poisoning deaths occurred less frequently. In 2011, "only" eleven thousand seven hundred Russians died from alcohol poisoning, quite a drop from the average of thirty-six thousand per year during Putin's eight years (2000–2008) but still some fifty times higher than in Europe and North America. Already by 2011, combined life expectancy for both men and women surpassed seventy years (64.3 for men, 76.1 for women) for the first time since 1986, during Gorbachev's anti-alcohol campaign.[32]

Dramatic demographic improvements also were the hallmark of the Gorbachev campaign—at least before crafty bootleggers and moonshiners eroded the progress. Similarly, sneaky entrepreneurs have circumvented Medvedev's anti-alcohol regulations. Even where nighttime sales are banned, companies have popped up that will deliver liquor to your door even in the dead of night—instead of buying the vodka, the customer extends the courier a loan, getting the courier's booze as collateral. As one such courier in Novosibirsk explained to Vedomosti, it is always possible to give back the collateral for a refund, "but he had never heard of anyone actually doing that."

Similar schemes have emerged across Russia. In Moscow you can join a local "social organization" for a set fee and receive a complimentary bottle of booze as a welcoming gift. Other companies will sell you (overpriced) trinkets and souvenirs accompanied by a "free" bottle of vodka. Still other online sites circumvent sales restrictions by having the customer sign a brief contract to "rent" booze. The contract expires the following day at 8 a.m.[33]

At the end of 2011 the health ministry warned that, despite meaningful progress, the new rules were "often not followed," with problematic implications for health. While alcohol poisonings were down, the gap in life expectancy—the most telling indicator of dangerous patterns of alcohol consumption—was still the highest in the world, with Russian men dying twelve years before their widows. Kids were drinking earlier and earlier, with seventy-seven percent of all underaged teenagers (15–17) regularly drinking vodka—upwards of ninety percent in rural areas. Even with the anti-alcohol campaign in full swing, 2.5 million Russians applied for alcoholism treatment in 2010. Another 28 million people claimed they either "misuse alcohol" or are "addicted" to it.[34] In other words, there are more alcoholics in Russia than there are Texans in Texas.

More worrisome are recent indicators suggesting that the anti-alcohol movement may be losing momentum. Particularly telling are the statistics on accidental alcohol poisonings, which fell a whopping thirty-two percent from 2009 to 2010—reflecting the first full year of the alcohol restrictions. The year 2011 added an additional 18.8 percent drop. By contrast, preliminary figures from 2013 suggest only a 1.4 percent yearly decrease in accidental alcohol poisonings. Similarly, slowing rates of improvement in all manner of alcohol-related mortality suggests diminishing returns to public health from the sobriety initiative.[35]

Moreover, market watchers have sounded the alarm over the additional thirty-three percent increase on vodka excise taxes imposed on January 1, 2013. The tax hike has brought more rubles into the treasury, but has decimated legal vodka producers, who have seen their output drop by more than a third from just the year before. And while legal vodka production is plummeting, after a few years of declining, per-capita vodka consumption is actually back on the rise as bootleggers, smugglers, and black-marketers bribe corrupt regulators to look the other way while their cheaper wares and dangerous alcohol surrogates flood the market—and all predictably to the detriment of public health.[36]

Taken together, these are troubling signs, as it has been the same pattern—overly strident alcohol restrictions combined with institutionalized corruption that lead to an explosion of unregulated, underground vodka and deadly surrogates that erode benefits to public health—that has ultimately doomed every previous attempt to rein-in vodka. Whether the Kremlin maintains a flexible approach and a focus on improving public health, or whether it succumbs to the ghosts of vodka history, only time will tell.

The Other Side of the Coin

Despite Russia's history of revolutionary upheavals, if there is one constant across the past five centuries it is that public well-being is almost *never* the Kremlin's foremost concern, especially when the greater good clashes with the financial needs of the state or those well-connected to it. Consequently, there have only been two kinds of anti-alcohol campaigns in Russian history. The most common is the half-hearted, populist overture to improving health and economic productivity, which invariably is eroded by the insatiable desire to maximize vodka profits. The other kind—as we have seen in the cases of Nicholas II and Gorbachev—zealously sacrificed state finance in the interest of social health only to blow a massive hole in the budget, thereby hastening the demise of both the tsarist and Soviet empires.[37] In either case, the outcome has been the same: failure (though of a far more spectacular variety in the latter case). So when leaders talk of putting the people before of the bottle, they are met with skepticism, if not outright trepidation. Would Medvedev's efforts fare any better?

There is reason for optimism that current efforts won't be of the disastrous, second variety. Unlike Nicholas's dry law, Russia is not embroiled in a debilitating war, and unlike the collapse in world oil prices under Gorbachev, the treasury is flush thanks to the high world price of oil and gas. The massive rents from these exports—and Putin's low, workable flat tax—mean that the present-day Russian Federation isn't nearly as reliant on alcohol to make ends meet. Instead of making up one quarter to one-third of all state revenues as in the tsarist and

Soviet eras, vodka's contribution to the federal budget is now only two to four percent (in addition to contributions to the regional governments).[38] Eschewing autocratic, shock-troop methods in favor of incrementally ratcheting up restrictions also bodes well for avoiding the worst-case scenario.

If the regime-implosion scenario isn't likely, all that remains is the half-hearted, temporary concession. As mentioned, there have been some troubling signs suggesting this possible outcome. But if these turn out to be just bumps in the road, could Medvedev actually have initiated the first truly successful sobriety campaign in all of Russian history, and finally buried Russia's long tradition of autocratic vodka politics?

Early on, there was certainly room for hope. From praising Gorbachev's anti-drink crusade to putting Russia's "traditional vices of bribery, larceny, sloth and drunkenness" in the crosshairs through his *Russia, Forward!* manifesto, Medvedev certainly "talked the talk." The incremental restrictions and willingness to bread with the usual vodka-soaked banquets and high-level intrigues that marked Russian politics from Ivan the Terrible to Boris Yeltsin made it look like he could also "walk the walk."[39]

Still, the core dynamics of Russian vodka politics are tenacious. While vodka's relative budgetary importance has waned, selling liquor to Russians is still very easy money, making the vodka trade a breeding ground for institutionalized corruption. Indeed, it seems that the temptation of trillions of rubles in alcohol revenues has proven too strong for the Kremlin and state-backed entrepreneurs—especially in the midst of a global economic crisis that transformed Russia's budget surpluses into a debt of some seven percent of GDP. In assessing the new anti-alcohol initiative, "It's not clear what the goal is," claimed Renaissance Capital analyst Natalya Zagvozdina in 2009, "to decrease alcohol consumption or to raise money for the budget."[40]

That summer, while his protégé Medvedev was drumming up support for an epic showdown with alcohol, Prime Minister Putin and his cabinet were noticeably subdued. "We [Russians] should drink less," was his most energetic statement on the matter. Putin critics, including former chess grandmaster-turned-dissident Garry Kasparov, suggested that his frigid response was business related: heavily invested in Rosspirtprom, Putin's friend and former judo partner Arkady Rotenberg stood to lose millions from slashing vodka. Indeed, this was one of the most damning accusations of corruption against Putin in a widely circulated exposé titled simply *Putin. Corruption.* "Why would Putin raise taxes on his friends' business?" asked the report's authors, including opposition politicians Boris Nemtsov and Vladimir Ryzhkov. "The lower the price, the higher the sales. And so, while people across this vast country are drinking themselves to death—it is simply not considered a problem for this government."[41]

A necessary corollary is that, if the state were to raise taxes on vodka (either in the name of public health or state finance), it'd also likely find a way to protect the business interests of the well-connected members of the ruling *sistema*. It seems that is precisely what it has done.

In 2008, the Kremlin formed *Rosalkogolregulirovanie* (RAR), a new government bureaucracy ostensibly meant to streamline oversight and control over the vodka market. But instead of the usual bluster about promoting public health, First Deputy Prime Minister Viktor Zubkov—whom Putin had personally entrusted with the new vodka authority—has focused almost exclusively on revenues being lost to the black market. Just like Arkady Rotenberg and Vasily Anisimov—the billionaires controlling the national champion company Rosspirtprom—Zubkov also had ties to Putin's elite judo club Yawara-Neva, as member of its board of trustees and chair of its audit committee. What's more, Zubkov was also a long-time board member of Rosspirtprom itself—one of the companies RAR was now in charge of regulating. Ignoring any conflict of interests, many of the RAR executives simply emigrated with Zubkov from Rosspirtprom. And perhaps not surprisingly, these omnipotent government regulators have been selectively wielding their licensing power primarily to rebuild Rosspirtprom's market share at the expense of domestic and foreign competitors, with reducing public drunkenness a mere afterthought.[42]

Of course, the protection of these vested interests in vodka works at cross-purposes to the promotion of public health and wellbeing. If the farce of RAR wasn't enough, these misplaced priorities are evident even among others tabbed with promoting the public good. Take, for instance, pronouncements by Putin's Minister of Health and Social Development, Tatyana Golikova, who has focused on alcohol and the plight of Russia's youth. And with good reason: with *more than half* of all recent high school graduates projected to die before they reach retirement age, the children truly are Russia's demographic future.[43] Yet inexplicably, instead of targeting vodka—the potent tipple that comprises the vast majority of the Russian alcohol market—she instead took aim at beer. "Some 33% of young men and 20% of females drink alcohol, including beer, every day or in a day, while regular beer drinkers account for 76% of the population." This was an unusual tactic, since it is common knowledge among health experts that distilled spirits like vodka have a far more damaging impact on health than fermented wines and beers.[44]

Golikova was trained as an economist, not a physician or epidemiologist—curious qualifications for the nation's top health authority. She previously served as first deputy finance minister under her mentor, Alexei Kudrin. As health minister, Golikova was besieged by allegations of corruption, starting with Navalny's probes. Investigators have alleged her complicity in the embezzlement of hundreds of millions of dollars allocated for health ministry purchases. Potentially more damning are accusations that she intentionally failed to regulate the dangerous, highly addictive narcotic called desomorphine—known as "kroko-dil" due to the scaly, rotted appearance of the flesh around injection spots—manufactured by a company where her stepson works, effectively making Russia's health minister also its "main drug dealer," in the words of opposition journalists.[45] Time will tell whether such damning accusations have merit.

Golikova's demonization of beer rather than the more potent vodka fore-shadowed Duma legislation in 2009 that proposed a ten to thirty-five percent increase in taxes on vodka (which made up seventy percent of the market) while increasing levies on beer by *two hundred* percent. "200% tax is not enough," declared United Russia representative Viktor Zvagelsky, deputy chairman of the Duma's powerful Committee for Economic Policy, who wanted to see the beer levy increased by an additional eighty percent. His reasoning? "The risk of alco-hol dependence among consumers of beer is higher than that of consumers of wine or hard liquor." Flying in the face of all epidemiological research and his-torical experience in Russia and abroad, Zvagelsky claims: "Beer alcoholism is, in some cases, more dangerous than distilled spirits."[46]

"I find it very hard to understand the logic behind the disproportionate increase of excise duty on beer compared to strong alcohol," replied Anton Artemiev, chief executive of Baltika, Russia's largest brewery. "It will inevitably favor the consumption of hard alcohol, including vodka, and is bound to have a negative effect on alcohol abuse in the Russian society."[47]

Cynics saw the logic of vodka politics all too clearly. "The motivating fac-tor behind the proposal was as old as they come: taxes," wrote Tim Wall of the *Moscow News* in 2009. In addition to its vodka problem, Russia had also become the world's third-largest beer market, behind only China and the United States, a major difference being that fully four-fifths of the beer consumed in Russia was made by foreign-owned brewers while almost the entire vodka market was either in state or private Russian hands. Slapping such a hefty tax on beer would not only bring in another two billion dollars; it would also bolster the position of (domestic) vodka producers vis-à-vis their (foreign) beer rivals—all ostensibly in the name of the public interest. "The Kremlin is just doing what governments do when they're short of cash," Wall concluded, "roll the drunks for a few rou-bles, dollars, pounds or euros. And Russia's federal budget will be seriously short of funds in the next couple of years, particularly if the oil price falls."[48]

Despite the vocal protests of beer manufacturers, the measure passed, severely damaging multinational producers like Carlsberg and SABMiller with their extensive investments in Russia. The predictions came true, of course: beer sales dropped between five and fifteen percent by 2012 while domestic manu-facturing of the more potent vodka expanded by roughly the same amount.[49]

The counterintuitive crusade against beer continued in 2011, when a bill from Medvedev's original 2009 anti-alcohol plan came before the Duma, intent on re-categorizing beer as an "alcoholic beverage"—meaning it could no longer be advertised on television or be purchased at any of Russia's ubiquitous kiosks. The original bill focused primarily on the more potent, higher alcohol brews. Proposed exemptions covered weaker beers under five percent alcohol by volume, which comprised the lion's share of beer sales. Yet somewhere between the first and second reading (and quick passage) of the bill, the five percent exemption mysteriously disappeared: effectively imposing a total ban on *all* beer in kiosks, dealing a major blow to brewers and retailers alike.[50] In the process, an originally sensible, incremental restriction was transformed into a drastic, sweeping imposition, similar in spirit to the failed autocratic sobriety measures of the past.

As with the previous anti-beer legislation championed by United Russia deputy Viktor Zvagelsky—who (according to articles linked on his official website) has authored most of the legislation related to the alcohol industry—this was not so much a benevolent move in the defense of public health, but rather a blatant attempt to defend the market share of domestic vodka manufacturers against predominantly foreign beer companies. Did I mention that before entering the Duma in 2007, Zvagelsky was deputy CEO of Rosspirtprom, and founder of at least three highly lucrative vodka production and distribution companies that would profit handsomely from driving beer out of the alcohol market?[51]

The picture is becoming clear: Rosspirtprom, the RAR, Duma, and the ministry of health have effectively hijacked another well-intentioned public initiative to serve the private financial interests of high-ranking members of the autocratic *sistema*, thereby perverting the very intent of an anti-alcohol campaign. If the past 500 years of top–down alcohol control in Russia is any guide, recent increases in the consumption of vodka and dangerous surrogates—even while the Kremlin claims to be fighting against them—are worrying signs that the time-tested pattern of financial interests trumping the wellbeing of Russian society is primed to repeat itself again. And that is even before considering the entrenched interests of the treasury itself.

Since vodka politics has always been about the centrality of alcohol to Russia's state finances, its ultimate defenders have always been its finance ministers. From Sergei Witte and Vladimir Kokovtsov in the imperial era to Vasily Garbuzov under the Soviets, the ministers of finance fastidiously defended the state's coffers against all comers. Thanks to the steadily increasing alcohol taxes levied under president Medvedev's anti-alcohol campaign, by 2012, the treasury was swimming in over two hundred and fifty billion rubles ($8 billion) annually from liquor taxes, more than twice the amount collected in 2007.[52]

The finance minister overseeing this vodka windfall was Alexei Kudrin, who had capably directed Putin's ministry of finance since 2000, and had been a Putin loyalist from their time in St. Petersburg many years earlier. This was the same

Alexei Kudrin whom Putin left out of the loop about establishing the national champion Rosspirtprom in 2000, which he was forced to bail out in 2006 after Putin's botched consolidation (chapter 22). Instead of splurging Russia's incredible oil and gas windfall of the Putin years, the fiscally conservative Kudrin built up the monetary reserves that helped Russia weather the global financial crisis. Still, his defense of the treasury—and of vodka politics—continued under Medvedev, despite growing tensions. It was Kudrin whom Medvedev called out over Twitter for not addressing spending on "national priority" social issues.

In early 2010—while Russia was still being lashed by the global financial crisis—Prime Minister Putin announced sixteen billion in new spending on healthcare. Critics saw it as a populist splurge ahead of the 2012 elections. Admittedly "disappointed," Kudrin vocally opposed the healthcare plan. "I think we will have to hold serious discussions," he said, hoping the government would reconsider. When the Kremlin refused, Kudrin looked to make up the expense with cigarette and alcohol taxes.[53]

What followed was perhaps the most audacious defense of the basic tenets of Russia's autocratic vodka politics—*ever*. Completely undercutting Medvedev's anti-alcohol campaign, in September 2010 Kudrin brazenly declared that Russians "should smoke more and drink more" in the interests of state finance. "People should understand: Those who drink, those who smoke are doing more to help the state," Kudrin claimed, by "giving more to help solve social problems such as boosting demographics, developing other social services and upholding birth rates."[54]

Flabbergasted opponents quickly pointed out to the finance minister that budgets don't work that way: expenditures on health and social projects aren't linked to tobacco and alcohol excise taxes. "Nevertheless," continued an article in the communist opposition newspaper, *Pravda*: "Minister Kudrin transferred the message accurately: the state will take advantage of smokers and alcohol consumers."[55] Bemused bloggers joked that Kudrin should at least be awarded the Nobel Prize for Honesty. Instead, the following month the austere Kudrin—who helped Russia weather the Great Recession—was honored as *Euromoney* magazine's 2010 Finance Minster of the Year.[56]

The tensions only increased the following year, as the 2011 Duma elections inched closer, followed by the crucial presidential elections of March 2012. Kudrin proposed dramatically quadrupling the vodka tax. Following public outcry that such heavy-handed measures would lead to the same doom as Gorbachev's and Nicholas II's efforts—namely by fueling the underground vodka economy of dangerous surrogates and counterfeits—Kudrin drew a strong rebuke from Putin himself. "You know my attitude to the alcoholization of the population: we have, of course, to fight that. But there is no simple, linear solution," Putin declared. Kudrin's plans were dialed back accordingly.[57]

Yet the biggest confrontation was yet to come. In September 2011—a week after Medvedev announced he would step aside so that Putin could again run for president, Russia's outgoing president threw down the gauntlet. Perhaps frustrated by the entrenched vodka opposition to his reforms from all levels of government including the treasury, Medvedev gave Kudrin a public dressing-down for his vocal opposition to social spending and publicly second-guessing his competence.

Before a bank of television news cameras at a ministerial meeting, an emotionless Medvedev announced that Kudrin's "insubordination" was "inappropriate and inexcusable." He went on.

> Mr. Kudrin: if you don't agree with the president's policies—and it is the president's policies that the government implements—you have only one choice, and you know yourself what that is: you should tender your resignation. So I will ask you right here: if you think that your view on the economic agenda differs from those of the president, you are welcome to write a letter of resignation. Naturally, I expect you to give an answer here and now. Are you going to resign?

Turning on his microphone, the stunned but steady finance minster replied: "Mr. President: indeed there are differences between you and me on some issues." Figuring that he held the trump card by way of his strong personal relationship with Putin, Kudrin defiantly added: "But I will make a decision on your proposal after I consult with the Prime Minister."

"You know what?" Medvedev continued, unbowed. "You can consult anyone you like, including the Prime Minister—but as long as I am president, decisions such as this one are up to me." Medvedev added that, until his term as president ended and Putin's began,"I'll be the one making all the necessary decisions. I hope this is clear to everyone."[58]

And with that, the most audacious modern defender of Russia's autocratic vodka politics, the reigning finance minister of the year, was gone by the end of the day.

24

An End to Vodka Politics?

"Drunken hooligans and thugs, every one"—the neighborhood thugs were always loitering in the courtyard where Vladimir Putin grew up. "Unwashed, unshaven guys with cigarettes and bottles of cheap wine. Constant drinking, swearing, fistfights—and there was Putin in the middle of it all." Putin essentially grew up in Leningrad's *Fight Club*, where the scrappy kid held his own against the biggest and the baddest. "If anyone ever insulted him in any way, Volodya would immediately jump on the guy, scratch him, bite him, rip his hair out by the clump."[1]

Coming from the mean, drunken streets, Putin developed an affinity for judo and sambo at a young age and the human cockfight that is mixed martial arts (MMA) later in life. When, in 2007, Russian heavyweight sambo champion Fedor "the Last Emperor" Emelianenko finally fought in Putin's hometown of St. Petersburg, Putin sat ringside flanked by "the Muscles from Brussels"—Belgian kickboxing actor Jean Claude Van Damme—and Silvio "the Italian Rapscallion" Berlusconi. Putin, Van Damme, and Emelianenko later reconnected to kick off the Mixed Fight European Championship in Sochi in 2010, and when the Russian champ Emelianenko looked to end a three-fight slump against American Jeff "the Snowman" Monson at a packed Olympic Stadium in Moscow in late 2011, Putin again looked on approvingly from the front row.

Beamed live on the Rossiya-2 television channel, the no-holds-barred battle between these "two enormous sacks of rocks" (as David Remnick artfully described them), lasted the entire three rounds. An early-round kick broke Monson's leg. Another ruptured a tendon, further limiting his mobility. A flurry of punches caused the fight to be stopped to tend to the blood pouring from the American contender's mouth, which poured all over his anarchist and anticapitalist tattoos. Still, online MMA aficionados panned the fight as "a bit of a snoozer."[2]

Each fighter's corner was conspicuously emblazoned with the VTB logo of the fight's primary corporate benefactor, Vneshtorgbank. At the end, both returned to their corners as trainers tended to their injuries—Monson's being far more apparent than Emelianenko's—before the latter won by unanimous decision. Only then did Prime Minister Putin climb through the ropes to congratulate "the genuine Russian hero," Emelianenko. What happened next was a shock to the cocksure Putin, who just two months earlier declared his intention to return to the presidency in the 2012 elections. Unexpectedly, yet unmistakably, Russia's most powerful man was *booed*. Taken aback, Putin puzzled momentarily before continuing his judo kudos. During the previous twelve years in power Putin had never been booed by his own people. Now it seemed that his return for at least one (and, more likely, two) newly extended six-year presidential terms did not sit well with some. Something had definitely changed.

Suddenly, the global media took an interest in MMA, trying to gauge what just happened. Were they booing a bad fight, as Putin's spokesman claimed? Were they booing the pre-fight singer, as the organizers claimed? Or were they booing the long lines at the bathrooms, as the pro-Putin youth movement *Nashi* claimed? As far as I can tell, MMA blogger Michael David Smith has never been one to take sides in Kremlin politics—or any politics for that matter—but it was clear even to him that "No one floating those alternate explanations has explained why, if that's what the fans were booing about, they began their booing at the exact moment Putin began talking. And if the fans weren't booing Putin, it's hard to understand why Russian state television broadcasts felt the need to edit out the booing."[3]

From the other side of the blogosphere, anti-corruption activist Alexei Navalny claimed that the booing heralded "the end of an epoch." Navalny's campaigns had brought him toe to toe with Putin's regime: his re-branding of United Russia as "the party of crooks and thieves" resonated with a wide swath of a new Russian middle class that had grown tired of duplicity, corruption, and the bizarre, neo-feudal system of Putinism. The erosion of support could not have come at a worse time for the Kremlin: the December 2011 Duma elections were already upon them. Despite ratcheting up both nationalist rhetoric and pressure on independent monitors and critics, United Russia received only forty-nine percent of the votes—the party's first ever backward step. Despite the frigid Moscow winter, first thousands, and then hundreds of thousands, of protestors condemned the vote rigging, ballot-stuffing, and biased media coverage that marked the "dirtiest elections in post-Soviet history"—suggesting that even United Russia's forty-nine percent was a greatly inflated figure.[4] Even more telling, tens of thousands of Russians—part of an increasingly active civil society— trained to become election observers in polling stations throughout the country.

These "for fair elections" protests were the largest Russia had seen since the collapse of communism, leading many to wonder whether the autocratic regime would respond with repression and bloodshed. Thankfully, it did not. Despite a sizable security presence looming nearby, the largest protests between the

December 2011 Duma elections and the March 2012 presidential elections all passed without confrontation. Other signs of accommodation followed: the protests were reluctantly covered on state-run TV, and once-blacklisted opposition figures were allowed to air their grievances.[5] Outgoing President Dmitry Medvedev met with opposition leaders and even proposed liberalizing reforms, such as reinstating the direct election of governors. The state even promised greater transparency in the presidential elections by installing webcams to monitor each of Russia's nearly one hundred thousand polling stations.

Whether the webcams deterred the widespread voter fraud of previous elections or simply pushed it off camera is still unclear. What is clear is that Vladimir Putin easily won the 2012 election, due primarily to his enduring popularity beyond the capital and the lack of an opponent who could unite the diverse streams of anti-Putin discontent. Nationalist posturing and promises of increased social spending further bolstered his appeal.

But while the opposition did not sink Putin, they certainly fired a warning shot across his bow. Where Russia goes in Putin's third term and beyond will largely be determined by whether the Kremlin heeds the shot or ignores it.

History's Revenge

With Satan at its center, the deepest circle of hell in Dante's *Divine Comedy* is reserved for traitors. Just one step up in the eighth circle are the fraudsters: crooks, thieves, and corrupt politicians boiling in the sticky pitch of their own dark secrets. Alongside them are prognosticators and false prophets—their heads twisted backward, forever looking back on their failed predictions. So while we should perhaps tread lightly in making bold political prognostications, we can at least understand the constraints imposed on the Kremlin by Russia's demographic past.

In 2010 the United Nations released its new long-term population projections. Despite such recent improvements as increased fertility and decreased mortality under Medvedev and Putin, Russia's population will likely shrink from 143 million today to roughly 125 million by 2050 (figure 24.1). This would drop Russia from the seventh most populous nation to the eleventh—barely beating out Vietnam.[6]

How do they come up with estimates so far into the future, and how can they possibly be reliable? Well, demographers consider fertility and mortality statistics for all age cohorts, figure in migration, and calculate a range of optimistic, pessimistic, and likely scenarios. As it turns out, these projections hit the mark ninety-four percent of the time.[7] When they miss, it usually is due to big surprises: the unexpected baby boom after World War II made earlier American projections look foolishly low. The grim reality of the HIV/AIDS epidemic

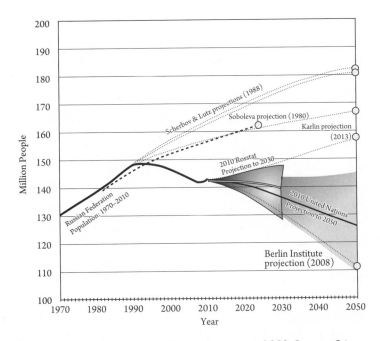

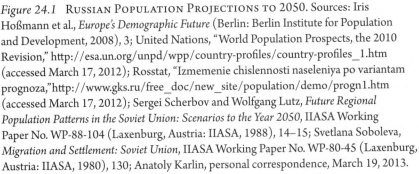

Figure 24.1 Russian Population Projections to 2050. Sources: Iris Hoßmann et al., *Europe's Demographic Future* (Berlin: Berlin Institute for Population and Development, 2008), 3; United Nations, "World Population Prospects, the 2010 Revision," http://esa.un.org/unpd/wpp/country-profiles/country-profiles_1.htm (accessed March 17, 2012); Rosstat, "Izmemenie chislennosti naseleniya po variantam prognoza," http://www.gks.ru/free_doc/new_site/population/demo/progn1.htm (accessed March 17, 2012); Sergei Scherbov and Wolfgang Lutz, *Future Regional Population Patterns in the Soviet Union: Scenarios to the Year 2050*, IIASA Working Paper No. WP-88-104 (Laxenburg, Austria: IIASA, 1988), 14–15; Svetlana Soboleva, *Migration and Settlement: Soviet Union*, IIASA Working Paper No. WP-80-45 (Laxenburg, Austria: IIASA, 1980), 130; Anatoly Karlin, personal correspondence, March 19, 2013.

made African population projections from the 1980s look far too rosy. And as figure 24.1 shows, demographers from the 1980s could not foresee the demodernization that decimated Russia and its heavy-drinking post-Soviet neighbors.

Unlike the African AIDS epidemic, however, Russia's demographic wounds were self-inflicted: the culmination of centuries of bad governance through vodka politics. The exhaustive 2009 study in *The Lancet* concluded that, were it not for vodka, Russia's mortality figures would look more like those of Western Europe instead of resembling war-torn areas of sub-Saharan Africa.[8] Were it not for vodka, Russia could have at least escaped the gut-wrenching post-communist transitions of the 1990s with a healthier population—more like the Hungarians with their wine or the Czechs with their beer—instead of being mired in demographic decay.

Consider Poland: a neighboring hard-drinking Slavic nation with its own storied vodka traditions. Poland also suffered the pain of post-communist transition. Yet while Yeltsin and Putin ignored the vodka epidemic in the 1990s and
2000s, Poland consistently increased excise taxes on the far more potent vodka
as part of a concerted effort to migrate to safer, fermented wines and beers. Partly
as a consequence, Poland has not suffered the same demographic calamity that
has befallen Russia. When communism collapsed in Poland, sixty-one percent
of alcohol consumed was in the form of distilled spirits. By 2002, it was down to
twenty-six percent. Even despite the "stress" of transition, male life expectancy in
Poland jumped four full years. In Estonia, the proportion of alcohol consumed
in the form of vodka dropped from seventy-two to thirty-three percent over the
same time frame. Male life expectancy increased 1.5 years. Meanwhile, in the
absence of a real alcohol policy in Russia, vodka's share of alcohol consumption
increased from sixty-six to seventy-one percent and male life expectancy plummeted by five years. Today, Poles and Estonians still drink a lot, but far less of it
is in distilled forms like vodka. As a consequence, male life expectancy for both
Polish and Estonian men is north of seventy years or a full decade longer than
their vodka-soaked neighbors in Russia.[9]

Meanwhile, the Kremlin seems content to settle for band-aid solutions that
treat symptoms of vodka politics rather than the disease. Even while the government undertakes yet another well-intentioned campaign against alcohol, it
hypocritically promotes increased vodka production by well-connected insiders. Meanwhile, the finance ministry implores citizens to impale themselves on
the bottle for the greater glory of the state.

At some point, this madness must end.

Even if we limit ourselves to just the last two decades since the collapse
of communism, clearly the single greatest obstacle to a normal, healthy, and
wealthy Russia is the legacy of the state's own vodka politics. Despite improvements under Medvedev, Russia still loses some fifteen thousand people every
year to alcohol poisoning—that's more than the number of soldiers sacrificed
during the Soviets' entire ten-year debacle in Afghanistan (1979–89). Since the
Soviet Union collapsed, some six hundred thousand people have died directly
as a result of vodka: more than the total number of military deaths in imperial
Russia's nine eighteenth-century wars.

Alternatively we can look to the projections of what Russia would have been
were it not for the vodka-laced demodernization of the 1990s. In 1988 Sergei
Scherbov and Wolfgang Lutz projected that the population of the Russian
Republic—then within the Soviet Union—would be some one hundred eighty
million by the year 2050 (figure 24.1).[10] If we subtract the reasonable, mid-range
estimate of the United Nations of 125 million from what *should have been* around
180 million, it leaves a difference of 55 million people. That is more than three

times the number of soldiers killed in every Russian war, *ever*. In other words, by 2050 the Russian population will only be two-thirds of *what it should have been* were it not for the alcoholization and demodernization of the past twenty years—all legacies of vodka politics.

This, then, is what Russia could have been—or what economists would call the "opportunity cost" of vodka. To this lost fifty-five million since the collapse of communism, one could add perhaps hundreds of millions more lost to the bottle over the five-hundred-plus years since the tsars first started pushing the more lucrative and more potent distilled alcohol over the lighter beers, ales, meads, and wines indigenous to Russia.

Just consider what Russia could have been—how great it could have been—had its rulers not consistently encouraged the people to drink such a potent concoction to benefit the state. Consider the combined economic contributions of another fifty-five million people—especially if one-third of them were *not* getting drunk at work.[11] Consider the potential contributions to commerce, science, or the arts that another healthy fifty-five million people would bring. As Russia's population would have expanded, so too would its wealth, its tax base, and its capacity to innovate and modernize. It would have no problem staffing its military and would not have to rely on immigrants to bolster its demographic prospects. But that is all gone—Russia's potential and ambitions have been drowned at the bottom of the bottle, by its own unwitting government.

Instead, Russia's once-and-future president Vladimir Putin confronts a bleak future on the vodka front—one that he did precious little to fix during his previous two terms. The government's own statistics project that, even with generous immigration from the other former Soviet republics, by 2030 the number of Russians between the ages of fifteen and sixty-five will shrink from 102.2 million to 91.1 million. The dwindling working-age population will put a brake on economic growth, since there will be far fewer productive workers. We know that younger employees are especially important to technological innovation—but with fewer younger workers, the Russian economy will be even more hamstrung by the old, outmoded, and corrupted labor patterns of the past, putting it at a further competitive disadvantage with the rest of the world. Under normal circumstances, the policy response would be to invest in modernization and growing the productive capital stock—but this option is stymied by Russia's rampant, systemic corruption, which is itself a legacy of vodka politics (chapter 8). Encouraging research and development would be another option, but according to Russian scientists, fundamental science in the country is in a "catastrophic" condition—still largely isolated from international research trends.[12] The picture is bleak: without profound change, the Russian economy will become less dynamic and less productive, reinforcing the country's reliance on selling off its mineral, oil, and gas wealth, with well-placed oligarchs investing the profits from them in more attractive locations abroad. And—if this journey has taught us anything—if there is another crisis in these lucrative resource sectors, the Kremlin will increasingly revert to vodka revenues, making the situation even worse.

As we've seen, Russians did not always drink vodka: when Prince Vladimir of Kiev famously declared that "drinking is the joy of the Rus', we cannot exist without it,"[13] he wasn't talking about vodka. The traditional drinks of Russia were naturally fermented beers, ales, meads, and *kvas*. The imposition of the more potent, artificial, distilled spirits came only with the imposition of the modern autocratic state, which used vodka to siphon off society's wealth into the treasury, making vodka the central pillar of Russian autocratic statecraft. Vodka, autocracy, and corruption in Russia have been inseparably intertwined ever since.

Russia is a nation that has achieved greatness despite vodka, certainly not because of it. If Russia truly wants to regain its place among the great world powers, it will have to confront its greatest challenge ever: the deeply rooted traditions of vodka politics itself. How great could Russia be without this debilitating political curse?

One Final History Lesson

One of the great virtues of historical investigation is to use the past to inform the politics of the present with an eye to the future. Yet history is not simply populated by events and people, but also by ideas and innovations forgotten as we haughtily bask in the wisdom of the present. Especially when it comes to the struggle with alcohol, it may be time to dust off some lessons of the past. Consider, if you will, the following account from 1904, which traces the origins of public drunkenness to autocratic edicts...

> which made the distilling and selling of spiritous liquors a State monopoly, and one of the principal sources of public revenue. The consumption of spirits was encouraged in every way in order to increase the receipts of the Treasury. Public servants knew they might count upon favour by inducing people to drink by every means in their power. Tea and coffee were prohibited to prevent undesirable competition; beer was unknown, wine rare; and the Government produce reigned supreme. As a writer of the time puts it: "A stream of cheap liquor was made to flow over the country, and was poured down the throats of the people, making every Swede a drunkard, and of drunkenness a national blemish."[14]

Wait...did he say *Swede*?

Yes! While today Sweden is one of the healthiest and least corrupt countries on earth—chock full of pragmatic, blonde, Volvo-driving, post-industrial progressives—just one hundred and fifty years ago it was written off as a backward country, full of drunken blonde peasants hopelessly mired in a swamp of state-sponsored distilled *brännvin*. If the astronomical rates of vodka consumption in Russia today have any historical parallel, it would certainly be with the Swedes of old. With per capita consumption rates north of twelve liters of pure alcohol per year, Sweden had "the sad distinction of being the most drunken country in Europe."[15]

Beyond the social and economic losses caused by widespread drunkenness, Swedish modernization suffered under a corrupt royal autocracy. While there was widespread recognition of the alcohol problem, any grass-roots response was consistently undermined by both the state and the alcohol producers, who combined to safeguard their financial benefits from drunkenness. Sound familiar?

Yet by the early twentieth century the Swedish economy was growing steadily, along with an increasingly vibrant civil society. Swedish healthcare facilities were thriving, and the death rate was "probably the lowest in the world, or at all events in Europe." Foreign commenters hailed the halving of Swedish alcohol consumption as nothing less than "one of the greatest victories of a nation over itself."[16]

What happened?

For one, there was widespread popular concern over mass drunkenness. From humble beginnings as a mutual support community like Alcoholics Anonymous, the Swedish Temperance Society (*Svenska Nykterhetssällskapet*) began lobbing for tighter government restrictions on alcohol, culminating in the Licensing Act of 1855.[17]

Arguably, an even more important innovation arose that same year: Sweden's second largest city, Gothenburg, adopted a municipal liquor-dispensary system that quickly gained global fame as a supremely effective tool against societal drunkenness. The genius of this so-called Gothenburg System was that it did not take aim at drunks themselves or even the social harms they created. Instead, it focused on the ever-present allure of tremendous profits that encouraged the state, liquor producers, and the saloon keepers to keep harmful liquor flowing down the peoples' throats.

Here's how it worked: the village would charter a private company—normally headed by the town's most respected citizens—with the charge of regulating the local liquor traffic in the interest of the community. For their investment, the company shareholders received a strictly limited return of five percent yearly, with the bulk of the profits turned over to local agricultural and philanthropic organizations that promoted community well-being. Not only did the system enable temperance-minded citizens to have a real, tangible impact on community sobriety, but the greater resources flowing into civic organizations led to a blossoming of local grass-roots activism.[18]

The system was a resounding success. Thanks to the Licensing Act, alcohol was restricted in accordance with the wishes of the local population—with some rural governments even voting themselves dry by refusing to issue any liquor licenses at all. Prices were gradually raised and availability restricted in the interest of local sobriety, leading to a steady decrease in alcohol consumption and its antecedent ills. Alcohol revenues helped expand health, welfare, agricultural, and community services that benefited drinkers and nondrinkers alike while also encouraging greater civic engagement.

Hoping to emulate Gothenburg's successes, cities and towns throughout Scandinavia adopted the system of "disinterested" municipal dispensary by the 1870s. News of reduced drunkenness, crime, and bootlegging, along with the prosperity and moral rejuvenation of Swedish communities, spread across Europe and North America, where more and more cities and states adopted the system. As early as 1859, even the Russian revolutionary democrat Nikolai Chernyshevsky advocated dumping the drunkenness- and corruption-inducing vodka tax farm for a system of local control like in Sweden.[19] Across the Atlantic, various American states had experimented with outright prohibition since the "Maine Law" of 1851—most were plagued by illegal moonshining, corruption, and disrespect for the rule of law, often leading to repeal. Disillusioned by prohibition's obvious failures, many American temperance advocates looked to the Gothenburg System as a practical blueprint for advancing sobriety. (Why the United States later doubled down on a well-known policy failure by adopting nationwide prohibition is one underlying puzzle of my previous book, *The Political Power of Bad Ideas*.[20])

You can probably see where I am going with this. Without question, the anti-alcohol initiatives begun under President Dmitry Medvedev have been well-intentioned (as have most previous, failed, anti-alcohol measures). We can only applaud the continuing efforts to raise alcohol prices, limit hours of sale, control advertising, and expand awareness through modern public relations campaigns. But even beyond the hurdles presented by the financial needs of the state and the vested interests of entrenched cronies, the effectiveness of such reforms will inherently be limited by the fact that they only address the symptom of widespread drunkenness rather than the disease of Russia's autocratic vodka politics. Russia's drinking problem is the product of a centralized state that historically debauches and disempowers its own people. If the Kremlin is truly serious about overcoming vodka politics—and its resulting depopulation and decline that bedevils Russia's future ambitions—they first have to be aware of those dynamics. Then they have to do something meaningful about it.

Ever since Boris Yeltsin did away with the Soviet vodka monopoly in 1992, virtually every Russian alcohol-policy debate has revolved around resurrecting it in the interest of state finance—and always in the guise of defending public health. In 1997 Yeltsin pleaded that "if people spend money on vodka, that money should go to the treasury, not to crooks." His ambitious Foreign Minister Evgeny Primakov then quickly proposed a vodka monopoly. The Kremlin aspirations of Moscow mayor Yury Luzhkov the following year also included renationalizing vodka.[21] When Vladimir Putin instead ascended to the presidency in 2000, he built Rosspirtprom to establish monopoly control over the vodka market, though his attempts to consolidate its position backfired spectacularly (chapter 22). Still, the siren beckons: when alcohol poisonings spiked in 2006, United Russia leaders called for a monopoly. When Medvedev launched his anti-alcohol campaign, his top health official, Gennady Onishchenko, lobbied for the vodka monopoly, shortsightedly arguing that "the budget would benefit and counterfeit alcohol would cease to exist. When there is a state monopoly, this area can be regulated in a tougher and more effective way."[22] Even in the contentious 2012 elections, Putin's conservative opposition—the nationalist Vladimir Zhirinovsky and the communist Gennady Zyuganov—agreed about the necessity of a vodka monopoly in order to restore the former glory of the Russian state.[23]

Populist rhetoric aide, time after time the traditional vodka monopoly has *always* put the financial interests of the state ahead of the welfare of its people. Always. When Ivan the Terrible instituted Russia's first retail monopoly through his *kabaks* in the sixteenth century, it was in the interest of state revenue. When Sergei Witte rebuilt the imperial monopoly in 1894, it was done in the name of reducing out-of-control vodka consumption. Yet once the treasury was hooked up to a stronger dose of vodka revenues, it encouraged alcohol consumption to skyrocket from eight liters per capita to fourteen on the eve of the Great War. Following the disastrous prohibition of Nicholas II—continued by Aleksandr Kerensky and Vladimir Lenin—Joseph Stalin again resurrected the vodka monopoly in 1924, ostensibly to protect the peoples' health from dangerous bootleg vodka. The result? An even more pervasive alcoholization of Soviet society, with consumption rising virtually unimpeded for some sixty years and with vodka again contributing one-quarter to one-third of all state revenues.[24] Now, there are worrying signs that even Russia's present anti-alcohol initiative may be falling victim to this same pattern (chapter 23).

So even paying lip service to the greater good, why would we expect that resurrecting the traditional vodka monopoly today would have any different outcome today than the iron-clad dynamics of vodka politics past? It wouldn't. If there is an answer to the so-called alcohol question beyond incremental retail restrictions and other band-aid measures, it is to be found not in monopolization, but in *municipalization* akin to the Swedish experience—an idea that is beginning to gain greater traction within Russia's public health community.[25]

A Russian Gothenburg System of disinterested management would be a boon to communities throughout Russia by promoting local activism. Temperance-minded individuals would be empowered to oversee the local alcohol restrictions. Local governments would be empowered to adopt restrictions as deemed appropriate by the community instead of waiting for Kremlin dictates that never seem to come.[26] What's more, the windfall vodka revenues could help empower local civic organizations, such as those interested in promoting a clean environment, healthy lifestyles, agriculture, education, and beyond as well as care for the elderly, the disabled and orphans. Money could also be funneled into the chronically cash-strapped healthcare infrastructure, rehabilitation centers, and orphanage systems. Ironically, when former Finance Minister Alexei Kudrin suggested that heavy drinkers do more to support the government's provision of social services, his opponents lampooned his disingenuousness, since vodka revenues and social spending were in no way linked. In a system of disinterested management they actually *would* be linked, empowering local representatives to address their community's greatest needs. Such local autonomy would help make the Russian Federation into an *actual* federation, where policy decisions are divided among the national, regional, and local authorities and the Kremlin is freed from its micro-managing tendencies.

Of course there will be objections. I can already hear them: this system may work for the Swedes or Canadians, but it would never work in Russia. Russia just isn't ready: there isn't enough grass-roots activism. The cultures are just too different. It is too impractical. And with Russia's systemic corruption, it would be impossible to find honest administrators who could resist the temptation for personal enrichment.

As it turns out, the Russian government already poo-pooed the idea in exactly those terms. After extensive research into the Gothenburg System and prolonged debate within the quasi-official "Commission on the Question of Alcoholism" comprising bureaucrats, physicians, economists, and policy experts, the ministry of finance openly admitted that, while "the system is theoretically better than ours," similar results could not be expected in Russia because of the "insufficiently cultured society" and the inability to find honest administrators.[27] The author was Ivan Mintslov—the Russian finance ministry's resident specialist on the vodka economy. The year was 1898. In the decades before the outbreak of the Great War and Tsar Nicholas's disastrous prohibition decree in 1914, Russia's alcohol experts were unified in acknowledging that the municipal system was "the best legislative weapon in the fight against alcoholism" but that the Russian people were unfit culturally, educationally, and administratively.[28] Russian society simply could not be trusted to put its own welfare first. As the long history of vodka politics has demonstrated, Russia's autocratic leaders were even less trustworthy with such a charge.

In the intervening hundred-plus years since the tsarist Commission on the Question of Alcoholism panned the disinterested municipal dispensary in favor of the traditional autocratic monopoly, that "question of alcoholism" has effectively been put to bed as an issue of high politics in every other industrialized country. Meanwhile in Russia, the imperial and Soviet autocratic monopolies not only did not solve Russia's alco-woes; it made them far worse. But since monopolization remains the only alternative that Russia has ever known, both policy makers and critics naively look to it as the solution rather than the problem.

Monopolization relies on the autocratic assumption that the people don't know what is in their own best interest. While that may have been true for the illiterate peasantry of the nineteenth century, Russia today boasts one of the most highly educated populations on earth. Moreover, the growth and stability of the Putin and Medvedev years produced a middle class that is increasingly affluent, increasingly connected, and—as the protests of 2011–12 demonstrated—increasingly impatient with systemic corruption and their inability to influence governance. Anachronistic arguments about reverting to monopoly control are not only wrongheaded; they are an insult to the Russian people themselves.

Russians know alcohol is a problem, thank you very much. For years opinion polls have ranked alcohol abuse as Russia's top political challenge, even ahead of terrorism, economic crisis, and human rights issues.[29] And yet, the entrenched financial interests of the state and politically influential businessmen; the systemic corruption; an autocratic system that impedes grass-roots activism and local governance; and the national culture of inebriation that these factors all helped create conspire to prevent the Russian people from tackling their most enduring political challenge.

The Kremlin today has a unique window of opportunity to finally move beyond band-aid solutions and directly address Russia's autocratic vodka politics and the subordination of public welfare to the financial interests of the state.

First, while vodka revenues are still significant, in percentage terms they aren't nearly as vital today as they once were. One upside of the government's increased reliance on oil, gas, and mineral exports—as well as a series of effective tax reforms under Putin—is that vodka's relative contribution to the federal budget has diminished to some two to four percent of revenues rather than the twenty to forty percent under the tsars and Soviets. Swearing off vodka revenues today would be tough, but it would not be fatal as in the past. This alone suggests that the time is ripe for the Kremlin to go cold turkey and finally divorce itself from the toxic legacies of vodka politics.

Second, it is not as though foregone revenues would simply disappear—instead they would fund the cash-strapped social and medical organizations the state has chronically neglected. Instead of the occasional (and much-bally-hooed) infusions of a few billion rubles here and there, a system of disinterested management would provide localities with a steady and reliable revenue stream that would finally allow healthcare and other services to thrive.[30] And if revenues diminished over time, it would be due primarily to reduced alcohol consumption, which would mean better health and less stress on the healthcare system itself.

Third, Russia is already waging another anti-alcohol campaign, nominally in the interest of the welfare of its people. What clearer signal could there be that the Kremlin is sincere about *finally* putting the people before both the government and its cronies than swearing off Russia's autocratic vodka politics once and for all? Bringing Russia's astronomical alcohol-related mortality in line with that in other European countries would help Russia avoid the worst-case demographic forecasts and build a healthier, stronger, and more prosperous country.

Finally, the Gothenburg option may promote genuine democratization in Russia by empowering local civic organization and activism. Beyond the widespread public concern over societal alcoholism, networks of grass-roots organizations and concerned individuals ready to act on the alcohol issue have been denied an opportunity to do so.[31] "If society's problems are to be solved, it is essential that social responsibilities be shared by the state and local governments," declares Lilia Shevtsova. "The latter must be given the authority to provide the basic services needed by individuals and their families: schooling, medical care, public services, and cultural activities. For this to be possible the Kremlin will need to abandon its efforts to embed local government in the state structure; it must develop local self-government and allow local authorities to raise their own revenues."[32] In his first State of the Nation address upon returning to the presidency in 2012, Vladimir Putin encouraged Russia's regions to draw up and implement their own health and demographic policies to supplement federal initiatives.[33] Here, too, the Gothenburg option is well suited to answer the president's call.

Moreover, a Gothenburg System could also build on the pervasive anti-corruption sentiment that rose to the surface during the protests of 2011–12. What better place to begin a concerted grass-roots fight against systemic corruption than with vodka, which bred such widespread corruption in the first place?[34]

At the end of a recent conference of Russian and international health specialists, noted expert Andrei Demin concluded that "in the present conditions, the possibility of securing the interests of public health, overcoming the shadow market and other endemic problems can only develop through the systematic control over the alcohol market under the control of civil society."[35] In other words: Russia can put the vodka question to bed only in the same way it was laid to rest in almost every other industrialized country: a Gothenburg-type system of disinterested civic management. Would the Kremlin ever attempt such a bold move? Fundamentally, it should be a clear choice of promoting the interests of society over those of the state, health over misery, moderation over drunkenness, honesty over corruption, and empowerment over autocracy. The very future of Russia itself largely hangs in the balance.

Parting Thoughts…

At the height of American prohibition in the 1920s, Hollywood actor, vaudeville performer, humorist, and "cowboy philosopher" Will Rogers went on a worldwide speaking tour as unofficial goodwill ambassador from the United States. Denied entry to Russia by the new Bolshevik regime, Rogers instead went to Paris, where he was welcomed by affluent Russian émigrés who had fled the revolution. It was in one of their well-to-do restaurants that America's most famous celebrity first encountered this exotic drink known as vodka.

"It was the most innocent-looking thing I ever saw," Rogers later explained (in his folksy style) to an American audience that had never heard of it. "They all said just drink it all down at one swig; nobody can sip Vodka. Well, I had no idea what the stuff was, and for a second I thought that somebody had loaded me up with molten lead, and I hollered for water." Thinking that the clear liquid in the tabletop carafe must have been water, Rogers gulped it down quick, only to find that it too was vodka!

The cowboy from Oklahoma slowly regained his composure after a few panicked moments that surely amused his Russian hosts. "How they can concentrate so much insensibility into one prescription is almost a chemical wonder," Rogers recounted. "One tiny sip of this Vodka poison and it will do the same amount of material damage to mind and body that an American strives for for hours."[36]

Since then, Americans have become well-acquainted with the concentrated insensibility of Russia's foremost cultural export, which has become the world's top-selling liquor. And while a small segment of discriminating connoisseurs claim to appreciate the subtle distinctions between this or that top-shelf brand, the vast majority of drinkers are more interested in vodka's mind-blasting effects. Yet even as drinkers of the world raise a toast to vodka, we should all be reminded of its dark past: the generations of Russians who found not only consolation at the bottom of the bottle but also grief, illness, and death. We must remember that such incredible human costs were—and still are—attributable not just to the lowly drunkard, but to the autocratic political system that reaped unimaginable profits from the people's misery, generation after generation.

With history in mind, the cowboy philosopher's alcoholic musings sound even more fitting: "Now that is the whole story to Vodka," Rogers surmised. "Nobody in the world knows what it is made out of, and the reason I tell you this is that the story of Vodka is the story of Russia. Nobody knows what Russia is made out of, or what it is liable to cause its inhabitants to do next."[37]

The story of vodka truly is the story of Russia: not just its culture and society, but its history and statecraft as well. Whether it can ever break free of the shackles of vodka politics—and the autocratic system that nurtures it and is nurtured by it—may well be the most fundamental political question facing the future of Russia.

NOTES

Preface

1. *Chto-to pro medvedei i balalaiki zabyli.* "'N'yu Iork Taims' ne unimaetsya," http://politics. d3.ru/comments/469696 (accessed Aug. 28, 2013). This in response to my op-ed on the LGBT Russian vodka boycotts: Mark Lawrence Schrad, "Boycotting Vodka Won't Help Russia's Gays," *New York Times*, Aug. 21, 2013, A19.
2. Valerii Melekhin, "Nuzhno vybirat' trezvost'," *Soratnik*, January 2010, 2, http://video.sbnt. ru/vl/Newspapers/Soratnik/Soratnik_167.pdf; "Obshchestvennoe mnenie," Radio svoboda, Nov. 17, 2002, http://archive.svoboda.org/programs/vp/2002/vp.111702.asp (both accessed Jan. 8, 2011).; Aleksandr Nemtsov, *Alkogol'naya istoriya Rossii: Noveishii period* (Moscow: URSS, 2009), 6. On the image of Russian alcoholism more generally, see Irina R. Takala, "Russkoe p'yanstvo kak fenomen kul'tury," in: *Alkogol' v Rossii: Materialy pervoi mezhdunarodnoi nauchno-prakticheskoi konferentsii* (Ivanovo, 29–30 oktyabrya 2010), ed. Mikhail V. Teplyanskii (Ivanovo: Filial RGGU v g. Ivanovo, 2010), 12–21.
3. This is not to claim that economic fears are unimportant: "inflation," "living standards" and "employment" all consistently place in the 40–50 percent range. Respondents can choose up to seven of the twenty-six issues listed. VTsIOM, "What Russians Are Afraid Of: Press Release No. 1299," *Russian Public Opinion Research Center* 1299 (2010), and "August Problem Background: Press Release No. 1383," *Russian Public Opinion Research Center* 1383 (2011), http://wciom.com/index.php?id=61&uid=411 (accessed Feb. 2, 2012).
4. AFP, "Kremlin-Bound Putin Tells Russians to Have More Children," *AhramOnline*, April 11, 2012, http://english.ahram.org.eg/NewsContent/2/9/39030/World/International/ Kremlinbound-Putin-tells-Russians-to-have-more-chi.aspx (accessed April 12, 2012). See also Vladimir Putin, "Annual Address to the Federal Assembly," May 10, 2006, http:// archive.kremlin.ru/eng/speeches/2006/05/10/1823_type70029type82912_105566. shtml (accessed Nov. 1, 2010).
5. Nicholas Eberstadt, *Russia's Peacetime Demographic Crisis: Dimensions, Causes, Implications* (Seattle, Wash.: National Bureau of Asian Research, 2010), 89; 2009 Life Tables at World Health Organization (WHO), "Life Tables for WHO Member States," http://www.who.int/ healthinfo/statistics/mortality_life_tables/en/ (accessed Jan. 22, 2013).
6. Mark Lawrence Schrad, "Moscow's Drinking Problem," *New York Times*, April 17, 2011, and "A Lesson in Drinking," *Moscow Times*, March 4, 2011.
7. Charles van Onselen, "Randlords and Rotgut 1886–1903: An Essay on the Role of Alcohol in the Development of European Imperialism and Southern African Capitalism, with Special Reference to Black Mineworkers in the Transvaal Republic," *History Workshop* 1, no. 2 (1976): 84; Frederick Douglass, *Narrative of the Life of Frederick Douglass: An American Slave* [1845] (New York: Cambridge University Press, 2011), 74–76. Many thanks to Emmanuel

Akyeampong for this reference. On Russia see David Christian, "Traditional and Modern Drinking Cultures in Russia on the Eve of Emancipation," *Australian Slavonic and East European Studies* 1, no. 1 (1987): 61–84.

8. Examples include Nicholas Ermochkine and Peter Iglikowski, *40 Degrees East: An Anatomy of Vodka* (Hauppauge, N.Y.: Nova, 2003); Patricia Herlihy, *Vodka: A Global History* (London: Reaktion Books, 2012); Vladimir Nikolaev, *Vodka v sud'be Rossii* (Moscow: Parad, 2004); Gennadii M. Karagodin, *Kniga o vodke i vinodelii* (Chelyabinsk: Ural, 2000).

9. David Christian, *Living Water: Vodka and Russian Society on the Eve of Emancipation* (Oxford: Clarendon, 1990); Patricia Herlihy, *The Alcoholic Empire: Vodka and Politics in Late Imperial Russia* (New York: Oxford University Press, 2002); Kate Transchel, *Under the Influence: Working-Class Drinking, Temperance, and Cultural Revolution in Russia, 1895–1932* (Pittsburgh, Pa.: University of Pittsburgh Press, 2006); Vladimir G. Treml, *Alcohol in the USSR: A Statistical Study*, Duke Press Policy Studies (Durham, N.C.: Duke University Press, 1982); Stephen White, *Russia Goes Dry: Alcohol, State and Society* (New York: Cambridge University Press, 1996); Aleksandr Nemtsov, *A Contemporary History of Alcohol in Russia*, trans. Howard M. Goldfinger and Andrew Stickley (Stockholm: Södertörns högskola, 2011). The works of Boris Segal and Irina Takala also are worthy of mention in this vein. Boris Segal, *Russian Drinking: Use and Abuse of Alcohol in Pre-Revolutionary Russia* (New Brunswick, N.J.: Rutgers Center of Alcohol Studies, 1987) and *The Drunken Society: Alcohol Use and Abuse in the Soviet Union* (New York: Hippocrene Books, 1990); Irina R. Takala, *Veselie Rusi: Istoriia alkogol'noi problemy v Rossii* (St. Petersburg: Zhurnal Neva, 2002).

10. W. J. Rorabaugh, *The Alcoholic Republic: An American Tradition* (New York: Oxford University Press, 1979), 5, 30, 49; Cedric Larson, "The Drinkers Dictionary," *American Speech* 12, no. 2 (1937): 87–92.

Chapter 1

1. Andrei Bitov, "The Baldest and the Boldest," in *Memoirs of Nikita Khrushchev, vol. 1: Commissar, 1918–1945*, ed. Sergei Khrushchev (University Park: Pennsylvania State University Press, 2004), xxxiv.

2. Sergei Khrushchev, ed., *Memoirs of Nikita Khrushchev, vol. 1: Commissar, 1918–1945* (University Park: Pennsylvania State University Press, 2004), xxiii; Jerrold L. Schecter, "Introduction," in *Khrushchev Remembers: The Last Testament*, ed. Strobe Talbott (Boston, Mass.: Little, Brown, 1974), xi.

3. It is worth noting that Vissarion Dzhugashvili, father of a young Joseph Dzhugashvili (Stalin), was a violent, alcoholic semi-itinerant cobbler who routinely beat his wife and children. Simon Sebag Montefiore, *Young Stalin* (New York: Vintage Books, 2007), 25.

4. Khrushchev, *Memoirs of Nikita Khrushchev*, 1:79. See also Seweryn Bialer, *Stalin's Successors: Leadership, Stability, and Change in the Soviet Union* (New York: Cambridge University Press, 1980), 33.

5. Khrushchev, *Memoirs of Nikita Khrushchev*, 1:79, 1:287.

6. Anastas Mikoyan, *Tak bylo: razmyshleniia o minuvshem* (Moscow: Vagrius, 1999), 353. Nadezhda Segeevna Alliluyeva died on November 9, 1932. On the events surrounding her death see Roman Brackman, *The Secret File of Joseph Stalin: A Hidden Life* (London: Routledge, 2000), 231; Miklós Kun, *Stalin: An Unknown Portrait* (Budapest: Central European University Press, 2003), 207; Donald Rayfield, *Stalin and His Hangmen: The Tyrant and Those Who Killed for Him* (New York: Random House, 2005), 240; Khrushchev, *Memoirs of Nikita Khrushchev*, 1:290. On the outbreak of war see Peter Kenez, *A History of the Soviet Union from the Beginning to the End*, 2nd ed. (New York: Cambridge University Press, 2006), 139. On Stalin's alcoholic father and the role of alcohol in his upbringing see Aleksandr Nikishin, *Vodka i Stalin* (Moscow: Dom Russkoi Vodki, 2006), 119–21.

7. Khrushchev, *Memoirs of Nikita Khrushchev*, 1:385. Stalin's daughter, Svetlana Allilueva, confirms this observation in *Only One Year*, trans. Paul Chavchavadze (New York: Harper & Row, 1969), 385.

8. Sergei Khrushchev, ed., *Memoirs of Nikita Khrushchev, vol. 2: Reformer, 1945–1964* (University Park: Pennsylvania State University Press, 2006), 43. See also Khrushchev, *Memoirs of Nikita Khrushchev,* 1:288; Kun, *Stalin,* 335.

9. Milovan Djilas, *Conversations with Stalin,* trans. Michael B. Petrovich (New York: Harcourt, Brace, 1962), 76–78; Simon Sebag Montefiore, *Stalin: The Court of the Red Tsar* (New York: Alfred A. Knopf, 2004), 521. See also Yoram Gorlizki, "Stalin's Cabinet: The Politburo and Decision Making in the Post-War Years," *Europe-Asia Studies* 53, no. 2 (2001): 295–98.

10. Khrushchev, *Memoirs of Nikita Khrushchev,* 2:43.

11. Laurence Rees, *World War II Behind Closed Doors: Stalin, the Nazis and the West* (New York: Random House, 2009), 32; I. Joseph Vizulis, *The Molotov-Ribbentrop Pact of 1939: The Baltic Case* (Ann Arbor: University of Michigan Press, 1990), 15.

12. Anthony Read and David Fisher, *The Deadly Embrace: Hitler, Stalin and the Nazi-Soviet Pact, 1939–1941* (New York: W. W. Norton, 1988), 354; William L. Shirer, *The Rise and Fall of the Third Reich: A History of Nazi Germany* (New York: Simon & Schuster, 1960), 540.

13. Read and Fisher, *Deadly Embrace,* 354. Stalin shared the secret with other Nazi delegates at the signing ceremony. Piers Brendon, *The Dark Valley: A Panorama of the 1930s* (New York: Random House, 2000), 682–83.

14. Gustav Hilger and Alfred Mayer, *Incompatible Allies: A Memoir-History of German-Soviet Relations, 1918–1941* (New York: Macmillan, 1953), 301, 13–14.

15. Winston Churchill, *The Second World War, vol. 6: Triumph and Tragedy* (New York: Houghton Mifflin, 1953), 348–49.

16. Documents from the National Archives (U.K.), catalog no. fo/1093/247; http://filestore.nationalarchives.gov.uk/documents/fo-1093-247.pdf. Cited in Tommy Norton, "Winston...Was Complaining of a Slight Headache," National Archives (U.K.) blog, May 22, 2013; http://blog.nationalarchives.gov.uk/blog/winston-was-complaining-of-a-slight-headache/ (accessed May 22, 2013). These documents also allude to a similarly intoxicated banquet for Franklin D. Roosevelt's ambassador-at-large, Wendell Willkie. See also Wendell Lewis Willkie, *One World* (New York: Simon & Schuster, 1943), 58–62, 92–93.

17. Montefiore, *Stalin,* 477; Charles de Gaulle, *The Complete War Memoirs of Charles de Gaulle,* trans. Richard Howard, 3 vols. (New York: Da Capo, 1964), 3:752. On the arrest of Khrulev's wife see Harrison E. Salisbury, *The 900 Days: The Siege of Leningrad* (New York: Harper & Row, 1969), 487n1.

18. Montefiore, *Stalin,* 477. On the fate of Novikov see Michael Parrish, *Sacrifice of the Generals: Soviet Senior Officer Losses, 1939–1953* (Lanham, Md.: Scarecrow, 2004), 270; Brian D. Taylor, *Politics and the Russian Army: Civil-Military Relations, 1689–2003* (New York: Cambridge University Press, 2003), 177.

19. Montefiore, *Stalin,* 314.

20. Ibid., 477. On Kaganovich and the terror-famine see Robert Conquest, *The Harvest of Sorrow: Soviet Collectivization and the Terror-Famine* (New York: Oxford University Press, 1986), 328; Robert Gellately, *Lenin, Stalin, and Hitler: The Age of Social Catastrophe* (New York: Vintage Books, 2007), 229. On the interrogation of Mikhail Kaganovich see Brackman, *Secret File of Joseph Stalin,* 349–50; Roy A. Medvedev, *Let History Judge: The Origins and Consequences of Stalinism* (New York: Alfred A. Knopf, 1971), 310. Also see David Remnick, *Lenin's Tomb: The Last Days of the Soviet Empire* (New York: Random House, 1993), 34.

21. Montefiore, *Stalin,* 477–78.

22. Brackman, *Secret File of Joseph Stalin,* 411; William Taubman, *Khrushchev: The Man and His Era* (New York: W. W. Norton, 2003), 211, 14–15; Montefiore, *Stalin,* 521; Adam B. Ulam, *Stalin: The Man and His Era* (New York: Viking, 1973), 436; Allilueva, *Only One Year,* 385; James Graham, *Vessels of Rage, Engines of Power: The Secret History of Alcoholism* (Lexington, Va.: Aculeus, Inc., 1993), 188.

23. Khrushchev, *Memoirs of Nikita Khrushchev,* 1:289. Khrushchev continues on this point: "People might ask me: 'What are you saying? That Stalin was a drunk?' I can answer that he was and he wasn't. That is, he was in a certain sense. In his later years, he couldn't get by without drinking, drinking, drinking. On the other hand, sometimes he didn't pump

himself full as he did his guests; he would pour a drink for himself in a small glass and even dilute it with water. But God forbid that anyone else should do such a thing. Immediately, he would be 'fined' for deviating from the norm, for 'trying to deceive society.' This of course was a joke, but you had to do some serious drinking as a result of the joke." Ibid., 1:291.

24. Mikoyan, *Tak bylo*, 353.

25. Montefiore, *Stalin*, 520. On Khrushchev's brutality see, for instance, Gellately, *Lenin, Stalin, and Hitler*, 388.

26. Khrushchev, *Memoirs of Nikita Khrushchev*, 1:289. Also see Aleksei Adzhubei, *Kruzhenie illiuzii* (Moscow: Interbuk, 1991), 166–68; Montefiore, *Stalin*, 521.

27. Khrushchev, *Memoirs of Nikita Khrushchev*, 1:291. Also see Nikishin, *Vodka i Stalin*, 167.

28. Montefiore, *Stalin*, 521.

29. Khrushchev, *Memoirs of Nikita Khrushchev*, 2:42.

30. Ibid., 2:43 (emphasis added).

31. Khrushchev, *Memoirs of Nikita Khrushchev*, 1:80. See also Kees Boterbloem, *The Life and Times of Andrei Zhdanov, 1896–1948* (Montreal: McGill-Queens University Press, 2004), 259.

32. Montefiore, *Stalin*, 326. After being demoted in 1942 and expelled from the Central Committee, Kulik allegedly became critical of Stalin, which sealed his fate. Apparently he was arrested in 1947, and after three years of inquiry and torture, he was executed in 1950. Kun, *Stalin*, 430.

33. Allilueva, *Only One Year*, 386; Montefiore, *Stalin*, 521–22; Gorlizki, "Stalin's Cabinet." Poskrebyshev was often forced to hold lighted "New Year's candles" of rolled-up paper, Stalin delighting in watching Poskrebyshev's pain as the fiery paper burned his hands. Graham, *Vessels of Rage*, 189. Poskrebyshev arranged many show trials of the 1930s and was removed under pressure from Beria as part of the so-called doctors' plot in 1952 but not before condemning his own wife to the gulags. Helen Rappaport, *Joseph Stalin: A Biographical Companion* (Santa Barbara, Calif.: ABC-CLIO, 1999), 210.

34. Maureen Perrie, *The Cult of Ivan the Terrible in Stalin's Russia* (New York: Palgrave, 2001), 172. On the paternalism of the tsars see Georg Brandes, *Impressions of Russia*, trans. Samuel C. Eastman (Boston: C. J. Peters & Son, 1889), 38.

35. Khrushchev, *Memoirs of Nikita Khrushchev*, 1:80.

36. Bialer, *Stalin's Successors*, 34–35; Gorlizki, "Stalin's Cabinet," 295–98; Robert Service, *Stalin: A Biography* (Cambridge, Mass.: Harvard University Press, 2004), 575; Vladislav B. Aksenov, *Veselie Rusi, XX vek: gradus noveishei rossiiskoi istorii ot "p'yanogo byudzheta" do "sukhogo zakona"* (Moscow: Probel-2000, 2007), 24–25. On atomization see Hannah Arendt, *The Origins of Totalitariansim, pt. 3: Totalitarianism* (New York: Harvest/HBJ, 1968), 9–20. With regard to alcohol see Therese Reitan, "The Operation Failed, but the Patient Survived. Varying Assessments of the Soviet Union's Last Anti-Alcohol Campaign," *Communist and Post-Communist Studies* 34, no. 2 (2001): 255–56.

37. See chapter 10. Also see Friedrich Engels, *The Condition of the Working Class in England in 1844* (London: Swan Sonnenschein & Co., 1892), 127–29; Mark D. Steinberg, *Voices of Revolution, 1917* (New Haven, Conn.: Yale University Press, 2001), 24–25; Vladimir I. Lenin, *Polnoe Sobranie Sochinenii*, vol. 43 (Moscow: Political Literature Publishers, 1967), 326. More generally see Charles van Onselen, "Randlords and Rotgut 1886–1903: An Essay on the Role of Alcohol in the Development of European Imperialism and Southern African Capitalism, with Special Reference to Black Mineworkers in the Transvaal Republic," *History Workshop* 1, no. 2 (1976).

38. A. Krasikov, "Commodity Number One (Part 2)," in *The Samizdat Register*, vol. 2, ed. Roy A. Medvedev (New York: W. W. Norton, 1981), 163.

39. Walter G. Moss, *A History of Russia: To 1917* (London: Anthem, 2005), 259, 302.

40. Mikhail Gorbachev, "O zadachakh partii po korennoi perestroike upravleniya ekonomikoi: doklad na Plenume TsK KPSS 25 iyunya 1987 goda," in *Izbrannye rechi i stat'i*, vol. 5 (Moscow: Izdatel'stvo politicheskoi literatury, 1988), 158. On Europe see Stephen Smith, "Economic Issues in Alcohol Taxation," in *Theory and Practice of Excise Taxation: Smoking, Drinking, Gambling, Polluting and Driving*, ed. Sijbren Cnossen (New York: Oxford University Press, 2005), 57–60.

41. Krasikov, "Commodity Number One (Part 2)," 169.
42. Viktor Erofeev, *Russkii apokalipsis: opyt khudozhestvennoi eskhatologii* (Moscow: Zebra E, 2008), 19–20; English version reprinted as Victor Erofeyev, "The Russian God," *New Yorker*, Dec. 16, 2002. On the relationship to Vladimir Erofeyev, Stalin's translator, see "Stalin's Translator Dead at 90," *Moscow Times*, July 20, 2011, http://www.themoscowtimes.com/news/article/stalins-translator-dead-at-90/440793.html#axzz1SaU9kXl7 (accessed July 20, 2011.).
43. Erofeev, *Russkii apokalipsis*, 20–21.

Chapter 2

1. Alexander Nemtsov, "Alcohol-Related Human Losses in Russia in the 1980s and 1990s," *Addiction* 97 (2002): 1413; Judyth Twigg, "What Has Happened to Russian Society?" in *Russia after the Fall*, ed. Andrew Kuchins (Washington, D.C.: Carnegie Endowment, 2002), 172.
2. Aleksandr Nemtsov, *Alkogol'nyi uron regionov Rossii* (Moscow: Nalex, 2003); quoted in Daria A. Khaltourina and Andrey V. Korotayev, "Potential for Alcohol Policy to Decrease the Mortality Crisis in Russia," *Evaluation & the Health Professions* 31, no. 3 (2008): 273.
3. Melvin Goodman, *Gorbachev's Retreat: The Third World* (New York: Praeger, 1991), 100.
4. Jay Bhattacharya, Christina Gathmann, and Grant Miller, *The Gorbachev Anti-Alcohol Campaign and Russia's Mortality Crisis.* NBER Working Paper Series No. 18589 (Cambridge, Mass.: National Bureau of Economic Research, 2012), 2; "Vladimir Putin on Raising Russia's Birth Rate," *Population and Development Review* 32, no. 2 (Documents) (2006): 386; Aleksandr Nemtsov, "Tendentsii potrebleniya alkogolya i obuslovlennye alkogolem poteri zdorov'ya I zhizni v Rossii v 1946–1996 gg.," in *Alkogol' i zdorov'e naseleniya Rossii: 1900–2000*, ed. Andrei K. Demin (Moscow: Rossiiskaya assotsiatsiya obshchestvennogo zdorov'ya, 1998), 105; David Zaridze et al., "Alcohol and Cause-Specific Mortality in Russia: A Retrospective Case-Control Study of 48,557 Adult Deaths," *The Lancet* 373 (2009): 2201–14.
5. Pravitel'stvo Rossiiskoi Federatsii (Government of the Russian Federation), "Kontseptsiia realizatsii gosudarstvennoi politiki po snizheniiu masshtabov zloupotrebleniia alkogol'noi produktsiei i profilaktike alkogolizma sredi naseleniia Rossiiskoi Federatsii na period do 2020 goda" (Concept for the implementation of a state policy to reduce the scale of alcohol abuse and prevention of alcoholism in the population of the Russian Federation for the period until 2020), order no. 2128-r, December 30, 2009.
6. Murray Feshbach, "Potential Social Disarray in Russia Due to Health Factors," *Problems of Post-Communism* 52, no. 4 (2005): 22, and "The Health Crisis in Russia's Ranks," *Current History*, October, 2008, 336; Dar'ya A. Khalturina and Andrei V. Korotaev, "Vvedeniye: alkogol'naya katastrofa; kak ostanovit' vymiranie Rossii," in *Alkogol'naya katastrofa i vozmozhnosti gosudarstvennoi politiki v preodolenii alkogol'noi sverkosmertnosti v Rossii*, ed. Dar'ya A. Khalturina and Andrei V. Korotaev (Moscow: Lenand, 2010).
7. Mark Lawrence Schrad, "Moscow's Drinking Problem," *New York Times*, April 17, 2011.
8. Pravitel'stvo Rossiiskoi Federatsii, "Kontseptsiia realizatsii gosudarstvennoi politiki."
9. James C. Scott, *Seeing Like a State: How Certain Schemes to Improve the Human Condition Have Failed* (New Haven, Conn.: Yale University Press, 1998), 194–95. Orwell's *1984* was premised on the dystopian Russian novel *We* by Evgeny Zamyatin completed in 1921.
10. Maria Lipman, "Stalin Lives," *Foreign Policy*, March 1, 2013, http://www.foreignpolicy.com/articles/2013/03/01/stalin_lives (accessed March 3, 2013).
11. Scott, *Seeing Like a State*, 2. See also Charles Tilly's four functions of states: war making, state making, protection, and extraction. Both approaches emphasize extracting resources from society, monopolizing violence, and ensuring state security. Charles Tilly, "Warmaking and Statemaking as Organized Crime," in *Bringing the State Back In*, ed. Peter Evans, Dietrich Rueschmeyer, and Theda Skocpol (New York: Cambridge University Press, 1985), 181. See also Francis Fukuyama, *The Origins of Political Order: From Prehuman Times to the French Revolution* (New York: Farrar, Straus and Giroux, 2011), 389.

12. Sheila Fitzpatrick, *The Russian Revolution, 1917–1932* (New York: Oxford University Press, 1982), 119; Stephen Kotkin, *Magnetic Mountain: Stalinism as a Civilization* (Berkeley: University of California Press, 1995).

13. Vladimir I. Lenin, "X vserossiiskaya konferentsiya RKP(b)," in *Sochineniya, tom 32: dekabr' 1920–avgust 1921* (Moscow: Gosudarstvennoe izdatel'stvo politicheskoi literatury, 1951), 403.

14. 30 million *pud* of grain translates into 491 million kilograms or 1.08 billion pounds annually. See f. 374 (Narodnyi komissariat raboche-krest'yanskoi inspektsii SSSR), op. 15, d. 1291, l.18–22, Gosudarstvennyi Arkhiv Rossiskoi Federatsii (State archive of the Russian Federation), Moscow. See also Gregory Sokolnikov et al., *Soviet Policy in Public Finance: 1917–1928* (London: Oxford University Press, 1931), 194; Anton M. Bol'shakov, *Derevnya, 1917–1927* (Moscow: Rabotnik prosveshcheniya, 1927), 339–41. On alcoholism in the party see T. H. Rigby, *Communist Party Membership in the U.S.S.R., 1917–1967* (Princeton, N.J.: Princeton University Press, 1968), 121–25.

15. Alexander Hamilton's Tariff Act of 1789 and the federal tax of 1791 both disproportionately focused on alcohol. The ensuing Whiskey Rebellion is a reminder of its contentiousness. Still, the inability to raise federal revenues is commonly cited as the main reason for the failure of the Articles of Confederation. Mark Lawrence Schrad, "The First Social Policy: Alcohol Control and Modernity in Policy Studies," *Journal of Policy History* 19, no. 4 (2007): 433–34. See also W. J. Rorabaugh, *The Alcoholic Republic: An American Tradition* (New York: Oxford University Press, 1979), 50–55; Charles van Onselen, "Randlords and Rotgut 1886–1903: An Essay on the Role of Alcohol in the Development of European Imperialism and Southern African Capitalism, with Special Reference to Black Mineworkers in the Transvaal Republic," *History Workshop* 1, no. 2 (1976).

16. James C. Scott, *Domination and the Arts of Resistance: Hidden Transcripts* (New Haven, Conn.: Yale University Press, 1990), 121.

17. David Christian, "The Black and the Gold Seals: Popular Protest against the Liquor Trade on the Eve of Emancipation," in *Peasant Economy, Culture, and Politics of European Russia, 1800–1921*, ed. Esther Kingston-Mann and Jeffrey Burds (Princeton, N.J.: Princeton University Press, 1991), 273–77.

18. Carl Friedrich and Zbigniew Brzezinski, *Totalitarian Dictatorship and Autocracy* (New York: Praeger, 1956), 33.

19. Scott, *Seeing Like a State*, 5. In Russian history see Allen C. Lynch, *How Russia Is Not Ruled: Reflections on Russian Political Development* (New York: Cambridge University Press, 2005), 7–8, 18–21; Tim McDaniel, *The Agony of the Russian Idea* (Princeton, N.J.: Princeton University Press, 1996), 14.

20. Michel Foucault, *Discipline and Punish: The Birth of the Prison* (New York: Random House, 1975).

21. Alexander Barmine, *One Who Survived: The Life Story of a Russian under the Soviets* (New York: G. P. Putnam's Sons, 1945), 214. At the conclusion of World War II, Stalin seized the extensive film catalogue once owned by Hitler's minister of propaganda, Joseph Goebbels. Beyond domestic films, Stalin particularly enjoyed westerns, detective and gangster films, and anything with Charlie Chaplin. Svetlana Alliluyeva, *Only One Year*, trans. Paul Chavchavadze (New York: Harper & Row, 1969), 389.

22. Richard Stites, *Russian Popular Culture: Entertainment and Society since 1900* (New York: Cambridge University Press, 1992), 94–95; Neya Zorkaya, *The Illustrated History of Soviet Cinema* (New York: Hippocrene Books, 1991), 109.

23. Richard Taylor, *Film Propaganda: Soviet Russia and Nazi Germany* (New York: I. B. Tauris, 1998), 64.

24. J. Hoberman and Jonathan Rosenbaum, *Midnight Movies* (New York: Da Capo, 1991), 231.

25. Peter Kenez, *Cinema and Soviet Society from the Revolution to the Death of Stalin* (London: I. B. Tauris, 2001), 179.

26. Scott, *Domination and the Arts of Resistance*, 18.

27. Joan Neuberger, *Ivan the Terrible: The Film Companion* (New York: I. B. Tauris, 2003), 22; Maureen Perrie, *The Cult of Ivan the Terrible in Stalin's Russia* (New York: Palgrave, 2001), 176. The award was a surprise, as the Stalin Prize committee had previously excluded Eisenstein's

film from consideration. The prize had instead been awarded at Stalin's personal insistence. Leonid Kozlov, "The Artist and the Shadow of Ivan," in *Stalinism and Soviet Cinema*, ed. Richard Taylor and D. W. Spring (London: Routledge, 1993), 126; Orlando Figes, *Natasha's Dance: A Cultural History of Russia* (New York: Macmillan, 2003), 497. On Eisenstein's premonitions see Richard Taylor, "Eisenstein, Sergei," FilmReference.com, http://www.filmreference.com/Directors-Du-Fr/Eisenstein-Sergei.html.

28. Herbert Marshall, *Masters of the Soviet Cinema: Crippled Creative Biographies* (London: Routledge, 1983), 9; Kozlov, "The Artist and the Shadow of Ivan," 122.

29. Mikhail Romm, *Besedy o kino* (Moscow: Iskusstvo, 1964), 91. See also Marshall, *Masters of the Soviet Cinema*, 229.

30. Perrie, *The Cult of Ivan the Terrible in Stalin's Russia*, 177.

31. Kozlov, "The Artist and the Shadow of Ivan," 123.

32. Leonid K. Kozlov, "'Ten' Groznogo i khudozhnik," *Kinovedcheskie zapiski* 15 (1992): 38; Figes, *Natasha's Dance*, 497.

33. Kozlov, "The Artist and the Shadow of Ivan," 127.

34. Marshall, *Masters of the Soviet Cinema*, 221; Donald Rayfield, *Stalin and His Hangmen: The Tyrant and Those Who Killed for Him* (New York: Random House, 2005), 433; David Sillito, "Hamlet: The Play Stalin Hated," BBC, April 22, 2012, http://www.bbc.co.uk/news/magazine-17770170 (accessed April 22, 2012).

35. Romm, *Besedy o kino*, 91.

36. Richard Taylor, "Sergei Eisenstein: The Life and Times of a Boy from Riga," in *The Montage Principle: Eisenstein in New Cultural and Critical Contexts*, ed. Jean Antoine-Dunne and Paula Quigley (Amsterdam: Rodopi, 2004), 40–41; Kenez, *Cinema and Soviet Society*, 197; Grigorii Mar'yamov, *Kremlevskii tsenzor: Stalin smotrit kino* (Moscow: Konfederatsiya soyuzov kinomatografistov 'Kinotsentr', 1992), 84–91; an English transcript can be found at http://www.revolutionarydemocracy.org/rdv3n2/ivant.htm. For Eisenstein's remark see Kozlov, "The Artist and the Shadow of Ivan," 129.

37. On Eisenstein's note taking see Taylor, "Sergei Eisenstein: The Life and Times of a Boy from Riga," 40. On not altering the film see Kozlov, "The Artist and the Shadow of Ivan," 248 n91.

38. Rostislav N. Yurenev, ed., *Eizenshtein v vospominaniyakh sovremennikov* (Moscow: Iskusstvo, 1974), 283.

39. Kozlov, "The Artist and the Shadow of Ivan," 130.

40. Robert Conquest, *Stalin: Breaker of Nations* (New York: Penguin Books, 1991), 312; Rayfield, *Stalin and His Hangmen*, 466–67.

41. Albert J. LaValley and Barry P. Scherr, *Eisenstein at 100: A Reconsideration* (New Brunswick, N.J.: Rutgers University Press, 2001), 117, 42–43.

42. Sergey Radchenko, *Two Suns in the Heavens: The Sino-Soviet Struggle for Supremacy, 1962–1967* (Washington, D.C.: Woodrow Wilson Center Press, 2009), 135, 225. On Khrushchev see also Steve LeVine, *The Oil and the Glory: The Pursuit of Empire and Fortune on the Caspian Sea* (New York: Random House, 2007), 51.

43. Paul R. Bennett, *Russian Negotiating Strategy: Analytic Case Studies from Salt and Start* (Commack, N.Y.: Nova, 1997), 64–65; James Humes, *Nixon's Ten Commandments of Leadership and Negotiation* (New York: Touchstone, 1998), 49. On Brezhnev's alcoholism see Donald Trelford, "A Walk in the Woods with Gromyko," *Observer*, April 2, 1989; Richard Ned Lebow and Janice Gross Stein, *We All Lost the Cold War* (Princeton, N.J.: Princeton University Press, 1994), 478.

44. Anatoly Dobrynin, *In Confidence: Moscow's Ambassador to America's Six Cold War Presidents (1962–1986)* (New York: Times Books, 1995), 373.

45. Ibid., 281–82.

46. Aleksandr Nemtsov, *Alkogol'naya istoriya Rossii: noveishii period* (Moscow: URSS, 2009), 66. On *Kto kogo?* see Christopher Read, *Lenin: A Revolutionary Life* (New York: Routledge, 2005), 248.

Chapter 3

1. Stephen Graham, *Ivan the Terrible: Life of Ivan IV of Russia* (New Haven, Conn.: Yale University Press, 1933), 4.

2. Arthur Voyce, *The Moscow Kremlin: Its History, Architecture, and Art Treasures* (Berkeley: University of California Press, 1954), 19; Graham, *Ivan the Terrible*, 5.

3. Nathan Haskell Dole, *Young Folks' History of Russia* (New York: Saalfield Publishing Co., 1903), 271. See also R. E. F. Smith and David Christian, *Bread and Salt: A Social and Economic History of Food and Drink in Russia* (New York: Cambridge University Press, 1984).

4. Dole, *Young Folks' History of Russia*, 271. Also see Freiherr Sigmund von Herberstein, *Description of Moscow and Muscovy: 1557* (New York: Barnes & Noble, 1969), 65.

5. H. Sutherland Edwards, "Food and Drink," in *Russia as Seen and Described by Famous Writers*, ed. Esther Singleton (New York: Dodd, Mead & Co., 1906), 260–61; James Billington, *The Icon and the Axe: An Interpretive History of Russian Culture* (New York: Alfred A. Knopf, 1966), 86.

6. Dole, *Young Folks' History of Russia*, 271.

7. M. P. Alekseev, "Zapadnoevropeiskie slovarnye materialy v drevnerusskikh azbukovni-kakh XVI–XVII vekov," in *Akademiku Viktoru Vladimirovichu Vinogradovu k ego shestid-esyatiletiyu: sbornik statei*, ed. Akademiya nauk SSSR (Moscow: Izdatel'svto akademii nauk SSSR, 1956), 41; cited in Billington, *Icon and the Axe*, 86. On the importance of foreign accounts to medieval Russian history see Vasilii O. Klyuchevskii, *Skazanie inostrantsev o moskovskom gosudarstve* (Moscow: Universitetskoi Tipografiya Katkov i Ko., 1866); August Ludwig von Schlözer, *Nestor: Ruskiia lietopisi na drevleslavenskom iazykie*, 3 vols. (St. Petersburg: Imperatorskaya Tipografiya, 1816), 2:295–96.

8. As with later visitors to Moscow, the Russian leader not only received toasts; he also doled them out. Von Herberstein recounted the grand prince's toasts to Holy Roman Emperor Maximilian, proclaiming that "you shall drain it too and all the others afterwards in token of our affection for our brother Maximilian etc., and you shall tell him what you have seen." Von Herberstein, *Description of Moscow and Muscovy: 1557*, 67.

9. Ibid., 66–67.

10. Janet Martin, *Medieval Russia, 980–1584*, 2nd ed. (New York: Cambridge University Press, 2007), 364–69.

11. By all accounts it was the thirteen-year-old prince Ivan himself who had the boyar Andrei Shuisky eaten alive by wild dogs. Ibid., 370; Henri Troyat, *Ivan the Terrible* (New York: E. P. Dutton, 1984), 16.

12. This was from the opening of the Stoglav Council of 1551. Troyat, *Ivan the Terrible*, 16, 27. See also: J. L. I. Fennell, ed., *Prince A. M. Kurbsky's History of Ivan IV* (Cambridge: Cambridge University Press, 1965), 19.

13. Isabel de Madariaga, *Ivan the Terrible: First Tsar of Russia* (New Haven, Conn.: Yale University Press, 2005), 360; Troyat, *Ivan the Terrible*, 106.

14. Troyat, *Ivan the Terrible*, 16. On Ivan's inebriate youth see James Graham, *Vessels of Rage, Engines of Power: The Secret History of Alcoholism* (Lexington, Va.: Aculeus, 1993), 165.

15. Kazemir Valishevskii, *Ivan Groznyi, 1530–1584* (Moscow: Obshchestvennaya pol'za, 1912), 142–43. There is much debate over the origins of the word *tsar*. Some suggest that it is of Tatar origins while most associate its use in the slavic languages as being derived from Caesar—laying claim to both the rank of emperor and a deep, rich imperial tradition.

16. Sergei F. Platonov, *Ivan the Terrible*, trans. Joseph Wieczynski (Gulf Breeze, Fla.: Academic International, 1974), 104; de Madariaga, *Ivan the Terrible*, 148, 361.

17. Troyat, *Ivan the Terrible*, 133.

18. Fennell, *Prince A. M. Kurbsky's History of Ivan IV* and *The Correspondence between Prince A. M. Kurbsky and Tsar Ivan IV of Russia, 1564–1579* (Cambridge: Cambridge University Press, 1963).

19. Fennell, *Prince A. M. Kurbsky's History of Ivan IV*, 163–65.

20. Ibid., 165.

21. Troyat, *Ivan the Terrible*, 193.

22. Ibid., 134.

23. de Madariaga, *Ivan the Terrible*, 148.

24. Fennell, *Prince A. M. Kurbsky's History of Ivan IV*, 181.

25. Ibid., 291.

26. Paul Bushkovitch, *Peter the Great: The Struggle for Power, 1671–1725* (New York: Cambridge University Press, 2001), 38.

27. George Backer, *The Deadly Parallel: Stalin and Ivan the Terrible* (New York: Random House, 1950). See in particular Alexander Yanov, *The Origins of Autocracy: Ivan the Terrible in Russian History*, trans. Stephen Dunn (Berkeley: University of California Press, 1981), 59–60.

28. Giles Fletcher, *Of the Russe Commonwealth: 1591*, facsimile ed. (Cambridge, Mass.: Harvard University Press, 1966), 43–44. See also chapters 6 and 7 herein.

29. Troyat, *Ivan the Terrible*, 106. Indeed, from afar, Prince Kurbsky's denunciations more frequently were addressed to Ivan's henchmen for their nefarious influence rather than on the tsar himself. de Madariaga, *Ivan the Terrible*, 148. See for instance: Fennell, *Prince A. M. Kurbsky's History of Ivan IV*, 131, 57, 65.

30. Troyat, *Ivan the Terrible*, 169.

31. Graham, *Vessels of Rage*, 165; Platonov, *Ivan the Terrible*, 36, 108; Troyat, *Ivan the Terrible*, 123–34, 220; Richard Hellie, "In Search of Ivan the Terrible," in *S. F. Platonov's Ivan the Terrible*, ed. Joseph Wieczynski (Gulf Breeze, Fla.: Academic International, 1974), xx, xxvi–xxvii; de Madariaga, *Ivan the Terrible*, 178–83; Robert Nisbet Bain, *Slavonic Europe: A Political History of Poland and Russia from 1447 to 1796* (Cambridge: Cambridge University Press, 1908), 121.

32. Platonov, *Ivan the Terrible*, 128;. Troyat, *Ivan the Terrible*, 222.

33. Graham, *Ivan the Terrible*, 296.

34. Caroline Brooke, *Moscow: A Cultural History* (New York: Oxford University Press, 2006), 15.

35. Martin, *Medieval Russia, 980–1584*, 365–66.

36. Graham, *Ivan the Terrible*, 314. There is some discrepancy as to the actual events of Ivan's death: original accounts end with the calling of physicians, and "in the mean, he was strangled and stark dead." Whether he had been physically strangled or was choking or otherwise not breathing is unclear. de Madariaga, *Ivan the Terrible*, 352–58.

37. Fennell, *Prince A. M. Kurbsky's History of Ivan IV*, 289.

Chapter 4

1. Samuel Collins, *The Present State of Russia, in a Letter to a Friend at London; Written by an Eminent Person Residing at the Great Czars Court at Mosco for the Space of Nine Years* (London: John Winter, 1671), 63–64. On the tavern revolts of 1648 see chapter 5.

2. Lindsey Hughes, *Peter the Great: A Biography* (New Haven, Conn.: Yale University Press, 2004), 12; Robert K. Massie, *Peter the Great: His Life and World* (New York: Alfred A. Knopf, 1980), 118.

3. Joseph T. Fuhrmann, *Tsar Alexis, His Reign and His Russia* (Gulf Breeze, Fla.: Academic International, 1981), 195.

4. Eugene Schuyler, *Peter the Great, Emperor of Russia: A Study of Historical Biography* (New York: Charles Scribner's Sons, 1890), 14.

5. Philip Longworth, *Alexis, Tsar of All the Russias* (London: Secker & Warburg, 1984), 219.

6. Hughes, *Peter the Great*, 11.

7. Early foreign travelers often referred to what we now know as vodka as brandy—the closest type of distilled spirits with which they previously were familiar. Schuyler, *Peter the Great*, 57.

8. Ibid., 59.

9. Lindsey Hughes, *Sophia: Regent of Russia, 1657–1704* (New Haven, Conn.: Yale University Press, 1990), 68–69. See also ibid., 58. Schuyler, *Peter the Great*, 68; Lindsey Hughes, "Sophia Alekseyevna and the Moscow Rebellion of 1682," *Slavonic and East European Review* 63, no. 4 (1985): 536.

10. Hughes, *Sophia*, 231–37.

11. Schuyler, *Peter the Great*, 325–29. Jakob von Staehlin presents anecdotes concerning the *streltsy*'s alcohol-fueled attempts to assassinate Tsar Peter in *Original Anecdotes of Peter the Great: Collected from the Conversation of Several Persons of Distinction at Petersburgh and Moscow* (London: J. Murray, 1788), 31–32.

12. John Barrow, *The Life of Peter the Great* (Edinburgh: William P. Nimmo & Co., 1883), 96; Dmitrii N. Borodin, *Kabak i ego proshloe* (St. Petersburg: Vilenchik, 1910), 45, cited in Boris Segal, *Russian Drinking: Use and Abuse of Alcohol in Pre-Revolutionary Russia* (New Brunswick, N.J.: Rutgers Center of Alcohol Studies, 1987), 72.

13. Literally translated as "new Transfiguration," the residence was not located far from where the Moscow Lokomotiv soccer stadium stands today. Ernest A. Zitser, *The Transfigured Kingdom: Sacred Parody and Charismatic Authority at the Court of Peter the Great* (Ithaca, N.Y.: Cornell University Press, 2004), 4.

14. Philip John von Strahlenberg, *An Historico-Geographical Description of the North and Eastern Parts of Europe and Asia; but More Particularly of Russia, Siberia and Great Tatary* (London: J. Brotherton, J. Hazard, W. Meadows, T. Cox, T. Astley, S. Austen, L. Gilliver, and C. Corbet, 1738), 238; Paul Bushkovitch, *Peter the Great: The Struggle for Power, 1671–1725* (New York: Cambridge University Press, 2001), 194. In Russian, *nemetskii* has the double meaning of both "German" and "foreign," so the *nemetskaya sloboda* were not exclusively populated by Germans, but by foreigners of many varieties.

15. Robert Nisbet Bain, *Slavonic Europe: A Political History of Poland and Russia from 1447 to 1796* (Cambridge: Cambridge University Press, 1908), 324.

16. Borodin, *Kabak i ego proshloe*, 45, cited in Segal, *Russian Drinking*, 72. Lindsey Hughes, *Russia in the Age of Peter the Great* (New Haven, Conn.: Yale University Press, 1998), 418–19. See also Derek Wilson, *Peter the Great* (New York: St. Martin's, 2010), 41.

17. Hughes, *Peter the Great*, 36; Wilson, *Peter the Great*, 40.

18. Massie, *Peter the Great*, 116–17; Yaroslav E. Vodarskii, "Peter I," in *The Emperors and Empresses of Russia: Rediscovering the Romanovs*, ed. Donald J. Raleigh and A. A. Iskenderov (Armonk, N.Y.: M. E. Sharpe, 1996), 12.

19. On Lefort having "a great Share in Debauching the *Czar*" see von Strahlenberg, *Russia, Siberia and Great Tatary*, 238, 43; James Cracraft, *The Revolution of Peter the Great* (Cambridge, Mass.: Harvard University Press, 2003), 5. Leibniz quotation from Massie, *Peter the Great*, 118.

20. "Peter the Great in England," *The Living Age* 47, no. 11 (1855): 468. On general impacts see Arthur MacGregor, "The Tsar in England: Peter the Great's Visit to London in 1698," *The Seventeenth Century* 19, no. 1 (2004); Anthony Cross, *Peter the Great through British Eyes: Perceptions and Representations of the Tsar since 1698* (New York: Cambridge University Press, 2000), 20.

21. "Peter the Great in England," 471. See also MacGregor, "Tsar in England"; Wilson, *Peter the Great*, 55. On the monkey incident see Barrow, *Life of Peter the Great*, 88; Leo Loewenson, "Some Details of Peter the Great's Stay in England in 1698: Neglected English Material," *Slavonic and East European Review* 40, no. 95 (1962): 434.

22. Zitser, *Transfigured Kingdom*, 46; Massie, *Peter the Great*, 118.

23. Massie, *Peter the Great*, 118.

24. von Strahlenberg, *Russia, Siberia and Great Tatary*, 249; Alfred Rambaud, *Russia*, 2 vols. (New York: P. F. Collier & Son, 1902), 2:51–52.

25. von Staehlin, *Original Anecdotes of Peter the Great*, 354; see also John Banks, *Life of Peter the Great*, 2 vols. (Boston: Houghton, Mifflin, 1882), 2:220–21; Cross, *Peter the Great through British Eyes*, 44. Anthony Cross' anecdotes of Peter the Great forcing even his heartiest sailors to get drunk with him originate with a letter of 20 August 1702 from Thomas Hale, a British merchant in Arkhangelsk, found in the British Library, Add. Mss. 33,573, Hale Papers, Correspondence vol. 11 (1661–1814), f. 178.

26. Walter K. Kelly, *History of Russia, from the Earliest Period to the Present Time*, 2 vols. (London: Henry G. Bohn, 1854), 1:260; Philippe-Paul (comte de) Ségur, *History of Russia and of Peter the Great* (London: Treuttel and Würtz, Treuttel, Jun. and Richter, 1829), 270; Bushkovitch, *Peter the Great*, 233.

27. Friedrich Wilhelm von Bergholz, *Dnevnik kammer-iunkera Berkhgol'tsa, vedennyi im v Rossii v tsarstvovanie Petra Velikago, s 1721–1725 g.*, trans. I. Ammon, 2nd ed. (Moscow: Tipograpfiya Katkova i Ko., 1858), 2:349. See also Massie, *Peter the Great*, 119.

28. von Strahlenberg, *Russia, Siberia and Great Tatary*, 240; Vladislav B. Aksenov, *Veselie Rusi, XX vek: gradus noveishei rossiiskoi istorii ot "p'yanogo byudzheta" do "sukhogo zakona"* (Moscow: Probel-2000, 2007), 32–33.

29. Massie, *Peter the Great*, 119–20. Such a scene is reminiscent of Pieter Bruegel's (in)famous 1559 oil painting depicting *The Fight between Carnival and Lent*.

30. Kelly, *History of Russia*, 338–39. On Zotov's Bible see James Cracraft, *The Church Reform of Peter the Great* (Palo Alto, Calif.: Stanford University Press, 1971), 11.

31. Just Juel, "Iz zapisok datskogo poslannika Iusta Iulia," *Russkii arkhiv* 30, no. 3 (1892): 41; Hughes, *Russia in the Age of Peter the Great*, 258. Even Voltaire's history of Peter makes mention of Volkov; see M. de Voltaire, *The History of the Russian Empire under Peter the Great*, 2 vols. (Berwick, U.K.: R. Taylor, 1760), vol. 1, chap. 9, "Travels of Peter the Great."

32. Lindsey Hughes, "Playing Games: The Alternative History of Peter the Great," *SSEES Occasional Papers* 41 (1998): 13, and *Peter the Great*, 90.

33. Wilson, *Peter the Great*, 33; Hughes, *Peter the Great*, 73.

34. Borodin, *Kabak I Ego Proshloe*, 44; Hughes, *Peter the Great*, 157; H. Sutherland Edwards, "Food and Drink," in *Russia as Seen and Described by Famous Writers*, ed. Esther Singleton (New York: Dodd, Mead & Co., 1906), 260–61.

35. von Strahlenberg, *Russia, Siberia and Great Tatary*, 240–41; Segal, *Russian Drinking*, 72. Segal's accounts are based on Aleksei Tolstoi, *Pyotr Pervyi* (Moscow: Pravda, 1971), 335. See also Massie, *Peter the Great*, 117. Even Swedish playwright August Strindberg referenced Peter's house crashing, in *Historical Miniatures (1905)* (Middlesex, U.K.: Echo Library, 2006), 152.

36. Hughes, *Peter the Great*, 147.

37. On faulting Peter's upbringing see von Strahlenberg, *Russia, Siberia and Great Tatary*, 238. On the need for entertainment see Rambaud, *Russia*, 27. For the cultural backlash argument see Hughes, *Russia in the Age of Peter the Great*; Wilson, *Peter the Great*, 34. On the use of parody to discredit tradition see Zitser, *Transfigured Kingdom*, 3–9.

38. von Strahlenberg, *Russia, Siberia and Great Tatary*, 240–41.

39. Kelly, *History of Russia*, 289. See also Orlando Williams Wight, *Life of Peter the Great*, 2 vols. (Boston: Houghton, Mifflin, 1882), 1:223–25.

40. Peter himself sailed to meet the first merchant vessel to approach his new capital. Peter then piloted the Dutch vessel, with its cargo of salt and wine, to port, paying the skipper five hundred ducats out of pocket and decreeing the ship forever free from tolls. Nathan Haskell Dole, *Young Folks' History of Russia* (New York: Saalfield Publishing Co., 1903), 391.

41. Massie, *Peter the Great*, 119. Indeed, much official business was run through "unofficial" channels. All petitions and memorials addressed to the tsar wound up with Romodanovsky. If one were to complain about any particular outcome to the tsar, he would pass the blame: "It is not my fault; all depends on the czar of Moscow," Romodanovsky. Kelly, *History of Russia*, 271–72.

42. Juel, "Iz zapisok datskogo poslannika Iusta Iulia," 37.

43. Kelly, *History of Russia*, 298. Also see Walter J. Gleason, *Empress Anna: Favorites, Policies, Campaigns* (Gulf Breeze, Fla.: Academic International, 1984), 194; Hughes, *Peter the Great*, 91, and "Playing Games," 13. The reverse of this dynamic also had tragic consequences, as Russian ambassadors often took their inebriety with them. Adam Olearius recounted how, in 1608, the Russian ambassador to Swedish King Charles IX drank so much that he was found dead in bed. Samuel H. Baron, ed., *The Travels of Olearius in Seventeenth-Century Russia* (Palo Alto, Calif.: Stanford University Press, 1967), 144. See also Vladimir P. Nuzhnyi, *Vino v zhizni i zhizn' v vine* (Moscow: Sinteg, 2001), 24.

44. "Peter the Great as Peter the Little," in *Review of Reviews*, vol. 5, January–June, ed. W. T. Stead (London, Mowbray House: 1892), 172; Juel, "Iz zapisok datskogo poslannika Iusta Iulia," 30, 32, 42–44. See also Hughes, *Russia in the Age of Peter the Great*, 266.

45. Hughes, *Russia in the Age of Peter the Great*, 266. The quote is from Juel, "Iz zapisok datskogo poslannika Iusta Iulia," 43–44.

46. Cracraft, *Church Reform of Peter the Great*, 13. See also Banks, *Life of Peter the Great*, 2:222–23. Banks cites a handwritten manuscript of Dr. Birch housed in the Sloane papers in the British Museum.

47. Bergholz, *Dnevnik kammer-iunkera Berkhgol'tsa*, 1:257. See also ibid., 1:237; Banks, *Life of Peter the Great*, 216.

48. Barrow, *Life of Peter the Great*, 116; Kelly, *History of Russia*, 254–55.

49. Ségur, *History of Russia and of Peter the Great*, 381; von Strahlenberg, *Russia, Siberia and Great Tatary*, 241–42.

50. Kelly, *History of Russia*, 254–55. On Romodanovsky's bear see Friederich Christian Weber, *The Present State of Russia* (London: W. Taylor, 1722), 137. See also Kelly, *History of Russia*, 271–72; Robert Coughlan, *Elizabeth and Catherine: Empresses of All the Russias* (New York: G. P. Putnam's Sons, 1974), 17. Other noteworthy accounts of Peter's drunken cruelty can be found in the works of novelist Alexei Tolstoy. In his well-researched *Peter the First*, Tolstoy depicts Peter's Jolly Company emasculating members of the old boyar class: "Prince Belosel'sky was stripped naked and eggs were broken against his bare butt.... They stuck a candle into Prince Volkonsky's anus and chanted prayers over him until they collapsed with laughter. They pitched and tarred people and made them stand on their heads. They even used a bellows to pump air into Courtier Ivan Akakievich's anus, which caused his subsequent speedy death." Tolstoi, *Pyotr Pervyi*, 214; English translation from Segal, *Russian Drinking*, 72.

51. Rambaud, *Russia*, 27; von Strahlenberg, *Russia, Siberia and Great Tatary*, 248.

52. Ségur, *History of Russia and of Peter the Great*, 443.

53. Bushkovitch goes on to note that in the ensuing drinking "Menshikov got so drunk he lost a jewel-encrusted order of knighthood, a present from the King of Prussia. Fortunately a common soldier found it the next day and returned it to him." Bushkovitch, *Peter the Great*, 344–46. On the little people see Hughes, *Russia in the Age of Peter the Great*, 259. Of course, the birth of Alexei also was celebrated with alcohol. Hughes, *Peter the Great*, 29.

54. Evgenii Viktorovich Anisimov, *The Reforms of Peter the Great: Progress through Coercion in Russia*, trans. John T. Alexander (Armonk, N.Y.: M. E. Sharpe, 1993), 278–79.

55. On the law of succession and the crowning of Catherine see Anisimov, *Reforms of Peter the Great*, 279; Cracraft, *Revolution of Peter the Great*, 66–67. On the Drunken Synod and Peter's death see Kelly, *History of Russia*, 338–39.

Chapter 5

1. Vasilii O. Klyuchevskii, *A Course in Russian History: The Time of Catherine the Great*, vol. 2, trans. Marshall Shatz (Armonk, N.Y.: M. E. Sharpe, 1997), 15–16.

2. Robert Nisbet Bain, *The Daughter of Peter the Great: A History of Russian Diplomacy and of the Russian Court under the Empress Elizabeth Petrovna, 1741–1762* (London: Archibald Constable & Co., 1899), 106; Mark Cruse and Hilde Hoogenboom, "Preface: Catherine the Great and Her Several Memoirs," in *The Memoirs of Catherine the Great*, ed. Mark Cruse and Hilde Hoogenboom (New York: Modern Library, 2005), xv.

3. Catherine II, *The Memoirs of Catherine the Great*, trans. Mark Cruse and Hilde Hoogenboom (New York: Modern Library, 2005), 4–5.

4. Klyuchevskii, *A Course in Russian History*, 17–18; Samuel Smucker, *Memoirs of the Court and Reign of Catherine the Second, Empress of Russia* (Philadelphia: Porter & Coates, 1855), 24; Catherine II, *Memoirs of Catherine the Great*, 74.

5. Catherine II, *Memoirs of Catherine the Great*, 120; Robert K. Massie, *Catherine the Great: Portrait of a Woman* (New York: Random House, 2011), 159; Henri Troyat, *Catherine the Great*, trans. Joan Pinkham (New York: E. P. Dutton, 1980), 86, 99–100.

6. Catherine II, *Memoirs of Catherine the Great*, 82–84.

7. Ibid., 184.

8. Klyuchevskii, *Course in Russian History*, 16–17.

9. Samuel M. Smucker, *The Life and Reign of Nicholas the First, Emperor of Russia* (Philadelphia: J. W. Bradley, 1856), 25.

10. Charles Geneviève Louis Auguste André Timothée d'Eon de Beaumont, *Lettres, mémoires & négociations particulieres du Chevalier d'Éon, ministre plénipotentiaire de France aupres du roi de la Grande Bretagne; avec M. M. les ducs de Praslin, de Nivernois, de Sainte-Foy, & Regnier de Guerchy ambassadeur extraordinaire, &c. &c. &c.* (London: Jaques Dixwell, 1764); for an English translation see Troyat, *Catherine the Great,* 26–27. See also Jean-Henri Castéra, *The Life of Catharine II. Empress of Russia,* 3rd ed., 3 vols. (London: T. N. Longman & O. Rees, 1799), 1:124. Henri Troyat, *Terrible Tsarinas: Five Russian Women in Power,* trans. Andrea Lyn Secara (New York: Algora, 2000), 153. On the need to balance Peter and Elizabeth see Cruse and Hoogenboom, "Catherine the Great and Her Several Memoirs," xvi.

11. C. C. J., "Russian Court Life in the Eighteenth Century," *Littell's Living Age* 23, no. 1777 (1878): 762.

12. Troyat, *Catherine the Great,* 133.

13. Smucker, *Catherine the Second,* 38–39.

14. Troyat, *Catherine the Great,* 133–34.

15. Klyuchevskii, *Course in Russian History,* 17–18.

16. Harford Montgomery Hyde, *The Empress Catherine and Princess Dashkov* (London: Chapman & Hall, 1935), 29; Klyuchevskii, *A Course in Russian History,* 22–23; Troyat, *Catherine the Great,* 136–37.

17. Klyuchevskii, *Course in Russian History,* 22–23.

18. Valerie A. Kivelson, "The Devil Stole His Mind: The Tsar and the 1648 Moscow Uprising," *American Historical Review* 98, no. 3 (1993): 733; Dmitry Shlapentokh, "Drunkenness in the Context of Political Culture: The Case of Russian Revolutions," *International Journal of Sociology and Social Policy* 14, no. 8 (1994): 18; Paul Miliukov, Charles Seignobos, and Louis Eisenmann, *History of Russia, vol. 1: From the Beginnings to the Empire of Peter the Great* (New York: Funk & Wagnalls, 1968), 151. Adam Olearius vividly described the sorrowful fate of those too drunk to escape the flames; see Samuel H. Baron, ed., *The Travels of Olearius in Seventeenth-Century Russia* (Palo Alto, Calif.: Stanford University Press, 1967), 208–13.

19. Robert Coughlan, *Elizabeth and Catherine: Empresses of All the Russias* (New York: G. P. Putnam's Sons, 1974), 32. On Catherine I and alcohol see Sergei Romanov, *Istoriya russkoi vodki* (Moscow: Veche, 1998), 117–18. Also see Troyat, *Terrible Tsarinas,* 15–18.

20. Troyat, *Terrible Tsarinas,* 69.

21. Troyat, *Terrible Tsarinas,* 82–85; Evgenii Viktorovich Anisimov, "Empress Anna Ivanovna, 1730–1740," in *The Emperors and Empresses of Russia: Rediscovering the Romanovs,* ed. Donald J. Raleigh and A. A. Iskenderov (Armonk, N.Y.: M. E. Sharpe, 1996), 45–53.

22. Coughlan, *Elizabeth and Catherine,* 37–38; Bain, *Daughter of Peter the Great,* 92.

23. Klyuchevskii, *Course in Russian History,* 23.

24. Ibid., 22; Alfred Rambaud, *Russia,* 2 vols. (New York: P. F. Collier & Son, 1902), 2:85.

25. Klyuchevskii, *Course in Russian History,* 23–24, 204; Walter K. Kelly, *History of Russia, from the Earliest Period to the Present Time,* 2 vols. (London: Henry G. Bohn, 1854), 1:463.

26. Troyat, *Catherine the Great,* 143–48.

27. Ibid., 148–49.

28. Ibid., 149.

29. Ekaterina Romanovna Dashkova, *The Memoirs of Princess Dashkova,* trans. Kyril Fitzlyon (Durham, N.C.: Duke University Press, 1995), 82; Massie, *Catherine the Great,* 268–69. On the rumors see Virginia Rounding, *Catherine the Great: Love, Sex, and Power* (New York: Macmillan, 2006), 147.

30. Klyuchevskii, *Course in Russian History,* 26. Claims of losses from the celebration totaled roughly 105,000 rubles. Rounding, *Catherine the Great,* 147. Walter Kelly suggests that even foreign ambassadors contributed to the celebrations. Kelly, *History of Russia,* 466.

31. Dashkova, *Memoirs of Princess Dashkova,* 81. Klyuchevskii suggests that Peter also requested Elizabeth Vorontsova, who was instead dispatched to Moscow to marry Alexander Poliansky. Klyuchevskii, *A Course in Russian History,* 26.

32. Robert Nisbet Bain, *Peter III, Emperor of Russia: The Story of a Crisis and a Crime* (London: Archibald Constable & Co., 1902), 182–84; Kelly, *History of Russia,* 475.

33. Kelly, *History of Russia,* 473.

34. J. M. Buckley, *The Midnight Sun, the Tsar and the Nihilist* (Boston: D. Lothrop & Co., 1886), 168–71.
35. Smucker, *Catherine the Second*, 268–69.
36. Edvard Radzinsky, *Alexander II: The Last Great Tsar*, trans. Antonina W. Bouis (New York: Free Press, 2006), 16–17.
37. Smucker, *Life and Reign of Nicholas the First*, 69; Radzinsky, *Alexander II*, 32–34.
38. See, for instance, Stephen Kotkin, *Armageddon Averted: The Soviet Collapse, 1970–2000* (New York: Oxford University Press, 2008), 99; Stephen White, *Russia's New Politics: The Management of a Postcommunist Society* (New York: Cambridge University Press, 2000), 29–30.

Chapter 6

1. See, for instance: Linda Himelstein, *The King of Vodka: The Story of Pyotr Smirnov and the Upheaval of an Empire* (New York: HarperCollins, 2009), 287–338; K. V. Smirnova et al., *Vodochnyi korol' Petr Arsen'evich Smirnov i ego potomki* (Moscow: Raduga, 1999), 85–118. On international disputes arising from such Russian imagery see Boris S. Seglin, "Russkaya vodka v mezhdunarodnykh sudakh," *Biznes-advokat*, no. 1 (2005); http://www.bestlawyers.ru/php/news/newsnew.phtml?id=370&idnew=14983&start=0 (accessed Feb. 8, 2013).
2. *Vice Magazine* journalist Ivar Berglin goes on a similar expedition into the origins of vodka in his Vice Guide to Travel documentary "Wodka Wars," http://www.youtube.com/watch?v=SR_37f6hHTE (accessed July 21, 2013).
3. The biographical material on Vilyam Pokhlebkin was culled from the Russia 1 television documentary "Smert' kulinara: Vil'yam Pokhlebkin," http://www.rutv.ru/video.html?vid=39680&cid=5079&d=0.
4. "Vodka," in *Bol'shaia sovetskaia entsiklopediia* (Big Soviet Encyclopedia) (English translation), ed. A. M. Prokhorov (New York: Macmillan, 1974), 545.
5. Daniel J. Malleck, "Whiskies," in *Alcohol and Temperance in Modern History: An International Encyclopedia*, ed. Jack S. Blocker Jr., David M. Fahey, and Ian R. Tyrrell (Oxford: ABC-CLIO, 2003), 2:650; Birgit Speckle, *Streit ums Bier in Bayern: Wertvorstellungen um Reinheit, Gemeinschaft und Tradition* (Münster: Waxman Verlag, 2001), 80–81.
6. Artur Tabolov, *Oligarkh: Prestupleniya i raskayanie* (Moscow: EKSMO, 2008); cited in Boris V. Rodionov, *Bol'shoi obman: Pravda i lozh' o russkoi vodke (Grand Deception: Truth and Lies about Russian Vodka)* (Moscow: Izdatel'stvo AST, 2011), 58–63.
7. Vilyam Vasilevich Pokhlebkin, *Istoriya vodki* (Moscow: Tsentpoligraf, 2000), 11–15. On Stolichnaya and Pepsi see Charles Levinson, *Vodka Cola* (London: Gordon & Cremonesi, 1978), 94; Vladislav Kovalenko, "Vodka—vse ravno chto vechnyi dvigatel'," *Kompaniya* 197, no. 1 (2002), http://ko.ru/articles/3858 (accessed Feb. 10, 2013); Igor Shumeiko, *10 mifov o russkoi vodke* (10 myths about Russian vodka) (Moscow: Yauza, 2009), 30–35.
8. Shumeiko, *10 mifov o russkoi vodke*, 35 (emphasis in original).
9. "Smert' kulinara: Vil'yam Pokhlebkin," http://www.rutv.ru/video.html?vid=39680&cid=5079&d=0.
10. Yuliya Azman and Oleg Fochkin, "Za chto ubili pisatelya Pokhlebkina?" *Moskovskii Komsomolets*, April 18, 2000; Aleksandr Evtushenko, "…A telo prolezhalo v kvartire tri nedeli," *Komsomol'skaya pravda*, April 21, 2000; "Ubit znamenityi geral'dist i kulinar," *Moskovskii Komsomolets*, April 15, 2000; James Meek, "The Story of Borshch," *The Guardian*, March 15, 2008.
11. Azman and Fochkin, "Za chto ubili pisatelya Pokhlebkina?"; "Smert' kulinara: Vil'yam Pokhlebkin," http://www.rutv.ru/video.html?vid=39680&cid=5079&d=0; Evtushenko, "…A telo prolezhalo v kvartire tri nedeli."
12. Viktor Erofeev, *Russkii apokalipsis: opyt khudozhestvennoi eskhatologii* (Moscow: Zebra E, 2008), 15; Victor Erofeyev, "The Russian God," *New Yorker*, Dec. 16, 2002.
13. "Smert' kulinara: Vil'yam Pokhlebkin," http://www.rutv.ru/video.html?vid=39680&cid=5079&d=0. Some sources that retell the Pokhlebkin case include Shumeiko, *10 mifov o russkoi vodke*, 34–35; Anatolii Sheipak, *Istoriya nauki i*

tekhniki: Materialy i tekhnologii, 2nd ed. (Moscow: Izdatel'stvo MGIU, 2009), 1:141; Mikhail Timofeev, *Rossiya: Nezavershennyi proekt* (Ivanovo: Ivanovskii Gos. Universitet, 2000), 34.

14. Aleksandra Verizhnikova, "Narodnyi kulinar Pokhlebkin," *Vechernyaya Moskva*, April 22, 2003.

15. See, for instance, Nicholas Ermochkine and Peter Iglikowski, *40 Degrees East: An Anatomy of Vodka* (Hauppauge, N.Y.: Nova, 2003), 42–43; Yurii Ivanov, *Kniga o vodke* (Smolensk: Rusich, 1997), 44; V. Z. Grigor'eva, *Vodka izvestnaya i neizvestnaya: XIV–XX veka* (Moscow: Enneagon, 2007), 6–8; Sergei Romanov, *Istoriya russkoi vodki* (Moscow: Veche, 1998), 29; Vitalii Krichevskii, *Russian vodka: Pis'ma moemu shveitsarskomu drugu* (St. Petersburg: Dean, 2002), 7–13; Vladimir Nikolaev, *Vodka v sud'be Rossii* (Moscow: Parad, 2004), 148–49; V. B. Aksenov, *Veselie Rusi, XX vek: Gradus noveishei rossiiskoi istorii ot 'p'yanogo byudzheta' do 'sukhogo zakona'* (Moscow: Probel-2000, 2007); Gennadii M. Karagodin, *Kniga o vodke i vinodelii* (Chelyabinsk: Ural, 2000), 44; Vadim V. Zolotaryov, *Pod znakom orla i lebedya* (Moscow: Krugozor-Nauka, 2003), 14–16.

16. David Christian, "Review: A History of Vodka by William Pokhlebkin," *Slavic Review* 53, no. 1 (1994): 245.

17. Pokhlebkin, *Istoriya vodki*, 55, 118–19; Rodionov, *Bol'shoi obman*, 152. In this context Pokhlebkin is speaking of a Genoese diplomatic delegation to Moscow in the year 1429 (mistranslated as 1426 in the English version, p. 57) to the court of "Vasily III Temnyi." In the 1420s, Muscovy was ruled by Vasily II Temnyi, so the difference between "II" and "III" appears to be a typo in the original Russian. However, the English translation drops the "the Blind" to suggest that "the Genoese displayed further samples of *aqua vitae* to the court of Vasily III" (p. 57). Additional errors include (p. 55) dating a Genoese visit to Moscow to 1386, citing Gavriil Uspenskii, *Opyt povestvovaniya o drevnostyakh russkikh*, 2 vols. (Kharkov: Tipografiya Imperatorskago Khar'kovskago Universiteta, 1818), 78. Unfortunately, Uspensky provides no such date, only mentioning that the Genoese fled an invasion in 1389. Perhaps accordingly, in his chronology, Pokhlebkin (p. 298) dates the Genoese arrival as "1386–1398." Rodionov also enumerates Pokhlebkin's errors in terms of chemical composition and history of the distillation process. See Rodionov, *Bol'shoi obman*, 23–33.

18. Christian, "Review: *A History of Vodka* by William Pokhlebkin," 256. Similar accusations were made by Rodionov, though it appears that Rodionov never read Christian's review. Rodionov, *Bol'shoi obman*, 80.

19. The documentary is available at http://www.rutv.ru/video.html?tvpreg_id=101763&cid=5 079&d=0&mid=14.

20. See the PCA case list at http://www.pca-cpa.org/upload/files/Consolidated%20Annexes. pdf; the ICJ case list at http://www.icj-cij.org/docket/index.php?p1=3&p2=2 (accessed Jan. 11, 2011).

21. Peter Maggs. Personal correspondence with author. Nov. 13, 2010.

22. Howard A. Tyner, "Poles Say They Made Vodka First," *Chicago Tribune*, Feb. 1, 1978, 4; "Vodka Credit Goes to Poles," *Hartford Courant*, Aug. 25 1970, 16. On the legal disputes over champagne, cognac, etc., see Alfred Phillip Knoll, "Champagne," *International and Comparative Law Quarterly* 19, no. 2 (1970).

23. We enlisted the help of researchers both at the Library of Congress and the Law Library of Congress, yet all of their findings referred back to Pokhlebkin's unsubstantiated claims. *Pravda* and *Izvestiya* archives provided by EastView.

24. Rodionov, *Bol'shoi obman*, 6, 64–66. Many thanks to Adrianne Jacobs for bringing Rodionov's recent work to my attention, even late in the final stages of review and revision.

25. Kovalenko, "Vodka."

26. The present-day Hotel Moskva on Manezh Square across from the Kremlin in Moscow is a replica of the original hotel built in the 1930s, which stood on the same site. The new Moskva even reproduces the noteworthy merging of two separate architectural styles. Viewing the hotel from Manezh Square, the ornate edifice and rounded-top windows of the left protrusion are completely different from the square, simpler edifice on the right side. The most popular explanation faults architect Alexei Shchusev for submitting to Stalin two alternative blueprints side by side with a line down the middle to distinguish the different styles. Apparently not realizing that he was being asked to choose, Stalin simply signed off on the

plans. Fearing the consequences of second-guessing Stalin, the architects and builders simply built the structure as he authorized. The presence of the Moskva on the Stoli label is
reportedly attributable to Lavrenti Beria himself. Aleksandr Nikishin, *Vodka i Gorbachev*
(Moscow: Vsya Rossiya, 2007), 51.

27. Peter Maggs. Personal correspondence with author. Nov. 13, 2010. See also Michael
Blakeney, "Proposals for the International Regulation of Geographical Indications," *Journal
of World Intellectual Property* 4, no. 5 (2001). This is not to be confused with more recent
disputes (the so-called vodka war of 2006) within the European Union over what *ingredients*
of distillation beyond the traditional grains and potatoes can legally be classified as vodka.
See Dan Bilefsky, "A Spirited War: The Search for the Real Vodka," *New York Times*, Nov.
23, 2006, http://www.nytimes.com/2006/11/23/world/europe/23iht-vodka.3648566.
html (accessed Oct. 18, 2010.) The so-called Schnellhardt compromise (after the German
rapporteur) now states that products made from something other than traditional grains or
potatoes must be clearly labeled as "vodka produced from…" European Parliament, "Vodka
War May Soon Be at an End" (June 26, 2007). http://www.europarl.europa.eu/sides/get-
Doc.do?language=EN&type=IM-PRESS&reference=20070131STO02626 (accessed Oct.
24, 2010).

28. Peter Maggs. Personal correspondence with author. Nov. 13, 2010.

29. See The Truth about Vodka in Black & White, http://www.vodkasobieski.com/2010/the_
truth.php (accessed Oct. 26, 2010). On Polish vodka history see Hillel Levine, "Gentry, Jews,
and Serfs: The Rise of Polish Vodka," *Review (Fernand Braudel Center)* 4, no. 2 (1980): 223.
The Polish Spirits Industry association (Polski Przemysł Spirytusowy) claims that the word
vodka first appeared in court documents dated 1405 from the Palatinate of Sandomierz reg-
istry; see http://www.pps.waw.pl/9,43,55_history_of_polish_vodka.html (accessed Oct.
26, 2010); see also Exposition Universaelle des Vins et Spir023itueux, "About Vodka," http://
www.euvs.org/en/collection/spirits/vodka (accessed Oct. 26, 2010); "Vodka Credit Goes
to Poles"; Tyner, "Poles Say They Made Vodka First."

30. Richard Pipes, *Russia under the Old Regime* (New York: Charles Scribner's Sons, 1974),
157. On pot stills see David Christian, *Living Water: Vodka and Russian Society on the Eve of
Emancipation* (Oxford: Clarendon, 1990), 26. On the Mongolian still see Joseph Needham,
*Science and Civilisation in China, vol. 5: Chemistry and Chemical Technology, pt. 4: Spagyrical
Discovery and Invention: Apparatus, Theories and Gifts* (New York: Cambridge University
Press, 1980), 48–62. On skepticism see George Snow, "Vodka," in *Alcohol and Temperance in
Modern History: An International Encyclopedia*, ed. Jack S. Blocker Jr., David M. Fahey, and Ian
R. Tyrrell (Oxford: ABC-CLIO, 2003), 2:636.

31. See Yu. I. Bobryshev et al., *Istoriya vinokureniya, prodazhi pitei, aktsiznoi politiki Rusi i Rossii
v arkheologicheskikh nakhodkakh i dokumentakh XII–XIX vv.* (Moscow: Krugozor-nauka,
2004), 37–41; Zolotaryov, *Pod znakom orla i lebedya*, 34–35.

32. Jos Schaeken, Leiden University, the Netherlands, personal correspondence with the
author, Oct. 24, 2010. On the present interpretation of *vodja* as alluding to marriage see
A. A. Zaliznyak, *Drevnenovgorodskii dialekt*, 2nd ed. (Moscow: Yazyki slavyanskoi kul'tury,
2004). On birchbark linguistic study see Jos Schaeken, "Line-Final Word Division in Rusian
Birchbark Documents," *Russian Linguistics* 19, no. 1 (1995); Willem Vermeer, "Towards a
Thousand Birchbark Letters," *Russian Linguistics* 19, no. 1 (1995). Unfortunately, Rodionov's
criticism of the Bobryshev et al. myth is far gentler than his handling of Pokhlebkin. See
Boris V. Rodionov, *Istoriya russkoi vodki ot polugara do nashikh dnei* (Moscow: Eksmo, 2011),
278–80, and *Bol'shoi obman*, 77–80.

33. Brian Hayden, Neil Canuel, and Jennifer Shanse, "What Was Brewing in the Natufian?
An Archaeological Assessment of Brewing Technology in the Epipaleolithic," *Journal of
Archaeological Method and Theory* 20, no. 1 (2013): 102–4; Maggie Fox, "At 6,000 Years
Old, Wine Press Is Oldest yet Found," *Reuters*, Jan. 11 2011, http://www.reuters.com/
article/idUSTRE70A0XS20110111 (accessed Jan. 11, 2011); Patrick E. McGovern, *Ancient
Wine: The Search for the Origins of Viniculture* (Princeton, N.J.: Princeton University Press,
2003). As I note elsewhere, paeans for temperance are almost as old as the discovery of alcohol itself. Mark Lawrence Schrad, "The First Social Policy: Alcohol Control and Modernity
in Policy Studies," *Journal of Policy History* 19, no. 4 (2007): 438.

34. The eighty-proof standard is often attributed to nineteenth-century Russian chemist, inventor, and founder of the periodic table of elements Dmitry Mendeleyev. Erofeyev, "The Russian God." Rodionov, however, suggests that even this is a false reading of history that has been elevated to the status of legend. Rodionov, *Bol'shoi obman*, 12–13, 348–70.

35. Bruce T. Moran, *Distilling Knowledge: Alchemy, Chemistry, and the Scientific Revolution* (Cambridge, Mass.: Harvard University Press, 2005), 12.

36. R. J. Forbes, *A Short History of the Art of Distillation: From the Beginnings up to the Death of Cellier*, 2nd ed. (Leiden: E. J. Brill, 1970), 57.

37. Ibid., 60–61; Uspenskii, *Opyt povestvovaniya o drevnostyakh ruskikh*, 1:77; Hugh Johnson, *Vintage: The Story of Wine* (New York: Simon & Schuster, 1989), 2:126.

38. Edward Gildemeister and Fr. Hoffman, *The Volatile Oils*, trans. Edward Kremers, 2nd ed. (New York: John Wiley & Sons, 1913), 1:30. Also see Rodionov, *Istoriya russkoi vodki*, 44.

39. Edward Gibbon Wakefield, *An Account of Ireland, Statistical and Political*, 2 vols. (London: Longman, Hurst, Rees, Orme & Brown, 1812), 1:727–28; Forbes, *Short History of the Art of Distillation*, 101.

40. Donald MacGillivray Nicol, *The Last Centuries of Byzantium, 1261–1453*, 2nd ed. (New York: Cambridge University Press, 1993).

41. Charles King, *The Black Sea: A History* (New York: Oxford University Press, 2004), 86; H. Sutherland Edwards, "Food and Drink," in *Russia as Seen and Described by Famous Writers*, ed. Esther Singleton (New York: Dodd, Mead & Co., 1906), 261–62.

42. Edwards, "Food and Drink," 261; Pero Tafur, *Travels and Adventures, 1435–1439* (London: RoutledgeCurzon, 2005), 134; Ivan Pryzhov, *Istoriya kabakov v Rossii* (Moscow: Molodiya sily, 1914), 44.

43. James Billington, *The Icon and the Axe: An Interpretive History of Russian Culture* (New York: Alfred A. Knopf, 1966), 86. Likewise, see N. A. Bogoyavlenskii, *Drevnerusskoe vrachevanie v XI–XVII vv.* (Moscow: Gosudarstvennoe izdatel'stvo meditsinskoi literatury medgiz, 1960), 81.

44. Pokhlebkin, *Istoriya vodki*, 55, 118–19. This highlights further factual errors in Pokhlebkin's account: Pokhlebkin (p. 55) dates the Genoese visit to Moscow to 1386, citing Uspensky's *Opyt povestvovaniya*, p. 78. Unfortunately, Uspensky provides no such date, only mentioning that the Genoese fled an invasion in 1389. Perhaps accordingly, in his chronology of alcohol, Pokhlebkin (p. 298) dates the Genoese arrival as "1386–1398." Furthermore, Pokhlebkin (p. 119) claims there was another Genoese diplomatic delegation to Lithuania in 1429. The English translation of Pokhlebkin's *A History of Vodka* (p. 57) mistakenly cites the date as 1426. See also note 17 above.

45. King, *Black Sea*, 100; Pokhlebkin, *Istoriya vodki*, 120. Here too there are discrepancies between Pokhlebkin's Russian text and the English translation: the former has the conquest of Kaffa in 1395, and its incorporation into the Crimean Khanate of Girei in 1465, whereas the latter merges the conquest and incorporation into a single event, deleting any mention of 1465. R. E. F. Smith and David Christian are skeptical that a trade in alcoholic beverages would have been permitted via this route following the the conversion of the Tatars to Islam in 1389—the *knowledge* of distillation, however, is another matter. R. E. F. Smith and David Christian, *Bread and Salt: A Social and Economic History of Food and Drink in Russia* (New York: Cambridge University Press, 1984), 88.

46. Billington, *Icon and the Axe*, 86.

47. Erofeyev, "The Russian God"; Erofeev, *Russkii apokalipsis*, 15. Here again we find more Pokhlebkin misinformation regarding the legend: suggesting Isidore was held under the command of Vasily III (pp. 163–64, Russian; pp. 83–84, English), apparently meaning Vasily II, since Vasily III—again—did not rule until 1503 (see note 17 above). In the end, even Pokhlebkin dismisses the legend. Pokhlebkin, *Istoriya vodki*, 163–64. Others who present the legend as fact include Sergei I. Shubin, *Severnyi vektor politiki Rossii: Problemy i perspektivy* (Arkhangel'sk: Pomorskii universitet, 2006), 190; Krichevskii, *Russian vodka*, 76; Anthony Dias Blue, *The Complete Book of Spirits: A Guide to Their History, Production, and Enjoyment* (New York: HarperCollins, 2004), 13; Bob Emmons, *The Book of Gins and Vodkas: A Complete Guide* (Peru, Ill.: Open Court Publishing, 1999), 101–2; Karagodin, *Kniga o vodke i vinodelii*, 44.

48. Anna L. Khoroshkevich, *Torgovlya Velikogo Novgoroda s Pribaltikoi i zapadnoi Evropoi v XIV–XV vekakh* (Moscow: Izdatel'stvo akademii nauk SSSR, 1963), 323–32; Smith and Christian, *Bread and Salt*, 88–89.

49. Rodionov, *Istoriya russkoi vodki*, 266.

50. Grigor'eva, *Vodka izvestnaya i neizvestnaya: XIV–XX veka*, 19. Another source of ongoing confusion in the history of vodka concerns the use of the word *vino*, which translates as *wine* but was often used in reference to grain-based distilled alcohol—vodka—rather than wine. Christian, *Living Water*, 26. Rodionov's central thesis is that early distilled "burnt wine" and *polugar* were substantively distinct from "modern" rectified vodka, which emerges only with Sergei Witte's vodka monopoly in 1895. Rodionov, *Bol'shoi obman*, 394–410; Rodionov, *Istoriya russkoi vodki*, 13–33.

Chapter 7

1. One noteworthy recent exception is Oliver Bullough, *The Last Man in Russia: The Struggle to Save a Dying Nation* (New York: Basic Books, 2013), who sees the roots of Russian intemperance in the post–World War II Soviet political system.

2. Charles de Secondat Montesquieu, *Esprit De Lois* (Paris: Libraire de firmin didot freres, 1856), 194.

3. William Hepworth Dixon, *Free Russia*, 2 vols. (Leipzig: Berhard Tauchnitz, 1872), 1:254. Similar notions can be found in the works of novelist Nikolai Gogol; see Lady Frances Verney, "Rural Life in Russia," in *Russia as Seen and Described by Famous Writers*, ed. Esther Singleton (New York: Dodd, Mead & Co., 1906), 247. See also D. MacKenzie Wallace, *Russia* (New York: Henry Holt & Co., 1877), 98.

4. Dar'ya A. Khalturina and Andrei V. Korotaev, "Vvedeniye: Alkogol'naya katastrofa: kak ostanovit' vymiranie Rossii," in *Alkogol'naya katastrofa i vozmozhnosti gosudarstvennoi politiki v preodolenii alkogol'noi sverkosmertnosti v Rossii*, ed. Dar'ya A. Khalturina and Andrei V. Korotaev (Moscow: Lenand, 2010), 24–25; Frank Jacobs, "442—Distilled Geography: Europe's Alcohol Belts," Strange Maps (blog), Jan. 30, 2010, http://bigthink. com/ideas/21495 (accessed Feb. 23, 2010). The term "geoalcoholics" is borrowed from Alex De Jonge, *Stalin and the Shaping of the Soviet Union* (New York: Morrow, 1986), 19–20.

5. The first Russian vineyards were planted in Astrakhan on the Caspian Sea in 1613, beginning a modest domestic trade in wine. H. Sutherland Edwards, "Food and Drink," in *Russia as Seen and Described by Famous Writers*, ed. Esther Singleton (New York: Dodd, Mead & Co., 1906), 260–61; Igor Smirennyi, Ivan Gorbunov, and Sergei Zaitsev, *Pivo Rossiiskoi Imperii* (Moscow: Ayaks, 1998), 9–14; Stanislav I. Smetanin and Mikhail V. Konotopov, *Razvitie promyshlennosti v krepostnoi Rossii* (Moscow: Akademicheskii proect, 2001), 169–71.

6. Nathan Haskell Dole, *Young Folks' History of Russia* (New York: Saalfield Publishing Co., 1903), 108.

7. The ninth-century Arabian traveler Ahmad Beh-Fodhlan Ibn al Abbas Ben-Assam Ben-Hammad even described the ubiquity of alcohol and drunkenness in Russian pagan rituals. Dole, *Young Folks' History of Russia*, 52.

8. Ivan Pryzhov, *Istoriya kabakov v Rossii* (Moscow: Molodiya sily, 1914), 10; Horace Lunt, "Food in the Rus' Primary Chronicle," in *Food in Russian History and Culture*, ed. Musya Glants and Joyce Toomre (Bloomington: Indiana University Press, 1997), 24.

9. René J. Dubos, *Pasteur and Modern Science*, ed. Thomas D. Brock (Washington, D.C.: American Society for Microbiology Press, 1998), 54–60.

10. See, for instance, Ernest H. Cherrington, ed., *Standard Encyclopedia of the Alcohol Problem*, 6 vols. (Westerville, Ohio: American Issue, 1926), 3:910–39.

11. "Flavored Vodka Fuels Vodka Volume and Sales," *Reuters*, Oct. 11, 2012, http://www. reuters.com/article/2012/10/11/idUS149559+11-Oct-2012+PRN20121011 (accessed Feb. 13, 2013).

12. Victor Erofeyev, "The Russian God," *New Yorker* Dec. 16, 2002; Viktor Erofeev, *Russkii apokalipsis: Opyt khudozhestvennoi eskhatologii* (Moscow: Zebra E, 2008), 19–20. Similarly, see Selina Bunbury, *Russia after the War*, 2 vols. (London: Hurst & Blackett, 1857), 2:156–57; Andrei Makarevich, *Zanimatel'naya narkologiya* (Moscow: Makhaon, 2005), 9–10.

13. Vladimir P. Nuzhnyi, *Vino v zhizni i zhizn' v vine* (Moscow: Sinteg, 2001), 15–16.

14. David Christian, *Living Water: Vodka and Russian Society on the Eve of Emancipation* (Oxford: Clarendon, 1990), 25.

15. George Vernadsky, "Feudalism in Russia," *Speculum* 14, no. 3 (1939): 301; K. V. Bazilevich, *Gorodskie vosstaniia v Moskovskom gosudarstve XVII v.: Sbornik dokumentov* (Moscoe: Gosudarstvennoe sotsial'no-ekonomicheskoe izdatel'stvo, 1936), 39–40; Richard Hellie, "Early Modern Russian Law: The Ulozhenie of 1649," *Russian History* 2, no. 4 (1988). On the importance of history to drinking patterns see V. A. Terekhina, ed., *Profilaktika p'yanstva i alkogolizma* (Moscow: Yuridicheskaya literaturna, 1983), 28.

16. This section draws largely from Christian, *Living Water*, 26–33; Pryzhov, *Istoriya kabakov v Rossii*, 27–40.

17. Rodionov suggests that this early distilled *polugar* was fundamentally different from "modern" rectified vodka, which he dates from 1895. Boris V. Rodionov, *Istoriya russkoi vodki ot polugara do nashikh dnei* (Moscow: Eksmo, 2011), 43–81. To avoid confusion I will refer to both distilled and rectified products as vodka.

18. Boris V. Rodionov, *Bol'shoi obman: Pravda i lozh' o russkoi vodke* (Moscow: Izdatel'stvo AST, 2011), 413; William Blackwell, *The Beginnings of Russian Industrialization: 1800–1860* (Princeton, N.J.: Princeton University Press, 1968), 26.

19. Vilyam Pokhlebkin, *Istoriya vodki (A History of Vodka)* (Moscow: Tsentpoligraf, 2000), 100. This becomes one of Pokhlebkin's arguments for the timing of vodka's birth, as the prosperity of the three-field system gave rise to vodka production, or vice versa. Ibid., 144, 51–54. Distilling as a primary link between state formation and economic prosperity has been borne out in historical comparison. Charles van Onselen, "Randlords and Rotgut 1886–1903: An Essay on the Role of Alcohol in the Development of European Imperialism and Southern African Capitalism, with Special Reference to Black Mineworkers in the Transvaal Republic," *History Workshop* 1, no. 2 (1976).

20. Boris Segal, *Russian Drinking: Use and Abuse of Alcohol in Pre-Revolutionary Russia* (New Brunswick, N.J.: Rutgers Center of Alcohol Studies, 1987), 30; Paul Bushkovitch, "Taxation, Tax Farming and Merchants in Sixteenth-Century Russia," *Slavic Review* 37, no. 3 (1978): 391.

21. Giles Fletcher, *Of the Russe Commonwealth: 1591*, facsimile ed. (Cambridge, Mass.: Harvard University Press, 1966), 43–44. The Russian novelist Alexei Tolstoi presents a remarkably similar description in *Petr Pervyi* (Kishinev: Kartya Moldovenyaske, 1970), 22.

22. On torture in early imperial Russia see Jean Chappe d'Auteroche, *Voyage en Sibérie, fait par ordre du roi en 1761, contenant les Mœurs, les Usages des Russes, & l'État actuel de cette Puissance; &c.* (Amsterdam: Marc Michel Rey, 1769), 193–94; Edward Peters, *Torture*, expanded ed. (Philadelphia: University of Pennsylvania Press, 1996), 95–96.

23. Samuel H. Baron, ed., *The Travels of Olearius in Seventeenth-Century Russia* (Palo Alto, Calif.: Stanford University Press, 1967), 198, 42.

24. Ibid., 144.

25. Christian, *Living Water*, 30–31, 39. See also Mikhail E. Saltykov, *Tchinovnicks: Sketches of Provincial Life, from the Memoirs of the Retired Conseiller de Cour Stchedrin (Saltikow)*, trans. Frederic Aston (London: L. Booth, 1861), 99. On indirect rule and Russian internal colonization see Alexander Etkind, *Internal Colonization: Russia's Imperial Experience* (Malden, Mass.: Polity, 2011), 145.

26. This is largely in line with Etkind's thesis on the state's "internal colonization" of early Russia. Etkind, *Internal Colonization*, 65. See also Mikhail Ya Volkov, *Ocerki istorii promyslov Rossii vtoraya polovina XVII–pervaya polovina XVIII v.* (Moscow: Nauka, 1979), 25–27; Richard Hellie, *Economy and Material Culture of Russia, 1600–1725* (Chicago: University of Chicago Press, 1999), 106; Christian, *Living Water*, 33, 36, 47.

27. McKee quoted in Richard Weitz, "Russia: Binge Drinking and Sudden Death," Eurasianet. org, Dec. 15, 2010, http://www.eurasianet.org/node/62577 (accessed Dec. 17, 2010). See also http://csis.org/event/new-insights-catastrophic-level-mortality-russian-men.

28. Iosaphat Barbaro, "Viaggio alla Tana," in *Barbaro i kontarini o Rossii: K istorii italo-russkikh svyazei v XV v.*, ed. Elizaveta Ch. Skrzhinskaya (Leningrad: Nauka, 1971), 133; V. Z. Grigor'eva, *Vodka izvestnaya i neizvestnaya: XIV–XX veka* (Moscow: Enneagon, 2007), 16.

29. Ambrogio Contarini, "Viaggio in Persia," in *Barbaro i kontarini o Rossii: K istorii italo-russkikh svyazei v XV v.*, ed. Elizaveta Ch. Skrzhinskaya (Leningrad: Nauka, 1971), 204–5.

30. Vladimir B. Bezgin, "Alkogol' v obydennoi zhizni russkogo sela (konets XIX–nachalo XX v.," *NB: Problemy obshchestva i politiki*, no. 3 (2013). http://www.e-notabene.ru/pr/article_549.html (accessed July 15, 2013). David Christian, "Traditional and Modern Drinking Cultures in Russia on the Eve of Emancipation," *Australian Slavonic and East European Studies* 1, no. 1 (1987): 66–67; R. E. F. Smith and David Christian, *Bread and Salt: A Social and Economic History of Food and Drink in Russia* (New York: Cambridge University Press, 1984), 84–85; Vera Efron, "Russia, Yesterday," in *Drinking and Intoxication: Selected Readings in Social Attitudes and Controls*, ed. Raymond G. McCarthy (New Haven, Conn.: Yale Center of Alcohol Studies, 1959), 131.

31. Quoted in: Paul Bushkovitch, "The Epiphany Ceremony of the Russian Court in the Sixteenth and Seventeenth Centuries," *Russian Review* 49, no. 1 (1990): 12–13.

32. Segal, *Russian Drinking*, 47–48.

33. Sergei M. Soloviev, *History of Russia, vol. 12: Russian Society under Ivan the Terrible*, trans. T. Allan Smith (Gulf Breeze, Fla.: Academic International, 1996), 211. The *Domostroi* also stipulated that women "must be preserved from intoxicating beverages" and only drink nonalcoholic beers and *kvas*. Ibid., 208–9. See also Grigor'eva, *Vodka izvestnaya i neizvestnaya: XIV–XX veka*, 18.

34. Carolyn Pouncy, *The "Domostroi": Rules for Russian Households in the Time of Ivan the Terrible* (Ithaca, N.Y.: Cornell University Press, 1994), 157.

35. Soloviev, *History of Russia*, vol. 12: *Russian Society under Ivan the Terrible*, 70. Similar practices were noted by Adam Olearius during his visits in the 1630s. Baron, ed., *Travels of Olearius in Seventeenth-Century Russia*, 270.

36. Samuel Collins, *The Present State of Russia, in a Letter to a Friend at London; Written by an Eminent Person Residing at the Great Czars Court at Mosco for the Space of Nine Years* (London: John Winter, 1671), 23–24. On the *Zemskii Prikaz* see John P. LeDonne, *Absolutism and Ruling Class: The Formation of the Russian Political Order, 1700–1825* (New York: Oxford University Press, 1991), 121–28.

37. Quoted in Erofeev, *Russkii apokalipsis*, 21. On Coyet see also Bushkovitch, "Epiphany Ceremony of the Russian Court."

38. Wallace, *Russia*, 98. See also Selina Bunbury, *Russia after the War*, 2 vols. (London: Hurst & Blackett, 1857), 1:102–3; Eustace Clare Grenville Murray, *The Russians of To-Day* (London: Smith, Elder & Co., 1878), 16; Georg Brandes, *Impressions of Russia*, trans. Samuel C. Eastman (Boston: C. J. Peters & Son, 1889), 39. Famed dramatist Anton Chekov depicts similar scenes in fiction: Anton Chekhov, "Peasants," in *The Oxford Chekhov*, ed. Robert Hingley (New York: Oxford University Press, 1965), 217–18.

39. Baron, *Travels of Olearius in Seventeenth-Century Russia*, 145. Similarly, see Collins, *Present State of Russia*, 19.

40. Esther Singleton, ed., *Russia as Seen and Described by Famous Writers* (New York: Dodd, Mead & Co., 1906), 249–50. I changed *Vodki* to vodka.

41. A. Preobrazhenskii, "Volost' Pokrovsko-Sitskaya Yaroslavskoi gubernii Molozhskago uezda," in *Etnograficheskii sbornik*, ed. Imperatorskoe russkoe geograficheskoe obshchestvo (St. Petersburg: Tipografiya Ministerstva vnutrennikh del, 1853–1864), 103–4; quoted in Christian, *Living Water*, 77. Similar vodka indoctrination persisted through the Soviet period. Gordon B. Smith, *Reforming the Russian Legal System* (New York: Cambridge University Press, 1996), 47. See also chapters 16 and 17.

42. Andrei P. Zablotskii-Desyatovskii, "O krepostnom sostoyanii," in *Graf P. D. Kiselev i ego vremya: Materialy dlya istorii Imperatorov Aleksandr I-go, Nikolaya I-go, i Aleksandra II* (St. Petersburg: Tipografiya M. M. Stasyulkvicha, 1882), 312. Many thanks to David Christian for this reference.

43. Cited in Christian, *Living Water*, 76.

44. Grant Podelco, "Holiday Sobriety: 'There Is No Worse Enemy for a Russian Than Himself'," Radio Free Europe/Radio Liberty, Dec. 28, 2012, http://www.rferl.org/content/russia-alcohol-vodka-holiday-smoking—drinking-abuse/24811093.html (accessed Jan. 2, 2013). See also Associated Press, "In Russia, New Year's Celebrations Last 10 Days," National Public

Radio, Jan. 7, 2011, http://www.npr.org/templates/story/story.php?storyId=132733640 (accessed Jan. 8, 2011); Agence France-Presse, "Russians Advised to Celebrate Dry New Year Holiday," *Inquirer.net*, Jan. 2, 2011, http://www.inquirer.net/mindandbody/health-beat/view.php?db=1&article=20110102-312131 (accessed Jan. 3, 2011).

45. Paul Goble, "Drunkenness a 'More Terrible' Threat to Russia Than Terrorism, Moscow Psychiatrist Says," Window on Eurasia (blog), Dec. 19, 2009, http://windowoneurasia.blogspot.com/2009/12/window-on-eurasia-drunkenness-more.html; Artem Serikov, "Pochemu P'yanstvo Strashnee Terrora?" WIN.ru (blog), Dec. 18, 2009, http://www.win.ru/topic/3053.phtml (both accessed Dec. 20, 2009). One could also add *pominki*, the remembrance service forty days after the passing of a love one, which was likewise "accompanied by great debauchery." J. M. Buckley, *The Midnight Sun, the Tsar and the Nihilist* (Boston: D. Lothrop & Co., 1886), 302.

46. Baron August Freiherr Haxthausen, *The Russian Empire: Its People, Institutions, and Resources*, trans. Robert Faire, 2 vols. (London: Chapman & Hall, 1856), 2:175. On *zapoi* see also David A. Leon, Vladimir M. Shkolnikov, and Martin McKee, "Alcohol and Russian Mortality: A Continuing Crisis," *Addiction* 104, no. 10 (2009): 1631–34; David A. Leon et al., "Hazardous Alcohol Drinking and Premature Mortality in Russia: A Population Based Case-Control Study," *The Lancet*, June 16, 2007, 2002–4; Nikolai G. Chernyshevskii, "Otkupnaya sistema (Sovremennik, 1858)," in *Izbrannye ekonomichesie proizvedeniya*, tom 1 (Moscow: Gosudarstvennoe izdatel'stvo politicheskoi literatury, 1948), 678.

47. E. Protas'ev, "O poroke, svoistvennom krest'yanam i prepyatstvuyushchem uluchsheniyu ikh byta," *Zhurnal zemlevladel'tsa* 9, no. 6 (1858): 7; translation in Christian, "Traditional and Modern Drinking Cultures in Russia on the Eve of Emancipation," 76; see also ibid., 62–63.

48. Murray, *Russians of To-Day*, 34–35.

49. Luigi Villari, *Russia under the Great Shadow* (New York: James Pott & Co., 1905), 231; Christian, *Living Water*, 95–96.

50. Pokhlebkin, *Istoriya vodki*, 104.

51. Christian, *Living Water*, 36; Etkind, *Internal Colonization*, 145–46.

52. Nikolai I. Pavlenko, "K voprosu Ob evolyutsii dvorianstva v XVII–XVIII vv," in *Voprosy genezisa kapitalizma v Rossii*, ed. Vladimir V. Mavrodin (Leningrad: Leningrad Universitet, 1960), 61–65.

53. Christian, *Living Water*, 37; van Onselen, "Randlords and Rotgut."

54. Christian, *Living Water*, 47.

Chapter 8

1. Julia Ioffe, "The End of Putin: Alexey Navalny on Why the Russian Protest Movement Will Win," *Foreign Policy*, Dec. 28, 2011, http://www.foreignpolicy.com/articles/2011/12/28/the_end_of_putin (accessed Jan. 1, 2012).

2. Carol J. Williams, "Russia Set to Make Olympic History—for Spending, Controversy," *Los Angeles Times*, Feb. 9 2013, http://www.latimes.com/news/world/worldnow/la-fg-wn-russia-olympics-costs-controversy-20130208,0,2858111.story (accessed Feb. 13, 2013). Julia Ioffe, "Net Impact: One Man's Cyber-Crusade against Russian Corruption," *New Yorker*, April 4, 2011, http://www.newyorker.com/reporting/2011/04/04/110404fa_fact_ioffe#ixzz1hrtTCJaa (accessed Jan. 1, 2012); Transparency International, "Corruption Perceptions Index, 2012," http://cpi.transparency.org/cpi2012/results (accessed Feb. 13, 2013); Friedrich Schneider, Andreas Buehn, and Claudio E. Montenegro, *Shadow Economies All over the World: New Estimates for 162 Countries from 1999 to 2007*, World Bank Policy Research Working Paper No. 5356 (Washington, D.C.: World Bank: 2010): 29.

3. Alena V. Ledeneva, *Can Russia Modernise? Sistema, Power Networks and Informal Governance* (New York: Cambridge University Press, 2013), 19–25; "57% Rossiian schitaiut narkomaniiu pervostepennoi' problemoi'," *Rossiiskaya gazeta*, Nov. 8, 2010, 13; Gregory Feifer, "Corruption in Russia, Part 2: Law Enforcers Often the Worst Offenders," Radio Free Europe/Radio Liberty, Nov. 28, 2009, http://www.rferl.org/articleprintview/1890104.html (accessed Oct. 22, 2010); Will Englund, "Russian Corruption Takes on a Life of Its

Own," *Washington Post*, Oct. 26, 2010, http://www.washingtonpost.com/wp-dyn/content/article/2010/10/26/AR2010102601429_pf.html.

4. See Mark Levin and Georgy Satarov, "Corruption and Institutions in Russia," *European Journal of Political Economy* 16, no. 1 (2000): 116; Andrei Shleifer and Robert W. Vishny, "Corruption," *Quarterly Journal of Economics* 108, no. 3 (1993): 615.

5. Leonid I. Brezhnev, "Otchetnyi dokad Tsentral'nago Komiteta KPSS, XVIV s'ezdu Kommunisticheskoi Partii Sovetskogo Soyuza. Doklad General'nogo sekretarya TsK tovarishcha L. I. Brezhneva, 30 marta 1971 goda," *Pravda*, March 31, 1971; Nikita Khrushchev, "Razvitie ekonomiki SSSR i partiinoe rukovodstvo narodnym khozyaistvom: Doklad tovarishcha N. S. Khrushcheva na plenume TsK KPSS 19 noyabrya 1962 goda," *Pravda*, Nov. 20 1962.

6. Steven Staats, "Corruption in the Soviet System," *Problems of Communism* 21 (Jan.–Feb. 1972): 47. *Kasha* is a traditional Russian cereal or porridge commonly made from buckwheat. See also Hedrick Smith, *The Russians* (New York: Quadrangle/New York Times Book Co., 1976), 120.

7. Samuel M. Smucker, *The Life and Reign of Nicholas the First, Emperor of Russia* (Philadelphia: J. W. Bradley, 1856); Petr A. Zaionchkovskii, *Pravitel'stvennyi apparat samoderzhavnoi Rossii v XIX v.* (Moscow: Mysl', 1978), 156.

8. This quote by President Dmitry Medvedev is in particular reference to Russia's "eternal corruption." Timothy Frye, "Corruption and Rule of Law," in *Russia after the Global Economic Crisis*, ed. Anders Åslund, Sergei Guriev, and Andrew Kuchins (Washington, D.C.: Peterson Institute for International Economics, 2010), 92.

9. Edward Crankshaw, *Russia without Stalin: The Emerging Pattern* (London: Viking, 1956), 74–75; Alena Ledeneva, Stephen Lovell, and Andrei Rogachevskii, "Introduction," in *Bribery and Blat in Russia: Negotiating Reciprocity from the Middle Ages to the 1990s*, ed. Stephen Lovell, Alena Ledeneva, and Andrei Rogachevskii (New York: St. Martin's, 2000), 5–9.

10. Leslie Palmier, "Bureaucratic Corruption and Its Remedies," in *Corruption: Causes, Consequences and Control*, ed. Michael Clarke (New York: St. Martin's, 1983), 207. Other commonly accepted definitions of corruption can be found in Joseph S. Nye, "Corruption and Political Development: A Cost-Benefit Analysis," *American Political Science Review* 61, no. 2 (1967): 421; Shleifer and Vishny, "Corruption," 599.

11. Samuel Collins, *The Present State of Russia, in a Letter to a Friend at London; Written by an Eminent Person Residing at the Great Czars Court at Mosco for the Space of Nine Years* (London: John Winter, 1671), 60. Similar numbers were reported by Olearius some four decades earlier. Samuel H. Baron, ed., *The Travels of Olearius in Seventeenth-Century Russia* (Palo Alto, Calif.: Stanford University Press, 1967), 198–99.

12. David Christian, *Living Water: Vodka and Russian Society on the Eve of Emancipation* (Oxford: Clarendon, 1990), 200. See also George Tennyson Matthews, *The Royal General Farms in Eighteenth-Century France* (New York: Columbia University Press, 1958), 11.

13. Linda T. Darling, *Revenue-Raising and Legitimacy* (Leiden: E. J. Brill, 1996), 119–20; Christian, *Living Water*, 31, 195. This section draws from *Living Water* and David Christian, "Vodka and Corruption in Russia on the Eve of Emancipation," *Slavic Review* 46, no. 3/4 (1987).

14. Paul Bushkovitch, "Taxation, Tax Farming and Merchants in Sixteenth-Century Russia," *Slavic Review* 37, no. 3 (1978): 390–91; Richard Pipes, *Russia under the Old Regime* (New York: Charles Scribner's Sons, 1974), 61; Christian, *Living Water*, 33.

15. Sergei M. Troitskii, *Finansovaia politika russkago absoliutizma v XVIII veke* (Moscow: Nauka, 1966), 214; Aleksandr P. Pogrebinskii, "Finansovaya reforma nachala 60-kh godov XIX veka v Rossii," *Voprosi istorii*, no. 10 (1951): 74–75, and *Ocherki istorii finanasov dorevolyutsionnoi Rossii (XIV–XX vv.)* (Moscow: Gosfinizdat, 1954), 99.

16. Mikhail E. Saltykov, *Tchinovnicks: Sketches of Provincial Life, from the Memoirs of the Retired Conseiller De Cour Stchedrin (Saltikow)*, trans. Frederic Aston (London: L. Booth, 1861), 97–98; Gordon B. Smith, *Reforming the Russian Legal System* (New York: Cambridge University Press, 1996), 12. On vodka revenues under Peter the Great see Friedrich Wilhelm von Bergholz, *Dnevnik kammer-iunkera Berkhgol'tsa, vedennyi im v Rossii v tsarstvovanie Petra*

Velikago, s 1721-1725-y god, trans. I. Ammon, 2nd ed. (Moscow: Tipograpfiya Katkova i Ko., 1858), 2:239.

17. Distillation was long a privilege reserved for the gentry, who sold their vodka to state wholesalers. Eustace Clare Grenville Murray, *The Russians of To-Day* (London: Smith, Elder & Co., 1878), 33.

18. "Koe chto ob otkupakh, *Kolokol* list 10, 1 marta 1858 g.," in *Kolokol: Gazeta A. I. Gertsena i N. P. Ogareva* (Moscow: Izdatel'stvo Akademii nauk SSSR, 1962), 79.

19. Vasilii A. Kokorev, "Ob otkupakh na prodazhu vina," *Russkii vestnik*, book 2, Sovremennaya letopis' (1858): 42; cited in Christian, "Vodka and Corruption," 481.

20. Christian, *Living Water*, 136.

21. *Ekonomicheskii ukazatel'* 41 (Oct. 1858); cited in Christian, "Vodka and Corruption," 473. See also Saltykov, *Tchinovnicks*, 98.

22. Zaionchkovskii, *Pravitel'stvennyi apparat*, 158; cited in Christian, "Vodka and Corruption," 474, 76.

23. Christian, *Living Water*, 150.

24. Gregory Feifer, "Corruption in Russia, Part 1: A Normal Part of Everyday Life," Radio Free Europe/Radio Liberty, Nov. 27, 2009, http://www.rferl.org/articleprintview/1889394.html (accessed Oct. 22, 2010).

25. *Russkii dnevnik*, no. 51 (March 7, 1859); cited in: Christian, "Vodka and Corruption," 482–83.

26. Quoted in Geoffrey Hosking, *Russia: People and Empire, 1552–1917* (Cambridge, Mass.: Harvard University Press, 1997), 104–5. On raiding roadside inns see *Svedeniia* 3:282; cited in Christian, "Vodka and Corruption," 483. On peasant extortion see Murray, *Russians of To-Day*, 31.

27. R. E. F. Smith and David Christian, *Bread and Salt: A Social and Economic History of Food and Drink in Russia* (New York: Cambridge University Press, 1984), 145.

28. "Koe chto ob otkupakh, *Kolokol* list 10, 1 marta 1858 g.," 79.

29. Ibid., 80. Natal'ya E. Goryushkina, " 'Imeyu chest' dolozhit', chot vzyatki polucheny': K voprosu ob otkupnom vzyatochnichestve v Rossii," in: *Alkogol' v Rossii: Materialy tret'ei mezhdunarodnoi nauchno-prakticheskoi konferentsii* (Ivanovo, 26-27 oktyabrya 2012), ed. Mikhail V. Teplyanskii (Ivanovo: Filial RGGU v g. Ivanovo, 2012), 127.

30. N. Herséwanoff, *Des Fermes d'eaux-de-vie en Russie (The Eaux-de-Vie Farms in Russia)* (Paris, Bonaventure: 1858), 22–23; cited in Christian, *Living Water*, 148.

31. This being one of Saltykov's favored euphemisms. Saltykov, *Tchinovnicks*, 95, 100.

32. *Svedeniya* 3:248; quoted in: Christian, *Living Water*, 136. For contemporary parallels see Ledeneva, *Can Russia Modernise?* 161.

33. *Svedeniya*, 1:35, from *Polnoe sobranie zakonov*, 2nd series, 12444; cited in Christian, *Living Water*, 106.

34. "Koe chto ob otkupakh, *Kolokol* list 10, 1 marta 1858 g.," 80.

35. Zaionchkovskii, *Pravitel'stvennyi apparat*, 155; cited in Christian, *Living Water*, 148–49.

36. Quote from "Koe chto ob otkupakh, *Kolokol* list 10, 1 marta 1858 g.," 80. On Nicolas's inquiry see Christian, *Living Water*, 154.

37. Alena Ledeneva, *How Russia Really Works: The Informal Practices That Shaped Post-Soviet Politics and Business* (Ithaca, N.Y.: Cornell University Press, 2006), 192.

38. V. Fedorovskii, "Podolsko-Vitebskii otkup," *Sovremennik* (1859), Mar. "Sovremennoe obozrenie," 1; cited in Christian, *Living Water*, 110. Tavern keeper regulations from 1841 can be found in ibid., 113. Also see Ivan Pryzhov, *Istoriya kabakov v Rossii* (Moscow: Molodiya sily, 1914), 59–74.

39. V. K— —ov, "Vopros o prodazhe vina," *Russkii mir*, no. 19 (May 15, 1859); cited in Christian, *Living Water*, 136. On "special vodkas" see *Vestnik promyshlennosti*, no.4 (Oct. 1858), 18; cited in Christian, "Vodka and Corruption," 481.

40. Hosking, *Russia*, 105.

41. Christian, *Living Water*, 62–63.

42. A. Korsak, "Nalogoi i vinnyi otkup," *Russkaya gazeta*, no. 9 (1858); cited in Christian, "Vodka and Corruption," 481–82.

43. Nikolai I. Turgenev, *Rossiya i russkie* (Moscow: Knigoizdatel'stvo K. F. Nekrasova, 1915), 212 Christian, *Living Water*, 114.

44. Baron August Freiherr Haxthausen, *The Russian Empire: Its People, Institutions, and Resources*, trans. Robert Faire, 2 vols. (London: Chapman & Hall, 1856), 2:408. See also H. Sutherland Edwards, "Russian Tea and Tea-Houses," in *Russia as Seen and Described by Famous Writers*, ed. Esther Singleton (New York: Dodd, Mead & Co., 1906), 277. Indeed, as Adam Olearius suggested in the mid-1600s, "the best cure among the common people…is vodka and garlic." Baron, *Travels of Olearius in Seventeenth-Century Russia*, 162.

45. Luigi Villari, *Russia under the Great Shadow* (New York: James Pott & Co., 1905), 169. See also Sergei Stepniak, *Russia under the Tzars* (New York: Charles Scribner's Sons, 1885), 20–21; Lady Frances Verney, "Rural Life in Russia," in *Russia as Seen and Described by Famous Writers*, ed. Esther Singleton (New York: Dodd, Mead & Co., 1906), 252. More generally see Alexander Etkind, *Internal Colonization: Russia's Imperial Experience* (Malden, Mass.: Polity, 2011), 145.

46. D. MacKenzie Wallace, *Russia* (New York: Henry Holt & Co., 1877), 541–42. See also Hosking, *Russia*, 209; Sir John Maynard, *The Russian Peasant and Other Studies* (New York: Collier Books, 1942), 66, 75.

47. Murray, *Russians of To-Day*, 24–26.

48. Stephen P. Frank, *Crime, Cultural Conflict, and Justice in Rural Russia, 1856–1914* (Berkeley: University of California Press, 1999), 213. On taking a sin on the soul see Wallace, *Russia*, 541–42. See also Hosking, *Russia*, 209. A stark parallel with the not-so-subtle influence of vodka on contemporary Russian jury trials can be found in the opening lines of Ellen Barry, "In Russia, Jury Is Something to Work Around," *New York Times*, Nov. 16, 2010, A1.

49. V. Polivanov, "Zapiski zemskogo nachal'nika," *Russkaya mysl'* 9–10 (1917): 32; cited in Frank, *Crime, Cultural Conflict, and Justice*, 213.

50. See f. 586, op. 1, d. 117, l.41; and f. 586, op. 1, d. 120, l.62, Gosudarstvennyi Arkhiv Rossiskoi Federatsii (GARF) (State archive of the Russian Federation), Moscow; cited in Frank, *Crime, Cultural Conflict, and Justice*, 213.

51. Frank, *Crime, Cultural Conflict, and Justice*, 221.

52. Sergei Stepniak, *The Russian Peasantry* (New York: Harper & Brothers, 1888), 202–5; similarly, see 176, 88.

53. Frank, *Crime, Cultural Conflict, and Justice*, 253–60; Stephen P. Frank, "Popular Justice, Community and Culture among the Russian Peasantry, 1870–1900," *Russian Review* 46, no. 3 (1987): 247–49.

54. Verney, "Rural Life in Russia," 246–47.

55. Murray, *Russians of To-Day*, 16, 34, 231. See also Wallace, *Russia*, 97–99.

56. Saltykov, *Tchinovnicks*, 99–100.

57. Stepniak suggests that corrupt clergy could use their "monopoly" on religious sacraments as an instrument of holy extortion. Stepniak, *Russian Peasantry*, 230–31.

58. Ioann S. Belliustin, *Description of the Clergy in Rural Russia: The Memoir of a Nineteenth-Century Parish Priest* (Ithaca, N.Y.: Cornell University Press, 1985), 129–30.

59. Ibid., 130–31.

60. Ibid., 139–40; Wallace, *Russia*, 97–98. Olearius related identical accounts in the 1630s, with some drinking until "the soul is given up with the draught." Baron, *Travels of Olearius in Seventeenth-Century Russia*, 143. See also William Richardson, *Anecdotes of the Russian Empire in a Series of Letters Written, a Few Years Ago, from St. Petersburg* (London: W. Strahan & T. Cadell, 1784), 61.

61. Baron, *Travels of Olearius in Seventeenth-Century Russia*, 144–46. Vladimir Lenin related similar tales of the rural clergy in the 1860s in "The Agrarian Programme of Social-Democracy in the First Russian Revolution 1905–1907 (1908)," in *Collected Works*, vol. 13: *June 1907–April 1908* (Moscow: Progress Publishers, 1972), 385.

62. Belliustin, *Description of the Clergy*, 114. See also Smucker, *The Life and Reign of Nicholas the First, Emperor of Russia*, 199; Stepniak, *Russia under the Tzars*, 58. The "All steal" proverb quoted in Georg Brandes, *Impressions of Russia*, trans. Samuel C. Eastman (Boston: C. J. Peters & Son, 1889), 148.

63. Nathan Haskell Dole, *Young Folks' History of Russia* (New York: Saalfield Publishing Co., 1903), 521.

64. "Koe chto ob otkupakh, *Kolokol* list 10, 1 marta 1858 g.," 79; Haxthausen, *Russian Empire*, 2:174–75; Hosking, *Russia*, 105–6. On "coercion-intensive" statecraft see Charles Tilly, *Coercion, Capital and European States, AD 990–1990* (Cambridge, Mass.: Blackwell Press, 1990), 87–91. On the importance of the article on agenda-setting: Christian, *Living Water*, 264–65.

65. Levin and Satarov, "Corruption and Institutions in Russia," 113–14. On the state and the ruling class in Russia see Donald Ostrowski, "The Façade of Legitimacy: Exchange of Power and Authority in Early Modern Russia," *Comparative Studies in Society and History* 44, no. 3 (2002): 536–39; John P. LeDonne, *Absolutism and Ruling Class: The Formation of the Russian Political Order, 1700–1825* (New York: Oxford University Press, 1991), 3–9.

66. See Ledeneva, *Can Russia Modernise?* 50–84.

67. Feifer, "Corruption in Russia, Part 1: A Normal Part of Everyday Life," and Part 3: How Russia Is Ruled," Radio Free Europe/Radio Liberty, Nov. 28 2009, http://www.rferl.org/articleprintview/1890170.html (accessed Oct. 22, 2010); Vladimir Shlapentokh, "Russia's Acquiescence to Corruption Makes the State Machine Inept," *Communist and Post-Communist Studies* 36, no. 2 (2003): 158; Michael Bohm, "Thieves Should Go to Jail!" *Moscow Times*, Oct. 8, 2010, http://themoscowtimes.com/opinion/article/thieves-should-go-to-jail/418993.html (accessed Oct. 11, 2010); Smith, *Reforming the Russian Legal System*, 12; Dev Kar and Sarah Freitas, *Russia: Illicit Financial Flows and the Role of the Underground Economy* (Washington, D.C.: Global Financial Integrity, 2013), 22.

68. David M. Herszenhorn, "Text of Navalny's Closing Remarks in Russian Court," *New York Times*, July 5, 2013, http://www.nytimes.com/2013/07/06/world/europe/text-of-navalnys-closing-remarks-in-russian-court.html (accessed July 6, 2013).

69. Ibid.

70. P. V. Berezin, *Na sluzhbe zlomu delu* (Moscow: I. N. Kyshnerev i Ko., 1900); Mikhail Fridman, *Vinnaya monopoliya, tom 2: Vinnaya monopoliya v Rossii*, 2 vols. (Petrograd: Pravda, 1916), 2:70–74. On the tenacity of bribery and corruption under Alexander III, see Dole, *History of Russia*, 521.

71. Hermann von Samson-Himmelstjerna, *Russia under Alexander III. And in the Preceding Period*, trans. J. Morrison, ed. Felix Volkhovsky (New York: Macmillan, 1893), xxii–xxiii (emphasis in original).

72. Ibid., xxiii.

73. Frye, "Corruption and Rule of Law," 94.

74. Quoted in Alena Ledeneva, *Russia's Economy of Favours: Blat, Networking and Informal Exchange* (New York: Cambridge University Press, 1998), 11.

75. Ledeneva, *How Russia Really Works*, 193.

76. Feifer, "Corruption in Russia, Part 1.

77. Levin and Satarov, "Corruption and Institutions in Russia," 130.

78. Ledeneva, *Can Russia Modernise?* 252–55. Different perspectives of Putin's ongoing anti-corruption campaign are provided in "Is Russia's Anti-Corruption Drive the Real Thing?" Voice of Russia Weekly Experts' Panel–13, Feb. 12, 2013, http://english.ruvr.ru/experts13 (accessed Feb. 15, 2013).

Chapter 9

1. See, for instance: Charles Tilly, *Coercion, Capital and European States, AD 990–1990* (Cambridge, Mass.: Blackwell, 1990), 65–95.

2. Geoffrey Hosking, *Russia: People and Empire, 1552–1917* (Cambridge, Mass.: Harvard University Press, 1997), 103; Arcadius Kahan, *The Plow, the Hammer and the Knout* (Chicago: University of Chicago Press, 1985), 316; David Christian, *Living Water: Vodka and Russian Society on the Eve of Emancipation* (Oxford: Clarendon, 1990), 186.

3. Janet Hartley, "Provincial and Local Government," in *Cambridge History of Russia: Imperial Russia, 1689–1917*, ed. Dominic Lieven (New York: Cambridge University Press, 2006), 473;

Sergei M. Troitskii, *Finansovaia politika russkago absoliutizma v XVIII veke* (Moscow: Nauka, 1966), 53.

4. Kahan, *Plow, the Hammer and the Knout*, 319–20; John P. LeDonne, "Indirect Taxes in Catherine's Russia, I: The Salt Code of 1781," *Jahrbücher für Geschichte Osteuropas* 23 (1975): 162–63.

5. John P. LeDonne, "Indirect Taxes in Catherine's Russia, II: The Liquor Monopoly," *Jahrbücher für Geschichte Osteuropas* 24, no. 2 (1976): 203.

6. Ibid; Troitskii, *Finansovaia politika*, 214.

7. Sergei F. Platonov, *Ivan the Terrible*, trans. Joseph Wieczynski (Gulf Breeze, Fla.: Academic International, 1974), 118; Johann Danckaert, *Beschrijvinge van Moscovien ofte Rusland* (Amsterdam, 1615), 63; cited in James Billington, *The Icon and the Axe: An Interpretive History of Russian Culture* (New York: Alfred A. Knopf, 1966), 86; Isabel de Madariaga, *Ivan the Terrible: First Tsar of Russia* (New Haven, Conn.: Yale University Press, 2005), 221.

8. Samuel H. Baron, ed., *The Travels of Olearius in Seventeenth-Century Russia* (Palo Alto, Calif.: Stanford University Press, 1967), 143.

9. William Coxe, *Travels in Poland, Russia, Sweden and Denmark, Interspersed with Historical Relations and Political Inquiries*, 3 vols. (Dublin: S. Price, 1784), 3:63–66.

10. Robert Ker Porter, "Excerpts from 'Travelling Sketches in Russia and Sweden,'" in *Seven Britons in Imperial Russia: 1698–1812*, ed. Peter Putnam (Princeton, N.J.: Princeton University Press, 1952), 312–13.

11. Hannibal Evans Lloyd, *Alexander I: Emperor of Russia; or, a Sketch of His Life, and of the Most Important Events of His Reign* (London: Treuttel & Würtz, 1826), 118–19.

12. Frederick Douglass, *Narrative of the Life of Frederick Douglass: An American Slave* [1845] (New York: Cambridge University Press, 2011), 74–76. Many thanks to Emmanuel Akyeampong for this reference.

13. Astolphe Custine, marquis de, *Empire of the Czar: A Journey through Eternal Russia: 1839* (New York: Doubleday, 1989), 437.

14. Baron August Freiherr Haxthausen, *The Russian Empire: Its People, Institutions, and Resources*, trans. Robert Faire, 2 vols. (London: Chapman & Hall, 1856), 2:174–75, 408–09. Also see Hosking, *Russia*, 106.

15. Audronė Janužyte, "Historians as Nation State-Builders: The Formation of Lithuanian University, 1904–1922" (academic diss., University of Tampere, 2005), 22. Likewise see Piotr S. Alekseev, *O p'yanstve s predisloviem gr. L. N. Tolstago* (Moscow: 1891), 93.

16. Alexis de Tocqueville, *Democracy in America*, ed. Richard D. Heffner, abridged ed. (New York: Mentor Books, 1956), 201. On the history of the transnational temperance movement see Mark Lawrence Schrad, *The Political Power of Bad Ideas: Networks, Institutions, and the Global Prohibition Wave* (New York: Oxford University Press, 2010), 31–61.

17. Henry M. Baird, *The Life of the Rev. Robert Baird, D.D.* (New York: A. D. F. Randolph, 1866), 195. See also Baird's correspondence from St. Petersburg to the American Sunday School Union, Oct. 20, 1840, in the Presbyterian Historical Society, American Sunday School Union Papers, 1817–1915, reel 45 series I, C:1840B, no. 200-202. On "religious sects" see Dawson Burns, *Temperance History: A Consecutive Narrative of the Rise, Development and Extension of the Temperance Reform*, (London: National Temperance Publication Depot, 1889), 120, 255; Eustace Clare Grenville Murray, *The Russians of To-Day* (London: Smith, Elder & Co., 1878), 19.

18. Egidijus Aleksandravičius, *Lietuvių atgimimo istorijos studijos, tom 2: Blaivybė Lietuvoje XIX amžiuje* (Vilnius: Sietynas, 1991), 61. On Bishop Motiejus Valančius and temperance in Kaunas guberniia see Janužyte, "Historians as Nation State-Builders," 21. In Poland and western Ukraine see Boris Savchuk, *Korchma: alkogol'na politika i rukh tverezosti v Zakhidnii Ukraini u XIX - 30-kh rokakh XX st.* (Ivano-Frankivs'k, Ukraine: Lileya-NV, 2001), 138–230. See also Barbara J. Falk, *The Dilemma of Dissidence in East-Central Europe* (Budapest: CEU Press, 2003), 18; Patrick Rogers, *Father Theobald Mathew: Apostle of Temperance* (Dublin: Browne & Nolan, 1943).

19. Aleksandravičius, *Blaivybė Lietuvoje XIX amžiuje*, 72; Christian, *Living Water*.

20. Christian, *Living Water*, 295; David Christian, "A Neglected Great Reform: The Abolition of Tax Farming in Russia," in *Russia's Great Reforms, 1855–1881*, ed. Ben Eklof, John Bushnell, and Larissa Zakharova (Bloomington: Indiana University Press, 1994), 105.

21. Christian, *Living Water*, 325–26; derived from reports in *Svedeniya* 2:235–237.

22. V. A. Fedorov, "Liquor Tax Rebellion (Trezvennoe dvizhenie)," in *Bol'shaia sovetskaia entsiklopediia*, ed. A. M. Prokhorov (New York: Macmillan, 1981), 101.

23. Ivan Pryzhov, *Istoriya kabakov v Rossii* (Moscow: Molodiya sily, 1914), 50–51; John Stearns, *Temperance in All Nations: History of the Cause in All Countries of the Globe* (New York: National Temperance Society and Publication House, 1893), 329–33.

24. D. MacKenzie Wallace, *Russia* (New York: Henry Holt & Co., 1877), 99. See also R. E. F. Smith and David Christian, *Bread and Salt: A Social and Economic History of Food and Drink in Russia* (New York: Cambridge University Press, 1984), 93.

25. *Moskovskie vedomosti*, no. 62, March 13, 1859; translated in Christian, *Living Water*, 314.

26. Murray, *Russians of To-Day*, 29–30. Similarly, see Fedorov, "Liquor Tax Rebellion (*Trezvennoe dvizhenie*)," 101.

27. Quoted in Christian, *Living Water*, 348.

28. Fedorov, "Liquor Tax Rebellion (*Trezvennoe dvizhenie*)," 101.

29. Christian, "A Neglected Great Reform," 107–9; Aleksandr P. Pogrebinskii, "Finansovaya reforma nachala 60-kh godov XIX veka v Rossii," *Voprosi istorii*, no. 10 (1951): 78–82; W. Bruce Lincoln, *The Great Reforms: Autocracy, Bureaucracy, and the Politics of Change in Imperial Russia* (Dekalb: Northern Illinois University Press, 1990), 62; Walter McKenzie Pinter, *Russian Economic Policy under Nicholas I* (Ithaca, N.Y.: Cornell University Press, 1967), 78.

30. Translated in Christian, *Living Water*, 357. See also ibid., 349; Christian, "A Neglected Great Reform," 108.

31. Quoted in: Christian, *Living Water*, 349.

32. Ibid., 350.

33. Ibid., 361–64; Irina R. Takala, *Veselie Rusi: Istoriia alkogol'noi problemy v Rossii* (St. Petersburg: Zhurnal Neva, 2002), 92–93.

34. Mikhail Fridman, *Vinnaya monopoliya, tom 2: Vinnaya monopoliya v Rossii*, 2 vols. (Petrograd: Pravda, 1916), 2:70–75; P. V. Berezin, *Na sluzhbe zlomu delu* (Moscow: I. N. Kyshnerev i Ko., 1900); Christian, *Living Water*, 374–79; Pinter, *Russian Economic Policy under Nicholas I*, 78–80.

35. Fridman, *Vinnaya monopoliya*, tom 2, 2:65–66. Perhaps the most detailed investigation of consumption is V. K. Dmitriev, *Kriticheskie issledovaniya o potreblenii alkogolya v Rossii* (Moscow: V. P. Ryabushinskii, 1911). See also Stanislav I. Smetanin and Mikhail V. Konotopov, *Razvitie promyshlennosti v krepostnoi Rossii* (Moscow: Akademicheskii proect, 2001), 184–90.

36. See Switzerland Bureau fédéral de statistique, *Question de l'alcoolisme. Exposé comparatif des lois et des expériences de Quelques états étrangers, par le Bureau fédéral de statistique* (Berne: Imprimerie K.-J. Wyss, 1884), esp. 672.

37. Murray, *Russians of To-Day*, 30–33.

38. Luigi Villari, *Russia under the Great Shadow* (New York: James Pott & Co., 1905), 250.

39. Georg Brandes, *Impressions of Russia*, trans. Samuel C. Eastman (Boston: C. J. Peters & Son, 1889), 144.

Chapter 10

1. Karl Marx and Friedrich Engels, *The Communist Manifesto* (New York: International Publishers, 1948), 9.

2. On the state see ibid., 11. On religion see Karl Marx, *Critique of Hegel's 'Philosophy of Right'* (New York: Cambridge University Press, 1970), 131.

3. See also Joseph R. Gusfield, "Social Structure and Moral Reform: A Study of the Woman's Christian Temperance Union," *American Journal of Sociology* 61, no. 3 (1955): 225. I have found no evidence that the passage originated with Karl Marx himself. Frank Harris, *Oscar Wilde: His Life and Confessions*, vol. 1 (New York: Brentano's Publishers, 1916), 166.

4. Karl Marx, *Capital, vol. 3: The Process of Capitalist Production as a Whole* (New York: Penguin Classics, 1991), 927.

5. Friedrich Engels, *The Condition of the Working Class in England in 1844* (London: Swan Sonnenschein & Co., 1892), 127–29.

6. David Christian, "Accumulation and Accumulators: The Metaphor Marx Muffled," *Science and Society* 54, no. 2 (1990), and, *Living Water: Vodka and Russian Society on the Eve of Emancipation* (Oxford: Clarendon, 1990), 37.

7. Orlando Figes, *A People's Tragedy: The Russian Revolution, 1891–1924* (New York: Viking, 1996), 129; Franz Mehring, *Karl Marx: The Story of His Life* (London: Routledge, 2003), 407; M. Grigoryan, "N. G. Chernyshevsky's World Outlook," in *N. G. Chernyshevsky: Selected Philosophical Essays* (Moscow: Foreign Languages Publishing House, 1953), 9.

8. Figes, *A People's Tragedy*, 135.

9. "Koe chto ob otkupakh, *Kolokol* list 10, 1 marta 1858 g.," in *Kolokol: Gazeta A. I. Gertsena i N. P. Ogareva* (Moscow: Izdatel'stvo Akademii nauk SSSR, 1962), 79.

10. Ibid; Baron August Freiherr Haxthausen, *The Russian Empire: Its People, Institutions, and Resources*, trans. Robert Faire, 2 vols. (London: Chapman & Hall, 1856), 2:174–75; Geoffrey Hosking, *Russia: People and Empire, 1552–1917* (Cambridge, Mass.: Harvard University Press, 1997), 105–6. On "coercion-intensive" statecraft see Charles Tilly, *Coercion, Capital and European States, AD 990–1990* (Cambridge, Mass.: Blackwell, 1990), 87–91.

11. Perhaps the sapient reader will agree. Joseph Frank, *Through the Russian Prism: Essays on Literature and Culture* (Princeton, N.J.: Princeton University Press, 1990), 187. See also Andrew M. Drozd, *Chernyshevskii's What Is to Be Done?: A Reevaluation* (Evanston, Ill.: Northwestern University Press, 2001), 13.

12. Figes, *A People's Tragedy*, 129.

13. Marshall Berman, *All That Is Solid Melts into Air: The Experience of Modernity* (New York: Verso, 1983), 215–16.

14. Robert H. Stacy, *Russian Literary Criticism: A Short History* (Syracuse, N.Y.: Syracuse University Press, 1974), 55.

15. Drozd, *Chernyshevskii's What Is to Be Done? A Reevaluation*, 13.

16. Joseph Frank, *Dostoevsky: The Stir of Liberation, 1860–1865* (Princeton, N.J.: Princeton University Press, 1986), 285; Frank, *Through the Russian Prism*, 188–89.

17. Georgii V. Plekhanov, *Izbrannye filosofskie proizvedeniia*, 5 vols. (Moscow: Gosudarstvennoe izdatel'stvo politicheskoi literatury, 1958), 4:159–60; Marx, *Capital*, 19; William F. Woehrlin, *Chernyshevskii: The Man and the Journalist* (Cambridge, Mass.: Harvard University Press, 1971), 216.

18. "Sombre Monsters—or, How to Blow up a Country," Nicky's What (Russian history blog), May 10, 2010, http://nickyswhat.wordpress.com/2010/05/10/sombre-monsters-or-how-to-blow-up-a-country (accessed March 17, 2011).

19. Nikolai G. Chernyshevskii, *A Vital Question; or, What Is to Be Done?* trans. Nathan Haskell Dole and S. S. Skidelsky (New York: Thomas Y. Crowell & Co., 1886), 2–3, 139. In what follows, I alternate between translations from different centuries to deliver what I feel to be the most accurate and accessible interpretation to a contemporary readership.

20. Nikolai G. Chernyshevskii, *What Is to Be Done?* trans. Michael R. Katz (Ithaca, N.Y.: Cornell University Press, 1989), 52, 64.

21. Chernyshevskii, *What Is to Be Done?* 12, 115–16, 18 (1886 edition).

22. Chernyshevskii, *What Is to Be Done?* 93 (1993 edition).

23. Chernyshevskii, *What Is to Be Done?* 116 (1886 edition).

24. Nikolai G. Chernyshevskii, "Otkupnaya sistema (Sovremennik, 1858)," in *Izbrannye ekonomichesie proizvedeniya*, tom 1 (Moscow: Gosudarstvennoe izdatel'stvo politicheskoi literatury, 1948), 668; the original was written under the pseudonym L. Pankrat'ev, "Otkupnaya sistema," *Sovremennik*, no. 10 (1858). See also Marc Lee Schulkin, "The Politics of Temperance: Nicholas II's Campaign against Alcohol Abuse" (Ph.D. diss., Harvard University, 1985), 28. On Pankrat'ev see: T. I. Pecherskaya, "Avtor v strukture syuzhetnogo povestvovaniya ("Povesti v povesti" N. G. Chernyshevskogo)," *Raznochintsy shestidesyatykh godov XIX veka. Fenomen samosoznaniya v aspekte filologicheskoi germenevtiki*, Jan. 28, 2004, http://rassvet.websib.ru/text.htm?no=15&id=11 (accessed May 11, 2011).

25. Chernyshevskii, "Otkupnaya sistema," 682.

26. Ibid., 670, 679

27. Ibid., 671–72.

28. Ibid., 678. See also chapter 7, note 46.

29. Ibid., 685–87.

30. Chernyshevskii, *What Is to Be Done?* 212 (1886 edition).

31. Nikolai G. Chernyshevskii, *Chto delat'? Iz rasskazov o novykh lyudyakh* (Moscow: Molodaya gvardiya, 1948), 242. Further clues are provided by Chernyshevsky's reference to the *grud'*—alternatively translated as "chest" or "lungs." At least a half-dozen times in the novel Chernyshevsky writes that the alcoholics (or reformed alcoholics) have (or once had) some unspecified sickness of the *grud'*. Yet rather than the tuberculosis of the lungs—the common diagnosis of heroines in nineteenth-century European literature—in the first sentences of his *Sovremennik* exposé on the tax-farm system, Chernyshevsky repeatedly invokes sicknesses and ulcers of the *grud'*, suggesting "in actuality, we have in our chest a very serious ulcer" (*v samom dele, u nas na grudi yazva dovol'no vrednogo kachestva*). Chernyshevskii, "Otkupnaya Sistema," 667.

32. See chapter 7, note 8.

33. Edvard Radzinsky, *Alexander II: The Last Great Tsar*, trans. Antonina W. Bouis (New York: Simon & Schuster, 2005), 161–62; Berman, *All That Is Solid Melts into Air*, 216; Michael Burleigh, *Earthly Powers: The Clash of Religion and Politics in Europe, from the French Revolution to the Great War* (New York: HarperCollins, 2007), 280–81.

34. Radzinsky, *Alexander II*, 162.

35. Kenneth Lantz, *The Dostoyevsky Encyclopedia* (Westport, Conn.: Greenwood, 2004), 58; Peter Sekirin, "Literary Journals and "Innocent" Novels: The Period of Transition," in *The Dostoyevsky Archive: Firsthand Accounts of the Novelist from Contemporaries' Memoirs and Rare Periodicals*, ed. Peter Sekirin (Jefferson, N.C.: McFarland & Co., 1997), 145; Frank, *Dostoevsky*, 155; Walter G. Moss, *Russia in the Age of Alexander II, Tolstoy and Dostoevsky* (London: Anthem, 2002), 80.

36. Lantz, *Dostoyevsky Encyclopedia*, 58.

37. Indeed, the first few dozen pages of the book present a veritable exposé on drunkenness in which the pawnbroker, the tavern keeper, and their drunken customers are explicitly interconnected. Fyodor Dostoevsky, *Crime and Punishment*, trans. Jessie Coulson, ed. George Gibian, 3rd ed. (New York: W. W. Norton, 1989), 6–23.

38. Donald Fanger, *Dostoevsky and Romantic Realism: A Study of Dostoevsky in Relation to Balzac, Dickens, and Gogol* (Evanston, Ill.: Northwestern University Press, 1998), 184–85; Robin Feuer Miller, *Dostoevsky's Unfinished Journey* (New Haven, Conn.: Yale University Press, 2007), 55–56.

39. Donald Fanger explicitly notes the important influence of the liquor debates on Dostoevsky's masterpiece in *Dostoevsky and Romantic Realism*, 184–85. See also Leonid P. Grossman, "Gorod i lyudi Prestupleniya i nakazaniya," in *Prestupleniya i nakazaniya*, ed. Fyodor Dostoevsky (Moscow: Goslitizdat, 1935), 23.

40. Dostoevsky's letter of June 8, 1865, is reprinted as an addendum in *Crime and Punishment*, 476.

41. Miller, *Dostoevsky's Unfinished Journey*, 55.

42. Cited in Patricia Herlihy, *The Alcoholic Empire: Vodka and Politics in Late Imperial Russia* (New York: Oxford University Press, 2002), 7–8.

43. Reprinted in Dostoevsky, *Crime and Punishment*, 487–88. See also Miller, *Dostoevsky's Unfinished Journey*, 57.

44. See Herlihy, *Alcoholic Empire*, 113–14.

45. To be fair, Tolstoy's *Tak chto zhe nam delat'?* ("Then what must we do?") is not quite identical to Chernyshevsky's *Chto delat'?* For Tolstoy on Chernyshevsky see Hugh McLean, *In Quest of Tolstoy* (Brighton, Mass.: Academic Studies, 2008), 110; Andrew Baruch Wachtel, *Plays of Expectations: Intertextual Relations in Russian Twentieth-Century Drama* (Seattle: University of Washington Press, 2006), 25 n.10. On Tolstoy's realism see György Lukács, "Tolstoy and the Development of Realism," in *Studies in European Realism: A Sociological Survey of the Writings of Balzac, Stendhal, Zola, Tolstoy, Gorki, and Others* (London: Merlin, 1972), 126–205. On Tolstoy and the Russian state see Fedor Stepun, "The Religious Tragedy of

Tolstoy," *Russian Review* 19, no. 2 (1960): 157–58. Ironically, Chernyshevsky often defended Tolstoy's early works against accusations of downplaying pressing social problems. Adam B. Ulam, *The Bolsheviks* (New York: Macmillan, 1965), 58.

46. Leo Tolstoy, *What Is to Be Done? and "Life"* (New York: Thomas Y. Crowell & Co., 1899), 60 (follow on to page 64).

47. Arguing how the state and the bourgeois class have conspired to invent "torpedoes, appliances for the use of the spirit-monopoly, and for privies." Tolstoy complains, "but our spinning-wheel, peasant-woman's loom, village plough, hatchet, flail, rake, and the yoke and bucket, are still the same that they were in the times of Rurik" back in the ninth century. Leo Tolstoy, *What Then Must We Do?* trans. Aylmer Maude (London: Oxford University Press, 1925), 295–96.

48. Henri Troyat, *Tolstoy* (New York: Doubleday, 1967), 378. See also Stepun, "Religious Tragedy of Tolstoy," 162.

49. Stepun, "Religious Tragedy of Tolstoy," 164; Anna A. Tavis, "Authority and Its Discontents in Tolstoy and Joyce," in *Leo Tolstoy*, ed. Harold Bloom (Broomall, Pa.: Chelsea House, 2003), 67.

50. Tavis, "Authority and Its Discontents in Tolstoy and Joyce," 66.

51. Quoted in: Herlihy, *Alcoholic Empire*, 111–12.

52. Leo Tolstoy, "Letter to A. M. Kuzminskii, November 13–15, 1896," in *Polnoe sobranie sochenenii* (Moscow: Gosudarstvennoe izdatel'stvo khudozhestvennoi literatury, 1954), 69:205–6; quoted in Herlihy, *Alcoholic Empire*, 15.

53. Troyat, *Tolstoy*, 567.

54. William Nickell, *The Death of Tolstoy: Russia on the Eve, Astapovo Station, 1910* (Ithaca, N.Y.: Cornell University Press, 2010), 75.

55. Jan Kucharzewski, *The Origins of Modern Russia* (New York: Polish Institute of Arts and Sciences in America, 1948), 162; Julio Alvarez del Vayo, *The March of Socialism* (London: Cape, 1974), 114.

56. Ivan S. Turgenev, *Virgin Soil*, trans. T. S. Perry (New York: Henry Holt & Co., 1877), 70–71. For an updated version see the New York Review of Books Classics edition (translated by Constance Garnett), 2000, 84. Some translate it as "brandy"; others, as "drink."

57. Turgenev, *Virgin Soil*, 240.

58. Here again I use the 1877 translation (ibid., 232–33), replacing "brandy" for "vodka," as is consistent with later translations. Turgenev, *Virgin Soil*, 266 (2000 edition).

59. Turgenev, *Virgin Soil*, 252.

60. Ibid., 254–55.

61. Ibid.

62. Figes, *A People's Tragedy*, 130.

63. Sue Mahan and Pamala L. Griset, *Terrorism in Perspective*, 2nd ed. (Thousand Oaks, Calif.: Sage, 2009), 40–41.

64. Philip Pomer, *Lenin's Brother: The Origins of the October Revolution* (New York: W. W. Norton, 2010), 127–28. Also noteworthy is the extent to which revolutionaries used smuggled vodka to bribe or dope prison guards upon their arrival in Siberian exile. Helen Rappaport, *Conspirator: Lenin in Exile* (New York: Basic Books, 2010), 195, 75–76.

65. See Pomer, *Lenin's Brother*; Adam B. Ulam, *Prophets and Conspirators in Prerevolutionary Russia* (New Brunswick, N.J.: Transaction, 1998), 392–93; Peter Julicher, *Renegades, Rebels and Rogues under the Tsars* (Jefferson, N.C.: MacFarland & Co., 2003), 222–23.

66. Burleigh, *Earthly Powers*, 280; Michael R. Katz and William G. Wagner, "Introduction: Chernyshevsky, What Is to Be Done? and the Russian Intelligentsia," in *What Is to Be Done?* ed. Nikolai G. Chernyshevskii (Ithaca, N.Y.: Cornell University Press, 1989), 32; quoted in N. Valentinov, "Chernyshevskii i Lenin," *Novyi zhurnal*, no. 27 (1951): 193–94.

67. Vladimir I. Lenin, "What Is to Be Done?" in *Essential Works of Lenin* (New York: Bantam Books, 1966). See also Lars T. Lih, *Lenin Rediscovered: What Is to Be Done? in Context* (Leiden: E. J Brill, 2006). For Lenin on Chernyshevsky see, for instance, Vladimir I. Lenin, "'The Peasant Reform' and the Proletarian-Peasant Revolution," in *Collected Works, vol. 17: December 1910–April 1912* (Moscow: Progress Publishers, 1963), 122–24; Valentinov, "Chernyshevskii i Lenin."

68. Rakhmetov famously even went so far as to sleep on a bed of nails so as to better endure torture by the state. Drozd, *Chernyshevskii's What Is to Be Done?: A Reevaluation*, 113–40.

69. Vladimir I. Lenin, "Socialism and Religion," in *Collected Works, vol. 10: November 1905–June 1906* (Moscow: Progress Publishers, 1962), 83–84. The original appeared in *Novaya zhizn'*, no. 28, Dec. 3, 1905. On Lenin's personal drinking habits see Rappaport, *Conspirator*, 195, 75–76; Robert Hatch McNeal, *Bride of the Revolution: Krupskaya and Lenin* (Ann Arbor: University of Michigan Press, 1972), 76. See also James D. Young, *Socialism since 1889: A Biographical History* (London: Pinter, 1988), 102. On Lenin and Krupskaya's temperate drinking habits when hosting the more intemperate Stalin see Robert Service, *Stalin: A Biography* (Cambridge, Mass.: Harvard University Press, 2004), 88–89.

70. Stephen Colbert, "The Red Lending Menace," *The Colbert Report*, Oct. 7, 2008, http://www.colbertnation.com/the-colbert-report-videos/187342/october-07-2008/the-red-lending-menace (accessed March 2, 2012).

71. Nadezhda Krupskaya, *Reminiscences of Lenin*, trans. Bernard Isaacs (New York: International Publishers, 1970), 40.

72. Vladimir I. Lenin, "The Development of Capitalism in Russia," in *Collected Works, vol. 3: The Development of Capitalism in Russia* (Moscow Progress Publishers, 1960), 290–91. The original appeared in Vladimir I. Lenin, *Razvitie kapitalizma v Rossii* (St. Petersburg: Tipo-litografiya A. Leiferta, 1899). For Lenin on alcohol and domestic violence see Christopher Read, *Lenin: A Revolutionary Life* (New York: Routledge, 2005), 38.

73. "Liquor Monopoly," in *Bol'shaia sovetsakaia entsiklopediia*, ed. A. M. Prokhorov (New York: MacMillan, Inc., 1974), 248; citing Vladimir I. Lenin, "Duma i utver-zhdenie byudzheta," in *Polnoe sobranie sochinenii, tom 15: Fevral'-iyun' 1907* (Moscow: Gosudarstvennoe izdatel'stvo politicheskoi literatury, 1961); the original appeared in *Nashe ekho*, no. 2, March 27, 1907.

74. Vladimir I. Lenin, "To the Rural Poor," in *Collected Works, vol 6: January 1902–August 1903* (Moscow: Progress Publishers, 1961), 400–401; originally published in Vladimir I. Lenin, *K derevenskoi bednote: Ob'yasnenie dlya krest'yan, chego khotyat sotsial'demokraty* (Geneva: Tipografiya ligi russkoi revolyutsionnoi sotsial'demokratii, 1903).

75. Vladimir I. Lenin, "The Serf-Owners at Work," in *Collected Works, vol. 5: May 1901–February 1902* (London: Lawrence & Wishart, 1961), 95; originally published in *Iskra*, no. 8, Sept. 10, 1901.

76. Vladimir I. Lenin, "Casual Notes," in *Collected Works, vol. 4: 1898–April 1901* (Moscow: Progress Publishers, 1972), 407–8; originally published in *Zarya* no. 1, April 1901.

77. *Pravda*, March 15, 1913; Vladimir I. Lenin, "Spare Cash," in *Collected Works, vol. 18: April 1912–March 1913* (Moscow: Gosudarstvennoe izdatel'stvo politicheskoi literatury, 1963), 601–2.

78. Vladimir I. Lenin, "Lessons of the Moscow Uprising," in *Collected Works, vol. 11: June 1906–January 1907* (Moscow: Progress Publishers, 1962), 174; the original appeared in *Proletary* No. 2, Aug. 29, 1906.

79. Vladimir I. Lenin, "Beat—But Not to Death!" in *Collected Works, vol. 4: 1898–April 1901* (Moscow: Progress Publishers, 1960); the original, "Bei, no ne do smerti," was published in the inaugural edition of *Zarya*, April 1901. See also Lih, *Lenin Rediscovered*, 206.

80. Ivan V. Strel'chuk, *Alkogolizm i bor'ba s nim* (Moscow: Molodaya gvardiya, 1954), 13. See also Clara Zetkin, "My Recollections of Lenin," in *On the Emancipation of Women*, ed. Vladimir I. Lenin (London: Pluto, 2003), 102–3.

Chapter 11

1. Nikolai G. Chernyshevskii, "Otkupnaya sistema (Sovremennik, 1858)," in *Izbrannye eko-nomichesie proizvedeniya*, tom 1 (Moscow: Gosudarstvennoe izdatel'stvo politicheskoi literatury, 1948), 670–72. On statecraft and European war making see Francis Fukuyama, *The Origins of Political Order: From Prehuman Times to the French Revolution* (New York: Farrar, Straus & Giroux, 2011), 389; Charles Tilly, *Coercion, Capital and European States, AD 990–1990* (Cambridge, Mass.: Blackwell, 1990), 74. See also Aleksandr E. Levintov, "Voina i vodka v Rossii," in: *Alkogol' v Rossii: Materialy tret'ei mezhdunarodnoi nauchno-prakticheskoi*

konferentsii (Ivanovo, 26–27 oktyabrya 2012), ed. Mikhail V. Teplyanskii (Ivanovo: Filial RGGU v g. Ivanovo, 2012), 12–19.

2. Nathan Haskell Dole, *Young Folks' History of Russia* (New York: Saalfield Publishing Co., 1903), 256.

3. Sergei M. Soloviev, *History of Russia, vol. 9: The Age of Vasily III* (Gulf Breeze, Fla.: Academic International, 1976), 55; Dole, *Young Folks' History of Russia*, 250. The establishment of the sixteenth-century Naloi (meaning "fill up") garrison, where the emperor's soldiers were fed beer and mead, likewise bears mention. See Freiherr Sigmund von Herberstein, *Description of Moscow and Muscovy: 1557* (New York: Barnes & Noble, 1969), 20.

4. This observation draws from Bruno S. Frey and Heinz Buhofer, "Prisoners and Property Rights," *Journal of Law and Economics* 31, no. 1 (1988).

5. Margaret Levi, *Consent, Dissent, and Patriotism* (New York: Cambridge University Press, 1997), 42.

6. Georg Brandes, *Impressions of Russia*, trans. Samuel C. Eastman (Boston: C. J. Peters & Son, 1889), 210–11. Little wonder that mercenary desertion was high. William C. Fuller Jr., "The Imperial Army," in *The Cambridge History of Russia, vol. 2: Imperial Russia, 1689–1917*, ed. Dominic Lieven (New York: Cambridge University Press, 2006), 532–33.

7. Isser Woloch, "Napoleonic Conscription: State Power and Civil Society," *Past & Present* 111 (1986).

8. Fuller, "Imperial Army," 537.

9. Ibid., 533; George Snow, "Alcoholism in the Russian Military: The Public Sphere and the Temperance Discourse, 1883–1917," *Jahrbücher für Geschichte Osteuropas* 45, no. 3 (1997): 419–21.

10. Richard A. Gabriel, *The New Red Legions: An Attitudinal Portrait of the Soviet Soldier* (Westport, Conn.: Greenwood, 1980), 153.

11. Hannibal Evans Lloyd, *Alexander I: Emperor of Russia; or, a Sketch of His Life, and of the Most Important Events of His Reign* (London: Treuttel & Würtz, 1826), 91, 95.

12. P. S. White and H. R. Pleasants, *The War of Four Thousand Years* (Philadelphia: Griffith & Simon, 1846), 183.

13. Aleksandr Nikishin and Petr Nechitailov, *Vodka i Napoleon* (Moscow: Dom russkoi vodki, 2008); Owen Connelly, *Blundering to Glory: Napoleon's Military Campaigns* (Lanham, Md.: Rowman & Littlefield, 2006), 172.

14. Consider Tolstoy's description in *War and Peace*, trans. Nathan Haskell Dole, 4 vols. (New York: Thomas Y. Crowell & Co., 1889), 3:382.

15. Adam Zamoyski, *Moscow 1812: Napoleon's Fatal March* (New York: HarperCollins, 2005), 300; Mary Platt Parmele, *A Short History of Russia* (Flint, Mich: Bay View Reading Circle, 1899), 182; Alfred Rambaud, *Russia*, 2 vols. (New York: P. F. Collier & Son, 1902), 2:186; Walter K. Kelly, *History of Russia, from the Earliest Period to the Present Time*, 2 vols. (London: Henry G. Bohn, 1854), 1:185–86.

16. August Fournier, *Napoleon I: A Biography*, 2 vols. (New York: Henry Holt & Co., 1911), 207–8. Petrovsky Palace is today located on Leningradskoe shosse, near Dinamo Stadium and the Khodynka Fields.

17. Napoleon Bonaparte, *Memoirs of the History of France during the Reign of Napoleon: Historical Miscellanies*, vol. 2 (London: Henry Colburn & Co., 1823), 101.

18. Tolstoy, *War and Peace*, 383. Tolstoy was suspicious of arson conspiracies since an unintentional ignition was also likely given the circumstances.

19. Fournier, *Napoleon I: A Biography*, 207–8. See also Zamoyski, *Moscow 1812*, 302. See also Letter of the Abbe Surrugues, curate of the parish of St. Louis in Moscow, quoted in Gaspard(?) Gourgaud, *Napoleon and the Grand Army in Russia; or a Critical Examination of Count Philip De Segur's Work* (Philadelphia: Anthony Finley, 1825), 169.

20. Quoted in Zamoyski, *Moscow 1812*, 302. Similarly, see C. Joyneville, *Life and Times of Alexander I: Emperor of All the Russias*, 3 vols. (London: Tinsley Brothers), 2:199.

21. Eugène Labaume, *Relation complète de la campagne de Russie, en 1812*, 5th ed. (Paris: Rey et Gravier, 1816), 226–27; Louis Florimond Fantin des Odoards, *Journal du général Fantin des Odoards* (Paris: E. Plon, Nourrit et Cie, 1895), 337.

22. Labaume, *Relation complète de la campagne de Russie, en 1812*, 240–42; Gourgaud, *Napoleon and the Grand Army in Russia*, 273, 313–14, 29; "The French Retreat from Moscow," *The Living Age* 95, no. 7 (1867): 475.

23. Gourgaud, *Napoleon and the Grand Army in Russia*, 160–61.

24. Fournier, *Napoleon I: A Biography*, 209.

25. Stephan Talty, *The Illustrious Dead: The Terrifying Story of How Typhus Killed Napoleon's Greatest Army* (New York: Three Rivers, 2009), 67–69.

26. Joyneville, *Life and Times of Alexander I*, 233–34.

27. J. M. Buckley, *The Midnight Sun, the Tsar and the Nihilist* (Boston: D. Lothrop & Co., 1886), 215–16.

28. Leo Tolstoy, *A Confession and Other Religious Writings* (New York: Penguin Classics, 1987), 23; cited in Patricia Herlihy, *The Alcoholic Empire: Vodka and Politics in Late Imperial Russia* (New York: Oxford University Press, 2002), 61.

29. A. N. Wilson, *Tolstoy* (New York: W. W. Norton, 1988), 117.

30. Robert A. Hodasevich, *A Voice from within the Walls of Sebastopol: A Narrative of the Campaign in the Crimea, and of the Events of the Siege* (London: John Murray, 1856), 57. On Menshikov and his ladies see Orlando Figes, *The Crimean War: A History* (New York: Macmillan, 2011), 206.

31. Hodasevich, *Voice from within the Walls of Sebastopol*, 57; Robert B. Edgerton, *Death or Glory: The Legacy of the Crimean War* (Boulder, Colo.: Westview, 1999), 60. The *charka* was officially 1/100 of a *vedro* (bucket) or about 3.3 ounces. See also Dominic Lieven, *Russia against Napoleon: The True Story of the Campaigns of War and Peace* (New York: Penguin, 2010), note 11.

32. Hodasevich, *Voice from within the Walls of Sebastopol*, 57.

33. Ibid., 86, 90.

34. Edgerton, *Death or Glory*, 84–85; Figes, *Crimean War*, 210, 16.

35. Figes, *Crimean War*, 218.

36. Edgerton, *Death or Glory*, 86.

37. William Simpson, "Within Sebastopol during the Siege," *The English Illustrated Magazine*, vol. 17 (April to September 1897): 302; Hodasevich, *Voice from within the Walls of Sebastopol*, 2. For vodka and corruption as an epidemic problem in the tsarist military see John Shelton Curtiss, *The Russian Army under Nicholas I: 1825–1855* (Durham, N.C.: Duke University Press, 1965), 194, 212–27.

38. Hodasevich, *Voice from within the Walls of Sebastopol*, 98–99; Figes, *Crimean War*, 234.

39. Hodasevich, *Voice from within the Walls of Sebastopol*, 99.

40. Ibid., 239, also 122, 184; Figes, *Crimean War*, 255; Edgerton, *Death or Glory*, 236; Leo Tolstoy, *Sebastopol*, trans. Frank D. Millet (New York: Harper & Brothers, 1887), 58–66, 191–97. On foreign perceptions see Lady Frances Verney, "Rural Life in Russia," in *Russia as Seen and Described by Famous Writers*, ed. Esther Singleton (New York: Dodd, Mead & Co., 1906), 247.

41. Robert H. G. Thomas, *The Russian Army of the Crimean War, 1854–56* (Oxford: Osprey, 1991), 3.

42. Henry Tyrrell, *The History of the War with Russia: Giving Full Details of the Operations of the Allied Armies*, 2 vols. (London: London Printing & Publishing Co., 1855), 2:197–98. On the drinking of the French and British see also Figes, *Crimean War*, 181, 396; Edgerton, *Death or Glory*, 227–28, 236–277.

43. Tyrrell, *History of the War with Russia*, 198.

44. Herlihy, *Alcoholic Empire*, 57. See also William Steveni, *The Russian Army from Within* (New York: Hodder & Stoughton, 1914), 44–45.

45. Snow, "Alcoholism in the Russian Military," 424–25. For more on "Was he drunk?" see Frederick McCormick, *Tragedy of Russia in Pacific Asia*, 2 vols. (New York: Outing Publishing Co., 1907), 2:281.

46. Frederic William Unger, *Russia and Japan, and a Complete History of the War in the Far East* (Wilmington, Del.: Scholarly Resources, 1905), 231–40.

47. Vinkentii V. Veresaev, *In the War: Memoirs of V. Veresaev*, trans. Leo Winter (New York: Mitchell Kennerley, 1917), 7–8; on suicides, 19–21.

48. Joshua A. Sanborn, *Drafting the Russian Nation: Military Conscription, Total War, and Mass Politics, 1905–1925* (DeKalb: Northern Illinois University Press, 2003), 13; Veresaev, *In the War*, 23.

49. Veresaev, *In the War*, 25.

50. On McCormick's first impressions see *Tragedy of Russia in Pacific Asia*, 1:27. See also ibid., 2:278–82; Ernest Barron Gordon, *Russian Prohibition* (Westerville, Ohio: American Issue, 1916), 8.

51. Eugene S. Politovsky, *From Libau to Tsushima: A Narrative of the Voyage of Admiral Rojdestvensky's Fleet to Eastern Seas, Including a Detailed Account of the Dogger Bank Incident*, trans. F. R. Godfrey (New York: E. P. Dutton, 1908), 11.

52. McCormick, *Tragedy of Russia in Pacific Asia*, 1:143. On the high levels of drunkenness among the officer class see V. E. Bagdasaryan, "Vinnaya monopoliya i politicheskaya istoriya," in *Veselie Rusi, XX vek: Gradus noveishei rossiiskoi istorii ot "p'yanogo byudzheta" do "sukhogo zakona*," ed. Vladislav B. Aksenov (Moscow: Probel-2000, 2007), 101–3.

53. McCormick, *Tragedy of Russia in Pacific Asia*, 1:180–81.

54. Ibid., 2:279.

55. Ibid., 2:281.

56. Richard Linthicum, *War between Japan and Russia* (Chicago: W. R. Vansant, 1904), 213.

57. Petr A. Zaionchkovskii, *The Russian Autocracy under Alexander III*, trans. David R. Jones (Gulf Breeze, Fla.: Academic International, 1976), 22.

58. Kevin Lee, "Dogger Bank: Voyage of the Damned," Hullwebs History of Hull (Kingston upon Hull city history website) (2004), http://www.hullwebs.co.uk/content/l-20c/disaster/dogger-bank/voyage-of-dammed.htm# (accessed March 21, 2009); Sydney Tyler, *The Japan-Russia War* (Philadelphia: P. W. Ziegler Co., 1905), 357.

59. Lee, "Dogger Bank: Voyage of the Damned."

60. Richard Michael Connaughton, *The War of the Rising Sun and Tumbling Bear: A Military History of the Russo-Japanese War, 1904–5* (New York: Routledge, 1991), 246.

61. Norman E. Saul, *Sailors in Revolt: The Russian Baltic Fleet in 1917* (Lawrence: Regents Press of Kansas, 1978), 64–66.

62. Connaughton, *War of Rising Sun and Tumbling Bear*, 246; Lee, "Dogger Bank: Voyage of the Damned"; Constantine Pleshakov, *The Tsar's Last Armada: The Epic Voyage to the Battle of Tsushima* (New York: Basic Books, 2003), 98.

63. Pleshakov, *Tsar's Last Armada*, 98–99; Tyler, *Japan-Russia War*, 364.

64. Gordon, *Russian Prohibition*, 9; Michael Graham Fry, Erik Goldstein, and Richard Langhorne, *Guide to International Relations and Diplomacy* (London: Continuum, 2002), 162.

65. J. Martin Miller, *Thrilling Stories of the Russian-Japanese War* (n.p., 1904), 449.

66. Veresaev, *In the War*, 259–60.

67. Ibid., 275.

68. Ibid., 259–60.

69. Reported in the *Vil'no voenno-listok*; cited in Snow, "Alcoholism in the Russian Military," 427.

70. McCormick, *Tragedy of Russia in Pacific Asia*, 2:280.

71. Pleshakov, *Tsar's Last Armada*, 192–93.

72. Ibid., 283, 86.

73. McCormick, *Tragedy of Russia in Pacific Asia*, 2:280. See also Pleshakov, *Tsar's Last Armada*, 324–25.

74. McCormick, *Tragedy of Russia in Pacific Asia*, 2:281.

75. W. Bruce Lincoln, *In War's Dark Shadow: The Russians before the Great War* (New York: Dial, 1983), 243, 59.

76. Quoted in Herlihy, *Alcoholic Empire*, 52; see also Ernest Poole, "Two Russian Soldiers," *The Outlook*, Sept. 2 1905, 21–22.

Chapter 12

1. Viktor P. Obninskii, *Poslednii samoderzhets, ocherk zhizni i tsarstvovaniia imperatora Rossii Nikolaia II-go* (Moscow: Respublika, 1992), 21–22.

2. Mark D. Steinberg and Vladimir M. Khrustalëv, *The Fall of the Romanovs: Political Dreams and Personal Struggles in a Time of Revolution* (New Haven, Conn.: Yale University Press, 1995), 5.

3. Robert K. Massie, *Nicholas and Alexandra* (New York: Atheneum, 1967), 19–20.

4. See Orlando Figes, *A People's Tragedy: The Russian Revolution, 1891–1924* (New York: Viking, 1996), 16; Valentina G. Chernukha, "Emperor Alexander III, 1881–1894," in *The Emperors and Empresses of Russia: Rediscovering the Romanovs*, ed. Donald J. Raleigh and Akhmed A. Iskenderov (Armonk, N.Y.: M. E. Sharpe, 1996), 359; Charles Lowe, *Alexander III of Russia* (New York: Macmillan, 1895), 277–89; Hermann von Samson-Himmelstjerna, *Russia under Alexander III. And in the Preceding Period*, ed. Felix Volkhovsky, trans. J. Morrison (New York: MacMillan and Co., 1893), xxi–xxii.

5. Petr A. Zaionchkovskii, *Rossiiskoe samoderzhavie v kontse XIX stoletiya* (Moscow: Mysl', 1970), 47–48.

6. James P. Duffy and Vincent L. Ricci, *Czars: Russia's Rulers for over One Thousand Years* (New York: Barnes & Noble Books, 1995), 331–32; Catherine Radziwill, *Nicholas II: The Last of the Tsars* (London: Cassell & Co., 1931), 100.

7. Zaionchkovskii, *Rossiiskoe samoderzhavie*, 51–52.

8. Mohammed Essad-Bey [Lev Nussimbaum], *Nicholas II: Prisoner of the Purple*, trans. Paul Maerker-Branden and Elsa Branden (New York: Funk & Wagnalls Co., 1936), 153. See also George Alexander Lensen, *Russia's Eastward Expansion* (New York: Prentice-Hall, 1964), 95; David Chavchavadze, *The Grand Dukes* (New York: Atlantic International, 1990), 224.

9. Mark D. Steinberg, "Russia's Fin De Siècle, 1900–1914," in *Cambridge History of Russia*, ed. Ronald G. Suny (New York: Cambridge University Press, 2006), 72. This wasn't the first time that a *festin du peuple* went horribly awry. Following Alexander II's coronation forty years earlier, a free dinner for a quarter-million guests was spoiled by rain and ravaged by crows. Moreover, the festivities were accidentally begun even before the new tsar arrived. Once the guests laid into the 1,252 *vedro*s of wine, 3,120 *vedro*s of beer, and untold quantities of vodka, they could not be stopped. Henry Tyrrell, *The History of the War with Russia: Giving Full Details of the Operations of the Allied Armies*, 2 vols. (London: London Printing & Publishing Co., 1855), 2:334–35.

10. Duffy and Ricci, *Czars*, 331; Massie, *Nicholas and Alexandra*, 58–59; W. Bruce Lincoln, *The Romanovs: Autocrats of All the Russias* (New York: Dial, 1981), 627. On the couple's charitable work see Christopher Warwick, *Ella: Princess, Saint and Martyr* (London: John Wiley & Sons, 2006), 167.

11. Alexander Mikhailovich Romanov, *Once a Grand Duke* (New York: Farrar & Rinehart, 1932), 139; Zaionchkovskii, *Rossiiskoe samoderzhavie*, 52, 136–37; Patricia Herlihy, *The Alcoholic Empire: Vodka and Politics in Late Imperial Russia* (New York: Oxford University Press, 2002), 24–28, 209n1.

12. Constantine Pleshakov, *The Tsar's Last Armada: The Epic Voyage to the Battle of Tsushima* (New York: Basic Books, 2003), 21–22. See also Zaionchkovskii, *Rossiiskoe samoderzhavie*, 51.

13. Mike Martin, *From Crockett to Custer* (Victoria, B.C.: Trafford, 2004), 172–73.

14. Dee Brown, *Wondrous Times on the Frontier* (Little Rock, Ark.: August House, 1991), 46–52.

15. Marc Ferro, *Nicholas II: Last of the Tsars* (New York: Oxford University Press, 1993), 49; Julia P. Gelardi, *From Splendor to Revolution: The Romanov Women, 1847–1928* (New York: Macmillan, 2011), n.p.

16. Pleshakov, *Tsar's Last Armada*, 21, 58, 98, 152.

17. The grand duchess subsequently retired to a convent and devoted herself to alleviating poverty and intemperance. Edith Martha Almedingen, *An Unbroken Unity: A Memoir of Grand-Duchess Serge of Russia, 1864–1918* (London: Bodley Head, 1964), 52; Lincoln, *Russia*, 651.

18. On his alcoholism see Obninskii, *Poslednii samoderzhets*, 21. As a scapegoat, see Ferro, *Nicholas II*, 47.

19. Alexander Polunov, *Russia in the Nineteenth Century: Autocracy, Reform and Social Change, 1814–1914*, trans. Marshall Shatz (Armonk, N.Y.: M. E. Sharpe, 2005), 219–21. On the vodka-fueled riots and pogroms see Kate Transchel, *Under the Influence: Working-Class Drinking, Temperance, and Cultural Revolution in Russia, 1895–1932* (Pittsburgh, Pa.: University of Pittsburgh Press, 2006), 36; V. E. Bagdasaryan, "Vinnaya monopoliya i

politicheskaya istoriya," in *Veselie Rusi, XX vek: Gradus noveishei rossiiskoi istorii ot "p'yanogo byudzheta" do "sukhogo zakona,"* ed. Vladislav B. Aksenov (Moscow: Probel-2000, 2007), 108–11.

20. V. Blagoveshchenskii, "Vred p'yanstva dlya obshchestva i gosudarstva," in *Pit' do dna— ne vidat' dobra. Sbornik statei protiv p'yanstva* (St. Petersburg: Tipografiya Aleksandro-Nevskago obshchestva trezvosti, 1911); N. N. Shipov, *Alkogolizm i revolyutsiya (Alcohol and Revolution)* (St. Petersburg: Grad., 1908), 35–42; W. Arthur McKee, "Sobering up the Soul of the People: The Politics of Popular Temperance in Late Imperial Russia," *Russian Review* 58, no. 2 (1999): 214; Herlihy, *Alcoholic Empire*, 61–62, 66–68. On the vodka boycotts see Transchel, *Under the Influence*, 36.

21. Marr Murray, *Drink and the War from the Patriotic Point of View* (London: Chapman & Hall, 1915), epigraph; Vladimir P. Nuzhnyi, *Vino v zhinzni i zhizn' v vine* (Moscow: Sinteg, 2001), 234; A. W. Harris, "A Compensation of the War," *Union Signal*, June 8, 1916, 5.

22. Mark Lawrence Schrad, *The Political Power of Bad Ideas: Networks, Institutions, and the Global Prohibition Wave* (New York: Oxford University Press, 2010), 141, 73–74. On the Kaiser's proclamation see "Kaiser Wilhelm Seeks to Curb Drink Evil," *Union Signal*, Sept. 25, 1913; James S. Roberts, *Drink, Temperance, and the Working Class in Nineteenth-Century Germany* (Boston: George Allen & Unwin, 1984), 68–69.

23. Aleskandr M. Korovin, "Vysochaishii manifest 17 oktabrya i bor'ba s p'yanstvom," *Vestnik trezvosti*, no. 130 (1905) cited and translated in Herlihy, *Alcoholic Empire*, 129. Indeed, America's pioneering expert on Russia, George Kennan, explained to temperance advocate Frances Willard that "drunkenness among the peasants is a result of the latter's poverty and wretchedness—that it is an attempt to escape for a time from the consciousness of hopeless misery caused by oppression and bad government." George Kennan to Frances Willard, Aug. 29, 1888, p. 2, folder 47—Correspondence, 1888: July–September (reel 15), Women's Christian Temperance Union Series, Temperance and Prohibition Papers, Evanston, Ill.

24. Quoted in Transchel, *Under the Influence*, 31. See also Irina R. Takala, *Veselie Rusi: Istoriia alkogol'noi problemy v Rossii* (St. Petersburg: Zhurnal Neva, 2002), 100–103. Evgenii V. Pashkov, "Kazennaya vinnaya monopoliya v Rossii kontsa XIX-nachala XX v." in: *Alkogol' v Rossii: Materialy vtoroi mezhdunarodnoi nauchno-prakticheskoi konferentsii* (Ivanovo, 28–29 oktyabrya 2011), ed. Nikolai V. Dem'yanenko (Ivanovo: Filial RGGU v g. Ivanovo, 2011), 72–9.

25. Sergei Witte, *The Memoirs of Count Witte* (Garden City, N.Y.: Doubleday, 1921), 54–57; Mikhail Fridman, *Vinnaya monopoliya, tom 2: Vinnaya monopoliya v Rossii* (Petrograd: Pravda, 1916), 120–31; Nikolai Osipov, *Vinnaya monopoliya: Ee osnovniya nachala, organizatsiya, i nekotoriya posledstviya* (St. Petersburg: P. P. Soikin, 1899), 9, 14 Alexis Raffalovich, "The State Monopoly of Spirits in Russia, and Its Influence on the Prosperity of the Population," *Journal of the Royal Statistics Society* 64, no. 1 (1901). Robert Hercod, *La prohibition de l'alcool en Russie* (Westerville, Ohio: American Issue, 1919), 4; Vladimir I. Lenin, "Casual Notes," in *Collected Works, vol. 4: 1898–April 1901* (Moscow: Progress Publishers, 1972), 407–8. Also see Vladimir I. Lenin, "Spare Cash," in *Collected Works, vol. 18: April 1912–March 1913* (Moscow: Progress Publishers, 1963), 601–2.

26. D. G. Bulgakovskii, *Ocherk deyatel'nosti popechitel'stv o narodnoi trezvosti za vse vremya ikh sushchestvovaniya, 1895–1909 G.*, 2 vols. (St. Petersburg: Otechestvennaya tipografiya, 1910); V. A. Hagen, *Bor'ba s narodnym p'yanstvom: Popechitel'stva o narodnoi trezvosti, ikh sovremennoe polozhenie i nedostatki* (St. Petersburg: Gosudarstvennaya Tipgrafiya, 1907); David Lewin, "Das Branntweinmonopol in Russland," *Zeitschrift für die gesamte Staatswissenschaft* 25 (1908).

27. See, for instance, I. Mordvinov, *Obshchestvo trezvosti, zhizn' i rabota v nem* (St. Petersburg: Tipografiya Aleksandro-Nevskago obshchestva trezvosti, 1911); John F. Hutchinson, "Medicine, Morality, and Social Policy in Imperial Russia: The Early Years of the Alcohol Commission," *Histoire sociale/Social History* 7 (1974): 204; George Kennan, "Results of the Russian Liquor Reform," *The Outlook*, Jan. 11, 1902; original manuscript is housed in the New York Public Library.

28. Quoted in Herlihy, *Alcoholic Empire*, 15.

29. Vladimir I. Gurko, *Features and Figures of the Past: Government and Opinion in the Reign of Nicholas II*, trans. Laura Matveev (Palo Alto, Calif.: Stanford University Press, 1939), 530; Marc Lee Schulkin, "The Politics of Temperance: Nicholas II's Campaign against Alcohol Abuse" (Ph.D. diss., Harvard University, 1985), 151–95. See also f. 115 (Soyuz 17-ogo Oktyabrya), op. 1, d. 111, l.3; f. 115, op. 1, d. 19, l.1–317; f. 115, op. 2, d. 16, l.1, 16; f. 115, op. 2, d. 18, l.1–63; f. 1779 (Kantselyariya vremennogo pravitel'stva, 1917), op. 1, d. 709, l.1, Gosudarstvennyi Arkhiv Rossiskoi Federatsii (GARF) (State archive of the Russian Federation), Moscow. On the evolution of temperance and the legislature, see Aleksandr L. Afanas'ev, "Trezvennoe dvizhenie 1907–1914 godov v Rossii: Etapy, kharakter, znachenie," in: *Alkogol' v Rossii: Materialy pervoi mezhdunarodnoi nauchno-prakticheskoi konferentsii* (Ivanovo, 29–30 oktyabrya 2010), ed. Mikhail V. Teplyanskii (Ivanovo: Filial RGGU v g. Ivanovo, 2010), 114–19.
30. GARF, f. 102 (Departament Politsii (4-oe deloproizvodstvo)), op. 1909, d. 194 (Vserossiiskii s''ezd' po bor'be s p'yanstvom), l.3–64; N. A. Lyubimov, *Dnevnik uchastnika pervago vserossiiskago s'ezda po bor'be s narodnym p'yanstvom. Sankt Peterburg, 28 dekabrya 1909 g.–6 yanvarya 1910 g.* (Moscow: Pechatnya A. I. Snegirevoi, 1911); Laura Phillips, *Bolsheviks and the Bottle: Drink and Worker Culture in St. Petersburg, 1900–1929* (DeKalb: Northern Illinois University Press, 2000), 12–17; Herlihy, *Alcoholic Empire*, 130–32; Transchel, *Under the Influence*, 55–65. On political opposition parties and temperance see Mikhail V. Teplyanskii, "Politicheskii aspekt trezvennogo dvizheniya v dorevolyutsionnoi Rossii," in: *Alkogol' v Rossii: Materialy tret'ei mezhdunarodnoi nauchno-prakticheskoi konferentsii* (Ivanovo, 26–27 oktyabrya 2012), ed. Mikhail V. Teplyanskii (Ivanovo: Filial RGGU v g. Ivanovo, 2012), 181.
31. Edvard Radzinsky, *The Last Tsar: The Life and Death of Nicholas II*, trans. Marian Schwartz (New York: Doubleday, 1992), 102–10; Sir John Maynard, *Russia in Flux* (New York: Macmillan, 1949), 171.
32. Cited in Vladimir N. Kokovtsov, *Out of My Past: The Memoirs of Count Kokovtsov*, trans. Laura Matveev (Palo Alto, Calif.: Stanford University Press, 1935), 444. See also Vladislav B. Aksenov, *Veselie Rusi, XX vek: Gradus noveishei rossiiskoi istorii ot "p'yanogo byudzheta" do "sukhogo zakona"* (Moscow: Probel-2000, 2007), 152–54.
33. Alexander M. Michelson, "Revenue and Expenditure," in *Russian Public Finance during the War*, ed. Alexander M. Michelson, Paul Apostol, and Michael Bernatzky (New Haven, Conn.: Yale University Press, 1928), 82. On alcohol consumption and temperance conversion see Boris V. Ananich and Rafail S. Ganelin, "Emperor Nicholas II, 1894–1917," ed. Donald J. Raleigh and Akhmed A. Iskenderov (Armonk, N.Y.: M. E. Sharpe, 1996), 390; W. Arthur McKee, "Taming the Green Serpent: Alcoholism, Autocracy, and Russian Society, 1881–1914" (Ph.D. diss., University of California, Berkeley, 1997), 522.
34. William Johnson, *The Liquor Problem in Russia* (Westerville, Ohio: American Issue, 1915), 191; Peter L. Bark, "Memoirs," Sir Peter Bark Papers, Leeds Russian Archive, Special Collections, Leeds University Library, n/d. See also Bernard Pares, "Sir Peter Bark," *Slavonic and East European Review* 16, no. 46 (1937): 191; Takala, *Veselie Rusi*, 167.
35. The minister of war, General Vladimir Sukhomlinov, likewise encouraged the prohibition measure. George Snow, "Alcoholism in the Russian Military: The Public Sphere and the Temperance Discourse, 1883–1917," *Jahrbücher für Geschichte Osteuropas* 45, no. 3 (1997): 428–29; Arthur Toombes, *Russia and Its Liquor Reforms: National Experiments in License, State Monopoly and Prohibition* (Brisbane: Queensland Prohibition League, 1920), 2.
36. Steinberg and Khrustalëv, *Fall of the Romanovs*, 6–8; Anna Viroubova, *Memories of the Russian Court* (London: Macmillan, 1923), 127.
37. GARF, f. 601 (Imperator Nikolai II), op. 1, d. 991, l.1–2. See also Johnson, *Liquor Problem in Russia*, 194; Stephen P. Frank, *Crime, Cultural Conflict, and Justice in Rural Russia, 1856–1914* (Berkeley: University of California Press, 1999), 296. See also A. S. Rappoport, *Home Life in Russia* (New York: Macmillan, 1913), 94; Ernest Barron Gordon, *Russian Prohibition* (Westerville, Ohio: American Issue, 1916), 41, 56; George Thomas Marye, *Nearing the End in Imperial Russia* (Philadelphia: Dorrance & Co., 1929), 38.
38. Denis Garstin, *Friendly Russia* (London: T. Fisher Unwin, 1915), 215–16.
39. GARF, f. 671 (v. kn. Nikolai Nikolaevich Romanov—mladschii), op. 1, d. 47, l.1. On policy influence of noble alcohol interests see Walter G. Moss, *A History of Russia, vol. 1: To*

1917 (Boston: McGraw Hill, 1997), 300–302. On entrenched financial interests preventing radical change see Dmitrii N. Borodin, "Vinnaya monopoliya," *Trudy kommissii po voprosu ob alkogolizm: Zhurnaly zasedanii i doklady III* (1899): 173; Mikhail N. Nizhegorodtsev, "Alkogolizm i bor'ba s nim," *Zhurnal russkago obshchestva okhraneniya narodnago zdraviya* 8 (1909) Bernard Pares, *Russia and Reform* (London: Archibald Constable & Co., 1907), 146–48, 420–23; M. Bogolepoff, "Public Finance," in *Russia: Its Trade and Commerce*, ed. Arthur Raffalovich (London: P. S. King & Son, 1918), 27; Alexis Raffalovich, "Some Effects of the War on the Economic Life of Russia," *Economic Journal* 27, no. 105 (1917): 105. On drinking in elite restaurants see Rowland Smith, "Despatch from His Majesty's Ambassador at Petrograd, Enclosing a Memorandum on the Subject of the Temperance Measures Adopted in Russia since the Outbreak of the European War," in *House of Commons: Accounts and Papers, 1914–1916* (London: Harrison & Sons, 1915), 154–55.

40. Bark, "Memoirs," chap. 10, pp. 29–30.

41. Murray, *Drink and the War from the Patriotic Point of View*, 16–17. See also Michelson, "Revenue and Expenditure," 146–52; John Newton, *Alcohol and the War: The Example of Russia* (London: Richard J. James, 1915), 10–11.

42. *Russkoe slovo* (Moscow), Oct. 7, 1914; reprinted in Johnson, *Liquor Problem in Russia*, 200. The same wording is found in the report of the tsar's council of ministers of the following day, September 13 (old style)/September 29, 1914 (new style): "No. 137. Osobyi zhurnal soveta ministrov. 13 sentyabrya 1914 goda: Ob usloviyakh svedeniya gosudarstvennoi rospisi dokhodov i raskhodov na 1915 god"; in *Osobye zhurnaly Soveta Ministrov Rossiiskoi Imperii. 1909–1917 gg./1914 god*, (Moscow: ROSSPEN, 2006), 364. See also W. Arthur McKee, "Sukhoi zakon v gody pervoi mirovoi voiny: Prichiny, kontseptsiya i posledstviya vvedeniya sukhogo zakona v Rossii: 1914-1917 gg.," in *Rossiya i pervaya mirovaya voina (Materialy mezhdunarodnogo nauchnogo kollokviuma)* (St. Petersburg: Izdatel'stvo 'Dmitrii Bulanin', 1999), 152–53.

43. Zaionchkovskii, *Rossiiskoe samoderzhavie*, 52.

44. From the text of a letter, written in English, dated Nov. 20, 1883, a young Tsarevich Nicholas refers to Konstantin as "dearest uncle Costy"; otherwise he refers to him as Kostya in correspondence. GARF, f. 660 (V. Kn. Konstantin Konstantinovich Romanov), op. 2, d. 195, l.1.

45. See Konstantin's letters to the tsar on behalf of the VTSKhT: GARF, f. 601 (Imperator Nikolai II), op. 1, d. 1268, l.179–180, 184. See also GARF, f. 579 (Pavel N. Milyukov), op. 1, d. 2571, l.1–4; Herlihy, *Alcoholic Empire*, 120.

46. Johnson, *Liquor Problem in Russia*, 166–67.

47. Charlotte Zeepvat, *The Camera and the Tsars: The Romanov Family in Photographs* (Stroud, U.K.: Sutton, 2004); GARF, f. 660, op. 1, d. 65.

48. John Curtis Perry and Konstantin Pleshakov, *The Flight of the Romanovs: A Family Saga* (New York: Basic Books, 2001), 124.

49. Nicholas II Romanov, *Dnevniki imperatora Nikolaya II* (Moscow: Orbita, 1991), 489; Letter from Konstantin Konstantinovich to Tsar Nicholas II: GARF, f. 601 (Imperator Nikolai II), op. 1, d. 1268, l.182–183.

50. GARF, f. 601, op. 1, d. 262, l.22–26. See also Almedingen, *Unbroken Unity*, 87.

51. Richard Pipes, *The Russian Revolution* (New York: Vintage Books, 1990), 779–80. Given the proximity, time, and similarity of execution, it is widely thought that the murderers in both instances were the same. See Great Britain Foreign Office, *A Collection of Reports on Bolshevism in Russia* (London: H.M. Stationery Office, 1919), 26.

Chapter 13

1. Based on archival materials: f. 6996 (Ministerstvo Finansov Vremennogo Pravitel'stva), op. 1, d. 345, l.28, Gosudarstvennyi Arkhiv Rossiskoi Federatsii (GARF) (State archive of the Russian Federation), Moscow.

2. Bark's authoritative accounts are reprinted in Ernest Barron Gordon, *Russian Prohibition* (Westerville, Ohio: American Issue, 1916), 11; William Johnson, *The Liquor Problem in Russia* (Westerville, Ohio: American Issue, 1915), 213, as well as throughout Anglo-American temperance periodicals.

3. John Newton, *Alcohol and the War: The Example of Russia* (London: Richard J. James, 1915), 5.
4. Alfred Knox, *With the Russian Army, 1914–1917*, 2 vols. (London: Hutchinson & Co., 1921), 1:39.
5. Peter L. Bark, "Memoirs," Sir Peter Bark Papers, Leeds Russian Archive, Special Collections, Leeds University Library (n/d), chap. 9, p. 21.
6. Letter from General Alexei Andreevich Polivanov to William E. Johnson, September 26, 1915, William E. "Pussyfoot" Johnson papers, Special Collections #180, New York State Historical Association, Cooperstown.
7. GARF, f. 102, (Departament politsii, 4-oe deloproizvodstvo), op. 1914, d. 138, "Obezporyadkakh zapisnykh nishnikh chinov prizvannykh na voinu," l.24–120. Similarly see V. L. Telitsyn, "Pervaya mirovaya i pervach," in *Veselie Rusi, XX vek: Gradus noveishei rossiiskoi istorii ot "p'yanogo byudzheta" do "sukhogo zakona,"* ed. Vladislav B. Aksenov (Moscow: Probel-2000, 2007), 122–27.
8. GARF, f. 102, op. 1914, d. 138, l.35–38.
9. GARF, f. 102, op. 1914, d. 138, l.100–105. Joshua Sanborn finds similar coverage in the Russian State Historical Archives (RGIA), f. 1292, op. 1, d. 1729; cited in Joshua A. Sanborn, *Drafting the Russian Nation: Military Conscription, Total War, and Mass Politics, 1905–1925* (DeKalb: Northern Illinois University Press, 2003), 31.
10. Joshua A. Sanborn, "The Mobilization of 1914 and the Question of the Russian Nation: A Reexamination," *Slavic Review* 59, no. 2 (2000): 277.
11. GARF, f. 102, op. 1914, d. 138, l.116.
12. Quoted in Marc Ferro, *Nicholas II: Last of the Tsars* (New York: Oxford University Press, 1993), 71.
13. Sanborn, *Drafting the Russian Nation*, 30–32, 214; Vladimir I. Gurko, *Features and Figures of the Past: Government and Opinion in the Reign of Nicholas II*, trans. Laura Matveev (Palo Alto, Calif.: Stanford University Press, 1939), 537.
14. Francis B. Reeves, *Russia Then and Now: 1892–1917* (New York: G. P. Putnam's Sons, 1917), 110.
15. GARF, f. 579, op. 1, d. 2598, l. 1; GARF, f. 579, op. 1, d. 2549, l.1–2. See also Stephen P. Frank, *Crime, Cultural Conflict, and Justice in Rural Russia, 1856–1914* (Berkeley: University of California Press, 1999), 296; A. S. Rappoport, *Home Life in Russia* (New York: Macmillan, 1913), 94.
16. Bark, "Memoirs," chap. 10, pp. 1–2, 8–16; Sergei G. Belyaev, *P.L. Bark i finansovaya politika Rossii, 1914–1917 gg.* (St. Petersburg: Izdatel'stvo S.-Peterburgskogo universiteta, 2002), 162–64. See also Alexander M. Michelson, "Revenue and Expenditure," in *Russian Public Finance during the War*, ed. Alexander M. Michelson, Paul Apostol, and Michael Bernatzky (New Haven, Conn.: Yale University Press, 1928), 146–52.
17. Bark, "Memoirs," chap. 10, pp. 16, 21–22.
18. See, for instance, the report of A. Shingarev of the Finance Ministry on "War, Temperance and Finances" in GARF, f. 579, op. 1, d. 2547, l.1.
19. Mikhail P. Ironshnikov, Lyudmila A. Protsai, and Yuri B. Shelayev, *The Sunset of the Romanov Dynasty* (Moscow: Terra, 1992), 192; Bernard Pares, *The Fall of the Russian Monarchy* (New York: Alfred A. Knopf, 1939), 459–71; Tsuyoshi Hasegawa, *The February Revolution: Petrograd, 1917* (Seattle: University of Washington Press, 1981), 503–7.
20. Of the voluminous theoretical literature on revolutions see Jack Goldstone, "Toward a Fourth Generation of Revolutionary Theory," *Annual Review of Political Science* 4 (2001); Eric Selbin, "Revolution in the Real World: Bringing Agency Back In," in *Theorizing Revolutions*, ed. John Foran (London: Routledge, 1997); Theda Skocpol, *Social Revolutions in the Modern World* (New York: Cambridge University Press, 1994) and *States and Social Revolutions: A Comparative Analysis of France, Russia and China* (New York: Cambridge University Press, 1979).
21. See, for instance, Arthur Mendel, "On Interpreting the Fate of Imperial Russia," in *Russia under the Last Tsar*, ed. Theofanis George Stavrou (Minneapolis: University of Minnesota Press, 1969); Mark von Hagen, "The Russian Empire," in *After Empire: Multiethnic Societies and Nation-Building*, ed. Karen Barkey and Mark von Hagen (Boulder, Colo.: Westview, 1997).

22. Kate Transchel, *Under the Influence: Working-Class Drinking, Temperance, and Cultural Revolution in Russia, 1895–1932* (Pittsburgh, Pa.: University of Pittsburgh Press, 2006), 70.

23. GARF, f. 601, *(Imperator Nikolai II)*, op. 1, d. 991, l.1–2. On the flood of media support for prohibition see Gordon, Russian Prohibition, 41; Robert Hercod, *La prohibition de l'alcool en Russie* (Westerville, Ohio: American Issue, 1919), 5.

24. D. N. Voronov, *O samogone* (Moscow, 1929), 6; cited in Transchel, *Under the Influence*, 70. On moonshine, surrogates, and poisonings see: GARF, f. 1779, op. 1, d. 716, l. 1b, 41; Andrei M. Anfimov, *Rossiiskaia derevnia v gody pervoi mirovoi voiny: 1914–fevral' 1917 G.* (Moscow: Izdatel'stvo sotsial'no-ekonomicheskoi literatury, 1962), 243; V. Bekhterev, "Russia without Vodka," in *The Soul of Russia*, ed. Winifred Stephens (London: Macmillan, 1916), 273; Ol'ga A. Chagadaeva, "'Sukhoi zakon' v rossiiskoi imperii v gody pervoid mirovoi voiny (po materialam Moskvy i Petrograda)," in: *Alkogol' v Rossii: Materialy vtoroi mezhdunarodnoi nauchno-prakticheskoi konferentsii* (Ivanovo, 28–29 oktyabrya 2011), ed. Nikolai V. Dem'yanenko (Ivanovo: Filial RGGU v g. Ivanovo, 2011), 83–4; David Christian, "Prohibition in Russia 1914–1925," *Australian Slavonic and East European Studies* 9, no. 2 (1995): 102; Mikhail Friedman, "The Drink Question in Russia," in *Russia: Its Trade and Commerce*, ed. Arthur Raffalovich (London: P. S. King & Son, 1918), 439, 47; Hasegawa, *February Revolution*, 201.

25. Doreen Stanford, *Siberian Odyssey* (New York: E. P. Dutton, 1964), 31.

26. J. Y. Simpson, *The Self-Discovery of Russia* (London: Constable & Co., 1916), 84.

27. Dmitry Shlapentokh, "Drunkenness in the Context of Political Culture: The Case of Russian Revolutions," *International Journal of Sociology and Social Policy* 14, no. 8 (1994): 38. See also Dmitry Shlapentokh, "Drunkenness and Anarchy in Russia: A Case of Political Culture," *Russian History/Histoire Russe* 18, no. 4 (1991): 477.

28. Shlapentokh, "Drunkenness and Anarchy in Russia," 483. Ironically, in a battle with the Prussians in 1758, Russian forces allegedly lost a battle after drinking a large alcohol supply, leading to the capture of some twenty thousand soldiers. Boris Segal, *Russian Drinking: Use and Abuse of Alcohol in Pre-Revolutionary Russia* (New Brunswick, N.J.: Rutgers Center of Alcohol Studies, 1987), 75.

29. Dmitri P. Os'kin, *Zapiski soldata* (Moscow: Federatsiya, 1929), 274–76. See also Karen Petrone, *The Great War in Russian Memory* (Bloomington: Indiana University Press, 2011), 101. More generally see "Soldatskie pis'ma v gody mirovoi voiny, s predisloviem O. Chaadaevoi," *Krasnyi arkhiv* 4–5, no. 65–66 (1934): 118–63.

30. Emile Vandervelde, *Three Aspects of the Russian Revolution* (London: George Allen & Unwin, 1918), 131–32.

31. GARF, f. 1779, op. 1, d. 705, l. 5; GARF, f. 1779, op. 2, d. 299, l.1–7; GARF, f. 6996 (Ministerstvo Finansov Vremennogo Pravitelistva, 1917), op. 1, d. 293, l.5, 6, 17, 28, 33–38; GARF, f. 6996, op. 1, d. 296, l.17; GARF, f. 6996, op. 1, d. 299, l.5; GARF, f. 6996, op. 1, d. 300, l.1–244

32. Shlapentokh, "Drunkenness and Anarchy in Russia," 482.

33. *The Russian Diary of an Englishman: Petrograd, 1915–1917* (New York: Robert M. McBride & Co., 1919), 15.

34. W. Arthur McKee, "Taming the Green Serpent: Alcoholism, Autocracy, and Russian Society, 1881–1914" (Ph.D. diss., University of California, Berkeley, 1997), 534.

35. Allan Wildman, "The February Revolution in the Russian Army," *Soviet Studies* 22, no. 1 (1970).

36. GARF, f. 579 (Milyukov, Pavel Nikolaevich), op. 1, d. 2547 (Tezisy k dokladu A. I. Shingareva "Voina, trezvost' i finansy"), l.1; for an English translation see Michael T. Florinsky, *The End of the Russian Empire* (New York: Collier Books, 1961), 44.

37. W. Arthur McKee, "Sukhoi zakon v gody pervoi mirovoi voiny: Prichiny, kontseptsiya i posledstviya vvedeniya sukhogo zakona v Rossii: 1914–1917 gg.," in *Rossiya i pervaya mirovaya voina (Materialy mezhdunarodnogo nauchnogo kollokviuma)* (St. Petersburg: Izdatel'stvo 'Dmitrii Bulanin', 1999), 149; M. Bogolepoff, "Public Finance," in *Russia: Its Trade and Commerce*, ed. Arthur Raffalovich (London: P. S. King & Son, 1918), 346; Olga Crisp, *Studies in the Russian Economy before 1914* (New York: Barnes & Noble, 1976), 27; Alexis Raffalovich, "Some Effects of the War on the Economic Life of Russia," *Economic Journal* 27, no. 105 (1917).

On the decrease in revenues see Alexander M. Michelson, "Revenue and Expenditure," in *Russian Public Finance during the War*, ed. Alexander M. Michelson, Paul Apostol, and Michael Bernatzky (New Haven, Conn.: Yale University Press, 1928), 45; R. W. Davies, *Development of the Soviet Budgetary System* (New York: Cambridge University Press, 1958), 65.

38. Transchel, *Under the Influence*, 72. On contemporary alarms see Sergei N. Prokopovich, *Voina i narodnoe khozyaistvo*, 2nd ed. (Moscow: Tipografiya N. A. Sazonovoi, 1918), 115.

39. GARF, f. 579 (Milyukov, Pavel Nikolaevich), op. 1, d. 2547 (Tezisy k dokladu A. I. Shingareva "Voina, trezvost' i finansy"), l.1.

40. See, for instance, Boris Bakhmeteff, "War and Finance in Russia," *Annals of the American Academy of Political and Social Science* 75 (1918): 192–98. On Bark's (and Witte's) public pronouncements belittling the financial impact of prohibition, see Marr Murray, *Drink and the War from the Patriotic Point of View* (London: Chapman & Hall, 1915), 16–17; Newton, *Alcohol and the War*, 10–11; Arthur Sherwell, *The Russian Vodka Monopoly* (London: S. King & Son, 1915), 7. On the continued faith in the solvency of the imperial treasury despite all evidence to the contrary see Peter L. Bark, "Doklad P. L. Barka Nikolayu II o rospisi dokhodov i raskhodov na 1917 god, s predisloviem B. A. Romanova," *Krasnyi arkhiv* 26, no. 4 (1926); Bogolepoff, "Public Finance," 348; Friedman, "The Drink Question in Russia," 449; Stephen Graham, *Russia in 1916* (New York: Macmillan, 1917), 120–25; D. N. Voronov, *Zhizn' derevni v dni trezvosti* (St. Petersburg: Gosudarstvennaya tipografiya, 1916). Some have cited the so-called accounting effect (*bukhgalterskii effekt*), whereby war expenditures were kept separate from the normal operating budget, as the root of the financial problem. "Finansovoe polozhenie Rossii pered oktyabr'skoi revolutsiei, s predisloviem B. A. Romanova," *Krasnyi arkhiv* 25, no. 6 (1927): 4–5.

41. Quoted in: Vladimir N. Kokovtsov, *Out of My Past: The Memoirs of Count Kokovtsov*, trans. Laura Matveev (Palo Alto, Calif.: Stanford University Press, 1935), 473.

42. Bark, "Memoirs," chap. 10, pp. 29–30.

43. Aleksandr P. Pogrebinskii, *Ocherki istorii finanasov dorevolyutsionnoi Rossii (XIX–XX vv.)* (Moscow: Gosfinizdat, 1954), 126–28.

44. Michelson, "Revenue and Expenditure," 35.

45. See, for instance, GARF, f. 1779, op. 1, d. 705, l.5.

46. On the Bukhov case see GARF, f. 6996, op. 1, d. 345, l.8, 28. For additional cases from Voronezh, Ekaterinoslav, Tomsk, and other *gubernii* see GARF, f. 6996, op. 1, d. 345, l.9–21 and 39–46.

47. Anton M. Bol'shakov, *Derevnya, 1917–1927* (Moscow: Rabotnik prosveshcheniya, 1927), 338.

48. GARF, f. 6996, op. 1, d. 346, l.5–397, esp. 51–52; Christian, "Prohibition in Russia 1914–1925," 107.

49. GARF, f. 1779, op. 1, d. 705, l.5; GARF, f. 1779, op. 2, d. 299, l.1–7; GARF, f. 6996 (Ministerstvo Finansov Vremennogo Pravitelistva, 1917), op. 1, d. 293, l.5, 6, 17, 28, 33–38; GARF, f. 6996, op. 1, d. 296, l.17; GARF, f. 6996, op. 1, d. 299, l.2–376; GARF, f. 6996, op. 1, d. 300, l.1–245; GARF f. 6996, op. 1, d. 340, l.1–4; GARF, f. 6996, op. 1, d. 342, l.1–8.

50. Orlando Figes, *A People's Tragedy: The Russian Revolution, 1891–1924* (New York: Viking, 1996), 307; Patricia Herlihy, *The Alcoholic Empire: Vodka and Politics in Late Imperial Russia* (New York: Oxford University Press, 2002), 142–44; Kimitaka Matsuzato, "Interregional Conflicts and the Collapse of Tsarism: The Real Reason for the Food Crisis in Russia after the Autumn of 1916," in *Emerging Democracy in Late Imperial Russia*, ed. Mary Schaeffer Conroy (Niwot: University Press of Colorado, 1998), 244.

51. "The Distressed Condition of the Russian Alcohol Industry," *Pure Products* 11, no. 6 (1915): 279.

52. GARF, f. 1779, op. 1, d. 706, l.1–16; GARF, f. 6996, op. 1, d. 343, l.14, 27, 46; GARF, f. 6996, op. 1, d. 344, l.1–8.

53. Graham, *Russia in 1916*, 130.

54. "The Distressed Condition of the Russian Alcohol Industry," 279. It is doubtful that these plans were ever realized, as the Russians were pushed out of Galicia in the summer of 1915. It is evidence of gentry distillers' plans to sell alcohol during prohibition and the willingness of the state to assist them.

55. GARF, f. 6996, op. 1, d. 343, l.50, 69–71, 87.
56. Arkadii L. Sidorov, *Ekonomicheskoe polozhenie Rossii nakanune velikoi oktyabr'skoi sotsial-isticheskoi revolutsii: Dokumenty i materialy*, 3 vols. (Moscow: Izdatel'stvo akademii nauk SSSR, 1967), 3:131. On continued private distillation see: Alexis Antsiferov et al., *Russian Agriculture during the War* (New Haven, Conn.: Yale University Press, 1930), 164. On the traditional trade between peasants and distillers see Francis Palmer, *Russian Life in Town and Country* (New York: G. P. Putnam's Sons, 1901), 86–88.
57. Christian, "Prohibition in Russia 1914–1925," 113.
58. Sergei S. Ol'denburg, *Tsarstvovanie imperatora Nikolaya II*, 2 vols. (Munich: Izdanie obshchestva rasprostraneniya russkoi natsional'noi i patrioticheskoi literaturoi, 1949), 2:154–55. Likewise see Comptroller Kharitonov's declarations in Johnson, *Liquor Problem in Russia*, 211.
59. Rappoport, *Home Life in Russia*, 94.
60. John Hodgson, *With Denikin's Armies* (London: Temple Bar Publishing Co., 1932), 79; cited in Herlihy, *Alcoholic Empire*, 152.

Chapter 14

1. Speech reprinted in *Rabochaya gazeta*, Jan. 13, 1926; quoted in Kate Transchel, *Under the Influence: Working-Class Drinking, Temperance, and Cultural Revolution in Russia, 1895–1932* (Pittsburgh, Pa.: University of Pittsburgh Press, 2006), 75.
2. Based on f. 1779 (Kantselyariya vremennogo pravitel'stva), op. 2, d. 206, l.1–5, Gosudarstvennyi Arkhiv Rossiskoi Federatsii (GARF) (State archives of the Russian Federation), Moscow. See also Joseph Barnes, "Liquor Regulation in Russia," *Annals of the American Academy of Political and Social Science* 163 (1932): 228.
3. Ian F. W. Beckett, *The Great War: 1914–1918*, 2nd ed. (New York: Pearson-Longman, 2007), 521–25.
4. Richard Pipes, *The Russian Revolution* (New York: Vintage Books, 1990), 307–17.
5. Orlando Figes, *A People's Tragedy: The Russian Revolution, 1891–1924* (New York: Viking, 1996), 316–21.
6. Edward T. Heald, *Witness to Revolution: Letters from Russia, 1916–1919*, ed. James B. Glidney (Kent, Ohio: Kent State University Press, 1972), 59. See also Orlando Figes and Boris Kolonitskii, *Interpreting the Russian Revolution: The Language and Symbols of 1917* (New Haven, Conn.: Yale University Press, 1999), 34; James L. Houghteling Jr., *A Diary of the Russian Revolution* (New York: Dodd, Mead & Co., 1918), 146; R. H. Bruce Lockhart, *The Two Revolutions: An Eye-Witness Study of Russia, 1917* (Chester Springs, Pa.: Dufour Editions, 1967), 51; Emile Vandervelde, *Three Aspects of the Russian Revolution* (London: George Allen & Unwin, 1918), 29–30.
7. GARF, f. 1779, op. 2, d. 206, l.1–5. See also Arkadii L. Sidorov, ed., *Ekonomicheskoe polozhenie Rossii nakanune velikoi oktyabr'skoi sotsialisticheskoi revolutsii: Dokumenty i mate-rialy*, 3 vols. (Moscow: Izdatel'stvo akademii nauk SSSR, 1957), 2:432; Barnes, "Liquor Regulation in Russia," 228. Indeed, not even the most radical provisional government pro-posal to mend the state's finances included reintroducing alcohol. Robert Paul Browder and Alexander F. Kerensky, eds., *The Russian Provisional Government, 1917: Documents*, 3 vols. (Palo Alto, Calif.: Stanford University Press, 1961), 2:492–522. On the institutional paraly-sis see Vladimir D. Nabokov, *The Provisional Government* (New York: John Wiley & Sons, 1970), 30–31.
8. See Mark D. Steinberg, *Voices of Revolution, 1917* (New Haven, Conn.: Yale University Press, 2001), 100–101, 230, 88–89. Also see Dmitry Shlapentokh, "Drunkenness and Anarchy in Russia: A Case of Political Culture," *Russian History/Histoire Russe* 18, no. 4 (1991): 477–79.
9. "Like a plague bacillus from Switzerland into Russia," as Winston Churchill famously described it. Winston Churchill, *The World Crisis, vol. 5: The Aftermath* (New York: Charles Scribner's Sons, 1957), 63.
10. Peter Kenez, *A History of the Soviet Union from the Beginning to the End*, 2nd ed. (New York: Cambridge University Press, 2006), 28.
11. Vladimir D. Bonch-Bruevich, *Na boevykh postakh fevral'skoi i oktyabr'skoi revolyutsii*, 2nd ed. (Moscow: Federatsiya, 1931), 183.

12. Bessie Beatty, *The Red Heart of Russia* (New York: The Century Co., 1918), 333–34.

13. John Reed, *Ten Days That Shook the World* (New York: Random House, 1935), 321. See also John H. L. Keep, *The Russian Revolution: A Study in Mass Mobilization* (London: Weidenfeld & Nicholson, 1976), 332; Beatty, *Red Heart of Russia*, 330–31. Strong interviewed Trotsky, who preferred selling the liquor abroad. Anna Louise Strong, *The First Time in History: Two Years of Russia's New Life (August 1921 to December 1923)* (New York: Boni & Liveright, 1924), 156; Igor' V. Narskii, "Alkogol' v russkoi revolyutsii (1917–1922 gg.)," in: *Alkogol' v Rossii: Materialy pervoi mezhdunarodnoi nauchno-prakticheskoi konferentsii* (Ivanovo, 29–30 oktyabrya 2010), ed. Mikhail V. Teplyanskii (Ivanovo: Filial RGGU v g. Ivanovo, 2010), 28–31.

14. Meriel Buchanan, *Petrograd, the City of Trouble: 1914–1918* (London: W. Collins Sons & Co., 1919), 231–32.

15. See Boris Segal, *The Drunken Society: Alcohol Use and Abuse in the Soviet Union* (New York: Hippocrene Books, 1990), 30. On Gorky's criticism of the tsarist alcohol monopoly see his *Bystander* (New York: Jonathan Cape & Harrison Smith, 1930), 538.

16. Buchanan, *Petrograd*, 233–34. Narkompros was the agency in charge of education and censorship.

17. Yuri S. Tokarev, "Dokumenty narodnykh sudov (1917-1922)," in *Voprosy istoriografii i istochnikovedeniia istorii SSSR: Sbornik statei*, ed. Sigismund N. Valk (Leningrad: Izdatel'stvo Akademii nauk SSSR, 1963), 153.

18. Dmitrii A. Chugaev, ed., *Petrogradskii voenno-revoliutsionnyi komitet; Dokumenty i materialy*, 3 vols. (Moscow: Nauka, 1967), 3:276–78; Buchanan, *Petrograd*, 231; Reed, *Ten Days That Shook the World*, 321; Steinberg, *Voices of Revolution, 1917*, 24–25. On Dzerzhinsky, vodka, and the Cheka see Neil Weissman, "Prohibition and Alcohol Control in the USSR: The 1920s Campaign against Illegal Spirits," *Soviet Studies* 38, no. 3 (1986): 350; Bonch-Bruevich, *Na boevykh postakh fevral'skoi i oktyabr'skoi revolyutsii*, 183–84. Value conversion from 1917 dollars to 2013 dollars, courtesy of the US Inflation Calculator, http://www.usinflationcalcula-tor.com (accessed Aug. 20, 2013).

19. Strong, *First Time in History*, 157.

20. Reed, *Ten Days That Shook the World*, 309. See also Anatolii I. Razgon, *VTsIK Sovetov v pervye mesyatsy diktatury proletariata* (Moscow: Nauka, 1977), 215–38.

21. Helena Stone, "The Soviet Government and Moonshine, 1917–1929," *Cahiers du Monde Russe et Soviétique* 27, nos. 3–4 (1986): 359.

22. Vladimir A. Antonov-Ovseyenko, *Zapiski o grazhdanskoi voine*, 4 vols. (Moscow: Gosudarstvennoe izdatel'stvo, Otdel voennoi literatury, 1924), 1:19–20; cited in Stephen White, *Russia Goes Dry: Alcohol, State and Society* (New York: Cambridge University Press, 1996), 18.

23. Rex A. Wade, *Red Guards and Workers' Militias in the Russian Revolution* (Palo Alto, Calif.: Stanford University Press, 1984), 316; Christopher Williams, "Old Habits Die Hard: Alcoholism under N.E.P. and Some Lessons for the Gorbachev Administration," *Irish Slavonic Studies* No. 12 (1991): 74–75; Stone, "Soviet Government and Moonshine," 359; Robert Gellately, *Lenin, Stalin, and Hitler: The Age of Social Catastrophe* (New York: Vintage Books, 2007), 53.

24. Vladimir I. Lenin, "Our Tasks and the Soviet of Workers' Deputies," in *Collected Works, vol. 10: November 1905–June 1906* (Moscow: Progress Publishers, 1962), 26–27. See also Vladimir I. Lenin, "Lessons of the Moscow Uprising," in *Collected Works, vol. 11: June 1906–January 1907* (Moscow: Progress Publishers, 1962), 174; originally published in *Proletary* no. 2, Aug. 29, 1906.

25. Vladimir I. Lenin, "Casual Notes," in *Collected Works, vol. 4: 1898–April 1901* (Moscow: Progress Publishers, 1972), 406; originally published in *Zarya* No. 1, April 1901. See chapter 10. Also see George Snow, "Socialism, Alcoholism, and the Russian Working Classes before 1917," in *Drinking: Behavior and Belief in Modern History*, ed. Susanna Barrows and Robin Room (Berkeley: University of California Press, 1991), 244, 50.

26. Lenin, "Casual Notes," 404–5.

27. Weissman, "Prohibition and Alcohol Control in the USSR," 350; David Christian, "Prohibition in Russia 1914–1925," *Australian Slavonic and East European Studies* 9, no. 2

(1995): 95–96. See also f. 733 (Tsentral'noe upravlenie i ob"edinenie spirtovoi promyshlennosti, Gosspirt), op. 1, d. 4433, Rossiiskii Gosudarstvenni Arkhiv Ekonomiki (RGAE) (Russian State Archive of the Eeconomy), Moscow.

28. A. G. Parkhomenko, "Gosudarstvenno-pravovye meropriyatiya v bor'be s p'yanstvom v pervye gody sovetskoi vlasti," *Sovetskoe gosudarstvo i pravo* 4 (1984): 114; Grigory G. Zaigraev, *Obshchestvo i alkogol'* (Moscow: Ministry of Internal Affairs, 1992), 32–33; W. Bruce Lincoln, *Red Victory: A History of the Russian Civil War* (New York: Simon & Schuster, 1989), 59–60; Bertrand M. Patenaude, *The Big Show in Bololand: The American Relief Expedition to Soviet Russia in the Famine of 1921* (Palo Alto, Calif.: Stanford University Press, 2002), 430.

29. Evan Mawdsley, *The Russian Civil War* (New York: Pegasus Books, 2007), 285–88. See also Kenez, *History of the Soviet Union*, 41–48; Laura Phillips, *Bolsheviks and the Bottle: Drink and Worker Culture in St. Petersburg, 1900–1929* (DeKalb: Northern Illinois University Press, 2000), 28–29.

30. Quoted in Benjamin M. Weissman, *Herbert Hoover and Famine Relief to Soviet Russia, 1921–1923* (Stanford, Calif.: Hoover Institution, 1974), 2–3.

31. Patenaude, *Big Show in Bololand*, 1–3.

32. I. Gofshtetter, "Vodka ili khleb?" *Russkoe bogatstvo* (1891): 180–84; Hermann von Samson-Himmelstjerna, *Russia under Alexander III. And in the Preceding Period*, ed. Felix Volkhovsky, trans. J. Morrison (New York: Macmillan, 1893), xxi–xxii; George S. Queen, "American Relief in the Russian Famine of 1891–1892," *Russian Review* 14, no. 2 (1955): 140; Figes, *People's Tragedy*, 158–62.

33. Cited in Richard G. Robbins Jr., *Famine in Russia, 1891–1892* (New York: Columbia University Press, 1975), 131. See also Stephen Dunn and Ethel Dunn, *The Peasants of Central Russia* (New York: Holt, Rinehart & Winston, 1967), 29.

34. Patenaude, *Big Show in Bololand*, 429.

35. Amartya Sen, *Development as Freedom* (New York: Random House, 1999), n.p.

36. Tovah Yedlin, *Maxim Gorky: A Political Biography* (Westport, Conn.: Praeger\, 1999), 134–36.

37. Michael Barnett, *Empire of Humanity: A History of Humanitarianism* (Ithaca, N.Y.: Cornell University Press, 2011), 87.

38. Patenaude, *Big Show in Bololand*, 433; also, 440, 443, 450. Patenaude's account has been made into an excellent PBS documentary, *The Great Famine*: http://video.pbs.org/video/1853678422/.

39. Patenaude, Big Show in Bololand, 440–41.

40. Ibid., 441.

41. George H. Nash, *The Life of Herbert Hoover, vol. 3: Master of Emergencies, 1917–1918* (New York: W. W. Norton, 1996), 532 n.19.

42. Daniel Yergin and Joseph Stanislaw, *The Commanding Heights: The Battle between Government and the Marketplace that Is Remaking the Modern World* (New York: Simon & Schuster, 1998), 12. In response to the Kronstadt Uprising, Resolution 12 of the Tenth Party Congress outlawed dissenting factions within the party itself, thus eliminating any remaining opposition to bolshevism.

43. Vladimir I. Lenin, "X vserossiiskaya konferentsiya RKP(b)," in *Sochineniya, tom 32: dekabr' 1920–avgust 1921* (Moscow: Gosudarstvennoe izdatel'stvo politicheskoi literatury, 1951), 403; T. P. Korzhikhina, "Bor'ba s alkogolizmom v 20-kh—nachale 30-kh godov," *Voprosi istorii* no. 9 (1985): 22.

44. Anton M. Bol'shakov, *Derevnya, 1917–1927* (Moscow: Rabotnik prosveshcheniya, 1927), 337–48; V. M. Lavrov, *Sibir' v 1923–24 godu* (Novonikolaevsk: Sibrevkom, 1925), 210–15. *Pravda* reports from Weissman, "Prohibition and Alcohol Control in the USSR," 351; Strong, *First Time in History*, 159. Moscow vignettes from Transchel, *Under the Influence*, 78. See also S. A. Pavlyuchenkov, "Veselie Rusi: Revolyutsiya i samogon," in *Veselie Rusi, XX vek: Gradus noveishei rossiiskoi istorii ot "p'yanogo byudzheta" do "sukhogo zakona"*, ed. Vladislav B. Aksenov (Moscow: Probel-2000, 2007).

45. Cited in S. A. Smith, *Red Petrograd: Revolution in the Factories, 1917–1918* (New York: Cambridge University Press, 1983), 93.

46. Dmitri P. Os'kin, *Zapiski soldata* (Moscow: Federatsiya, 1929), 318–19; cited in Christian, "Prohibition in Russia 1914–1925," 104.

47. Keep, *Russian Revolution*, 256; Strong, *First Time in History*, 160.

48. Patenaude, *Big Show in Bololand*, 432.

49. Ian D. Thatcher, "Trotsky and Bor'ba," *Historical Journal* 37, no. 1 (1994): 116–17; originally published in Anon, 'Gosudarstvo i narodnoe khozyaistvo', *Bor'ba*, no. 2, pp. 3–8; reprinted in Leon Trotsky, *Sochineniya*, tom 4: *Politicheskaya khronika* (Moscow: Gosudarstvennoe izdatel'stvo, 1926), 525–33.

50. Leon Trotsky, "Vodka, tserkov', i kinematograf," *Pravda*, July 12, 1923.

51. Walter Connor, "Alcohol and Soviet Society," *Slavic Review* 30, no. 3 (1971): 580.

52. Trotsky, "Vodka, tserkov', i kinematograf."

53. A. M. Aronovich, "Samogonshchiki," in *Prestupnyi mir Moskvy*, ed. M. N. Gernet (Moscow: MKhO "Liukon", 1924), 174; Konstantin Litvak, "Samogonovarenie i potreblenie alkogolya v rossiiskoi derevne 1920-kh godov," *Otechestvennaya istoriya* no. 4 (1992): 76; Lars T. Lih, *Bread and Authority in Russia, 1914–1921* (Berkeley: University of California Press, 1990), 238.

54. British Trade Union Delegation to Russia and Caucasia, *Russia Today: The Official Report of the British Trade Union Delegation* (New York: International Publishers, 1925), 69.

55. Weissman, "Prohibition and Alcohol Control in the USSR," 351; Stone, "Soviet Government and Moonshine," 367.

56. Bol'shakov, *Derevnya, 1917–1927*, 339–41; Litvak, "Samogonovarenie i potreblenie alkogolya v rossiiskoi derevne 1920-kh godov," 76; Barnes, "Liquor Regulation in Russia," 229.

57. Yakov A. Yakovlev, *Derevnya kak ona est': Ocherki Nikol'skoi volosti*, 4th ed. (Moscow: Gosudarstvennoe izdatel'stvo, 1925), 106; quoted in Transchel, *Under the Influence*, 76.

58. Yakovlev, *Derevnya kak ona est'*, 109–10; quoted in Transchel, *Under the Influence*, 76.

59. Vladimir I. Lenin, "XI s'ezd RKP(b): 21 marta–2 aprelya 1922 g.," in *Sochineniya, tom 33: avgust 1921–mart 1923* (Moscow: Gosudarstvennoe izdatel'stvo politicheskoi literatury, 1955), 279.

60. E. Shirvindt, F. Traskovich, and M. Gernet, eds., *Problemy prestupnosti: Sbornik*, vol. 4 (Moscow: Izdatel'stvo narodnogo komissariata vnutrennikh del RSFSR, 1929), 116. NKVD statistics taken from *Vlast' sovetov* no. 31 (1925): 26–27; both quoted in Weissman, "Prohibition and Alcohol Control in the USSR," 350, 52–53.

61. Churchill, *World Crisis*, 66. On the circumstances of Lenin's death see Gina Kolata, "The Death of Lenin: Tracking a Suspect," *New York Times*, May 8, 2012, D5, http://www.nytimes.com/2012/05/08/health/research/lenins-death-remains-a-mystery-for-doctors.html (accessed May 8, 2012).

Chapter 15

1. Will Rogers, *There's Not a Bathing Suit in Russia & Other Bare Facts* (New York: Albert & Charles Boni, 1927), 110–11.

2. Yu. Chanin, "Po staroi, po nikolaevskoi," *Pravda*, Sept. 13, 1922, 5. See also A. L'vov, "Eto ne proidet," *Pravda*, Sept. 7, 1922, 1, and "Nuzhno li sokhranit' vinokurennuyu promyshlennost'?" *Pravda*, Sept. 8, 1922, 1; "Samogonshikov von iz rabochikh domov!" *Pravda*, Sept. 13, 1922, 5.

3. Vladimir I. Lenin, "Letter to the Congress (December 23–31, 1922) [Lenin's 'Testament']," in *The Structure of Soviet History: Essays and Documents*, ed. Ronald Grigor Suny (New York: Oxford University Press, 2003), 119–20.

4. Leon Trotsky, "Vodka, tserkov', i kinematograf," *Pravda*, July 12, 1923, 1. On the 1923 Central Committee meeting see Aleksandr Nemtsov, *Alkogol'naya istoriya Rossii: Noveishii period* (Moscow: URSS, 2009), 61.

5. Anna Louise Strong, *The First Time in History: Two Years of Russia's New Life (August 1921 to December 1923)* (New York: Boni & Liveright, 1924), 158–59.

6. L'vov, "Eto ne proidet," 1; an English version (with emphasis) from Strong, *First Time in History*, 162–63.

7. Strong, *First Time in History*, 164–65 (emphasis in original); see also 161.
8. Joseph Stalin, "Pis'mo Shinkevichu (20 marta 1927 g.)," in *Sochineniya, tom 9: dekabr' 1926–iyul' 1927* (Moscow: Gosudarstvennoe izdatel'stvo politicheskoi literatury, 1948), 191.
9. Helena Stone, "The Soviet Government and Moonshine, 1917–1929," *Cahiers du Monde Russe et Soviétique* 27, nos. 3–4 (1986): 372. See also Marie-Rose Rialand, *L'alcool et les Russes* (Paris: Institut d'études slaves, 1989), 108; Gregory Sokolnikov et al., *Soviet Policy in Public Finance: 1917–1928* (London: Oxford University Press, 1931), 195–96.
10. William Henry Chamberlin, *Russia's Iron Age* (New York: Little, Brown, 1934), 351–52.
11. Strong, *First Time in History*, 158.
12. Stalin, "Pis'mo Shinkevichu (20 marta 1927 g.)," 191–92. See also Joseph Stalin, "Beseda s inostrannymi rabochimi delegatsiyami: 5 noyabrya 1927 g.," in *Sochineniya, tom 10: 1927 avgust–dekabr'* (Moscow: Gosudarstvennoe izdatel'stvo politicheskoi literatury, 1952), 232.
13. Translated version in Strong, *First Time in History*, 168.
14. Stalin, "Pis'mo Shinkevichu (20 marta 1927 g.)," 192.
15. Stalin, "Beseda s inostrannymi rabochimi delegatsiyami," 232–33.
16. Ibid., 233–34.
17. Quoted in Ellen Barry, "Bulldogs under the Rug? Signs of a Putin-Medvedev Rift," *New York Times*, May 9, 2011, A6.
18. Peter Kenez, *A History of the Soviet Union from the Beginning to the End*, 2nd ed. (New York: Cambridge University Press, 2006), 84.
19. On the economic needs for vodka see f. 733 (Tsentral'noe upravlenie i ob"edinenie spirtovoi promyshlennosti, Gosspirt), op. 1, l.107–108; f. 733, op. 1, d. 1, l.1–56, Rossiiskii Gosudarstvennyi Arkhiv Ekonomiki (RGAE) (Russian State Archive of the Economy), Moscow. On the five-year plans for increased vodka output see RGAE, f. 733, op. 1, d. 143a, l.1–156; RGAE, f. 733, op. 1, d. 144, l.1–216; Ivan Viktorov, *Spirtovaya promyshlennost' SSSR* (Moscow: Snabtekhizdat, 1934), 15.
20. Stalin, "Beseda s inostrannymi rabochimi delegatsiyami," 232–33. See also R. W. Davies, *Development of the Soviet Budgetary System* (New York: Cambridge University Press, 1958), 121–24.
21. Emmanuil I. Deichman, *Alkogolizm i bor'ba s nim* (Moscow: Moskovskii rabochii, 1929), 143.
22. RGAE, f. 733, op. 1, d. 144, l.1; translated in Kate Transchel, *Under the Influence: Working-Class Drinking, Temperance, and Cultural Revolution in Russia, 1895–1932* (Pittsburgh, Pa.: University of Pittsburgh Press, 2006), 93.
23. Kenez, *History of the Soviet Union*, 93. See also S. A. Smith, *Red Petrograd: Revolution in the Factories, 1917–1918* (New York: Cambridge University Press, 1983), 93–94.
24. See f. 5515 (Narodnyi komissariat truda), op. 20, d. 7, l.29, 32, 43, 46, 48, 50, 52–53, 117, Gosudarstvennyi Arkhiv Rossiskoi Federatsii (GARF) (State archive of the Russian Federation), Moscow. See also GARF, f. 5467 (TsK Profsoyuza derevoobdeloinikov), op. 11, d. 179, l.1–14; GARF, f. 5467, op. 14, d. 108, l.17–20. On alcoholism statistics see RGAE, f. 1562 (TsSU pri Sovete Ministrov SSSR), op. 1, d. 490, l.9–10.
25. Transchel, *Under the Influence*, 112; T. H. Rigby, *Communist Party Membership in the USSR, 1917–1967* (Princeton, N.J.: Princeton University Press, 1968), 120–25.
26. The high caliber of the founding members signaled a high level of government and party support. Neil Weissman, "Prohibition and Alcohol Control in the USSR: The 1920s Campaign against Illegal Spirits," *Soviet Studies* 38, no. 3 (1986): 360–61.
27. See concluding speech of E. I. Deichman, "Vsesoyuznyi sovet protivoalkogol'nykh obshchestv v SSSR," in *Bor'ba s alkogoloizmom v SSSR* (Moscow: Gosudarstvennoe meditsinskoe izdatel'stvo, 1929), 87–88; also see Deichman, *Alkogolizm i bor'ba s nim*, 164–200. See also Leo M. Glassman, "Russia's Campaign to Keep Ivan Sober," *New York Times Magazine*, March 5, 1933, 6–7; Association against the Prohibition Amendment Papers, Library of Congress Manuscripts Division, box 4, Glassman File.
28. Irina R. Takala, *Veselie Rusi: Istoriia alkogol'noi problemy v Rossii* (St. Petersburg: Zhurnal Neva, 2002), 209–16; Transchel, *Under the Influence*, 90. Relatively little is known about the OBSA, as its archives were destroyed during the siege of Moscow in World War II: bombed and sunk while being evacuated by boat down the Moscow River.

29. Transchel, *Under the Influence,*, 146–47. K. V. Beregela, "Obshchestvo bor'by s alkogoliz-mom: poslednii etap syshchestvovaniya (1929–1932 gg.)" in: *Alkogol' v Rossii: Materialy tret'ei mezhdunarodnoi nauchno-prakticheskoi konferentsii* (Ivanovo, 26–27 oktyabrya 2012), ed. Mikhail V. Teplyanskii (Ivanovo: Filial RGGU v g. Ivanovo, 2012), 182–4.

30. Letter 62: Sept. 1, 1930; see Joseph Stalin, *Pis'ma I.V. Stalina V.M Molotovu, 1925–1936 gg.: Sbornik dokumentov* (Moscow: Rossiya molodaya, 1995), 209–10; an English transla-tion is in Lars T. Lih, Oleg V. Naumov, and Oleg V. Khlevniuk, eds., *Stalin's Letters to Molotov* (New Haven, Conn.: Yale University Press, 1995), 208–9. On completely abolishing the monopoly see Stalin, "Beseda s inostrannymi rabochimi delegatsiyami," 233.

31. Lih, Naumov, and Khlevniuk, *Stalin's Letters to Molotov*, xiv, 209.

32. Stone, "Soviet Government and Moonshine," 374. See also *Izvestiya*, March 9, 1923, p. 1; quoted in Weissman, "Prohibition and Alcohol Control in the USSR" 362. On the "scissors crisis" see Robert Service, *Trotsky: A Biography* (Cambridge, Mass.: Harvard University Press, 2009), 304.

33. Chamberlin, *Russia's Iron Age*, 352.

34. *Alkogolizm—put' k prestupleniyu*, ed. A. Gertsenzon (Moscow: Yuridicheskaya literatura, 1966), 21–23; cited in Walter Connor, "Alcohol and Soviet Society," *Slavic Review* 30, no. 3 (1971): 572. See also Davies, *Development of the Soviet Budgetary System*, 91–92.

35. Rogers, *There's Not a Bathing Suit in Russia*, 111.

36. GARF, f. 374 (Narodnyi komissariat raboche-krest'yanskoi inspektsii SSSR), op. 15, d. 1291, l.18–22. See also Sokolnikov et al., *Soviet Policy in Public Finance: 1917–1928*, 194.

37. Stone, "Soviet Government and Moonshine," 374. On Stalin at Potsdam see Helen Rappaport, *Joseph Stalin: A Biographical Companion* (Santa Barbara, Calif.: ABC-CLIO, 1999), 53. While accurate figures are scarce, a general scholarly consensus is forming around a combined death toll from collectivization, dekulakization, famine, and disease of around ten to 12 million. See Alec Nove, "Victims of Stalinism: How Many?" in *Stalinist Terror: New Perspectives*, ed. J. Arch Getty and Roberta T. Manning (New York: Cambridge University Press, 1993), 268.

38. Kenez, *History of the Soviet Union*, 86; Rappaport, *Joseph Stalin*, 43. This association actually goes back even farther, to the imperial period. See Olga Semyonova Tian-Shanskaia, *Village Life in Late Tsarist Russia*, trans. David L. Ransel (Bloomington: Indiana University Press, 1993), 154.

39. V.Ts.I.K. decree 35, art. 468. See Boris Segal, *The Drunken Society: Alcohol Use and Abuse in the Soviet Union* (New York: Hippocrene Books, 1990), 45.

40. Yakov M. Sverdlov, "O zadachakh sovetov v derevne: Doklad na zasedanii VTsIK 4–go sozyva 20 maya 1918 goda," in *Izbrannye proizvedeniya*, tom 2 (Moscow: Gosudarstvennoe izdatel'stvo politicheskoi literatury, 1959), 216.

41. Quoted in Peter Kenez, *Cinema and Soviet Society from the Revolution to the Death of Stalin* (London: I. B. Tauris, 2001), 82. More generally see Seema Rynin Allan, *Comrades and Citizens* (London: Victor Gollancz, 1938), 117; Lewis Siegelbaum and Andrei Sokolov, *Stalinism as a Way of Life*, abridged ed. (New Haven, Conn.: Yale University Press, 2004), 39.

42. Mariya Degtyareva, "Sobor novomuchenikov, v butovo postradavshikh," Pravmir.ru, May 21, 2010, http://www.pravmir.ru/sobor-novomuchenikov-v-butovo-postradavshix-2 (accessed May 12, 2012); Segal, *Drunken Society*, 40; Orlando Figes, *The Whisperers: Private Life in Stalin's Russia* (New York: Metropolitan Books, 2007), 84; David Satter, *It Was a Long Time Ago, and It Never Happened Anyway: Russia and the Communist Past* (New Haven, Conn.: Yale University Press, 2011), 59. Exiled kulaks were often given drunken public sendoffs. Sheila Fitzpatrick, *Stalin's Peasants: Resistance and Survival in the Russian Village after Collectivization* (New York: Oxford University Press, 1994), 58.

43. Lynne Viola, "The Second Coming: Class Enemies in the Soviet Countryside, 1927–1935," in *Stalinist Terror: New Perspectives*, ed. J. Arch Getty and Roberta T. Manning (New York: Cambridge University Press, 1993), 65. The great dissident writer Solzhenitsyn describes a similar situation: Aleksandr Solzhenitsyn, *The Gulag Archipelago, 1918–1956*, 3 vols. (New York: Harper & Row, 1976), 3:359.

44. Alec Nove, *An Economic History of the U.S.S.R.* (Baltimore: Penguin, 1969), 168. See also Piers Brendon, *The Dark Valley: A Panorama of the 1930s* (New York: Random House, 2000), 136.

45. Report to Kolkhoz Center on collectivization in Belorussia, Sept. 26, 1930, f. 7486s, op. 1, d. 102, ll.226–25 ob, Rossiiskii Gosudarstvennyi Arkhiv Ekonomiki (RGAE) (Russian State Archive of the Economy), Moscow; cited in Siegelbaum and Sokolov, *Stalinism as a Way of Life*, 49. This too was a repeat of the practices of War Communism. Robert Conquest, *The Harvest of Sorrow: Soviet Collectivization and the Terror-Famine* (New York: Oxford University Press, 1986), 46.

46. Rappaport, *Joseph Stalin*, 48. On livestock sere Jerry F. Hough and Merle Fainsod, *How the Soviet Union Is Governed* (Cambridge, Mass.: Harvard University Press, 1979), 151.

47. Geoffrey Hosking, *The First Socialist Society: A History of the Soviet Union from Within*, 2nd ed. (Cambridge, Mass.: Harvard University Press, 1993), 161.

48. Joseph Stalin, "Golovokruzhenie ot uspekhov. K voprosam kolkhoznogo dvizheniya (2 marta 1930 g.)," in *Sochineniya, tom 12: aprel' 1929–iyun' 1930* (Moscow: Gosudarstvennoe izdatel'stvo politicheskoi literatury, 1952), 199.

49. Kenez, *History of the Soviet Union*, 117; Transchel, *Under the Influence*, 152.

50. Tom Brokaw, *The Greatest Generation* (New York: Random House, 1998), xxxviii.

51. Vadim Erlikhman, *Poteri narodonaseleniya v XX veke* (Moscow: Russkaya panorama, 2004), 20–21; Anne Leland and Mari-Jana Oboroceanu, "American War and Military Operations Casualties: Lists and Statistics" (Washington D.C.: Congressional Research Service, 2010), 2, http://www.fas.org/sgp/crs/natsec/RL32492.pdf (accessed July 28, 2011).

52. Lilian T. Mowrer, *Rip Tide of Aggression* (New York: William Morrow & Co., 1942), 165; Aleksandr Nikishin, *Vodka i Stalin* (Moscow: Dom Russkoi Vodki, 2006), 170–71.

53. Quoted in Gabriel Gorodetsky, *Grand Delusion: Stalin and the German Invasion of Russia* (New Haven, Conn.: Yale University Press, 1999), 198.

54. Quoted in ibid.

55. Robert Gellately, *Lenin, Stalin, and Hitler: The Age of Social Catastrophe* (New York: Vintage Books, 2007), 429.

56. Charles W. Sutherland, *Disciples of Destruction* (Buffalo, N.Y.: Prometheus Books, 1987), 354; Bob Carroll, *The Battle of Stalingrad* (San Diego, Calif.: Lucent Books, 1997), 42.

57. Segal, *Drunken Society*, 73.

58. Constantine Pleshakov, *Stalin's Folly: The Tragic First Ten Days of World War II on the Eastern Front* (Boston: Houghton Mifflin, 2005), 11.

59. For wartime vodka production figures, see Nikishin, *Vodka i Stalin*, 226; Segal, *Drunken Society*, 71; Dmitri Volkogonov, *Autopsy for an Empire: The Seven Leaders Who Built the Soviet Regime* (New York: Simon & Schuster, 1999), 119; Takala, *Veselie Rusi*, 245–49. See also chapter 22.

60. Quoted in Laurence Rees, *War of the Century: When Hitler Fought Stalin* (New York: New Press, 1999), 86.

61. Bradley Lightbody, *The Second World War: Ambitions to Nemesis* (London: Routledge, 2004), 109.

62. Segal, *Drunken Society*, 73.

63. "British Open 'Second-Best Front' in Hot Libyan Desert as Nazis Smash at Moscow in Winter Gales," *Life*, Dec. 1, 1941, 30.

64. Anthony Eden, *The Reckoning*, vol. 2 of the *Memoirs of Anthony Eden* (Boston: Houghton Mifflin, 1965), 350–51. On Voroshilov see Hugh Dalton, *The Second World War Diary of Hugh Dalton, 1940–45*, ed. Ben Pimlott (London: Cape, 1986), 341.

65. Geoffrey Roberts, *Stalin's Wars: From World War to Cold War, 1939–1953* (New Haven, Conn.: Yale University Press, 2006), 131.

66. Personal communication reported in Segal, *Drunken Society*, 74.

67. Yitzhak Arad, *In the Shadow of the Red Banner: Soviet Jews in the War against Nazi Germany* (Jerusalem: Gefen, 2010), 180.

68. Segal, *Drunken Society*, 75.

69. Erlikhman, *Poteri narodonaseleniya v XX veke*; Robert Conquest, *The Great Terror: A Reassessment, 40th Anniversary Edition* (New York: Oxford University Press, 2008), xvi.

70. Joseph Stalin, "Vystuplenie tovarishcha I. V. Stalina na priyome v kremle v chest' komanduyushchikh voiskami Krasnoi Armii (24 maya 1945)," in *O Velikoi Otechestvennoi voine Sovetskogo Soyuza* (Moscow: Gosudarstvennoe izdatel'stvo politicheskoi literatury, 1946), 173–74. Also see Robert Service, *Comrades! A History of World Communism* (Cambridge, Mass.: Harvard University Press, 2007), 224.

Chapter 16

1. Peter Kenez, *A History of the Soviet Union from the Beginning to the End*, 2nd ed. (New York: Cambridge University Press, 2006), 166–71.

2. Max Hayward and Edward L. Crowley, eds., *Soviet Literature in the Sixties: An International Symposium* (New York: Praeger, 1964), 191.

3. David Burg and George Feifer, *Solzhenitsyn* (New York: Stein & Day, 1972), 49. See also Michael Scammell, *Solzhenitsyn: A Biography* (New York: W. W. Norton, 1984), 431, 604.

4. Aleksandr Solzhenitsyn, "Matryona's House (1959)," in *Stories and Prose Poems* (New York: Farrar, Straus & Giroux, 1970), 35–40.

5. Aleksandr Solzhenitsyn, *The Cancer Ward*, trans. Rebecca Frank (New York: Dial, 1968), 267–68.

6. Ibid., 209.

7. Alexander Elder, *Rubles to Dollars: Making Money on Russia's Exploding Financial Frontier* (New York: New York Institute of Finance, 1999), 70–71.

8. Donald Trelford, "A Walk in the Woods with Gromyko," *Observer*, April 2, 1989, 23. See also Anatoly Dobrynin, *In Confidence: Moscow's Ambassador to America's Six Cold War Presidents (1962–1986)* (New York: Times Books, 1995), 281.

9. Anatoly S. Chernyaev, "The Unknown Brezhnev," *Russian Politics and Law* 42, no. 3 (2004): 47.

10. David Aikman, *Great Souls: Six Who Changed the Century* (Boston: Lexington Books, 2003), 177. See also Aleksandr Solzhenitsyn, *Invisible Allies* (Washington, D.C.: Counterpoint, 1995).

11. Aleksandr Solzhenitsyn, *Letter to the Soviet Leaders* (New York: Harper & Row, 1974), 34–35.

12. Ibid., 41. See also Donald R. Kelley, *The Solzhenitsyn–Sakharov Dialogue: Politics, Society, and the Future* (Westport, Conn.: Greenwood, 1982), 91; Christopher Moody, *Solzhenitsyn*, rev. ed. (New York: Harper & Row, 1975), 27d.

13. Andrei Sakharov, *Memoirs*, trans. Richard Lourie (New York: Alfred A. Knopf, 1990), 650. See also Jay Bergman, *Meeting the Demands of Reason: The Life and Thought of Andrei Sakharov* (Ithaca, N.Y.: Cornell University Press, 2009), 183.

14. Andrei Sakharov, *Sakharov Speaks* (New York: Alfred A. Knopf, 1974), 42–43, 148. See also Andrei Sakharov, *My Country and the World*, trans. Guy V. Daniels (New York: Alfred A. Knopf, 1976), 23, 44.

15. Sakharov, *Memoirs*, 54.

16. Ibid., 274; see also 109, 362, 480, 506.

17. Ibid., 506. This echoes the anti-alcohol sentiments conveyed in his 1970 plea to Brezhnev. Denny Vågerö, "Alexandr Nemtsov's Pioneering Work on Alcohol in Modern Soviet and Russian History," in *A Contemporary History of Alcohol in Russia*, ed. Aleksandr Nemtsov (Stockholm: Södertörns högskola, 2011), 18.

18. Andrei Sakharov, "Sakharov's Reply to Solzhenitsyn," *War/Peace Report* 13, no. 2 (1974): 3. They were hardly alone in this respect, as Oliver Bullough shows in his investigation of dissident priest Father Dmitri Dudko, who likewise railed against the alcoholic system. Oliver Bullough, *The Last Man in Russia: The Struggle to Save a Dying Nation* (New York: Basic Books, 2013), 83–88.

19. Alexander Nazaryan, "Susan Orlean, David Rembick, Ethan Hawke, and Others Pick Their Favorite Obscure Books," *Village Voice*, Dec. 3, 2008, http://www.villagevoice.com/2008-12-03/books/susan-orlean-david-remnick-ethan-hawke-and-others-pick-their-favorite-

obscure-books (accessed Aug. 8, 2011). Apparently Venedikt Vasilievich is of no relation to the other two V. Erofeyevs mentioned thus far in this book: Viktor and Vladimir.

20. Venedikt Erofeyev, *Moscow to the End of the Line* (New York: Taplinger Publishing, 1980), 24.

21. Ibid., 35–36.

22. I. I. Lukomskii, "Alcoholism," in *Bol'shaia sovetskaia entsiklopediia*, ed. A. M. Prokhorov (New York: MacMillan, 1973), 218. See also Walter Connor, "Alcohol and Soviet Society," *Slavic Review* 30, no. 3 (1971): 571.

23. A. Krasikov, "Commodity Number One (Part 1)," in *The Samizdat Register*, ed. Roy A. Medvedev (New York: W. W. Norton, 1977), 102.

24. Cullen Murphy, "Watching the Russians," *Atlantic Monthly*, February 1983, 48–49.

25. From *Poiski* No. 3 (1978); quoted in Mikhail Baitalsky, *Notebooks for the Grandchildren: Recollections of a Trotskyist Who Survived the Stalin Terror*, trans. Marilyn Vogt-Downey (Atlantic Highlands, N.J.: Humanities Press, 1995), 431. Other biographical details are drawn from ibid., xii–xiii.

26. Tat'yana Prot'ko, *V bor'be za trezvost': Stranitsy istorii* (Minsk: Nauka i tekhnika, 1988), 130. Baitalsky bans drinking in his own home in *Notebooks for the Grandchildren*, 105.

27. Krasikov, "Commodity Number One (Part 1)," 94–95. On the disappearance of Soviet infant mortality statistics see Christopher Davis and Murray Feshbach, "Rising Infant Mortality in the USSR in the 1970s," in *United States Bureau of the Census*, Series P-95, No. 74 (Washington, D.C.: US Bureau of the Census, September 1980), 4.

28. See also Krasikov, "Commodity Number One (Part 1)," 101.

29. A. Krasikov, "Tovar nomer odin (II)," in *Dvadtsatyi vek: Obshchestvenno-politicheskii i literaturnyi al'manakh*, ed. Roy A. Medvedev (London: TCD Publications, 1977), 118–19; A. Krasikov, "Commodity Number One (Part 2)," in *The Samizdat Register*, ed. Roy A. Medvedev (New York: W. W. Norton, 1981), 175–76. On homebrew see: Arkadii T. Filatov, *Alkogolizm vyzvannyi upotrebleniem samogona* (Kiev: Zdorovya, 1979).

30. Krasikov, "Commodity Number One (Part 1)," 101; Baitalsky, *Notebooks for the Grandchildren*, 113; Krasikov, "Tovar nomer odin (II)," 128. For similar economic assessments see R. W. Davies, *Development of the Soviet Budgetary System* (New York: Cambridge University Press, 1958), 286–88.

31. Krasikov, "Commodity Number One (Part 1)," 105–6.

32. Ibid., 109. In a follow-up article Baitalsky upped these estimates to 26 billion rubles spent on alcohol every year, with 19.2 billion going to the state or roughly eleven percent of the entire operating budget of the Soviet state. Krasikov, "Commodity Number One (Part 2)," 171; Krasikov, "Tovar nomer odin (II)."

33. V. A. Bykov, "Videt' problemu vo vsei ee slozhnosti: Sotsial'nye fakory p'yanstva i alkogolizma," *EKO*, no. 9 (1985): 26; cited in Daniel Tarschys, "The Success of a Failure: Gorbachev's Alcohol Policy, 1985–88," *Europe-Asia Studies* 45, no. 1 (1993): 9.

34. See Krasikov, "Tovar nomer odin (II)," 138–39.

35. Krasikov, "Commodity Number One (Part 1)," 114.

36. Krasikov, "Commodity Number One (Part 2)," 188. Similarly see Robert G. Kaiser, *Russia: The People and the Power* (New York: Atheneum, 1976), 82.

37. Krasikov, "Tovar nomer odin (II)," 147–48. See also Baitalsky, *Notebooks for the Grandchildren*, 396.

38. Baitalsky, *Notebooks for the Grandchildren*, 238–39. Similarly see Krasikov, "Tovar nomer odin (II)," 150.

39. On seating arrangements atop the rostrum see Stephen Kotkin, "The State—Is It Us? Memoirs, Archives, and Kremlinologists," *Russian Review* 61, no. 1 (2002): 49.

40. Murphy, "Watching the Russians," 34.

41. Ibid.: 42. See also "Murray Feshbach Discusses Quality of Life in the Soviet Union," C-Span.org, Feb. 11, 1985, http://www.c-spanvideo.org/program/PoliticalDiscussion254 (accessed Aug. 23, 2011.)

42. See "Murray Feshbach Discusses Quality of Life in the Soviet Union" and Laurie Garrett, *Betrayal of Trust: The Collapse of Global Public Health* (New York: Hyperion, 2000), 128–37.

43. Murphy, "Watching the Russians," 35.

44. See, for instance, "Murray Feshbach Discusses Quality of Life in the Soviet Union."

45. Davis and Feshbach, "Rising Infant Mortality in the USSR in the 1970s," 6, 11. See also Murray Feshbach, "The Soviet Union: Population Trends and Dilemmas," *Population Bulletin* 37, no. 3 (1982). These estimates were later reprinted in the USSR during *glasnost*: B. M. Guzikov and A. A. Meiroyan, *Alkogolizm u zhenshchin* (Leningrad: Meditsina, 1988); Vladimir V. Dunaevskii and Vladimir D. Styazhkin, *Narkomanii i toksikomanii* (Leningrad: Meditsina, 1988), 66–72.

46. Murphy, "Watching the Russians," 38; "Murray Feshbach Discusses Quality of Life in the Soviet Union." More generally see John Dutton Jr., "Causes of Soviet Adult Mortality Increases," *Soviet Studies* 33, no. 4 (1981): 548–52.

47. Murphy, "Watching the Russians," 38.

48. On estimates and corroboration, see Vladimir Treml, *Alcohol in the U.S.S.R.: A Statistical Study, Duke Press Policy Studies* (Durham, N.C.: Duke University Press, 1982), 47–60; Prot'ko, *V bor'be za trezvost'*, 135; Stanislav Strumilin and Mikhail Sonin, "Alkogolnie poteri i bor'ba s nimi," *EKO*, no. 4 (1974): 37. See also Vladimir Treml, "Alcohol in the Soviet Underground Economy," Berkeley–Duke Occasional Papers on the Second Economy in the USSR No. 5, December (Berkeley: University of California Press, 1985): 4.

49. Murphy, "Watching the Russians," 38. Per 100,000 population, the percentage of Soviet alcohol-poisoning deaths was around 19.05, as compared to 0.17 in the United States. See also Anatolii Kapustin, *Alkogol'—vrag zdorov'ya* (Moscow: Meditsina, 1976), 38–42.

50. Aleksandr Nemtsov, *Alkogol'naya istoriya Rossii: Noveishii period* (Moscow: URSS, 2009), 205.

51. See letter from Vladimir Treml to Murray Feshbach, Oct. 23, 1981, p. 2, Murray Feshbach alcoholism archive (author's personal collection).

52. Vladimir Treml, "Alcohol in the U.S.S.R.: A Fiscal Dilemma," *Soviet Studies* 27, no. 2 (1975): 166. Also see Connor, "Alcohol and Soviet Society," 586; Tsentral'noe statisticheskoe upravlenie SSSR, *Narodnoe khozyaistvo SSSR v 1959 g.* (Moscow: Finansy i statistika, 1959), 646; Tsentral'noe statisticheskoe upravlenie SSSR, *Narodnoe khozyaistvo SSSR v 1962 g.* (Moscow: Finansy i statistika, 1962), 520; Prot'ko, *V bor'be za trezvost': Stranitsy istorii*, 130. Also see Raymond Hutchings, *The Soviet Budget* (Albany: SUNY Press, 1983), 36; Hedrick Smith, *The Russians* (New York: Quadrangle/New York Times Book Co., 1976), 121–22.

53. See, for instance, "Murray Feshbach Discusses Quality of Life in the Soviet Union."

54. Nemtsov, *Alkogol'naya istoriya Rossii*, 66. See also David Powell, "Soviet Union: Social Trends and Social Problems," *Bulletin of the Atomic Scientists* 38, no. 9 (1982): 24.

55. Nikita Khrushchev, *Khrushchev Remembers: The Last Testament*, trans. Strobe Talbott (Boston: Little, Brown, 1974), 145. See also Eduard Babayan, "Ne ostupis' . . . " *Izvestiya*, Oct. 16 1982, 3; Igor Birman, *Secret Incomes of the Soviet State Budget* (Boston: Martinus Nijhoff, 1981), 158.

56. *Pravda*, April 14, 1970; cited in "Alcoholism in the Soviet Union," Radio Liberty Dispatch, June 1, 1970, 1, Murray Feshbach alcoholism archive.

57. Kathryn Hendley, "Moscow's Conduct of the Anti-Alcohol Campaign: A Comparative Analysis, 1972–1986" (M.A. thesis, Georgetown University, 1987), 30–68; Krasikov, "Tovar nomer odin (II)."

58. Leonid I. Brezhnev, "Rech' na XVIII s'ezde Vsesoyuznogo Leninskogo Kommunisticheskogo Soyuza Molodezhi, 25 aprelya 1978 goda," in *Izbrannye proizvedeniya, tom 3: 1976—Mart 1981* (Moscow: Izdatel'stvo politicheskoi literatury, 1981), 302. More generally see Pavel V. Romanov, *Zastol'naya istoriya gosudarstva rossiiskogo* (St. Petersburg: Kristall, 2000), 413.

59. See Trelford, "A Walk in the Woods with Gromyko," 23; Viktor Erofeev, *Russkii apokalipsis: Opyt khudozhestvennoi eskhatologii* (Moscow: Zebra E, 2008), 12; Aleksandr Nikishin, *Vodka i Gorbachev* (Moscow Vsya Rossiya, 2007), 244. Even Gorbachev recounts the story, in his *Memoirs* (New York: Doubleday, 1995), 220–21.

60. See chapter 7, note 8.

Chapter 17

1. Rolf H. W. Theen, "Party and Bureaucracy," in *The Soviet Polity in the Modern Era*, ed. Erik P. Hoffman and Robbin F. Laird (Hawthorne, N.Y.: Aldine de Gruyter, 1984), 147.

2. Edwin Bacon, "Reconsidering Brezhnev," in *Brezhnev Reconsidered*, ed. Edwin Bacon and Mark Sandle (New York: Palgrave Macmillan, 2002), 9–11; Ben Fowkes, "The National Question in the Soviet Union under Leonid Brezhnev: Policy and Response," in *Brezhnev Reconsidered*, ed. Edwin Bacon and Mark Sandle (New York: Palgrave Macmillan, 2002), 70.

3. Christopher Andrew and Vasili Mitrokhin, *The Sword and the Shield: The Mitrokhin Archive and the Secret History of the KGB* (New York: Basic Books, 1999), 5–7, 251.

4. Martin Ebon, *The Andropov File* (New York: McGraw-Hill, 1983), 30; Vladimir Solov'ev and Elena Klepikova, *Yuri Andropov: A Secret Passage into the Kremlin* (New York: Macmillan, 1983), 250.

5. "Vopros o tom, kto budet sleduyushchim gensekom, reshalsya nad telom umershego Brezhneva," *Loyd*, Nov. 9, 2007, http://loyd.com.ua/articles/item-1973.html (accessed May 5, 2012); Larissa Vasilieva, *Kremlin Wives* (New York: Arcade Publishing, 1994), 209–11; Peter Reddaway and Dmitri Glinski, *The Tragedy of Russia's Reforms: Market Bolshevism against Democracy* (Washington, D.C.: United States Institute of Peace Press, 2001), 115; Robert Service, *A History of Twentieth-Century Russia* (Cambridge, Mass.: Harvard University Press, 1998), 384, 426–28.

6. Yuri V. Andropov, "Vstrecha s moskovskimi stankostroitelyami, 31 yanvarya 1983 goda," in *Izbrannye rechi i stat'i* (Moscow: Izdatel'stvo politicheskoi literatury, 1983), 221–30; Nicholas Daniloff, "Kremlin's New Battle against Drunks and Slackers," *U.S. News and World Report*, Jan. 31, 1983, 32.

7. Kathryn Hendley, "Moscow's Conduct of the Anti-Alcohol Campaign: A Comparative Analysis, 1972–1986" (M.A. thesis, Georgetown University, 1987), 73–79.

8. Vladimir Treml, "Price of Vodka Reduced for Economic and Health Reasons," Radio Liberty Research, RL 450/83, Nov. 30, 1983, 2; Aleksandr Nikishin, *Vodka i Gorbachev* (Moscow Vsya Rossiya, 2007), 87; Archie Brown, *The Gorbachev Factor* (New York: Oxford University Press, 1996), 4.

9. Archie Brown, *Gorbachev Factor*, 66.

10. Konstantin U. Chernenko, "Vysokii grazhdanskii dolg narodnogo kontrolera: Rech' na Vsesoyuznom soveshchanii narodnykh kontrolerov 5 oktyabrya 1984 goda," in *Po puti sovershenstvovaniya razvitogo sotsializma* (Moscow: Izdatel'stvo politicheskoi literatury, 1985), 264.

11. Vladimir Solov'ev and Elena Klepikova, *Behind the High Kremlin Walls* (New York: Dodd, Mead & Co., 1986), 42; Ilya Zemtsov, *Chernenko: The Last Bolshevik* (New Brunswick, N.J.: Transaction, 1989), 172; Archie Brown, *Seven Years That Changed the World: Perestroika in Perspective* (New York: Oxford University Press, 2007), 55.

12. Lawrence K. Altman, "Succession in Moscow: A Private Life, and a Medical Case; Autopsy Discloses Several Diseases," *New York Times*, March 12, 1985.

13. Ronald Reagan, *An American Life* (New York: Simon & Schuster, 1990), 611.

14. Mikhail Gorbachev, *Memoirs* (New York: Doubleday, 1995), 37. Also see Nikishin, *Vodka i Gorbachev*, 82-83.

15. See Mikhail Gorbachev, "Sel'skii trudovoi kollektiv: Puti sotsial'nogo razvitiya (iz stat'i opublikovannoi v zhurnale 'Kommunist' No. 2 Za 1976 God")," in *Izbrannye rechi i stat'i*, tom 1 (Moscow: Izdatel'stvo politicheskoi literatury, 1987), 131–32; and "Sovershenstvovat' rabotu s pis'mani trudyashchikhsya: Iz doklada na Stavropol'skogo kraikoma KPSS 4 aprelya 1978 goda," in *Izbrannye rechi i stat'i*, tom 1 (Moscow: Izdatel'stvo politicheskoi literatury, 1987), 168. On Kulakov see Valerii I. Boldin, *Krushenie p'edestala: Shtrikhi k portretu M. S. Gorbacheva* (Moscow: Respublika, 1995), 228.

16. Mikhail Gorbachev, "Zhivoe tvorchestvo naroda: Doklad na Vsesoyuznoi nauchno-prakticheskoi konferentsii 'Sovershenstvovanie razvitogo sotsializma i ideologicheskaya rabota partii v svete reshenii iyun'skogo (1983 g.) Plenuma TsK KPSS,' 10 dekabrya 1984 goda," in *Izbrannye rechi i stat'i*, tom 2 (Moscow: Izdatel'stvo politicheskoi literatury, 1987), esp. 71–82; Brown, *Gorbachev Factor*, 78–81; Eduard Shevardnadze, *The Future Belongs to Freedom*, trans. Catherine A. Fitzpatrick (New York: Free Press, 1991), 37.

17. Jerry F. Hough, *Democratization and Revolution in the USSR: 1985–1991* (Washington, D.C.: Brookings Institution, 1997), 69. On Thatcher see Margaret Thatcher, *The Downing Street Years* (New York: HarperCollins, 2009), 453.

18. Thatcher, *Downing Street Years,* 453; Rupert Cornwell, "Obituary—Grigory Romanov: Gorbachev's Chief Rival for Power," *The Independent,* June 9, 2008, http://www.independent.co.uk/news/obituaries/grigory-romanov-gorbachevs-chief-rival-for-power-842814.html (accessed September 11, 2011).

19. Gorbachev, *Memoirs,* 145.

20. Angus Roxburgh, *The Second Russian Revolution: The Struggle for Power in the Kremlin* (New York: Pharos Books, 1992), 29.

21. Yegor Ligachev, *Inside Gorbachev's Kremlin* (New York: Pantheon, 1993), 56.

22. Roxburgh, *Second Russian Revolution,* 29. Also see Dusko Doder and Louise Branson, *Gorbachev: Heretic in the Kremlin* (New York: Viking-Penguin, 1990), 100. See also former U.S. diplomat Dick Combs' description of how "Romanov's true colors emerged" during a misunderstanding over a toast after "a fair amount of alcohol was consumed" in *Inside the Soviet Alternate Universe: The Cold War's End and the Soviet Union's Fall Reappraised* (University Park: Pennsylvania State University Press, 2008), 77.

23. Brown, *Gorbachev Factor,* 141.

24. Donald Trelford, "A Walk in the Woods with Gromyko," *Observer,* April 2, 1989, 23. Andrei Gromyko, *Memoirs,* trans. Harold Shukman (New York: Doubleday, 1989), 6; Ligachev, *Inside Gorbachev's Kremlin,* 76.

25. Gromyko, *Memoirs,* 342; Brown, *Gorbachev Factor,* 87.

26. David Christian, *Imperial and Soviet Russia: Power, Privilege, and the Challenge of Modernity* (New York: St. Martin's, 1997), 405–6. See also Moshe Lewin, *The Gorbachev Phenomenon* (Berkeley: University of California Press, 1988).

27. Stephen F. Cohen, "Introduction: Gorbachev and the Soviet Reformation," in *Voices of Glasnost: Interviews with Gorbachev's Reformers,* ed. Stephen F. Cohen and Katrina vanden Heuvel (New York: W. W. Norton, 1989), 22; Ilya Zemtsov and John Farrar, *Gorbachev: The Man and the System* (New Brunswick, N.J.: Transaction, 1989), xiii.

28. "O merakh po preodoleniyu p'yanstva i alkogolizma," *Pravda,* May 17, 1985, 1.

29. Nicholas Daniloff, "Gorbachev's 100 Days—New Vigor in the Kremlin," *U.S. News & World Report,* June 24, 1985, 27. Also see Celestine Bohlen, "Drunkenness Crackdown Gets Off to Early Start," *Washington Post,* June 1, 1985, A17.

30. "Utverzhdat' trezvyi obraz zhizni," *Pravda,* Sept. 26, 1985, 3; Hendley, "Moscow's Conduct of the Anti-Alcohol Campaign," 98; Celestine Bohlen, "Anti-Alcohol Drive," *Washington Post,* Aug. 2, 1986, A12; Stephen White, *Russia Goes Dry: Alcohol, State and Society* (New York: Cambridge University Press, 1996), 76–78.

31. Anders Åslund, *Gorbachev's Struggle for Economic Reform, 1985–88* (Ithaca, N.Y.: Cornell University Press, 1989), 75. On the continuity in tactics see Daniel Tarschys, "The Success of a Failure: Gorbachev's Alcohol Policy, 1985–88," *Europe-Asia Studies* 45, no. 1 (1993): 18–19.

32. Tarschys, "The Success of a Failure," 19.

33. White, *Russia Goes Dry,* 74–75, 88.

34. "Vospitanie lichnosti," *Pravda,* Aug. 25, 1985, 3; translation in Hendley, "Moscow's Conduct of the Anti-Alcohol Campaign," 92–93.

35. See, for instance, "O merakh po preodoleniyu p'yanstva i alkogolizma," 1; "O ser'eznykh nedostatkakh v organizatsii vypolneniya v gorode Permi postanovlenii partii i pravitel'stva o preodolenii p'yanstva i alkogolizma," *Pravda,* Aug. 6, 1985, 2; Nikolai Ryzhkov, "Ob osnovnykh napreavleniyakh ekonomicheskogo i sotsial'nogo razvitiya SSSR na 1986–1990 gody i na period do 2000 goda," *Pravda,* March 4, 1986, 2.

36. Gorbachev, *Memoirs,* 181. On Romanov in Hungary see Roy A. Medvedev, "The Kremlin and the Bottle," *Russian Life* 41, no. 4 (1998): 20; Roxburgh, *Second Russian Revolution,* 29.

37. Peter Kenez, *A History of the Soviet Union from the Beginning to the End,* 2nd ed. (New York: Cambridge University Press, 2006), 254.

38. On plan fulfillment see "Novyi krupnyi shag v razvitii ekonomiki: Ob itogakh vypolneniya gosudarstvennogo plana ekonomicheskogo i sotsial'nogo razvitiya SSSR v 1985 gody," *Pravda,* Jan. 26, 1986, 2. On forecasts to 2000 see Ryzhkov, "Ob osnovnykh napravleniyakh," 2–5.

39. White, *Russia Goes Dry*, 38.

40. Ibid. Tat'yana Prot'ko, *V bor'be za trezvost': Stranitsy istorii* (Minsk: Nauka i tekhnika, 1988), 132.

41. David Powell, "Soviet Union: Social Trends and Social Problems," *Bulletin of the Atomic Scientists* 38, no. 9 (1982): 24; Aleksandr Nemtsov, "Tendentsii potrebleniya alkogolya i obuslovlennye alkogolem poteri zdorov'ya i zhizni v Rossii v 1946–1996 gg.," in *Alkogol' i zdorov'e naseleniya Rossii: 1900–2000*, ed. Andrei K. Demin (Moscow: Rossiiskaya assotsiatsiya obshchestvennogo zdorov'ya, 1998), 98–99.

42. Marshall I. Goldman, "Gorbachev's Risk in Reforming the Soviet Economy," *Technology Review* (1986): 19. See also Basile Kerblay, *Gorbachev's Russia* (New York: Pantheon, 1989), 13; David Joel Fishbein, "Do Dna: Alcoholism & the Soviet Union," *Journal of the American Medical Association* 266, no. 9 (Sept. 4, 1991): 1211; Igor' Urakov, *Alkogol': Lichnost' i zdorov'e* (Moscow: Meditsina, 1986), 18–21; Padma Desai, *Perestroika in Perspective: The Design and Dilemmas of Soviet Reform* (Princeton, N.J.: Princeton University Press, 1989), 28.

43. Mikhail Gorbachev, "O zadachakh partii po korennoi perestroike upravleniya ekonomikoi: Doklad na Plenume TsK KPSS 25 iyunya 1987 goda," in *Izbrannye rechi i stat'i*, tom 5 (Moscow: Izdatel'stvo politicheskoi literatury, 1988), 158; Tarschys, "Success of a Failure," 10.

44. Roxburgh, *Second Russian Revolution*, 33. On his expulsion from Russia and subsequent return months later see Angus Roxburgh, "From the Archive: Exiled by the KGB Just as Russia Dares to Be Free (June 4, 1989)," *Sunday Times*, Aug. 30, 2009, http://www.timesonline.co.uk/tol/news/world/europe/article6815093.ece (accessed Sept. 10, 2011.) In perhaps the crowning irony, Roxburgh would return to Russia as a Kremlin public relations advisor under Vladimir Putin. Angus Roxburgh, *Strongman: Vladimir Putin and the Struggle for Russia* (New York: Palgrave Macmillan, 2012), xi–xii.

45. See, for instance, Archie Brown, "Gorbachev: New Man in the Kremlin," *Problems of Communism* 34, no. 3 (1985): 1–23; Marshall I. Goldman, "What to Expect from Gorbachev," *Bulletin of the Atomic Scientists* 41, no. 4 (1985): 8–9; Serge Schmemann, "The Emergence of Gorbachev," *New York Times Magazine*, March 3, 1985, 40–46.

46. See Raisa Gorbacheva, *Ya nadeyus'* (Moscow: Kniga, 1991), 38; Nikishin, *Vodka i Gorbachev*, 402. On Stavropol influence see Viktor Erofeev, *Russkii apokalipsis: Opyt khudozhestvennoi eskhatologii* (Moscow: Zebra E, 2008), 14. For other speculation centered on Gorbachev see Nikishin, *Vodka i Gorbachev*, 199.

47. "Tak dal'she zhit' nel'zya"; quoted in Gorbacheva, *Ya nadeyus'*, 13.

48. Erofeev, *Russkii apokalipsis*, 12–13; for an English version see Victor Erofeyev, "The Russian God," *New Yorker*, Dec. 16, 2002. See also Aleksandr Nemtsov, *Alkogol'naya istoriya Rossii: Noveishii period* (Moscow: URSS, 2009), 73; Gorbachev, *Memoirs*, 220; Lev Ovrutsky, "Impasses of Sobering Up," in *Gorbachev & Glasnost': Viewpoints from the Soviet Press*, ed. Isaac J. Tarasulo (Wilmington, Del.: Scholarly Resources, 1989), 195; originally published in *Sovetskaya kultura*, July 16, 1988.

49. Nikolai Ryzhkov, *Perestroika: Istoriya predatel'stv* (Moscow: Novosti, 1992), 361.

50. Gorbachev, *Memoirs*, 220.

51. Mikhail S. Solomentsev, "O praktike raboty i zadachakh organov partiinogo kontrolya: Doklad na soveshchanii predsedatelei Partiinykh Komissii pri TsK kompartii soyuznykh respublik, kraikomakh i obkomakh KPSS 19 noyabrya 1984 goda," in *Vremya reshenii i deistvii: Izbrannye rechi i stat'i* (Moscow: Izdatel'stvo politicheskoi literatury, 1985), 533–34. On earlier policy suggestions see Mikhail S. Solomentsev, "Sotsial'no-ekonomicheskoe razvitie Rossiiskoi Federatsii na sovremennom etape: Iz stat'i opublikovannoi v zhurnale 'Istoriya SSSR' No. 6, 1981 God," in *Vremya reshenii i deistvii: Izbrannye rechi i stat'i* (Moscow: Izdatel'stvo politicheskoi literatury, 1985), 370–71. On "cognac" funds see also Konstantin Simis, *USSR: The Corrupt Society; The Secret World of Soviet Capitalism* (New York: Simon & Schuster, 1982), 130.

52. Gromyko, *Memoirs*, 343.

53. "V politbyuro TsK KPSS," *Pravda*, April 5, 1985, 1.

54. Anatoly S. Chernyaev, *Shest' let s Gorbachevym* (Moscow: Kul'tura, 1993), 39. On Solomentsev and the work of the commission see Anatoly S. Chernyaev, *My Six Years with*

Gorbachev, trans. Robert D. English and Elizabeth Tucker (University Park: Pennsylvania State University Press, 2000), 17; Roxburgh, *Second Russian Revolution*, 28; White, *Russia Goes Dry*, 68, 210 n. 66; Ligachev, *Inside Gorbachev's Kremlin*, 336.

55. Gorbachev, *Memoirs*, 220. See also Trelford, "Walk in the Woods with Gromyko," 23.

56. Chernyaev, *Shest' let s Gorbachevym*, 39.

57. Ligachev, *Inside Gorbachev's Kremlin*, 336. On shutting down liquor stores in Tomsk see Roxburgh, *Second Russian Revolution*, 28; White, *Russia Goes Dry*, 67–68.

58. Yegor Ligachev, "Aprel'skii Plenum TsK KPSS—Glavnoe soderzhanie vsei nashei raboty: Doklad na partiinom sobranii otdela organizatsionno-partiinoi raboty TsK KPSS 5 maya 1985 goda," in *Izbrannye rechi i stat'i* (Moscow: Izdatel'stvo politicheskoi literatury, 1989), 86.

59. Ligachev, *Inside Gorbachev's Kremlin*, 335–36; Gorbachev, *Memoirs*, 221; Chernyaev, *Shest' let s Gorbachevym*, 39.

60. Ryzhkov, *Perestroika*, 94–95. Also see Leon Aron, "Everything You Think You Know about the Collapse of the Soviet Union Is Wrong," *Foreign Policy*, July/August 2011, 66–67.

61. Roxburgh, *Second Russian Revolution*, 28.

62. Ryzhkov, *Perestroika*, 95; Chernyaev, *Shest' lets Gorbachevym*, 39. In terms of Ryzhkov's supporters we may add Vladimir Dolgikh, Vitaly Vorotnikov, Haydar Aliyev, Ivan Kapitonov, Viktor Nikonov, Vasily Garbuzov, and presumably Grigory Romanov. Nemtsov, *Alkogol'naya istoriya Rossii*, 73.

63. Chernyaev, *Shest' let s Gorbachevym*, 39.

64. White, *Russia Goes Dry*, 68; Medvedev, "Kremlin and the Bottle," 20. Garbuzov reportedly died shortly after his dismissal in 1985. Brown, *Gorbachev Factor*, 141.

65. Shevardnadze, *Future Belongs to Freedom*, 3.

66. Steve LeVine, *The Oil and the Glory: The Pursuit of Empire and Fortune on the Caspian Sea* (New York: Random House, 2007), 177–78; Arkady Vaksberg, *The Soviet Mafia* (New York: St. Martin's, 1991), 178, 82; Nikishin, *Vodka i Gorbachev*, 75.

67. Roxburgh, *Second Russian Revolution*, 28–29. Also see White, *Russia Goes Dry*, 68. Nikishin, *Vodka i Gorbachev*, 214.

68. LeVine, *Oil and the Glory*, 178. On Gorbachev's position see Gorbachev, *Memoirs*, 144.

Chapter 18

1. Ben Lewis, *Hammer and Tickle* (New York: Pegasus Books, 2009), 260.

2. See "Hammer and Tickle" (video), http://www.youtube.com/watch?v=CEgRit8dxDY (accessed Aug. 8, 2011).

3. Garry Wills, *Reagan's America: Innocents at Home* (New York: Penguin, 2000), xv.

4. See the Reagan documentary *In the Face of Evil: Reagan's War in Word and Deed*, http://www.inthefaceofevil.com/inthefaceofevil/story.html (accessed Aug. 8, 2011). On moral resolve and defense spending see Jeffrey W. Knopf, "Did Reagan Win the Cold War?" *Strategic Insights* 3, no. 8 (2004), http://www.nps.edu/Academics/centers/ccc/publications/OnlineJournal/2004/aug/knopfAUG04.html (accessed Aug. 17, 2011).

5. This has become a standard example of "how not to do" historical research. Martha Howell and Walter Prevenier, *From Reliable Sources: An Introduction to Historical Methods* (Ithaca, N.Y.: Cornell University Press, 2001), 79.

6. Stephen White, *Russia Goes Dry: Alcohol, State and Society* (New York: Cambridge University Press, 1996), 43. On "counter-modernization" see Victor Zaslavsky, "The Soviet Union," in *After Empire: Multiethnic Societies and Nation-Building*, ed. Karen Barkey and Mark von Hagen (Boulder, Colo.: Westview, 1997), 73.

7. Aleksandr Nemtsov, "Mnogo pit', vse-taki vredno," *EKO*, no. 281 (1997): 179–81. I conducted a similar analysis in "A Lesson in Drinking," *Moscow Times*, March 5, 2011.

8. Igor' Lanovenko, Aleksandr Svetlov, and Vasilii Skibitskii, *P'yanstvo i prestupnost': Istoriya, problemy* (Kiev: Naukova dumka, 1989), 6–7; White, *Russia Goes Dry*, 44.

9. "80 millionov alkogolikov k 2000 godu?" *Russkaya mysl'*, Dec. 27, 1984. See also chapter 16; Vladimir V. Dunaevskii and Vladimir D. Styazhkin, *Narkomanii i toksikomanii* (Leningrad: Meditsina, 1988), 24; White, *Russia Goes Dry*, 40–45.

10. Barimbek S. Beisenov, *Alkogolizm: Ugolovno-pravovye i kriminologicheskie problemy* (Moscow: Yuridicheskaya literatura, 1981), 36; quoted, along with statistics, in White, *Russia Goes Dry*, 45–48.

11. White, *Russia Goes Dry*, 50–52; Boris Segal, *The Drunken Society: Alcohol Use and Abuse in the Soviet Union* (New York: Hippocrene Books, 1990), 368–69.

12. This is broadly resonant with Leon Aron's argument about the collapse of the Soviet Union as resulting from attempts to reform its "moral decay." Leon Aron, "Everything You Think You Know about the Collapse of the Soviet Union Is Wrong," *Foreign Policy*, July/August 2011, 66.

13. Aleksandr Nemtsov, *Alkogol'naya istoriya Rossii: Noveishii period* (Moscow: URSS, 2009), 80–81; White, *Russia Goes Dry*, 102.

14. Nemtsov, "Mnogo pit', vse-taki vredno," 179; Thomas H. Naylor, *The Gorbachev Strategy* (Lexington, Mass.: Lexington Books, 1988), 194.

15. Alain Blum, "Mortality Patterns in the USSR and Causes of Death: Political Unity and Regional Differentials," in *Social Change and Social Issues in the Former USSR*, ed. Walter Joyce (New York: St. Martin's, 1992), 92; Vladimir Treml, "Drinking and Alcohol Abuse in the U.S.S.R. in the 1980s," in *Soviet Social Problems*, ed. Anthony Jones (Boulder, Colo.: Westview, 1991), 124; White, *Russia Goes Dry*, 103–4.

16. Aleksandr Nemtsov, "Tendentsii potrebleniya alkogolya i obuslovlennye alkogolem poteri zdorov'ya i zhizni v Rossii v 1946-1996 gg.," in *Alkogol' i zdorov'e naseleniya Rossii: 1900–2000*, ed. Andrei K. Demin (Moscow: Rossiiskaya assotsiatsiya obshchestvennogo zdorov'ya, 1998), 102, and "Smertnost' naseleniya i potreblemiye alkogolya v Rossii," *Zdravookhranenie Rossiiskoi Federatsii* (1997): 33. Others estimate a 24 percent decline in the crude death rate or about 1.61 million fewer deaths in the late 1980s. Jay Bhattacharya, Christina Gathmann, and Grant Miller, *The Gorbachev Anti-Alcohol Campaign and Russia's Mortality Crisis*, NBER Working Paper No. 18589 (Cambridge, Mass.: National Bureau of Economic Research, 2012), 23.

17. Mikhail Gorbachev, *Memoirs* (New York: Doubleday, 1995), 222.

18. Viktor Erofeev, *Russkii apokalipsis: Opyt khudozhestvennoi eskhatologii* (Moscow: Zebra E, 2008), 14. See also "Hammer and Tickle" (video); Joy Neumeyer, "Exhibits Grapple with Gorbachev, Yeltsin's Legacies," *Moscow Times*, Jan. 28, 2011.

19. Leonid Ionin, "Chetyre bedy Rossii," *Novoe vremya* No. 23 (1995): 16–17; translated in Leon Aron, *Yeltsin: A Revolutionary Life* (New York: St. Martin's, 2000), 180–81.

20. Angus Roxburgh, *The Second Russian Revolution: The Struggle for Power in the Kremlin* (New York: Pharos Books, 1992), 28; "Veni, Vidi, Vodka," *Economist*, Dec. 23, 1989, 52; Fred Coleman, *The Decline and Fall of the Soviet Empire* (New York: St. Martin's, 1996), 234.

21. Many articles to this effect followed major holidays. See E. Sorokin, "8 marta bez shampan-skogo?" *Pravda*, March 5, 1990, 2; Yu. Petrov, "Bezalkogolnyi pososhok," *Trud*, Nov. 8, 1990, 2. On queues see White, *Russia Goes Dry*, 140.

22. Celestine Bohlen, "Drunkenness Crackdown Gets Off to Early Start," *Washington Post*, June 1, 1985, A17.

23. Gorbachev, *Memoirs*, 221–22; Aron, *Yeltsin*, 180.

24. Gorbachev, *Memoirs*, 221. I explore this more fully in *The Political Power of Bad Ideas: Networks, Institutions, and the Global Prohibition Wave* (New York: Oxford University Press, 2010), 135–43. See also White, *Russia Goes Dry*, 100–104, and more generally Karl W. Ryavec, *Russian Bureaucracy: Power and Pathology* (New York: Rowman & Littlefield, 2003).

25. White, *Russia Goes Dry*, 107.

26. Vitalii Vorotnikov interview transcript, May 26, 1990; in ibid. See also Gorbachev, *Memoirs*, 221.

27. Gorbachev, *Memoirs*, 221–22.

28. Yegor Ligachev, *Inside Gorbachev's Kremlin* (New York: Pantheon, 1993), 337.

29. Dale Pesmen, *Russia and Soul: An Exploration* (Ithaca, N.Y.: Cornell University Press, 2000), 182.

30. See Gorbachev, *Memoirs*, 221; Ligachev, *Inside Gorbachev's Kremlin*, 336–38.

31. Vladislav M. Zubok, *A Failed Empire: The Soviet Union in the Cold War from Stalin to Gorbachev* (Chapel Hill: University of North Carolina Press, 2008), 268.

32. Mikhail Korchemkin, "Russia's Oil and Gas Exports to the Former Soviet Union," in *Economic Transition in Russia and the New States of Eurasia*, ed. Bartłomiej Kamiński (Armonk, N.Y.: M. E. Sharpe, 1996), 123; Anders Åslund, *How Capitalism Was Built: The Transformation of Central and Eastern Europe, Russia, and Central Asia* (New York: Cambridge University Press, 2007), 20; Paul Klebnikov, *Godfather of the Kremlin* (New York: Harcourt, 2000), 48–50.

33. Treml, "Drinking and Alcohol Abuse in the U.S.S.R. in the 1980s," 131; Gus Ofer, "Budget Deficit and Market Disequilibrium," in *Milestones in Glasnost and Perestroyka*, vol. 1: *The Economy*, ed. Ed A. Hewett and Victor H. Winston (Washington, D.C.: Brookings Institution, 1991), 292; Stephen White, *Gorbachev and After* (New York: Cambridge University Press, 1992), 132.

34. Ed A. Hewett, "Perestroyka and the Congress of People's Deputies," in *Milestones in Glasnost and Perestroyka*, vol. 1: *The Economy*, ed. Ed A. Hewett and Victor H. Winston (Washington, D.C.: Brookings Institution, 1991), 318.

35. Daniel Tarschys, "The Success of a Failure: Gorbachev's Alcohol Policy, 1985–88," *Europe-Asia Studies* 45, no. 1 (1993): 10. On budget estimates see Treml, "Drinking and Alcohol Abuse in the U.S.S.R. in the 1980s," 131; Ofer, "Budget Deficit and Market Disequilibrium," 280, 86, 306; Basile Kerblay, *Gorbachev's Russia* (New York: Pantheon, 1989), 107.

36. Gorbachev, *Memoirs*, 221.

37. *Krokodil* No. 15 (1988); reproduced in White, *Russia Goes Dry*, 123; Nikolai Ryzhkov, *Perestroika: Istoriya predatel'stv* (Moscow: Novosti, 1992), 95. On the upsurge in homebrew see Marshall I. Goldman, *What Went Wrong with Perestroika?* (New York: W. W. Norton, 1992), 138; James H. Noren, "The Economic Crisis: Another Perspective," in *Milestones in Glasnost and Perestroyka*, vol. 1: *The Economy*, ed. Ed A. Hewett and Victor H. Winston (Washington, D.C.: Brookings Institution, 1991), 379; Gertrude E. Schroeder, " 'Crisis' in the Consumer Sector: A Comment," in *Milestones in Glasnost and Perestroyka*, vol. 1: *The Economy*, ed. Ed A. Hewett and Victor H. Winston (Washington, D.C.: Brookings Institution, 1991), 410.

38. Cited in Vladimir Treml, "Alcohol in the Soviet Underground Economy," *Berkeley–Duke Occasional Papers on the Second Economy in the USSR* No. 5 (1985): 12.

39. Abel Aganbegyan, "Economic Reforms," in *Perestroika 1989*, ed. Abel Aganbegyan (New York: Charles Scribner's Sons, 1988), 102. Similarly see Lev Ovrutsky, "Impasses of Sobering Up," in *Gorbachev & Glasnost': Viewpoints from the Soviet Press*, ed. Isaac J. Tarasulo (Wilmington, Del.: Scholarly Resources, 1989), 201.

40. Quoted in Arnold Beichman and Mikhail S. Bernstam, *Andropov: New Challenge to the West* (New York: Stein & Day, 1983), 3.

41. Igor' Urakov, *Alkogol': Lichnost' i zdorov'e* (Moscow: Medistina, 1986), 7; Igor' Bestuzhev-Lada, "Piteinye traditsii i 'alkgol'nye tsivilizatsii'," in *Bezdna: P'yanstvo, narkomaniya, SPID*, ed. Sergei Artyukhov (Moscow: Molodaya gvardiya, 1988), 25; "Veni, Vidi, Vodka," 52; Dunaevskii and Styazhkin, *Narkomanii i toksikomanii*, 99–103.

42. John Barron, *Mig Pilot* (New York: McGraw Hill, 1980), 97; Nomi Morris, "War on Soviet Alcoholism," *MacLean's*, Jan. 19, 1987, 48; Erofeev, *Russkii apokalipsis*, 13–14. On drug use see A. Mostovoi, "Kogda zatsvetaet mak..." *Komsomol'skaya pravda*, June 8, 1986, 2; E. Borodina, "Vovremya ostanovit'sya," *Moskovskaya pravda*, June 12, 1986. See also John M. Kramer, "Drug Abuse in the USSR," in *Social Change and Social Issues in the Former USSR*, ed. Walter Joyce (New York: St. Martin's Press, 1992), 61.

43. Erofeev, *Russkii apokalipsis*, 14. See also Gorbachev, *Memoirs*, 222.

44. Ministerstvo vnutrennikh del SSSR, *Prestupnost' i pravonarusheniya 1990: Statisticheskii sbornik* (Moscow: Finansy i statistika, 1991), 15. See also Vladimir Volkov, "Mnogolikoe chudovishche," in *Bezdna: P'yanstvo, narkomaniya, SPID*, ed. Sergei Artyukhov (Moscow: Molodaya gvardiya, 1988), 62.

45. Nikolai Shmelev, "Novye trevogi," *Novyi mir* 4 (1988), 162–163; translated in Tarschys, "Success of a Failure," 21; On Aganbegyan's estimate see Aganbegyan, "Economic Reforms," 102. See also György Dalos, *Lebt wohl, Genossen! Der Untergang des sowjetischen Imperiums* (Munich: Verlag C. H. Beck, 2011), 58–59.

46. Ruslan Khasbulatov, *The Struggle for Russia: Power and Change in the Democratic Revolution* (London: Routledge, 1993), 116.

47. Segal, *Drunken Society*, xxi.

48. Erofeev, *Russkii apokalipsis*, 15; Jane I. Dawson, *Eco-Nationalism: Anti-Nuclear Activism and National Identity in Russia, Lithuania, and Ukraine* (Durham, N.C.: Duke University Press, 1996), 3–8; Zaslavsky, "Soviet Union," 84–91; Aleksandr Nikishin, *Vodka i Gorbachev* (Moscow Vsya Rossiya, 2007), 213–14.

49. Cited in Thomas de Waal, *Black Garden: Armenia and Azerbaijan through Peace and War* (New York: NYU Press, 2004), 17.

50. Erofeev, *Russkii Apokalipsis*, 13; Aleksandr Konobov, "Vnosyatsya korrektivy," *Trud*, Oct. 6, 1988, 2. Jeffrey Lamont, "Perestroika, Monopoly, Monoposony, and the Marketing of Moldovan Wine," *International Journal of Wine Making* 5, nos. 2–3 (1993): 49. See also V. Vasilets, "Tsekh menyaet profil'," *Pravda*, Aug. 1, 1985, 3; Aron, *Yeltsin*, 179; Pavel Palazchenko, *My Years with Gorbachev and Shevardnadze: The Memoir of a Soviet Interpreter* (University Park: Pennsylvania State University Press, 1998), 29.

51. Richard E. Ericson, "Soviet Economic Structure and the National Question," in *The Post-Soviet Nations: Perspectives on the Demise of the USSR*, ed. Alexander J. Motyl (New York: Columbia University Press, 1992), 260.

52. Gorbachev, *Memoirs*, 221–22. Likewise see Yevgeny Yevtushenko, *Fatal Half-Measures: The Culture of Democracy in the Soviet Union*, trans. Antonina W. Bouis (New York: Little, Brown, 1991), 131–34.

53. Paul Kengor, "Predicting the Soviet Collapse," *National Review Online*, July 14, 2011, http://www.nationalreview.com/articles/print/271828 (accessed Aug. 17, 2011).

54. The original memo, "Why Is the World So Dangerous?," from Herbert E. Meyer to the director of central intelligence, Nov. 30, 1983, can be found at http://www.foia.cia.gov/docs/DOC_0000028820/DOC_0000028820.pdf (accessed Aug. 30, 2011).

55. Ibid..

56. Personal correspondence, Aug. 19, 2011.

Chapter 19

1. Lilia Shevtsova, *Russia—Lost in Transition: The Yeltsin and Putin Legacies* (Washington, D.C.: Carnegie Endowment for International Peace, 2007), 1, 5; Peter Kenez, *A History of the Soviet Union from the Beginning to the End*, 2nd ed. (New York: Cambridge University Press, 2006), 284–85, 293.

2. Mikhail Gorbachev, *Memoirs* (New York: Doubleday, 1995), 632; Jonathan Steele, "Gennady Yanayev Obituary," *The Gaurdian*, Sept. 26, 2010, http://www.guardian.co.uk/world/2010/sep/26/gennady-yanayev-obituary-communist-gorbachev (accessed Oct. 11, 2011); Jerrold M. Post and Robert S. Robins, *When Illness Strikes the Leader: The Dilemma of the Captive King* (New Haven, Conn.: Yale University Press, 1995), 74; Dmitrii Yazov, "Interrogation of Defense Minister Dmitrii Yazov on August 22, 1991," in *Russia at the Barricades: Eyewitness Accounts of the August 1991 Coup*, ed. Victoria E. Bonnell, Ann Cooper, and Gregory Freidin (Armonk, N.Y.: M. E. Sharpe, 1994), 58–59.

3. Yazov, "Interrogation of Defense Minister Dmitrii Yazov on August 22, 1991," 62; Gorbachev, *Memoirs*, 632; Nikolai Vorontsov, "Between Russia and the Soviet Union—With Notes on the USSR Council of Ministers Meeting of August 19, 1991," in *Russia at the Barricades: Eyewitness Accounts of the August 1991 Coup*, ed. Victoria E. Bonnell, Ann Cooper, and Gregory Freidin (Armonk, N.Y.: M. E. Sharpe, 1994), 194. For Pavlov's account see Valentin Pavlov, "Interrogation of Soviet Prime Minister Valentin Pavlov, August 30, 1991," in *Russia at the Barricades*, 64–65.

4. Jonathan Aitken, *Nazarbayev and the Making of Kazakhstan* (New York: Continuum, 2009), 94–95; Aleksandr Korzhakov, *Boris El'tsin: Ot rassveta do zakata* (Moscow: Interbuk, 1997), 80–82.

5. Aitken, *Nazarbayev and the Making of Kazakhstan*, 97–98.

6. Aleksandr Lebed', *Za derzhavu obidno . . .* (Krasnoyarsk: Chest' i Rodina, 2004), 415. Curiously, this paragraph is completely omitted from the English translation: Alexander Lebed, *My Life and My Country* (Washington, D.C.: Regnery, 1997), 293. See also Conor O'Clery, *Moscow, December 25, 1991: The Last Day of the Soviet Union* (New York: PublicAffairs, 2011), 144;

Daniel Treisman, *The Return: Russia's Journey from Gorbachev to Medvedev* (New York: Simon & Schuster, 2011), 35–36.

7. William E. Odom, *The Collapse of the Soviet Military* (New Haven, Conn.: Yale University Press, 2000), 358.

8. Donald J. Raleigh, "A View from Saratov," in *Russia at the Barricades: Eyewitness Accounts of the August 1991 Coup*, ed. Victoria E. Bonnell, Ann Cooper, and Gregory Freidin (Armonk, N.Y.: M. E. Sharpe, 1994), 136–37. On the general sobriety of the resistance see: Lauren G. Leighton, "Moscow: The Morning of August 21, 107, and Iain Elliot, "Three Days in August: On-the-Spot Impressions," 291, both in *Russia at the Barricades: Eyewitness Accounts of the August 1991 Coup*, ed. Victoria E. Bonnell, Ann Cooper, and Gregory Freidin (Armonk, N.Y.: M. E. Sharpe, 1994). On the press conference see "The Press Conference of the State Committee for the State of Emergency, August 19, 1991," in *Russia at the Barricades*, 49–50.

9. Peter Vincent Pry, *War Scare: Russia and America on the Nuclear Brink* (Westport, Conn.: Greenwood, 1999), 79–80; Post and Robins, *When Illness Strikes*, 74.

10. Yazov, "Interrogation," 61.

11. David Remnick, *Resurrection: The Struggle for a New Russia* (New York: Random House, 1997), 27.

12. Ibid., 3–4.

13. Leon Aron, *Yeltsin: A Revolutionary Life* (New York: St. Martin's, 2000), 7–8; Timothy J. Colton, *Yeltsin: A Life* (New York: Basic Books, 2008), 35, 551 n. 69.

14. Aron, *Yeltsin*, 112–13.

15. Viktor Manyukhin, *Pryzhok nazad: O El'tsine i o drugikh* (Ekaterinburg: Pakrus, 2002), 177.

16. Colton, *Yeltsin*, 88–89.

17. Ibid., 117–18.

18. Dimitri K. Simes, *After the Collapse: Russia Seeks Its Place as a Great Power* (New York: Simon & Schuster, 1999), 51.

19. Ibid., 51–52.

20. Colton, *Yeltsin*, 310.

21. Ibid., 310–13. Yuri M. Baturin et al., *Epokha El'tsina: Ocherki politicheskoi istorii* (Moscow: Vagrius, 2001), 515; Aleksandr Nikishin, *Vodka i Gorbachev* (Moscow Vsya Rossiya, 2007), 235; Remnick, *Resurrection*, 277, 328.

22. See chapter 21, Aleksandr Nemtsov, "Tendentsii potrebleniya alkogolya i obuslovlennye alkogolem poteri zdorov'ya i zhizni v Rossii v 1946–1996 gg.," in *Alkogol' i zdorov'e naseleniya Rossii: 1900–2000*, ed. Andrei K. Demin (Moscow: Rossiiskaya assotsiatsiya obshchestvennogo zdorov'ya, 1998), 101–5.

23. Celestine Bohlen, "Yeltsin Deputy Calls Reforms 'Economic Genocide'," *New York Times*, Feb. 9, 1992, http://www.nytimes.com/1992/02/09/world/yeltsin-deputy-calls-reforms-economic-genocide.html?pagewanted=all&src=pm (accessed Oct. 21, 2011).

24. Remnick, *Resurrection*, 52–53. See also Stephen White, *Understanding Russian Politics* (New York: Cambridge University Press, 2011), 107.

25. Remnick, *Resurrection*, 49, 58–59; also 244.

26. Colton, *Yeltsin*, 311.

27. Remnick, *Resurrection*, 58–59.

28. Donald Murray, *A Democracy of Despots* (Boulder, Colo.: Westview, 1996), 177. That tea was meant as a signal that he was not drunk was made explicit by CNN and the international press. See http://www.youtube.com/watch?v=ioXt3RT5ueA (accessed Feb. 17, 2009).

29. Remnick, *Resurrection*, 64.

30. Peter Reddaway and Dmitri Glinski, *The Tragedy of Russia's Reforms: Market Bolshevism against Democracy* (Washington, D.C.: United States Institute of Peace Press, 2001), 426.

31. Korzhakov, *Boris El'tsin*, 195–98. For a counterpoint see Martha Howell and Walter Prevenier, *From Reliable Sources: An Introduction to Historical Methods* (Ithaca, N.Y.: Cornell University Press, 2001), 76–77.

32. Baturin et al., *Epokha El'tsina*, 515.

33. Colton, *Yeltsin*, 311; Korzhakov, *Boris El'tsin*, 217–18.

34. Baturin et al., *Epokha El'tsina*, 521.

35. Ibid., 522–24.

36. Strobe Talbott, *The Russia Hand: A Memoir of Presidential Diplomacy* (New York: Random House, 2002), 46.

37. Ibid., 45–47; Colton, *Yeltsin*, 310.

38. George Stephanopoulos, *All Too Human: A Political Education* (Boston: Little, Brown, 2000), 139–40; Colton, *Yeltsin*, 310–11.

39. Simes, *After the Collapse*, 104.

40. James M. Goldgeier and Michael McFaul, *Power and Purpose: U.S. Foreign Policy toward Russia after the Cold War* (Washington, D.C.: Brookings Institution, 141; Talbott, *Russia Hand*, 89, 185. Thomas Friedman went further, opining in the April 16, 1999, edition of the *New York Times* that "even a half-dead, stone-cold-drunk Boris Yeltsin is still an enormous asset for the U.S." See Boris Kagarlitsky, *Russia under Yeltsin and Putin: Neo-Liberal Autocracy* (New York: Pluto, 2002), 226.

41. Taylor Branch, *The Clinton Tapes: Wrestling History with the President* (New York: Simon & Schuster, 2009), 198. Branch mistakenly attributed the year of the visit to 1995, an error the Russian press has used to discredit the entire account. "Bill Clinton and His Tapes: Lies, Lies, Lies," *Pravda*, Oct. 2 2009, http://english.pravda.ru/world/americas/02-10-2009/109635-bill_clinton-0 (accessed Nov. 11, 2011). Clinton advisor Strobe Talbott confirmed a slightly different take of the pizza event but dated it more precisely at September 26–27, 1994. Talbott, *Russia Hand*, 135.

42. Nikolai Kozyrev, "The President Failed to Show…" *International Affairs* 53, no. 4 (2007): 169. Ambassador Kozyrev is no relation to Andrei Kozyrev, then Yeltsin's minister of foreign affairs.

43. Ibid.: 170–71.

44. Ibid.: 169–71; Korzhakov, *Boris El'tsin: Ot rassveta do zakata*, 204–5; Mark Franchetti, "The Sober Truth behind Boris Yeltsin's Drinking Problem," *Sunday Times* March 7, 2010, http://www.timesonline.co.uk/tol/news/world/europe/article7052415.ece (accessed March 8, 2010); Colton, *Yeltsin*, 315, 552–53 n. 93; Aron, *Yeltsin*, 578. See also "Reynolds Tells of Yeltsin's Favours after Shannon Snub," Breakingnews.ie, April 23, 2007, http://www.break-ingnews.ie/ireland/reynolds-tells-of-yeltsins-favours-after-shannon-snub-307635.html (accessed Nov. 11, 2011); Remnick, *Resurrection*, 250; also 328, 33–34.

45. *Lipetskaya gazeta*, March 2, 1995, 2; quoted in White, *Understanding Russian Politics*, 108. On media reception see Kozyrev, "President Failed to Show…," 171.

46. Anatol Lieven, *Chechnya: Tombstone of Russian Power* (New Haven, Conn.: Yale University Press, 1998), 86.

47. Georgie Anne Geyer, *Predicting the Unthinkable, Anticipating the Impossible: From the Fall of the Berlin Wall to America in the New Century* (New Brunswick, N.J.: Transaction, 2011), 230–31.

48. Andrew Higgins, "Grozny Rebels Braced for Final Assault," *The Independent*, Jan. 13, 1995; Charles King, *The Ghost of Freedom: A History of the Caucasus* (New York: Oxford University Press, 2008), 235; O'Clery, *Moscow, December 25, 1991*, 282–83.

49. Emma Gilligan, *Terror in Chechnya: Russia and the Tragedy of Civilians in War* (Princeton, N.J.: Princeton University Press, 2009), esp. 26–27.

50. Lieven, *Chechnya*, 50.

51. O. P. Orlov and Aleksandr Cherkasov, *Rossiya—Chechnya: Tsep' oshibok i prestuplenii* (Moscow: Zven'ia, 1998); an English translation was published as "Russia and Chechnya: A Chain of Errors and Crimes," *Russian Studies in History* 41, no. 2 (2002): 88–89. The commander was apparently incorrect—marine depth charges were not used; instead, concrete-piercing, high-explosive bombs that had the same effect. See also Iu. Kazakov, "Voina zakonchilas', no mir re nastupil," *Nezavisimaya gazeta*, June 25, 1997. Similarly, regarding the Second Chechen War, see Amelia Gentleman, "82 Civilians Feared Dead in Chechen Massacre," *The Guardian*, Feb. 22, 2000, http://www.guardian.co.uk/world/2000/feb/23/chechnya.ameliagentleman (accessed Dec. 20, 2011). On alcohol and barter see Pavel Baev, "Enforcing 'Military Solutions' in the North Caucasus: Accumulated Experiences in Conflict (Mis)Management," in *Russian Power Structures: Present and Future Roles in Russian Politics*, ed. Jan Leijonhielm and Fredrik Westerlund (Stockholm: FOI, Swedish Defense Research Agency, 2007), 50.

52. Lieven, *Chechnya*, 17–18, 49–50, 286.
53. Henry E. Hale, *Why Not Parties in Russia? Democracy, Federalism and the State* (New York: Cambridge University Press, 2006), 68; Vladimir Petrovich Kartsev and Todd Bludeau,!*Zhirinovsky! An Insider's Account of Yeltsin's Chief Rival & 'Bespredel'* (New York: Columbia University Press, 1995), 81; Kevin Fedarko, "A Farce to Be Reckoned With," *Time*, Dec. 27, 1993.
54. Remnick, *Resurrection*, 305–6; Steven Levitsky and Lucan A. Way, *Competitive Authoritarianism: Hybrid Regimes after the Cold War* (New York: Cambridge University Press, 2010), 194; Colton, *Yeltsin*, 315.
55. Michael McFaul, *Russia's 1996 Presidential Election: The End of Polarized Politics* (Stanford, Calif.: Hoover Institution, 1997), 23–24. Remnick, *Resurrection*, 102, 334.
56. McFaul, *Russia's 1996 Presidential Election*, 23.
57. Colton, *Yeltsin*, 438–39; Michael McFaul, "Evaluating Yeltsin and His Revolution," in *Russia after the Fall*, ed. Andrew C. Kuchins (Washington, D.C.: Carnegie Endowment for International Peace, 2002), 22.
58. Colton, *Yeltsin*, 316; Franchetti, "The Sober Truth behind Boris Yeltsin's Drinking Problem."

Chapter 20

1. Anders Åslund, *How Russia Became a Market Economy* (Washington, D.C.: Brookings Institution, 1995), 64; Peter Reddaway and Dmitri Glinski, *The Tragedy of Russia's Reforms: Market Bolshevism against Democracy* (Washington, D.C.: United States Institute of Peace Press, 2001), 270–73.
2. Åslund, *How Russia Became a Market Economy*, 69.
3. Harley Balzer, "Human Capital and Russian Security in the Twenty First Century," in *Russia after the Fall*, ed. Andrew C. Kuchins (Washington, D.C.: Carnegie Endowment for International Peace, 2002), 175; Judyth Twigg, "What Has Happened to Russian Society?" in *Russia after the Fall*, ed. Andrew C. Kuchins (Washington, D.C.: Carnegie Endowment for International Peace, 2002), 149.
4. Reddaway and Glinski, *Tragedy of Russia's Reforms*, 249–51.
5. Steven Rosefielde, "Premature Deaths: Russia's Radical Economic Transition in Soviet Perspective," *Europe-Asia Studies* 53, no. 8 (2001): 1162; Vladimir M. Shkolnikov, Martin McKee, and David A. Leon, "Changes in Life Expectancy in Russia in the Mid-1990s," *The Lancet* 357 (2001); Anatoly Karlin, "Demography II—Out of the Death Spiral," Da Russophile (blog), April 14, 2008, http://darussophile.com/2008/04/14/out-of-the-death-spiral (accessed May 5, 2012).
6. Richard C. Paddock, "Patient Deaths Point to Depth of Russian Crisis," *Los Angeles Times*, March 13, 1999, http://articles.latimes.com/1999/mar/13/news/mn-16823 (accessed Nov. 14, 2011).
7. Colin McMahon, "Shortages Leave Russia's East out in the Cold," *Chicago Tribune*, Nov. 19, 1998. See also Stephen F. Cohen, *Failed Crusade: America and the Tragedy of Post-Communist Russia*, updated ed. (New York: W. W. Norton, 2001), 47; Naomi Klein, *The Shock Doctrine: The Rise of Disaster Capitalism* (New York: Henry Holt & Co., 2007), 301.
8. Cohen, *Failed Crusade*, 169; Peter Kenez, *A History of the Soviet Union from the Beginning to the End*, 2nd ed. (New York: Cambridge University Press, 2006), 288.
9. Cohen, *Failed Crusade*, 169 (emphasis added).
10. Michael Specter, "The Devastation," *New Yorker*, Oct. 11, 2004, 59. This is not to say that "demodernization" has never been used. In terms of alcoholization see Andrei V. Podlazov, "Demograficheskaya demodernizatsiya i alkogolizatsiya Rossii," in *Alkogol'naya katastrofa i vozmozhnosti gosudarstvennoi politiki v preodolenii alkogol'noi sverkhsmertnosti v Rossii*, ed. Dar'ya A. Khalturina and Andrei V. Korotaev (Moscow: Lenand, 2010), 133. On grass-roots connotations see Oleg Yanitsky, *Russian Greens in a Risk Society: A Structural Analysis* (Helsinki: Kikimora, 2000), 3, 267. On the rural-resource connotation see Stephen K. Wegren, *Land Reform in Russia: Institutional Design and Behavioral Responses* (New Haven, Conn.: Yale University Press, 2009), 162. Regarding capacity for civic organization see Valerii Aleksandrovich Tishkov, *Chechnya: Life in a War-Torn Society* (Berkeley: University of

California Press, 2004), 14. Still, none of these have the same connotation as the retrograde economic, social, and political development I propose here.

11. See, for instance, Hans Rosling's "200 Countries, 200 Years, 4 Minutes" presentation on gapminder.org, http://www.gapminder.org/videos/200-years-that-changed-the-world-bbc (accessed Nov. 25, 2011).

12. Irina Rozenberg, "Proizvoditeli podpol'noi vodki mogut pereiti na legal'noe polozhenie," *Segodnya*, Nov. 6, 1996, 6.

13. Alexander Elder, *Rubles to Dollars: Making Money on Russia's Exploding Financial Frontier* (New York: New York Institute of Finance, 1999), 40; Stephen White, *Russia Goes Dry: Alcohol, State and Society* (New York: Cambridge University Press, 1996), 168. Kosmarskaya calculates that all excise taxes contributed only 8.3 percent of state revenue in 1997. T. Kosmarskaya, "Problemy gosudarstvennogo regulirovaniya rynka alkogol'noi produktsii," *Voprosi ekonomiki* (1998): 140; Irina R. Takala, *Veselie Rusi: Istoriia alkogol'noi problemy v Rossii* (St. Petersburg: Zhurnal Neva, 2002), 272–74.

14. A. Krasikov, "Commodity Number One (Part 2)," in *The Samizdat Register*, ed. Roy A. Medvedev (New York: W. W. Norton, 1981), 164.

15. Victor Erofeyev, "The Russian God," *New Yorker*, Dec. 16, 2002).

16. Daniel Treisman, "Death and Prices: The Political Economy of Russia's Alcohol Crisis," *Economics of Transition* 18, no. 2 (2010): 281–82. In 1990, the average Soviet monthly wage was equal to sixteen liters of vodka. By 1993 it could buy thirty-three liters. Relative to foodstuffs, the price of vodka fell over 70 percent from 1990 to 1994. Aleksandr Nemtsov, *Alkogol'naya istoriya Rossii: Noveishii period* (Moscow: URSS, 2009), 99.

17. N. V. Molina, "Vino tochit'—chto zolotuyu monetu chekanit'," *EKO*, no. 298 (1999): 178; Sonni Efron, "Grim Prognosis," *Los Angeles Times*, Nov. 12, 1995, 1; Jay Bhattacharya, Christina Gathmann, and Grant Miller, *The Gorbachev Anti-Alcohol Campaign and Russia's Mortality Crisis*, NBER Working Paper No. 18589 (Cambridge, Mass.: National Bureau of Economic Research, 2012).

18. On the roles of money see William Stanley Jevons, *Money and the Mechanism of Exchange* (New York: D. Appleton & Co., 1901), 14–38. Vodka in Russia has fulfilled most of these roles (not a widely recognized standard of value), making it, at best, a "preferred medium of barter" in the terms described by Paul Einzig in *Primitive Money: In Its Ethnological, Historical and Economic Aspects* (London: Eyre & Spottiswoode, 1949), 328.

19. Boris Pasternak, *Doctor Zhivago* (New York: Pantheon, 1958), 175. Similarly see Kenez, *History of the Soviet Union*, 58.

20. Stephen Handelman, *Comrade Criminal: Russia's New Mafiya* (New Haven, Conn.: Yale University Press, 1995), 77; Konstantin Simis, *USSR: The Corrupt Society; The Secret World of Soviet Capitalism* (New York: Simon & Schuster, 1982), 130, 256. On bartering for Pepsi see Charles Levinson, *Vodka Cola* (London: Gordon & Cremonesi, 1978). See also Caroline Humphrey and Stephen Hugh-Jones, *Barter, Exchange and Value: An Anthropological Approach* (New York: Cambridge University Press, 1992), 5.

21. "Of Aeroflot, Volgas and the Flu: Some Joys and Sorrows of the Soviet Way," *Time*, June 23, 1980, 88. See also Nicholas Daniloff, "Kremlin's New Battle against Drunks and Slackers," *U.S. News & World Report*, Jan. 31, 1983, 32. More generally see Kenez, *History of the Soviet Union*, 217.

22. I. Gerasyuk, "Butylka za uslugu," *Sovetskaya Belarussiya*, Oct. 12 1984, 4; "(A Bottle for a Favor—Or Why Does Grandma Marya Make Home Brew?)," abstract in *Current Digest of the Soviet Press*, vol. 37, no. 3, Feb 13, 1985, p. 11; abstract also available in *USSR: Political and Sociological Affairs*, JPRS-UPS-84-098, Nov. 13, 1984, 27.

23. Even during the anti-alcohol campaign, "compared to money, not to mention gratitude, a bottle has far more clout." Ivan Yaskov, "Alcohol Is the Enemy of Society: Don't Step into the Abyss," *Selskaya zhizn'*, May 14, 1985, 4; translated in *Current Digest of the Soviet Press* 37, no. 20 (1985): 7.

24. Michael Specter, "Russia Takes Aim at Vodka Bacchanalia: Bootlegger's Dream/A People Drowning in Drink," *International Herald Tribune*, Jan. 22 1997, A3; David Hoffman, "Yeltsin Cracks Down on Alcohol Industry," *Washington Post*, Dec. 26, 1996, 27; Caroline Humphrey, "How Is Barter Done? The Social Relations of Barter in Provincial Russia," 277,

and Jayasri Dutta, "Some Lasting Thing: Barter and the Value of Money," 17, both in *The Vanishing Rouble: Barter Networks and Non-Monetary Transactions in Post-Soviet Societies*, ed. Paul Seabright (New York: Cambridge University Press, 2000); Grigory G. Zaigraev, "The Russian Model of Noncommercial Alcohol Consumption," in *Moonshine Markets: Issues in Unrecorded Alcohol Beverage Production and Consumption*, ed. Alan Haworth and Ronald Simpson (New York: Brunner-Routledge, 2004), 38.

25. White, *Russia Goes Dry*, 168; Andrei Demin, ed., *Alkogol' i zdorov'e naseleniya Rossii: 1900–2000* (Moscow: Rossiiskaya assotsiatsiya obshchestvennogo zdorov'ya, 1998), 298. Also see Rosalko chief Vladimir Yarmosh, "Russian Vodka Outpriced at Home," *Business in Russia/ Deolvye lyudi* 63 (1996): 7.

26. Michael A. Hiltzik, "Russia Thirsts for Vodka Plants' Profits," *Los Angeles Times*, Nov. 30, 1998, 1; Sergei Gornov, "A Sobering Thought for Russia's Distillers," *Business in Russia/ Deolvye lyudi* 69 (1996): 88–89, and "Quotas: To Be or Not to Be?" *Business in Russia/ Deolvye lyudi* 69 (1996): 94.

27. Nemtsov, *Alkogol'naya istoriya Rossii*, 104–6. See also Goskomstat Rossii, *Prodovol'stvennyi rynok Rossii: Statisticheskii sbornik* (Moscow: Goskomstat, 2000), 116–52.

28. Alla Alova, "Rossiiskie pogranichniki prishchemili khvost 'zelenomu zmiyu,'" *Obshchaya gazeta*, July 31–Aug. 6, 1997; Viktor Zubanyuk, "Ukraine's Rivers of Alcohol Hit the Shallows," *Business in Russia/Deolvye lyudi* 74 (1997): 72–73. See also Nikolai Styazhkin, "Attempt to Smuggle Alcohol from Georgia to Russia Thwarted," ITAR-TASS News Agency, Jan. 15, 2000; Valerii Shanaev, "Russian Border Guards Continue to Thwart Alcohol Smugglers," ITAR-TASS News Agency, Jan. 3, 1998; Anatolii Yurkin, "Azeri Train Carrying Alcohol Detained on Russian Border," ITAR-TASS News Agency, Jan. 5, 1998, and "Border Chief Coordinates with Georgia on Alcohol Smuggling," ITAR-TASS News Agency, Jan. 5 1998; Nemtsov, *Alkogol'naya istoriya Rossii*, 115–18.

29. Nemtsov, *Alkogol'naya istoriya Rossii*, 102. On the NFS see El'mar Guseinov, "Poslednyaya afera NFS?," *Izvestiya*, June 22, 1996, 2; Andrei Grekov, "Drinking and Sport Don't Mix," *Business in Russia/Deolvye lyudi* 69 (1996): 91–92. See also "Chernomyrdin Signs Resolution on Licensing Imported Alcohol," ITAR-TASS News Agency, Jan. 31, 1997; Augusto López-Claros and Sergei V. Alexashenko, *Fiscal Policy Issues during the Transition in Russia* (Washington, D.C.: International Monetary Fund, 1998), 16–20. On the Orthodox Church see Robert C. Blitt, "How to Entrench a De Facto State Church in Russia: A Guide to Progress," *Brigham Young University Law Review*, no. 3 (2008): 722; Maxim Shevchenko, "Smoking Is Not Harming the Soul," *Nezavisimaya gazeta*, Feb. 18, 1997, http://www2.stetson.edu/~psteeves/relnews/tobacco1802eng.html (accessed Jan. 13, 2012).

30. Rozenberg, "Proizvoditeli podpol'noi vodki mogut pereiti na legal'noe polozhenie," 6.

31. On the "transition" in taxation and fiscal policy see Jorge Martinez-Vazquez, Mark Rider, and Sally Wallace, *Tax Reform in Russia* (Northampton, Mass.: Edward Elgar, 2008), 144–45; Andrei Shleifer and Daniel Treisman, *Without a Map: Political Tactics and Economic Reform in Russia* (Cambridge, Mass.: MIT Press, 2001), 113–30.

32. Rozenberg, "Proizvoditeli podpol'noi vodki mogut pereiti na legal'noe polozhenie," 6.

33. Hiltzik, "Russia Thirsts for Vodka Plants' Profits," 1.

34. Goskomstat Rossii, *Russia in Numbers: Concise Statistical Handbook* (Moscow: Goskomstat, 1999), 275.

35. Nemtsov, *Alkogol'naya istoriya Rossii*, 108; for an English translation see Aleksandr Nemtsov, *A Contemporary History of Alcohol in Russia*, trans. Howard M. Goldfinger and Andrew Stickley (Stockholm: Södertörns högskola, 2011), 138.

36. Boris Yeltsin, "Perekryt' kran spirtovoi kontrabande: Radioobrashchenie prezidenta Rossiiskoi Federatsii B. N. El'tsina," *Rossiiskaya gazeta*, Sept. 13, 1997, 1–2. See also "Return of the State Monopoly on Alcohol," *Business in Russia/Deolvye lyudi* 64 (1996): 94.

37. See Joel S. Hellman, "Winners Take All: The Politics of Partial Reform in Postcommunist Transitions," *World Politics* 50, no. 2 (1998). Also see Nemtsov, *Alkogol'naya istoriya Rossii*, 101–3.

38. Shleifer and Treisman, *Without a Map*, 117.

39. Nemtsov, *Alkogol'naya istoriya Rossii*, 131. Also see Sergei Gornov, "Alcohol Producers Set Their Sights on the Regions," *Business in Russia/Deolvye lyudi* 67 (1996): 66; Dar'ya

A. Khalturina and Andrei V. Korotaev, "Vvedeniye: Alkogol'naya katastrofa: Kak osta-novit' vymiranie Rossii," in *Alkogol'naya katastrofa i vozmozhnosti gosudarstvennoi politiki v preodolenii alkogol'noi sverkosmertnosti v Rossii*, ed. Dar'ya A. Khalturina and Andrei V. Korotaev (Moscow: Lenand, 2010), 29; Tomila V. Lankina, *Governing the Locals: Local Self-Government and Ethnic Mobilization in Russia* (Lanham, Md.: Rowman & Littlefield, 2004), 154. For the situation in Yaroslavl see Beth Mitchneck, "The Changing Role of the Local Budget in Russian Cities: The Case of Yaroslavl," in *Local Power and Post-Soviet Politics*, ed. Theodore H. Friedgut and Jeffrey W. Hahn (Armonk, N.Y.: M. E. Sharpe, Inc., 1994), 82–84.

40. Scott Gehlbach, *Representation through Taxation: Revenue, Politics, and Development in Postcommunist States* (New York: Cambridge University Press, 2008), 9.

41. Ibid., 3, 7–16, 131.

42. Seguey Braguinsky and Grigory Yavlinsky, *Incentives and Institutions: The Transition to a Market Economy in Russia* (Princeton, N.J.: Princeton University Press, 2000), 234.

43. Anders Åslund, *How Capitalism Was Built: The Transformaton of Central and Eastern Europe, Russia, and Central Asia* (New York: Cambridge University Press, 2007), 136.

44. Humphrey, "How Is Barter Done?" 270; Alena Ledeneva, *How Russia Really Works: The Informal Practices That Shaped Post-Soviet Politics and Business* (Ithaca, N.Y.: Cornell University Press, 2006), 177–81.

45. See Khristina Narizhnaya, "As Business Becomes More Civil, So Do Its State Relations," *Moscow Times*, Jan. 12, 2012, http://www.themoscowtimes.com/business/article/as-busi-ness-becomes-more-civil-so-do-its-state-relations/450927.html (accessed Jan. 12, 2012).

46. Humphrey, "How Is Barter Done?" 273.

47. Padma Desai and Todd Idson, *Work without Wages: Russia's Nonpayment Crisis* (Cambridge, Mass.: MIT Press, 2000), 185. Similarly, see Andrei Sinyavsky, *The Russian Intelligentsia* (New York: Columbia University Press, 1997), 40–41.

48. Humphrey, "How Is Barter Done?" 279.

49. David G. Anderson, "Surrogate Currencies and the 'Wild Market' in Central Siberia," in *The Vanishing Rouble: Barter Networks and Non-Monetary Transactions in Post-Soviet Societies*, ed. Paul Seabright (New York: Cambridge University Press, 2000), 339.

50. Leonid Nevzlin, quoted in David Hoffman, *The Oligarchs: Wealth and Power in the New Russia*, revised and updated (New York: PublicAffairs, 2011), 118.

51. Clifford G. Gaddy and Barry W. Ickes, "Russia's Virtual Economy," *Foreign Affairs* 77, no. 5 (1998); Thane Gustafson, *Capitalism Russia-Style* (New York: Cambridge University Press, 1999), 203; Ledeneva, *How Russia Really Works*; Sergei Guriev and Barry W. Ickes, "Barter in Russia," in *The Vanishing Rouble: Barter Networks and Non-Monetary Transactions in Post-Soviet Societies*, ed. Paul Seabright (New York: Cambridge University Press, 2000). On strengthening the regions see David Woodruff, *Money Unmade: Barter and the Fate of Russian Capitalism* (Ithaca, N.Y.: Cornell University Press, 1999), 5.

52. Clifford G. Gaddy and Barry W. Ickes, *Russia's Virtual Economy* (Washington, D.C.: Brookings Institution, 2002), 248.

53. Such as the Kristall distillery in Moscow. See chapter 22. According to *Goskomstat*, excise tax arrears from the alcohol sector comprised only 1.2 percent of all budgetary arrears, further suggesting that vodka producers were fairly reliable taxpayers. Goskomstat Rossii, *Rossiiskii statisticheskii ezhegodnik: Statisticheskii sbornik* (Moscow: Goskomstat, 1998), 654.

54. See, for instance, Anders Åslund, "Ten Myths about the Russian Economy," in *Russia after the Fall*, ed. Andrew C. Kuchins (Washington, D.C.: Carnegie Institute for International Peace, 2002), and *Russia's Capitalist Revolution: Why Market Reform Succeeded and Democracy Failed* (Washington, D.C.: Peterson Institute for International Economics, 2007).

55. Åslund, *How Capitalism Was Built*, 186–87, 90–91.

56. Ibid., 188. On the demographic deterioration in Russia, the Baltics, and Western CIS, see Khalturina and Korotaev, "Alkogol'naya katastrofa," 7.

57. Åslund, *How Capitalism Was Built*, 188. See also Åslund, "Ten Myths about the Russian Economy," 119. For Ingushetia and Dagestan see Khalturina and Korotaev, "Alkogol'naya katastrofa," 8. For more in-depth demographic comparisons see Dar'ya A. Khalturina and Andrei V. Korotaev, *Russkii krest: Faktory, mekhanizmy i puti preodoleniia demograficheskogo krizisa v Rossii* (Moscow: KomKniga, 2006). This also bridges the divide between economic

factors (privatization) and increased mortality; see John S. Earle and Scott Gehlbach, "Did Post-Communist Privatization Increase Mortality?" *Comparative Economic Studies* 53 (2011).

58. Åslund, *How Capitalism Was Built*, 188; repeated again on 205.

59. Here I admittedly overlook the interwar independence of the Baltic republics. On alcohol consumption patterns see country reports in World Health Organization (WHO), *Global Status Report on Alcohol and Health* (Geneva: WHO, 2011), http://www.who.int/substance_abuse/publications/global_alcohol_report/en (accessed March 11, 2011). Likewise, see the "mortality belt" in Elizabeth Brainerd and David M. Cutler, "Autopsy on an Empire: Understanding Mortality in Russia and the Former Soviet Union," *Journal of Economic Perspectives* 19, no. 1 (2005): 107.

60. Wendy Carlin et al., "Barter and Non-Monetary Transactions in Transition Economies: Evidence from a Cross-Country Survey," in *The Vanishing Rouble: Barter Networks and Non-Monetary Transactions in Post-Soviet Societies*, ed. Paul Seabright (New York: Cambridge University Press, 2000), 240–41. Note the similarities in Ukraine: Viktor Zubanyuk, "Ukraine Takes the Strain," *Business in Russia/Deolvye lyudi* 69 (1996): 98–99.

61. Åslund, *How Capitalism Was Built*, 205. Khalturin and Korotaev dismiss simple pessimism as the primary factor in the demographic crisis: Khalturina and Korotaev, "Alkogol'naya katastrofa," 13.

62. Hilary Pilkington, *Migration, Displacement and Identity in Post-Soviet Russia* (New York: Routledge, 1998), 170.

63. Ronald Inglehart and Christian Welzel, *Modernization, Cultural Change, and Democracy: The Human Development Sequence* (New York: Cambridge University Press, 2005), 300; see also 16–47.

64. Vladimir Shlapentokh, "Trust in Public Institutions in Russia: The Lowest in the World," *Communist and Post-Communist Studies* 39, no. 2 (2006): 154–55; Nicholas Eberstadt, *Russia's Peacetime Demographic Crisis: Dimensions, Causes, Implications* (Seattle, Wash.: National Bureau of Asian Research, 2010), 270; Ronald Inglehart and Wayne E. Baker, "Modernization, Cultural Change, and the Persistence of Traditional Values," *American Sociological Review* 65, no. 1 (2000): 40–41, 46–48. For World Values Survey data see http://www.wvsevsdb.com/wvs/WVSAnalizeStudy.jsp (accessed Nov. 27, 2011); Daniel Treisman, *The Return: Russia's Journey from Gorbachev to Medvedev* (New York: Simon & Schuster, 2011), 374, 86.

65. Inglehart and Welzel, *Modernization, Cultural Change, and Democracy*, 263. For more confirmation see European Bank for Reconstruction and Development (EBRD), *Life in Transition: After the Crisis* (London: EBRD Publications, 2011), 98. See also Richard Rose, William Mishler, and Neil Munro, *Russia Transformed: Developing Popular Support for a New Regime* (New York: Cambridge University Press, 2006), 128.

Chapter 21

1. Michael Specter, "The Devastation," *New Yorker*, Oct. 11, 2004, 67–68. See also Cullen Murphy, "Watching the Russians," *Atlantic Monthly*, February 1983); Murray Feshbach, "The Soviet Union: Population Trends and Dilemmas," *Population Bulletin* 37, no. 3 (1982). See also chapters 16 and 18.

2. "Fact of Life in Russia," *60 Minutes*, CBS News, May 19, 1996; Mark G. Field, "The Health and Demographic Crisis in Post-Soviet Russia: A Two-Phase Development," in *Russia's Torn Safety Nets: Health and Social Welfare during the Transition*, ed. Mark G. Field and Judyth L. Twigg (New York: St. Martin's, 2000), 11.

3. I largely agree with blogger Anatoly Karlin's reservation—not that Russia's demographic situation in the 1990s was particularly rosy, but that such apocalyptic pronouncements of Russia's demographic demise have continued through the present, overshadowing marked improvements over that time. See Anatoly Karlin, Da Russophile (blog), http://darussophile.com/category/demography (accessed May 5, 2012).

4. Dar'ya A. Khalturina and Andrei V. Korotaev, *Russkii krest: Faktory, mekhanizmy i puti preo-doleniia demograficheskogo krizisa v Rossii* (Moscow: KomKniga, 2006), 5. On origins of the term *Russkii krest* see Anatolii G. Vishnevskii, "Russkii krest," *Novye izvestiya*, Feb. 26, 1998. A more optimistic assessment can be found in Anatoly Karlin, "Russia Demographic Update VOO," Da Russophile (blog), Oct. 24, 2011, http://darussophile.com/2011/10/24/russia-demographic-update-7 (accessed May 5, 2012).

5. Dar'ya A. Khalturina and Andrei V. Korotaev, "Vvedeniye: Alkogol'naya katastrofa: Kak ostanovit' vymiranie Rossii," in *Alkogol'naya katastrofa i vozmozhnosti gosudarstvennoi poli-tiki v preodolenii alkogol'noi sverkosmertnosti v Rossii*, ed. Dar'ya A. Khalturina and Andrei V. Korotaev (Moscow: Lenand, 2010), 23; Nicholas Eberstadt, "The Dying Bear," *Foreign Affairs* 90, no. 6 (2011): 96. A comparison of percentage of population lost can be found in Daniel Treisman, *The Return: Russia's Journey from Gorbachev to Medvedev* (New York: Simon & Schuster, 2011), 368–69.

6. Khalturina and Korotaev, "Alkogol'naya katastrofa," 25; Eberstadt, "Dying Bear," 96.

7. "Fact of Life in Russia," *60 Minutes*, CBS News, May 19, 1996. Similarly see Laurie Garrett, *Betrayal of Trust: The Collapse of Global Public Health* (New York: Hyperion, 2000), 127.

8. Nicholas Eberstadt, *Russia's Peacetime Demographic Crisis: Dimensions, Causes, Implications* (Seattle, Wash.: National Bureau of Asian Research, 2010), 135–38.

9. Nicholas Eberstadt, "Drunken Nation: Russia's Depopulation Bomb," *World Affairs* 171, no. 4 (2009): 59; David E. Powell, "The Problem of AIDS," in *Russia's Torn Safety Nets: Health and Social Welfare during the Transition*, ed. Mark G. Field and Judyth L. Twigg (New York: St. Martin's, 2000), 124–25; Alexander Winning, "Fight against TB Plagued by Shortfalls," *Moscow Times*, June 9, 2012, http://www.themoscowtimes.com/news/article/fight-against-tb-plagued-by-shortfalls/460119.html (accessed June 9, 2012).

10. See Andrei Demin, ed., *Alkogol' i zdorov'e naseleniya Rossii: 1900–2000* (Moscow: Rossiiskaya assotsiatsiya obshchestvennogo zdorov'ya, 1998); Andrei Vroublevsky and Judith Harwin, "Russia," in *Alcohol and Emerging Markets: Patterns, Problems and Responses*, ed. Marcus Grant (Ann Arbor, Mich.: Edwards Brothers, 1998), 213. On "Disease #3" see Vladimir Solovyov, "The Paradox of Russian Vodka," *Michigan Quarterly Review* 21, no. 3 (1982): 407; David Powell, "Soviet Union: Social Trends and Social Problems," *Bulletin of the Atomic Scientists* 38, no. 9 (1982): 24. On Russia's alcohol-related mortality being the highest in the world see Andrew Stickley et al., "Alcohol Poisoning in Russia and the Countries in the European Part of the Former Soviet Union, 1970–2002," *European Journal of Public Health* 17, no. 5 (2007): 447.

11. "Fact of Life in Russia," *60 Minutes*, CBS News, May 19, 1996; Daria A. Khaltourina and Andrey V. Korotayev, "Potential for Alcohol Policy to Decrease the Mortality Crisis in Russia," *Evaluation & the Health Professions* 31, no. 3 (2008): 273.

12. Stickley et al., "Alcohol Poisoning," 446–47; Mark Lawrence Schrad, "A Lesson in Drinking," *Moscow Times*, March 5, 2011.

13. This is why famed Swedish doctor-turned-alcohol-reformer Ivan Bratt declared that absolute consumption statistics are "utterly valueless." Marquis W. Childs, *Sweden: The Middle Way* (New Haven, Conn.: Yale University Press, 1936), 112. In this section I refer to a standard half-liter bottle of 80-proof vodka, conventional 750 milliliter bottles of wine at 12 percent alcohol, and international standard 0.35 liter bottles of beer at 5 percent alcohol. Stickley et al., "Alcohol Poisoning," 446–47; Schrad, "Lesson in Drinking."

14. Khalturina and Korotaev, "Alkogol'naya katastrofa," 21; Vladimir P. Nuzhnyi and Sergei A. Savchuk, "Nelegal'nyi alkogol' v Rossii: Sravnitel'naya toksichnost' I vliyanie na zdorov'e naseleniya," in *Alkogol'naya katastrofa i vozmozhnosti gosudarstvennoi politiki v preodole-nii alkogol'noi sverkosmertnosti v Rossii*, ed. Dar'ya A. Khalturina and Andrei V. Korotaev (Moscow: Lenand, 2010), 227.

15. Garrett, *Betrayal of Trust*, 137.

16. Aleksei Mitrofanov, "Prazdnik teper' vsegda s toboi," *Izvestiya*, Feb. 17, 1999, 8; Murray Feshbach, "Russia's Population Meltdown," *Wilson Quarterly* 25, no. 1 (2001): 19; Hedrick Smith, *The Russians* (New York: Quadrangle/New York Times Book Co., 1976), 121. On the traditional Russian drinking culture see chapter 7 and Walter Connor, *Deviance in*

Soviet Society: Crime, Delinquency and Alcoholism (New York: Columbia University Press, 1972), 39–42.

17. Richard Weitz, "Russia: Binge Drinking and Sudden Death," Eurasianet.org, Dec. 15, 2010, http://www.eurasianet.org/node/62577 (accessed Dec. 17, 2010). Higher death rates among Russian men is based on a 2010 presentation by Martin McKee, co-director of the European Center on Health and Societies in Transition; the audio podcast can be found at http://csis.org/event/new-insights-catastrophic-level-mortality-russian-men.

18. Aleksandr Nemtsov, *Alkogol'naya istoriya Rossii: Noveishii period* (Moscow: URSS, 2009), 241; Francis C. Notzon et al., "Causes of Declining Life Expectancy in Russia," *Journal of the American Medical Association* 279, no. 10 (1998): 798.

19. Martin McKee, "Zdorov'e rossiyan: Chto nuzhno predprinyat', chtoby izmenit' situatsiyu k luchschemu," in *Alkogol'naya katastrofa i vozmozhnosti gosudarstvennoi politiki v preodolenii alkogol'noi sverkosmertnosti v Rossii*, ed. Dar'ya A. Khalturina and Andrei V. Korotaev (Moscow: Lenand, 2010), 141; Martin McKee et al., "The Composition of Surrogate Alcohols Consumed in Russia," *Alcoholism: Clinical and Experimental Research* 29, no. 10 (2005): 1887–88; Vladimir M. Shkol'nikov, Evgenii M. Andreev, and Dmitrii A. Zhdanov, "Smertnost' trudosposobnogo naseleniya, alkogol' i prodolzhitel'nost' zhizni v Rossii," in *Alkogol'naya katastrofa i vozmozhnosti gosudarstvennoi politiki v preodolenii alkogol'noi sverkosmertnosti v Rossii*, ed. Dar'ya A. Khalturina and Andrei V. Korotaev (Moscow: Lenand, 2010), 98.

20. David A. Leon et al., "Nepit'evoi alkogol' v Rossii: Potreblenie i vozdeistvie na zdorov'e. Chto nam izvestno?" in *Alkogol'naya katastrofa i vozmozhnosti gosudarstvennoi politiki v preodolenii alkogol'noi sverkosmertnosti v Rossii*, ed. Dar'ya A. Khalturina and Andrei V. Korotaev (Moscow: Lenand, 2010), 156, 59.

21. Garrett, *Betrayal of Trust*, 136; Eberstadt, "Drunken Nation," 61. During the 1990s alcohol directly killed 31 out of every 100,000 people in Russia and 54 out of every 100,000 men. Nuzhnyi and Savchuk, "Nelegal'nyi alkogol' v Rossii," 271; Aleksandr Nemtsov, "Mnogo pit', vse-taki vredno," *EKO*, no. 281 (1997): 187; Vroublevsky and Harwin, "Russia," 213.

22. A. M. Harkin, ed., *Alcohol in Europe—A Health Perspective* (Copenhagen: W.H.O. Regional Office for Europe, 1995); Vladimir S. Moiseev, *Alkogol'naya bolezn': Porazheniya vnutrennikh organov pri alkogolizme* (Moscow: Izdatel'stvo Universiteta druzhby narodov, 1990), 18–20, 54–55.

23. Nicholas Eberstadt, "Russia: Too Sick to Matter?" *Policy Review*, no. 95 (1999): 9; Larry Husten, "Global Epidemic of Cardiovascular Disease Predicted," *The Lancet*, Nov. 7, 1998, 352; Sonni Efron, "Grim Prognosis," *Los Angeles Times*, Nov. 12, 1995, 1.

24. Eberstadt, "Russia: Too Sick to Matter?" 9.

25. Khalturina and Korotaev, "Alkogol'naya katastrofa," 17–19; William Alex Pridemore, "Vodka and Violence: Alcohol Consumption and Homicide Rates in Russia," *American Journal of Public Health* 92, no. 12 (2002): 1921; Eberstadt, "Drunken Nation," 60–61; "Fact of Life in Russia," *60 Minutes*, CBS News, May 19, 1996.

26. Shkol'nikov, Andreev, and Zhdanov, "Smertnost' trudosposobnogo naseleniya," 98; Goskomstat Rossii, *Sotsial'noe polozhenie i uroven' zhizni naseleniya Rossii: Statisticheskii sbornik* (Moscow: Goskomstat Rossii, 1998), 310.

27. Average life expectancy among Russian men bottomed out at 57.6 years in 1994. Aleksandr Nemtsov, "Tendentsii potrebleniya alkogolya i obuslovlennye alkogolem poteri zdorov'ya i zhizni v Rossii v 1946–1996 gg.," in *Alkogol' i zdorov'e naseleniya Rossii: 1900–2000*, ed. Andrei K. Demin (Moscow: Rossiiskaya assotsiatsiya obshchestvennogo zdorov'ya, 1998), 105; Anders Åslund and Andrew Kuchins, *The Russia Balance Sheet* (New York: Petersen Institute for International Economics, 2009), 86.

28. Khalturina and Korotaev, "Alkogol'naya katastrofa," 24–25. Every additional liter of alcohol consumed per year reduces a man's life expectancy by 10.5 months but only 4 months for a woman. Andrei V. Podlazov, "Demograficheskaya demodernizatsiya i alkogolizatsiya Rossii," in *Alkogol'naya katastrofa i vozmozhnosti gosudarstvennoi politiki v preodolenii alkogol'noi sverkosmertnosti v Rossii*, ed. Dar'ya A. Khalturina and Andrei V. Korotaev (Moscow: Lenand, 2010), 116. The widest Soviet sex differential between 1980 and 1983 was 10.2 years. W. Ward Kingkade and Eduardo E. Arriaga, "Sex Differentials in Mortality in the Soviet Union,"

in *Social Change and Social Issues in the Former USSR*, ed. Walter Joyce (New York: St. Martin's, 1992), 115.

29. Feshbach, "Russia's Population Meltdown," 16–17; Eberstadt, "Drunken Nation," 54. TFR and other demographic data can be found at the website of Goskomstat Rossii, the state statistical agency: http://www.gks.ru/dbscripts/Cbsd/DBInet.cgi?pl=2403012 (accessed Jan. 14, 2012.)

30. "Fact of Life in Russia," *60 Minutes*, CBS News, May 19, 1996.

31. Feshbach, "Russia's Population Meltdown," 16–17; Eberstadt, "Drunken Nation," 54. Relatedly, "90 Percent of Russian Men Suffer from Erectile Dysfunction," *Pravda*, Jan. 11, 2012, http://english.pravda.ru/health/11-01-2012/120204-erectile_dysfunction-0 (accessed Jan. 12, 2012).

32. Garrett, *Betrayal of Trust*, 135. See also Victoria I. Sakevich and Boris P. Denisov, "The Future of Abortions in Russia," Paper presented at the European Population Conference 2008, July 9–12, in Barcelona, Spain, http://epc2008.princeton.edu/download. aspx?submissionId=80419 (accessed Feb. 2, 2012).

33. Nikita Mironov, "Rossiya vymiraet, potomu chto v strane ne ostalos' muzhchin," *Komsomol'skaya pravda*, June 24 2009, http://www.kp.ru/daily/24316.3/508858 (accessed Nov. 5, 2010); Paul Goble, "High Mortality among Men Undercuts Moscow's Pro-Birth Policies," *Moscow Times*, June 30, 2009; "Endangered Species," in Nemtsov, *Alkogol'naya istoriya Rossii*, 294. 2010 census figures are available at http://www.perepis-2010.ru/results_ of_the_census (accessed Feb. 1, 2012). Murray Feshbach is quoted in Garrett, *Betrayal of Trust*, 130.

34. Khalturina and Korotaev, "Alkogol'naya katastrofa," 19.

35. Ibid., 18; Eberstadt, "Drunken Nation," 55; Nemtsov, *Alkogol'naya istoriya Rossii*, 108.

36. Judyth Twigg, "What Has Happened to Russian Society?" in *Russia after the Fall*, ed. Andrew C. Kuchins (Washington, D.C.: Carnegie Endowment for International Peace, 2002), 152–53.

37. Khalturina and Korotaev, "Alkogol'naya katastrofa," 18; Jake Rudnitsky, "Bleak House," *The eXile*, Jan. 22, 2003, http://exile.ru/articles/detail.php?ARTICLE_ID=6802&IBLOCK_ ID=35 (accessed Jan. 2, 2013); Eberstadt, "Dying Bear," 100; Eric Rosenthal et al., "Implementing the Right to Community Integration for Children with Disabilities in Russia," *Health and Human Rights* 4, no. 1 (1999): 83; Garrett, *Betrayal of Trust*, 138.

38. Twigg, "What Has Happened to Russian Society?" 151. Also see Fred Weir, "Russia's Shrinking Population Mars Putin's Superpower Ambitions," *Global Post*, Nov. 3, 2011, http://www.globalpost.com/dispatch/news/regions/europe/russia/111102/russia-popu- lation-superpower-health-soviet-union?page=0,2 (accessed Feb. 2, 2012). This is why I find it important to support organizations like the Russian Orphan Opportunity Fund, which provides educational and vocational development: http://www.roofnet.org/mission.

39. Garrett, *Betrayal of Trust*, 139–40.

40. Richard Galpin, "Russia's Disabled Suffer Neglect and Abuse," BBC News, Oct. 12, 2009, http://news.bbc.co.uk/2/hi/8302633.stm (accessed June 26, 2011); Rimma Avshalumova, "Finding Work Is Difficult for Disabled," *Moscow Times*, Feb. 14, 2012, http://www. themoscowtimes.com/business/article/finding-work-is-difficult-for-disabled/453103. html (accessed Feb. 14, 2012); Rosenthal et al., "Implementing the Right to Community Integration for Children with Disabilities in Russia." One in nine families with disabled children reports familial strife with regard to alcohol. Ethel Dunn, "The Disabled in Russia in the 1990s," in *Russia's Torn Safety Nets: Health and Social Welfare during the Transition*, ed. Mark G. Field and Judyth L. Twigg (New York: St. Martin's, 2000).

41. Laurie C. Miller et al., "Fetal Alcohol Spectrum Disorders in Children Residing in Russian Orphanages: A Phenotypic Survey," *Alcoholism: Clinical and Experimental Research* 30, no. 3 (2006): 531. Likewise, see Khalturina and Korotaev, "Alkogol'naya katastrofa," 19; Tatiana Balachova et al., "Women's Alcohol Consumption and Risk for Alcohol-Exposed Pregnancies in Russia," *Addiction* 107, no. 1 (2012): 109.

42. Feshbach, "Russia's Population Meltdown," 15; Twigg, "What Has Happened to Russian Society?" 150; Garrett, *Betrayal of Trust*, 130. See also "Teenagers' Health Worsens—Rf Chief Pediatrician," ITAR-TASS Daily, May 12, 2012.

43. "Fact of Life in Russia," *60 Minutes*, CBS News, May 19, 1996.

44. *Doklad o sostoyanii zdorov'ya detei v Rossiiskoi Federatsii (po itogam Vserossiiskoi dispanserizatsii 2002 goda)* (Moscow: 2003), 31–59; cited in Murray Feshbach, "The Russian Military: Population and Health Constraints," in *Russian Power Structures: Present and Future Roles in Russian Politics*, ed. Jan Leijonhielm and Fredrik Westerlund (Stockholm: FOI, Swedish Defense Research Agency, 2007), 138–42; personal correspondence with Murray Feshbach, Feb. 18, 2012. Also see "Russia's Alcohol Consumption More Than 100% above Critical Level," RIA Novosti, Sept. 24, 2009. http://en.rian.ru/russia/20090924/156238102. html (accessed Sept. 28, 2009).

Chapter 22

1. Moscow Distillery Cristall webpage, http://www.kristall.ru/page.php?P=1 (accessed Nov. 8, 2010). On the history of Stolichnaya see also Vladimir Ul'yanov, "Vodka Stolichnaya: Kak vse nachinalos," Popsop.ru, May 27, 2008, http://popsop.ru/2155 (accessed Nov. 8, 2010); Viktor Erofeev, *Russkii apokalipsis: Opyt khudozhestvennoi eskhatologii* (Moscow: Zebra E, 2008), 26.

2. Aleksei Sivov and Igor' Ivanov, "U 'Kristalla' dvoitsya," *Izvestiya*, Aug. 5, 2000, 2.

3. Nikolai Pavlov, "Violent DTS at Kristall," *Current Digest of the Russian Press* 33, no. 52 (2000): 13; originally published in the *Rossiiskaya gazeta*, Aug. 15, 2000, 2.

4. Nikolai Petrov, "Kak v kaple vodki: Politika, finansy, regionalizm," in *Regiony Rossii v. 1999 g.: Ezhegodnoe prilozheniye k politicheskomu almanakhu Russii*, ed. Carnegie Center Moscow (Moscow: Gendal'f, 2000), 143; Sophie Lambroschini, "Stand-Off at Vodka Distillery Continues," Radio Free Europe/Radio Liberty, Aug. 8, 2000, http://www.rferl.org/content/article/1094494.html (accessed Feb. 2, 2012).

5. "Putin's Inauguration Speech," BBC News, May 7, 2000, http://news.bbc.co.uk/2/hi/world/monitoring/media_reports/739432.stm (accessed Nov. 5, 2010).

6. Nikolai Chekhovskii, "Gosmonopoliya na zhidkuyu valyutu," *Segodnya*, Sept. 9, 2000, 2; AFI, "Aktsii 'Kristalla' perevedeny v federal'nuyu sobstvennost'," *Segodnya*, Sept. 13, 2000, 5.

7. Marshall I. Goldman, *Petrostate: Putin, Power, and the New Russia* (New York: Oxford University Press, 2008), 98–99.

8. "Natsional'nyi proekt 'Dostupnyu alkogol'," *Ekspert Sibir'*, Feb. 19, 2007, http://expert.ru/siberia/2007/07/rynok_alkogolya_editorial/ (accessed Aug. 27, 2013); translated in: Anna Bailey, "Explaining Rosalkogol'regulirovaniye. Why Does Russia Have a New Federal Alcohol Regulator?" in: *Alkogol' v Rossii: Materialy vtoroi mezhdunarodnoi nauchno-prakticheskoi konferentsii (Ivanovo, 28-29 oktyabrya 2011)*, ed. Nikolai V. Dem'yanenko (Ivanovo: Filial RGGU v g. Ivanovo, 2011), 105.

9. Jim Heintz, "Vodka Dispute Shows Russia Chaos," Sept. 26, 2000, AP News Archive, http://www.apnewsarchive.com/2000/Vodka-Dispute-Shows-Russia-Chaos/id-d45f0cd-2f85248828e5368441009fcf0 (accessed Aug. 6, 2013); Fred Weir, "In Russia, Hostile Takeover Takes on a New Meaning," Christian Science Monitor, Aug. 8, 2000, http://www.csmonitor.com/2000/0808/p7s2.html (accessed Feb. 12, 2012).

10. Pavlov, "Violent DTS at Kristall," 14; Aleksei Sivov, "Ognennoi vodoi ne razlit'," *Izvestiya*, Aug. 7, 2000, 20.

11. Lambroschini, "Stand-Off at Vodka Distillery Continues."

12. Ibid.; Aleksandr Nikonov, "Kristall'nyi vopros," *Ogonek*, Aug. 14, 2000, 20; Ekaterina Kats, "Kristal'no gryaznyi skandal," *Segodnya*, Aug. 7, 2000, 1–2; Il'ya Khrennikov and Nikolai Chekhovskii, "Operatsiya 'burya v stakane'," *Segodnya*, Aug. 10, 2000, 2.

13. Heintz, "Vodka Dispute Shows Russia Chaos."

14. Lambroschini, "Stand-Off at Vodka Distillery Continues."

15. Chekhovskii, "Gosmonopoliya na zhidkuyu valyutu," 2; Dmitrii Khitarov, "Dobro i kulaki," *Itogi*, Oct. 24, 2000, 4.

16. Aleksei Makarkin, "Sdavaite vodku, grazhdane," *Segodnya*, May 30, 2000, 2.

17. The Gusinsky raid took place May 11, 2000—predating the similar raid on Kristall. David Hoffman, *The Oligarchs: Wealth and Power in the New Russia*, revised and updated (New York: PublicAffairs, 2011), 477–78.

18. Ol'ga Kryshtanovskaya and Stephen White, "The Sovietization of Russian Politics," *Post-Soviet Affairs* 25, no. 4 (2009): 287.

19. Masha Gessen, "The Wrath of Putin," *Vanity Fair*, April 2012, http://www.vanityfair.com/politics/2012/04/vladimir-putin-mikhail-khodorkovsky-russia (accessed May 5, 2012).

20. Angus Roxburgh, *Strongman: Vladimir Putin and the Struggle for Russia* (New York: Palgrave Macmillan, 2012), 289; Robyn Dixon, "Business Rivals Don't Mix in Standoff at Vodka Plant," *Los Angeles Times*, Aug. 8, 2000, http://articles.latimes.com/print/2000/aug/08/news/mn-629 (accessed Feb. 12, 2012). On the organization of raids under Putin and Medvedev see Daniel Treisman, *The Return: Russia's Journey from Gorbachev to Medvedev* (New York: Simon & Schuster, 2011), 140–41.

21. Alena V. Ledeneva, *Can Russia Modernise? Sistema, Power Networks and Informal Governance* (New York: Cambridge University Press, 2013), 188–92.

22. See ibid., 96, 113.

23. See chapter 1; Richard Sakwa, *Putin: Russia's Choice*, 2nd ed. (New York: Routledge, 2008), 2.

24. Andrew Jack, *Inside Putin's Russia* (New York: Oxford University Press, 2006), 51; Vladimir Putin, *First Person: An Astonishingly Frank Self-Portrait by Russia's President* (New York: PublicAffairs, 2000), 19.

25. Interview with Lyudmila Putina, in Putin, *First Person*, 150.

26. "Russian Politicians Learn to Say Goodbye to Vodka," *Pravda*, March 19, 2008, http://english.pravda.ru/history/19-03-2008/104564-russian_vodka-0 (accessed Feb. 10, 2010).

27. Boris El'tsin, *Prezidentskii marafon* (Moscow: Izdatel'stvo ACT, 2000), 315.

28. Some contend the bombings were actually part of a FSB coup d'etat to bring Putin to the presidency. Putin's foremost accuser, former FSB whistleblower Aleksandr Litvinenko, was poisoned with radioactive polonium-210 in London in November 2006. Aleksandr Litvinenko and Yuri Felshtinsky, *Blowing up Russia: The Secret Plot to Bring Back KGB Terror* (New York: Encounter Books, 2007).

29. Emma Gilligan, *Terror in Chechnya: Russia and the Tragedy of Civilians in War* (Princeton, N.J.: Princeton University Press, 2009), 31–32.

30. Lilia Shevtsova, *Russia—Lost in Transition: The Yeltsin and Putin Legacies* (Washington, D.C.: Carnegie Endowment for International Peace, 2007), 36–41.

31. The connotation obviously depends on the position of the author. See Treisman, *Return*, 232; Anders Åslund, "Putinomics," *Peterson Institute for International Economics*, Dec. 3, 2007, http://www.iie.com/publications/opeds/oped.cfm?ResearchID=852 (accessed Feb. 14, 2012). Also see Sean Guillory, "A Genealogy of 'Putinism,'" Sean's Russia Blog, Dec. 23, 2007, http://seansrussiablog.org/2007/12/23/a-genealogy-of-putinism (accessed Dec. 12, 2010). On Russian "semi-feudalism" see Vladimir Shlapentokh, "Russia's Acquiescence to Corruption Makes the State Machine Inept," *Communist and Post-Communist Studies* 36, no. 2 (2003): 158.

32. Mark R. Beissinger, *Nationalist Mobilization and Collapse of the Soviet State* (New York: Cambridge University Press, 2002), 265.

33. Consider the "notorious" Nenets distiller, Aleksandr Sabadash: Aleksei Vasilevetskii, "V Sovet Federatsii prishla bol'shaya vodka," *Kommersant'*, June 26, 2003, http://kommersant.ru/doc/391593 (accessed March 17, 2013).

34. Virginie Coulloudon, "Putin's Russia: A Confusing Notion of Corruption," Working Paper, Liechtenstein Institute on Self-Determination at Princeton University, August 2003, 10–11.

35. Nikolai Petrov and Darrell Slider, "The Regions under Putin and After," in *After Putin's Russia: Past Imperfect, Future Uncertain*, ed. Stephen K. Wegren and Dale R. Herspring (Lanham, Md.: Rowman & Littlefield, 2010), 66–70.

36. Yulia Latynina, "Inside Russia: Heavyweights Still Waging Centralization," *Moscow Times*, Sept. 20, 2000; cited in: Anna Bailey, "Explaining Rosalkogol'regulirovaniye," 105. See also Nina Petlyanova, "Soobrazili na svoikh," *Novaya gazeta*, March 4, 2011, http://www.novaya-gazeta.ru/politics/6856.html (accessed Aug. 27, 2013).

37. New State Ice Co. v. Liebmann, 285 U.S. 262, 311 (1932) (Brandeis, J., dissenting).

38. Ekaterina Zhuravskaya, "Federalism in Russia," in *Russia after the Global Economic Crisis*, ed. Anders Åslund, Sergei Guriev, and Andrew Kuchins (Washington, D.C.: Peterson Institute for International Economics, 2010), 61. On the weakness of *samoupravlenie*, or local

self-government, see Tomila V. Lankina, *Governing the Locals: Local Self-Government and Ethnic Mobilization in Russia* (Lanham, Md.: Rowman & Littlefield, 2004), 141–43; Peter Reddaway and Robert W. Orttung, eds., *The Dynamics of Russian Politics: Putin's Reform of Federal-Regional Relations*, 2 vols. (Lanham, Md.: Rowman & Littlefield, 2005); Vladimir Gel'man, "The Politics of Local Government in Russia: The Neglected Side of the Story," *Perspectives on European Politics and Society* 3, no. 3 (2002).

39. Artyom Gil et al., "Alcohol Policy in a Russian Region: A Stakeholder Analysis," *European Journal of Public Health* (2010): 1. More generally see Judyth Twigg, "Health Care under the Federal Reforms," in *The Dynamics of Russian Politics: Putin's Reform of Federal-Regional Relations*, ed. Peter Reddaway and Robert W. Orttung (Lanham, Md.: Rowman & Littlefield, 2005), 420–22.

40. Gil et al., "Alcohol Policy in a Russian Region," 3–4.

41. Ibid., 5–6.

42. Michele A. Berdy, "Chernomyrdin's Linguistic Legacy," *Moscow Times*, Nov. 12, 2010.

43. David Satter, *Darkness at Dawn: The Rise of the Russian Criminal State* (New Haven, Conn.: Yale University Press, 2003), 60; Kaj Hobér, *The Impeachment of President Yeltsin* (Huntington, N.Y.: Juris, 2004), 60–71.

44. Satter, *Darkness at Dawn*, 61–63.

45. Kryshtanovskaya and White, "Sovietization of Russian Politics," 290–91; Shevtsova, *Russia—Lost in Transition*, 48.

46. Mikhail Myagkov, Peter C. Ordeshook, and Dimitri Shakin, *The Forensics of Election Fraud: Russia and Ukraine* (New York: Cambridge University Press, 2009), 71–137; M. Steven Fish, *Democracy Derailed in Russia: The Failure of Open Politics* (New York: Cambridge University Press, 2005), 30–81; Shevtsova, *Russia—Lost in Transition*, 299–300.

47. Shevtsova, *Russia—Lost in Transition*, 25.

48. Sakwa, *Putin*, 103–4; Vicki L. Hesli, "Parliamentary and Presidential Elections in Russia: The Political Landscape in 1999 and 2000," in *The 1999–2000 Elections in Russia: Their Impact and Legacy*, ed. Vicki L. Hesli and William M. Reisinger (New York: Cambridge University Press, 2003), 15–16.

49. Daniel Treisman, "Russian Politics in a Time of Economic Turmoil," in *Russia after the Global Economic Crisis*, ed. Anders Åslund, Sergei Guriev, and Andrew Kuchins (Washington, D.C.: Peterson Institute for International Economics, 2010), 46–51.

50. Richard Stengel, "Choosing Order before Freedom," *Time*, Dec. 31, 2007, 45.

51. Kathryn Hendley, "The Law in Post-Putin Russia," in *After Putin's Russia: Past Imperfect, Future Uncertain*, ed. Stephen K. Wegren and Dale R. Herspring (Lanham, Md.: Rowman & Littlefield, 2010), 87–93; Shevtsova, *Russia—Lost in Transition*, 295.

52. Richard Sakwa, "Putin's Leadership," in *Putin's Russia*, ed. Dale R. Herspring (Lanham, Md.: Rowman & Littlefield, 2007), 24–29; Alexandr Dugin, "The World Needs to Understand Putin," *Financial Times*, March 12, 2013, http://www.ft.com/cms/s/0/67fa00d2-874b-11e2-9dd7-00144feabdc0.html (accessed March 12, 2013).

53. Allen C. Lynch, *How Russia Is Not Ruled: Reflections on Russian Political Development* (New York: Cambridge University Press, 2005), 7; Shevtsova, *Russia—Lost in Transition*, 294.

54. Kryshtanovskaya and White, "Sovietization of Russian Politics," 293; Sakwa, "Putin's Leadership," 29; Shevtsova, *Russia—Lost in Transition*, 63.

55. Nikolai Troitsky, "Viktor Chernoymrdin: The End of Two Eras," RIA-Novosti, Nov. 3, 2010, http://en.rian.ru/analysis/20101103/161203286.html (accessed Feb. 29, 2012).

56. See, for instance, Anders Åslund, *How Capitalism Was Built: The Transformation of Central and Eastern Europe, Russia, and Central Asia* (New York: Cambridge University Press, 2007), 189.

57. Alcohol poisonings in Russia in 2008 were 16.9 per 100,000, according to Goskomstat: http://www.gks.ru/free_doc/new_site/population/demo/dem5_bd.htm/.

58. Michael Specter, "The Devastation," *New Yorker*, Oct. 11, 2004, 61.

59. "Russians Lose a Centimeter," *Moscow Times*, May 23, 2007; Tom Parfitt, "Spin Doctors Reinvent the 'Nano-President'," *The Observer*, March 1, 2008; Murray Feshbach, "The Russian Military: Population and Health Constraints," in *Russian Power Structures: Present and Future Roles in Russian Politics*, ed. Jan Leijonhielm and Fredrik Westerlund (Stockholm: FOI,

Swedish Defense Research Agency, 2007), 138–47; "Teenagers' Health Worsens—RF Chief Pediatrician," ITAR-TASS Daily, May 12, 2012.

60. Vladimir Putin, "Annual Address to the Federal Assembly," May 10, 2006, http://archive. kremlin.ru/eng/speeches/2006/05/10/1823_type70029type82912_105566.shtml (accessed Nov. 11, 2011).

61. Ibid.; Fred Weir, "Russia's Shrinking Population Mars Putin's Superpower Ambitions," Global Post, Nov. 3, 2011, http://www.globalpost.com/dispatch/news/regions/europe/russia/111102/russia-population-superpower-health-soviet-union (accessed Nov. 12, 2011.)

62. Cited in Graeme P. Herd, "Russia's Demographic Crisis and Federal Instability," in Russian Regions and Regionalism: Strength through Weakness, ed. Graeme P. Herd and Anne Aldis (New York: RoutledgeCurzon, 2003), 46. See also Aleksandr Nemtsov, Alkogol'naya istoriya Rossii: Noveishii period (Moscow: URSS, 2009), 136.

63. Ibid., 281–82.

64. Ibid., 288.

65. Shevtsova, Russia—Lost in Transition, 54.

66. "Arkady Rotenberg," thishousewillexist.org, http://thishousewillexist.org/arkadyrotenberg. php (accessed Feb. 20, 2012); Simon Shuster, "Vladimir Putin's Billionaire Boys Judo Club," Time, March 1, 2011, http://www.time.com/time/world/article/0,8599,2055962,00.html (accessed Nov. 11, 2011).

67. Erofeev, Russkii apokalipsis, 27.

68. Evgeniya Al'bats and Anatolii Ermolin, "Korporatsiya "Rossiya"," Novoe vremya: The New Times, Oct. 31, 2011, http://newtimes.ru/articles/detail/45648/ (accessed Nov. 11, 2011). Also see Richard Sakwa, The Crisis of Russian Democracy: The Dual State, Factionalism and the Medvedev Succession (New York: Cambridge University Press, 2011), 209.

69. Erofeev, Russkii apokalipsis, 28. Petlyanova, "Soobrazili na svoikh."

70. Ibid.; "Rosspirtprom to Become Federal Brand," Kommersant', Nov. 22, 2006, http://www. kommersant.com/p723749/vodka_Rosspritprom (accessed Nov. 15, 2010.) On Zivenko see http://www.forbes.com/finance/lists/75/2004/LIR.jhtml?passListId=75&passYear=2004&passListType=Person&uniqueId=L23U&datatype=Person (accessed Feb. 20, 2012); Alex Nicholson, "New Shot Fired in Vodka Battle," SPI Group Media Stories, Jan. 14, 2004, http://www.spi-group.com/about-spi-group/company-news/media_stories/new-shot-fired-in-vodka-battle-the-moscow-times-14-01-2004 (accessed Feb. 20, 2012). see also: Petlyanova, "Soobrazili na svoikh."

71. Yuliya Yarosh and Il'ya Bulavinov, "Arkadii Rotenberg: Nikto ne mozhet skazat', chto ya kogo-to unizil, u kogo-to chto-to otnyal," Kommersant', April 28, 2010, http://www.kommersant.ru/doc/1361793 (accessed Feb. 20, 2012).

72. See http://www.forbes.com/profile/arkady-rotenberg (Accessed Feb. 20, 2012).

73. Ledeneva, Can Russia Modernise? 96; specific to the alcohol industry see 56–60, 217.

74. Andrew Osborn, "Will Russia's Putinka Outlast the President?" Wall Street Journal, May 29, 2007, http://online.wsj.com/article/SB118039981514116698.html (accessed Aug. 14, 2009). See also "'Crystal' Has Suspended Production of 'Putinka'," WineLiquorMart (blog), April 19, 2011, http://wineliquormart.wordpress.com/2011/04/19/crystal-has-suspended-production-of-putinka/ (accessed Jan. 14, 2012). On brand loyalty see Petrov, "Kak v kaple vodki," 148.

75. Marya Levintova, "Russian Alcohol Policy in the Making," Alcohol and Alcoholism 42, no. 5 (2007): 502.

76. Nemtsov, Alkogol'naya istoriya Rossii, 286.

77. Claire Bigg, "Russia: Alcohol Reform Blamed for Outbreak of Poisonings," Radio Free Europe/Radio Liberty, Oct. 30, 2006, http://www.rferl.org/content/article/1072399.html (accessed Dec. 8, 2008); Levintova, "Russian Alcohol Policy in the Making," 502.

78. Valery P. Goreglyad, "Otchet o rezul'tatakh kontrol'nogo meropriyatiya 'proverka effektivnosti ispol'zovaniya federal'noi sobstvennosti, peredannoi federal'nomu gosudarstvennomu unitarnomu predpriyatiyu Rosspirtprom, za 2005–2006 gody'," Byletten' Schetnoi palaty Rossiiskoi Federatsii 124, no. 4 (2008), http://www.budgetrf.ru/Publications/Schpalata/2008/ACH200805211952/word/ACH200805211952_000.zip/.

79. Ibid.

80. Howard Amos, "Fast VTB Growth Raises Eyebrows," *Moscow Times*, Jan. 19 2012, http://www.themoscowtimes.com/business/article/fast-vtb-growth-raises-eyebrows/451249.html (accessed Jan. 23, 2012); "VTB Sues Rosspirtprom," PMR, Feb. 11, 2010, http://www.russiaretail.com/81995/VTB-sues-Rosspirtprom.shtml (accessed March 7, 2012); Julia Ioffe, "Net Impact: One Man's Cyber-Crusade against Russian Corruption," *New Yorker*, April 4, 2011, http://www.newyorker.com/reporting/2011/04/04/110404fa_fact_ioffe?currentPage=all (accessed April 11, 2011). For Alexei Navalny on VTB see http://navalny.livejournal.com/tag/ВТБ; also, Fond bor'by s korruptsiei, *Fit for International Financial Markets? A Closer Look at VTB Group's Practices* (London: Henry Jackson Society 2012). Of course, it also helped that members of the board of directors of Kristall and other Rosspirtprom holdings, like Igor' Kriskovets, were also on the board of directors of VTB. Nina Petlyanova, "Soobrazili na svoikh," *Novaya gazeta*, March 4, 2011, http://www.novaya-gazeta.ru/politics/6856.html (accessed Feb. 20, 2012).

81. Goreglyad, "Proverka effektivnosti." Rosspirtprom was not alone: Russia's largest factory, Istok in North Ossetia—like manufacturers throughout the country—also was struggling. Nina Petlyanova, "Soobrazili na svoikh."

82. Petlyanova, "Soobrazili na svoikh"; Dmitry Sergeyev, "Russian Bank VTB Gets Control of 11 Distilleries," Reuters, Oct. 5, 2009, http://www.reuters.com/article/2009/10/05/vtb-vodka-idUSL53868020091005 (accessed Nov. 11, 2009).

83. Andrew Scott Barnes, *Owning Russia: The Struggle over Factories, Farms, and Power* (Ithaca, N.Y.: Cornell University Press, 2006), 119.

84. Peter Rutland, "The Oligarchs and Economic Development," in *After Putin's Russia: Past Imperfect, Future Uncertain*, ed. Stephen K. Wegren and Dale R. Herspring (Lanham, Md.: Rowman & Littlefield, 2010), 172.

85. Phoebe Eaton, "How Much Is That in Rubles?" *New York*, May 21, 2005, http://nymag.com/print/?/nymetro/news/people/features/9873 (accessed Nov. 11, 2011.)

86. Elena Tokareva, "Gruzinskii skandal rossiiskogo oligarkha," *Stringer*, Jan. 26, 2011, http://www.stringer.ru/publication.mhtml?Part=48&PubID=15616 (accessed Jan. 12, 2012); Petlyanova, "Soobrazili na svoikh."

87. Oleg Trutnev and Kristina Bus'ko, "Vasilii Anisimov predskazal po 'Kristallu'," *Kommersant'*, May 31, 2011, http://www.kommersant.ru/doc/1650972 (accessed Feb. 24, 2012). See also Oleg Trutnev, " 'Rosspirtprom' i polyaki mutyat vodki," *Kommersant'*, Sept. 15, 2011, http://www.kommersant.ru/doc/1773740 (accessed Feb. 24, 2012). See also Rinat Sagdiev, "Vasiliyu Anisimovu i 'Rosspirtpromu' vodochnye kompanii dostalis' bez chasti aktivov i s predstavitelyami struktur Arkadiya Rotenberga v sovetakh direktorov," Kompromat.ru, Feb. 18, 2010, http://www.compromat.ru/page_28855.htm (accessed Nov. 5, 2011).

88. Oleg Trutnev, " 'Kristall' ne nalivaet," *Kommersant'*, Jan. 18, 2012, http://www.kommersant.ru/doc/1853092 (accessed Jan. 19, 2012).

Chapter 23

1. Dmitrii Medvedev, "Rossiya, vpered!" Kremlin.ru, Sept. 10, 2009, http://news.kremlin.ru/news/5413 (accessed March 1, 2012). See Richard Sakwa, *The Crisis of Russian Democracy: The Dual State, Factionalism and the Medvedev Succession* (New York: Cambridge University Press, 2011), 347–50.

2. Mezhduregionalnoye dvizhenie 'Edinstvo' or MeDvEd.

3. Which in turn is borrowed from a description of Sergei Witte. Daniel Treisman, *The Return: Russia's Journey from Gorbachev to Medvedev* (New York: Simon & Schuster, 2011), 123, 419.

4. Andrei Vandenko, "Prostye istiny," *Itogi*, Feb. 18, 2008, http://www.itogi.ru/russia/2008/8/3759.html (accessed March 7, 2012). Medvedev grew up on Western rock bands like Pink Floyd, Led Zeppelin, Deep Purple, and Black Sabbath—which is not important politically but is definitely an upgrade over Putin's unhealthy fixation with the Swedish super group ABBA. " 'Money, Money, Money' for Putin," *Moscow Times*, Feb. 6, 2009. See also http://www.youtube.com/watch?v=ahnZYdjd7Ww (accessed March 2, 2012).

5. Treisman, *Return*, 137; Sakwa, *Crisis of Russian Diplomacy*, 98–101.

6. Leonid Abalkin, "Razmyshleniya o dolgosrochnoi strategii, nauke i demokratii," *Voprosi ekonomiki* 12 (2006): 15; quoted in Stephen White, *Understanding Russian Politics* (New York: Cambridge University Press, 2011), 148. See also ibid., 105–6; Jason Bush, "Russia's New Deal," *Bloomberg Businessweek*, March 29, 2007, http://www.businessweek.com/globalbiz/content/mar2007/gb20070329_226664.htm?chan=search (accessed Feb. 29, 2012).

7. Cable 08MOSCOW558, "Medvedev and Russia's National Priority Projects—All Hat, No Cattle?" Feb. 28, 2008, http://wikileaks.ch/cable/2008/02/08MOSCOW558.html; Cable 06MOSCOW12764, "Russians Still Cynical about National Priority Projects," Dec. 4, 2006, http://wikileaks.org/cable/2006/12/06MOSCOW12764.html (accessed March 3, 2012).

8. Stephen K. Wegren and Dale R. Herspring, "Introduction," in *After Putin's Russia: Past Imperfect, Future Uncertain*, ed. Stephen K. Wegren and Dale R. Herspring (Lanham, Md.: Rowman & Littlefield, 2010), 5.

9. Stephen Colbert, "Un-American News: Financial Edition," *The Colbert Report*, Oct. 6, 2008, http://www.colbertnation.com/the-colbert-report-videos/187306/october-06-2008/un-american-news—financial-edition, and "Cold War Update: Russia,"*The Colbert Report*, May 12, 2008, http://www.colbertnation.com/the-colbert-report-videos/168292/may-12-2008/cold-war-update—russia (accessed March 2, 2012).

10. Wegren and Herspring, "Introduction," 6–7. On loyalty and trust being the most important values in the ruling *sistema* see Alena V. Ledeneva, *Can Russia Modernise? Sistema, Power Networks and Informal Governance* (New York: Cambridge University Press, 2013), 39.

11. Sergei Guriev and Aleh Tsyvinski, "Challenges Facing the Russian Economy after the Crisis," in *Russia after the Global Economic Crisis*, ed. Anders Åslund, Sergei Guriev, and Andrew Kuchins (Washington, D.C.: Peterson Institute for International Economics, 2010), 13–17.

12. Ronald D. Asmus, *A Little War That Shook the World: Georgia, Russia, and the Future of the West* (New York: Palgrave Macmillan, 2010), 49; for the role of alcohol in the war see, 33, 151.

13. Guriev and Tsyvinski, "Challenges Facing the Russian Economy," 16–30.

14. Il'ya Barabanov, "Luchshaya rol' vtorogo plana," *Novoe vremya/New Times*, May 11, 2009, http://newtimes.ru/articles/detail/3161 (accessed March 3, 2012); Treisman, *Return*, 140–41. See also President of Russia, official web portal, http://archive.kremlin.ru/eng/text/news/2009/04/214779.shtml.

15. Maria Levina, "National Projects under Crisis Watch," *Moscow Times*, Nov.14, 2008, http://www.themoscowtimes.com/news/article/national-projects-under-crisis-watch/372358.html (accessed March 2, 2012); Treisman, *Return*, 138.

16. "Medvedev Angered by Officials' Demagogy," RT.com, July 29, 2010, http://rt.com/news/sci-tech/medvedev-national-projects-council (accessed Aug. 15, 2010). Also see Sakwa, *Crisis of Russian Diplomacy*, 312.

17. Julia Ioffe, "Net Impact: One Man's Cyber-Crusade against Russian Corruption," *New Yorker*, April 4, 2011, http://www.newyorker.com/reporting/2011/04/04/110404fa_fact_ioffe?currentPage=all (accessed April 10, 2011). On the resignation of "Mr. Unibrow," Oleg Simakov, see "Glava departamenta informatizatsii Minzdravsotsrazvitiya Simakov ushel v otstavku," *Gazeta.ru*, Oct. 13, 2010. http://www.gazeta.ru/news/lastnews/2010/10/13/n_1559346.shtml (accessed March 6, 2012).

18. Tom Balmforth and Gregory Feifer, "Russian Health Care Provides No Real Safety Net," *Radio Free Europe/Radio Liberty*, Aug. 14, 2011, http://www.rferl.org/content/russian_healt_car_provides_no_real_safety_net/24296527.html (accessed Feb. 11, 2012); Reuters, "Russians Wrongly Think They're Healthy," *Moscow Times*, April 27, 2011, http://www.themoscowtimes.com/news/article/russians-wrongly-think-theyre-healthy/435851.html (accessed April 28, 2011).

19. Balmforth and Feifer, "Russian Health Care Provides No Real Safety Net."

20. Ibid.

21. Ibid.

22. "More Than 80 Percent of Russian Teenagers Take Alcohol," *ITAR-TASS Daily*, Oct. 9, 2010, http://dlib.eastview.com/browse/doc/22613353 (accessed Oct. 11, 2010). See also Aleksandr Nemtsov, *Alkogol'naya istoriya Rossii: Noveishii period* (Moscow: URSS,

2009), 288–90; Grigory G. Zaigraev, "The Russian Model of Noncommercial Alcohol Consumption," in *Moonshine Markets: Issues in Unrecorded Alcohol Beverage Production and Consumption*, ed. Alan Haworth and Ronald Simpson (New York: Brunner-Routledge, 2004), 38. Also see chapter 21, note 44.

23. Nemtsov, *Alkogol'naya istoriya Rossii*, 295 (author's translation); for an English-language edition see Aleksandr Nemtsov, *A Contemporary History of Alcohol in Russia*, trans. Howard M. Goldfinger and Andrew Stickley (Stockholm: Södertörns högskola, 2011), 320. On the life-expectancy discrepancy between the sexes see chapter 21, note 27.

24. "Medvedev Urges More Steps to Curb Alcohol Threat," *RIA Novosti*, Aug. 12, 2009, http:// en.rian.ru/russia/20090812/155791576.html (accessed Nov. 5, 2009); Maria Ermakova, "Russia May Ban Beer Sales at Kiosks, Markets, Ministry Says," Bloomberg, Sept. 29, 2009, http://www.bloomberg.com/apps/news?pid=newsarchive&sid=afmjcxsVo0Hc (both accessed Nov. 5, 2009).

25. Guy Faulconbridge, "Russia's President Calls Time on Vodka 'Disaster'," Reuters, Aug. 12, 2009, http://www.reuters.com/article/2009/08/12/us-russia-vodka-idUS-TRE57B4KC20090812; "Medvedev against Ban on Alcohol, Will Fight Problem Differently," RIA Novosti, July 4, 2009, http://en.rian.ru/russia/20090704/155431427. html (both accessed Sept. 11, 2009); David Zaridze et al., "Alcohol and Cause-Specific Mortality in Russia: A Retrospective Case-Control Study of 48,557 Adult Deaths," *The Lancet* 373 (2009): 2201. See also N. F. Izmerov and G. I. Tikhonova, "Problemy zdorov'ya rabotayushchego naseleniya v Rossii," *Problemy prognozirovaniya* 3 (2011): 56.

26. Oleg Shchedrov, "Medvedev Praises Anti-Alcohol Drive," *Moscow Times*, July 20, 2009.

27. "Medvedev Urges More Steps to Curb Alcohol Threat."

28. Megan K. Stack, "Foreign Exchange: Russian President Takes out after Alcohol," *Los Angeles Times*, Sept. 3, 2009, http://articles.latimes.com/2009/sep/03/world/fg-russia-booze3; Maria Antonova and Anna Malpas, "Medvedev Puts Limits on Alcohol," *Moscow Times*, Sept. 14, 2009, http://www.themoscowtimes.com/news/article/383100/index.html (accessed Sept. 15, 2009).

29. Richard Weitz, "Global Insights: Russia's Demographic Timebomb," *World Politics Review*, Feb. 15, 2011, http://www.worldpoliticsreview.com/articles/7888/global-insights-russias-demographic-timebomb (accessed Feb. 17, 2011).

30. Pavel Butorin, " 'Squirrel from Hell' Takes on Russian Alcoholism," *Radio Free Europe/Radio Liberty*, Dec. 22, 2010, http://www.rferl.org/content/squirrel_from_hell_takes_on_rus-sian_alcoholism/2255880.html (accessed Dec. 25, 2010); for the "Squirrel from Hell," see "Adskaya belochka," http://www.youtube.com/watch?v=73cjNp7n75o (Nov. 25, 2010); "Adskaya belochka 2: Tolyan-bratan," http://www.youtube.com/watch?v=3JtdhvAjXtM (Dec. 19, 2011); "Zolotaya Manufaktura" vodka company, http://rsg.org.ru/en/belochka.

31. Seth Meyers, "Weekend Update," *Saturday Night Live*, Nov. 7, 2009, http://www.hulu. com/watch/107514/saturday-night-live-taylor-swift#s-p12-so-i0 (at 35:5; accessed March 7, 2012). See also Andrew Osborn, "Kremlin Encourages Russia to Drink More Wine," *Telegraph*, Sept. 7, 2011, http://www.telegraph.co.uk/news/worldnews/europe/russia/8747419/Kremlin-encourages-Russia-to-drink-more-wine.html (accessed Sept. 11, 2011).

32. Ekaterina Shcherbakova, "Demograficheskie itogi 2011 goda (chast' II)," *Demoskop Weekly*, February 20–March 4, 2012, http://demoscope.ru/weekly/2012/0499/barom03.php (accessed March 8, 2012). Putin-era average is author's estimation based on Scherbakova's data. Alexandra Koshkina, "Alcohol Consumption in Russian Cities Decreasing," *Gazeta. ru*, Aug. 23, 2011, http://rbth.ru/articles/2011/08/23/alcohol_consumption_in_rus-sian_cities_decreasing_13282.html (accessed Aug. 24, 2011); "Booze Kills Seven Per Cent Fewer Muscovites," RT.com, March 9, 2012, http://rt.com/news/prime-time/booze-mos-cow-statistcis-down-211 (accessed March 10, 2012).

33. Vedomosti, "Russian Ingenuity Conquers Alcohol Sale Restrictions," *Moscow Times*, Feb. 8, 2012, http://www.themoscowtimes.com/business/article/alcohol-delivered-after-hours/452672.html (accessed Feb. 10, 2012).

34. Igor' V. Ponkin, "Monitoring i profilaktika potrebleniya alkogol'nykh napitkov v sis-teme obrazovaniya," in *Alkogol'naya katastrofa i vozmozhnosti gosudarstvennoi politiki v*

preodolenii alkogol'noi sverkosmertnosti v Rossii, ed. Dar'ya A. Khalturina and Andrei V. Korotaev (Moscow: Lenand, 2010), 332–34; Natalya Krainova, "Report: Adults Drink Less, Teens More," *Moscow Times*, Nov. 16, 2011, http://www.themoscowtimes.com/news/article/report-adults-drink-less-teens-more/447989.html (accessed Nov. 18, 2011.) For an on-the-ground take see Jeffrey Tayler, "Russian Hangover: A Moscow Apartment Block's Tenants Turn over, One Vodka Binge at a Time," *The Atlantic*, Oct. 11, 2011, http://www.theatlantic.com/magazine/archive/2011/11/russian-hangover/8665/ (accessed Oct. 11, 2011).

35. 2010 figures from Ekaterina Shcherbakova, "Demograficheskie itogi 2010 goda (chast' II)," *Demoskop Weekly*, March 7–20, 2011 http://demoscope.ru/weekly/2011/0457/barom03.php (accessed Aug. 29, 2013). 2011 figures from Ekaterina Shcherbakova, "Demograficheskie itogi 2011 goda (chast' II)." Figures for the first half of 2013 from Rosstat, "Estestvennoe dvizhenie naseleniya v razreze sub'ektov Rossiiskoi Federatsii za yanvar'-iyul' 2013 goda," Aug. 27, 2013, http://www.gks.ru/free_doc/2013/demo/edn07-13.htm (accessed Aug. 28, 2013).

36. Lyudmila Alexandrova, "Legal Output of Vodka Sliding in Russia but Russians Drinking as Much as Always," *ITAR-TASS*, July 19, 2013, http://www.itar-tass.com/en/c39/813821.html (accessed July 24, 2013); Isabel Gorst, "Russia's Vodka Tax: Backfiring," *Financial Times* (beyondbrics blog), July 17, 2013, http://blogs.ft.com/beyond-brics/2013/07/17/russias-vodka-tax-backfiring/ (accessed July 17, 2013); "Legal Vodka Production Falls by One-Third in Russia," *RT.com*, June 24, 2013, http://rt.com/business/russia-vodka-production-falls-158/ (accessed July 17, 2013).

37. Walter Joyce, "The Battle Continues: Gorbachev's Anti-Alcohol Policies," in *Social Change and Social Issues in the Former USSR*, ed. Walter Joyce (New York: St. Martin's, 1992), 99.

38. Arina Petrova, "Alkogol'naya sostavlyayushchaya reforma," *Kommersant'*, June 29, 2011, http://www.kommersant.ru/doc/1665297 (accessed Aug. 27, 2013). Many thanks to Anna Bailey for this reference. Earlier estimates have vodka contributing 7–8 percent of the budget. Nemtsov, *Alkogol'naya istoriya Rossii*, 288–90; Zaigraev, "Russian Model," 38. On the flat tax see Jorge Martinez-Vazquez, Mark Rider, and Sally Wallace, *Tax Reform in Russia* (Northampton, Mass.: Edward Elgar, 2008), 38–52.

39. "Medvedev, Putin Toast Each Other with Milk," AFP, Oct. 2, 2010, http://www.google.com/hostednews/afp/article/ALeqM5gpVfhA2SZ4Dh5fxvOo5-QQcXdrLQ?docId=CNG.4db59b76c2daef9f84b5eea831b965fa.441 (accessed Oct. 4, 2010).

40. Antonova and Malpas, "Medvedev Puts Limits on Alcohol." See also Polya Lesova, "Russia Targets Beer, Not Vodka, to Tackle Alcoholism," *Wall Street Journal MarketWatch*, Oct. 9, 2009, http://www.marketwatch.com/story/russia-targets-beer-not-vodka-vs-alcoholism-2009-10-09 (accessed Oct. 11, 2009).

41. "Za zdorov'e: Putin posovetoval rossiyanam men'she pit'," Kasparov.ru, June 26, 2009, http://www.kasparov.ru/material.php?id=4A44AC95792B2 (accessed July 3, 2009); Vladimir Milov et al., eds., *Putin. Korruptsiya* (Moscow: Partiya narodnoi svobody, 2011), 22–24, http://www.putin-itogi.ru/f/Putin-i-korruptsiya-doklad.pdf.

42. Anna Bailey, "Explaining Rosalkogol'regulirovaniye. Why Does Russia Have a New Federal Alcohol Regulator?" in: *Alkogol' v Rossii: Materialy vtoroi mezhdunarodnoi nauchno-prakticheskoi konferentsii (Ivanovo, 28–29 oktyabrya 2011)*, ed. Nikolai V. Dem'yanenko (Ivanovo: Filial RGGU v g. Ivanovo, 2011), 105. On ties to Yawara-Neva and Rosspirtprom, see Nina Petlyanova, "Soobrazili na svoikh," *Novaya gazeta*, March 4, 2011, http://www.novayagazeta.ru/politics/6856.html (accessed Aug. 27, 2013).

43. Faulconbridge, "Russia's President Calls Time on Vodka 'Disaster.'"

44. "Medvedev Urges More Steps to Curb Alcohol Threat."

45. Stanislav Belkovskii, "Kak nam posadit' federal'nykh ministrov," *Moskovskii Komsomolets*, April 22, 2011, http://www.mk.ru/politics/article/2011/04/21/583254-kak-nam-posadit-federalnyih-ministrov.html; Yulia Latynina, "The 3rd Opium War," *Moscow Times*, April 20, 2011, http://www.themoscowtimes.com/opinion/article/the-3rd-opium-war/435388.html (accessed April 24, 2011); "Will Golikova Be Shown the Door?" Rumafia.com, Dec. 12, 2011, http://rumafia.com/news.php?id=470 (accessed Dec. 15, 2011).

46. Zvagelsky on increasing the tax: Malcolm Borthwick, "Russian Beer Sales Suffering Tax Hike," *BBC News*, May 31, 2011 http://www.bbc.co.uk/news/mobile/business-13604311 (accessed June 2, 2011). Beer more dangerous than vodka, see Irina Novoselova, "Deputatskaya artel'," *Vek*, April 29, 2010, http://wek.ru/ekonomika/17636-deputatskaya-artel.html (accessed June 2, 2011).

47. Lesova, "Russia Targets Beer, Not Vodka, to Tackle Alcoholism."

48. Tim Wall, "Beer, Death and Taxes," *Moscow News*, Oct. 5, 2009, http://themoscownews.com/proetcontra/20091005/55389702.html (accessed Oct. 11, 2009).

49. Isabel Gorst, "Russia: Downing Fewer Pints," *Financial Times* (BeyondBRICs blog), Nov. 9, 2011, http://blogs.ft.com/beyond-brics/2011/11/09/russia-downing-fewer-pints/#axzz1dcREZv7H (accessed Nov. 10, 2011); Evgeniya Chaykovskaya, "Russia Produced Record Quantity of Vodka," *Moscow News*, July 17, 2012, http://themoscownews.com/russia/20120717/189970216.html (accessed July 20, 2012); Il'ya Khrennikov, "Russian Beer Output Falls on Restrictions, Fueling Vodka Gains," Bloomberg, Oct. 17, 2012, http://www.bloomberg.com/news/2012-10-17/russian-beer-output-falls-on-restrictions-fueling-vodka-gains.html (accessed October 18, 2012).

50. Anna Bailey, "Protecting the Public, or Protecting Vodka? How Beer was Banished from Russian Kiosks," unpublished manuscript, University College London, 2013.

51. On authoring alcohol legislation: Anna Levinskaya, "U gastronomov v regionakh otzyvayut alkogol'nye litsenzii," *RBK Daily*, Feb. 13, 2013 http://rbcdaily.ru/market/562949985714936 (accessed Aug. 13, 2013), linked from Zvagelsky's homepage, http://www.zvagelskiy.ru/. On ties to Rosspirtprom and other vodka companies, see "Zvagel'skii, Viktor Fridrikhovich," *Lobbying.ru* http://www.lobbying.ru/persons.php?id=2722 (accessed May 28, 2013); "A byl li uchreditel'?" *Novaya gazeta*, July 12, 2010, http://www.novayagazeta.ru/politics/2727.html (accessed May 28, 2013).

52. Alina Lobzina, "Alcohol Consumption Fills Russian Budget," *Moscow News*, Nov. 29, 2012, http://themoscownews.com/business/20121129/190929807.html (accessed Dec. 1, 2012).

53. Anatoly Medetsky, "In a Populist Move, Putin Promises $16bln for Health Care," *Moscow Times*, April 21, 2010, http://www.themoscowtimes.com/news/article/in-a-populist-move-putin-promises-16bln-for-health-care/404405.html (accessed April 23, 2010); Darya Korsunskaya, "Interview: More Government Spending Won't Help Russian Economy— Finance Minister," Reuters, June 16, 2010, http://af.reuters.com/article/energyOilNews/idAFLDE65F13020100616?sp=true (accessed July 11, 2010).

54. "'People Should Smoke and Drink More,' Says Russian Finance Minister," *Telegraph*, Sept. 1, 2010, http://www.telegraph.co.uk/news/worldnews/europe/russia/7975521/People-should-smoke-and-drink-more-says-Russian-finance-minister.html (accessed Sept. 11, 2010).

55. Anatoly Miranovsky, "Kuril'shchiki i p'yanitsy zaplatyat 'nalog' na vrednye privichki," *Pravda*, Sept. 2, 2010, http://www.pravda.ru/economics/finance/02-09-2010/1047661-tax-0 (accessed Sept. 11, 2010).

56. M. J. Akbar, "Wanted: A Nobel Prize for Honesty," *Arab News*, Sept. 11, 2010, http://arab-news.com/opinion/columns/article134636.ece?comments=all (accessed Sept. 11, 2010); "Kudrin: Finance Minister of the Year," RT.com, Oct. 11, 2010, http://rt.com/news/kudrin-euromoney-award-2010 (accessed Nov. 5, 2010).

57. Anatoly Karlin, "The Uncertain Future of Cheap Russian Booze," *Sublime Oblivion*, April 28, 2011, http://www.sublimeoblivion.com/2011/04/28/future-of-russian-booze (accessed April 30, 2011); Mark Lawrence Schrad, "Moscow's Drinking Problem," *New York Times*, April 16, 2011, W8, http://www.nytimes.com/2011/04/17/opinion/17Schrad.html?_r=1&hpw (accessed April 18, 2011); "Vladimir Putin Speaks out against Sharp Rises in Prices on Alcohol in Russia," BCM News Portal, April 1, 2011, http://www.newsbcm.com/doc/725 (accessed April 2, 2011).

58. Michael Schwirtz, "Russian President Ousts Finance Minister, a Putin Ally, for Insubordination," *New York Times*, Sept. 27, 2011, A4; For RT.com video coverage see http://www.youtube.com/watch?v=gpCVLv-1mpA/.

Chapter 24

1. Oleg Blotskii, *Vladimir Putin: Istoriya zhizny* (Moscow: Mezhdunarodnaya otnosheniya, 2001), 68–69; cited in Masha Gessen, *The Man without a Face: The Unlikely Rise of Vladimir Putin* (New York: Riverhead Books, 2012), 48–49.

2. David Remnick, "The Civil Archipelago: How Far Can the Resistance to Vladimir Putin Go?" *New Yorker*, Dec. 19, 2011, http://www.newyorker.com/reporting/2011/12/19/111219fa_fact_remnick?currentPage=all (accessed Dec. 25, 2011). On the fight being a "bit of a snoozer," see Steve Barry, "M-1 Global 'Fedor vs. Monson' Results: Fedor Emelianenko Snaps Three-Fight Losing-Streak," *MMA Convert*, Nov. 20, 2011, http://www.mmaconvert.com/2011/11/20/m-1-global-fedor-vs-monson-results-fedor-emelianenko-snaps-three-fight-losing-streak (accessed March 16, 2012).

3. Michael David Smith, "Booing of Putin at Fedor Fight Draws International Interest," MMAFighting.com, Nov. 21, 2011, http://www.mmafighting.com/2011/11/21/booing-of-putin-at-fedor-fight-draws-international-interest (accessed March 17, 2012); Remnick, "Civil Archipelago."

4. Vladimir Ryzhkov, "The Dirtiest Elections in Post-Soviet History," *Moscow Times*, Dec. 2, 2011. http://www.themoscowtimes.com/opinion/article/the-dirtiest-elections-in-post-soviet-history/449079.html/ (accessed Dec. 3, 2011); AP, "An Insider's Account of Vote Rigging," *Moscow Times*, Dec. 7, 2011, http://www.themoscowtimes.com/news/article/an-insiders-account-of-vote-rigging-for-putin/449455.html (accessed Dec. 8, 2011).

5. Nikolaus von Twickel, "Media Thaw's Staying Power Hotly Debated," *Moscow Times*, March 16, 2012, http://www.themoscowtimes.com/news/article/media-thaws-staying-power-hotly-debated/454836.html (accessed March 16, 2012).

6. Iris Hoßmann et al., *Europe's Demographic Future: Growing Imbalances* (Berlin: Berlin Institute for Population and Development, 2008), 3; United Nations, Department of Economic and Social Affairs, Population Division, Population Estimates and Projections Section, "World Population Prospects, the 2010 Revision," http://esa.un.org/unpd/wpp/country-profiles/country-profiles_1.htm (accessed March 17, 2012). See also Howard Amos, "Russia's Ghost Towns," *Global Post*, July 26, 2011, http://www.globalpost.com/dispatch/news/regions/europe/russia/110720/russia-rural-population-demographics (accessed July 28, 2011).

7. John Bongaarts and Rodolfo A. Bulatao, eds., *Beyond Six Billion: Forecasting the World's Population* (Washington, D.C.: National Academy Press, 2000), 278; Jeremy Singer-Vine, "Crowded, with a Chance of Overcrowded," *Slate*, Jan. 27, 2011, http://www.slate.com/articles/news_and_politics/explainer/2011/01/crowded_with_a_chance_of_overcrowded.html (accessed Jan. 28, 2012).

8. David Zaridze et al., "Alcohol and Cause-Specific Mortality in Russia: A Retrospective Case-Control Study of 48,557 Adult Deaths," *The Lancet* 373 (2009): 2213.

9. Belarusian trends largely conform to the Russian experience. Anatolii G. Vishnevskii, "Rossiya pered demograficheskim vyborom," 74–75; Dar'ya A. Khalturina and Andrei V. Korotaev, "Vvedeniye: Alkogol'naya katastrofa: Kak ostanovit' vymiranie Rossii," 43, both in *Alkogol'naya katastrofa i vozmozhnosti gosudarstvennoi politiki v preodolenii alkogol'noi sverkhsmertnosti v Rossii*, ed. Dar'ya A. Khalturina and Andrei V. Korotaev (Moscow: Lenand, 2010).

10. Sergei Scherbov and Wolfgang Lutz, *Future Regional Population Patterns in the Soviet Union: Scenarios to the Year 2050*, IIASA Working Paper No. WP-88–104 (Laxenburg, Austria: IIASA, 1988), 14–15. See also Svetlana Soboleva, *Migration and Settlement: Soviet Union*, IIASA Working Paper No. WP-80-45 (Laxenburg, Austria: IIASA, 1980): 130.

11. Elena Arakelyan, "Kazhdyi tretii rossiyanin vypivaet na rabote," *Komsomol'skaya pravda*, March 22, 2012, http://amur.kp.ru/daily/25855.4/2823658/ (accessed March 23, 2012).

12. Philip Hanson, "The Russian Economy and Its Prospects," in *Putin Again: Implications for Russia and the West* (London: Chatham House, 2012), 22–29.

13. See text accompanying note 8 of chapter 7. On vodka politics and beer see David M. Herszenhorn, "New Beer Law Draws Cautious Support, with Notes of Pessimism," *New York Times*, Jan. 7, 2013, A8, http://www.nytimes.com/2013/01/07/world/europe/russian-beer-law-draws-support-and-some-pessimism.html (accessed Jan. 7, 2013).

14. O. G. von Heidenstam, *Swedish Life in Town and Country* (New York: G. P. Putnam's Sons, 1904), 193–94.
15. Ibid., 193. For Swedish consumption statistics see Statens folkhälsoinstitut (Swedish National Institute of Public Health), *Försäljning av spritdrycker, vin och öl i Sverige under åren 1861–1999* (Stockholm: Statens folkhälsoinstitut), 12–16; Switzerland Bureau fédéral de statistique, *Question de l'alcoolisme. Exposé comparatif des lois et des expériences de quelques états étrangers, par le bureau fédéral de statistique* (Berne: Imprimerie K.-J. Wyss, 1884), 672.
16. von Heidenstam, *Swedish Life in Town and Country*, 187, 93. See also Victor Nilsson, *Sweden* (New York: Co-Operative Publication Society, 1899), 387.
17. Johan Pontén, *Historia kring alkoholen: Från Syndafloden till dagens Sverige* (Stockholm: Natur och kultur, 1967), 72–88; Hanna Hodacs, "Det civiliserade, protestantiska och nyktra Europa: Om nykterhetstankens spridning i det tidiga 1800-talets Sverige," *Spiritus*, no. 4 (2002): 14–16; Nykterhetskommittén, *Betänkande VI, 1: Redogörelse för lagstiftningen i Sverige om rusdryckers försäljning, 1800–1911* (1914), 9341 Arbetarrörelsens arkiv och bibliotek, Stockholm, 14–22. Temperance membership data from Carl-Goran Andræ and Sven Lundkvist, Swedish Popular Movement Archive (Folkrörelsearkivet), 1881–1950; Swedish Social Science Data Service (Svensk Samhällsvetenskaplig Datatjänst), http://snd.gu.se (accessed Feb. 29, 2012).
18. John Bergvall, *Restriktionssystemet: Hur det kommit till, hur det arbetar, vad det uträttat* (Norrtelje: Nortelje Tidnings Boktryckeri AB, 1929), 9; Nykterhetskommittén, *Betänkande VI, 1*, 41–42; Olov Kinberg, "Temperance Legislation in Sweden," *Annals of the American Academy of Political and Social Science* 163 (1932); Per Frånberg, "Den svenska supen," in *Den svenska supen*, ed. Kettil Bruun and Per Frånberg (Stockholm: Prisma, 1985), 34.
19. L. Pankrat'ev, "Vinnyi aktsiz," in *Sovremennik: Zhurnal literaturnyi i politicheskii (s 1859 goda)*, ed. Ivan Panaev and Nikolai Nekrasov (St. Petersburg: Tipografiya Karla Vul'fa, 1859), 106.
20. Mark Lawrence Schrad, *The Political Power of Bad Ideas: Networks, Institutions, and the Global Prohibition Wave* (New York: Oxford University Press, 2010), 151–55.
21. Boris Yeltsin, "Enough of Our Drinking Vodka Made Who Knows Where," *Current Digest of the Russian Press* 49, no. 37 (1997): 11–12; Paul Klebnikov, "Who Will Be the Next Ruler of Russia?" *Forbes.com*, Nov. 16, 1998, http://www.forbes.com/forbes/1998/1116/6211152a.html (accessed Nov. 5, 2010).
22. Interfax News Agency, "State Monopoly Necessary to Tackle Alcoholism in Russia—Public Health Chief," Johnson's Russia List (JRL) No. 2009-171, Sept. 14, 2009, http://www.russialist.org/2009-171-19.php (accessed Aug. 8, 2013).
23. Margarita Bogdanova, "Russian Presidential Campaign Nears Final Stage," Press TV, Feb. 26, 2012, http://www.presstv.ir/detail/228813.html (accessed Feb. 27, 2012). Also see Gleb Bryanski, "Russian Communists Flirt with Medvedev," Reuters, Nov. 7, 2009, http://www.reuters.com/article/2009/11/07/us-russia-communists-medvedev-idUS-TRE5A60VO20091107 (accessed Feb. 27, 2012); Mark Lawrence Schrad, "Kicking the Vodka Habit," *Moscow Times*, Nov. 3, 2006.
24. Schrad, "Kicking the Vodka Habit."
25. Sturla Nordlund, "Alkogol'naya politika skandinavskikh stran: Nauchnye osnovaniya, empiricheskie issledovaniya i perspektivy," 297; Esa Osterberg, "Kakie mekhanizmy bor'by s alkogolem yavlyayutsya effektivnymi i ekonomicheski tselesoobraznymi," 271; and Øyvind Horverak, "Chto nuzhno dlya uspekha alkogol'noi politiki: Opyt Norvegii," all in *Alkogol'naya katastrofa i vozmozhnosti gosudarstvennoi politiki v preodolenii alkogol'noi sverkosmertnosti v Rossii*, ed. Dar'ya A. Khalturina and Andrei V. Korotaev (Moscow: Lenand, 2010); Ol'ga Kostenko and Syuzanna Gadzhieva, "Kak ne propit' Rossiyu," *Argumenty i fakty*, May 10, 2012, http://www.aif.ru/society/article/51901 (accessed May 12, 2012).
26. Artyom Gil et al., "Alcohol Policy in a Russian Region: A Stakeholder Analysis," *European Journal of Public Health* (2010): 6.
27. Ivan R. Mintslov, "Monopoliya torgovli spirtnymi napitkami v nekotorykh inostrannykh gosudarstvakh i v Rossii," *Trudy Komissii po Voprosu ob Alkogolizm: Zhurnaly zasedanii i doklady* 1 (1898): 73; Vladislav D. Shidlovskii, "Obzor deyatel'nosti, napravlennoi na bor'bu s p'yanstvom v Severnoi Amerike i Zapadnoi Evrope," *Trudy Komissii po Voprosu ob Alkogolizm: Zhurnaly zasedanii i doklady* 3 (1899): 86; Irina R. Takala, *Veselie Rusi: Istoriia*

alkogol'noi problemy v Rossii (St. Petersburg: Zhurnal Neva, 2002), 146–53. On Russian impressions of the Gothenburg system more generally, see I. A. Krasnov, "Luchshe men'she ne luchshe. 'Gottenburgskaya sistema' i polemika o piteinoi kul'ture v Rossii na rubezhe XIX-XX veka," in: *Alkogol' v Rossii: Materialy pervoi mezhdunarodnoi nauchno-prakticheskoi konferentsii* (Ivanovo, 29-30 oktyabrya 2010), ed. Mikhail V. Teplyanskii (Ivanovo: Filial RGGU v g. Ivanovo, 2010), 22–26.

28. Mikhail Fridman, *Vinnaya monopoliya*, tom 1: *Vinnaya monopoliya v inostrannykh gosudarstvakh* (St. Petersburg: Pravda, 1914), 548. See also John F. Hutchinson, "Science, Politics and the Alcohol Problem in Post-1905 Russia," *Slavonic and East European Review* 58, no. 2 (1980): 241–42. On Russian interest in the Gothenburg System see also f. 586 (Plevhe, Vyacheslav K.), op. 1, d. 275 (Stat'ya iz gazety "Morning Post" o prodazhe spirtnykh napitkov v Anglii), l.1, Gosudarstvennyi Arkhiv Rossiskoi Federatsii (GARF) (State archive of the Russian Federation), Moscow; Alexis Raffalovich, "The State Monopoly of Spirits in Russia, and Its Influence on the Prosperity of the Population," *Journal of the Royal Statistics Society* 64, no. 1 (1901): 24–28; Dmitrii N. Borodin, "Vinnaya monopoliya," *Trudy Kommissii po Voprosu ob Alkogolizm: Zhurnaly zasedanii i doklady* 3 (1899); L. K. Dymsha, "Kazennaya vinnaya monopoliya i eya znachenie dlya bor'by s p'yanstvom," *Trudy Kommissii po Voprosu ob Alkogolizm: zhurnaly zasedanii i doklady* 4 (1900).

29. VTsIOM, "What Russians Are Afraid Of: Press Release No. 1299," *Russian Public Opinion Research Center* 1299 (2010), and "August Problem Background: Press Release No. 1383," *Russian Public Opinion Research Center* 1383 (2011), http://wciom.com/index. php?id=61&uid=411 (accessed Feb. 2, 2012). Anna Bailey, "Russian Public Opinion on Alcohol: What the Opinion Polls Tell Us, and What They Don't," in: *Alkogol' v Rossii: Materialy tret'ei mezhdunarodnoi nauchno-prakticheskoi konferentsii* (Ivanovo, 26-27 oktyabrya 2012), ed. Mikhail V. Teplyanskii (Ivanovo: Filial RGGU v g. Ivanovo, 2012), 121. See also note 3 of the preface.

30. Irina Filatova, "'Millionaire' Doctors Part of Solution to Demographic Problem," *Moscow Times*, Jan. 27, 2013, http://www.themoscowtimes.com/business/article/millionaire-doctors-part-of-solution-to-demographic-problem/474606.html (accessed Jan. 28, 2013).

31. Gil et al., "Alcohol Policy in a Russian Region," 6; Richard Sakwa, *The Crisis of Russian Democracy: The Dual State, Factionalism and the Medvedev Succession* (New York: Cambridge University Press, 2011), 361.

32. Lilia Shevtsova, *Russia—Lost in Transition: The Yeltsin and Putin Legacies* (Washington, D.C.: Carnegie Endowment for International Peace, 2007), 158.

33. Vladimir Putin, "Poslaniye Prezidenta Federal'nomu Sobraniyu," Kremlin.ru, Dec. 12, 2012, http://news.kremlin.ru/transcripts/17118 (accessed Dec. 12, 2012).

34. Martha Wexler, "Young Russian Politician Fights from the Bottom Up," NPR, March 19, 2012, http://www.npr.org/2012/03/19/148924951/young-russian-politician-fights-from-the-bottom-up (accessed March 19, 2012).

35. Andrei K. Demin and Irina A. Demina, "Opyt grazhdanskogo obshchestva v reshenii problem zloupotrebleniya alkogolem v Rossiiskoi Federatsii: Deyatel'nost' Rossiiskoi Assotsiatsii Obshchestvennogo Zdorov'ya," in *Alkogol'naya katastrofa i vozmozhnosti gosudarstvennoi politiki v preodolenii alkogol'noi sverkhsmertnosti v Rossii*, ed. Dar'ya A. Khalturina and Andrei V. Korotaev (Moscow: Lenand, 2010), 368.

36. Will Rogers, *There's Not a Bathing Suit in Russia & Other Bare Facts* (New York: Albert & Charles Boni, 1927), 25–31. In a similar vein see Hedrick Smith, *The Russians* (New York: Quadrangle/New York Times Book Co., 1976), 120.

37. Rogers, *There's Not a Bathing Suit in Russia*, 31.

INDEX